D1156699

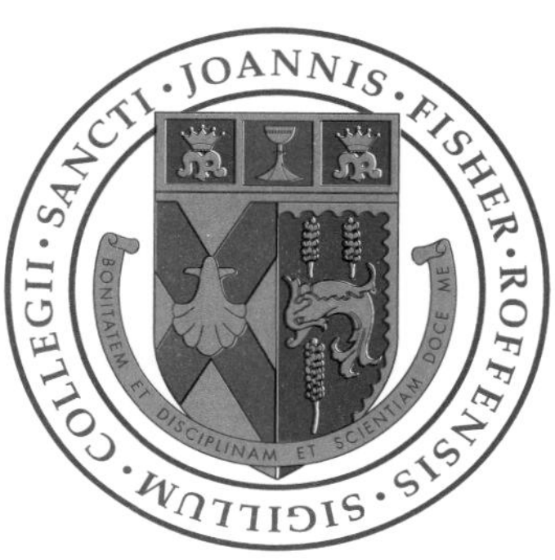
SANCTI·JOANNIS·FISHER·ROFFENSIS·SIGILLUM·COLLEGII
BONITATEM ET DISCIPLINAM ET SCIENTIAM DOCE ME

STALIN

AN UNKNOWN PORTRAIT

STALIN

AN UNKNOWN PORTRAIT

By Miklós Kun

Central European University Press
Budapest New York

First published in Hungarian as
Az ismeretlen Sztálin
in 2002 by PolgART and Athenaeum 2000

English edition published in 2003 by

Central European University Press

An imprint of the
Central European University Share Company
Nádor utca 11, H-1051 Budapest, Hungary
Tel: +36-1-327-3138 or 327-3000
Fax: +36-1-327-3183
E-mail: ceupress@ceu.hu
Website: www.ceupress.com

400 West 59th Street, New York NY 10019, USA
Tel: +1-212-547-6932
Fax: +1-212-548-4607
E-mail: mgreenwald@sorosny.org

ISBN 963 9241 19 9 cloth

Library of Congress Cataloging-in-Publication Data

Kun, Miklós, 1946–
[Az ismeretlen Sztálin. English]
Stalin: an unknown portrait / by Miklós Kun.
p. cm.
Includes bibliographical references and index. Illustrated.
ISBN
1. Stalin, Joseph, 1879–1953. 2. Heads of state—Soviet
Union—Biography. 3. Soviet Union—Politics and government—1917–1936.
4. Soviet Union—Politics and government—1936–1953. I. Title.
DK268.S8K86513 2003
947.084'2'092—dc21

2003000054

Cover design by Anna Benkő
Preprint by Attributum Stúdió, Budapest
Printed in Hungary by
Akadémiai Nyomda, Martonvásár

Table of Contents

To the loving memory of
my mother, Olga

Acknowledgements

I wish to acknowledge the support of the following institutions and individuals: the Library of the Hungarian Academy of Sciences; the CEU Library and its head, Mária Szlatky; the Library and Archives of the Hoover Institution at Stanford University; the Ministry of Foreign Affairs of the Republic of Hungary and former Minister of Foreign Affairs, János Martonyi; the Ministry of Education of the Republic of Hungary and former Minister of Education, Zoltán Pokorni; the Twentieth Century Institute and Mária Schmidt; the Hungarian Foreign Trade Bank, Ltd. and its Chairman and CEO, Tamás Erdei; the Open Society Institute and the Open Society Archives at Central European University; the Viktória Légrády and Co., Ltd.; the Hungarian Book Foundation and the Sándor Demján Foundation.

I am indebted to those who helped the shaping of the book with their reminiscences, ideas and advice: Vladimir Antonov-Ovseyenko (Moscow), Margarita Balmaceda (Princeton), Vladimir Bukovsky (Cambridge), Réka Szemerkényi (Budapest), Helène Carrère d'Encausse (Paris), Alfred Rieber (Budapest), David Bronstein (Moscow), Yury Felstinsky (Boston), Sándor Csoóri (Budapest), Kirill Henkin (Munich), Aleksandr Yakovlev (Moscow), György Granasztói (Budapest), Irina Deskova (Moscow), Nadezhda Yoffe (New York), Tatyana Litvinova (London), Stephen Koch (New York), Sergo Mikoyan (Moscow), Irina Pavlova (Novosibirsk), Zsuzsa Király (Budapest), Natalya Rikova (Moscow), Sergei Udartsev (Almati), László Iván (Budapest), Manana Saladze (London) and János Horváth (Budapest).

Special thanks to Alex Bandy
for his valuable assistance and observations.

Illustrations by courtesy of
the David King Collection, London.

PREFACE
In Stalin's Shadow

As Tolstoy famously said, all happy families resemble one another, each unhappy family is unhappy in its own way. In the same way, the chronicle of Stalin's many biographies is long and unending. They range from unscrupulous apologies to personal diatribes of hatred. Bulky Stalin biographies that are still quoted today by some writers frequently use "double entry bookkeeping" that forgives the Soviet dictator's genocide—or even justifies it. There are also after-the-fact explanations by former leading Soviet politicians who for decades worked with the Master of the Kremlin, and who likewise have bloody hands.

Joseph Stalin, the Master (Khozyain) of the Kremlin

Just as varied is the phylogenesis of Stalin biographies; they have been created for many different personal reasons, more reasons than usual for historiography. At first glance, this book which puts a number of unpublished documents from the dictator's archives into the reader's hands, is similar to its predecessors. I was eight years old, living in a small Russian town called Orekhovo-Zuyevo, when I read Aleksei Tolstoy's *Peter the First.* I was enthralled. In many ways, it was this book, full of monumental battle scenes and unexpected adventures, that helped me decide to become a historian. Of course, at that point I didn't know that the "Soviet Count", had brazenly lifted some of the best parts of the book from the works of the noted Russian writer, Dmitry Merezhkovsky, who had been forced into emigration. Nor did I know the that the descriptions of the *tsar* had been covered with a gloss of class warfare—that this, too, had been made to fit the wishes of Joseph Stalin. The tableaux created by Aleksei Tolstoy, like a Byzantine picture, were made to illustrate political points, and, thereby, humble the reader. Anyone who has picked up *Peter the First* comes face to face with the similarities between the empire-building tsar and the man who, from a pockmarked Georgian Seminary student, became the Generalissimo who expanded the Soviet Empire to the Vistula and Bug rivers. The parallels probably hit me in the little school in Orekhovo-Zuyevo, too, since I carefully pasted a small photograph of Joseph Stalin on the title page. In large letters I scrawled "December 21st, 1879". This was the Soviet dictator's official birthday, a day celebrated each year by millions. I am proud that, decades later, I was able to successfully piece together how Stalin and his circle changed this from the original date, December 6th, 1878.

However, for a long time I was convinced that I had seen the Master of the Kremlin myself. At the end of April 1952, when I was six year old, to my great delight I was able to go to Moscow. I left my parent's sewerless wooden house, which was built next to and owned by the penniless rural hospital. And I went to a metropolis, ornamented with brilliant skyscrapers and shinning holiday decorations. I went riding on the shoulders of a doctor colleague of my father's, to take part in the May Day parade. My memories of the colorful group of party leaders, quite a few of them uniformed, waving from the Lenin mausoleum, are cloudy. But I would have been ready to swear that the one in the middle, with his army cap in his hand, the "Master," waved to me.

Not long ago, I talked again with that "young" doctor, who had since emigrated. I realized I had been living half a century with the wrong impression. My old acquaintance, who is a retired professor living in New York, said that when he carried me on his shoulders to Red Square in 1952, Stalin—who was having trouble breathing and had suffered several smaller cerebral hemorrhages—was no longer on the podium. He had gone into a small waiting room that had been set up for him in one of the wings of the mausoleum. And so I found that the story of my life was one legend the lesser.

These things went through my mind when I finished my book, *Stalin: An Unknown Portrait* [Az ismeretlen Sztálin]. I breathed a sigh of relief that day: May 4th, 2001. For decades I had felt that this man, who had ruled with an iron hand both his own subjects as well as those outside the Soviet border, had hardly left me in peace. I had spent years dusting off documents that had never been published or had been unavailable for so long. One by one, I had knocked on the doors of the ancient, desiccated people who had worked with him. I went to the homes of those who had survived the Gulag, the Soviet death camps. For days I talked with the descendents of the pre-war Soviet elite, an elite now almost vanished. I must confess that this was sometimes emotionally taxing, and for I while I shut several chapters, which had become as convoluted as the coils of a snake, in the drawer of my desk. There they joined the unpublished (even in Russian), letters between Stalin and Kliment Voroshilov, the unmistakable evidence of senility of the ageing "Master", the fight amongst his subordinates for succession and the post-war Soviet trials. These chapters are still waiting to be published.

This book is also built on hundreds of previously unknown documents. It consists of two closely related sections. *Prolonged Youth* covers the events of Stalin's life chronologically. For this section, I relied heavily on resources of the American and the then-Soviet archives. These chapters deal with episodes in the life of Iosif Dzhugashvili—known also as Soselo, Soso, Koba and finally Stalin—before 1917, episodes that foreshadowed the character of the Soviet tyrant. I touch on the succession of conflicts with his violent-tempered, alcoholic father and his double life, a life of endless lies. I write about the overage student's flight from a Tiflis Seminary, a flight that happened strangely close to the end of his studies; his early absorption into a pointless, dissolute lifestyle. His dreary private life, which only increased his original frustration. These are important moments that have not been emphasized enough even in the most detailed of biographies.

The primary reason for this is Stalin himself. He methodically and systematically obliterated many sources that could blacken or contradict the picture he had created of himself. As this book proves, he handpicked the numerous important documents that were allowed to be published. He also burned pictures from his past if they showed him to a disadvantage. Photos that were not burned were retouched. The writers of his hagiographies, though, were rewarded with benefits both at home and at work. Even by the middle of the thirties, the institutes and research groups studying Stalin's life were already hard at work on their subject.

The ill-tempered revengeful politician with the piercing glance was an unparallelled master at creating legends. He invented, for example, the fact that by 1903 he had, as an anonymous Georgian party worker, already begun a secret relationship with Lenin, "the golden eagle", who was living in exile. Stalin's collected works were rewritten by editors and secretaries, trembling like aspen leaves before him, on the pretext of translating from Georgian the articles he'd written when he was young. After this rather skimpy collected works didn't fit the picture of the "passionate revolutionary", he and Beria, "governor" of Georgia and later the feared head of the NKVD, scraped together documents that could prove his alleged acts of heroism. But he did not even trust his fellow Georgians who outdid each other in slavishness. In the end, the effusions and

This picture was taken in the summer of 1922 in a cottage in Gorky by the sister of the terminally ill Lenin, Maria Ulyanova. In this picture, Stalin looks more confident and also much taller than his teacher.

embellishments—in which it is hard to find any credible details that in any way match the truth—were gone over by strict censors.

The years of censorship are responsible for the increasing number of strange gaps I came across in the volumes about Stalin edited by Tiflis and Moscow historians. That is why I turned to earlier editions. I realized that the "Beria group" created the final, fictional versions of Stalin's memoirs, which were very primitive to begin with. After that, I tried to take a look at the original manuscripts, which sometimes held surprises for me. My research in the west, beyond the reach of the Soviet dictator, gathering evidence from contemporaries in other countries, proved more useful. Of course, these were also biased memoirs, mostly anti-Stalin. In the eyes of the writers forced to emigrate, Joseph Stalin was a despised tyrant, who had cruelly forced them to flee their homeland. Therefore, from the beginning I had reservations about these emigré reminiscences (which were full of contradictions, and included things like the Master of the Kremlin robbing mail-coaches in his youth). Another reason I had to be suspicious about these resources was that after the Bolsheviks got into power, many politicians—but not Stalin—boasted about those robberies (they were referred to euphemistically as " expropriation", which sometimes took the life of innocents). "Comrade Koba", however, consistently denied that he had anything to do with these. Since he was, in fact, a coward, it is possible that he never personally took part in the armed raids that were fairly common in the Caucasians at the beginning of the 1900s. He usually also denied that he was the puppeteer behind the legendary Semyon Ter-Petrosyan, better known as Kamo, whom an example to the most vicious Caucasian terrorists. This book is the first to demonstrate incontrovertibly—based on court records—that Stalin's illegal life did include being party to terrorism and mail-coach robbery.

The lord of one-sixth of the planet was very careful in making sure this would not come to light. He never said anything incriminating about his days of exile and illegality to his foreign visitors. It was not in his interest that posterity know that much about the years of his prolonged youth. One incident particularly bothered the grand master of power plays and political intrigue. In the early spring of 1912, just past his thirty-third birthday, he was promoted by Lenin and Zinovyev, the two leaders of the exiled Bolsheviks, and coopted into the Central Committee. Barely one year later, Stalin was arrested and sent to Siberia, banished to the Artic Circle, and both of his patrons completely forgot about him. He was deeply upset and disappointed. For long months he pined, with nothing to do, in a tiny little place called Kureyka, in the company of Yakut hunters and Ostyak fishermen. He had so much retreated into his shell that he didn't even take part in the Siberian events of the decisive 1917 revolution. There were no indications that hardly five years later, when Lenin was still alive, he would reach the height of power. However, the sources my book is based on show that in undeveloped, unstructured, authoritarian Russia, outside of accidental circumstances, the rise of the man born in a small Georgian town, who had an enormous hunger for power, went very much according to the rules.

I had to find out how this tyrant, who had ruined the lives of millions was able

Gorky (X), who was lured to Moscow from his Sorrento villa, Voroshilov (XX) and Stalin at an air show in Moscow. The fate of the three famous men is known, but what happened to the members of their guard, the air force officers in the first line and the people staring?

David King, my friend and collaborator from London.

to carry out his tragic decisions so easily. How was he able to stay in power for so many decades? Why did these once proud Soviet leaders go so compliantly and humbly to the slaughterhouse? What made them call their best friends, or even themselves, "enemies of the people"? And this was not only under interrogation, when horrible forms of torture were used, but also people who were free. I had to go to the scenes of events to find the answers. To the beautiful, lacy walls of the Kremlin, which went from the population of a small town to an empty place after the years of the Great Terror. To the Moscow "House on the Embankment", powerful symbol of the "new class", which housed the Soviet elite from the beginning of the 1930s. I had to talk to the last surviving eyewitnesses of the life of the new class, in palatial villas tucked away on the coast of the Black Sea. It became apparent that Stalin sometimes ran the country from there for months, using couriers. I had to look for the intelligentsia, artists and stakhanovite workers who had attended the exclusive receptions. Some of them can hardly understand how they applauded the tyrant so thunderously who had been manipulating them for so many years. In fact, there was a lot less idealism in Stalin than in the other learned, bespectacled Bolshevik leaders. He figured out much quicker than Kamenev, Trotsky, Bukharin and Rykov that "all the Soviet world is a stage". And on this stage there was one playwright, one star, one director, one set designer, one theater critic and one person watching from the best box.

Finally, in my thoughts I moved into the middle of that dense forest near Moscow, to the Zubalovo resort in that sunny valley where Stalin often went to relax. Previously, with the large Alliluyev-Redens-Svanidze clan, whose members were dispersed or even killed by Stalin during the Great Terror. Later, he stopped going there, and by the 1940s had moved into a *dacha* in Kuntsevo, also near Moscow. On March 1st, 1953, it was there he had his last cerebral hemorrhage.

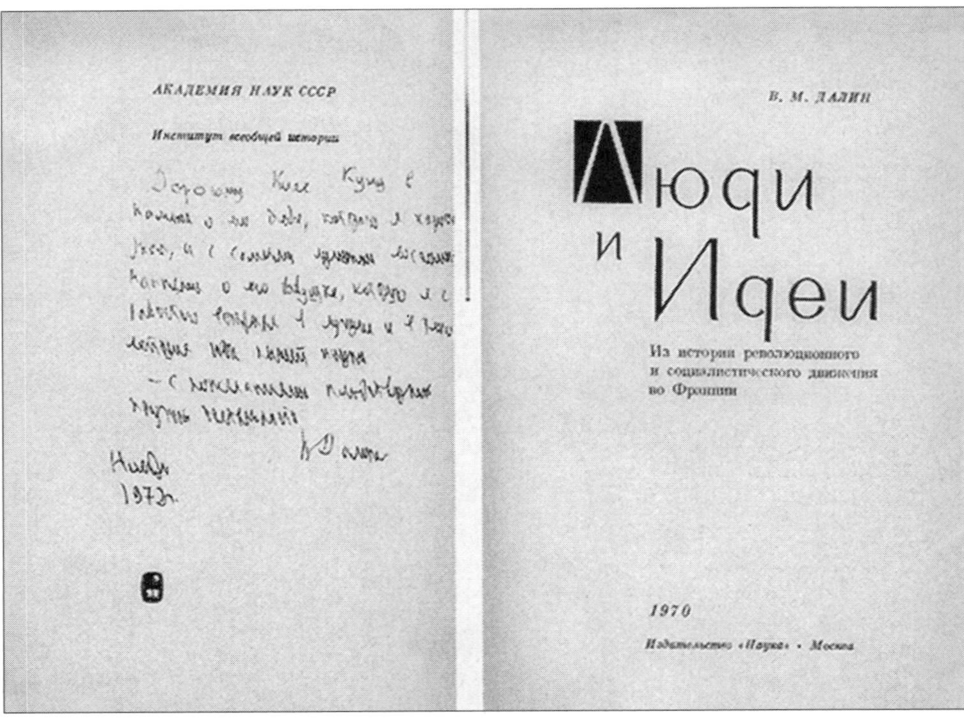

АКАДЕМИЯ НАУК СССР

Институт всеобщей истории

В. М. ДАЛИН

Люди и Идеи

Из истории революционного и социалистического движения во Франции

1970

Издательство «Наука» · Москва

My late mentor, Viktor Dalin when he was a Trotskyist and after he was released from his long imprisonment.

Only after I had completed the book did I learn that it was Lenin's idea to settle Zubalovo with reliable people. Lenin made this plan at the beginning of the 1920s in order to create a place where he could not only relax, but also hold secret discussions with Stalin and other trusted men. This is a reminder that there was continuity between "Lenin's golden age" and "the day of reckoning" known, since Robert Conquest's famous book, as the Great Terror.

Part of that continuity is the fact that the Soviet nomenclatura (which after a period of trying its wings became confident) could only pacify its subjects with the bayonet. The millions of muzhiks shared the same fate as the Cossaks, the people of minority regions, the Nepmans, the "bourgeois" intellectuals, whose lives were broken and often destroyed on the altar of the Soviet Utopia.

In the meantime, Joseph Stalin, who made a place for himself at the top of the pyramid and the new elite. This is what the second part of the book is about: *The "Master's" Friends and Enemies*. From a thematic point of view, it opens a window on the secret life of the Soviet dictator and his circle. In this section I relied even more on new documentary sources. I was also able to introduce, through pictures, the stars of this stage, thanks mainly to the large collection of early Soviet photographs belonging to my long-term collaborator, David King. It does not mean so much to read in some contemporary memoir that Stalin prepared the Tukhachevsky show trial with the help of his best friend and ally, Voroshilov. The simple slip of paper that I found in the Moscow Voroshilov estate says more than any text. On this paper, before a meeting of the military court, the people's commissar for military affairs (Voroshilov) wrote down a list of who would be the judges, presumably after having checked with Stalin. I was able to find the list of the victims of the show trial, too, chosen beforehand by Stalin and Voroshilov. This document showed that they originally wanted different people for roles in the show trial of "the traitor Tukhachevsky's spy ring". This led to the Red Army, deprived of an experienced leader, fleeing in panic. And this in turn brought tragedy to millions when Nazi Germany invaded the Soviet Union.

Stalin made a different impression in a smaller domestic circle than he did on western visitors. A series of horrific events and an insignificant petty bourgeois family life drift by in front of us. Our knowledge of this story, which was largely unknown, has been expanded. Stalin later hated his second wife, Nadezhda Alliluyeva, who died in tragic circumstances. He kept up a correspondence with definite Freudian undertones with his daughter Svetlana, the "little princess." He was harsh to his two sons, Yakov and Vasily, one of whom he pushed into an unsuccessful suicide, the other he turned into an alcoholic good-for-nothing. A host of important details connected to these events are now presented for the first time, including some scenes of the tragedy of the Alliluyev family, who became a victim of the Stalinist anti-Semitic policy after the Second World War. At this point I decided to end the work and will at some point continue.

There are only a few people left who can give truly personal information about Joseph Stalin and his time. Not everybody was ready to help me. From the Soviet dictator's right-hand man, Lazar Kaganovich, for example, I received only a "moving" dedication, and help with identifying the faces of executed Bolshevik party members in photographs. However, Nikolay Baybakov, who had been the Oil Industry Minister in Stalin's post-war government and played a key role in the military-industrial complex run by Beria, painted for me an extraordinarily detailed picture of the Master of the Kremlin and his circle.

I received help on some of the more important episodes of those turbulent times from people whose fates read more like novels than reality, some of whom have become my close friends. Among them was Viktor Dalin, the renowned historian of the 1789 French revolution. He spent more than 15 years languishing in the Gulag, then was exiled. I was one of his favorite students, and not long before his death he admitted that charges brought against him by the NKVD were partly true. At the end of the 1920s, he was in fact one of the leaders of the illegal Trotskyist youth group in the Soviet Union. Boris Sapir, the "last of the Menshevik mohicans", drew my attention to the emigré literature on the subject of Stalin, especially the estate of Nicolaevsky, located at Stanford. Sapir who was imprisoned on the Soviet death island because of his Social Democratic views at the beginning of the 1920s, dissolved the Menshevik party a good forty years later when one by one the last emigré comrades died. Sapir lived to see *perestroika*, but never truly believed in the Gorbachev type of openness. He warned me against nourishing illusions about "the human face of socialism". I heard the same warning from Abdurakhman Avtorkhanov, when we were sitting in his peaceful home near Munich. He was, however, possibly the best analyst at America's Russian-language Liberation (later Liberty) Radio during the years of the Cold War. Despite the fact that he was a militant anticommunist, he respected the "Jacobin" Dalin, whom he knew from Moscow's "Red professorate". He often sent messages through me to Sapir, whom, however, he considered a "flabby social democrat". All three of them encouraged me to write my book about the Stalin era.

Levon Saumyan, whose father died as a martyr in 1918 in the Baku Commune, also played a large role helping this book see the light of day. At the end of the 1960s, as a student of Budapest's Eötvös Loránd University, I had already visited his Moscow home several times, "following traces of the past". He gave me a thick notebook upon which he had written, "Stalin, as he was". Saumyan also told me colorful stories of Kremlin life. "Be careful, because a lot of it I don't remember properly anymore", he used to say, after our long conversations. When I later compared what I'd heard from him with documents dredged from the bottom of archives, I was surprised to see how good a memory, this elderly historian and editor of encyclopedias.

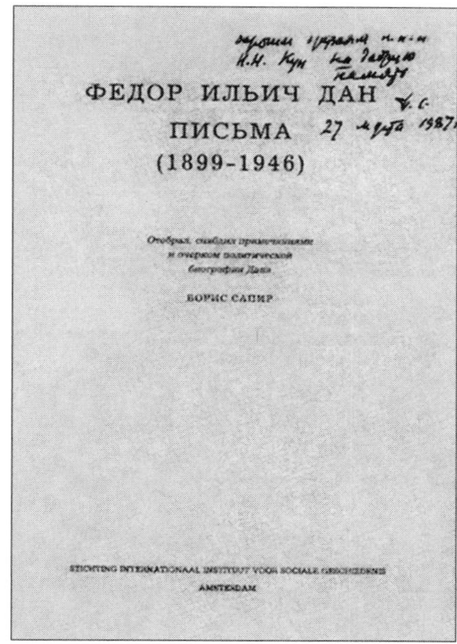

ФЕДОР ИЛЬИЧ ДАН
ПИСЬМА
(1899-1946)

БОРИС САПИР

Boris Sapir, the "last of the Menshevik mohicans" who was sent to the infamous Solovky death island at the beginning of the 1920s.

I am incredibly grateful to many friends and acquaintances, both at home and abroad, who have provided help with this book. I have been encouraged many anonymous people who have stopped me on the street to tell me how much they were looking forward to the book coming out. Among my colleagues abroad, most particularly I thank Maya Dvorkina, a librarian in Moscow, who generously put her half-century's experience with archives and libraries at my disposal. I am also grateful to the archives of Russia and the United States and to the historians in the Netherlands who are in charge of part of the Trotsky estate. I also include Jaap Kloosterman, the director of the International Institute of Social History in Amsterdam, who has helped me with my research for decades. Last but not least, I would like to thank the ever-accommodating Maciej Siekierski and Helen Danielson, archivists at Stanford's Hoover Institute; and Gábor Szényi, the former editor of *Magyar Nemzet*.

So after many years, the book that never ended was finally complete. To my great happiness, two publishing houses, Athenaeum 2000 Kiadó and PolgArt Kiadó, agreed to take part in publishing the Hungarian version of my book. I would also like to thank Krisztina Kós at CEU Press and Anna Benkő, the designer and type-setter of the book for their thorough work. Last, but certainly not least, I thank my wife, Ágnes Gereben, with whom I discussed the text from beginning to end, her comments about the last chapters of the book were particulary valuable—at that time she was working on her book, *Antisemitism in the Soviet Union*, so we could exchange ideas about these questions on a daily basis. They all, like me, breathed a sigh of relief that the work was over. Only my mother, Olga, wasn't happy about it: "Why can't you leave Stalin and his people alone? Even from beyond the grave he's capable of taking revenge!" This she said more than once. "And they weren't so different, those who got rid of them. They would have got kicked out of the Garden of Eden."

She truly has no reason to say a good word for the Soviet *nomenclatura*. Her father, an accomplished typographer, was put in prison by OGPU, the Soviet political police. This happened even though he, the descendent of Polish aristocrats and Byelorussian muzhiks, enthusiastically took part in overthrowing the "great white tsar," even earning, in March, 1917, a yellow medal with a woman in a Phrygian hat from the local Soviet. He was not an enemy of the new, post-November 1917 system, either, but found the work norms too high. Moreover, some leather-jacketed neighbor, who worked at the political police, had his eye on the apartment. So they put him in prison, where he was beaten to death. The family was only told that he had hanged himself in his cell. From this point until the Second World War, my grandmother lived in fear that she would be fired from her job as a humble administrator at the College of Architecture during the next period of "rationalization". When my mother grew up, she had to keep her father's fate shrouded in secrecy on countless forms and papers. She didn't even have a photograph of him. When I read her some of the letters of Molotov, Bukharin, Voroshilov, Kaganovich and Mikoyan, she sighed. "Real Stalinism was the things that happened to simple people without reprisals, not these people devouring each other in the Kremlin like scorpions." There is a lot of truth in this. Nevertheless, using these unknown documents, I have tried to expose the story of Stalin and his times in a way that my mother would also find interesting. While I was correcting the proofs of the English version of my book, my mother died at the age of eighty three after long suffering. This book is dedicated to her memory.

January 28, 2003, Budapest

Kun Miklós

PART I

PROLONGED YOUTH

"Stalin once alluded to his Siberian dog, Tishka, but he never referred to a mistress, a wife, or a friend in his early life."

EDWARD ELLIS SMITH

"I am not a European man but an Asian, a Russified Georgian."

JOSEPH STALIN

CHAPTER 1
The Childhood of Soso

In Soviet reference works and memoirs published before the early 1930s and dealing with the beginning of the twentieth century in Russia, the name of Joseph Stalin is scarcely mentioned.[1] Although this reflected the actual role of the politician, it still offended the former "Soso" or "Soselo" Dzhugashvili.* One of his fellow countrymen, Lavrenty Beria, the head of the Georgian party organization, realized the opportunity offered, in terms of his future career, by an improvement in this situation. He therefore ordered a vast team of historians and party workers to begin to map out Stalin's career prior to 1917. The work began with a thorough examination of the archives in the more important locations in the young Iosif Dzhugashvili's life. At the same time, all over Georgia and Azerbaijan they began to carry out oral history research in places where he had once lived.

For Beria, however, who even had problems with spelling, the management of this huge team proved too complex a task and he had the job carried out by some of the more erudite party workers in Tiflis (now Tbilisi). As a result, he was able to deliver a long speech summarizing the history of the Bolshevik Party organizations in Transcaucasia during the marathon session of the Tiflis party congress, held on July 21 and 22, 1935. In the speech, which *Pravda* published in several installments, Beria canonized once and for all Stalin's activities in Georgia and Azerbaijan. At the same time, he labeled the majority of the famous Bolshevik leaders from the Caucasus as "deviationists", Menshevik agents, Trotskyite traitors, and mischief-makers. In 1952 this same speech, which by this time had evolved into a thick volume, was reprinted for the ninth time.[2]

In parallel with this, research work into the earlier activities in Azerbaijan of the Master of the Kremlin was conducted in Baku by another favorite of Stalin, Mirzafar Bagirov, head of the Azerbaijani party organization. He shared his "findings" with the world for the first time at the Baku party congress, held on December 19 and 20, 1939 in honor of Joseph Stalin's sixtieth birthday.[3] Even today we still do not know for sure whether the former Soselo Dzhugashvili was aware of the enormous pile of documents concerning his youth that had been accumulated, by the late 1930s, by the new "Stalinologists". We can only surmise that an insignificant number of these documents actually made their way to his desk prior to the publication of the various books. While the dictator had previously been frustrated by his "obscurity", interestingly, by the end of the 1930s, he occasionally showed signs of dissatisfaction at the publication of such sources.

The young Soso in 1896.

This may be the reason why there is scarcely any trace of the documents collected by Beria and Bagirov in the pages of Stalin's official biography.[4] Initially, the dictator was not even willing to read the manuscript. In December 1939, when the first version of the"great work" had been completed, he wrote to the two authors, Mark Mitin and Pyotr Pospelov: "I have no time to read it. Send it to the Marx-Engels-Lenin Institute! J. St[alin]."[5] Later, however, he changed his mind. He thoroughly re-edited and extensively amended his own biography. His attitude was similar when it came to the publication of his Collected Works. From behind the scenes he encouraged the team of authors to be ready as soon as possible with the first volume. At the end of the 1930s, however, he talked dismissively about his own early writings. "It's not worth publishing. The article is of no significance", he wrote on February 3, 1932 with respect to a study he had written in 1908 on the national issue, to Ivan Tovstukha, who was in charge of Stalin research for many years. On November 27 the same year Stalin learned that some of his writings had been found from the period of illegality. He was asked whether he consented to their publication. Again he refused: "To Comrade Adoratsky [director of the Marx-Engels-Lenin Institute]. In my opinion the letters are of no special significance. Thus *it is not worth publishing them.* J[oseph] Stalin."[6]

Only a fraction of the material produced by the "Beria brigade" was published. Until today the most vivid details have remained in manuscript form. For example, it remained unknown for a long time how a railway conductor by the name of Mshviobadze smuggled Soso Dzhugashvili, then hiding from the police, from Batum to Tiflis. As the conductor recalled: "The representative of the illegal Batum Social Democratic organization committee appeared at the agreed time with a young man whom he addressed as Soso. I decided that I would dress him up as a conductor so that he would not arouse suspicion. I gave Soso the uniform and the hat to go with it. It was evening, so I gave him a lantern to hold as well. The night passed without incident. This is how I delivered Comrade Stalin [to the agreed place]."[7] The censors occasionally found less significant details unworthy of the dictator. However, it is hard to understand what it was they found to object to in the recollections of Sonya Todria (Simakova), the Russian wife of a Georgian Social Democrat: "Comrade Stalin was terribly thin. He had a swarthy complexion. The whiteness of his teeth made an immediate impression when one looked at him."[8] Any tentative suggestions of physical defect in the dictator—that is, the comment that one of his arms was slightly deformed, showed signs of paralysis, and was shorter than his left—were omitted from the recollections of Vera Shweitzer, one of Stalin's fellow exiles in Siberia: "Me and my husband, Suren Spandarian, paid a visit to Stalin. [...] He was wearing a jacket, but he had only one of his arms through the sleeve. Later I realized that he likes to dress in such a way that his right arm remains free."[9]

☆ On the basis of the folktale-like recollections of the childhood and youth of Joseph Stalin, a countless number of published sources, hagiographic biographies, long narrative poems, filmstrips and paintings were produced. The former acquaintances of the young Soselo tried to dig up even the smallest episodes from the depths of their memories. They even remembered how their young friends elected the future party General Secretary—allegedly an excellent swimmer, who could shoot with a catapult further than any of the others, who surpassed everyone else in drawing and singing, and who was witty and clever—to the role of "sultan" or "tsar" in the course of their childhood games.[10] They also recalled how the son of the poor cobbler was top of the class in the Church School in Gori and won the respect of both teachers and classmates.[11] There were also recollections of how cunningly, while adhering strictly to the rules of conspiracy, he created several illegal Marxist study circles at the same time within the old walls of the theological Seminary in Tiflis.[12] According to the legends, while attending the Seminary the young revolutionary even had time to train manual workers, working in the railway depots, as future barricade fighters.[13] Several former fellow students of his remembered how the teenage Soso had impressed the gray-haired editors of the Tiflis papers with his poems.[14]

There may well have been some truth in the latter stories; it was not easy for a teenager from the provinces to get his work published in the Georgian press of the time, and Soso, who began writing poetry in Gori, did indeed outdo his contemporaries in this respect. He was only seventeen when his lyrical poems, written in the tradition of classical Georgian poetry, appeared in print. Five of his poems were published in *Iveria,* a Georgian-language Tiflis daily, in 1895, without the permission of his priest teachers. In the following years one of his poems appeared in *Kvali,* a quality publication. "I lost my interest in writing poetry", he told Levon Shaumyan, "because it requires the whole of one's attention and a hell of a lot of patience. And in those days I was like quicksilver."

In later life Stalin occasionally felt a certain nostalgia for writing poetry. He made corrections to the Russian translation of the Georgian national epic, *The Knight in the Panther's Skin,* by the great Georgian poet Shota Rustaveli. During the Second World War he slightly re-edited the text of the new Soviet national anthem, which replaced the *Internationale.* One of the lines—the "unbreakable union of freeborn republics/Great Russia has welded forever to stand"—which displays how Russian chauvinism was becoming a state ideology, is his work. Towards the end of his life he wondered on several occasions whether or not his early poems should be translated into Russian. According to Semyon Lipkin, the doyen of Russian translators, in the second half of the 1940s, before the dictator's seventieth birthday, a few famous Russian poets and translators had already begun the work using literal drafts. However, someone from party headquarters very soon stopped the publication, which promised to be a sensation.[15]

Without speaking Georgian it is hard to judge whether the author of the poems, which appeared in the 1890s and which were signed "Soselo" or "I. Dzh-vili", abandoned poetry because he realized his own dilettantism, or because the Muses smiled on him only for a short while. Fact is that at the beginning of the century a few poems by Stalin had been included in anthologies. For example, the poem "Morning", which was published in *Iveria* in June 1895, was used in 1916 by Gogebashvili, the editor of a textbook for students, without mention of the author's name. Stalin's sentimental poem "To the Moon", which was also published in *Iveria* in November 1895, was quoted in full four years later by the famous Georgian literary historian Kalendzheridze, in his *Literary Theory*. Also in 1899 young Iosif Dzhugashvili's work on his favorite poet Prince Eristavi, which had appeared four years earlier, was included in the literary annual published in honor of the great contemporary Georgian poet.[16]

As Stalin grew older he recalled his memories of Georgia more and more often. For example, several months before the outbreak of the Second World War he had brought to him by airplane the former apprentice of his shoemaker father Beso, a man by the name of Data Gasitashvili, who was then almost eighty. Although Stalin kept the old man waiting for weeks in one of the government *dachas* near Moscow, he subsequently organized a real Georgian feast for him and revealed why he had been summoned: "Tell me, Data, is that enormous stone in Hidistavi, at the bend in the road that leads from Gori to Atheni, still there?"[17] If we are to believe Georgy "Bichigo" Egnatoshvili, the son of one of Stalin's childhood friends, who took part in the feast on 6 May 1940, the old man, who had long ago taken care of Soso as a child, responded to the question with the exclamation: "Your God be a dog! What a memory you have!" Stalin laughed at this and, twirling his mustache, "in a Gori accent corrected Data [in Georgian] 'Your Christ is a dog! Why do you curse my God?'" However, according to the recollection the elderly Data stood firm: "'Do you think that you are Stalin to me as you are to others?! To me, you are the same little boy I

This photograph of Mirzafar Bagirov and Lavrenty Beria was taken in the 1930s. After Stalin's death, both of them were executed. The bearded Filipp Makharadze, turning towards them, was a target of their attacks. It is a wonder that he died as an old man, of natural causes, in 1941.

held in my arms. And if you carry on, I'll pull your trousers down and spank your bottom until it's redder than your flag!' Stalin, however, just laughed."[18]

It is doubtless down to these sentimental bursts of nostalgia that Stalin, following the example of the old Georgian feudal lords who often bestowed gifts on their vassals, occasionally surprised his relatives and acquaintances in Georgia with smaller or larger sums of money, or with honors.[19] Discovered in his archive was a medium-sized envelope marked "To Misha Monoselidze from Soso", containing a letter written in Georgian: "Greetings to Misha! I received your letter. As to the scholarship, I have talked to the relevant people. I will let you know what happens. I have given five thousand rubles to Sasha *[Sashiko Svanidze, the wife of the addressee, who, as a result of Stalin's first marriage, was the dictator's sister-in-law—M. K.]*. For the moment this will be enough for both of you. I have no more money, otherwise I would send it. These are the fees I have received for my articles and speeches. In other words, there is nothing more. But this should remain between ourselves (you, me and Sasha). No one else should get to know about it, otherwise my other relatives and acquaintances will begin to pursue me and will never leave me alone. So this is how it must be. Misha! Live happily for a thousand years! Give my greetings to our friends! Your Soso. February 19, 1935. P. S. If you meet my mother, give her my greetings."[20]

As a rule, when Joseph Stalin visited his native land as General Secretary of the party he did not receive his old acquaintances except for a few occasions.[21] His childhood Georgian friends, however, despite their legendary pride, besieged their fellow countryman who was attempting to hide from them. They would sometimes ask his mother, who was living in Tiflis, to intervene on their behalf. On other occasions they inundated their "little Soso" with petitions and letters. Stalin even kept a few of the humble applications received on his visit to Tiflis in 1926. All of them were written in Georgian: "My brother Soso! I have learned from the newspaper that you have arrived in Tiflis. If it is possible please set aside a time and a place where we can meet. I would very much like to see you," appealed Oniashvili, the clerk of the local Elektrobank. Iosif Imedashvili, the editor of the Russian-language theater journal *Teatr i Zhizn* (Theater and Life), at first only sent his card to the place where his famous fellow countryman was staying, the palace of Count Vorontsov, the former governor in tsarist times. He may have thought that his namesake would remember him. Nevertheless, the next day he reminded Stalin of their previous encounters in a letter: "Greetings, my old friend, my brother Soso! Remember the old second-hand bookshop that stood opposite the Alexander Gardens. Think of [...] my bible in those days, Jules Renan's *Life of Christ*, which was then distributed illegally, and how my possessions were completely ransacked *[by the teachers in the Seminary —M. K.]* in an attempt to find it. But you were saved by Filo Laprashvili, who hid the book [in the Seminary] under the rector's pillow.[22] Remember the little bookshop, how we thought and whispered there about great, unanswerable questions. Remember the kind of Soselo you were. And then you will remember me!" Following this sentimental introduction Iosif (Soso) Imedashvili came to the point: "I don't want to bother you but [...] first of all I would like to meet with you in person. Secondly, I would like to talk to you about an important social, cultural issue. Please spare me five minutes. Your old friend, who will always respect you."

The other letters followed the same pattern. Iosif Lomouri, for example, who had studied together with Stalin in the Church School in Gori, wanted to move to Moscow and asked for the help of "Comrade Soso". Sandro Tsikhitatrishvili, also a former schoolmate of the dictator and the son of Stalin's godfather, had little confidence that he would be received by the Master of the Kremlin, thus after Stalin had arrived in Tiflis Tsikhitatrishvili asked his old friend in a telegraph to send him an answer to the local post office.

"I have been to the [Vorontsov] palace three times but I have never been admitted, although I was hoping that you would fulfill my request." This was how one of Stalin's Abkhazian colleagues in the Social Democratic movement turned to him with respectful circumlocutions. "[...] My name is Ivliam Shapatava, and in 1901 to 1902 I controlled and guarded the illegal printing press in my home. I hope you will answer my letter."[23] In the mid-1930s, however, after several people had written down their memories of the operation of the conspiratorial press in Batumi, according to the official version it was Stalin who had directed the illegal printing house *on his own*. The name of Shapatava was simply "forgotten" by those reminiscing.[24]

The majority of petitioners could be grateful that during the years of the Great Terror Stalin did not simply do away with them as eye-witnesses of his youth in Georgia. He had done just this in the case of several old Bolshevik Party members in Moscow and St. Petersburg, who, according to the reports of the NKVD and the political police, had done no more than shake their heads in disbelief on hearing the newly emerging legends regarding "Comrade Koba".[25] However, towards the end of his life Stalin was not always pleased on reading the recollections of his Georgian friends and their enthusiastic praise of him: "The *Recollections* contain many fabricated and completely inaccurate elements. They should not be published. J. St[alin]." Such was the angry comment that he wrote on the first page of the Russian-language pamphlet by Pyotr (Petre) Kapanadze, *Recollections of the Childhood and Youth of the Leader*. As to Kapanadze, we know that he died in 1947 and that he had been awarded the Order of Lenin and given the title of "Eminent Pedagogue".[26] Stalin refused to support Kapanadze's publication despite the fact that the author used to be regarded as an intimate member of the circle that surrounded the dictator—so much so that the subordinates of the General Secretary of the party always had to forward messages from him, whatever the circumstances. If they failed to do so, Stalin would not hesitate to show his anger. A telegraph sent on December 7, 1933 reads: "Express telegraph. To Pyotr Kapanadze, schoolmaster. I received your letter the day before yesterday with two months' delay. Your request is granted. Greetings, Stalin."[27]

In contrast, the official biography of the Soviet dictator contains one section in which the young seminarian, Dzhugashvili, some time at the end of the nineteenth century, exclaimed: "I must meet him at any cost!" This rare wish was expressed with respect to an author by the name of Tulin, one of whose studies had made great waves among leftist Russian economists at the end of the nineteenth century. However, the study reached only a limited audience since the tsarist censors had the economic-political volume pulped almost immediately after publication. Understanding this work on the peculiarities of Russian capitalism, dense with figures and Latin technical terms, required a great deal of expertise. This kind of reading matter, if it had come into his hands at all, would obviously have been indigestible for a young Georgian in the provinces. However, by means of this story Pyotr Kapanadze—or someone from Beria's circle who was guiding his pen—was aiming to suggest that Dzhugashvili, then attending an Orthodox Seminary, was already on the side of Tulin, who in fact was none other than the young Vladimir Ulyanov, later Lenin, in as early as the second half of the 1890s.[28]

☆ As a student, Joseph Stalin was himself a master of obscurantism. After a while, however, he began to fabricate stories for their own sake and without any logical reason. It remains unclear, for example, why he falsified the year and date of his birth. Fortunately, contemporary ecclesiastical documents have survived, according to which his mother Yekaterina (Keke) Geladze gave birth to her third son on December 6, 1878. Eleven days later, on December 17, Stalin's godfather, Father Mikhail Tsikhitatrishvili, an old friend of the family and a witness at the marriage of Beso Dzhugashvili, gave the biblical name Joseph to the baby in the presence of the Armenian-born archdeacon Khakhanov and sub-deacon Kvinikidze.[29]

By the time the young Soso had become a "red tsar" by the name of Stalin, the subjects of the Soviet Empire, and later the whole of "progressive mankind", were obliged to regard December 21, 1879 (December 9, according to the ancient Russian calendar) as his date of birth. It is a miracle that the Master, who on other occasions—with the help of Beria—preferred to make any sources unpleasant for him disappear, did not destroy those archive documents that contained his true date of birth.

Perhaps Stalin even found it amusing to think that, following in the footsteps of Raskolnikov in *Crime and Punishment*, he could grant himself anything he wanted. In the last third of the nineteenth century the Dostoevskyan principle of *vse dozvoleno*, "everything is permitted", had become deeply rooted among the Narodnik revolutionaries, and through them had found a place among the Social Democrats. However, it is also possible that for Soso Dzhugashvili—who had been humiliated by many for years, who had had to cope with the sarcastic remarks of his teachers and with harassment by the authorities, and who had later suffered as a result of the intellectual superiority of his own comrades—it was a way of avenging the past. Perhaps he wanted to "erase once and for all" certain unpleasant episodes of his past. The fact remains that before 1920—the year in which Joseph Stalin referred to 1878 as the year of his birth for the last time during an interview with the Swedish newspaper *Folkets Dagblad Politiken*—he himself had rarely set down on paper data linked to events in his life. In his youth this was done mainly by the tsarist police and investigating magistrates.

Gori was built on rolling hills and in charming valleys. The little Soso, however, lived in the poorest, dustiest neighborhood of the small town.

In such circumstances a particular mistake might be transferred from one file to another in the course of the years. In official documents—arrest warrants and police files—filled in on the basis of his confessions, completely different dates were entered each time as Iosif Dzhugashvili's date of birth, ranging between 1878 and 1882.

Other biographical data also changed over the years. On December 9, 1911, for example, when Stalin was giving his personal details for the completion of an official record that he personally signed, he declared himself to be a *peasant* in response to a question about his "social position". This was, at the very least, a half-truth. His father was, for a long time, a worker in the Adelkhanov brothers' factory in Tiflis, after which he became a deliveryman in Gori for the Armenian entrepreneur Baramov, who was related to the factory owners. He subsequently became an independent artisan in Gori.[30] However, in the meantime he remained a member of the peasant commune of his native village, Didi-Lilo, and never officially asked to be released from it. According to contemporary law, since his son Iosif had become marginalized as a result of ceasing his studies at the Seminary in Tiflis and had not taken up a profession later on, nor even paid taxes, the definition "peasant" remained valid for him, too—as late as February 1917—even though he had no connection at all with agriculture. In the same document he also declared himself to be thirty-one years old, even though he was two years older than this at the time.[31]

Almost a decade later, in a questionnaire handed out to delegates attending the national Ukrainian Communist party conference held between March 17 and 23, 1920, Stalin declared himself to be forty years old, that is, two years younger than his real age. On this occasion he entered his profession as "writer (publicist)".[32] In another document, a hospital data sheet dated March 26, 1921, the politician again gave a false date of birth to his surgeon, Dr. Nikolai Rosanov. Stalin, who had been admitted for a serious abdominal operation, gave his age as forty years old. This time he had cheated by almost three years.[33]

Not long after this Joseph Stalin created even greater confusion, falsifying even the day of his birth. The decisive moment was December 15, 1925: it was on this day that Ivan Tovstukha, his "scribe" at the time, presented him with a sheaf of biographical papers. Stalin looked through the typed pages and made certain corrections. It was after this that his new, official, date of birth became December 21, 1879.[34]

Nor is it clear how many brothers Soso Dzhugashvili had. This subject was taboo by default, and in Georgia any family acquaintances who might have remembered whether, in the 1870s, Yekaterina Geladze had given birth to three boys or four, have all died. Not even the Soviet dictator's mother was a reliable source of information, since as an old woman she would tell conflicting stories to her visitors. What is certain is that her first-born, Mikhail (Misho), who was born on February 14, 1875, was baptized on February 20, and died on the following day. Georgy (Glach), whom Keke named after her father, was born on December 24, 1876. The little boy was christened, relatively late by contemporary standards, on February 17, 1877. However, he died in the summer of that year, on June 19, 1877, in one of the measles epidemics that regularly decimated the children of Gori. Seven-month-old Georgy was buried on the following day.[35] Among the documents of the Gori Orthodox church no traces of other Dzhugashvili children remained. However, in the early 1950s authentic copies—thanks, among others, to Yelena Chakaya, a local historian—made their way into the special Stalin collection of the central Soviet party archives.[36]

The Master of the Kremlin knew, of course, that he had had older brothers who had died before he was born. However, he tried to keep quiet about the fact until the end of his life. He did, however, make a revealing comment showing how the loss of his brothers affected him on one occasion when, on July 29, 1924, he received a letter from a certain Blokhin[37], a member of Komsomol (the 'Communist Union of Youth') who lived in a village in the north of Russia. The young man asked him whether, following the contemporary trend for changing one's name, he might assume the name Stalin: "In the newspaper *Smena*, to which I subscribe, I read that you are the favorite disciple of Lenin. This made me really excited because I thought Lenin did not have a favorite disciple. [...] After Lenin died I wanted to assume his name instead of Blokhin, but I did not think I was worthy of it. Now I think I would like to ask for your name, that is, Stalin." Judging from the tone of his reply the General Secretary of the party was deeply moved: "I have no objection to you using the name Stalin. And I am very pleased at the idea. At least I will have a younger brother, since I have no brothers. I have never had one."[38]

☆ At least according to sources that have become public, Stalin had never spoken about the origin of his family. The true story of his name also remained obscure for a long time. Dzhugashvili means "son of Dzhuga". However, genealogists maintain that there is no such old Georgian name. In 1939 academician Dzhvakhishvili wrote an essay about the semantic origin of the name, which has remained unpublished. He suggested that Stalin's peasant ancestors might have originally been called Besoshvili and later they moved to the village called Dzhugaavi in Kahetia, whence the name Dzhugashvili.[39]

It has also been suggested that the family came from Southern Ossetia. According to this version Stalin's ancestors were Ossetian peasants, whence their original name Dzhogisvili ('son of the herd').[40] The first Dzhugashvili, who incidentally was called Iosif, was mentioned in sources first in 1819. This is the year when his son Vano—Stalin's grandfather—was born. Vano was also mentioned as Ivan or Mily in the documents. He had three children: Beso—Stalin's father, Georgy and Pelageya. We do not know anything about the latter, Stalin's aunt, whereas Georgy was allegedly killed by bandits.[41] For a long time the hard fate of

Keke Geladze, Stalin's mother was not known either. At sixteen, the girl, who was orphaned at a young age, was married off to Beso Dzhugashvili by mediation of a matchmaker. Her acquaintances held her much more refined than her husband, since she had learned to read before her marriage.[42]

Nor was Stalin keen to talk about his relationship with his parents at various stages in his life. When he was forced to, he tried to idealize the past. "Although they were unskilled people they did not treat me badly at all," he said on December 13, 1931 to Emil Ludwig, who besieged him with questions for hours in the Kremlin. The German journalist, who specialized in interviewing famous personalities, had asked whether Stalin had become a professional revolutionary in tsarist Russia because his parents had beaten him as a child.[43]

Ludwig, who knew the works of Sigmund Freud and his disciples by heart, was completely on target with his question. The recollections of Soso Dzhugashvili's childhood acquaintances reveal that the dictator had not been a well-balanced child. "He would express his satisfaction in the most peculiar way," wrote Pyotr Kapanadze. "If he was pleased about something he would snap his fingers, yell loudly, and jump around on one leg."[44] Soso had also had some quite traumatic experiences as a child. Once, for example, he and his friends had witnessed a hanging. The little Soselo was not aware, of course, that standing in the crowd near him, watching the death throes of the two condemned thieves, was Maksim Gorky, who reported on the event to the Russian daily papers. On another occasion, on January 6 (a holiday in the Georgian Orthodox Church to commemorate the baptism of Jesus in the River Jordan) a carriage accidentally drove into the crowd. The Seminary students who were standing behind the military cordon

Stalin could be grateful, above all, to his mother, Keke, for becoming a "learned" man.

This picture of the dictator's birthplace became known to the public in the 1930s.

Later, on the site of the desolate hut, a lavish museum was built.

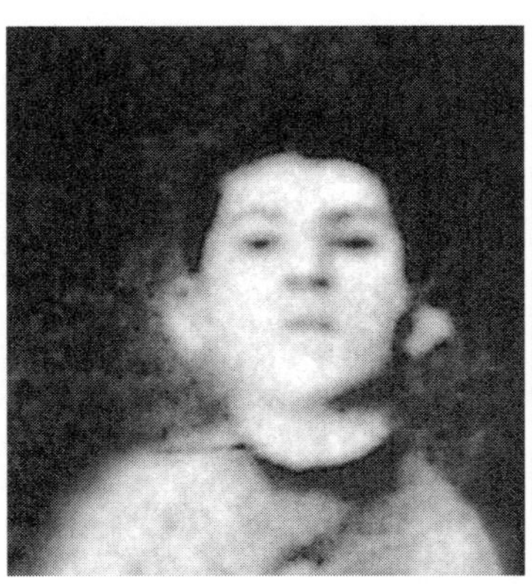

Soso, who started his schools later than most of his peers, was one of the smallest children of his class.

began to move backwards and then ran away. Only Iosif was not scared by the wild horses. He tried to run in front of the carriage, but slipped and fell. He was confined to bed for two weeks as a result.[45] This accident traumatized him for a long time. "In the presence of children he spoke a great deal about his childhood. As he said, he was sensitive and cried a lot. He had had a terrible childhood", was the comment made later by the armed guard, named Merzlyakov, who had charge of him during the First World War, while he was in exile in Siberia.[46]

According to acquaintances of the young schoolboy, Soso would often pick up a book and become engrossed in it entirely, after which he would become once again "like quicksilver". When in a fight, if he really lost his temper he could be merciless. "He knew such painful holds that he always overcame his opponents", revealed Vano Kechoveli, the brother of Lado Kechoveli, a well-known Georgian Social Democrat, in his recollections of Stalin that he began writing in 1934.[47]

In terms of psychology, the blame for Stalin's sudden and dramatic changes of mood between depression and euphoria in adulthood would lie with the use of "slapping as a pedagogical device", as used by an ambitious mother who surrendered everything for the career of her son. Keke was indeed easily provoked to slap her son. Furthermore, the slightly built boy was beaten by his father as well, when he was at home. On the other hand, Iosif revolted very early and very passionately against his environment. "He was a stubborn little boy," remembered Masho Abramidze, Soso's wet-nurse. "When his mother called him and he didn't feel like responding, he didn't stop playing."[48] "Indeed, little Soso misbehaved a lot as a child. He liked to shoot with arrows that he had made. And to use a catapult. He caused his mother a great deal of sorrow as a result," recalled Georgy Elisabedashvili, later a witness at Stalin's wedding, in his mostly unpublished memoirs.[49] This reference to the politician's excessive behavior and his wild and nervous disposition in his youth was left out of the published version of the recollections.[50]

Later, by way of a cautionary tale, Joseph Stalin told his own children that his parents used to beat him.[51] Svetlana Alliluyeva heard from someone else as well that his father "used to fight as a child and often misbehaved. Once he threw a brick into the fireplace through the chimney, which frightened the people there, who burned themselves. "Evidently Soso was beaten cruelly for this. On the other hand, the story that the boy, who loved his mother dearly, protected her from his father by "throwing a knife at him,"[52] should be rather considered a family myth. Stalin talked emotionally to his ideologically committed French biographer, Henri Barbusse, about his father, the good old Beso, and how keen he had been that his only son should go on to receive further education. Under the pen of the world-renowned French writer—or perhaps thanks to Alfred Kurella, the émigré German Communist who collected material for Barbusse for his biography of Stalin and, at the same time, "selected" it—quite a sweet story emerged: "[Vissarion] was a poor, uneducated, honest, and good man. He sent Stalin to the school in Gori […] then to the Seminary in Tiflis. That is, he really did do everything that he could for his son with the means at his disposal."[53]

In contrast to this quotation from Barbusse, it is worth taking note of seventeen-year-old Soso Dzhugashvili's petition, written in ornate handwriting: "To Archimandrite Serafim, the Very Reverend Rector of the Tiflis Orthodox Seminary. From the second-grade student of the said Seminary, Iosif Dzhugashvili. Request. Your Reverence knows all about the pitiful circumstances of my mother, who takes care for me. My father has not provided for me for three years. This is his way of punishing me for continuing my studies against his wishes. […] It is for this reason that I am applying to Your Reverence for the second time. I beg you on my knees to help me. August 25, 1895. Iosif Dzhugashvili, supplicant."[54]

The unschooled Beso had already been outraged by the fact that his wife, in his absence and without his consent, had enrolled their son in the "elite school of Gori", the Russian-language four-grade (in reality seven-grade) Church School, even though he was too old. Due to a long-term childhood illness and complications, Soso began his elementary schooling at the age of eight and a half. Besides, his wife's initiative wounded Beso's pride by creating the opportunity for the young Soso to become a man of the clergy, and thereby to break away from his background and rise above his father.

☆ The Russian-language Church School in Gori comprised four basic and three preliminary grades, "lower", "medium", and "upper". Georgian children learned Russian in the upper classes. However, there were more diligent pupils who contracted their preliminary classes. Soso Dzhugashvili appears to have been among them. However, due to his serious illness he was obliged to miss one year of school. What he had gained by amalgamating the classes he lost through illness. Thus he was already sixteen and a half years old by the time he finished his studies at the Gori Church School, which defined his social connections in subsequent years.

A report which appeared in March 1891 about the Gori Church School reveals that its staff consisted of surprisingly well trained pedagogues. There were many Russians among them, who had university or ecclesiastical Seminary education. The Russian, church Slav, and Greek languages played an important role in the curriculum. Unlike in similar Russian Church Schools, modern languages and Latin were not taught in Gori. Interestingly, in the Orthodox

Seminary in Tiflis these subjects were also absent, although the institution, in terms of status, was a crossover between a secondary school and a college. Joseph Stalin suffered from this omission throughout his life. As revealed by his school report card of June 1891, Soselo negotiated the obstacles well. Despite this, he unexpectedly found himself in difficulties. He was expelled from the Church School in Gori[55] since his family had "failed to pay the money that would entitle him to continue his studies."[56] Soon, however, an acquaintance—perhaps their wealthy neighbor, the wine grower Yakov Egnatoshvili—was found to come to the rescue of the Dzhugashvili family. Soso's school report of June 1892, written by the Exarch *[the head of the Georgian church—M. K.]*, mentions him as an outstanding pupil among those entering the third grade. The priest teachers on the school board voted to grant him a scholarship of three rubles a month and to exempt him from the obligation to pay school fees.[57] As known from other sources, in summer 1893, Soselo completed his exams at the end of the school-year with excellent results. Then, in July, the following year, the staff of the Church School in Gori unanimously recommended continuation of his studies at the Orthodox Seminary in Tiflis.[58]

At that time, Soso had an important ally at the Gori Church School, in the person of his own mother. Yekaterina Geladze, who was willing to do anything to provide for the further education of her son, had taken a job as a cleaner at the school for ten rubles a month. This can have done little to raise Soso's social prestige since, in this patriarchal semi-rural context, a Georgian woman doing menial work among strange men was regarded as living on the threshold of immorality. However, the Dzhugashvili family had to live on something. Beso was reputed to have drunk away his meager wages more and more frequently as the years passed. Nothing was left of Keke's income, earned by embroidering, ironing, cleaning, and taking in washing from the neighbors from dawn to dusk, once they had paid the owner, an Ossetian artisan, the rent on their small, damp ground-floor apartment and bought food.[59]

Vissarion, who had failed, in the eyes of his wife, as the head of the family, was annoyed that Iosif's childhood had gone on for too long. According to the recollections of Masho Abramidze, a neighbor of the Dzhugashvili couple, "Soso was attending the second grade when Beso began saying that he would remove him from the Church School and take him to Tiflis to learn his trade. My husband and Yakov Egnatoshvili *[another neighbor, the main supporter of Iosif and, according to the allegations of some, Yekaterina's lover—M. K.]* explained to him in vain the pointlessness of what he was intending to do. He, however, remained adamant..."[60] Another neighbor, Semyon Goglichidze, remembered the quarrel that could be heard from behind the closed doors of the Dzhugashvili apartment: "'Do you want my son to become a metropolitan?! Over my dead body! I'm a shoemaker, and my son will be one too. He will have to be, and that's that', yelled Vissarion at his wife. Although her husband worked and lived in Tiflis [...], Keke was permanently afraid: 'What if Vissarion turns up again one day?!' she said. 'He will take the boy and tear him away from his studies for good.'"[61]

Her maternal fears were soon realized. Beso did indeed drag his son by force to Tiflis, in order to "mold him into a working man" in the workshop of Adelkhanov, an Armenian tradesman. The eleven-year-old boy, who on the previous day had been a brilliant pupil and one of the acknowledged leaders of the student community in Gori's most prestigious educational institutions, was bound to feel that his wicked father had made his life hell. The Adelkhanov factory, which specialized in processing raw leather, was one of the filthiest factories in

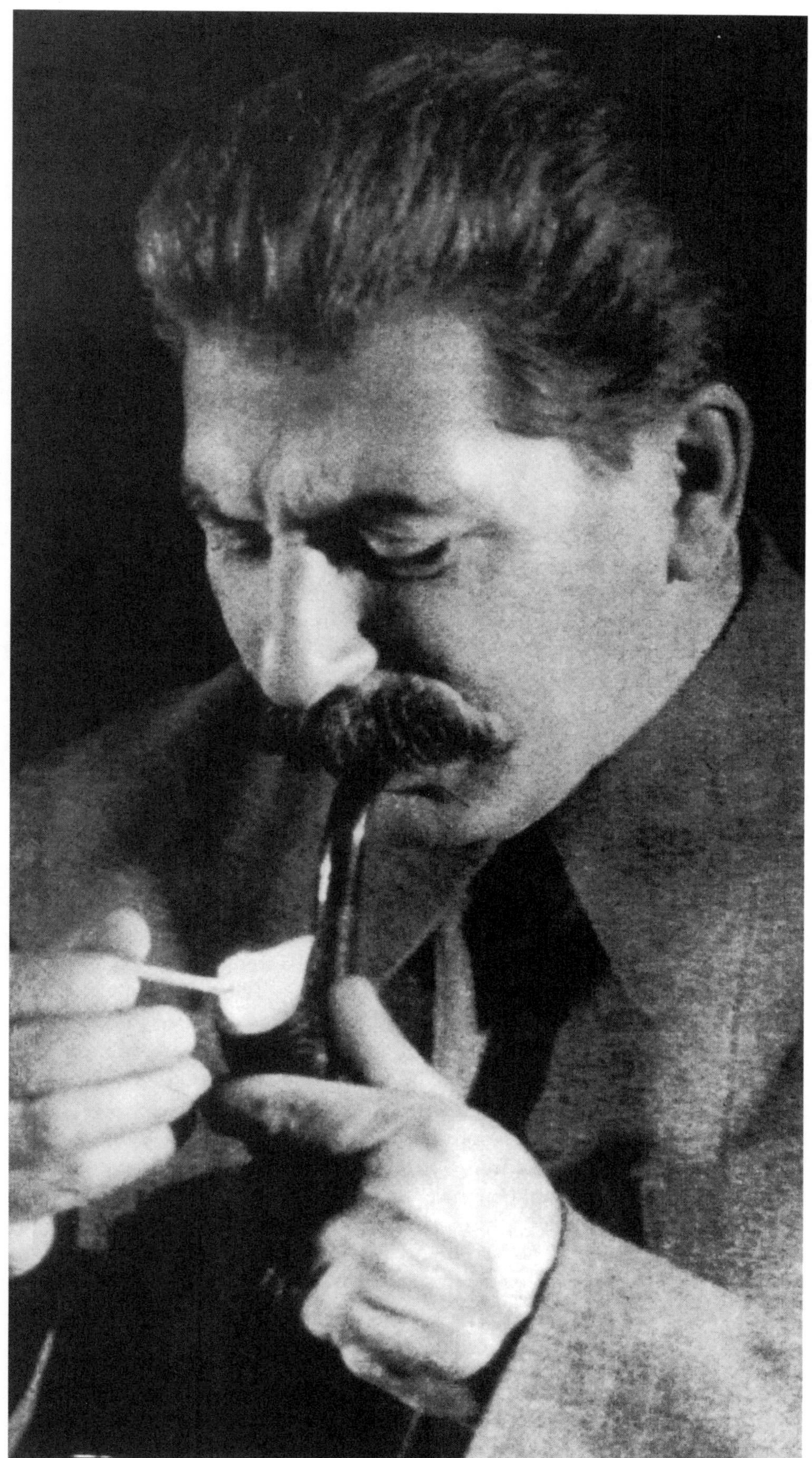

"Our Leader is the very image of his father."

Tiflis, and all the workshops reeked appallingly. The employees would often arrive at work drunk and were cruel to their younger colleagues, who then in turn relieved their anger on the youngest of all, Soso Dzhugashvili, who was at everyone's beck and call, carrying the rope for the baling and obeying the orders of the older workers.[62]

Beso Dzhugashvili, who was generally known as being foul-mouthed and bad-tempered, must have been happy to get Soso away from his mother. But the stubborn and vain Keke refused to accept defeat. With great determination she traveled to Tiflis where, according to Goglichidze, she turned to one of the entourage of the head of the church in Georgia for help against her husband. Eventually, one of the church dignitaries must have forced Beso to let the boy go back to Gori. Goglichidze's recollections, apparently a more reliable source than the other villagers, state that "the entourage of the exarch even offered Stalin's mother to find a place for the boy in the choir of the cathedral in Tiflis. She, however, would not even hear of the possibility, and returned with her son to Gori as soon as she could..."[63]

Keke Geladze was unable talk calmly about this episode, even as an old woman. "My son was an excellent student, but his father, the late Vissarion, decided to take him out of school and have him trained as a shoemaker. I resisted as far as I could. There was a continuing feud between us," she poured out to the journalist who visited her in October 1935, and who published what was said word for word in *Pravda*.[64] According to Levon Shaumyan, who was well acquainted with the leading staff members at the central party daily at the time, on reading the article Stalin harshly reprimanded Lev Mekhlis, the editor in chief. (At around the same time he berated Nikolai Bukharin, the editor in chief of *Izvestia,* for daring to mention his childhood name Soso in the pages of the paper.[65])

This, despite the fact that Keke had idealized the truth in the interview. She had omitted to mention the fact that, soon after these events, Vissarion Dzhugashvili, who had been humiliated in front of his acquaintances, finally left his family. In around 1892 he left the Adelkhanov factory and for a short while made a living doing casual work. He then traveled to Tiflis, where he opened a small shoe-mending workshop in the Armenian bazaar. Later, his situation became so bad that he took to begging in the bars on the outskirts of the city. On other occasions he took to the road and traveled through half of Georgia to squeeze money out of his acquaintances, old and new. This, at least, is the story told to Abdurahman Avtorkhanov about Beso by the old Georgian Menshevik emigrants whom the Chechen political scientist found still living after the Second World War when collecting data for his book on Stalin, a work which remained unfinished.[66]

The local tsarist authorities were probably soon aware of the conflict in the Dzhugashvili family. In the early 1900s the police often had occasion to harass Keke on account of her son. However, we know of no attempts to question "the drunkard Vissarion", as he was referred to by his friends. One member of the Baku gendarmerie, on May 23, 1908, wrote: "Vissarion Ivanov [that is, the son of Vano], shoemaker, lives in the city of Tiflis, and his wife, who is separated from him, lives in Gori."[67]

On February 27, 1909, in Solvychegodsk, northern Russia, where Stalin spent his time in exile, the police recorded that the Bolshevik politician "has a father, Vissarion Ivanov, aged fifty-five, and a mother, Yekaterina Klarovna *[in reality Glakhovna—M. K.]*, aged forty-five." However, there was never any talk of needing to trace Beso. On August 19 another police report, the authentic copy

Pablo Picasso saw the Georgian peasant in Stalin, his one-time idol. The drawing stirred up a scandal in the Kremlin because the Soviet politicans took it for a caricature.

of which has been preserved in the archives of the Hoover Institute in Stanford, characterized Beso as follows: "Vissarion Ivanovich lives as a vagrant."[68] A gendarmerie report dated November 16, 1911 in St. Petersburg stated that Stalin's father was no longer alive: "He is dead. His mother [that is, Stalin's mother] lives in the town of Gori." A warrant signed by the chief of police in Vologda on March 1, 1912 contains a similar reference: "His father is no longer alive. His mother is fifty-five years old and lives in Gori." Finally, on a document dated May 4, 1912, held in the archives of the St. Petersburg secret police, appears the real date of the death of Vissarion Dzhugashvili: 1909.[69]

The writings of Russian authors, including the official Stalin biography massively amended by the Master of the Kremlin himself, were usually vague about the date of Beso's death. The American author Robert C. Tucker, relying on the recollections of Georgian emigrants, also accepts the year 1890. In the Russian version of his book, which appeared based on archival research he carried out in Moscow, he says: "We know for certain that Beso was a stubborn and hot-headed character, who was very fond of drink. He eventually died in a pub brawl."[70] In her first book to appear in the West, Svetlana Alliluyeva gave very few details about the circumstances of the death of her paternal grandfather. Even the details she did give were inaccurate: "[...] He died in the course of a drunken brawl. He was stabbed."[71]

In Moscow in the mid-1990s, when browsing through the never-ending sea of Stalin documents, I came across a note of a few lines on a funeral that took place at the Orthodox chapel of St. Michael's Hospital in Tiflis. This document corresponds with the spoken testimony of Yagor Neladze, an old shoemaker, dating from the mid-1930s. (It was Neladze who had closed Beso's eyes.)

According to two corresponding sources Beso Dzhugashvili died on August 12, 1909 of cirrhosis of the liver, a disease common among alcoholics, in a hospice for the poor. He was buried two days later. This same date is mentioned in Yelena Chakaya's unpublished note, dated January 28, 1951. Her father, Mikhail Iluridze, was a young teacher at the Gori Church School in the 1890s. According to his former pupils he had a deep-rooted hatred for the little Soso. Despite this, from 1935 his ambitious daughter undertook a study of the sources relating to Stalin's childhood. In the course of her research she managed to reconstruct the story of Beso, who had died far from his family. Furthermore, she handed over some very important documents to the "Beria brigade" on the sufferings of Iosif Dzhugashvili. According to her, the young man was expelled from the Seminary in Tiflis for not paying his school fees and, apparently, for not sitting the necessary exams. Her facts, however, are so different from the official image of the Dzhugashvili family that Beria preferred quietly to forget about them, although formerly he had encouraged Yelena to collect as much previously unknown biographical data regarding the Great Compatriot as possible.[72]

On around the sixtieth birthday of Joseph Stalin the Tiflis party historians allegedly sent him a telegraph in which they promised that in the course of their "Stakhanovist" research *[Stakhanovism, named after Aleksei Stakhanov, a coal miner whose team had increased its output by a more efficient division of labor, was a method used in the Soviet Union for increasing production by rewarding individual initiative.—Trans.]* they would trace the life of his father. In response, they received an angry message telling them to leave the old man to rest in peace.[73] One reason was perhaps that the dictator did not want to bring Beso into the limelight, since in the meantime his similarity to his father had become more and more apparent. According to David Papitashvili, who had clear memories of Gori at the end of the century: "Vissarion, the father of the Leader [...] was a thin man, taller than average. He had a long face and a long nose and neck. He wore a mustache and beard, and his hair was jet-black. As I recall he did not have a single gray hair." In his largely unpublished recollections Papitashvili continues: "In the course of my many years of scientific and medical activity, and based on my observations, I have come to the conclusion that eighty per cent of children resemble their mothers in outward appearance. Our Leader, however, is the very image of his father, the only difference being that in the course of the years Comrade Soso has noticeably begun to gain weight. This fact also suggests that physical changes are not only inherited but are dependent on other factors."[74]

* We use the name Iosif Dzhugashvili when when referring to the main character of the book before 1910. After that the name Joseph Stalin is used to refer to the same person.

1 Trotsky, 1985, I. 55–56, 107, 175.
2 Beria, 1952, 3–7, 20, 23–27, 35–36, 43–44, 63–64, 80–83, 98–111, 123, 150–151,168–181, 219–220. On the role an educated party functionary, a certain Bedia played in the compilation of the Beria book, see Knight, 1993, 57–64.
3 Bagirov, 1948, 36–38, 70–80, 88–95, 103–122, 132–142, 193–200, 202–213.
4 Iosif Vissarionovich Stalin, 1951, 5, 8–11, 15–20.
5 *RGASPI (Russian National Archive for Social and Political History)*, fond. 558, op. 1, d. 43. The book, which ran two-and-a-half printed sheets, was nevertheless published at that time. The revised and enlarged version of 1951 expanded to 15 printed sheets. Zhukov, 2000, 95.
6 *RGASPI*, fond. 558, op. 1, d. 3045.
7 *RGASPI*, fond. 558, op. 1, d. 655.
8 *RGASPI*, fond. 558, op. 1, d. 647.
9 *RGASPI*, fond. 17, op. 1, d. 647.
10 *Molodaya Gvardia*, 1939, no. 12, 29–33.
11 *Rasskazi starikh rabochikh*, 1937, 13–14, 34.
12 Beria, 1952, 22–24.
13 *Rasskazi starikh rabochikh*, 1937, 42, 47–49.
14 *Molodaya Gvardia*, 1939, no. 12, 43, 69–70.
15 One of the biographers claims that these poems played an important role in making Stalin a "cultured person". See Payne, 1965, 45, 52. Another resarcher argues that it is not even sure Stalin himself was the author of these oft-mentioned poems. Smith, 1967, 38–44.
16 *RGASPI*, fond. 558, op. 1, d. 647.
17 Loginov, 1999, 14.
18 *Ibid.*, 14–15.
19 *RGASPI*, fond. 558, op. 2, d. 190.
20 *RGASPI*, fond. 558, op. 1, d. 5099.
21 The former seminarist, Feofan Gogiberidze was one of the exceptions. In September 1928, he learned that Stalin spends his vacation in the Black Sea resort of Sochi, and somehow found a way to see him. "Among other things, I asked him why [the daily *Pravda*] did not publish my memories [of him]. Stalin responded that he had not even received the article. Then he added that I should send it again, and it will be published," reads Gogiberidze's letter, which he sent to the editors of *Pravda. RGASPI*, fond. 558, op. 1, d. 665.
22 This incident appeared in the later writings on Stalin in a different form: as if he himself owned the banned Renan book, and he lent it to his friends in the Seminary.
23 All cited letters can be found in *RGASPI*, fond. 558, op. 4, d. 676.
24 *Rasskazi starikh rabochikh*, 1937, 114–126.
25 Trotsky, 1985, I. 104, 209, 240, 301.
26 *RGASPI*, fond. 558, op. 1, d. 5378.
27 *Ibid.*
28 Iosif Vissarionovich Stalin, 1951, 8. Soso's another classmate, Pankhadze, in the Seminary proved to be even more imaginative. He claimed to had "directly encountered the works of Marx, Engels, and Lenin" in the company of Iosif Dzhugashvili in the second half of the 1890s. Yaroslavsky, 1939, 9.
29 *RGASPI*, fond. 71, op. 10, d. 275.
30 An elderly resident in Gori, Gasitashvili recalled that at the turn of the 1860s and 70s, a certain Iosif Baramov (Baramyants) was entrusted by the Gori garrison to make footwear for the soldiers. Later he invited twenty-five shoemakers into town to work for him, including Beso Dzhugashvili.
31 *RGASPI*, fond. 558, op. 1, d. 4353.
32 *RGASPI*, fond. 558, op. 1, d. 675.
33 *RGASPI*, fond. 558, op. 1, d. 675.
34 Tovstukha, who had prepared to write Stalin's biography for years, did not prove to be an accurate philologist on other occasions either. During the mid-twenties, he wrote the lexicon entry that contained numerous errors in the introduction of the future dictator to the readers of the biographical lexicon published by the Granat Brothers Publishing House. Dyeyateli SSSR, 1989, 110–114.
35 *RGASPI*, fond. 71, op. 10, d. 275.
36 *RGASPI*, fond. 71, op. 10, d. 275.
37 "Talking name", it means "the one full of fleas".
38 *Istochnik*, 1996, no. 2, 156–158.
39 *Geneaologichesky Zhurnal*, 2001, no. 1, 39.
40 *Ibid.*, 40. For a list of literature that argues for Stalin's Ossetian origin on his father's side, see Torchinov-Leontyuk, 2000, 181–183. Other studies have more recently argued for Stalin' Armenian origin, but without sufficient proof. See Ayvazian, 2000, 623-625.
41 *Molodaya Gvardia*, 1939, no. 12, 24.
42 *Geneaologichesky Zhurnal*, 2001, no. 1, 45.

43 Stalin, 1951, XIII, 113.
44 *RGASPI*, fond. 558, op. 4, d. 665.
45 *RGASPI*, fond. 558, op. 4, d. 662.
46 *Molodaya Gvardia*, 1939, 12, 37.
47 *RGASPI*, fond. 558, op. 4, d. 665.
48 *RGASPI*, fond. 558, op. 4, d. 665.
49 *RGASPI*, fond. 558, op. 4, d. 665.
50 *Rasskazi starikh rabochikh*, 1937, 31–33.
51 Alliluyeva, 1981, 145.
52 Alliluyeva, 1970, 313.
53 Barbusse, 1936, 16. The book, which was originally published in French in 1935, soon became an efficient tool of the Soviet propaganda machinery: it was released in three Russian editions in 1936 and two more in 1937, each time in significant number of copies. Soon, however, it was put on the list of indexed books. In the years of the Great Terror, most of the members of Stalin's inner circle—the "chorus" around the "ancient Hero", as Barbusse depicted him for his friends from Moscow —disappeared from politics and perished in the executions.
54 *RGASPI*, fond. 558, op. 1, d. 4325.
55 *RGASPI*, fond. 71, op. 10, d. 275.
56 *RGASPI*, fond. 558, op. 4, d. 665.
57 In the ecclesiastical schools laymen and former seminarists also taught but they had a somewhat inferior role compared to the priest teachers.
58 *RGASPI*, fond. 71, op. 10, d. 275.
59 Trotsky, 1985, I. 26–27.
60 *Molodaya Gvardia*, 1939, no. 12, 43–44.
61 *Ibid.*, 44.
62 *Ibid.*, 44–45.
63 *Ibid.*, 45.
64 *Pravda*, October 27, 1935.
65 Larina, 1989, 32–33.
66 Some details of the book, however, were eventually published. See Avtorkhanov, 1959, 216–228; Avtorkhanov, 1973, I, 124–125, 164–205; Avtorkhanov, 1976, 82–95, 204–211, 230–252, 282–302, 459–485, 549–560.
67 *RGASPI*, fond. 71, op. 10, d. 275.
68 Smith, 1967, 28–29.
69 *Ibid.*
70 Tucker, 1991, 76, 78.
71 Alliluyeva, 1981, 145.
72 *RGASPI*, fond. 71, op. 10, d. 275.
73 A subconscious attachment to his violent father may explain one of Iosif Dzhugashvili's pseudonyms: Besoshvili, or "Beso's son".
74 *RGASPI*, fond. 558, op. 4, d. 665.

CHAPTER 2
Why Soso Dzhugashvili Dropped out of the Seminary

Tiflis, later Tbilisi, the seat of the Caucasian military province from the beginning of the nineteenth century, was Russia's most important gateway to Anatolia and the Near East. Its role as the capital of historical Georgia was no less significant, although the number of Georgian residents of the ancient settlement was eventually surpassed by its Armenian and Russian immigrants. The metropolis with its population of 160,000 according to the census of 1897 was home to many officials, army officers, traders, and artisans, but relatively few intellectuals. This was mostly due to the fact that Tiflis had never had a university. This role was fulfilled by the Theological Seminary, run by the Georgian Orthodox Church, where teaching was carried out mainly in the Russian language. The six-grade Seminary, which was attended by several hundred students at the end of the nineteenth century, also functioned as a teacher-training college. The students at this stronghold of Russification were the sons of Georgian and Russian Orthodox popes, and sometimes the sons of impoverished Georgian noble families.[1] Later, the children of middle-class citizens and artisans, and even the sons of rich peasant families, applied in increasing numbers. Many of them regarded the Seminary as a springboard and did not have the least intention of being ordained into the priesthood following their final exams in the sixth grade. This was naturally a source of irritation to the priests at the head of the exarchate, who found it embarrassing that so many graduates turned their backs on the church in spite of the expensive education they had received. In the early twentieth century certain Orthodox theologians also recognized that the tuition provided was of poor quality. Russification was so pronounced that in around 1905 the Seminary had virtually no Georgian Orthodox students.[2]

The internal problems faced by the institution are well illustrated by the fact that between 1874 and 1878 a total of eighty-three students were expelled on the grounds of "unreliability". Some of them joined the Russian Narodnik movement; others continued their studies abroad. A number of small, conspiratorial study circles existed within the Seminary itself. In the 1880s and 1890s, before Soso Dzhugashvili had moved to Tiflis, several disturbances occurred among the students. These mostly took the form of demonstrations against the poor living conditions and against the cruel, military-style behavior of the teachers. Many of the students also protested against the dominance of the Russian language, demanding the establishment of a department of Georgian language and literature. In 1885, in this troubled atmosphere, one of the student leaders, Silvestr (Silva) Dzhibladze, who was later one of the young Stalin's mentors in the Social Democratic movement, physically attacked the rector, Chudetsky. The following year another student, Lagiashvili, attacked one of the widely unpopular teachers with a dagger. As a result the police closed the institution for a while and several subversives were expelled from the Seminary. However, the position of the institution had been stabilized by the time the future Soviet dictator was accepted at the Orthodox Seminary. At the same time, admission to the Seminary became increasingly difficult, especially for those who did not belong to the church "caste".[3]

Iosif Dzhugashvili was a typical "outsider" when, in the summer of 1894, he traveled to Tiflis accompanied by his mother and successfully sat the entrance exam covering eight subjects. However, in this same year a high number of sons of Orthodox popes also applied for places, thus Soso's admission looked uncertain. He had every reason to believe that he would be exempt from the payment of tuition fees, as he had been in Gori. His application was heard at the beginning of the academic year, but the rector of the Seminary granted him exemption from only half the tuition fees, which were to be paid by the Georgian Treasury.[4] In the mid-1930s one of his childhood friends, Dormidont Gogokhia, remembered this as the reason why the young Soso Dzhugashvili had dropped out of the Seminary at the very beginning of his studies.[5]

His mother came to his aid. She knew some of the teachers at the Tiflis Seminary through her connection with the Church School in Gori, and she appealed to them on behalf of her son.[6] According to Soso's fellow student Parkadze, another benefactor also spoke up for Dzhugashvili: "This was Fyodor Dzhordania, the historian and archaeologist", recalled the former Seminary student, who eventually became the director of the Tiflis Revolutionary Museum. "He knew from [Stalin's] teachers and his dentist Sologov that Soso was a talented student."[7] Thanks to this intervention the young Iosif was able to take up his place for five years in the four-storey building, where every dormitory was home to twenty to thirty students.

The dormitory was initially something of a shock to the young man: "We led monotonous and uneventful lives in the Seminary," wrote Gogokhia decades later. "We woke at six in the morning. First there was prayer time, then we were given some tea. When the bell rang we made our way to the classrooms. The student monitor read a prayer and then the lessons began. We had lunch at three o'clock and afterwards were sometimes allowed to go into the town. At five o'clock an attendance register was called, and once this had been done students required special permission if they wished to leave the building."[8]

Later on evening prayer was introduced at the Seminary, the reading of secular newspapers[9] was banned, and it was forbidden to attend theater performances. At eight o'clock in the evening the students were given tea, after which they studied in their classrooms. According to Glurdzhidze, another former seminarian, unless they had been given leave of absence the students devoted their Saturdays and Sundays to prayer and liturgical song in the Seminary church. At night the supervisors made random checks on the teenage students to ensure that they were not indulging in "self-pollution" or reading in secret by candlelight. On other occasions the supervisors searched the wooden boxes next to the beds for secular publications. "At ten o'clock it was lights out, as if we were walled inside rock. We felt like prisoners," burst out the Megrail Gogokhia.[10]

Compared to his years at the school in Gori this was doubtless an enormous change for Soso, who even at a young age was unable to bear being shut in anywhere. According to the recollections of his schoolmates, in Gori he would spend hours out of doors. When, in late October 1894, he traveled home for the first time since beginning his studies at the Seminary, according to David Papitashvili he did nothing but "slander conditions at the Seminary and talk disparagingly about the hypocritical behavior and despicable lifestyle of the priests."[11] Nevertheless, at the beginning of his studies in Tiflis he still took seriously his mother's strict admonitions. And no matter how full of hostility he was, during the first two years he obviously made attempts to fit in. That is why the petitions addressed by him to his superiors were so humble in tone. "Tiflis Theological Seminary. To the Most Reverend Archemandrite Seraphim, Rector and Father,[12] the humble petition of the first-grade student of the Seminary above mentioned, Iosif Dzhugashvili. Having completed my studies at the Gori Church School as the best student, with the permission of Your Reverence I presumed to take the entrance examination for the Tiflis Theological Seminary even though I do not have the money to continue my studies. I was fortunate to be successful in this examination and was admitted among the students of the Theological Seminary. However, since my parents are unable to provide for me in Tiflis I am appealing with great humility to Your Reverence to admit me among those students who have half their tuition fees paid for them. I presume to mention here that throughout my studies at the Gori Church School I received assistance from the school funds. Iosif Dzhugashvili, first-grade student at the Tiflis Theological Seminary. October 1894."[13]

This is how the seminarist Iosif Dzhugashvili looked like. The photograph is taken from a group picture, and then drastically retouched.

Some of Soso's petitions were written after he had taken leave without permission. Every boarder at the Seminary was regularly granted leave of absence, mainly at weekends and on longer church holidays. Due to contemporary methods of transportation, however, traveling to and from Gori took almost two days. Perhaps this explains why Iosif Dzhugashvili occasionally failed to appear at classes following his weekend leave. This led to him being threatened with severe punishment, and he was obliged to provide explanations: "F[ather] Supervisor! I would not have presumed to write to you but would like to clarify why I did not keep my word. I had promised that I would return to the Seminary on Monday. This is why I have decided to write to you," was how Soso appealed to the monk Yoanaky in an undated letter. "The story is as follows. I arrived in Gori on Sunday. The deceased *[possibly a relative of the Dzhugashvili family—M. K.]*

had apparently stated in his will that he was to be buried next to his father near the village of Sveneti. The body was taken there on the Monday and the burial took place on the Tuesday. I wanted to return on Tuesday night, but circumstances were such that even the strongest person's hands would have been tied. The mother of the deceased, who had suffered so greatly at the cruel hand of fate, begged me with tears in her eyes to be a son to her, even if just for a week. I simply could not reject the appeal of a weeping mother. I hope you will forgive me but I decided to stay. After all, the Father Supervisor usually allows leave to those who intend to travel home. I[osif] Dzhugashvili, student." This letter was published in a collection of sources that illustrate the life of the Soviet dictator mostly in cheerful colors. Although the collection is full of philological errors it appears to be authentic. It was discovered in the Saratov state archive among the documents of Bishop Germogen, the former supervisor and subsequently rector of the Tiflis Theological Seminary.[14]

The petition reveals that at this time Iosif still tried to travel home as often as possible, despite the fact that what he found there was by no means uplifting. His mother, who had almost lost her eyesight because of the sewing work she constantly undertook, had already abandoned her job at the local Church School; once Soso had left she saw no point in continuing to work there. Uncharacteristically for a Georgian woman, however, she continued to take jobs as a cleaner. She worked in the houses of the wealthy to raise money for her son's education. Nevertheless, the money that Keke scraped together was not sufficient to cover even half the tuition fees. Thus, in response to her desperate request, Yakov Egnatoshvili, the godfather of Keke's son Georgy, who died of measles in 1877, took Soso under his wing. Surviving members of Egnatoshvili's family claim that it was the rich vine plantation owner and wine merchant who made it possible for his favorite "clever little Soselo" to study in Tiflis. However, this could only happen after Beso Dzhugashvili had left Gori. Thus Keke did not need to find excuses before her neighbors as to why she took the job of "housekeeper" with the neighboring household.[15]

In a small town like Gori, with a population of between eight and twelve thousand people, such things were regarded as scandalous. It could not be kept secret. Some "well-informed" people soon began to whisper that the real father of Soso, who was then studying in Tiflis, was not the vagrant, foul-mouthed Beso Dzhugashvili but Yakov Egnatoshvili, who had a reputation as a rich and generous man and whose wealth set him far above the poor people of the neighborhood. It is not impossible that this gossip reached Iosif, who was very vulnerable from his early childhood.

However, the Soviet dictator treated his mother with the greatest respect before the world. Their correspondence, loaded with archaic Georgian phrases, bears witness to this.[16] However, in the mid-1930s one of Stalin's early biographers, Boris Souvarine, who later dramatically turned his back on his Communist past, talked to Menshevik emigrants in Paris, according to whom Soso was hard, insensitive, and disrespectful towards his mother. They quoted some quite brutal stories to support their allegations.[17] In the second half of the 1940s Abdurakhman Avtorkhanov visited the aged Caucasian acquaintances of the dictator, who also talked to him a great deal about Stalin's cruelty. They recalled that in the early years of the century he had had fits of rage in the presence of his mother. However, none of them explained this as resulting from Soso's jealousy of his mother's supposed relationship. Nor was there any indication that the boy, who felt himself to be a half-orphan, hated "Uncle Yakov". Quite the contrary.

He obviously regarded the strong, wealthy man, who commanded respect by his sheer appearance, as a surrogate father.

The fact that in 1907, when in hiding from the police, the Bolshevik politician gave the name Yakov to his firstborn son suggests that there was a good relationship between the two families. After he had become the Master of the Kremlin he supported the Egnatoshvili family for years. In the Soviet era, of all his fellow countrymen in Gori it was only the sons of his surrogate father who achieved high positions. Vasily (Vaso), who was seven years younger than Stalin, became the dictator's "eyes and ears" in Georgia. The one-time "neighborhood kid" first became the deputy editor of the Georgian-language Tiflis party newspaper *Kommunisti*, then the secretary of the Georgian Supreme Soviet. Whenever Vaso visited the Soviet capital city Stalin always received him at his home or *dacha*. His elder brother Aleksandr (Sandro, or Sasho) Egnatoshvili, a commander of the government guard, was an eyewitness to these conversations. Although at the time Stalin was already suspicious of him, soon before Egnatoshvili's death in 1948 Stalin promoted his fellow countryman to the rank of lieutenant general.[18]

In the middle of the 1940s Stalin removed almost all Georgians from his environment. This included Sandro Egnatoshvili, who, via his father Yakov, was aware of several secrets concerning the two families who had once lived in the same neighborhood. After his fall the much-decorated one-time neighbor became the supervisor of the government resorts on the coast of the Black Sea. This was regarded as a major demotion, since earlier "good old Sandro" had lived in Stalin's immediate circle in the Kuntsevo *dacha* where his duties included taking care that the dictator was not poisoned—in the presence of the Master's guests he would often taste in advance the food and drink that was offered. Although his brother Vaso had managed to avoid Stalin's ire, following the dictator's death he was immediately arrested on the orders of Beria.[19]

The Egnatoshvili boys also enjoyed the patronage of Stalin's aged mother Keke. In a still-unpublished letter dated April 28, 1934 Aleksandr called her "my spiritual mother" *(dukhovaya maty)*: "I am sending you my greetings on the occasion of the forthcoming First of May celebrations," he wrote in Georgian, "and I wish you many happy returns of the day in the company of your son and grandson. Yesterday evening I visited Soso and we had a long talk. He looked very well. He had put on weight and had become more handsome than you can imagine. I cannot remember seeing him in such good shape during the past four years."

According to this letter the son of Uncle Yakov and the one-time Soso shared much laughter that evening: "He is very precious to me" Egnatoshvili wrote, "if only I could assume the burdens weighing on his shoulders [...] How happy I would be then! I wish he always felt cheerful and content! And that he, to whom our people owe their prosperity, might live for many long years to frustrate our enemies." The colorful phrases continue: "Who told you that he has grown old? This is not true at all. He is livelier, more cheerful, and younger than he was a year ago. Nobody would put him at more than forty...or perhaps forty-eight.[20] The heart beats merrily and old age sounds the retreat when things are going well." At the end of his letter Yekaterina's "spiritual son" inquired if she received enough meat from his godfather Saliko, who was a rural economist. Of Yakov Dzhugashvili, Stalin's elder son, he wrote: "He has grown tall, he looks like a giant. He is also in good health. He studies a great deal; the poor soul has hardly any leisure time." He also assured the old woman that life was sill patriarchal in the Kremlin, since Soso was planning to visit Saliko the next time he was in Georgia, that is, during his holiday at the Black Sea coast.[21]

☆ But all that belongs to a different story. Rather than considering a seaside holiday, the seminarian Soso Dzhugashvili was troubled by far more mundane problems such as a lack of money. However, in order to alleviate the hardships caused by his tuition fees he had other solutions available than relying on his overworked and worn-out mother Keke and his "Uncle Yakov", who had been promoted to the rank of "surrogate father". It would have helped, for example, if he had been a much more diligent student and less aggressive towards his teachers: working alongside the Orthodox Church Seminary was a minor order named after St. Andrew, whose members raised significant donations during the 1890s to support indigent students. However, their grants were mostly awarded to those seminarians who were rather more tractable. Iosif, who was far from his home roots and who found it difficult to get by without his mother's guidance, was never given this grant. According to still-unpublished documents his grades and his conduct fluctuated considerably during his five years at the Seminary. In the first academic year the average mark achieved by the sixteen-year-old boy rarely exceeded four. He was awarded a five only in Georgian language and was given a three for composition.[22]

His results were similar in the academic year 1895 to 1896. Having an excellent memory Soso could still rely to a certain degree on knowledge he had acquired at the Gori Church School. Although he was not an outstanding student—he received a five only in "Slavic singing"—the only three he was given, the mark usually awarded to the dullest students, was for Greek language in his end-of-term report.[23] As the Seminary statistics reveal, however, most of his one-time fellow students who were furthering their studies in Tiflis found it even more difficult to cope with the school's requirements. At the end of the first grade the young Stalin came eighth out of twenty-nine students, while in the second year he was fifth.[24]

In 1896, just before his eighteenth birthday when, following the summer recess, the increasingly unbalanced teenager returned from his hometown to Tiflis, the situation changed. He became a mediocre student overnight. For two and a half years there are hardly any fours in his school reports.[25] Gogokhia, or one of the censors who "stylized" his memoirs in an attempt to embellish the party leader's biography, made a virtue of this fact: "Iosif no longer cared about his classes. He was given threes and remembered only as much of what he was taught as was needed in order to pass his exams. He did not waste time and energy memorizing the legends of the Holy Scripture. Iosif had been interested in world literature and socioeconomic issues since his first year at the Seminary. [...] In the space of a year he had developed so much politically that in his second year he formed an [illegal] circle from among his seminarian friends."[26]

In reality things did not happen exactly like this. Iosif's "enlightenment" occurred much later. In spring 1897 he was awarded a two for his composition in secular history—by no means an ecclesiastical subject—which at the Tiflis Seminary was regarded as an unsatisfactory mark.[27] From then on until the early spring of 1899 his grades further deteriorated. In his end-of-year report for 1898 he received a four only for "ecclesiastical Slavic singing". For all other subjects he was awarded threes, and he failed both the written and the oral exams for Holy Scripture studies.[28] The eminent student of the Gori Church School was already among the poorest seminarians. At the end of the third grade he ranked sixteenth out of twenty-four students. At the beginning of the fifth grade he was only twentieth out of twenty-three.[29]

Soso must have felt more and more frequently that he had come to a dead-end. On such occasions he reverted to his old strategy of writing humble petitions. "To the Most Reverend Archemandrite Seraphim, Rector and Father of the Tiflis Theological Seminary. June 1898. The petition of the fourth-grade student of the Seminary above mentioned, Iosif Dzhugashvili. Due to my lung problems I require prolonged periods of rest. I have been suffering from this disease, which became more serious during the examination period, for some time. I need extended relief from work and exertion and appropriate medical treatment. Therefore I humbly ask Your Holiness to grant me exemption from the repeat examination in Holy Scripture studies. This would make it possible for me to have some relief from this disease, which has been undermining my strength since the first grade. I[osif] Dzhugashvili, petitioner. June 3, 1898."[30]

This is the fate the one-time seminarist had in store for Bryukhanov, the Bolshevik government's people's commissar for finances. In 1938 the terrible caricature became reality: Bryukhanov was tortured and executed on Stalin's order.

Although the rector's answer has not been preserved in the Stalin archives, we know that his problems were eventually solved: Soso did not drop out of the Seminary at this stage. Nevertheless, in the next grade, the fifth, at the age of twenty he remained among the worst students in the community. Besides the gaps in his study of the Holy Scriptures he had to take repeat examinations in the more theoretical "foundations of theology" as well. The future publicist of the Bolshevik party and the acknowledged poet of the Seminary strangely had near-failure marks in composition and in a subject known as "argumentation against anti-church sects". He received only one four for didactics. All his other marks were threes.[31] In nineteenth-century Russian seminaries such students were ridiculed as "*Kamchatkans*", since according to the seating order that was based on academic results they were placed furthest from the teacher's desk at the far end of the classroom.

Bearing this in mind it is ironic that his one-time fellow students mention him as a "Renaissance man" in their recollections: "I attended the same school as Iosif for thirteen years. I have been working as a teacher for thirty-five years, but never in my life have I met such a talented, conscientious student as he was," Pyotr Kapanadze remembered. "He learned to draw excellently, although this subject was not even part of the curriculum. I remember him drawing the portraits of Shota Rustaveli and other Georgian writers. During his school years he read almost every book in the Gori library. [...] 'We must learn and learn', he kept saying, 'so that we can help the peasants'. [...] He never boasted about being more talented than we were, but he came to our aid in every possible way. He helped us to draw maps and to solve arithmetical problems. [...] At the Tiflis Seminary he took part in the work of illegal circles, and he read a great deal. He studied geology, then he became engrossed in chemistry. He began to read the works of Marx."[32]

Other seminarians who were interviewed by the "Beria Brigade" were perhaps more reserved, but also embellished the truth when they talked about the outstanding achievements of the young Iosif Dzhugashvili. However, all of them made mention of Stalin's pleasant tenor voice. Soso was indeed one of the pillars of the Seminary 's church choir, as he had been in Gori but by the end of his studies he was no longer particularly interested in singing.[33]

According to archive resources the conduct of the future Soviet dictator was also changeable during the last two years at the Seminary. The rigorous supervisors meticulously recorded transgressions committed by the students in a special book. According to this book, in 1895 Iosif Dzhugashvili received written warnings on only three occasions. These were for childish acts of misdemeanor, even though Soso, who was older than the other students in his year, behaved in a more mature manner outside the walls of the Seminary than most of his fellows. From summer 1895 he had published his poems without permission in the newspaper *Iveria*. He was fortunate, however, that his teachers had no idea about this. Thus they were content to warn him every now and then for lurking around with the others following evening prayer instead of getting on with his homework. On another occasion Soso annoyed the day supervisor by being late for church and talking loudly in the dining hall. It is also recorded that the stubborn teenager did not agree to have his long hair cut.

In the following year, 1896, the number of warnings doubled. Nevertheless, unlike some of his classmates, Iosif was still not among the major troublemakers. According to the transgressions recorded he giggled in church, missed five classes without permission, climbed through the window into the dormitory during the afternoon, and once failed to take off his cap in the classroom. When it turned out that he had read two works by Victor Hugo that he had borrowed from the city library he was sentenced to spend time in a darkened cell.

In 1897, however, Soso received nine supervisor's warnings: he was apparently rebelling against everything and everyone. Like other students he chatted in class, was late for morning tea, and once took off his cap in the classroom only after being warned. For offenses such as these it was not usual at the Seminary to give a reprimand or lengthy punishment in a darkened cell. Soso, however, who according to his fellow students was increasingly outspoken by then, was demonstratively late for the evening litany and the *akathistos*, the long Orthodox hymn to the Virgin, for which he again received a warning. On one occasion he did not turn up for evening prayer, which was regarded as a major offense at the Orthodox Seminary. In the mid-1890s it even happened that Iosif Dzhugashvili, who had still been God-fearing in Gori, declared himself to be an atheist on several occasions among his closest circle of friends, and trotted out of the common morning prayer in order to gain attention. Last but not least, in order to annoy his supervisors he always kept at hand books by his favorite novelist, Victor Hugo, as well as cheap editions of other popular works of natural and social science.[34]

These books were published with the permission of the tsarist censors in Russia. Upper-grade students at the Moscow and St. Petersburg church colleges were not banned from reading them. It would therefore be a mistake to overestimate the significance of the fact that Stalin, at around the age of twenty, became acquainted with certain works by Dostoyevsky, Tolstoy, and Darwin, which were passed around at the Seminary and which even deeply religious students who were preparing for the priesthood thought it important to read. The supervisors, who searched the students' boxes in the dormitories extremely frequently for secular books, and who took detailed records of what they found, never came across illegal revolutionary brochures or foreign publications that could be regarded as subversive among the possessions of Soso and his closest friends. The very cautiously circulated handwritten student journal *Shtroma* ('Work'), in which Iosif Dzhugashvili apparently played a part in editing, provoked the wrath of the teaching staff, and the men of the Tiflis political police soon learned about its existence. Nevertheless, no severe punishments were inflicted since the publication was typical of the study circles.[35]

Until his last months at the Seminary in the early spring of 1899 Iosif Dzhugashvili was given warnings on eleven occasions and was often in confrontation with various members of the staff, especially with the supervisors whom he feared less and less. Once Father Dmitry, who before his ordination had been known as Prince David Abashidze and who came from one of the noblest families of Georgia, sneaked up on Soso while he was immersed in reading. According to Elisabedashvili "he craftily snatched the book from Stalin's hands, and Stalin immediately took it back. Outraged, Father Dmitry exclaimed: 'Don't you see who I am?' Stalin rubbed his eyes, gazed at him, and answered: 'I can only see a big black blob. Nothing else.'"[36]

Despite these confrontations the priest teachers and supervisors did not propose the immediate expulsion of Iosif Dzhugashvili. Nevertheless, it was obvious to them that closing him in a dark cell or depriving him of leave was not effective enough in his case. Over the years a system of punishments had been elaborated at the Tiflis Theological Seminary. If someone was late for Mass he would be shut in for at least half an hour. This happened to the young Stalin on several occasions. Once he returned from leave three days late and as a result the supervisor on duty sentenced him to five hours' confinement. At the end of the year the members of staff added up the punishments received. Anyone who had been punished too frequently, as Soso had been at the end of his career at the Seminary, was given a three for conduct. In Soso's case the situation was made more serious by the fact that after lights out he had read to his fellow students from forbidden, even if not revolutionary, books. After a time Stalin refused to acknowledge one of his teachers, by the name of Murakhovsky, who frequently censured his behavior. As a result he was referred to as a "cruel and disrespectful" student in one of the staff end-of-year record books.[37]

Iosif Dzhugashvili was not the only disobedient student at the Seminary. What distinguished him from others was the fact that in around 1898 he got into contact with a revolutionary communitiy named *Mesame Dasi* (the 'Third Group'), founden in 1892 by twenty young men and the editorial board of *Kvali,* which regularly published the writings of the outstanding representatives of the Georgian Left. The editorial board was headed by Noi Zhordania, the future Menshevik leader of independent Georgia.[38] If the rector, who was in close touch with the political police, or one of the supervisors had realized that Soso was one of the organizers of the Marxist circles at the Tiflis Seminary, he would no doubt have been expelled from the institution with a certificate of misconduct *(volchy bilet).*

The informers among the students, however, had no idea why Iosif Dzhugashvili sometimes gathered with some of his fellow students in the farthest corner of the dormitory or the courtyard, nor what kind of inflammatory speeches were being made at these gatherings. Since they received no reports from the informers the leaders of the Seminary did not realize that the, at first mediocre, then substandard, student had been leading a double life for years. The young Stalin pretended to be an indifferent, cynical student, thus leading his teachers by the nose. As a result he was never seriously punished, right up to the late spring of 1899 when he dropped out of the Seminary of his own accord.

☆ In all the official biographies of Stalin mention is made of the fact that the Bolshevik politician , as the organizer of several Marxist circles, already acted as a "fervent agitator" in Tiflis. It was for this reason that the "clerical reactionaries", in order to take revenge on his revolutionary stance, removed him from the Seminary. Elisabedashivli, who provides several fascinating details about Soso's youth, gets completely carried away on this point: "On Stalin's orders, and under his leadership, we created a Social Democratic student committee. Between 100 and 125 young men belonged to those [illegal] circles, which were united by this committee. They all paid a membership fee of ten to fifteen kopecks a month. This money was intended to be sent, through my intermediation, to the [Social Democratic] party committee."[39]

According to Beria, "Comrade Stalin alone controlled more than eight Social Democratic circles" in Tiflis between 1898 and 1900. The author even lists the factories to which the young seminarian went regularly in order to spread Socialist tenets: the railroad workshop, the Bozadzhants tobacco factory, a second tobacco factory, a building industry plant, Adelkhanov's tannery, where Beso Dzhugashvili had worked at one time, the Mirzoyev textile works, the Tolle oil processing plant, and a number of printers and smaller workshops. The young agitator had supposedly found time for all this during his two-hour leave in the early afternoons, in the middle of the working day at the factories. In addition, Soso was said to have managed to direct two large Marxist circles in the Seminary.[40]

Contrary to the above claims the study circle, which in reality operated at the Seminary under Marxist influence, cannot have had many members or Iosif Dzhugashvili and his fellow students would have been caught very quickly. Even so, the governors of the Seminary suspected that trouble was finally being fomented within the walls of the old building, and they tried to uncover the revolutionary agitators. On October 18, 1897, for example, they forwarded a list of students in the last four years to the Tiflis provincial gendarmerie. However, no reliable contemporary source suggests that they knew that Iosif Dzhugashvili was among the student conspirators.

Nor had they any idea about another "transgression" on the part of Stalin. Some of the fourth- and fifth-grade students rented a small apartment on the outskirts of the town, near David Hill. The five rubles rental fee was raised by the wealthier members of the small student group. According to the recollections of Gogokhia, the young Stalin had no money at all at the time. Nevertheless, it was he who suggested renting the apartment and visiting the hideout once or twice a week.[41]

The authors of the memoirs that were written at the request of the "Beria Brigade" portrayed the lodging as some kind of "secret base", where the opposition-minded seminarians took part in "systematic revolutionary training" under Soso's direction. The two-hour leave cannot have been long enough for this, although students who lived outside Tiflis and did not travel home for the weekend could use the place all day. However, it is by no means certain that the young men studied only the Russian edition of Marx's *Das Kapital.*[42] The apartment at the foot of David Hill could easily have served as a love nest for the young adult seminarians in their early twenties, who, lacking the company of other women, were known to follow the prostitutes outside Tiflis' red-light district. Soso and his friends, however, exposed themselves to many dangers when seeking sexual relations. The supervisors would try and track them down in the neighborhood of brothels, as well as in the corridors of Tiflis theaters, in cafeterias and confectioneries. The official recollections remained just as silent on this point as about Iosif Dzhugashvili's nights out during the summer vacation. According to Abdurakhman Avtorkhanov, the Georgian Menshevik émigrés, including the one-time Tiflis seminarians, clearly remembered debaucheries in women's company even half a century later.

Nevertheless, we have no evidence about the early love life of young Stalin. Only Elisabedashvili makes a vague reference to it in one of the unpublished versions of his memoirs: "In his youth Comrade Soso felt some sympathy towards a certain person [...] but it did not last for too long."[43] The romance must have taken place in Gori, where the young Stalin could move relatively freely. In Tiflis, however, he had to watch his step in this respect since, apart from a few exceptions, those students who were found guilty of the sin of "lust" were expelled from every Orthodox Seminary.

Seminarians therefore soon learned to dissimulate. According to the recollections of Talakvadze, one of Soso's fellow students, they had a friend called Grisha Makhatadze who liked to read out humorous poems from a notebook that he always carried with him: "The informers reported this to Abashidze, who silently sneaked to the door *[behind which the young men were laughing—M. K.]*. He heard every word. He ran into the room and tore the notebook from Makhatadze's hands. As far as I can remember Comrade Soso tried to get it back from the supervisor but could not. Father Dmitry drove both Soso and Makhatadze to his own apartment. He ushered them into the kitchen, brought in some paraffin, and forced the unclean souls to burn the subversive writings."[44]

All the above-mentioned acts of misdemeanor are typical student pranks without any political content. It would therefore be a mistake to claim that the young Stalin was "labeled as a Marxist agitator" and expelled from the Seminary as a result. Nor could his deteriorating academic results be the reason, especially because two months before the Theological Seminary staff meeting of 29 May he had sorted himself out and had improved his marks in almost all subjects, again reaching an average of four. His conduct must have improved dramatically as well, or he would not have received an excellent mark after so much time. The "copy of the final certificate" bears witness to this. It was granted to him at his special request four months following his dismissal from the Seminary: "Iosif Dzhugashvili, student at the Tiflis Theological Seminary, the son of Vissarion, a peasant living in the town of Gori in the province of Tiflis, who was born on the sixth day of December in the year 1878, having completed the course of studies at the Gori Church School was admitted to the Tiflis Theological Seminary in the month of September 1894. He studied at the aforesaid institution until the twenty-ninth day of May 1899, and in addition to excellent conduct (5) he achieved the following results:

Exegesis of the Holy Script – very good (4)
History of the Bible – very good (4)
Ecclesiastical history – good (3)
Homiletics – good (3)
Liturgics
Russian literature – very good (4)
History of Russian literature – very good (4)
Universal secular history – very good (4)
Russian secular history – very good (4)
Algebra – very good (4)
Geometry – very good (4)
Easter liturgy – very good (4)
Physics – very good (4)
Logic – outstanding (5)
Psychology – very good (4)
Ecclesiastical Georgian subjects – very good (4)
Greek language – very good (4)
Latin language – not studied
Ecclesiastical singing: Slavic – outstanding (5)
in Georgian language – very good (4)."

In keeping with the decree passed on May 29, 1899 by the pedagogical assembly of the Seminary's governors, acknowledged by His Eminence Archbishop Flavialos, the Exarch of Georgia, the named Iosif Dzhugashvili has been expelled from the Tiflis Theological Seminary. It has been taken into account that he had accomplished the fourth grade and had begun the fifth. Due to his expulsion he is not entitled to the privileges enjoyed by those students who have completed their studies at the Seminary. [...] If, on the other hand, he were to be conscripted as a soldier he would be entitled to the privileges enjoyed by the students of educational institutions of the first category.[45] To certify this we have issued this document for the aforesaid Dzhugashvili, complete with the proper signatures and with the seal of the council, in the name of the council of the Tiflis Theological Seminary. The city of Tiflis, June 1899. October 2.[46] Archemandrite Germogen, Rector. Dmitry, ordained monk, supervisor at the Seminary. The members of the council. The secretary of the council."[47] The document, which has so far escaped the attention of Stalin researchers, is completed by a short decree by the staff. According to this the immediate reason for the expulsion was that Iosif Dzhugashvili, "for reasons unknown", did not turn up for his final exams in his fifth year.[48]

On December 22, 1939, the Soviet Academy coopted Joseph Stalin as one of its members, disregarding the fact that he did not have a postsecondary degree.

This was not an entirely rational decision by Soso. It would have been more logical for him to accomplish the sixth grade and, in possession of a final degree certificate, which went along with several privileges, to transfer to a Russian university. However, the nerve of the seminarian, who was older than the other students in his year, had begun to give way. By that time he had been tormented for months by a desire to escape. According to Noi Zhordania Soso visited him somewhere around the end of 1898 at the editorial offices of *Kvali.* He spoke of his intention to leave the Seminary and asked for advice as to what he should do. The future head of the Georgian government suggested that he should stay at the Seminary for another year. Iosif Dzhugashvili promised to consider this advice.[49]

It seems, however, that by the spring of 1899 he could not bear to remain at the Seminary any longer. He spent the Easter vacation at home but when he was due to return to Tiflis he remained in Gori on the pretext of chronic pneumonia. He did not even return the books he had borrowed from the student library of the Tiflis Seminary. All the above were regarded as severe individual transgressions. According to an undated draft document the council of the Seminary was still demanding the cost of the books—eighteen rubles and fifteen kopecks—the following autumn.[50]

A further transgression was that Soso had not settled his dues before April 15, the date on which the deadline for payment of the last third of the tuition fees for the academic year 1898/1899 expired. This fact was also mentioned at the staff session on May 29, although it did not weigh as heavily as his several weeks of absence and the fact that he had not appeared for his exams.

The offender was informed by letter in early June about the strict decision taken by the Seminary council. Soso, however, in contrast to the past, did not submit an appeal as he had dropped out of the Seminary of his own accord. In the meantime the members of staff may have realized that they had gone too far since, according to his report in the early spring, Iosif Dzhugashvili had fought his way back among the so-called first-class students. Thus the rectorate offered to make peace with him: in a letter they suggested that he should take a temporary church post or that he should become a teacher in a lower level church institution. Had he been regarded as politically unreliable, this suggestion would, of course, never have been made. The offer was made so that Soso would not be obliged to

Stalin visited his mother for the last time in 1935, in her home in the Tiflis building that had been the Governor's Palace before the 1917 February revolution.

repay almost four hundred rubles which had been transferred to him by the Georgian Treasury over almost five years, and which was a huge sum for him.[51]

Iosif Dzhugashvili, however, did not have the slightest intention of returning as a "prodigal seminarian". Rather, he continued to hide from his priest teachers, who, after a while, wrote off both him and the money spent on his education—although, because of his debts, they could have caused a great deal of trouble for him. These facts, however, did not fit the biography of the later party leader. In his official biography, penned in the mid-1920s and personally overseen by him, the following can be read: "In 1893 Stalin completed his studies at the Gori Church School and in the same year was admitted to the Tiflis Orthodox Seminary.[52] This institution was at the time the hotbed of all liberating ideas from Narodnik nationalism to Marxist Internationalism. Several such circles operated within the Seminary. In 1897 Stalin became the leader of the Marxist study circles. In the same year he established a connection with the illegal Tiflis Social Democratic organization, from which he received illegal literature. He took part in the workers' meetings at the Tiflis railroad workshops. In 1898 he was officially admitted to the Russian Social Democratic Workers' Party.[53] At the time he was carrying out propaganda activities in the city's factory and railroad workers' districts. At the Seminary, where they investigated suspicious students, they realized that Stalin was undertaking illegal work. Thus he was expelled as *unreliable.*"[54]

As the years passed the Soviet dictator did not find this wording sufficiently worthy. Thus in 1931, as the representative of the district of the Soviet capital named after him *(Stalinsky rayon)*, he wrote in response to a questionnaire: "I was expelled from the Orthodox Church Seminary due to Marxist propaganda activities."[55]

A few years later his one-time fellow students enthusiastically embellished this laconic sentence in their recollections about Stalin. According to Gogokhia his work in the Marxist circle affected his academic results: "Iosif, however, was accepted into the next grade easily, without much effort on his part.[56] This success proved short-lived, however. Abashidze, a cruel and savage monk, began to realize why the intellectually advanced and talented Dzhugashvili, who had a very good memory, had become a mediocre student. [...] He spoke of this at the session of the Seminary council. He reported how much we were concerned with politics and that Dzhugashvili played a leading role in this. Thus Abashidze brought about his expulsion from the Seminary."[57] Talakvadze, another former

H. R. Knickerbocker, the famous American reporter, managed to learn bits of details about the past of the Dzhugashvili family.

seminarian, came up with a slightly different version: "Soso had a serious confrontation with the supervisor Abashidze, who had caught him reading illegal books. As a result Soso was expelled from the Seminary. Abashidze, on the other hand, was promoted: he became the rector of the Ardon Seminary."[58] The obviously false story was illustrated with a genuine socialist realist picture by the painter Bagratiani. In the picture a repulsive-looking monk and a typical tsarist *chinovnik* torment Iosif Dzhugashvili, who stands up proudly at the session of the council—although in reality he had been killing time in Gori for several weeks by the time the council met.

It was Leon Trotsky who first recognized the impossibility of this story when working on Stalin's biography in the late 1930s. "Iosif Dzhugashvili did not fulfill his mother's dreams by becoming a priest, nor did he even make it as far as the final exam. This might have opened up for him the gates of certain provincial universities. According to the recollections of Abel[59] Yenukidze, written in 1929, Iosif began to read subversive books at the Seminary. The Argus-eyed supervisor caught him, and the dangerous student was 'thrown out of the Seminary'. According to Beria, the official Caucasian historian, Stalin was 'expelled on a charge of unreliability' from the institution. There is nothing extraordinary in this, of course, since at the time such expulsions were by no means rare. The only strange aspect is that the Seminary's documents relating to this matter have still not been published, despite the fact that they have not been destroyed, nor did they disappear in the chaos of the revolutionary years. [...] Nevertheless they are shrouded in complete silence. Is this not the case because they contain unfavorable facts? Or do they contradict certain later legends?"[60]

At the end of the 1930s an elderly historian, Ivan Knizhnik-Vetrov, tried to find out the truth. The one-time Tolstoyan anarchist and acknowledged researcher of the Narodnik movement certainly doubted the canonized words of Lavrenty Beria, the much-dreaded head of the NKVD, concerning Joseph Stalin. Although he had no access to secret archive sources, he realized from the official reports of the Georgian exarchate that in May 1899 the Leader had himself to thank for his expulsion and the governors of the Seminary had seen no political dimension to the case. The courageous researcher wrote a lengthy study on Soso's student years and sent it to the *Istorik-Marksist* journal of the Soviet Institute of Historical Science. On February 13, 1940 he received a short admonishing letter from the deputy editor in chief, Rostovsky: "We are not publishing the article. [...] The facts it contains are partly widely known. At the same time there are some incorrect statements in what you write. For example, you claim that Comrade Stalin left the Seminary of his own accord."[61] A copy of the article and the editorial letter eventually ended up at the bottom of the Stalin archive. As a reward for his efforts the conscientious researcher was jailed—but only for a short time.

After some time even Stalin's mother, Keke Geladze, remembered a similar story about her son's expulsion. Until the end of her life she was unable to come to terms with the fact that her darling Iosif, for whom she had sacrificed everything, had not only not become an eloquent metropolitan but had not even become a simple village priest. Her disappointment was not alleviated by the fact that in the meantime Stalin had become the Master *(Hozyain)* of an entire country, that he lived in the Kremlin in Moscow—he even received her there on one occasion—and that he had created a home for her in the Tiflis palace of Prince Vorontsov.

On one occasion she told an American guest, H. R. Knickerbocker, who published a sensational article about their meeting in the *New York Evening Post* on

December 1, 1930, that it was she who had taken Iosif home for health reasons. "When he began his studies at the Seminary he was as strong as other boys of his age, but around the age of eighteen he became exhausted by the strains of his studies.[62] The doctors said that he was at risk from tuberculosis, so I took him out of school. He did not want to leave but I insisted since he was my only son."[63]

When Stalin's mother died the Tbilisi department of the Soviet Press Agency made a short report but the text could at first be read only in the so-called *Internal Report*. This states that the mother of the Soviet dictator died in her apartment in the Vorontsov palace on June 4, 1937 at 11.05 p.m. According to the five-member medical council the cause of death was heart failure. *Pravda* later published a report on the funeral, at which Joseph Stalin was represented by the Berias since the trials, in the form of public and secret calling to account, were well underway in Moscow and the one-time Soso preferred to remain at the helm. He nevertheless sent a wreath with a black and red ribbon, on which was written: "For his dear and beloved mother from her son Iosif Dzhugashvili (Stalin)." Keke's death certificate, the inventory of her property, and her personal papers were almost immediately sent to Moscow. From the still mostly unpublished documents it turns out that Keke Geladze, who was born on February 5, 1860, did not leave a significant estate. The majority of her furniture belonged to the treasury. On one of the iron beds hung a small tag with the inscription "Property of the NKVD". The majority of the personal effects were inherited by Maria (according to other documents Margo) Kvinkadze, one of the two "lady's companions" who had been close to Stalin's mother at all times. A detailed inventory was made of these items on August 15, 1937.[64] The "heir" had apparently lived together with Keke in Gori. In one of the letters a cousin by the name of Anichka is mentioned as having wished for a better apartment.[65] However, she inherited nothing.

1 *Molodaya Gvardia*, 1939, no. 12, 64–65.
2 *Ibid.*
3 Makharadze, 1927, 57–58.
4 In the academic year of 1894–95, Iosif Dzhugashvili filed another petition, in which he requested warm clothing. On other occasions, he received textbooks for free. *RGASPI*, fond. 71, op. 10, d. 275.
5 *Rasskazi starikh rabochikh*, 1937, 14.
6 This is what Goglichidze recalled, who was Soso's favorite teacher in the Church School. *RGASPI*, fond. 558, op. 4, d. 665.
7 *Ibid.* Sologov's original Georgian name was Aleksandr Sologoshvili. Only later did he become a dentist. Ostrovsky, 2002. 108.
8 *Rasskazi starikh rabochikh*, 1937, 15.
9 In the Georgian capital of the time illustrated magazines in Georgian, Armenian, Russian, even French were published. Their copies could be read in coffee shops and bookstores for free.
10 *Rasskazi starikh rabochikh*, 1937, 14–15, 28–29.
11 *Molodaya Gvardia*, 1939, no. 12, 65.
12 Father Serafim, Professor of theology, was the rector of the Seminary twice, between 1894–1895 and 1897–1899. In 1896 temporarily Father Dmitry substituted for him; then on July 18, 1898 Father Germogen (Georgy Dolganov) was named as his replacement, who later became famous for his fanaticism as the Metropolitan of Tsaritsyn. Father Germogen also turned against his own creation, Grishka Rasputin, the horse stealer, who became a not exactly pious *starets*. *RGASPI*, fond. 558, op. 4, d. 665.
13 *RGASPI*, fond. 558, op. 1, d. 4325.
14 Stalin, 1951, 30–31.
15 Loginov, 1999, 15–19, 23, 27, 55–57. The author, who was biased in favor of Stalin, managed to talk to Yakov Egnatoshvili's grandson, Georgy ('Bichigo') at almost the very last moment, as his interviewee was more than eighty years old.
16 *Iosif Stalin v obyatiakh semyi*, 1993, 5–21.
17 Souvarine, 1939, 3.
18 Loginov, 1999, 25.
19 *Ibid.*
20 At that time Stalin was well beyond 55.

21 *RGASPI*, fond. 558, op. 11, d. 1549.
22 *RGASPI*, fond. 558, op. 4, d. 21.
23 *RGASPI*, fond. 558, op. 4, d. 29.
24 *RGASPI*, fond. 558, op. 4, d. 665.
25 *RGASPI*, fond. 558, op. 4, d. 37.
26 *Rasskazi starikh rabochikh*, 1937, 17–18.
27 The authors of the thoroughly censored biographies remember differently, though: "Iosif liked secular history. [...] From this subject he always earned the best grades," wrote one of his oldest acquaintances, Gluridzhidze. *Ibid.*, 30.
28 *RGASPI*, fond. 558, op. 4, d. 48.
29 *RGASPI*, fond. 558, op. 4, d. 665.
30 *RGASPI*, fond. 558, op. 1, d. 4327.
31 *RGASPI*, fond. 558, op. 4, d. 64.
32 *Rasskazi starikh rabochikh*, 1937, 34–36.
33 The contemporary documents of the Seminary mention Soso as "the first tenor of the choir's right wing ." *RGASPI*, fond. 71, op. 10, d. 404.
34 *RGASPI*, fond. 71, op. 1, d. 275.
35 *Ibid.*
36 *Rasskazi starikh rabochikh*, 1937, 32–33.
37 *RGASPI*, fond. 71, op. 10, d. 404.
38 Souvarine, 1939, 15–16; Trotsky, 1985, I, 50–51.
39 *Rasskazi starikh rabochikh*, 1937, 33.
40 Beria, 1952, 23–24. Here we can also learn who were the seminarists whom Soso taught "revolutionary Marxism" in 1896–97. Ivan Knizhnik-Vertov, however, showed in 1940 that some of these fellow students were not yet enrolled at the Tiflis Seminary at this time. *RGASPI*, fond. 558, op. 4, d. 665.
41 *Molodaya Gvardia*, 1939, no. 12, 12, 73.
42 According to one of the biggest myth-makers, Paradze, Stalin and his friends made a hand-written duplicate of the only available copy of *Das Kapital* in Tiflis. It is not clear from this account which library or whose private collection the book belonged to. *Ibid.*, 71.
43 *RGASPI*, fond. 558, op. 4, d. 665.
44 *Molodaya Gvardia*, 1939, no. 12, 85.
45 That is, universities, as well as religious and secular colleges.
46 This latter date refers to the date of publication of the copy.
47 *RGASPI*, fond. 558, op. 4, d. 65.
48 *RGASPI*, fond. 71, op. 10, d. 275. See also Tucker, 1991, 92.
49 Smith, 1967, 52–53.
50 *RGASPI*, fond. 558, op. 4, d. 65.
51 *Ibid.*
52 In fact this happened a year later, in September 1894.
53 Stalin himself gave this date on December 11, 1920, when he filled out an official form. Here he also wrote that "I have sympathized RSDLP already before 1898." *RGASPI*, fond. 558, op. 1, d. 4507.
54 *Dyeyateli SSSR*, 1989, 107. It is worth it to compare the lines with Stalin's statement made on March 15, 1913, in front of the St. Petersburg gendarme: "I entered the Seminary, which I left *(otkuda vyshel)* in 1899 because of a lack of funds *(po nemeniu sredstv)* when the state took away my scholarship." *RGASPI*, fond 558. op. 4. d. 214.
55 Yaroslavsky, 1939, 14.
56 In fact, he did not even show up for the final exams in the spring of 1899.
57 *Rasskazi starikh rabochikh*, 1937, 48.
58 *Molodaya Gvardia*, 1939, no. 12, 86.
59 Correctly: Avel.
60 Trotsky, 1985, I, 42–43.
61 *RGASPI*, fond. 558, op. 4, d. 665.
62 In fact, at that time Stalin was almost 21.
63 Smith, 1967, 54.
64 *RGASPI*, fond. 558, op. 11, d. 1549.
65 *Ibid.*

CHAPTER 3
"Comrade Koba" Enters the Scene

"I cannot claim to have been attracted to socialism as early as the age of six. Nor had I reached this stage even by the time I was ten or twelve. I was fifteen when I joined the revolutionary movement. It was then that I came into contact with the illegal Russian Marxist groups [in Tiflis]. [...] They had a huge influence on me. They encouraged me to read illegal Marxist literature." Stalin made this somewhat dubious claim, without turning a hair, when talking to the German journalist Emil Ludwig on December 13, 1931.[1]

In reality, at the age of fifteen he was still a pupil at the Gori Church School and had not even taken the entrance exam for the Tiflis Seminary. Nevertheless, his Soviet biographers attempted to corroborate the preposterous statement: "By the time Stalin was expelled from the Seminary [in May 1899] [...] he had four years' experience of illegal Marxist activity."[2] However, there is not a single authentic source verifying that Soso was indeed connected to the small group of Russian Marxists working in Georgia before he moved to Tiflis. Nor can one be certain that he had even heard of Marx and Engels in the small provincial town of Gori. It is also difficult to believe that the young seminarian began his studies with the reading of Marx. Nevertheless, the Menshevik Iosif Iremashvili, usually a reliable source, claims that during their studies in Tiflis he himself and Soso would read such books during worship and prayers. "The Bible would be open in front of us on the table *[in the dormitory—M.K.]*, but meanwhile we were reading the works of Darwin, Marx, Plekhanov, and Lenin, which we kept hidden on our laps."[3]

So who are we to believe? At that time the works of Darwin, Marx, and Plekhanov were, in theory, accessible to the leftist Tiflis intelligentsia. However, the works of Lenin were not. For the official historians of Stalin, such minor details were not important. What was important was the creation of a myth that would strengthen Stalin's machinery of state. It was for this reason that the dictator had a tendency to embroider the truth when talking to Western visitors about his youth, a period not otherwise abounding in significant events. This was made all the more easy for him, since he knew that in the secretive Soviet world foreigners had no access to books or archive resources that would contradict his stories. In Tiflis, where there were still many who had known him personally as a young man, he apparently measured his words very carefully when talking about this period of his life. This was certainly the case on 10 June 1926, when, during a visit to the town, he toured the local railway workshops. The gray-haired General Secretary of the party, an imposing figure who commanded respect by his very presence, was suddenly transformed back into the tall, unshaven young man he had once been. With a theatrical gesture he claimed: "I remember clearly the year 1898. It was then that I was first put in charge of a railway workers' circle *[by the Tiflis Social Democratic leadership—M. K.]*. The progressive Tiflis workers taught me a lesson in practical party work. Compared to them I was a complete greenhorn. Perhaps I was a little more erudite than most of the comrades there, but as a practical party worker I was undoubtedly a total beginner. [...] Here, among my comrades, I became the apprentice of the revolution."[4]

Employees of the OGPU *[the "Unified State Political Directorate", a forerunner of the NKVD.—Trans.]*, who closely supervised the festive gathering, had carefully vetted the list of participants several days in advance. However, probably not even this selected audience would have greeted Stalin's speech with such huge applause had he not addressed them so humbly. Tiflis was not easy to conquer. The former seminarian, who spent most of his working time involved in political intrigue,[5] knew only too well that there were still many Menshevik strongholds throughout Georgia. In 1921 these Mensheviks could only be removed from power by the bayonets of the Soviet-Russian Red Army. In this scene of his youth Stalin was also made cautious by the fact that many well-known Georgian orthodox Bolsheviks sided with Leon Trotsky in the intensifying factional struggles. Most of the members of the old Tiflis party leadership, almost all of whom were sacked following the death of Lenin, were among them. The elite of the small Soviet republic of Georgia was further put out by the fact that Sergo Ordzhonikidze, an unlearned army doctor and Stalin's best friend, was appointed as the Kremlin's governor in Tiflis. He was generally known as a man who was ready to slap people in the face–and not just in the political sense.[6]

Iosif Dzhugashvili, who had once ignominiously left the Tiflis Seminary, had to take all this into account. It was no easy task for him to increase the number of his Georgian followers on such uncertain ground. It was for this reason that he addressed such blandishments to the group of workers who had been ordered to listen to him. They, on the other hand, despite being momentarily moved by the speech, could not forget that "Comrade Soso", who had turned up to address them after quarter of a century, had not played such a decisive role in the Georgian labor movement in the early twentieth century as was suggested by the official Bolshevik press from the mid-1920s.

In a further gesture to those present Joseph Stalin mentioned in his speech the famous Menshevik Silvester (Simbistro, Silva) Dzhibladze, who had once been his mentor in the revolutionary movement.[7] However, the grateful disciple had apparently forgotten the tragic fate that later befell this veteran of the Georgian Social Democratic movement. When the region was Sovietized, the popular Georgian politician did not emigrate. He remained in Tiflis in order to coordinate the illegal Menshevik circles, as he had done in tsarist times. However, the years of hardship eventually undermined his health and he died suddenly in February 1922. His friends took his body home from the "conspiratorial apartment", but members of the Tiflis political police, led by the young Lavrenty Beria, then turned up to take away Silva's remains. Even today the location of his unmarked grave remains unknown.[8]

Iosif Dzhugashvili in 1905–06.

The Georgian workers listening to the former "Comrade Koba" could recall many similarly tragic fates. Joseph Stalin, however, talked instead about the poor districts of the capital of Azerbaijan which were home to oil workers and where he himself had spent part of his life: "I remember the years 1905 to 1906 when the party ordered me to work in Baku.[9] That is where I underwent my second revolutionary baptism of fire. I became an assistant in the revolutionary movement. Allow me here to express my sincere, comradely thanks to my teachers in Baku." In the cleverly structured speech there then followed a formal nod in the direction of the Bolshevik workers of St. Petersburg, although at the time of the speech in the mid-1920s, Stalin was already busy pursuing the former "illegals" living in this city on the banks of the river Neva. At that time they formed the core of the "Leningrad opposition" that confronted him, led by Zinovyev, Kamenev, and Nadezhda Krupskaya. Finally, when talking about 1917, Stalin absurdly referred to Leningrad as the former capital of the tsars. According to the

speech he, a Bolshevik party worker "who had been languishing in prison and in exile", had been sent there by some abstract force—again "the party's orders". "That is where I understood for the first time," he stated proudly, "what it meant to be one of the leaders of the great party of the working class."

Just like a character in a folktale, after the former student from Tiflis had undergone his "revolutionary baptism of fire" in St. Petersburg for the third time, in his own words he became one of the "masters of the revolution". The speech, which was otherwise full of unnecessary digressions, ended with recollections of these three occasions: "After becoming an apprentice (Tiflis), and later a journeyman (Baku), I rose to the rank of one of the masters of our revolution (Leningrad). See, comrades, such was my revolutionary schooling. And this is the authentic picture, comrades, of what I was and what I became. I can say this with a clear conscience, without any exaggeration."[10]

At the end of the speech Joseph Stalin once again stepped out of the role of the former Soso, making quarter of a century of his life appear as if it had been a homogeneous process without major obstacles. This was another serious exaggeration, since, after leaving the Seminary in spring 1899, the former seminarian disappeared for several months from among his old acquaintances—as well as from his biographers, who later tried to reconstruct his career. According to his official biography he initially made a living by giving private tuition. However, it is not clear from the context whether he was living in Gori or Tiflis.[11]

Perhaps Soso was indeed giving lessons, although we know that before 1917 he does not appear to have been particularly keen on working in spite of permanent financial problems. Unlike most of his companions in misfortune, during the long years in which he was in exile at various times he simply preferred to go without rather than give lessons, not to mention undertake any physically demanding work. When he returned to Tiflis in late 1899 he had to face the fact that to rent an apartment would cost money. The devious Soso, however, rented a room together with one of his wealthy friends, his then best friend Mikhail (Misho) Davitashvili, who paid his bills. In his recollections Dmitry Kalandarashvili, his landlord at the time, mentions nothing as mundane as the payment of rent: "In 1899/1900 I lived in a three-room apartment in the former Michael Boulevard, number 110. Comrade Soso Dzhugashvili, now Comrade Stalin, the great leader of the world's proletariat, lived in one of the best rooms. His friend Misho Davitashvili lived with him. Simbistro Dzhibladze had recommended us to him, since we were regarded as a reliable family."[12]

In December 1899 Stalin was nevertheless forced to take a job as a clerk at the Tiflis Geophysical Observatory, which operated under the aegis of the Tiflis Institute of Physics. Besides the modest salary, the auxiliary staff were provided with accommodation. Soso was mainly responsible for taking weather-related measurements. However, because of the shortage of personnel his tasks occasionally included cleaning the yard, shoveling snow in winter and sweeping up the suffocating dust in summer.[13] One of his collegauges at the time, Dombrovsky, in his recollections, written down in January 1934, concerns a conflict between Comrade Soso, the recognized leader of the proletarians in Tiflis, and one of the officials working at the observatory. According to the story Dombrovsky and Stalin were living in the basement of a house, the mansard of which was occupied by their supervisor. On one occasion the latter brought a live pig into the apartment: "The animal was rampaging around for days up there, causing a great deal of disturbance to the people living below. Iosif Vissarionovich, however, did not hesitate. He asked the owner of the animal to do something with it, thus restoring calm. Such an action was regarded at the time as unusually brave," writes the author of the recollections, adding "Iosif Vissarionovich did not hesitate for a moment. He demanded his [human] rights and the right to peace and quiet. On such occasions he was afraid of no one."[14]

Soso did not have to live with the threat of revenge by his bosses: on March 28, 1901 he left his job suddenly, without handing in his notice. The Tiflis gendarmerie suspected him of taking part in spreading illegal publications and searched the observatory in his absence.[15] This brought an end to Stalin's "conformist period", during which he had mostly lived on his own salary.

From then on, until as late as autumn 1917 when he was appointed as people's commissar for nationalities in the first Bolshevik government led by Lenin—that is, for almost sixteen years—*other people supported Stalin financially.* Travel expenses for trips connected with party work were usually covered by one of the regional illegal party committees. His rare foreign trips were financed by the leaders of the Bolshevik emigration. During his periods in exile the tsarist authorities "took care" of him, transferring a monthly sum "which was not enough to live on, but enough to keep him alive". This sum was usually augmented by the trustees of a foundation called the Political Red Cross, the forerunner of Red Aid. In the early 1910s, when Stalin became, for a short time, one of the key figures in the Bolshevik movement, he was entitled to a relatively substantial allowance from the secret foreign fund handled by Lenin and his circle. Stalin also earned a few rubles from the nationwide Social Democratic press by his publications. This did not amount to much, although he kept track of his dues and immediately collected whatever he was entitled to.[16]

In the meantime, Stalin became adept at making money without working. He inundated his acquaintances with letters, asking them to send food parcels and used clothes. If one of his bills was settled by someone else on his behalf, he acknowledged it without turning a hair. During one of his periods of exile in Siberia a number of typical "lamentations" were included in his correspondence with Tatyana Slovatinskaya, his sweetheart at the time.[17] In one of the three letters intercepted by the tsarist postal censors, Stalin wrote on December 1, 1913: "Tatyana Aleksandrovna! I have no choice but to mention this: necessity compels it. I have no money and have even run out of food."[18]

His addressee apparently took the hint, since Stalin's next letter is full of expressions of gratitude: "December 12. Dearest darling Tatyana Aleksandrovna! I received your parcel, but you really didn't need to buy new undergarments. I asked only for my old ones to be sent. Yet you bought me a new set, spending money you yourself can ill afford. I don't know how I can repay you, my darling sweetheart!"[19]

However, his third letter, dated December 20, is once again full of his misery: "My darling, my need is increasing hour by hour. I am in dire straits. To make things worse, I have even fallen ill. I have a permanent cough. I need milk, but… that would take money, and I have none. My darling, if you can get hold of a little money, please forward it to me at once. I have no strength to wait any longer…"[20]

Like Tatyana Slovatinskaya, several of Stalin's comrades helped him regularly. However, before the revolution in October 1917 he accepted support mostly from wealthy "class alien" acquaintances of Georgian and other nationalities, and sometimes from their friends. According to Abdurakhman Avtorkhanov, who often heard stories on this subject from old Georgian emigrants, one of the favorite sayings of the dictator was: "Let the rich pay!" Nor was such "cadging" an alien concept to other militants in the Russian revolutionary movement.[21] However, some truly novelistic stories are known about these years in the life of Stalin. In 1904 a wealthy Georgian lawyer by the name of Bibineishvili, who came from a noble Georgian family,[22] apparently sent fifty rubles, a warm overcoat, and "a fine pair of felt boots with red decoration and white wool lining" to his fellow countryman who was then in prison. In the letter that accompanied the gift he offered further help in the future. In reply, the young Stalin sent him a note that read: "My grateful thanks! I have no need of anything else. Your offer truly moved me."

At the end of the 1930s the lawyer, by then very old and ill, was a prisoner in the Gulag. In his utter desperation he had a letter, addressed to the Soviet dictator, smuggled out during visiting time. As if talking to the former Soselo he requested the return of the warm clothes along with money corresponding to the new exchange rates, since when he had given his gift he had used his own money rather than party funds. The Master of the Kremlin, who by that time had arranged for the disappearance of several unwelcome witnesses of his career in the revolutionary movement, surprisingly gave orders for the old man to be released. However, according to the Georgian writer Chubua Amiredzhibi, the prisoner survived for only a few days after his release.[23]

The Bibineishvili story is supported by Georgy Bezirgani, one of the Georgian researchers into Stalin's youth, who met relatives of the lawyer. His is a less romantic version, however. According to him the elderly prisoner who was released from the Gulag was at one time a Bolshevik militant himself. His byname in the movement was the "Baron", a reference to his noble origins.[24] According to other sources, however, amongst others, the memoirs of the "Baron" himself, Bibineishvili's father was a simple peasant. This does not exclude the possibility that he supported the young Dzhugashvili. As a young man, Stalin's alleged benefactor participated in some "expropriations"—that is, armed mail-coach and bank robberies—carried out to further the aims of the Bolsheviks.[25]

☆ Whatever the generous lawyer's background, it remains true that Soso inherited the majority of his genes not so much from his industrious mother as from his vagrant father. For more than two decades he even demanded money from Keke, herself impoverished and ill. She, in return, was harassed in the meantime by the authorities because of her son. Later, however, a number of official documents mysteriously disappeared, including the statements made by the mother of the future General Secretary of the party and by his uncle, Glah (Georgy) Geladze, before the tsarist investigating magistrate.

The monitoring of Keke by the political police was stepped up after April 1902. Soso, who was then in detention in Batumi prison awaiting trial, had thoughtlessly thrown two notes out of his cell window in the hope that someone would find them and forward them to the addressee. In one of them he told Keke to make a confession confirming that her son, Soso, was with her in Gori throughout the summer and winter, up to March 15. However, the guards intercepted this note, along with the other, similarly compromising, letter.[26]

On May 18 and 20, 1902 the Gori gendarmes reported to their superiors in Tiflis that Keke "had left for an unknown destination". On June 16 they recorded that she had returned to Gori.[27] On November 3, 1911 Stalin's mother was summoned to the Gori gendarmerie to be questioned about her son who had been a fugitive.[28]

Interestingly, not a single letter has been found written by Keke Geladze to her son in the early years of the century. Thus we know only from the recollections of contemporaries that until the end of her life she called him by the nickname

Soso, or Soselo. However, his acquaintances referred more and more frequently to the emerging Social Democratic politician as "Koba". After a time the byname used in the movement began to appear in police documents. Occasionally, it can be found in rather odd compounds, such as "Soso-Koba", or "Koba (Soso)", and occasionally "Koba (S-so)", as if the two names were one.[29]

Iosif Dzhugashvili in 1903.

The origins of the name "Koba" have been general knowledge for decades. According to several concurring sources it can be traced back to one of the influential books read by Soso as a teenager—*The Parricide* (also known as *Nunu*), a novel by the popular Georgian writer Aleksandr Kazbegi.[30] The novel, from the beginning to the end, is built on black and white clichés. One of its central figures is the strong and muscular Koba. His skill with various weapons far surpasses that of his companions; he is a loyal friend and, despite being a Christian, sympathizes with the Muslim Chechen rebels. He has a deep hatred of the tsarist troops, the invaders of Caucasia, and ambushes the arrogant lords. After many moving love scenes Koba finally confronts those countrymen of his who have collaborated, and is overpowered by them. Although most of his comrades fall in the struggle, Koba breaks free from the surrounding enemy and at the end of the novel decides to take his revenge on the accomplices of the Russian invaders.

According to Stalin's friend in his youth, Iosif Iremashvili, Koba was young Soso's "ideal and the object of his dreams": "He wanted to be a second Koba, a hero fighting against his enemies, as famous as Koba was. He wanted Koba to come alive in him. [...] Whenever we called him 'Koba' his face would light up with pleasure and pride."[31]

Unlike the hero of his dreams, however, the real Soso would never be a loyal friend to anyone. He regularly dodged any potential dangers and was unwilling to get involved in direct confrontations. Perhaps it is only the romanticism surrounding the outlaw that has any echo in the career of Iosif Dzhugashvili. However, the money from the armed robberies that Stalin controlled from the wings during the period of the "bourgeois democratic" revolution of 1905–1907 was not shared among the needy Georgian peasants but was forwarded to the party's leaders. And when, in autumn 1917, the Bolshevik "Koba" became part of the establishment, unlike Kazbegi's hero he quickly forgot the deep-seated hatred felt by the Caucasian nations for their Russian oppressors. Before long it was Stalin himself who was accelerating the aggressive Russification of the region following the main lines of, and in certain details consciously imitating, the imperial policy of the "white tsars". He had the descendants of the Chechen freedom fighters, who were represented as positive heroes in the favorite novel of his youth, deported to central Asia along with members of other Caucasian, usually Muslim, nations.[32]

However, all this happened much later. Before the early 1910s several articles and letters written by Iosif Dzhugashvili, in which he criticized the nationality policy of the tsarist regime, were signed "Koba", "Ko...", "K. Kato" or "Koba Ivanovich".[33] In the early 1910s, when the politician assumed his new byname and became Joseph Stalin, for a while, rather than the first letter of his own Christian name he used the letter "K", for "Koba", before his new second name. He later did away with the movement byname that had been used in his youth—although his lingering sentimentalism is suggested by the fact that he tolerated the use of the name "Koba" by certain of his friends who had known him from the years of illegal activity, including Voroshilov, Bukharin, and Yenukidze.[34]

After a while the Master of the Kremlin began to avoid identifying himself not only with the byname but with the romantic hero as well. In the 1930s, within his family circle, he began to give vague explanations regarding the Turkish origin of the name "Koba". Evidence of this can be found in a letter written by Anna Alliluyeva, dated 13 December 1946, to Abulkasim Lakhuti, the most famous Soviet poet of the time, who wrote in Farsi: "Koba (also pronounced Kova and Kave) is the name of a hero of an ancient Oriental legend. It is the story of an honorable blacksmith who waved his leather apron aloft as a banner. [...] The name of the legendary blacksmith came to stand for the fearless hero, who revolts against the oppressors of his nation."[35] Anna, Stalin's sister-in-law, on the other hand, presents an entirely different explanation in her recollections, which appeared in the same year. Naming the, by then deceased, Bolshevik Georgian printer Sila Todria as her source, she claimed: "In Batumi, where Soso led the workers onto the streets to demonstrate *[on March 9, 1902—M. K.]*, he was named 'Koba', which in Turkish means 'invincible'."[36]

In the early years of the century, Iosif Dzhugashvili had another secret name besides "Koba", according to his compatriot Elisabedashvili. "We, his friends, would often see Soso wearing a blue or black satin shirt, a cap with the peak pulled down over his eyes, and short boots, pushing his left shoulder slightly forward, his right arm slightly bent, holding a cigarette in his hand, hurrying through the streets among the crowds. We called him 'Geza' because of his distinctive gait. He was given this nickname by Ambilarashvili, once a good friend of his, who died in 1911 and was buried in Gori. Apart from us no one knew this name, since otherwise he was called 'Koba'."[37]

This same recollection, with certain cuts, was published on the occasion of Stalin's sixtieth birthday. However, the censors substantially rewrote Elisabedashvili's text. In the final version Soso had neither a peaked cap nor a cigarette. The reference to his physical defects, to his waddling gait and the peculiar movement of his deformed arm, also disappeared, and even the word "Geza", which came from the Georgian dialect used around Gori, lost its original meaning. In the manuscript the author had defined it as "one with a waddling gait", whereas the ever-alert editors corrected the translation to "one with an upright bearing".[38]

It was not only his byname that Stalin changed during his remarkably long youth. Until the Bolshevik takeover of 1917 he had not really decided from which social stratum he came. He had always sought an intellectual context, but in such circles he was not keen to mention the fact that he had attended a Seminary. When he became General Secretary of the party, however, he no longer avoided the subject, especially in order to stress that he had revolted against his priest teachers. When talking to Emil Ludwig he compared his teachers in Tiflis to the Jesuits,[39] while up until the mid-1930s he posed as a man who had emerged from the lower classes. Following the outbreak of the Second World War, however, his relationship to the priesthood markedly changed. He eased up on his oppression of the Russian Orthodox Church, which until then had been almost forced underground. Nevertheless, he still got the NKVD, the political police to supervise the reorganized Patriarchate and to exercise comprehensive control over the senior priesthood. During the war, for instance, he told one of the best-educated officers of the Red Army, Marshal Vasilyevsky, who came from the family of an Orthodox pope and therefore was not promoted as quickly as others, that it was no problem for him to remain in contact with his father who lived in a parish in the country.[40]

It is apparent from many sources that Stalin occasionally played on his uneducated, cruel, "Asiatic" traits. Within the "inner circle" however, he often appealed for pity since, as the son of "a simple worker", he had missed out on so much during his life. Nevertheless, until as late as 1926 he did not mention that his shoemaker father was "a simple worker". He was probably afraid that, via his childhood acquaintances, half of Georgia knew that his father had had his own workshop in Gori. In the illegal Social Democratic, and later Bolshevik, organizations, it was for this reason, among others, that Iosif Dzhugashvili was not regarded by the manual laborers as one of their number. Besides, he was "the leader of the conspiratorial circle", "comrade newspaper editor", a "party intellectual", and perhaps even "the emissary of the center", that is, a *nachalnik.*

On the other hand, the tsarist authorities regarded Stalin as a "peasant". In September 1913, when a large group of St. Petersburg gendarmes raided the apartment of Sergei (Sergo) Kavtaradze on account of the young Bolshevik student,[41] they explained their action as follows: "We searched the apartment as a result of reports from external observers, according to which, in 1912, the said person was in contact with Iosif Vissarionovich Dzhugashvili (known as Koba), a peasant living in the jurisdiction of Tiflis."[42]

1 Stalin 1951, vol. XIII, 113. In most cases, the party secretary later thoroughly re-edited such interviews. And if the interviewer did not accept the text he corrected and signed—like the American agricultural expert, Campbell—he immediately reacted on the pages of the Moscow press. He found this so important that before his article appeared in *Pravda,* he sent it out to the members of the contemporary "inner circle": Andreyev, Voroshilov, Kaganovich, Kalinin, Kirov, Stanislav Kosior, Kuybishev, Mikoyan, Molotov, Ordzhonikidze, Petrovsky, Chubar, Rudzutak, and Postishev. *RGASPI,* fond. 558, op. 1, d. 2989. On other occasions, quite strangely, he even asked the Western visitors to write down the interview in a sketchy outline, he would even give them a type-writer, so that he can have it translated into Russian. See Lyons, 1937, 381–393. The Master of the Kremlin, however, enjoyed he conversation with Ludwig so much that apart from a few stylistic modifications, he did not change the text. For that matter, this one seems to be the best of Stalin's interviews.

2 Yaroslavsky, 1939, 14.

3 Tucker, 1991, 88.

4 *Molodaya Gvardia,* 1939, no. 12, 101. When this text was published in the Volume VIII of Stalin's Collected Works, the phrase "greenhorn" had already disappeared, and it was replaced by "young man". Stalin, 1948, vol. VIII, 174. More details from witnesses in: *RGASPI,* fond. 71, op. 10, d. 266 and fond. op. 4, d. 651.

5 Bazhanov, 1983, 145–154.

6 On his scandalous behavior, see Lenin, 1999, 330, 367.

7 *Molodaya Gvardia,* 1939, no. 12, 101.

8 Uratadze, 1968, 278.

9 Stalin was largely wrong in citing time. During the two years he referred to he worked mostly in Georgia. See Trotsky, 1990, I, 164–166.

10 Stalin, 1948, vol. VIII, 174–175.

11 Iosif Vissarionovich Stalin, 1951, 10. Crosschecking the sources leads us to the conclusion that in the fall of 1899, Stalin had to go to Tiflis to obtain the documents from the chancellery of the Exarchate in connection with his expulsion. I looked at some of these documents in Moscow. *RGASPI,* fond 558. op. 4. d. 65. I. and Molodaya Gvardia 1939, no. 12, 87.

12 *Molodaya Gvardia,* 1939, no. 12, 87. Davitashvili was a talented student of the Tiflis Seminary at the same time when Soso attended the school. He later emigrated to the West, and joined the Georgian Social Democratic community in Leipzig. According to his contemporary schoolmates, Misho was a somewhat happy-go-lucky, cheerful man. He was a good contrast to the boorish, rowdy, gimlet-eyed Iosif Dzhugashvili.

13 *RGASPI,* fond. 71, op. 10, d. 404. This is not true. However, archivists have revealed that Soso lived together with an opposition-minded one-time seminarist, a certain Vasily Berdzeneshvili (Berdzenev) in the official residence. Officially, Iosif Dzhugashvili started working at the Geophysical Observatory on December 28, 1899, and stayed there until March of 1901. He left his job, without resigning officially, when the police began to track him down. According to one of his coworkers from that time, Dombrovsky, Stalin's departure was in the beginning of March or the end of April, 1901. Some researchers quibble with this Ostrovsky 2002, 159–166. For my part, I accept the date of March 28, 1901, as the last day Stalin spent at the Observatory.

14 *RGASPI,* fond. 558, op. 4, d. 651.

15 *RGASPI,* fond. 71, op. 10, d. 404.

16 *Bolshevistkoye Rukovodstvo,* 1996, 17.

17 The grandmother of Yury Trifonov, the author of the famous book, *House on the Embankment.*

18 *RGASPI*, fond. 558, op. 4, d. 5392.
19 In the 1920s, the dictator arranged that Tatyana be hired to work in the party apparatus. She worked first in a secret department of the Central Committee, then became an office director at the party headquarters. Moreover, the Master of the Kremlin made sure that his ex-lover became a member of the Central Supervisory Committee. *Stalinskoye Politburo*, 1995, 307. Lazar Kaganovich, who knew their relationship well and was Slovatinskaya's immediate superior for a while, is wrong when he claims that Tatyana was ten years older than Stalin was. Tshuyev, 1992, 160. In fact, she was one year younger than the Master of the Kremlin. The gratitude towards Slovatinskaya did not last long, however. In 1937, Stalin arranged that Tatyana's daughter was sent to prison, her son-in-law executed, and she herself, together with two of her grandchildren, was kicked out of House on the Embankment, the home of the Soviet elite.
20 Smerch, 1998a.
21 Valentinov, 1993, 292–335.
22 Judging from some slips of his tongue, Stalin hated the Georgian nobility. Felstinsky, 1999, 172. Their money, however, he liked to accept.
23 Dombrovsky, 1989, 520-521, 553–563.
24 *Perspektivi*, 1991, 6, 55–56.
25 Bibineishvili, 1931, 85–110, 114, 126–133.
26 *RGASPI*, fond. 71, op. 10, d. 401. Keke requested the authorities in March 1902 or 1903 that his son be released from prison. *RGASPI*, fond. 558, op. 4, d. 405. Corroborating the latter date, there is the obituary published by *Zarya Vostoka*, the party daily in Tiflis, in 1937, which states that she visited Soso in the prison during the early spring of 1903. Perhaps what she saw then, prompted her to make her appeal.
27 *RGASPI*, fond. 71, op. 10, d. 404.
28 *RGASPI*, fond. 71, op. 10, d. 407.
29 *Krasny Arkhiv*, 1941, no. 2, 6, 9, 11.
30 Tucker, 1991, 82–83.
31 Iremaschwili, 1932, 18.
32 Bugay, 1995, 56–186.
33 Stalin, 1946, II, 13, 31, 77, 86, 145.
34 *RGASPI*, fond. 74, op. 2, d. 37, d. 5252, d. 41.
35 *RGASPI*, fond. 558, op. 4, d. 536.
36 Alliluyeva, 1946, 110.
37 *RGASPI*, fond. 558, op. 4, d. 665.
38 *Molodaya Gvardia*, 1939, no. 12, 86–87.
39 Stalin, 1951, vol. XIII, 113–114.
40 Vasilyevsky, 1975, 108.
41 Kavtaradze, an old acquaintance of Soso Dzhugashvili, was the head of the Georgian Soviet government in 1923–1924. In the 1920s, he became a supporter of Trotsky, and spent years in exile and prison. According to certain sources, at the beginning of the 1930s he informed the NKVD on the activities of the Trotskyist circles operating in the Soviet Union. Perhaps this is why Stalin granted a pardon to him before the war. He even visited Kavtaradze once, together with Beria, at his communal apartment, which has created a stir all over Moscow. Shortly after this, Kavtaradze was appointed Deputy Comissar for Foreign Relations, and later became the Soviet Ambassador to Bucharest. However, Stalin recalled him from duty in 1952, because he suspected, not without any reason, that he was biased towards one of the Romanian Communist leaders, Ana Pauker, who was imprisoned with the charge of "Jewish nationalism". (Kavtaradze did in fact fell in love with the woman.) After the death of the dictator, he was one of the few old guard party members, once living underground, who helped the researchers to understand how deep the roots of Soviet totalitarianism reach into the soil. Aleksandr Bek was also among them, who depicted the everyday life of the Soviet political leaders in his novel, *New Task*.
42 *RGASPI*, fond. 558, op. 4, d. 223.

CHAPTER 4
The Past Rewritten

The officials of the Okhrana *[the tsarist secret police—Trans.]*, who mentioned the future Soviet dictator as being a member of the Didi-Lilo village commune, could not have suspected that one day many local Bolshevik petty tyrants would compete as to which of them could tell the most fanciful story about the young Soso. The same is true, of course, for ordinary people. For example, Sila Todria attributes the following words of wisdom to Stalin: "He asked me what I was learning in Sunday school. When I told him that the teachers were explaining the course of the sun, he answered with a smile: 'You don't need to worry about the sun not keeping to its course. You should rather study the course of revolutionary affairs and help me create an illegal printing house.'"[1]

Kote Kalandarov, an elderly metalworker, told similar stories following this same pattern. According to his recollections, he gave a home to Iosif Dzhugashvili for two months in November 1901 when, on the orders of the party leadership—or, according to another version, after being rejected by his friends as a result of his conspiratorial nature—the underground party worker, then in hiding from the authorities, moved to Batumi. According to Kalandarov two workers, Kotrikadze and Kuridze, "recognized that Comrade Soso was wearing worn-out boots. They decided to buy him a new pair, but he refused their offer: 'I can only accept your gift', he said, 'if you buy a better pair of shoes for yourselves, too.'"[2]

A worker from Batumi by the name of Rodyon Korkia outdid everyone with his story. He recalled how he had awaited the coming of the new year on New Year's Eve 1901 along with a few colleagues and Soso. According to him the future leader greeted those present as follows: "Dawn is near! The sun will soon rise! It will shine on us! Believe in this, comrades!"[3]

These stories were raked together by members of the "Beria brigade". However, the Stalin cult in Georgia, based on "one-upmanship", was not started by the future chief of the NKVD. It was launched in the first half of the 1930s by Nestor Lakoba, a well-known member of the Caucasian Bolshevik movement, who was to experience the most dramatic fate.[4] The talented politician, who remains popular in his homeland even today, is remembered in the history of the region as the creator of the ephemerally short-lived independent Abkhazia *[now part of Georgia—Trans.]*. In spite of his efforts, as a result of a decision made in the Kremlin the subtropical region, rich in citrus trees and beautiful beaches, was annexed to Soviet Georgia in 1931, although its autonomous status remained. From then on the short, slightly reserved, and almost entirely deaf Lakoba had to travel to Tiflis regularly, since the fate of his homeland depended on the rapidly changing Georgian leadership, if only because of the lack of Abkhazian infrastructure and its geographical proximity. However, influential leaders from Moscow, whom the president of the Abkhazian soviet, based in Sukhumi, invited each year to the splendid government resorts on the Black Sea coast, were themselves fond of interfering in the internal affairs of Abkhazia.

Lakoba usually established good relationships with these politicians, and his wide range of acquaintances meant that he had some important connections in the Kremlin. Nicknamed "the deaf man", he very early on, from the beginning of the 1920s, ostentatiously maintained that he was an unconditional follower of Stalin.

As a sign of his loyalty he regularly sent crates of tangerines to the Kremlin. They were meant as a gift to the Caucasian clan in the Kremlin and to the Master himself. At the same time Lakoba welcomed in the province under his control those Moscow politicians who had fallen out of favor. Among them was the seriously ill Leon Trotsky, who later spoke very warmly of the two Lakoba brothers, Nestor and Mikhail, who was the Abkhazian minister of internal affairs and later of agriculture. In 1924 the two brothers looked after him for several months.[5]

According to the recollections of various contemporaries, whenever Stalin spent his holidays in Abkhazia or Georgia the first thing he did was to summon Nestor Lakoba. During lavish meals, punctuated by long toasts, that would last into the early hours and often ended in complete drunkenness, he is rumored to have forced the short Abkhazian, who had a reputation for being a good marksman, to produce his old Mauser rifle and, like some twentieth-century William Tell, to entertain the company with shooting tricks. In the meantime, Joseph Stalin reveled in stirring up quarrels between Lakoba, whom he showered with medals and expensive gifts, and his main rival, Lavrenty Beria.

For a while it seemed that the rivalry between these two politicians, which was by no means without risks, was evenly matched. However, it would eventually work out in favor of Beria, who was able to assimilate more quickly than others the—in many respects new—rules of the Great Terror. In December 1936, at a dinner he gave at his own home, Beria, the Georgian party leader, like some Oriental despot, poisoned "the deaf man". Feigning inconsolable grief he then organized a grand funeral for Lakoba, who was said to have died of a "heart attack". A year later, however, Beria targeted the family and clientele of his rival. The commando unit of the Tiflis NKVD—probably with Stalin's knowledge—traveled to Abkhazia where they staged a bloodbath that lasted for months among the relatives and followers of the dead party leader. No mercy was shown even to women and young children in their methodical elimination of the Abkhazian political elite, nor did they spare the mortal remains of Nestor Lakoba, who had in the meantime been labeled a spy and a saboteur. In Abkhazia even today there are several legends telling how Beria had the coffin of his rival removed from the cemetery.[6]

It was subsequently forbidden even to mention that it had been the posthumously "excommunicated" Lakoba who had "invented" Hashim Smirba, one of the important characters in Stalin's "shadow theater". The Abkhazian leader, Lakoba had made it appear that the illiterate old man had been an important helper of the young revolutionary Soso in his efforts to coordinate from the wings the conspiracy among the Batumi workers in 1902.

The underground party worker in 1905–06.

On the basis of his conversations with the garrulous old man, Nestor Lakoba had his colleagues produce a small pamphlet titled *Stalin and Hashim*, written in the style of a folktale. In the foreword Lakoba claimed simply to have set down in writing at the request of his acquaintances among the Abkhazian working peasants what had been preserved in the memory of the local population concerning "the politician; the practical executioner, the strategist, and the tactician of Bolshevism; the greatest figure of an entire era; the kind of man whom history produces only once in every one or two hundred years".[7] The promoter of Abkhazian autonomy included several tale-like motifs in the narrative. He described how young Iosif Dzhugashvili marched through the streets of Batumi at the head of a crowd of three thousand. He also recounted the advice that Dzhugashvili had given to the Batumi workers who were intending to protest in front of the state prison in the hope of setting their imprisoned comrades free. When the workers hesitated at the last moment, fearing that force would be used against them, Dzhugashvili urged

Hunting tour on a gunboat along the Abkhazian coast, the "Red Subtropics". Sitting next to Stalin is Nestor Lakoba (x), the ruler of the small Caucasian autonomous province.

them on: "The soldiers won't shoot at us. And don't be afraid of their commanders. Just strike them over the head! We will achieve freedom for our comrades."

The gray-uniformed tsarist troops, which were ordered from the inner provinces to the Black Sea coast, quashed the attack by the demonstrators. According to local historians fourteen workers died and another forty-six were wounded as a result of the volleys fired into the crowd in Batumi. According to Lakoba, Soso, who had left the scene in good time, hid in a nearby village at the home of Hashim Smirba.

However, to prove his steadfastness of purpose, he set up an illegal printing press there. "Once, when Comrade Soso was alone with Hashim, he said to him: 'Hashim, perhaps you are troubled by the fact that I am carrying out an activity in your home that may have serious consequences for you. Perhaps you do not want to be sent to prison with me, Hashim. I don't want to be a nuisance to you. If you think I should leave, I will go.'" Before answering, like any genuine folk hero Hashim sucked on his pipe for several minutes. Then he looked at Soso gravely before speaking: "You must have seen that I keep two fierce dogs in my yard. You can stay here. These two ferocious beasts won't let any strangers in." In another episode of the lengthy epic the host sighed: "'You could be a very good man, Soso! It's a pity you're not a Muslim.' 'Why would it be better if I were a Muslim?' asked Comrade Soso. 'Because if you adopted the Muslim faith I would find you seven beautiful women to marry. The kind you've never even dreamed of. So, do you want to be a Muslim?' Comrade Soso answered with a smile: 'Of course!', and shook Hashim by the hand."

"Hashim would never forget this exchange until his dying day," explained Nestor Lakoba to his fellow countrymen. "It was branded on his memory how tolerant Soso was of his old-fashioned philosophy. Soso hadn't laughed at the old man for proposing that he should convert to the Muslim faith."[8]

However, the long parable was still not finished. According to Lakoba, the next morning Hashim cheerfully addressed his friend Soso: "'Don't be afraid! […] Your cause will triumph.' 'How do you know?' asked Comrade Stalin. 'I had a dream, Soso. I dreamed that you set the whole of Caucasia free from the tsarist troops, and that we all lived at ease, in prosperity and freedom. You should be aware that this is a very good thing. This is a very good thing, Soso!'"[9]

Ivan Tovstukha, in spite of being one of the early initiators of the cult of Stalin, confided in a letter, dated March 11, 1934, to Lazar Kaganovich, then the deputy of the General Secretary of the party, that he had doubts concerning the Smirba tales: "Lazar Moyseyevich! I have held back the Hashim text for a while as I have been working on Stalin's new book. There were still things to correct and rewrite. Unfortunately, I have almost no material to rely on. I read through several books but have found only vague references. Not even copies of *Iskra*[10] from the time mention the events in Batumi. All that was published were some excerpts from the court hearing, but only after the trial. I still believe the book should be published. It promises to be interesting. But what shall I do about the foreword? I can't rewrite it. It should be thrown out. With Communist greetings!"[11]

The writer of the letter of course did not dare propose that the rest of the improbable tales by Lakoba be "thrown out" since he knew, better than anyone else, that this kind of byzantine legend-making took place with Stalin's consent and often even on his direct orders. Such naive stories were largely used to manipulate the less erudite stratum of the population.

☆ As he approached his sixtieth birthday, which was celebrated with massive pomp, Joseph Stalin came up with some new ideas. He ensured that his official biography be published continuously in huge print runs, along with the short history of the Bolshevik Party, the famous-infamous *Kratky Kurs*, and the volumes of his Collected Works. He considered it fitting that after working hours, or in the course of university lectures, the majority of the Soviet population should study these texts under the supervision of professional propagandists. He doubtless thought that in this way he could right an old injustice. Even though, from the beginning of the 1920s, Stalin had achieved prominence as General Secretary of the party, for a long time it was not his works that lined the bookshelves of the Soviet elite and of the libraries, but those of Lenin, Trotsky, Zinovyev, and Kamenev.[12] This was not, as Trotsky supposed, due to his weakness of style, which would force him to remain in the background. In this respect the Soviet dictator was no different from other Bolshevik political writers. Most Soviet party leaders, Trotsky himself, generally expressed their ideas in simplistic, long-winded, cliché language, especially when addressing a larger audience. Bearing this in mind, Stalin could in fact have published his Collected Works in the 1920s.[13] The truth was, however, that he had written relatively little. Among his thematic collections, *Concerning Questions of Leninism* and *On Opposition*, which were written in the heat of the power struggles, were nevertheless widespread,[14] and the combined print runs of smaller Stalin collections or pamphlets containing individual speeches amounted to several million.

Strangely enough, the chief opponent of the Master of the Kremlin, Trotsky, did not attribute any significance to this flood of publications: "Why doesn't a selected series of Stalin's speeches and writings and his Collected Works appear?" he asks in the pages of his book on Stalin. And he immediately answers his own question: "There can be little doubt that the idea of such an edition has arisen in the heads of young careerists willing to go to any lengths.[15] But Stalin had no option but to quash these plans in their embryonic stage. Nothing could have been more dangerous for him. The nine years he spent in a Church School have left an indelible trace on his personality. [...] The Russian language that he learned in scholastic theology classes remains a half-alien, artificial language for him, with a Seminary veneer. [...] Of course, no one could expect Stalin to have

Hashim Smirba adzhar peasant. We still do not know whether or not he wrote the stories praising Koba.

a writer's gift. His style, however, reveals the nature of his thoughts. As soon as he enters the realm of abstraction his language becomes uncertain and hesitant. [...] His sentences are connected artificially."[16]

Nevertheless, in his position at the top of the hierarchy such claims may have troubled Joseph Stalin very little. Perhaps all that is revealed by his correspondence is that in the Russian-language edition of his Collected Works he attempted to eliminate–or have eliminated by his colleagues–the rather slapdash wording of the original texts. It may have been this that held up for so long the publication of the first volume. The appearance of the small-format, brown-covered, typographically undistinguished book was originally planned by the joint editors for 1940. However, the first volume in the sixteen-volume series was eventually printed only in February 1946.[17] Since the book contained almost exclusively Stalin's Georgia-related early writings, the translation and editing, which was carried out simultaneously in Moscow and in Tiflis, took years to complete. In the 1930s Stalin thoroughly edited the Russian translations of his Georgian-language writings.[18] The suspicious dictator—at this time more or less justifiably—doubted the expertise of the historians and archivists working in Tiflis, even though the members of the editorial team were, from autumn 1934, already full-time employees at the richly subsidized local Stalin Institute in the Georgian capital. The "Beria brigade", which researched the biography of the "fervent warrior of the Caucasian proletariat", was recruited partly from among them.

"What a strange lot they are! The Institute is utterly deserted, no one seems to do anything there," wrote Ivan Tovstukha maliciously on September 28, 1934 to Mamia Orakhelashvili, a former Georgian party leader who was exiled to Moscow as a punishment where he was conducting research on the history of the party. "What is especially disturbing is the number of them employed there. Forty-seven people. [...] And this year, for instance, they say they have published *nine* works by Stalin. But which works? And did they do this with the permission of St[alin]?"[19]

Tovstukha did not speak Georgian and was therefore unable to supervise his colleagues in Tiflis properly. The Georgian Menshevik emigrants, however, who had once published their articles in the same local publications as "Comrade Soso", immediately recognized that the bogus researchers supervised by Beria were regularly falsifying, under the pretense of modernization, texts written by Stalin in the early years of the century.[20] In the 1950s the former Social Democrat journalist Arsenidze compared the original Stalin quotations used in the Georgian-language works of Beria with the Russian translations included in the first volume of the Collected Works of the Soviet dictator. He warned the exclusively Russian-speaking readers: "I found some very serious differences in the wording, in the line of thought, and in the argumentation."[21]

Irrelevant from the point of view of the later career of the young Koba, however, is the issue of how many texts were added to his works from among the writings of Georgian Social Democratic authors who published without signing what they had written.[22] What was more important during the period in which he was emerging as a politician were the character-forming influences to which he had been exposed in the stifling atmosphere of the conspiring circles, that is, how the somewhat dishonorable methods used during the period of underground activity were applied by Stalin in his struggle for total power as a mature politician and omnipotent dictator.[23]

From the recollections of Natrishvili, one of Stalin's classmates at the Seminary, written in the 1930s at the request of the "Beria brigade", it appears that

Keke Geladze, Beria (x), Lakoba (xx) and Stalin in 1935, in the home of the mortally ill old woman.

as early as April 1897 Stalin's presence created a split in the secret study circle at the Tiflis Orthodox Seminary. Before the arrival of Soso Dzhugashvili, the group had been led by Seid Davderiani, a student from one of the higher classes: "Initially, Seid appreciated Soso's contributions. Later, however, Soso gathered the students around himself and [...] gave the meetings a revolutionary focus. Seid disapproved. He became angry and called him 'nasty'. He said that Soso was undermining the cause of both the circle and the revolution."[24]

The reason for the conflict was not that Iosif Dzhugashvili was dissatisfied with the program of the conspiring study circle. He could not have been, since, according to other sources, it was Seid Davderiani who represented at the meetings the unique spirit of the first Georgian Marxists, that is, the editorial board of the *Kvali* periodical and the semi-legal movement known as Mesame-Dasi. Davderiani's mentors wrote a special course of study for him.[25] The debate was rather about who should be the leader of the secret study circle. Seid Davderiani and a few of his followers were in the end forced to leave. In the course of the final clash the offended Davderiani even called Soso "obnoxious".[26]

The writers of the official Stalin biographies welcomed the recollections of Natrishvili, since they radiated Stalin's "uncompromising revolutionary determination". At the same time, they must have been in some doubt as to what to do with Seid Davderiani's insults. Any expression—such as "nasty" or "obnoxious"—that might still have offended the Soviet dictator more than thirty years later, was omitted from the manuscript that was sent to the printers. On the other hand, the drastically abridged text was supplemented by a didactic explanation not present in the original manuscript: "Soso was of the opinion that the study circle existed in order to form conscious militant revolutionaries and staunch Marxists."[27]

Piecing together other parts of the jigsaw it turns out that the young Soso often antagonized his acquaintances, among them members of the editorial board of *Kvali* who were much older than he and who had earlier supported him. Along with a few fellow seminarians he had joined the periphery of the *Kvali* circle in late 1898, half a year before he left the Seminary. He was even entrusted with a task by the editors of the journal. He was asked to deliver lectures to workers at the Tiflis Railway Workshop. However, a few months later, in the early spring of 1899, an outraged "Silva" Dzhibladze told Noi Zhordania, a key figure in both the *Kvali* circle and Mesame-Dasi, that Soso did not agitate so much against tsarism as against them, the members of the two workers' study circles.[28]

The antagonisms between Soso and his first mentors in the movement were not so much down to ideological differences as to fairly banal personality clashes. From the recollections of his fellow seminarians it appears that the young Stalin was inordinately vain. The editors of *Kvali*, who published one of his poems in 1896, gravely offended him by not continuing to publish his writings. In his recollections, in which he recounts several minor but fascinating details of the youth of his friend, Elisabedashvili refers to this fact: "I remember how Soso was furious with the editors of *Kvali*. Noi Zhordania was the most influential person at the journal at that time. Comrade Filipp Makharadze and others also worked there.[29] Comrade Soso was very dissatisfied with the editorial board and with the *Kvali* circle. He was especially angry with Filipp Makharadze. As I remember, he refused to publish [...] one of Stalin's contributions."[30]

As the years passed, members of the editorial board of *Kvali*, which had ceased publication in the meantime, became, with the exception of Makharadze, prominent Georgian Mensheviks, although they were generally more radical than their Russian counterparts.[31] On a personal level, however, from the very beginning they clashed fiercely with Lenin and his Georgian followers. Thus Iosif Dzhugashvili, who was a faithful, even a "fanatical", Leninist—his Menshevik opponents mockingly referred to him as "Lenin's left foot"[32]—attacked them so savagely that the exchanges were reduced to little more than a wrestling match.[33]

Nevertheless, the old relationships were not severed for a long time, not even as a result of the particularly cruel outbursts between the Bolsheviks and the Mensheviks. Between 1905 and 1907, the years of the Russian "bourgeois democratic" revolution, the struggle against the common enemy—the military governor of Tiflis—unquestionably united the two camps to such an extent that the representatives of the most diverse Social Democratic trends occasionally wrote admiringly in their recollections about certain of their opponents. However, all the Mensheviks remembered Stalin as a troublemaker. According to Grigol Karadzhyan, who, using the pseudonym Arkhomed, was the first to write a history of the Caucasian labor movement, Soso Dzugashvili—whose name he does not mention, although he makes quite clear who he is referring to—as early as December 1901 "carried out hostile and disruptive agitation against the leadership of the Social Democratic Party organization in Tiflis".[34]

Even several years later Radzen Arsenidze, the stylistically sophisticated Menshevik political journalist, described the role played by the young Stalin in the increasingly cruel atmosphere. This text, which was not published in the author's lifetime, appears credible despite his bias, especially since other former renowned Georgian Social Democrats recorded similar memories of "Comrade Koba's" outbursts of anger, which would end in paroxysms of rage: "He spoke with cruelty and hostility. His cruelty, however, radiated energy. His words were imbued with raw power and determination. He was often sarcastic or ironical. His cruel witticisms were often extreme, like the lash of a whip. [...] Sometimes he would use harsh words or would curse obscenely. Only the protests of his outraged listeners could somewhat reduce the stream of invective. On such occasions he usually apologized, explaining that he was speaking the language of the proletariat who were taught neither subtle manners nor aristocratic eloquence. According to him, the manual laborers talked straightforwardly and bluntly, but they always told the truth. And he was following their example."[35]

In such situations Soso would often mention his Menshevik opponents and,

In the 1930s Joseph Stalin and Filipp Makharadze acted as if they had not been rivals at the beginning of the century.

according to the recollections of Arsenidze, did not hesitate to play the "Jewish card" against them: "I heard him speaking a couple of times during meetings of Georgian workers, at which Russian workers were also present. 'Lenin', said Koba, 'is outraged that God has cursed him with such comrades as the Mensheviks. And what people they are! Martov, Dan, Akselrod are all circumcised Jews, and there is that old hag Vera Zasulich. How can you work with such people? They cannot fight. Nor do they know how to enjoy themselves. They are simply cowardly money changers!'"[36] According to the recollections of the Georgian politician, the audience of workers was generally outraged by such references. However, Soso Dzhugashvili did not understand why: "Don't the Georgian workers know that the Jews are a cowardly lot? That they will be of no use when the time comes to fight?" Despite what he had heard, Arsendize did not regard the young Stalin as anti-Semitic. He wrote: "He was entirely neutral to the question of whether to stand up for the Jews or to turn against them. If the latter course of action was useful, he saw no reason why he shouldn't profit from it."[37]

In contrast, in his lengthy review of the RSDLP's London congress in 1907—at a time when bloody pogroms were sweeping through Russia—Stalin used a somewhat jocular tone: "The national composition of the congress was very interesting. According to the statistics, in the Menshevik faction Jews form the majority, followed by Georgians and Russians. In the Bolshevik faction, however, the Russians are in the majority [...] followed by the Jews, Georgians, etc. One of the Bolshevik delegates (I think it was Comrade Aleksinsky) jestingly remarked that the Mensheviks are Jewish while the Bolsheviks are a genuine Russian faction, thus it would do no harm if we Bolsheviks carried out a little pogrom within the party."[38]

Several former Georgian Social Democrats mentioned that Koba's character was marked by a love of intrigue, coupled with cruelty and vulgar behavior. According to Uratadze: "He was a very dry man. All emotion had dried up in him. For instance, when we were taken out for a walk *[in prison—M. K.]* we would all gather in one corner of the prison courtyard. But Stalin, with his typically short steps, would walk by himself. If someone addressed him he would shape his mouth into a cold smile and at best was willing to exchange only a few words with us. Everyone knew how surly he was. [...] He was a somber man, obdurate and vindictive. [...] He focused all his energy on trampling underfoot the local *[Social Democratic—M. K.]* organizations. He would balk at nothing in order to achieve this. He was incapable of cooperating with anyone. He trusted no one but himself. Of my many acquaintances he was the only one without a comrade or a good friend. He went from one organization to the other, but never stayed anywhere for long. And in every single party organization in which he turned up there was ultimately recourse to a disciplinary committee, first in Tiflis, then in Batumi, and finally in Baku."[39]

Noi Khomeriki, another well-known militant of the Caucasian Social Democrats, painted a no more flattering picture of Stalin than Uratadze.[40] During a house search at the apartment of Vera Hodzhashvili, the tsarist police confiscated one of Khomeriki's letters to her, dated 2 October 1904. The letter remained unpublished until the change of political system in Russia in 1991. Khomeriki wrote: "I am well aware of the worth of such people as this gentleman. However, I did not expect such 'courage' from him.[41] But apparently characters like him are capable of anything if the means are more important to them than the ends. [...] In other words, this base person has vain hopes of showing the people what a great man he is. [...] But since the Lord does not usually bestow sufficient talent on people such as him to turn their ideas into reality, he reverts to intrigue, lies, and other such pleasantries." Khomeriki warned Vera Hodzhashvili to be cautious with respect to "Koba-Don Quixote". It would be good, he wrote, if "such filthy characters were given a lesson when they smear our great and holy cause with dirt and excrement." (In the early years of the century this conflict apparently made great waves among the Georgian Social Democrats. When Lavrenty Beria, then fearful of Stalin's revenge, was collecting compromising material about the Master in the Soviet archives in 1950, he was keen to get hold of this letter. Serova, the younger sister of the infamous General Ivan Serov and the head of the reference service of the archive administration department, which worked under the aegis of the Soviet Ministry of Internal Affairs, made confidential inquiries at the central historical archives in Moscow as to whether they had the letter.)[42]

Naturally, in conflicts of this kind it was not necessarily Koba's opponents who were in the right. Besides, with the passage of time former opponents often judged their earlier conflicts through the prism of later political clashes. Also, the fierce quarrels were sometimes followed by theatrical acts of reconciliation. During one of my visits to Moscow I recorded the words of Levon Shaumyan, a researcher into the Caucasian labor movement, on this subject: no matter what grudges Joseph Stalin bore, in the early 1910s, when hiding illegally in St. Petersburg, he renewed his connections with the leading Georgian Mensheviks who had once excluded him, since "Perhaps one day they will be useful to me." Former students at the Tiflis Seminary, Noi Zhordania, Silva Dzhibladze, and Iosif Dzhugashvili had sat at the same classroom desks, although in different years. Thus, to a certain extent, they were united by common memories. Occasionally they even got together, sang Georgian songs, and drank to one another's health. However, according to Shaumyan they came no closer to one another than this once Koba recognized that he no longer needed them.

The authenticity of this information would seem to be supported by an unpublished archive source. "They are too old; one cannot agree with them." These words of Iosif Dzhugashvili on the subject of these meetings were quoted in the late 1940s by Sophia Simatsova, the widow of Sila Todria, a Georgian printer working in St. Petersburg. According to her, the meetings with Zhordania and Dzhibladze had taken place in her husband's apartment in St. Petersburg.[43]

1 *Rasskazi starikh rabochikh*, 1937, 44–45.
2 *Ibid.*, 73–74.
3 Yaroslavsky, 1939, 22. More than 25 people came to the gathering held at the home of the Lomdzharia brothers. *RGASPI*, fond 71. op. 10. d. 381.
4 Knight, 1993, 81, 242, 245.
5 Trotsky, 1991, 236–241. Besides the Lakoba brothers, Beria—who was quite young then—also visited him in Abkhazia. Immediately after Lenin's death, he also "interrogated" Trotsky—most likely following Stalin's and his insiders' order. Yagoda, 1997, 307–308.
6 Knight, 1993, 72, 81, 245.
7 Lakoba, 1934, 5.
8 Hashim's ancestors might have been adzhar peasants, who converted to Muslim religion during the period of Turkish occupation.
9 Lakoba, 1934, 34–35. Hashim Smirba was a sort of substitute father *(nazvanny otec)* for Silvester Lomdzharia. He filled the role of a kind of "adjutant" for Soso Dzhugashvili at that time. Ostrovsky 2002, 186.
10 A periodical published by Russian emigrant Social Democrats at the beginning of the century.
11 *RGASPI*, fond. 81, op. 3, d. 422. Tovstukha and other "Stalinologists" didn't dare say that the reason Soso Dzhugashvili, who was almost unknown in the Tiflis suburbs, became the leader of the incredibly weak local workers' movement in the spring, or perhaps summer, of 1901, was because the leaders of these local illegal Marxist circles were, almost without exception, away. They were either hiding outside the capital of Georgia, away from revengeful authorities, or in prison. Neither did Joseph Stalin have too much time to "rule" his comrades. According to one version, the authorities were already closing in on him. In the mean time, the other local social democratic "bellwethers" apparently hated him. At the end, his companions blackballed him from the Tiflis party leadership. Uratdze 1968, 66–67. 1. and *Poslednie Novosti* 1936, XII, 16. It is interesting that for the creators of the Stalin cult after the war, even "true to life" histories were forbidden to mention that an epithet for Soso in Batumi was Tsopur (Scabby). He was even mentioned in police documents under this name. Batumskaya Demonstratsia 1902 goda 1937, 246.
12 Lev Kamenev, the first caretaker of the party leader's archives, published Lenin's *Complete Works* in twenty volumes between 1923 and 1928. Two more editions followed the first before the beginning of the 1930s. The third one, which was published between 1927 and 1933, already consisted of 30 volumes. Trotsky's *Complete Works* were originally planned to consist of more than twenty volumes, but only half of them were published between 1925 and 1927, and even these not in chronological order. The "Zinovyev Complete", which also was intended to have twenty volumes, also came out incomplete, with ten volumes between 1923 and 1929. Lev Kamenev himself did not fare as well—he had time and opportunity to publish only six volumes of his own work. Postnikov, 1938, 100–101, 115, 121, 126.
13 On one occasion, he did make the effort: together with his assistants, he edited and published his newspaper articles from 1917. The book titled *Na putyah k Oktyabryu. Sztati i rechi. Mart-Oktyabr 1917 g.* (On the Road to October. Articles And Speeches, Moscow–Leningrad, GIZ, 1925) was published in two editions in the same year.
14 *Concerning Questions of Leninism* was published almost every year. By 1932, the more than 600-pages volume had appeared in nine unchanged editions and a year later a thin appendix also came out. This is how the author "streamlined" his thoughts that took shape during the fractional struggles. Postnikov, 1938, 127. From this time on, the employees of the Stalin secretariat revised and censored the successive new editions of *Concerning Questions of Leninism* even more carefully. The 1928 book titled *On opposition*, which contained Stalin's writings and speeches he made between 1921 and 1927, attacking mostly Trotsky's and Zinovyev's views, paradoxically was put on the list of indexed books ten years later because of its content—even though it was Stalin's work. In the following decades, the book was a sought-after rarity. For example, when Milovan Djilas visited Moscow in April 1946, he could get a copy for himself only with the help of a member of the Politburo, Georgy Malenkov. "Using the opportunity that our meeting offered, I asked him about Stalin's book *On opposition*, which was shelved because it contained numerous quotations from Trotsky, Bukharin, and others. The next day I received a copy, and it is still a precious addition to my library." Djilas, 1989, 101.
15 The author is wrong here. Ivan Tovstukha, the caretaker of Stalin's documents, Yemelian Yaroslavsky, the official historian of the Bolshevik Party, and Vladimir Adoratsky, who was the director of the Marx-Engels Institute between 1931 and 1939, proposed the idea to the dictator independently of each other. All three of them were elder members of the Soviet elite.
16 Trotsky, 1985, vol. I, 176–179. From one of Tovstukha's unpublished letters we can learn that Stalin himself considered publishing his *Complete Works* already in March 1931. *RGASPI*, fond. 71, op. 3, d. 81.
17 During Stalin's life, only the first thirteen volumes were published.
18 *RGASPI*, fond. 155, op. 1, d. 85.
19 *Ibid.*
20 Uratadze, 1968, 187–195.
21 *Novy Zhurnal*, 1963, no. 72, 226.

22 It seems unclear who was the author of the unsigned editorial introduction to the underground Social Democrat publication *Brdzola* (Struggle) that appeared in September 1901—even though the editors of Stalin's works credited him with writing it. But even if one granted that he is the author, it would mean that he made his debut in Marxist political writing quite late, at the age of almost 23. To alleviate this inconvenience, the editors mention in the formal introduction an article titled *The Agenda of Marxist Workers' Meetings*, which they dated to 1889 but had been "unable to find up until today." Stalin, 1946, I, X.

23 Iremaschvili, 1932, 21–22; Avtorkhanov, 1959, 152–153, 177–178; Avtorkhanov, 1973, I, 185–186, 691, 723; Avtorkhanov, 1973, II, 68–70, 300–307.

24 *RGASPI*, fond. 558, op. 1, d. 665. Davderiani left behind an interesting memoir, in which he mentions that it was on his recommendation that the young Iosif Dzhugashvili, in the fall of 1896, left the Tiflis Orthodox Seminary and joined an illegal circle. According to Davderiani, at the same time Soso became involved in politics, he completely gave up writing verse. He also says that a number of seminary students became ill around that time and were moved into private homes. Among them was Iosif Dzhugashvili. The two young men, Soso and Seid Davderiani (at least, according to Davderiani) became such good friends that they even visited each other during the holiday. They also argued about the circle's program. Their arguments were judged by Simbistro Dzhibladze and Filipp Makharadze, pioneers of Georgian Marxism. Ostrovsky 2002, 126–130.

25 Iremaschvili, 1932, 21.

26 *RGASPI*, fond. 558, op. 1, d. 665.

27 *Molodaya Gvardia*, 1939, no. 12, 72. The debate ended when Seid Davderiani was accepted to the Yuryev university, so there were no more obstacles for Soso Dzhugashvili. Ostrovsky, 2002, 147.

28 Tucker, 1991, 89–90. According to Iremaschwili, although Soso often visited the editors of *Kvali* to seek advice, behind their back he often ridiculed them.

29 Filipp Makharadze was a talented political writer, a key figure and a historian of the Georgian workers' movement. At the beginning of the century, his leftist comrades called him "rightist" and "conciliatory" within the underground Bolshevik circles. According to a contemporary sarcastic opinion, the main reason he joined Lenin was that Noi Zhordania, his archrival since the times they had spent together in the *Kvali* circle, was a Menshevik. In the 1920s Makharadze turned against Stalin and in the 1930s he was one of the main targets of Beria's political attacks. Still, he survived the Great Terror—what is more, he held high political offices up until his death.

30 *RGASPI*, fond. 558, op. 4, d. 665.

31 Uratadze, 1968, 207–208, 130–132, 151–159, 162, 197–198.

32 *Novy Zhurnal*, 1963, no. 72, 223.

33 "This fool does not understand that this is not the audience of *Kvali* he could gabble to," fulminated Stalin against Zhordania and his journal in a letter he sent to Leipzig in October 1904. Stalin, 1946, vol. I, 61.

34 Akromed, 1910, 55–56. At the end of the 1920s, the author was still able to publish the book in Tiflis, including the quotation that indisputably referred to Stalin.

35 *Novy Zhurnal*, 1963, no. 72, 220.

36 The word "money changer," clearly anti-Semitic in tone, which Koba used to describe the Mensheviks and the militant members of the Jewish Bund, seems to be a term that he borrowed from Rosa Luxemburg, the well-known figure of the German, Polish, and Russian workers' movements. Stalin, 1946, vol. II, 51.

37 *Novy Zhurnal*, 1963, no. 72, 220–221.

38 This part of the text was first published in *Bakinsky Proletariat*, a newspaper in Baku, on June 20, 1907, but the author found it necessary to republish it in his complete works, even after the Holocaust. Stalin, 1946, vol. II, 50–51.

39 Uratadze, 1968, 68, 208–210.

40 As a result of the conflicts Khomeriki had with his comrades, he declared himself a Menshevik as early as the beginning of 1905. Soon after this Stalin devoted an article to excluding him. Stalin, 1946, vol. I, 241–246.

41 The writer of the letter refers to the case when Stalin disintegrated the Kutaisi party committee from the inside by insinuating his comrades.

42 *Otechestvennie Arkhivi*, 1995, no. 4, 78–79.

43 *RGASPI*, fond. 558, op. 4, d. 647.

CHAPTER 5
Why Stalin was Called a "Mail-coach Robber"

In the second half of the nineteenth century and in the early twentieth century, time spent in prison or exile represented a decisive period in the life of any genuine Russian radical opponent of the tsarist government. The greatest suffering was endured by those held in dungeons, which were regarded as the lowermost circle of hell and where some prisoners were held for as much as two decades. Others were sent to *katorga*, the Siberian and Far-Eastern forced-labor camps described in the works of Dostoyevsky and Chekhov, where chained groups of prisoners were forced to build railways, quarry rock, work in tin mines, or clear the *taiga*, the dense Siberian coniferous forest.

Following the 1917 February Revolution in Russia, these former convicts were treated with enormous respect until the late 1920s. After this, however, since Stalin himself had not suffered to any great extent, time spent in the dungeons was no longer regarded as a special virtue in terms of one's revolutionary past. For the same reason the dictator preferred his court historians to treat the past histories of members of the Bolshevik elite as uniform. He himself talked belittlingly of his peers who had been in the *katorga*. On the other hand, as Anna Alliluyeva, Stalin's sister-in-law writes in her recollections, he liked to boast of how he had been imprisoned in dank, overcrowded, stinking prisons on half a dozen occasions, and how he had several times escaped from exile. Nevertheless, Joseph Stalin on November 23, 1902, with these obsequious words turned to Prince Golitsin, the governor of the Caucasus, to ask that he might possibly be set free: "A humble petition. My recurring cough is worsening. My old mother is in a hopeless *(bespomoshchnoye)* situation, her husband left her twelve years ago and she sees me as the support of her old age." This is my second attempt to turn to the governing *(glavnonachalstvuyushchy)* body to get my petition addressed and receive a response. Iosif Dzhugashvili, petitioner *(prositel)*, November 23, 1902." A petition such as this counted as a serious crime for a revolutionary in the first few years of the beginning of the century and was considered a reason for expulsion from the party.[1]

There is no authentic proof even today that Stalin was ever made to wear shackles connecting his wrists and ankles while in prison. What makes this somewhat surprising is the fact that, according to Yelizaveta Drabkina, one of the founders of the Soviet youth organization Komsomol, the Master of the Kremlin once spoke emotionally to the leaders of the organization describing how he knew of no better feeling than that of being able to straighten his back again after enduring this particular punishment. It is possible, however, that he was referring to the suffering that he underwent in the autumn of 1903, when his long period of detention on remand, spent in the Batumi and then in the Kutaisi prisons, finally came to an end. The story of his remand is full of blank spots. It is a fact that in April of 1903, Iosif Dzhugashvili was transferred from Batumi to a prison in the city of Kutaisi. Later he was taken back to Batumi. It was in that autumn that the authorities sent him into exile in eastern Siberia. To Levon Shaumyan Stalin boasted about that at the time shackles *(nozhnie kandali)* would have been fastened to his ankles to prevent escape. Locked with a key, the painful shackles were connected by a chain to which were attached a number of iron

Бакинское Губернское Жандармское Упр
ДЖУГАШВИЛИ
указательный
средний

balls, which further hindered the prisoner's movement. These were distressing weeks for Stalin, since this was the first long journey he had been forced to make. According to rumor his fellow prisoners brutally beat the future Master of the Kremlin several times in the course of the *etap* (the journey into exile)—a word which, in the Soviet era, was to become part of the everyday language. He soon realized that he could avoid some of his suffering if he could turn these aggressive, non-political prisoners against each other instead. In the late 1920s Levon Shaumyan heard the dictator telling the following story to members of his family: "During the *etap* it was my fate to come up against a psychotic safe-breaker *(medvezhatnik)*, a giant of a man, almost two meters tall. I made some harmless remark to him—perhaps I suggested that he shouldn't take so much tobacco from my tobacco pouch. The exchange ended in a fight. The idiot forced me to the ground, breaking several of my ribs. No one tried to help me. As I was coming round it occurred to me that a politician must always make efforts to win allies. I spent the remainder of the journey whispering to the other non-political prisoners what this particular individual had been saying about them to the guards in one of the transit prisons. One night, towards the end of the journey, he finally got what was coming to him. The prisoners I had been stirring up threw a coat over his head and proceeded to beat the hell out of him. The safe-breaker from Kharkov had no idea about the identity of his attackers. He had even less idea about who had put them up to it."

Later on, too, Stalin preferred to "remain in the background" and to act secretively. This is doubtless why he never wrote down the story of his long youth with all its scandals. He thus made the task of the Stalinologists even more difficult, since without facts it was extremely hard to edit the chronologies included at the end of the Stalin volumes. Even such incomplete facts as there were were then filtered by the censors. Once the text, with all its lacunae, had been prepared, first the vast brigade of censors comprising leaders from the Soviet party headquarters, then Stalin himself, weeded out from the chronology those entries regarded as unnecessary. Some of the changes are quite incomprehensible. It is difficult to see, for example, why the fact that Tsar Nikolai II approved—not by signature but with a stamp—the official order, dated 9 June 1903, exiling Iosif Dzhugashvili to eastern Siberia, should not have been included. Also omitted from the final version was the fact that the train transporting prisoners under armed guard made its way to its remote destination with a significant detour via Novorossysk, Rostov, Tsaritsyn, and Samara.[2]

Iosif Dzhugashvili in 1910.

Even today we do not know how much time Joseph Stalin spent in various transit prisons in the course of the journey. The official document concerning his forced journey across the country is dated August 17, 1903. This suggests that it was a particularly long *etap*, since "Comrade Koba" only arrived at the prison in Irkutsk in the late autumn of 1903. From there, armed guards escorted him to the settlement of Novaya Uda (in other documents Novo Udinskoye) in Balaginsk district. A number of documents relating to Stalin's exile have been preserved in the archives of the Irkutsk Okhrana. They reveal that Iosif Dzhugashvili did not give the town of Gori as his place of birth but rather the village of Didi-Lilo. He also stated that he was twenty-three years old, as usual subtracting one year from his true age.[3] The chronology compiled by rescarchers states that between November 27, 1903 and January 5, 1904 Stalin, the exiled Bolshevik politician did not leave the godforsaken village of Novaya Uda, home to Russian land-laboring settlers and Buryats who made a living by animal husbandry.[4]

According to local historians the settlement was a desolate backwater in the early twentieth century. There was no hospital for miles around, but alcohol was readily available in the settlement's five pubs, which the villagers regularly visited with the intention of getting drunk. In the middle of the settlement was an enormous wooden fortress, once built to control the rebellious Buryats. The streets converged in the square in front of the Orthodox church, creating a village center of a kind. Iosif Dzhugashvili did not rent a room here, but rather in the poorer quarter on the outskirts of the settlement, in the house of the peasant Marfa Litvintseva. Most of the space in the room was taken up by a huge Russian stove. These traditional stoves functioned either as saunas, if one climbed inside, or as warm places on which to sleep.[5]

Thirty years later the authors of the Stalin legendary tried to squeeze out of the inhabitants of Novaya Uda as much information as possible about the few weeks that "the Master" had spent in the settlement. Apart from several folkloristic tales, none of his one-time neighbors could remember anything meaningful about him. They merely recited a number of commonplaces, describing, for example, how the "warm-hearted" Iosif Dzhugashvili, on becoming aware of the needs of the villagers, had "helped them in any way he could". At the age of seventy-eight Nikolai Isakov, a former landless peasant who became a member of an agricultural collective *(kolkhoz)*, even unearthed from the depths of his memory how the black-bearded exile would tell stories in the presence of about eight villagers. They only learned many years later, he said—"when people were already working in *kolkhoz*"—that they had been entertained by the great Stalin. "Such an honest and good man had fate thrown to our faraway land", he added.[6]

The blacksmith in the *kolkhoz* in Novaya Uda, Mikhail Gulkin, recalled how he encountered the future Master of the Kremlin at the village grocery shop: "He went up to the counter and asked for a bag of tea or a pound of bread. He took the unwrapped goods and stood aside to listen to the talk of the poor peasants *(muzhiki)*. He stood and listened to the village gossip, then slipped away unnoticed."[7] The insignificant story continues: "In those days we poor peasants often talked to one another about our problems. [...] One could feel how Stalin yearned to [...] talk frankly with us about our hard fate. But it was difficult for him because he was closely watched. Besides the gendarmes the wealthy peasants *(kulaks)*, who were on good terms with the tsarist authorities, also watched his every word and step."[8]

However, it was Marfa Litvintseva, Stalin's former landlady, who could claim first prize among the narrators of such folkloristic stories. In January 1934, on the eve of the 17th Congress of the Bolshevik Party, school pupils from Novaya Uda wrote a letter to the General Secretary of the party, in which they referred to one of Marfa's stories: "The old lady visited our school, and when she looked at Your picture she said: 'I know this *muzhik*.' She meant You, Comrade Stalin. Then she continued: 'I can even remember that once, when he escaped, I gave him bread.' And we, in the name of our whole Pioneer troop, expressed our gratitude to her for that piece of bread."[9]

It is quite obvious that the long letter purporting to be from the village children, loaded with its byzantine turns, was in fact composed by their teachers or by members of the local party committee. "We congratulate You on the thirtieth anniversary of Your first escape from Siberia," continues the letter, which was published in a book edited by Konstantin Chernenko, the future General Secretary of the party. Stalin's reply is also included in this volume: "I wish you good health! Every success in your studies and your community work! I hope that you will complete your schooling successfully and will be the kind of zealous, well-prepared workers that our country needs. Along with Molotov, Voroshilov and Kaganovich I am sending you a little present, a radio and a record player with records. I hope this will be a useful addition to your school radio. Comrades Molotov, Voroshilov and Kaganovich send their greetings. I wish you all the best. J. Stalin."[10]

In the early years of the twentieth century the young Georgian was not in a position to give away such generous gifts in Novaya Uda. He tried to avoid meeting people but kept a keen eye open for lapses in the attention of the district chief of police who supervised the exiles. He tried to exploit the fact that, for some reason, the villagers had a deep antipathy for the head of the local police. This allowed him to persuade one of the deliverymen to take him to the faraway village of Zimnyaya on the pretext of making a complaint against the police chief. By way of fare he undertook to buy vodka at every stop for the owner of the troika, who did not even suspect that the exile was in fact intending to board the long-distance train on the outskirts of Zimnyaya, which ran on the same line as the trans-Siberian express.[11] "We traveled in temperatures of minus forty degrees", Stalin remembered later, clearly still envious of the strong physique of his driver. "I wrapped myself in furs. The driver, however, opened his coat while driving and let the bitter, freezing wind blow against his almost naked belly. Apparently the alcohol had completely warmed his body. What a healthy people they are! So, that's how I managed to escape."[12]

Several years later he told a somewhat different version of the story to his sister-in-law Anna Alliluyeva: "I decided to escape. At first I did not succeed because the village police chief kept a sharp eye on me. Then the freeze came. At first I waited for a while. I collected some winter clothes together and set off on foot. My face almost froze. But my furs were a great help."[13] A third version of the same story can be read in Sergei Alliluyev's recollections. As far as this rather elderly worker remembered, he met his future son-in-law for the first time in early 1904 when Stalin traveled to Tiflis to obtain equipment for an illegal printing house in Baku from his old friends: "I met Comrade Soso, a young Georgian (who was also known as Koba), at the apartment of Comrade Mikha Bocharidze. He had just arrived back from exile in east Siberia. [...] According to two comrades, Kalistrat (Gogua) and Yulia *[his wife for whom the exiled Stalin felt Platonic love—M. K.]*,[14] Comrade Soso had first tried to escape in November 1903. However, by the time he had got from the village of Uda to Balaginsk [the district seat] his face had frozen. It was hideously cold at the time and Soso was dressed lightly, as Caucasians normally are. That was why he got no further but returned to Novaya Uda."[15]

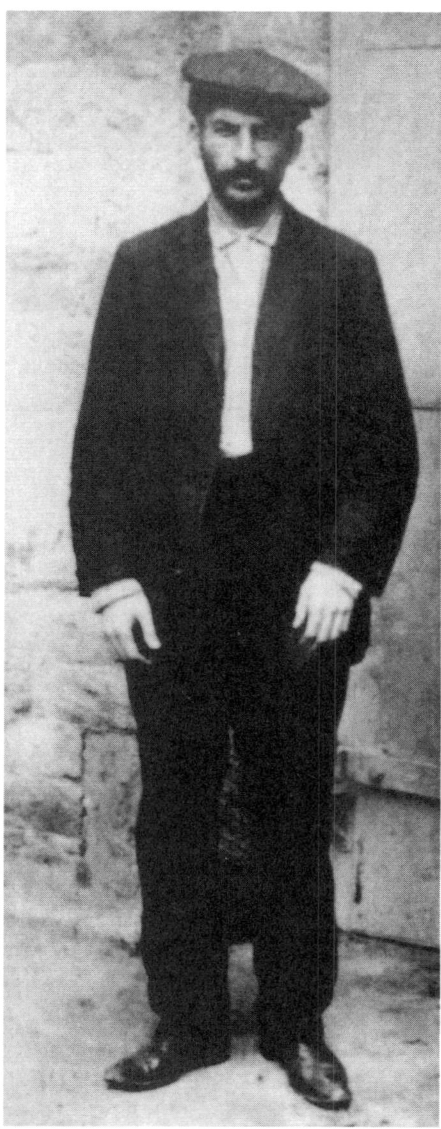

After his escape from Eastern Siberia, Iosif Dzhugashvili was wanted by the police for many years to come.

No matter what the true sequence of events, Iosif Dzhugashvili escaped on 5 January 1904. The local and Irkutsk authorities learned of it the very next day, but a warrant for his arrest was issued only nine days later in St. Petersburg.[16] Not that the informers hanging around in the railway stations in the vicinity of Irkutsk waited for this. They began approaching any passengers who resembled the escapee. Stalin, however, managed to avoid the trap. In the recollections of Domentia Vadachkoria, written down in the 1930s, we read: "I remember the stories told by Comrade Soso. Before he escaped he made an identity card, according to which he worked for one of the chiefs of police of a Siberian district. When he was on the train a suspicious character began to walk around near him. It must have been an informer. Comrade Soso was keen to get rid of him, so he got off at one of the stations, showed his false identity card to a gendarme, and demanded that the suspicious character be arrested. The gendarme did

Leon Trotsky with his fellow exiles. Like Stalin, he also escaped from eastern Siberia.

indeed arrest him. In the meantime, the train started off again and Comrade Soso was able to travel on in safety."[17]

This rather novelistic story might well have been true. However, publishing it rather harmed than helped Joseph Stalin. Georgian emigrants living in the West in the mid-1950s dug out the writings of Vadachkoria and wondered whether "perhaps Comrade Soso did not use a false secret policeman's identity card to escape from Siberia, but a real one. Perhaps he was helped by the local authorities."[18]

Such a claim is not supported by any reliable contemporary documents. An unproblematic and successful escape was not in fact unusual at the time. Several later political opponents of Stalin, including Leon Trotsky, managed to escape, even in more difficult circumstances. Shortly after these events Trotsky wrote down how he had escaped twice from Siberia, and later he included these accounts almost unchanged in his memoirs.[19] The Soviet dictator sometimes preferred to remain silent about his escape, but other times he would come out with unexpected stories about these episodes in front of his acquaintances. It is no wonder that it eventually occurred to many of them to wonder whether he could indeed have tricked the authorities or whether they had in fact helped him to escape in return for former services.

Because of the enormous secrecy surrounding the incident we still do not know where Iosif Dzhugashvili made for after he reached the Ural Mountains. According to one of the publications approved by the Soviet censors he appeared first in Leipzig rather than in his homeland, Georgia: "He met there with comrades with whom he had once worked in Transcaucasia. Later he traveled to Russia, then to Batumi […], and from there to Tiflis, where he assumed the leadership of the Caucasian committee of the Russian Social Democratic Labor Party (RSDLP).[20]

However, in most of the works on the life of the dictator the stay in Leipzig is not mentioned. On the other hand, several authors copied from Lavrenty Beria's "*chronicles*" the claim that, following his escape from eastern Siberia, Stalin assumed the leadership of the allied party committee *(soyuzny komitet)*—that is, the committee that included both Bolsheviks and Mensheviks—working illegally in the Caucasians. Contemporary documents do not support this version, either. The "Stalinologists", however, were able to rely on the help of Bolshevik veterans living in Baku and Tiflis. In theory "Comrade Koba" was supposed to cooperate with the representatives of the other Social Democratic trends represented in the allied committee. However, these stories reveal a completely different picture: most contemporaries, who had been coached by the "Beria brigade", emphasized the fact that instead of cooperation the fervent young leader unleashed his fury against the Mensheviks who opposed him: "I particularly remember one of Comrade Stalin's speeches. [...] Following the loud, aggressive Menshevik outbursts, he calmly exposed the practices *[of his Menshevik opponents—M. K.]* with a clear logic, the force of which never failed to shock and amaze his listeners", remembered Nina Aladzhalova about Iosif Dzhugashvili's "performance" in Baku.[21]

Her rather vague recollections do not even state precisely when these heated debates took place in Baku. What is certain is that before the revolution of 1905 Joseph Stalin could not have played a decisive role in the labor movement emerging in the capital of Azerbaijan, since, following his brief stay in Batumi, he settled in Tiflis.[22] From there he would disappear for long periods, traveling to some of the larger Russian cities and occasionally even abroad. He was driven not only by his restless, adventurous nature, but to a much greater extent by calculation. He needed to become personally acquainted with the movement elite in the two capital cities, St. Petersburg and Moscow, in order to obtain a place for himself in the Russian Social Democratic—and within that, the Bolshevik—hierarchy. From this point of view it was even more valuable for a professional party worker like him to travel abroad and be given an audience with a leader in exile, particularly Lenin. Such meetings were looked upon as personal tests, and eventually special rites and choreography were developed for them.[23]

☆ An important milestone in Stalin's career was his participation in the Russian Social Democratic conclave held in Tammerfors (now Tampere), Finland, in December 1905. At the time the young Georgian was known not only as "Comrade Koba". He had also assumed the byname "Ivanovich", which was the Russian version of the name of his paternal grandfather. Almost five months later, in April 1906, he also participated, under the same byname, in the 4th (unifying) Congress of the Russian Social Democrats in Stockholm. The division of power in the Caucasians was clearly reflected by the fact that he was the only Bolshevik in the large, eleven-member Tiflis delegation.[24]

In Tammerfors the young Tiflis delegate mostly sat in the back row during the sessions. In Stockholm, however, he spoke out during the debate on the agrarian issue. The former Tiflis Seminary student, who had never completed his studies, was only regarded as a peasant according to the contemporary tsarist law. He could have had no knowledge of the extensive literature written on agrarian affairs, yet despite this he presented his opinions on the land issue, which were fairly remote from the ideas of Lenin and his followers, based on radical nationalization. This, however, did not make the young Georgian any less of a faithful Leninist, as was suggested by Trotsky.[25]

These two foreign trips brought some color to Iosif Dzhugashvili's stay in Tiflis, which was otherwise made rather monotonous by the constraints imposed by illegality. The politician generally behaved more cautiously following his escape. He changed "conspiratorial apartment", byname, and false papers more frequently. Following his tribulations in Batumi and Kutaisi he obviously feared being caught by the Okhrana again. Even during the months of the 1905 revolution he remained in hiding, even though his comrades abandoned their underground life one after the other and walked freely. Stalin changed lifestyle only after 1907, when he suddenly and inexplicably abandoned his "hidden existence" and began provocatively attracting the attention of the police and street informers.

Following his escape from eastern Siberia he continued to live a somewhat parasitic life. He extorted money from his acquaintances, old and new. These were mostly wealthy sympathizers who were connected with the outer circle of the Georgian Marxists. Within his family circle, even decades later, he would describe with a mischievous smile how he had regularly pumped money from his former fellow seminarians, one of whom was his old friend Vasily Berdzeneshvili. This young man, who occasionally wrote his name as Berdzenyev, in the Russian style, had worked with Koba in 1901 at the Tiflis Geophysical Observatory. According to unpublished archive documents he rented two quiet rooms for the two of them on the outskirts of Tiflis: Misho's younger brother recalled later how the rooms "opened onto the courtyard. There was a separate flight of stairs leading to the apartment. In the smaller room were a small table, two chairs, and two wooden beds. It was there that Soso lived, and my brother lived there with him."[26]

In the 1930s the Georgian Institute of Party History, which employed local Tiflis historians, created a map tracing how Iosif Dzhugashvili changed "conspiratorial apartments". One of these apartments was on the corner of Sobachy (Dog) Street. On the wall of number 110 on the avenue that was named after Plekhanov in the years of Soviet power, there was, and still is, a memorial plaque stating that in the cellar workshop of the carpenter Mikha Chodrishvili Stalin held regular conspiratorial meetings and wrote his articles.[27] When the underground revolutionary could no longer bear to live like a hunted animal he escaped to the countryside from his forced confinement. His court historians, in retrospect, interpreted these short trips as being when "Comrade Koba" left Tiflis to carry out agitation among the rebellious land workers.[28]

The main circle of Iosif Dzhugashvili's acquaintances at the time, however, was made up not of "the common people", but of declassé intellectuals and the descendants of clerical and merchant families, who had become professional revolutionaries *(professionalnie revolyutsioneri).* During the underground period such people were the cogs in the machine, from whom the regional party leaders *(komitetchiki)* were selected following hard-fought internal struggles and fierce competition. Within this closed circle, in the early years of the century, a strictly vertical, rigid hierarchy was beginning to emerge, the top of which would later, in the Soviet era, be occupied by the former Soselo Dzhugashvili. The illegal apparatuses and party committees *(komiteti)* had a pyramid-like structure. These pyramids were mostly created from the top down. At the top was a clique comprising just a few members, although it might also be the case that a single person held the organization together and kept contact with the slightly mythologized party leadership abroad, that is, the Central Committee, and other bodies. Within the Russian Social Democratic movement the Bolsheviks, the Mensheviks, and the Social Democrats of the various nationalities, even following the 4th Congress in Stockholm that formally unified the various wings, retained their separate, secret vertical structures.[29]

Before the outbreak of the 1905 revolution "Comrade Koba" was somewhere in the middle of the pyramid. For a long time it did not seem possible that one day he might take over control of the whole Caucasian Social Democratic move-

As a consequence of Stalin's notorious secretiveness, we still do not know for sure whether following his escape he did manage to travel to Leipzig with false papers to visit his Georgian friends. The photograph shows a group of Georgians living in exile in Germany, Switzerland, and France. Soso Dzhugashvili was in regular correspondence with them.

ment, or at least control of the leading Bolshevik bodies in Tiflis or Baku. He had no hope of being, at any stage, as popular among the local workers as the much more experienced and erudite Mensheviks Chkheidze, Zhordania, or Tsereteli. However, in the early years of the century even Makharadze and Chakhaya (both Bolsheviks), who were much less significant figures than these three, were far more respected by the underground party workers than the "greenhorn" Soso Dzhugashvili, with his difficult personality.

Fortunately for him, however, such venerable figures emigrated one by one, or moved to European Russia from Tiflis, thus gradually clearing the way for "Comrade Koba". However, his path was then unexpectedly blocked by two highly talented Bolsheviks, the Georgian Budu Mdivani and the Armenian Stepan Shaumyan, who were roughly the same age as him. In the stormy months of the 1905 revolution it was partly they who prevented Joseph Stalin from "raising his profile" immediately on the outskirts of Tiflis and Baku. The ambitious and irreconcilable politician would never forgive them for this.[30]

The passing months, however, favored the future dictator. According to Noi Zhordania, who had known Stalin since his days at the Seminary, the assertive politician, as a result of his "outstanding ambition", his "perseverance", and "tenacity", finally made it to the forefront. From the end of 1905 he was, for almost four years, one of the most influential Caucasian *komitetchiki*. Furthermore, having brushed his rivals aside, he took over the editing of the Georgian Bolshevik publications one by one, thus emerging as a kind of regional ideologue.[31]

The fact that the majority of the Georgian Socialist publications remained permanently in Menshevik hands is a different issue.[32] The staff of the Bolshevik papers, which all had a fairly small print run, were permanently in competition with one another. According to the reliable Arsenidze, Joseph Stalin "surrounded himself exclusively with people who respected him unconditionally and gave into him on every issue. However, there were some people whom he could not stand and others who could not stand him, including some Bolsheviks as well. There were no well-known Bolshevik publicists, such as Makharadze or others, working for the illegal newspapers published by Stalin.[33] This was perhaps down to the fact that Soso insisted on the position of editor at any cost, even though he had no special literary abilities nor the erudition required."[34]

In his moments of clarity Stalin himself was aware of this fact. Thus while editing the Russian-language edition of his works he had the editors substantially rewrite his early Georgian-language publications, after which he made stylistic changes to the translations. One of his motives was doubtless his anger at the sarcastic comments of Trotsky, Bukharin, Zinovyev and others, who had become his opponents in the struggle for power and who criticized him for the fact that, in spite of being secretary-general, he had made no substantial contribution to universal Marxist theory. Thus as early as the late 1920s he attempted to resurrect texts intended as "theoretical", which he had written in the context of polemics with Georgian Mensheviks and anarchists.[35] In the 1940s these early articles were included in the collected edition of his works. They thus became compulsory reading in the Soviet educational system, despite the fact that their author, at the time they were written, had been content simply to paraphrase in Georgian a few popular Russian Marxist pamphlets of the time. This was certainly true of his long-winded series of articles *Anarchism or Socialism?*, which can be regarded as the best of his early publications. He used whole paragraphs taken from the work of Georgy Plekhanov, the father of Russian Marxism, criticizing anarchist theory, and from the translated articles of the French Socialist Paul Louis, who has been entirely forgotten in the meantime. He did not take the trouble to read through the works of Bakunin, Proudhon, Max Stirner, Malatesta, Elise Reclus, or the basic works of other anarchist theoreticians.[36]

The articles in the *Anarchism or Socialism?* series, like other early writings, appeared in obscure Georgian publications with small print-runs. In the 1920s Stalin was unable to find these peripheral publications in the Moscow libraries, thus in December 1929, as he approached his fiftieth birthday (which was celebrated throughout the country with great pomp), he passed this work on to members of his secretarial staff and to the Tiflis party historians. Since Ivan Tovstukha, who was given the task of supervising the research, spoke no Georgian, the gathering of the material progressed very slowly. It took these novice "Stalinologists" more than two years to complete the work. Tovstukha summarized the achievement as follows: "Comrade Stalin! I have attached a memo about the search for your articles. We have traced everything as far as October 1917. Please read it through and make your remarks. We will forward all the papers and material."[37]

From among the early-twentieth-century Caucasian papers the Master of the Kremlin immediately read through *Borba Proletariata*, the illegal, Russian-language paper which appeared between 1903 and 1905 in Tiflis, as well as *Gaitiadi*, *Elva*, and *Akhali Tshvoreba*, which were aimed at a Georgian reading public. Tovstukha, the head of Stalin's secretariat and his biographer, continued: "I am attaching all the issues of *Dro*, despite the fact that you have already read through them. The articles in question have all been found, but, according to the Caucasian researchers, there are several further articles also written by you. However, there were serious problems concerning the articles in the series *Anarchism or Socialism?*" Tovstukha was here referring to the fact that Stalin had published these articles at various times and in various publications between December 18, 1906 and April 10, 1907. He went on to remark: "Later (I have been unable to establish exactly when), extracts of these articles were published in the form of an individual pamphlet, under the title *Dialectical Materialism*, by Spartacus Publications in Kutaisi."[38]

☆ In the early twentieth century it was impossible to make a living from editing newspapers, however, especially since *Akhali Tshvoreba*, *Akhali Drosba*, *Mnatobi*, and *Chveni Tshvoreba* amounted to only seventy-eight issues altogether. These were the publications that Iosif Dzhugashvili was involved in editing and publishing in 1906–1907. He was therefore obliged to rely on "aid" and donations from sympathizers. In other words, his parasitic existence continued. "Comrade Koba" would sometimes travel distances of several hundred kilometers in order to obtain money. In 1905, for instance, an old friend of his, Otarashvili, who lived in Vladikavkaz, helped him in his quest for funds.[39]

Decades later Isaak Iluridze, a Jewish merchant in Vladikavkaz, said of Otarashvili: "He did a great job. If one of the "top dogs", Dzhugashvili, Yenukidze, or someone else, arrived, he immediately warned us: 'Boys, you mustn't breathe a word about him being here, but we must help him.' And we would collect and hand the money over to him. When the 1905 revolution was put down in Georgia, Dzhugashvili visited us and naturally stayed with Otarashvili. [...] Otarashvili summoned me and said: 'Isay, don't say a word to anyone, but a great man has arrived among us, our number one leader. We should raise some money for him.' [...] Dzhugashvili then stayed with us for nine or ten days until the money was raised. In those days things like this went very slowly, since life was hard."[40]

After a while, however, at least temporarily, "Comrade Koba" had to do without these hard-earned donations. He became one of the coordinators of the "expropriations" carried out by Caucasian Bolshevik terrorist squads, although he kept it a secret throughout his life that he had ever had anything to do, even indirectly, with terrorist actions. Nevertheless, in the 1920s and 1930s in the Soviet Union one could read a great deal about these "expropriations" in the pages of official publications, without exception with positive overtones. The Bolshevik political elite of the "heroic age"—including Lenin's widow Nadezhda Krupskaya; the famous economic expert and diplomat Leonid Krasin; the people's commissar of foreign affairs Maksim Litvinov; and Nikolai Semashko, the creator of the Soviet health system—like many other veterans of the Russian labor movement were proud of "the expropriations for the benefit of the movement", which were carried out in the Caucasians, in the Urals, in Ukraine, and elsewhere, by members of their special "combat squads". However, unlike them Stalin never admitted to having had anything to do with the "expropriations". Emil Ludwig once asked him: "Please excuse the question, which you might find somewhat strange [...], but in your biography there are some—how shall I put it?—'highwayman-like' incidents."[41] The Soviet dictator did not reply, although up until then he had given full answers to almost every question posed by the German writer and psychologist. Instead, he handed over a short pamphlet containing his biography, saying that in it Ludwig would find everything he wanted to know about his life.[42]

This was doubtless the thin, official biography written by the secretary-general's confidant, Tovstukha, which makes no mention of "highway robbery". According to Levon Shaumyan, Stalin was so unwilling to talk about these old issues, which he called "cops and robbers stories" *(kazaki-razboyniki)* that not even members of his immediate circle dared to mention them. Soviet historians and publicists were strictly forbidden to enter into a debate with foreign writers who called Stalin a "mail-coach robber" or "highwayman". In the 1930s such names found their way into the first English and German works on Stalin via the Russian- and Georgian-language émigré press. Western biographers relied mostly on a work of not particularly high quality by a former Tiflis-based Socialist Revolutionary political writer hiding behind the pen-name Essad-bey. The book was published in Riga in the Russian language. Later it became a bestseller in

A photograph of Semyon Ter-Petrosyan (alias 'Kamo') from the police files.

several countries. It depicts the General Secretary of the party as a ruthless Caucasian outlaw.

The emergence of a negative image of Stalin was a cause for concern for Willi Münzenberg, head of the propaganda work of the Comintern, the Communist international organization.[43] The Berlin-based politician felt it necessary to make rapid countermoves. On June 13, 1931 he turned for help first to Ivan Tovstukha: "Dear Comrade! In Germany several so-called Stalin biographies have appeared recently. Besides the book by Essad-bey [...] another called *Stalin* has been published. Its author is Boris Bazhanov, who claims to be Stalin's former personal secretary.[44] Furthermore, I have also been informed that other bourgeois publishers plan to issue several similarly useless books."[45]

As a result, a crisis management team was set up in Berlin. The German Communist officials planned an important role in their countermeasures for Ivan Tovstukha, who knew the life of Stalin better than anyone else: "Several comrades, including Heinz Neumann[46], have advised us to turn to you to ask you to write a biography of Stalin for our publisher as soon as possible. To help in this work we will be delighted to put all publications which have so far appeared about him at your disposal. I hope we will soon receive your initial consent and that we can begin discussing the concrete details."[47]

Tovstukha, however, was not given the consent of his much-feared boss. This was a great mistake on Stalin's part, since his deep silence gave further credence to the book by the imaginative Essad-bey, as well as to the writings of Georgian and Russian Mensheviks who had known Soso Dzhugashvili well at the beginning of the century. Although, unlike Essad-bey, they did not claim that Stalin had personally participated in the robberies, they wrote, independently from one another, that it was the aggressive and unscrupulous Koba who had coordinated the armed robberies of mail-coaches and trains carried out by Caucasian Bolsheviks. "I first met Stalin in May 1906 in Stockholm," recalled Rafail Abramovich, a prominent politician in the Menshevik wing of the RSDLP as well as in the Jewish Bund. "Under the byname Ivanovich he once even spoke *[at the congress of the Social Democratic parties—M. K.]*. However, his speech did not make much of an impression. As I remember, he spoke very badly. One year later he appeared in London at the (next) party congress. However, there was some problem qualifying with the mandate examination committee, since the Mensheviks questioned his license. They claimed that it was false.[48] When we negotiated in Stockholm and London with Lenin and with the Bolshevik leadership around him I did not meet Stalin. It was only after 1907, following the infamous Caucasian expropriations, that news began to spread about him in party circles. He had just returned from the London congress where expropriation had been strictly prohibited. Nevertheless, Stalin immediately began to organize the robbery of the Tiflis treasury. Koba did not carry out this 'heroic deed' openly, but hid behind the daredevil Kamo."[49]

What is the truth behind these claims? In the Russian Empire in the early years of the century, what was euphemistically known as "expropriation" was a fairly frequent occurrence. In fact it was nothing other than common armed robbery, which was carried out by members of "combat squads" at the command, or with the consent, of the radical parties opposing the tsarist system. In public they assumed responsibility for the assassination attempts on high-ranking tsarist officials, policemen, Cossacks, and the notoriously cruel prison guards. In Russia at that time the terrorist tradition of the nineteenth-century Narodnik movement was still very much alive, and certain strata of society approved of such actions.

Almost a century later it is becoming more and more difficult to judge the true motives behind these murders and attempted murders. The intended victims were usually governors and gendarme generals who had ordered their soldiers to shoot at peacefully demonstrating crowds, organized pogroms, and, after summary trials, ordered women and minors to be hung. Thus it is hard to tell when the attacks were inspired by the more abstract desire for social justice and when by revenge. Nor is it easy to judge the role played by a desire to make easy money. This desire occasionally tempted even the generally ascetic members of the "death brigades", who were also sometimes lured by a romantic vision of themselves as justice-seeking Robin Hoods—or, since we are dealing here with Russia, Stenka Razins. What is particularly important is the fact that in the nineteenth century the militants who had engaged in individual terror and those who had carried out expropriations had come mostly from the intellectual, noble, or merchant strata. In the early years of the twentieth century, however, more than fifty percent of them were born in poor laboring districts and had an entirely different attitude and philosophy. It is also striking that among those involved in armed robberies and assassinations the proportion of non-Russian nationals and women was extremely high.[50]

We know a great deal today about the era of armed revenge attacks in Russia. The figures are shocking: during the 1905 to 1907 revolution 3,611 high-ranking and other officials, porters, carriage drivers, etc. were killed by the terrorists. The number of civilian victims killed accidentally was at least as high. In the course of the attacks, including the expropriations, which were mostly carried out using revolvers and bombs, altogether more than 9,000 persons were wounded. After every incident the tsarist authorities retaliated heavily, and even carried out preemptive measures on occasion. To a certain extent the effects of this could be felt even in the few years preceding the First World War, when, following the collapse of the revolution, the clashes between power and opposition decreased. Nevertheless, the "revolutionary" terror was not eliminated even by the most severe retaliation, even though in 1906–1907 Prime Minister Pyotr Stolypin, the "strongman" of the contemporary tsarist system, using extreme cruelty did away with the members of the "armed squads" who had made an attempt on his life. A number of expressions from these times have been preserved in Russian folklore: "Stolypin's necktie" *(Stolipinsky galstuk)* is a euphemism for the noose, and "Stolypin's swing" *(Stolipinskie kacheli)* a euphemism for the gallows. In Russia, the freight wagons transformed for delivering prisoners by rail are, even today, called "Stolypin's wagons" *(Stolipinsky vagon).*

The terrorists attached to various political parties helped one another. On August 25, 1906 (according to the contemporary dating system August 12), Prime Minister Pyotr Stolypin was almost killed in a huge bomb explosion at his *dacha.* The attempt on his life was carried out by a commando of the Maximalist SR Party, which received the bombs from the Bolshevik Leonid Krasin and his men. Krasin, the talented engineer and succesful businessman, the darling of the intelligentsia, even tried to forge money, first in Russia and later in Germany.[51]

Armed robbery was at first only a byproduct of individual and collective terror in the early years of the twentieth century in Russia. However, it eventually became an increasingly separate "branch". The members of the armed squads *(boyevie gruppi)* largely explained the first bank robberies, jewelry shop break-ins, and mail-coach hold-ups as having been carried out in order to obtain arms against the instigators of the pogroms and the ruthless gendarmes. According to them the expropriated money was needed for carrying out justified revenge attacks and for bringing about popular justice, which had to be preceded by the purchase of arms.[52]

Aggression, however, bred further aggression. It was more and more frequently the case that the armed persons *(boyeviki)* began to act without special explanation. Moral support for them was provided by the fact that such activities appealed to some of the liberal and radical public, they could have had no idea of what had been revealed by the confidential survey carried out by the Russian Ministry of Finance, that is, that between the beginning of 1905 and the middle of 1906 almost one million rubles had been expropriated by armed squads from the state-owned banks alone, and had passed, via them, into the funds of various radical parties. Since it was the case that criminals also joined in with the "expropriators", it is certain that part of this amount, which was regarded as exorbitant at the time, ended up in the criminal underworld.[53] It is still not clear how the bank robbers apportioned the money stolen from the treasury. It is even more difficult to trace the fate of a further nine million rubles which the expropriators "borrowed" from private banks, mail-coaches, and the safes of private individuals. According to certain memoirs terrorists specializing in expropriation squandered part or all of the money and eventually became common highwaymen, while others claim that they left the money intended for the movement virtually untouched. Probably most members of the Caucasian squad led by Kamo (Semyon Ter-Petrosyan) belonged to the latter category. Apart from the leader of the group they dressed simply and they spent very little on food, although several of them suffered from serious tuberculosis.[54]

By 1905–1907 the "revolutionary terror" extended over a large part of the Russian Empire. In the homeland of Iosif Dzhugashvili, in Caucasia, the number of terrorist acts significantly exceeded the average. According to figures from the tsarist Ministry of Internal Affairs, after 1 January 1907 altogether 3,060 terrorist acts were carried out in the territory of the military province of Tiflis. Of these, 1,732 were robberies and highway hold-ups. In the course of the assassinations and expropriations 1,239 people died and 1,253 were wounded.[55] It is true that the statisticians often manipulated the figures with respect to their own interests at the time. On occasion they added the victims of Jewish pogroms provoked by the tsarist authorities, or the victims of the no less bloody Armenian/Tartar clashes, also fomented from above, to the victims of the armed revolutionary acts. Despite this, some modern researchers accept the statistics given by Prince Vorontsov-Dashkov, the Tiflis military governor, according to which 3,219 people in 1905 and 3,305 people in 1906 died or suffered serious injuries in the course of a series of attacks in Caucasia that he referred to as banditry.[56]

Contrary to public opinion, in the territory of this military province it was the activists of a relatively small party, the Armenian Socialist Dashnaktsutiun Party, who carried out the highest number of killings. On the other hand, it is the Georgian Bolsheviks and Mensheviks who are credited with the majority of expropriations. However, the number of such incidents somewhat decreased when, after spring 1907, the RSDLP, in a special congress resolution, banned individual acts of terror and expropriation.[57]

Following every armed attack the tsarist authorities conducted thorough investigations. The number of investigations into the most serious terrorist acts approached two hundred in 1905 alone. In recent years researchers have finally been given access to these documents. However, the name of Iosif Dzhugashvili has not been found among the "foot soldiers" who actually carried out the robberies and ambushes, even though many contemporaries knew that "Comrade Koba" had something to do with the armed actions. Tatyana Vulich, a Baku party activist who knew all the members of the Caucasian Bolshevik terrorist organization led by Kamo (Semyon Ter-Petrosyan), wrote in her unpublished recollections: "We, the members of the 'peaceful' *[Social Democratic—M. K.]* organizations, had no *[official—M. K.]* information about the combat squad. One was not expected to ask questions or inquire in any way about what they were doing. Despite this a lot of information did reach us, especially about certain members of the group. We knew that it was led by Kamo. [...] He was the link between the group and the local party organization after the Stockholm party congress had condemned expropriations, and, as a result, the members of the squad had left the *[Bolshevik—M. K.]* party. Nevertheless they regarded the party as their own and tried to keep up to date with party affairs. If the need for secrecy did not prevent them, they even attended party meetings. The highest leader of the combat organization was Stalin. Although he did not personally take part in the incidents, nothing important happened without his knowledge."[58] Menshevik historian Boris Nicolaevsky, who wrote an entire book, which remained unpublished for a long time, on the issues of expropriation and revolutionary terror, saw things differently. According to him: "The role played by Stalin in the activities of the Kamo group was subsequently exaggerated. As far as can be said, Stalin was aware of the activities of the group and visited the "conspiratorial apartment" in order to deliver political lectures. He shielded them from the local party organization but was never the leader of the terrorists.[...] Stalin played no part in the link *[between Kamo and the emigrant Bolshevik leadership—M. K.]*.[59]

We are unable to learn much more from the documents of the tsarist political police, which have recently been released for research. The Okhrana conducted a large-scale hunt for members of the Kamo group. They had individual files on politicians working in opposition parties who were suspected of terrorism. However, these documents are now obviously incomplete. It seems that certain files mysteriously disappeared in the course of sorting, in which the names Dzhugashvili, Soso, or Koba might have appeared in relation to the expropriations. In the period between 1905 and 1907 Joseph Stalin is not even mentioned in the remarkably comprehensive Okhrana files, even though the names of far less

Leonid Krasin, a man of the world and one of the most talented engineers of the Russian Empire, coordinated the raids of the Bolshevik "confiscating" troops. His clandestine bomb-making factor gave out explosives to the terrorists of other opposition groups as well. Paradoxically, after 1918, Krasin became the most moderate, "pacifist" member of Lenin's Bolshevik government.

significant "illegals" than the former prisoner and wanted exile are included in their lists.[60]

In the course of my research in Moscow, for a long time I did not find in the archives any credible contemporary documents proving that the future Master of the Kremlin had had anything to do with the expropriations carried out by the Kamo group, including the robbery of the Tiflis mail-coach that made such enormous waves at the time. Even the more recent archive publications do not imply that it was through the intermediation of "Comrade Koba" that Kamo, or anyone else, had contact with the Financial Group *(Finansovaya gruppa)* formed by Lenin, Aleksandr Bogdanov, and Leonid Krasin, which handled the money that flowed in from expropriations without the knowledge of the RSDLP's Central Committee and even the majority of the Bolshevik leadership. In the early 1910s, when the Financial Group finally split—after angry exchanges between Lenin, on one side, and Bogdanov and Krasin on the other—Kamo, who at the time was living in emigration in the West, put down a very accurate written account of the sums handed over to the party. However, the names Iosif Dzhugashvili and "Comrade Koba" do not appear in these documents.[61]

I was on the point of closing the historical investigation into Joseph Stalin's "mail-coach robbery" period, since I could not find any new documents, when, in the former Moscow party archives, I came across the official records of the party disciplinary committee. I found the name of Iosif Dzhugashvili in two, previously unpublished, documents. Both documents are connected to the party investigation carried out by the disciplinary committee of the RSDLP between February 15, 1908 and March 23, 1910 against Maksim Litvinov, one of the men who handled the secret Bolshevik money and the future Soviet people's commissar of foreign affairs.[62] It was he who, on Lenin's orders, had tried to change abroad the high denomination bank notes stolen by Kamo and his men, and as a result he had been arrested and held for a short time. Several similar secret financial dealings had already made him something of a thorn in the flesh of the Mensheviks, who made up the majority of the disciplinary committee.

They sent for records from the secret Tiflis Social Democratic party archives that would shed light on details of the robbery. On the basis of the previously entirely unknown documents of the investigatory trial held in secret in Tiflis *it is undeniable that from late 1904 or early 1905 Stalin took part in drawing up plans for expropriations*. It is now certain that he controlled from the wings the initial plans of the group that carried out the perhaps largest ambush of the era, the "Yerevan Square expropriation".

☆ Even the leftist public of Russia was shocked by the news that on June 12, 1907 (according to contemporary dating June 25), in Yerevan Square in the center of the Georgian capital Tiflis, surrounded by beautiful buildings, an armed group attacked two mail-coaches that were delivering money. The money was being guarded by the cashier of the State Bank, his colleague, five mounted Cossacks, and three uniformed armed guards. The attackers escaped with the stolen money amidst wild gunfire. The bombs used in the robbery were made with the help of Krasin, one of the leaders of the Bolshevik Party who was known as "the engineer of the revolution". These had exploded scattering vast amounts of shrapnel and killing several innocent bystanders. "Comrade Koba", one of the masterminds behind the attack, was not present at the scene.[63]

It is worth recalling in detail what happened on that day. According to reports in the contemporary press, in the morning, soon after half past ten, a crowd of people were milling around in the downtown area of Tiflis: gentlefolk out for a promenade, as well as children and street vendors. Thus no one noticed when a few small groups of nervous-looking people gathered, watching two open carriages drive into Yerevan Square. In one of them sat some well-dressed ladies, and in the other a mustached army officer. This was Kamo, the most daring Caucasian terrorist. The handsome man was born in Gori in 1882, the son of a rich Armenian merchant. He was therefore a compatriot of Iosif Dzhugashvili and in a certain sense his brainchild. Kamo's younger sister Dzhavaria Khutulushvili (Ter-Petrosyan) remembered towards the end of her life how "... my father asked furiously what on earth we saw in that penniless good-for-nothing, Stalin.[64] Were there no decent people in Gori? And we should mark his words, he said, nothing good would come of making friends with such a person. Koba, however, whom we then called Soso, drew us like a magnet. My brother Simiko *[Semyon—M. K.]* was completely enthralled by him."[65]

Soon after Iosif Dzhugashvili left the Tiflis Theological Seminary Kamo moved to the Georgian capital where "Comrade Koba" offered to teach him Russian so that he could apply to one of the educational establishments there. However, nothing came of this. Semyon Ter-Petrosyan, who made every effort to become assimilated—to the extent that towards the end of his life he assumed the Russian family name Petrov—continued to speak only broken Russian. Koba, however, turned him into a Bolshevik superman of a kind, able to impersonate a street fruit seller or a wealthy rural nobleman with equal brilliance. He was always ready to carry out highwayman-style hold-ups or bank robberies. In February 1906, for example, on the road to Kodzhoria, near Tiflis, with a few of his men he killed the driver of a mail-coach, seriously wounded the bank employee who was delivering the money, and got away with fifteen thousand rubles. The Tiflis Bolsheviks stuffed the money into empty wine bottles and sent it to St. Petersburg.[66]

The terrorists arriving in Yerevan Square were all, like Kamo, fanatical youths. They hoped that the money given to the party as a result of the expropriation would provide new impetus for the Russian revolutionary movement, which had

Thanks to the photographer of the tsarist police, we know what Maksim Litvinov looked like at the age of 25. The other picture taken in the 1930s shows him (x) in the company of Stalin and Molotov, when Litvinov was the people's comissar for foreign affairs.

lost its force. They tried to persuade one of their number, the seriously ill Eliso Lominadze, to return home to his native Guria for treatment. He, however, said that he was not willing to go until his great dream had become reality. His desire was to get hold of two or three hundred thousand rubles and to hand it over to Lenin with the impudent remark that the leader could do whatever he wanted with it. The two women in the carriage had apparently been sent along by the masterminds behind the robbery in order to divert attention. The attack was led by Kamo. Following long months of meticulous preparation the young Armenian and Georgian terrorists, who had been ordered at the last moment to Tiflis from the neighboring small towns and from Baku, attacked the convoy at a signal from Kamo.[67]

The robbers threw eight, or according to certain sources ten, bombs into the square in all directions. Then, moving quickly among the dead and wounded they seized the sealed linen money bags containing more than quarter of a million rubles.[68] Ten minutes after the explosion of the last bomb the money was in Kamo's hands. The terrorist got back into the carriage, shot into the air with his pistol like some hero from a western, then drove away to hide the booty in the Tiflis Geophysical Observatory where the expelled seminarian Soso Dzhugashvili had once been employed. Kamo and his men later smuggled the money out of Georgia and delivered it by train to Kuokkola, Finland, home to the illegal Bolshevik center.[69] Kamo was personally responsible for this as well and discussed with the Bolshevik leader plans for further expropriations.[70]

If the members of the Kamo group had been caught they would certainly have been hanged. However, they managed to scatter throughout Georgia and avoided punishment. Nevertheless, their fate still turned out to be tragic. Eliso Lominadze, following long exile in Siberia, died in 1918 of tuberculosis. Vano Shishmanov (Shishmanyan) was shot in 1908 in a "conspiratorial apartment" when he resisted the entry of the police. Khote Tsintsadze, who became the head of the Bolshevik political police after the Sovietization of Georgia, was exiled by Stalin in the late 1920s, to an area with one of the worst climates on the Crimean peninsula, for being a Trotskyite. He soon died of tuberculosis.[71]

There is every indication that, following the explosion in Yerevan Square, "Comrade Koba" simply "wrote off" the Kamo group, or at least this is what the consistently well-informed Arsenidze believes. Several years later the Menshevik politician carried out a zealous investigation into the kind of responsibilities Stalin had had for the fate of the terrorists who had followed him so blindly. "After he had exploited those around him he usually simply dropped them or sent them to their deaths without the least sign of pity. Thus the majority of his 'courtiers' [...] died ingloriously during the expropriations and robberies or ended up in forced-labor camps because of their role in these crimes. It is hard to forget the sad fate of Vano Kalandadze, Koridze, Eliso Lominadze, Intskrivali, and others. They were all young men who followed Stalin selflessly." Some of Arsenidze's further comments are reminiscent of George Orwell's *Nineteen Eighty-four*, where the ministry dealing with misinformation and brainwashing is called the Ministry of Truth. According to the Menshevik emigrant Stalin was very fond of such euphemisms. He used the term "expropriation", for example, in the sense of "filling the party coffers".[72]

Stalin also resembled Orwell's "Big Brother", the mysterious leader of the Inner party in *Nineteen Eighty-four*, and in the event of the slightest risk or danger he always tried to remain behind the scenes. This was what happened before the attack on Yerevan Square. It was Stalin who prepared the robbery, through the mediation of others. This is why until today it is generally believed that a postal clerk by the name of Gigo Kasradze had obtained the secret information for the Bolshevik combat group.[73]

Now that the documents of the Litvinov case have been found we can state for certain that, prior to the robbery, not only Kasradze but also a Bolshevik sympathizer by the name of Voznesensky, a good friend of Stalin who worked as a postal clerk, assumed the role of partner in crime *(navodchik)*. Following the great robbery he was made to give an explanation in Tiflis before a secret session of the three-member Social Democratic investigatory committee as to why he had taken part in the preparations for the bomb attack that had claimed the lives of so many innocent victims. The frightened "fellow traveler" defended himself, saying that a year before the Yerevan Square ambush Iosif Dzhugashvili had asked him to help the terrorist group in any way he could: "I went to school with Koba. I was at the Gori Church School [...]. We then attended the Tiflis Seminary where the students published a journal. Koba took part in this as well. He wrote a revolutionary poem on the death of Eristavi [the great Georgian poet]. The poem made a great impression on me", said Voznesensky on September 20, 1907 when the leaders of the Tiflis regional Social Democratic committee summoned him before a party committee in order to ascertain the details of the expropriation. He carried on: "Although I was expelled from the Seminary I still kept in touch with Koba. I often heard how much he excelled among his fellows with his knowledge and rapid progress. This made me truly glad."[74]

At the end of 1904 or at the beginning of the following year they met again in a milk bar. Iosif Dzhugashvili took along a comrade of his, presumably Vano Shishmanov. He immediately laid his cards on the table: "Koba asked for my help so that the Social Democratic Party could expropriate money delivered by the Tiflis post. The party needed money and the party program allowed for such actions."[75] It was also mentioned that the third person at this meeting was entirely reliable and could, if necessary, stand in for Koba as an intermediary.

Nothing happened for a long time. No one visited Voznesensky. It was he who spoke to Koba, his former schoolmate, when they met by chance: "You introduced me to your comrade, but I still don't know either his name or his address. Tell me who I am to turn to if I have to." Iosif Dzhugashvili said only that he should call at the editorial offices of the *Elva* newspaper and speak to Guryev, who would give him the address. The eager postal clerk did this, but at the newspaper office was told that Koba had gone to Stockholm to attend the party congress. Vano was somehow still able to get in touch with Voznesensky and introduced him to one of his fellow terrorists. The Kamo group could therefore still count on the "fellow traveler" who had been worked on by "Comrade Koba".[76]

In the meantime Voznesensky learned from the press that the Social Democratic Party had condemned expropriations. Despite this he still undertook to help the Kamo group. As he confessed to the Social Democratic investigatory committee, two weeks before the Yerevan Square incident "Vano visited me and asked me to support the party by way of the expropriation. He said 'We have to hurry, the party needs money.'" At the same time Vano introduced the clerk to Kamo. After this meeting Voznesensky was convinced that "this man is indeed capable of organizing the action". He added that during the period before the robbery Kamo often visited him: "He told me how poor the party was and how much the delegates at the Stockholm congress suffered as a result. He also told me that the comrades *[the members of the Bolshevik leadership—M. K.]* had criticized the men in Tiflis for their cowardice and passivity."[77]

"It will all be over in three minutes", the favorite disciple of "Comrade Koba" assured his partner in crime. Kamo also assured Voznesensky that he had drawn up a detailed plan for the attack. The last meeting took place in the home of an Armenian expropriator by the name of Didebulov, who rented an apartment with three other persons, including a woman called Varvara, in Goncharnaya Street. The clerk-cum-expropriator was also invited to the meeting, which was attended by ten people. As soon became clear Voznesensky kept his promise to Iosif Dzhugashvili. Keeping to the original script he informed Kamo's group exactly when the money delivery coach would set off. The otherwise extremely cautious Semyon Ter-Petrosyan already trusted Voznesensky to such an extent that later he even sent word to him telling him how they had distributed the money they had obtained: "They gave two hundred thousand to the Central Committee. They used twenty thousand for arms *[for the Kamo group—M. K.]*." And with the remainder they had covered their costs.[78]

However, the postal clerk then learned that the tsarist authorities had sent the serial numbers of the five hundred-ruble bank notes to foreign financial institutions. He immediately hurried to the hiding place in Goncharnaya Street. On hearing the disastrous news Didebulov proposed that they should burn the money, but Kamo did not agree.[79]

At the ad hoc hearing before the investigatory committee Voznesensky cooperated with obvious willingness. He was even ready to disclose the bynames of the terrorists who had taken part in the "expropriation" in contravention of the ban issued by the RSDLP's Central Committee. He also identified them from photographs. On January 10, 1908 the *chinovnik* (clerk), who by then was completely divided in his own mind about the events, was called as witness for a second time before the three-member Tiflis committee, which forwarded his confessions abroad to a higher disciplinary body. On this second occasion Voznesensky laid the blame on his long-time friend Iosif Dzhugashvili once again. According to the somewhat laconic records "he pointed out that he had only taken part in this [...] action because Koba had asked him to do so, and he had known him since his schooldays".[80]

In terms of the way in which the Yerevan Square robbery was received the date of the action is critically important. Had it happened a year, or even six months, earlier, the Central Committee would probably not have initiated an in-depth investigation. Only a little while before, such actions had been judged entirely differently. A significant proportion of Georgian society even spoke respectfully about the six-member Menshevik terrorist squad, which, on the orders of "Silva" Dzhibladze, on January 16, 1906, had blown up General Griaznov. The general had been in charge of the ruthless pacification of Georgian villages in his role as chief of staff of the Russian troops stationed in Caucasia. A bomb had been thrown at his carriage as it was passing by on the street by a young man called Dzhordzhiashvili, who was himself injured in the attack. This was the second attempt on the general's life, since on the previous occasion Griaznov's wife had been sitting behind him and the Menshevik terrorists had changed their minds. After a hasty decision taken at the summary proceedings Dzhordzhiashvili was executed the following day, although he remained a Georgian folk hero for years.[81]

An Armenian terrorist by the name of Magrabiants, who had directed the bomb attack, claimed in his recollections published in 1923 that "following the conquest of Georgia the Bolsheviks first claimed responsibility for this popular act themselves. They then claimed that Dzhordzhiashvili was a Bolshevik. Finally [...] they declared that Stalin had been the brains behind the attempt and that he had directed its execution".[82] This kind of story could only spread at the very beginning of the 1920s, since by the middle of the decade Stalin already preferred to distance himself from such incidents.

This is understandable since at the bomb attack on General Griaznov, in the Yerevan Square attack the members of Kamo's group paid no attention to the safety of innocent passers-by. Furthermore, they openly contravened the decree passed at the London congress which banned party members from taking part in armed expropriations, which were being carried out increasingly as ends in themselves.[83] (The fact that the congress itself was made possible partly by money expropriated by the "combat units" remains a moot point.[84])

The Yerevan Square action still came in useful to some extent to the Central Committee, which was elected in spring 1907 and which consisted mainly of Mensheviks and Bolshevik "Conciliators" who shied away from Lenin's radicalism. Also useful was the fact that well-known emigrant "Leninist" Bolsheviks were arrested one after the other when they tried to change the stolen five hundred-ruble notes in Western banks. Following the series of scandals the less extremist members of the Central Committee had indisputable evidence that there had been "Leninist" Caucasian party workers standing behind Kamo, who were acting in contravention of the London decree in as early as summer 1907. "Comrade Koba" was one of them. Nor was it a secret among the Caucasian

Stalin with Roosevelt. Roosevelt thought that he met a gentleman living in the Kremlin. But in truth this person was, according to many people, a Caucasian bandit in reality.

Social Democrats that at that time Iosif Dzhugashvili, like other radical Bolshevik politicians, was virtually a puppet of Lenin.[85]

☆ The series of internal investigations in the party began in the autumn of 1907 in Tiflis and Baku, and continued in the West European-based Russian Social Democratic emigration as late as spring 1910. It became one of the most important themes in the clashes between "moderate" and "radical" politicians. Following Stalin's accession to power, however, as a result of the purges that swept through the Soviet archives, several details were lost forever. We cannot therefore be certain whether "Comrade Koba" was excluded by the RSDLP's Caucasian committee (or one of its local party organizations) solely because of the Yerevan Square robbery.

It is possible that Iosif Dzhugashvili's party membership was only suspended temporarily until the conclusion of the investigation. "The committee of the Social Democratic Party's Transcaucasian organization set up an investigatory committee, led by S[ilva] Dzhibladze, to get to the bottom of the incident", recalled Arsendize, an influential member of the Georgian Menshevik leadership. "As a result of the committee's investigations the participants and organizers of the *[Yerevan Square—M. K.]* robbery, and Koba primarily, were expelled from the party. This decision, along with the relevant documents, was sent abroad to the Central Committee."[86] According to Boris Sapir, one of the outstanding Menshevik researchers on the subject, Stalin, as well as all the participants in the 1907 Tiflis expropriation, were expelled from the party by the RSDLP's regional committee. However, the session of the Central Committee held in 1909 made it possible for them to return to the party.[87]

The documents mentioned by Arsenidze are most probably identical with the unpublished archive sources, the records of the Voznesensky interrogations among them, which I found in the mid-1990s in the course of my research in Moscow. However, the text of the disciplinary decision condemning Iosif Dzhugashvili still has not been found. Perhaps it never will be, since the man in question, when he became General Secretary, preferred to get rid of any evidence against him, such as the Georgian-language works on party history that mentioned his "mail-coach robber" period. On Beria's orders the men of the NKVD pulped the copies of the earlier banned periodical *Revolutione Matiane* (Revolutionary Chronicle) that had remained in Georgian libraries, in which these texts were published. Even the yellowed issues of the periodical were confiscated from former subscribers.[88]

Only verbal recollections remained. These, however, with the exception of the vociferous Moscow press debate in 1918, never really harmed Stalin, since if any of his political enemies accused him of taking part in the Caucasian terrorist attacks and robberies he could respond by demanding that they produce documents backing up their charges. The scandal surrounding the Yerevan Square incident only arose for a second time following the October of 1917, when Iosif Dzhugashvili (Stalin)—who for a while still used his name in this form—became a member of the Council of Peoples' Commissars *(Sovnarkom)*, chaired by Lenin, the Soviet Russian government at the time. From then on he opposed his former Menshevik comrades even more fiercely. A significant part of his writings at the time were targeted at them.[89]

For as long as freedom of the press could be practiced the Menshevik politicians fought back. They produced floods of anti-Bolshevik articles in opposition publications, airing before the public all the dirty laundry of the past. In the Stalin archives in Moscow there is a whole collection devoted to the press polemics that Yuly Martov, the most respected Menshevik leader, launched against Stalin, the people's commissar for nationalities, in spring 1918. In the first exchange he attacked *Pravda*, the central Bolshevik organ, since it had compared the Mensheviks in government in Georgia to tsarist gendarmes and had accused them of shooting vast numbers of Georgian peasant revolutionaries. Martov reacted to this accusation on March 31, 1918 in the Menshevik paper *Vperyod*, which was published in the Soviet Russian capital, by targeting one of the front members of the Bolsehvik Party, Stalin: "As expected [...] Stalin refers to the heroic exploits of the robber gangs terrorizing the peasants as a peasants' revolt. However, these highwaymen wipe out whole families. They rob not only the landlords but others as well. The local Menshevik authorities have opposed these gangs with huge forces. This is why the anarchic Caucasian Bolsheviks accuse them of supporting the landlords. [...] But it was the Caucasian Bolsheviks themselves who *[in the early years of the century—M. K.]* took part in such glorious enterprises as expropriation. Mr. Stalin knows this very well, since in the past he was expelled by the party organization for his involvement in expropriations."

Stalin's reaction to the attack revealed his deep unease. He even went to extremes. Not only did he fiercely attack Martov through the columns of *Pravda*, he also passed on the case to the Moscow Revolutionary Tribunal, a court which had, among other things, rights over censorship.[90] At the same time, on April 1, 1918, he placed a short statement in the Bolshevik press: "In issue 51 of the newspaper *Vperyod*, an article appeared, signed by Martov [...], stating that Stalin was once expelled from the party for involvement in expropriations. I regard it as my duty [...] to declare that I, Stalin, was never called before the disciplinary committee of any party organization. In particular, I was never expelled from the party organization. I regard Martov's accusation as the contemptible action of an unbalanced man who has suffered total defeat in open political battle and who, in his despair, as a last resort falls back on filthy libel. I therefore request that proceedings be started against Martov."[91]

With this, events took a new turn. The ink had scarcely dried on the pen of the people's commissar for nationalities when Yuly Martov was summoned before the tribunal. The favorite of the old Social Democrats was aware that this body had the right to ban any publication if there was proof that it was spreading untruths. A few weeks earlier this had happened in the case of the opposition daily *Misl*, which, when criticizing the actions of the Bolshevik Council of Peoples' Commissars, had mistakenly claimed that Martov had been killed. While the person in question was naturally not happy to have been pronounced dead, Martov regarded as a far more serious problem the fact that the error was used as an excuse to practice censorship: "It is much easier and simpler to ban a newspaper for spreading news about the death of an opposition politician than to put an end to those circumstances due to which [...] such news emerges every day and appears quite credible", Martov wrote.[92]

In this atmosphere the Revolutionary Tribunal convened on April 5, 1918 before a "full house". In the room appeared Joseph Stalin himself. He was accompanied by another Bolshevik politician, Sosnovsky, who, in 1908, was a journalist in Baku. As a representative of the Caucasian proletariat a Georgian worker by the name of Filya was also with them. Yuly Martov also arrived with an escort. His "second" was a well-known Menshevik publicist, Lapinsky, who was also once a party worker in Baku. He was also accompanied by a laborer called Aleksandrovsky from the town of Tula.[93]

From the still unpublished records, which were at one time regarded as highly confidential, we learn that Yuly Martov objected because Stalin had not turned to the district judge competent in civilian disputes but had instead called him before a political jury. But the Bolsheviks did not accept this argument. Stalin stated that his honor had been attacked as part of a political campaign, and in such affairs "competence lies with such political institutions as the tribunal". The Bolshevik chairman of the tribunal brought the issue to a close by making a pre-judgment. "This is not a simple libel case", he declared. "This case concerns a libel in the press, thus it belongs within the competence of the Revolutionary Tribunal."[94]

However, the commissar for nationalities had little time to enjoy the obvious sympathy of the tribunal, since Martov was accusing him of something that could further damage his prestige. He asked the jury to call as witness Isidor Ramishvili[95], "a deputy in the First State Duma and president of the *[1908 disciplinary—M. K.]* court that met in Baku prison. The participants had examined [...] whether the Baku committee of the RSDLP, of which Stalin was a member, had indeed been involved in Baku in robbing the ship the *Nikolai I*."[96]

Neither then nor now did "Comrade Koba" give a meaningful answer in reply to this accusation. He merely turned to Martov with the words: "You are a wretched individual!" This gave the Menshevik politician the opportunity to come out with his third, no less serious, accusation. He claimed that he could prove by means of witnesses that Iosif Dzhugashvili had had a worker by the name of Zharikov (or, according to another version, Zhareny), who knew of his past affairs, beaten half-dead. Martov mentioned about half a dozen people who had been working in Baku at the time and who could have known about Stalin's dubious dealings, including Gukovsky, the commissar for finance in the Bolshevik government, and Martov's own brother, Yezhov (Tsederbaum).[97]

The Bolshevik politician perhaps realized at this point that he was in serious trouble. The old Social Democrats mentioned by Martov had indeed participated in the disciplinary hearing against Iosif Dzhugashvili, or, as Baku party workers, could have heard from others that in 1908 Stalin had been expelled from the local party organization. Instead of an answer, therefore, the future Master of the Kremlin dictated a list of his activities to the record clerk: "Since 1898 I have spent a total of six years in prison[98] and I have been abroad. Nowhere, whether as a free man, or in prison, or abroad, have I ever faced party proceedings. And by no means was I ever expelled. If you are unable to prove that I faced party proceedings I will be free to regard Martov as a common libeler."[99]

Yuly Martov then spoke again. The records read as follows: "At that time [...] the parties were working illegally and there were no written documents recording disciplinary decisions. He therefore recommended that witnesses mentioned by him should be heard next, who could have been involved in Stalin's expulsion."[100]

The discussion finally focused on the issue of how many days it would take to summon the eye-witnesses mentioned by Martov. Many of them lived in distant Baku and Tiflis, cut off from the Soviet Russian capital. However, there were some who lived in Petrograd and who were therefore within reach. It is hardly surprising that Joseph Stalin, who was extremely wary of the testimony of his Baku and Tiflis comrades, now wanted to put an end to the Revolutionary Tribunal as soon as possible. He also knew that it would go against him if the tribunal summoned as witness the former Menshevik Isidor Gukovsky. In 1908 in Baku prison Gukovsky had led the investigation against members of the local party committee, which included Stalin, who had been accused of conduct that was in breach of party discipline. Chances were good because Gukovsky lived in Moscow, as did Georgy Chicherin, a famous Menshevik politician, who, while living in emigration abroad, had held in his hands the various threads of the disciplinary proceedings in connection with expropriation. However, in the meantime both of Martov's key witnesses had become members of the Bolshevik Party and were part of the establishment: Gukovsky was the people's commissar for finances in the Lenin government and Chicherin was responsible for foreign affairs. Since they regularly took part, along with Joseph Stalin, in the meetings of the Soviet Russian government, they could not have been expected to disclose the earlier dealings of "Comrade Koba" lightheartedly. On the other hand they were both men of discipline and would certainly have answered the jury summons.

However, "due to lack of time" no such summons was issued. On the other hand, nor was Martov given a particularly severe punishment. There is every indication that the Bolshevik functionaries who were manipulating the Revolutionary Tribunal from the wings at first wanted to use the case as serious anti-Menshevik retaliation. The bulletin of the Smolensk soviet, for example, recorded that Martov "was sentenced to seven days in prison" even before the second phase of the trial had begun.[101]

In fact, the sentence turned out to be much more lenient: the Menshevik politician was merely given a reprimand. This was explained by the fact that Martov, as a public figure, had criticized the Bolshevik government and had thus proved himself to be "irresponsible". However, the inner Bolshevik party leadership regarded even this as excessive, even though, by that time, many of them had lost most of their sentimental feelings towards their one-time Menshevik allies. Despite the press polemics Lenin, along with the majority of the "founding fathers", still respected Martov. At the first opportunity they even voiced this attitude in the Central Executive Committee of the All-Russian Congress of Soviets, of which the Yuly Martov was a member. At a session of this body Nikolai Krylenko, the Bolshevik Party's legal expert who later became people's commissar of justice during the first show trials, came up with an unexpected proposal. He suggested that the case should be referred back to the Revolutionary Tribunal since, according to him, the judges had made several mistakes in matters of form.

Martov then stood up with the intention of supporting the truth of his claim with further facts. The chairman of the Central Executive Committee, Yakov

Sverdlov, however, did not allow him to speak, nor did he permit other Menshevik politicians to address the session. There was no further meeting of any committee in connection with the case. Thus several blank spots in the Tiflis and Baku life of "Comrade Koba" remain even today.[102]

☆ A curious omission from the old Tiflis and Baku underground activists whom, in spring 1918, Yuly Martov wished to summon to the trial, was Sergei Alliluyev, Stalin's future father-in-law, one of the founders of the Caucasian workers' movement. In one of his manuscripts we read: "I returned to Baku in April 1907 from exile in the North, but I was arrested again as early as May 5. After I left prison I met Comrade Dzhugashvili (Koba) for the second time. He had arrived in Baku after May 5, when most activists in our organization had been snatched by the police. The need *[in the local Bolshevik community—M. K.]* for fresh forces and a strong leadership was therefore greater than ever. Only a few comrades escaped arrest, like Alyosha Dzhaparidze, Suren Spandaryan, etc."[103] Pavel Sakhvarelidze, who at the time was also a good friend of Stalin, was another omission from the list of Martov's witnesses. Like the elderly Alliluyev he did not have a great career following the Bolshevik takeover, and he was among those who never came into conflict with the unpredictable "Comrade Koba". Stalin wrote: "I certify that in 1907/1908 Comrade Pavel Sakhvarelidze ("the Long Pavel") worked together with me, A. Dzhaparidze, S. Shaumyan, Spandaryan, and others in the Baku Social Democratic organization. He was a member of the higher leadership of the Baku organization, in which he was regarded as one of the most outstanding figures. J. Stalin, April 6, 1936. P. S. Perhaps it is worth mentioning that P. Sakhvarelidze became a member of the Social Democratic Party in 1902 and joined the party's Bolshevik wing at the time of its establishment. J. Stalin."[104]

Such a recommendation was as good as a letter of exemption in the period before the Great Terror. Its value was further increased by the fact that Stalin hated the movement from which he had started out in the early years of the century. In the second half of the 1930s former Tiflis and Baku party workers were taken away one after the other in the "black crows" *(chorny voron)*, the police vehicles used to transport prisoners. In the years of the Great Terror about two-thirds of the once underground Tiflis Bolshevik leadership, and at least half of the earlier leading Baku party workers, were killed.

There were many irrational elements in the way in which the Soviet dictator exterminated his former comrades in Caucasia, since in the 1930s they did not present much of a threat to him. By that time the majority of the more famous Baku and Tiflis Mensheviks had emigrated or were in prison in the Gulag. And the majority of the old Bolshevik leaders had been politically marginalized. They could regard themselves as fortunate to find shelter in some insignificant economic office.

Furthermore, Stalin's activity in Baku in 1908 was not such an obvious failure that he had to take revenge on his former acquaintances in order to erase it from the common memory. According to the already quoted Tatyana Vulich, the future Soviet dictator had won serious respect among the local Bolshevik community over the years: "It must be admitted that he had many followers, men who were unconditionally loyal to him, among the Caucasian Bolsheviks [...] and especially among the Georgian comrades. He was respected as the second member of the party, after Lenin, of course. At that time Stalin had no desire to appear as a theoretician. [...] However, he had an unquestionable influence over certain people, and he achieved a lot from them. There were some who were ready to do anything at one word from him. It is also true that the propagandists and people from a higher intellectual level liked and appreciated him less, but almost everyone admitted that in the whole of Caucasia he was one of the most zealous party members."[105]

Nevertheless, outside the region Dzhugasvili was obviously not regarded as a truly successful politician. Not even in 1907 was he really able to find his way to the forefront, even though, while commuting mostly between Tiflis and Baku, the two Caucasian metropolises, he left his homeland on two occasions on official affairs. It may appear important that he had taken part in the RSDLP's 5th Congress in London, and on returning home had published a detailed "Leninist" article in the illegal Baku Bolshevik press.[106] However, the delegates meeting in the English capital did not elect him onto any official body since the Caucasian Mensheviks, with whom he had arrived at the congress, queried the validity of his delegate's card. Nor was he included among the members of the highly secretive informal Bolshevik leadership, who worked in parallel with the reunited RSDLP's newly elected Central Committee.[107]

In addition, Iosif Dzhugashvili almost ended up behind bars during one of the breaks at the London Party Congress. He got into a fight in a London pub with some of the slightly inebriated customers. Maksim Litvinov, who was with him, came to the aid of the hot-tempered Georgian. Even decades later Stalin was grateful to him for his assistance: "Perhaps this was the reason why he let him live at the time of the mass executions", mused Litvinov's daughter during our meeting in England in the mid-1990s. "Even though he had him removed from the Central Committee and fired him from his job twice", she added. I have also heard from her that Stalin rewarded the commissar of foreign affairs with a royal gift when the Soviet Union became member of the League of Nations and established diplomatic relation with the USA: he gave him one of his *dacha*s. In addition an eight-member squad of bodyguards was ordered to guard him against terrorist attacks. And also to watch him round the clock.

From the early nineteen-twenties, for almost 25 years Stalin worked closely with Litvinov. He respected him for his knowledge of foreign languages and for his expertise. This, however did not mean that he would not be suspicious of Litvinov, who—apart from a few minor incidents—was loyal to Stalin. In the private correspondence of the dictator we find frequent nasty, occasionally vulgar remarks about Litvinov. (Not to mention the fact that the Soviet political police carried out several attempts—staged car accidents—on Maksim Litvinov's life. Once even Beria himself turned up to inspect the site of a planned "accident", which he would never have dared to do unless on Stalin's orders.[108])

Litvinov knew about these, but being a proud and daring man, did not care about Stalin's wrath.[109] His English wife refused to behave according to the unwritten rules of the "Bolshevik elite", she even took his favorite goat for walks in the city of Moscow on a leash.[110]

He behaved strangely also when, in the middle of the Second Word War, he was dismissed from his position of Soviet ambassador in Washington and for a second time he found himself on the periphery of political life. Although for years he strove to paint a positive picture of the Soviet system in the diplomatic circles he moved in, he dared twice to warn the Western elite not to trust Stalin and his associates. This, of course was promptly reported to the dictator through NKVD channels.[111]

Was it his fame that rescued the aged diplomat, or did Stalin still remember the incident in the London pub? Fact is that, when in 1948 Litvinov became severely ill and felt that he was dying, he again decided to speak his mind. According to his daughter Tatyana, he criticized the foreign policy of Molotov in a lengthy memo, which he locked up in his desk. Needless to say, the criticism was, of course, directed against Stalin.

Unfortunately I could not trace this document in the archives in Moscow. Maybe it has been destroyed. According to Tatyana Litvinova entire passages from this document could be identified in Khrushchev's foreign affairs doctrine of "thaw". I have found two important letters by Litvinov supporting the recollections of his daughter. In one of these, dated 24 October 1948, he asked "comrade Koba" to support his children. He wrote: "To J. V. Stalin, Head of the Council of Ministers of the Soviet Union. Dear Iosif Vissarionovich! I turn to you with a last wish before my death. Since I feel that my end is approaching, I am unable not to think about the fate of my family, especially my wife. My children, too, need support. So far practically they all had relied on me, so they will be unable to support their mother. Therefore, I would like to request at least a special pension for her and also, if possible, that my family may continue to live in our present flat, that is if they can afford it. I am dying with a clean conscience knowing that I made everything in my power for the communist cause and for our beloved country. It is not my fault if I could do no more. With this last message of mine, I wish you good health and a long life, M. M. Litvinov. October 24, 1948."[112]

However, Litvinov temporarily recovered from his severe cardiac condition. He died a few years later in December 1951. His flat was invaded by the political police, who found both documents mentioned above: the lengthy memo on Soviet foreign policy and the personal letter to Stalin. Tatyana Litvinova, having read this letter added the following note, entirely uncharacteristic of those times: "Dear Iosif Vissarionovich! I have learned about the contents of my father's letter which he wrote to you in 1948. I wish to add that we—his children Mikhail Maksimovich and Tatyana Maksimovna—have since grown up and are entirely capable of supporting ourselves. We do not want to give you the impression that we are imploring for support. Very best wishes: Tatyana Litvinova. December 31, 1951."[113] It is a miracle that Stalin did not imprison the two young Litvinovs in response.

☆ We know from indirect references that in 1907 "Comrade Koba", not long before the Yerevan Square "expropriation" met Litvinov in secret in the German capital. Litvinov was then one of the main handlers of the Bolshevik Party's secret funds. Even today this trip by Stalin, during which he even met with Lenin in great secrecy, remains rather obscure.[114] Nor can we be entirely certain if Lenin traveled to Berlin simply in order to meet Stalin, although this is generally regarded as axiomatic in the Stalin literature. It rather seems to be the case that Lenin traveled to the German capital independently of the visit by the Georgian Bolshevik, but that once he was there he ordered Koba to meet him, along with several others.

However, it is undeniable that in those months Iosif Dzhugashvili was one of the links between the Caucasian terrorists who were busy preparing new bank robberies, and the top-secret three-member Bolshevik Financial Group. Stalin's presence in Berlin is striking from this point of view, if, in the name of this group, it was in fact mainly Leonid Krasin who controlled Kamo's Caucasian terrorist community.[115]

Leon Trotsky, however, came up with a somewhat different version: "The London Party Congress ended on April 27 *[1907—M. K.]*. The Tiflis expropriation took place on June 12, one and a half months later. Between returning from abroad and the day of the expropriation Stalin was left with too little time to direct such a complicated enterprise personally. Besides, the members of the combat squad must have gelled together and familiarized themselves with one another in the course of previous dangerous enterprises. Some of the members were perhaps insecure about what Lenin thought *[following the ban issued at the congress—M. K.]* about expropriations. They were waiting for a sign, and following his return home Stalin may have given that sign."[116] This reasoning seems logical enough. However, the former Caucasian Mensheviks, and even several of the Bolsheviks, stated that Koba, in the year of the great "expropriation", was more than a simple courier. In the spring of 1907, at the time of his trip to Germany, he was regarded almost as "Lenin's extended arm" by the Caucasian Bolshevik terrorists. However, he never wrote down a word about his secret mission to Berlin, although he did let a few remarks slip out: "A long time ago in Germany they truly respected the law. In 1907, when I was forced to spend two or three months in Berlin, we Russian Bolsheviks often laughed at our German friends because of this", he said in April 1932 to Emil Ludwig. He also recounted an anecdote, according to which two hundred German Social Democrats missed a demonstration because, in the absence of the ticket collector, they did not dare to board the train without a ticket.[117]

In the Second World War Stalin also mentioned his stay in Germany when conversing with Churchill during a break in official negotiations. However, the Berlin trip was omitted from the biographical chronology at the end of the second volume of his Collected Works.[118] Nevertheless, the researchers who maintained the files in the Stalin archives containing biographical data recorded the Berlin trip twice.[119]

The chronology of the Soviet party leader's life also contains gaps at other points. Although recorded on the filing cards in the archives, the fact that in the summer of 1907 Iosif Dzhugashvili, who was then staying illegally in Baku, visited the oil wells owned by the oil baron Kokharev, where there had recently been a number of cases of arson, is not included in the printed version of the chronology. The later decision by the censors can readily be understood in this case: they did not wish to alert readers to the fact that "Comrade Koba" could have had anything to do with these incidents, which were referred to as "economic terror" by the Baku revolutionaries. The reference is also omitted from the book by Bagirov, which deals in great detail with Stalin's crucial role in the Baku workers' movement.[120]

The arson attacks were not characteristic of the situation in the "city of black gold". In early 1908, when Tiflis was on the verge of chaos, Baku was still relatively peaceful since the authorities and the oil barons wanted to come to terms with the revolutionaries who were carrying on a desperate rearguard action. According to the recollections of Tatyana Vulich the local propagandists "were acting openly. They often held their meetings in workers' hostels. The Bolshevik and Menshevik committees also met openly. The police were even happy to give out information as to when and where the committees would be meeting. These sessions usually took place in schools or other educational institutions. Shaumyan, Stalin, Budu Mdivani, Spandaryan, and others walked along the street quite openly. They would speak out at committee meetings as well as at public meetings and in private apartments."[121]

The local Menshevik leadership, which was far more militant than in Russia and which not much earlier had been in armed conflict with the tsarist authorities, was at that time willing to abandon its offensive tactics. The Mensheviks would readily have withheld strike action as well if, in return, the employers had made a collective contract with the oil workers and had improved their standard of living substantially. However, Stalin and his Bolshevik followers did everything they could to undermine the compromise that was taking shape. On the principle of "the worse it is the better it is", and on the basis of nationality, they turned the mostly Russian skilled workforce, who sympathized with the

Mensheviks, against the unskilled laborers, who had moved to Baku from the nearby Tatar and Azerbaijani villages and who were mostly illiterate and could barely speak Russian. Tatyana Vulich was told by her acquaintances that "Stalin wanted to obtain a majority, thus he herded along to the meetings *[where the decisions were made with respect to strike action and arson attacks—M. K.]* not only the elected delegates but everyone he met. I remember how surprised I was by the sight of the many Tatar Bolshevik delegates. They were obviously not active party members at all. The majority of them did not understand Russian and did not even know what was going on. They sat in one block. A Tatar student walked up and down near them; he was a member of the Bolshevik party organization and very loyal to Stalin. When it came to the vote, at his sign everyone raised their hand and thus with a majority of votes they defeated those decisions with which the Bolsheviks did not agree."[122]

Among the followers of "Comrade Koba" in Baku there were a few Russian Social Democrats as well, mostly people who, even at that time, were willing to give in to his will. Kliment Voroshilov, who had escaped from exile in northern Russia, was one of them, whom the party, in the phrasing of the time, "commanded" to Baku. The future red marshal mentioned his acquaintanceship with Stalin in an autobiographical text written in the early 1920s: "Between January and September 1908 I worked in Baku as the secretary of the oil industrial trade union. At the same time I was a member of the Baku party committee, along with comrades Shaumyan, Mdivani, Stalin, and others."[123] In another version of the autobiography almost the same names are mentioned in relation to his time in Baku: "I worked there with Shaumyan, Dzhaparidze, Stalin, Sosnovsky, and others, until the autumn (of 1908), after which I traveled to St. Petersburg."[124]

The old statesman, at the twilight of his life and with the help of his secretaries, edited his lengthy memoirs for publication and from this version left out the names of Mdivane and Sosnovsky. In the meantime both these men had been executed as Trotskyites. On the other hand he always wrote in glowing terms about the "Master" and his meetings with him at that time: "On one occasion J. V. Stalin learned that I had fallen ill. In the evening he came to visit me, even though he was an extremely busy man and at that time we were not even such good friends as we were to become later during the Civil War. By the time he arrived I was no longer confined to bed. He was very pleased about this. He joked a great deal. He said that poetry and music elevate the spirit, which is good for health." Then Stalin asked him if he enjoyed poetry. "When I answered that I did he asked me to recite a poem by Nekrasov. He called it an excellent poem that should be made known to as many workers as possible. Then we sang together the song 'I look up to the sky'. It turned out that he had a good voice and a fine ear for music."[125]

In the manuscript of his book, written at the end of the 1960s at a time of apparent re-Stalinization, Kliment Voroshilov wrote about Stalin as if he had directed the Bolshevik-oriented Baku workers *on his own*. In reality, however, following the Russian revolution of 1905–1907, at least two opposing groups were working in the Bolshevik community of the Azerbaijani capital: the "rightists" grouped around "Alyosha" Dzhaparidze, and the "leftists" sympathizing with "Koba" Dzhugashvili.[126] It would be a mistake to believe that these adjectives refer to major differences, since among the followers of Dzhaparidze there were similar ruthless terrorists as in the circle around Stalin.[127] However, relations became so poisonous between the two groups that the emigrant Bolshevik leadership had to send Grigory Aleksinsky, and later Rozalia Zemlyachka, to "restore order". Both of them came into conflict with Stalin almost immediate-

Who would think that the elegantly dressed, dashing and sophisticated Kliment Voroshilov (on the left) actually had finished only two grades in the elementary school and was a small-town locksmith when this picture was taken.

ly. Later, Zemlyachka traveled to Paris to make a complaint against the "troublemaker" Koba to Lenin. According to Tatyana Vulich the Bolshevik party leader himself called Iosif Dzhugashvili a "stupid Georgian" on that occasion.[128]

These internal struggles carried on in Baku for some time. Between the "leftist" and "rightist" Bolsheviks, Stepan Shaumyan, perhaps the most colorful and cultured personality in the local movement, occupied a position somewhere in the center. Even he regarded "economic terror" as a permissible tactic in the struggle, and even he "borrowed" money for the purposes of the movement from expropriators of the likes of Kamo. Despite this, his contemporaries, among them the most anti-Bolshevik Mensheviks, remembered him as a good-hearted and honest man. They recalled how Stalin was always jealous of the more popular Shaumyan and tried to remove him from his path, even using dishonorable and underhand methods. Exactly the same story was told by Shaumyan's former secretary, Olga Shatunovskaya. According to her still unpublished manuscript Iosif Dzhugashvili once deliberately gave away the address of Shaumyan's "conspiratorial apartment". On hearing the information the police went to the place and arrested Stalin's number one rival.[129]

It is hard to judge the credibility of this story. Shatunovskaya spent long years as a prisoner in Soviet concentration camps and desperately hated Stalin. In the period of political "meltdown" she became an advisor of Nikita Khrushchev and helped him to edit the final version of his famous "Secret Speech" delivered at a session of the 20th Congress of the Communist Party of the Soviet Union (CPSU). Shatunovskaya did everything she could to destroy the halo around the Soviet tyrant. She declared with conviction until the end of her life that Iosif Dzhugashvili had been a secret agent of the tsarist police. When I talked to her about this she referred to the mystical philosopher Gurdzhiev, who had emigrated to the West and who had studied with Soso Dzhugashvili at the Tiflis Seminary. Gurdzhiev, she claimed, was aware of Stalin's repulsive characteristics and, as far as he could tell, his one-time schoolmate who had made it to the top of the Russian Empire would have had no great difficulty in reconciling the roles of self-conscious revolutionary and agent of the tsarist Okhrana. Later she made a short memo about this.[130]

Stepan Shaumyan, the heart of the Bolshevik community in Baku, with his wife and two sons. The picture was taken in the courtyard of the local prison, as the family was sitting on the gallows. One of the boys, Levon (x), as an old man several decades later, told me many stories about the Master of the Kremlin and his environment. Levon Shaumyan was the first to tell me: "One day you will write a book about Stalin."

Many of those who talked to Shatunovskaya believed immediately—perhaps only because they wanted to—this story that continues to fascinate historians.[131] It was generally assumed that the highly respected old lady knew very well what was hidden behind the "blank spots" in the Stalin biography. For several years she was officially involved in the rehabilitation of old party members, and in the meantime got hold of a huge amount of information. On one occasion she read me the copy of a letter sent by Ivan Serov, which the leader of the KGB and the confidant of Khrushchev had written to the Supreme Soviet leadership. In this letter he told that Stalin had had a child from an underage girl in Kureyka, Siberia, during his last period in exile. The author of another document, Boris Ivanov, an old Bolshevik party member, had worked in the editorial offices of *Pravda* for a while. He wrote to Shatunovskaya that Stalin "behaved to his fellow exiles like a hooligan" and had once set a gang of common criminals on Yakov Sverdlov.[132]

The Stalinist *apparatchik*s were furious with Olga Shatunovskaya for coming out with such stories. It is hardly surprising that she was even sacked from the party archives after October 1964 when Khrushchev was ousted from his position as General Secretary. Nevertheless, she decided that once the opportunity for publication had been taken away from her she would at least set down on paper for posterity her memories in connection with the Baku Commune of 1918 and the conflict between Shaumyan and Stalin. The following fascinating passage is included in the latter: "Lenin sent military troops *[from Moscow—M. K.]* for the protection of Baku. A significant number of these, however, were held up on the orders of Stalin, who at the time was staying in Tsaritsyn. Thus from the large army, numbering almost 19,000, under the command of Petrov, 7,240 remained in Tsaritsyn. Shaumyan often said bitterly that 'Stalin will not help us'. He even protested to Lenin and the Military Revolutionary Committee of the Republic. Also on Stalin's orders the grain that was collected in the districts of northern Caucasia for the starving people in Baku was likewise directed to Tsaritsyn."[133]

There is a great deal of truth in this story. In the most reliable biography to date of Shaumyan, who died the death of a martyr, Ilya Dubinsky-Mukhadze, although without providing archival references, quotes word for word the relevant important archive sources supporting the claims of Olga Shatunovskaya.[134] Let's return to the early Baku period of Stalin's life. At the time the future Soviet dictator, in a period of revolutionary ebb, controlled at most a few dozen Baku party workers. Sometimes he participated in extremely dubious activities: "The party needed money. Stalin decided to collect money from the industrialists", we

After the end of the 1920s, the "Master" was always the center of attention.

read in the recollections of Tatyana Vulich. "They printed special certificates and the Baku Bolshevik committee strongly recommended various companies to pay a certain sum of money. (The sum was fixed according to the firm's liquidity.) The certificates were delivered by a courier, visibly carrying a weapon, to the offices of these firms. I remember one of them. He was a very strong, tall fellow. He was said to be Stalin's bodyguard. According to the comrades no one dared refuse his request."[135]

The blackmailing particularly enraged Aleksinsky and Zemlyachka who were investigating the activities of Stalin and his cronies.[136] According to Vulich's recollections, at the same time this blackmailing group forced those party members who did not please Stalin and his cronies to leave the oil producing regions: "I cannot judge the truth of this", we read in the closely typed manuscript, "but apparently they are said to have done away with certain people even more drastically. [...] For example, not long before my arrival Stalin accused a party member (a laboring man, if my memory serves me well) of being an agent provocateur. Although there was no definite proof of this he was taken out of the town, "tried", sentenced to death, and shot in the head."[137]

Then one day the police apprehended Stalin. Even today there are several versions as to why he was arrested on March 25, 1908. According to the Menshevik Arsenidze, during the previous days his comrades had initiated an investigation against Stalin, since they began to suspect why the authorities regularly received the addresses of underground party workers, written in block capitals. Curiously it was always those who had come into conflict with "Comrade Koba" who were snatched by the police. As a result of this investigation the party disciplinary committee held several sessions. Following one of them the judges, witnesses, and Stalin himself ended up in Baku's most infamous institution, the Baylov Prison.[138]

By that time the Okhrana had realized that they had caught a very important illegal Social Democrat leader. During a house search they found a two-page document, "The Decree of the Central Committee regarding the Split in the RSDLP's Baku Organization".[139] Nevertheless, the Bolshevik politician received a surprisingly lenient sentence: without a court hearing, as at other times, he was summarily exiled to northern Russia for a relatively short period.[140]

1 Alliluyeva, 1946, 37, 168. see also *RGASPI*, fond. 558, op. 4, d. 619.
2 *RGASPI*, fond. 71, op. 10, d. 404.
3 Chernenko, 1942, 22.
4 Stalin, 1946, vol. I, 420.
5 Chernenko, 1942, 24.
6 *Ibid.*, 24–25.
7 *Ibid.*, 24.
8 *Ibid.*, 25.
9 *Ibid.*, 24.
10 *Ibid.*, 37.
11 *Ibid.*, 32.
12 *Ibid.*, 32–33.
13 Alliluyeva, 1946, 37. One memoir-writer, Abram Gusinsky, wrote an entertaining if not too factual account of how he the fugitive Soso entered his home: "He was dressed foolishly for the Siberian cold…It was mainly his light, cordovan-lined hat and his short, white coat that were inappropriate for the bitter temperatures. My wife and children admired this coat, and with typical Caucasian generosity, Comrade Stalin gave it to them." *RGASPI*, fond 558. op. 11. d. 1494.
14 Later they both became well known Mensheviks. The man perished in a Bolshevik prison. Perhaps this is why Sergei Alliluyev did not mention their full names.
15 *RGASPI*, fond. 558, op. 1, d. 14.
16 *RGASPI*, fond. 558, op. 4, d. 92.
17 *Batumskaya Demonstratsia*, 1937, 11–112.
18 Felshtinsky, 1999, 6–8, 286, 382. It should be added that according to a noted Georgian party historian, the Mensheviks "claimed Stalin was a government agent and informer-spy." Talakvadze 1925. I. 117–118.
19 Trotsky, 1971, 138–146, 199–208.
20 Chernenko, 1942, 37–39. Stalin mentioned the mysterious "Leipzig stay" in his confession to interrogators on April 1, 1908, in Baku. There, too, he spoke obscurely when he answered that "I was in Leipzig in 1904 with the aim of hiding there…I lived in Leipzig for more than a year." *RGASPI*, fond 558. op. 4. d. 687. It's hardly necessary to mention that Stalin's assertion does not accord with the truth. It's hard to believe, but not impossible, that Stalin went to Leipzig in January of 1904, crossing the border with a fake passport. From there, after a relatively short period, he traveled to Tiflis. According to numerous sources, Soso Dzhugashvili was living deep in the underground in Tiflis in late winter and early spring. The writers of the memoirs in general do not name the exact day and month, or simply mistake it. The "blank spots" in Stalin's biography are connected precisely with the first two to two and a half months of 1904.
21 *RGASPI*, fond. 558, op. 4, d. 656. The writer of the memoir brought together Soso Dzhugashvili and one Ashot Tumanyan, an Armenian teacher, who "loaned" the hiding Bolshevik politician a passport.
22 *RGASPI*, fond. 558, op. 4, d. 92. In the December of 1904, the Tiflis branch of the Okhrana did mention Iosif Dzhugashvili's name when reporting on the rebirth of the Social Democrat organization in Baku. *RGASPI*, fond. 558, op. 4, d. 93.
23 Valentinov, 1993, 29–83. An important part of the "Stalin legend" is the confabulations about his early relationship with Lenin. Kentaur 1992/5–6, 58–79.
24 Trotsky, 1990, vol. I, 112.
25 *Ibid.*, 113–121.
26 *RGASPI*, fond. 558, op. 4, d. 651.
27 *RGASPI*, fond. 71, op. 10, d. 404.
28 *Sovetskaya Abkhazia*, 1947, vol. VI, 21.
29 Tyutyukin and Selohayev, 1996, 41–47, 78–91, 144–160.
30 Uratadze, 1968, 58–60, 66–70, 159–161, 208–210.
31 Nicolaevsky, 1965, 90. 4.
32 Uratadze, 1968, 197, 203–204.
33 Correctly, in the newspapers he *edited*, since as an underground party activist, he could not be the publisher of any printed media.
34 *Novy Zhurnal*, 1963, no. 72, 219.
35 Stalin, 1946, vol. I, 62–74, 241–247, 277–286.
36 *Ibid.*, 294–393.
37 *RGASPI*, fond. 155, op. 1, d. 66.
38 *Ibid.*
39 *RGASPI*, fond. 558, op. 4, d. 548.
40 *Ibid.*
41 Stalin, 1951, vol. XIII. 112.
42 Ludwig, 1942, 42–43. Strangely, Stalin did not really brag that in the beginning of 1905 he led in Baku the Bolshevik "battle squad" *(boyevaya druzhina)*, which was formed there. (This squad not only handled "expropriation" but also, armed, became involved in an ethnic conflict that took place in the Armenian and Tartar areas of Baku. The massacre was known of and in fact supported by local Tsarist authorities.) *RGASPI* fond 556. op. 4. d. 583. Not one of his acqua-

intances or biographers mentions that for a while he wracked his brains about whether it was possible to start an armed rebellion in Tiflis. Ostrovsky 2002, 243–244.

43 On Münzenberg's work, see Koch, 2000, 11–14, 17–35, 41–55, 61–76.

44 According to documents that survived in the Soviet archives, Bazhanov worked as a secretary at the Politburo meetings in the early 1920s. He also took part in the work of the Stalin secretariat.

45 *RGASPI*, fond. 155, op. 1, d. 81.

46 The second most important leader of the German communist at the time, and Stalin's favorite. He was a victim of the Great Terror. The NKVD handed over his wife to the Nazi authorities.

47 *RGASPI*, fond. 155, op. 1, d. 81.

48 At a price of several big scandals, Koba managed to participate in the work of the Congress, but he was present only in an advisory capacity. Trotsky, 1990, vol. I, 133–134.

49 *Socialistichesky Vestnik*, 1949, no. 12, 30, 215–216.

50 Geifman, 1997, 19–20, 35, 47.

51 Nicolayevskiy, 1995, 29.

52 Budnitsky, 2000, 323–327. On the purchase of arms and the operation of secret bomb-producing workshops, see the publication which is very hard to obtain nowadays: Sedova, 1927, 28–48.

53 Geifman, 1997, 222–225.

54 Nicolaevsky, 1965, 11, 207.

55 Geifman, 1997, 34–35.

56 *Ibid.*

57 Uratadze, 1968, 130–132, 163–167.

58 Nicolaevsky, 1965, 207, 11.

59 Nicolaevsky, 1995, 88.

60 Ostrovsky, a researcher discussing mostly these questions from St. Petersburg, based his findings mainly on unknown police records. In a facsimile manuscript, with the title *Kto stoyal za spinoy Stalina?* (Who stands behind Stalin?), he raises the possibility that Stalin was arrested twice, first during the course of 1905, then on January 29, 1906. Nevertheless, he luckily managed to escape on both occasions. An archivist in Moscow, Galina Gorskaya called my attention to this well-documented paper. Since the Hungarian version of this book was published, Ostrovsky's work—of which the quoted paper is an important chapter—has seen the light of day.

61 Bogdanov, 1995, vol. II, 120–142.

62 *Magyar Nemzet [a Hungarian daily—Trans.]*, September 14, 1996.

63 *Perspektivi*, 1991, no. 6, 51–57.

64 He must have said Dzhugashvili, of course.

65 *Ibid.*, 53. The younger sister of Kamo, mythologized by the Stalin propaganda machine, was imprisoned during the Great Terror, then sent to the Gulag. Ginzburg 1985, 295.

66 Geifman, 1997, 163.

67 Nicolaevsky, 1965, 207, 11.

68 This is the sum indicated in the most recent researches. Geifman, 1997, 164. The star witness, Martin Lyadov wrote that only a smaller part of this sum was smuggled to Western Europe in 500-ruble notes; the rest of the money was in smaller denominations. After many years passing, Lyadov wrote that Nadezhda Krupskaya sewed the banknotes into her vest in Lenin's home in Finland. According to other sources, there were 341,100 rubles in sacks in 500-ruble note packages. Wolfe, 1964, 393.

69 Wolfe, 1964, 393–394; Avtorkhanov, 1973, vol. I, 180–183; Geifman, 1997, 164.

70 Nicolaevsky, 1995, 28.

71 Nicolaevsky, 1965, 207, 7, 13.

72 *Novy Zhurnal*, 1963, no. 72, 220.

73 *Perspektivi*, 1991, no. 6, 51; Ostrovsky, 2002. 257.

74 *RGASPI*, fond. 332, op. 1, d. 53.

75 *Ibid.*

76 *Ibid.*

77 *Ibid.*

78 *Ibid.*

79 *Ibid.*

80 *Ibid.*

81 Uratadze, 1968, 130–131.

82 *Ibid.*, 132.

83 Avtorkhanov, 1973, vol. I, 183–186.

84 Budnitsky, 2000, 331.

85 *Ibid.*

86 *Novy Zhurnal*, 1963, no. 72, 232.

87 Dan, 1987, 101.

88 Uratadze, 1968, 190.

89 Stalin, 1946, vol. III, 383–386; Stalin, 1947, vol. IV, 33–37, 51–65.

90 *Ibid.*, 305.

91 *RGASPI*, fond. 558, op. 2, d. 42.

92 *Socialistichesky Vestnik*, 1939, no. 7–8, 86.

93 *RGASPI*, fond. 558, op. 2, d. 42.

94 *Ibid.*
95 In the records, here and elsewhere the name Megashvili appears. In other parts of the document, the stenographer wrote Ramishvili correctly when referring to the Georgian politician.
96 *RGASPI*, fond. 558, op. 2, d. 42. The incident occurred in Batumi. Bolshevik terrorists from the Caucasus did in fact rob the ship, on board of which the officials of the treasury, with armed escort, transported many hundred thousands of rubles.
97 *Ibid.*
98 In fact, four and a half years.
99 *RGASPI*, fond. 558, op. 2, d. 42.
100 *Ibid.*
101 Antonov–Ovseyenko, 1994, 13.
102 *Socialistichesky Vestnik*, 1939, no. 7–8, 88–89.
103 *RGASPI*, fond. 668, op. 1, d. 13.
104 *RGASPI*, fond. 558, op. 1, d. 3203.
105 Nicolaevsky, 1965, 134.
106 Stalin, 1946, vol. II, 46–77. Iosif Dzhugashvili was in the Russian capital on his way abroad from Baku. On this trip he only spent a few hours in St. Petersburg.
107 Trotsky, 1985, vol. I, 135–136. After the conference had finished, Stalin stayed for a short time in the English capital as his countryman and the one-time mentor of the workers' movement, Mikha Chakaya, had fallen ill, and somebody was needed to nurse him. *RGASPI*, fond 157. op. 1. d. 18. After that he passed through Paris and headed home. He spent close to a week in Paris, where he obtained the passport of a deceased Georgian emigrant, then went back to the Caucasus. Stalin also hid the fact that he had seen the Eiffel Tower. Later on he never talked about it to General Charles de Gaulle or other French guests.
108 Stolyarov, 1997, 277.
109 In the May of 1939, Joseph Stalin fired Litvinov to please Hitler, and put the majority of his assistants in prison. As a response, the former people's commissar of foreign relations frequently called the Soviet dictator a "mean fellow" and a "stupid politician", more often than not even in front of strangers.
110 Aroseva-Maksimova, 1999, 25.
111 *Sto storok besed s Molotovim*, 1991, 96–98
112 *RGASPI*, fond. 359, op. 1, d. 12.
113 *Ibid.*
114 Barbusse, 1936, 53.
115 Uratadze, 1968, 164–165; Avtorkhanov, 1973, vol. I, 176–184.
116 Trotsky, 1985, vol. I, 156.
117 Stalin, 1946, vol. XIII, 122. The Master of the Kremlin rounded up the numbers again. He spent not two-three months but only a couple of days in Berlin.
118 Stalin, 1946, vol. II, 408.
119 *RGASPI*, fond. 71, op. 10, d. 406. See the short note on the slip of paper in the third box. Every reference disappeared from the official chronicles of Stalin's life, which should have recorded some of the more important episodes, to the fact that he was involved in planning the armed robberies in Tiflis. The robbery was close in time to his secret trip to Germany. There are some unpublished memoirs that allow us to come to that conclusion. *RGASPI*, fond 558. op. 4. d. 583.
120 Bagirov, 1948, 80–102.
121 Nicolaevsky, 1965, 202, 9.
122 *Ibid.*
123 *RGASPI*, fond. 74, op. 2, d. 130.
124 *Ibid.*
125 *RGASPI*, fond. 74, op. 1, d. 240.
126 Stopanyi, 1923, 174
127 *Katorga i Silka*, 1927, no. 16, 103–104.
128 Nicolaevsky, 1965, 207, 9
129 *RGASPI*, fond. 558, op. 4, d. 671.
130 *Ibid.*
131 Felshtinsky, 1999, 3–21.
132 On both affairs, see *RGASPI*, fond. 558, op. 4, d. 671. Since then, General Ivan Serov's letter has been published in more than one place. For a copy of it, see *RGASPI*, fond 558. op. 1. d. 52
133 *Ibid.*
134 Dubinsky–Mukhadze, 1965, 301–306.
135 Independently of Vulich's account, one of the first biographers of the Soviet dictator reports the same story, and calls the money-acquiring actions of Stalin and his associates *vimogatelstvo*, or blackmailing. This biographer, however, does not reveal his/her sources. Souvarine, 1939, 111.
136 Nicolaevsky, 1965, 207, 9
137 *Ibid.* This could be the Zharikov-affair, which was also mentioned in the public debate with Martov conducted in the press in April, 1918.
138 *Novy Zhurnal*, 1963, no. 72, 224.
139 *RGASPI*, fond. 71, op. 10, d. 406.
140 Deutscher, 1990, 110.

Mikha Chakaya

Mikha Chakaya, a mentor of Iosif Dzhugashvili and the witness to Stalin's first wife at their wedding, was not killed during the Great Terror perhaps because he was a living legend and embodiment of the fin-de-siècle Georgian Bolshevik movement. The photograph was taken in Tiflis, around 1924–25.

Moscow, 1924. The 5th Congress of the Comintern is held. In this picture, in the first row from the left, there is the fifty-eight years old Boris Reinstein(X), a "Russian-American" politician; the sixty-seven years old Clara Zetkin (XX), the "founding mother" of the International Women's Day; the fifty-eight years old David Ryazanov, the famous researcher of Marx's work; and behind them the fifty-eight years old Mikha Chakaya. He gave the title "Four young workers" to this picture.

In the middle of the picture sits "Comrade Mikha", or Mikha Chakaya, and Serafima Gopner, a leading functionary of the Comintern, in the company of gray-haired veterans.

In the first half of the 1930s, Valeryan Kuybishev (X) was one of the main commanders of the Soviet economy. Although the high-spirited man liked drinking and "loved life", you could not tell that time eventually took its toll on him. Who would have guessed that he was going to die at the age of forty-seven, in 1935, under suspicious circumstances. Mikha Chakaya, who was twenty-five years older than Kuybishev, was going to die only in 1950.

CHAPTER 6
Escape and Love

I was told by several elderly people who were in prison in Vologda in the 1930s, how, during the Great Terror, one of the prison governors tortured those who, following the 1917 Bolshevik revolution, were regarded as "enemies of the people", using a phrase borrowed from the French Revolution. In the town of Vologda in northern Russia the armed men of the NKVD, in the style of the bloody Jacobin terror, herded the barefoot prisoners, who were dressed only in their undergarments, out into the prison yard in the middle of winter. There they hosed them with water until the miserable prisoners froze in the temperatures of minus thirty to thirty-five degrees. The prison doctor was then called, who certified that all the prisoners had died of "heart failure".

Some of the old Bolshevik Party members survived these dreadful times. Those who had earlier played an active role in the Red Terror were sometimes tortured by their consciences. Without exception they commented how much better the enemies of the system were treated during the—by no means easy—years of tsarist rule. Things that took place in the tsarist prisons, which at the time were regarded as hellish torments, could only be seen as mild at the end of the 1930s. Semyon Vereshchak, a Socialist Revolutionary emigrant who was in prison along with Stalin in Baku, described how Stalin tried to break down the door of his cell with the lid of the slop bucket while the other prisoners were attacking the soldiers and guards who were beating them.[1]

While in the Vologda prison "Comrade Koba" and a few of his fellow prisoners tried to channel their anger by lifting their food tins high and pouring the hot soup on the ground in the presence of the guards. One such confrontation took place after an imprisoned student knocked down a guard, then simply walked out of his cell and escaped. "Needless to say, the prison governor and the prosecutor were there within an hour," remembered a worker by the name of Fyodor Blinov, who, on December 23, 1929, wrote an emotional letter to Stalin on the occasion of his fiftieth birthday. "We were lying on our beds, and Comrade Koba merely said to us: 'Don't get up.' But the guards ordered us to stand up. Comrade Koba replied that we didn't feel like it. 'If you want to take a roll call, count the legs you can see under the blankets. [...] He really didn't obey anyone. He only retreated when they used force against him... "[2]

These early recollections, despite their evident enthusiasm for Stalin, were characterized by a rather unpolished style, which is why the majority remained in manuscript form. Yet without such "folktales" witnessing to the heroism of the Soviet dictator, a picture could emerge that Stalin had done nothing of significance between November 1908 and February 1912 in Solvychegodsk, where he was exiled, or in Vologda, where he was forced to live. Apparently he had been entirely preoccupied by events in his private life. There is certainly nothing to prove the statement of Bagirov, who was head of the party in Azerbaijan during Stalin's rule, that until summer 1909 Koba "was constantly in touch with the Baku Bolshevik party organization and directed its work" from Solvychegodsk.[3] "We do not know how Koba spent those nine months in Solvychegodsk, what he was doing, what he was thinking about. No documents have appeared to clarify this. There are no writings or diary records by him," wrote a perplexed Leon Trotsky. "In the local police files in connection with the Iosif Dzhugashvili case, under the column 'conduct', we read: 'Cruel, outspoken, disrespectful towards superiors.' 'Disrespect' was a common characteristic among revolutionaries, but cruelty was an individual trait."[4]

In recent years, in the Moscow and Stanford archives, I have checked out the majority of the still unpublished documents, mentioned as lacking by Trotsky, concerning Joseph Stalin's exile in northern Russia. These documents suggest that the naturally morose Koba, far from his Caucasian environment in Solvychegodsk, was subject to depression. He arrived at the place of his exile, on February 27, 1909, weakened by the typhoid he had contracted en route, during an epidemic. The journey had included a slight detour via the Butirki prison in Moscow and Vyatka, since, as a result of his illness, he had been taken under guard to Vyatka hospital on February 8, 1909. Twelve days later he was delivered to the local prison.[5]

Time seemed to have stood still in Solvychegodsk, which consisted almost entirely of wooden houses. It was dusty in summer, covered in mud in spring and autumn, and buried in thick snow in winter. In its tiny center, however, there were a few stone and brick buildings, such as the enormous two-storey house belonging to the merchant Piankov. It was here that the most important offices, the police station, the savings bank, and the post office, were to be found. The local prison was stylishly located in the basement and cellars of a large porticoed house. Opposite this building stood a sixteenth-century masterpiece of Russian national architecture, the Church of the Annunciation of the Blessed Virgin Mary. Iosif Dzhugashvili, the former seminarian, liked to walk around the church square in the evenings, and he told his fellow exiles how much he appreciated medieval Russian church architecture. Later, however, he obviously forgot about this: he allowed, and occasionally prompted, the local authorities in the northern provinces of his empire, which spread from Arkhangelsk to Vologda, to blow up or turn into barns such beautiful ancient churches as part of the "atheist struggle against the clerical past".

Within a few weeks Stalin had become acquainted with the local exile colony, which was a cross-section of all the Russian opposition parties and trends. The forced exiles often quarreled with one another. The frustrations of those exiles, whom the locals referred to simply as "politicals", were increased by the fact that in Solvychegodsk, referred to as "an open-air prison without bars", the local chief of police was a petty tyrant who delighted in making their lives wretched. On the day of their departure for Solvychegodsk they were told that no more than five of them were permitted to be in the street together at the same time. They were not allowed to put on amateur dramatic performances, nor could they even watch them. They could not visit the skating rink either. According to a later order they were not permitted to go rowing in the summer, nor were they allowed to pick mushrooms in the forest around the town. Any contravention of such orders was a punishable offense. On one occasion Iosif Dzhugashvili was imprisoned for a few days for taking part in the organization of an illegal reading. On another occasion he attended a theater performance, for which the local chief of police deducted the price of the twenty-five kopeck entry ticket from his monthly allowance of seven rubles and forty kopecks.[6]

It seems that the political exile Iosif Dzhugashvili also sought the company of exiled common criminals in Solvychegodsk. "Sometimes he would tell us about this," remembered Nikita Khrushchev. "He would say: 'What fine fellows those common criminals were compared to the exiles! I made friends with them. They were good men. I remember how we would go into a bar and produce whatever money we had. One ruble or three rubles. We stuck the notes against the window, ordered wine, and drank until all the money had gone. 'Today I pay, tomorrow you pay, then I'll pay again.' That was our principle. Those criminals were real community-minded people. In contrast, there were some absolute villains among the politicals. They convened a court of honor and summoned me to appear before it because I used to drink with the common criminals."[7]

According to later recollections "Comrade Koba" arrived in Solvychegodsk without any warm clothing. The dictator's contemporaries used even this insignificant detail to heap praise on him: "Once the comrades let us know that a group of ours was setting off into exile. Stalin was to be among them," remembered a Baku laborer called Ivan Vatsek, who knew Koba very well. "This happened in the autumn. We knew that Stalin did not have winter clothes or footwear. He usually wore a satin shirt and soft shoes. We bought him a short winter coat, boots, and some other warm garments. However, he only accepted them after much persuasion."[8] Stepan Shaumyan, however, remembered the journey of the exiled Stalin somewhat differently in a contemporary letter: "...We were informed that K[oba] had been exiled to the north and that he didn't have a single kopeck. Nor did he have a coat, or even a warm suit. We couldn't get hold of any money for him [...], and we weren't even able to get him a second-hand suit."[9]

Once Stalin had recovered from his illness he decided to escape. However, he divulged his plan to his new girlfriend, Tatyana Sukhova, also an exile, only at the last moment: "I often visited him in his room," we read in the recollections of the young teacher. "He lived in poverty. In the window was a wooden crate covered with planks and a bag of a straw. On top of it were a flannel blanket and a pink pillowcase. Comrade Osip Koba[10] would spend the night on that bed. But I often found him half lying there even during the daytime. Since he was very cold he lay in his coat and surrounded himself with books. [...] In his spare time Comrade Koba joined in our walks more and more often. We even went rowing. He would joke a lot, and we would laugh at some of the others. Comrade Koba liked to laugh at our weaknesses."[11]

On June 24, 1909, "Osip Koba" secretly left Solvychegodsk with Tatyana. Two other Bolshevik exiles, Sergei Shkarpetkin and Anton Bondarev, accompanied them as far as the small town of Kotlas. All four of them crossed the forest and forded a small river, the Vychegda. Then they traveled southwest on the wide Northern Dvina River. Whenever they saw a boat they pulled into the bank and hid for a short while in the bushes. Eventually they managed to get Stalin away. He boarded a train at the first station and continued on his way alone while his three comrades returned to Solvychegodsk. "Before his departure it turned out that Comrade Osip Koba had no money," recalled Sukhova.[12] "Sergei and Anton got hold of some money for him and I gave him a few handkerchiefs for the trip. Comrade Osip Koba took them, and smiling remarked: 'One day I will give you a silk handkerchief in return.'"[13]

The next important stop on Stalin's escape route was St. Petersburg. There he looked up his old acquaintance and future father-in-law, Sergei Alliluyev, who rented two rooms for his large family in one of the suburbs. The bearded, gray-haired electrician asked one of the relatives of the concierge of the house, a man by the name of Melnikov, to hide the escapee who had appeared so unexpectedly. According to his own statement this relative, an unemployed man, had nothing to do with the labor movement: "I was not a party member and still am not," he declared on October 2, 1937 in response to questions posed by an

One of the half a dozen wooden huts in Solvychegodsk, in which Iosif Dzhugashvili lived his somber life under strict police surveillance.

archivist. "Comrade Alliluyev arrived in the evening with a young man who had black hair, a swarthy complexion, and a mustache. He was dressed very badly. I gave him some underwear and a shirt to put on. [...] Alliluyev warned me that this person was staying there illegally. He was his comrade and I was told to help him if he wanted to go outside into the street: I should always have a look round before he went out to check there were no informers hanging around the gate."[14]

Sergei Alliluyev also asked the owner of the apartment, Kanon Savchenko, to help Koba. Savchenko obtained papers for the escapee, in other words, a domestic "passport" that functioned as ID. After this Kuzma, Kanon's brother, who lived in the cavalry barracks, sheltered "Comrade Koba".[15] From time to time he gave food to the hungry Iosif Dzhugashvili, who would hurry past the mounted guardsmen parading in front of the barracks, a book under his arm, on his way towards the guard-post at the gate. Sometimes Melnikov accompanied the Bolshevik escapee. However, almost thirty years later, when asked what they had talked about while eating, this simple man who had been promoted to the rank of historical witness was incapable of remembering anything. He only recalled that at the time he had told Stalin that he was looking for a job.[16]

Another of Koba's "guides" in the Russian capital was an old acquaintance, Sila Todria. Sofia Simakova, the wife of this Georgian party worker who died at a relatively early age of lung cancer, remembered their meeting as follows: "I was not feeling well that day and didn't go to work. My husband was working in the printing house and rushed home during working hours. He told me to prepare something to eat as he had met an old friend, Comrade Soso, the leader of our Georgian organization. At the time I had no idea who Soso was. My husband said that he would buy a bottle of wine and would bring Soso for lunch."[17]

Following the modest lunch, consisting of a few potatoes, herrings, and salted cucumber, the guest asked to have a rest. This led to a minor disagreement with his host: "Stalin refused to lie down on our bed. He said that that was our place and he would rather lie on the ground," Todria's wife remembered emotionally. "I objected, but he insisted that I should make a bed for him on the floor. I swept the floor, of course, and then put down a blanket and gave Soso a pillow. He lay down, lit a cigarette, and began asking us about our life in Finland..."[18] Sila Todria, along with a few other Georgian printers, had worked in a secret typesetting workshop in Viborg, which at the time was part of Grand Duchy of Finland.

According to the recollections of Vera Shweitzer it was also Todria who accompanied Stalin to the apartment of Nikolai Poletayev, a worker poet and a Bolshevik representative in the State Duma. This is quite possible. The rest of the story, however, is less credible. Shweitzer writes that at this meeting a decision was taken about the launch of a countrywide daily newspaper under the title *Zvezda*. However, the paper first appeared months later, only at the very end of 1910, and not as a result of the decision of Stalin and Poletayev but at the instigation of Lenin and Zinovyev. Nevertheless, the version of the story told by Shweitzer was useful in suggesting that Joseph Stalin, even before 1912, was not simply an illegal party worker but "a decisive figure and great strategist" in the Russian labor movement.[19]

Within the Bolshevik leadership at the beginning of the 1910s the idea had arisen several times to publish a radical countrywide daily. Iosif Dzhugashvili, along with several others, had supported the idea. In his article "Letters on Caucasia", which appeared in *Sotsial-Demokrat*, a journal published abroad that gave equal space to the views of Lenin and the Mensheviks Yuly Martov and Fyodor Dan, Stalin explained his conviction that an all-Russian party congress should be organized and a countrywide organ published. This did not mean that at the time he could make an individual decision in affairs of such importance. Despite this, Beria, in his role as biographer, concluded that "Stalin's proposal made great waves. Nine months after the appearance of the article, on December 10, 1910, the first issue of the daily *Zvezda* appeared, which was initially a joint publication of the Bolsheviks and party-building Mensheviks. Later, from autumn 1911, it became an exclusively Bolshevik organ."[20]

☆ Soon after the meeting with Poletayev, Iosif Dzhugashvili bade farewell to his acquaintances in St. Petersburg and traveled on to Baku. The local police were almost immediately aware that a Social Democrat by the name of "Koba" or "Soso" had appeared in the city. They thought mistakenly that he had arrived from Siberia. The Okhrana were then informed that his comrades would, in all likelihood, soon assign a more important task to the new arrival, what actually did happen.

According to the August 1909 report of the Baku political police, Koba began writing articles for the illegal Bolshevik newspaper, the *Bakinsky Proletary*. In September they were also given the information that he was a member of the local illegal party committee. He would often appear at doctors' surgeries attended by workers. In his free time he was looking for people to start up an illegal printing house.[21] The Bolshevik politician can only have moved around with such self-confidence in the "city of black gold" because his comrades obtained a passport for him in the name of an Armenian merchant, Oganes Totomyants. With this document he visited his birth place, Tiflis, several times, where on one occasion he chaired the city's party conference which was convened in great secrecy.[22]

The political police in Baku, which employed dozens of informers, naturally learned about this immediately. From the official documents it also appears that the authorities were annoyed that Koba commuted regularly between Baku and

Iosif Dzhugashvili in 1912. The tsarist police tried in vain to find out who is behind the pseudonym "Soso", "Koba", or sometimes even "Osip Koba".

Tiflis. However, for more than eight months they failed to arrest him. Four or five informers in turn followed "Mr. Totomyants" on the street. They carefully recorded whom the "Milkman"—the name by which Stalin was mentioned in the police records—met and where he went. The escapee's real name, however, remained a mystery to them. Strangely, the investigators in the political police failed to realize that the short, pock-marked, morose, rather dirty man, who always wore the same broad-rimmed black hat and crumpled, checked shirt, was one and the same person as "Iosif Vissarionovich Dzhugashvili, the peasant from the Didi-Lilo village community", who had escaped from Solvychegodsk and who had been a wanted man throughout the country since August 1909.[23]

The police, who even intercepted some of his letters, failed to decipher anything from the lines written to Tatyana Sukhova, which he wrote on November 30, 1909 on a picture postcard depicting King David before the Arc of the Covenant: "I remember how many times I promised to write, but I haven't even sent a postcard until now. What a beast I am. There's no getting away from it. I beg your for-give-ness. Be content with my greetings. It seems that I live well, even very well."[24] Tatyana left the Vologda province soon after this. The next time she met Stalin was entirely by accident in 1912 in St. Petersburg: "I was on my way to teach on Staro-Nevsky Avenue. Suddenly I felt a man's hand on my shoulder. It made me jump, but then a familiar voice addressed me: 'Don't be afraid, Comrade Tatyana, it's me.' And there was Comrade Osip Koba standing next to me, in the same clothes and boots but without the old, short winter coat. [...] We met that same evening at a workers' meeting. As we walked past the refreshment counter Comrade Koba took a red carnation and gave it to me."[25] This was a very cautious hint at her earlier brief romance with "Comrade Koba".

☆ Iosif Dzhugashvili disclosed his real name only on March 23, 1910, during the second (or according to another version the first) interrogation following his arrest. When apprehended by the police another false passport was confiscated from him. He had been using the identity of an Armenian called Zakar Melikiants, who was registered in the Yelizavetpol province.[26]

As the police files reveal the Caucasian, and even the national, authorities benefited greatly from the several-month-long cat-and-mouse chase they had played with "Comrade Koba". The ambitious Bolshevik politician, as so many times in his life within the movement, had, from the very first moment he arrived in Baku, ignored even the most basic rules of conspiracy. Although he realized that he was being followed, he visited several institutions and factories in order to "build the party". His mail arrived at the Invalid Association, which worked in conjunction with the oil industry's workers' sick benefit society. He himself used every opportunity to criticize the former leaders of the Baku Bolshevik organization, mentioning concrete names and addresses. Stalin made no secret of the fact that he had arrived in the city to revitalize the local labor movement, which had become increasingly dispirited following the defeat of the revolution of 1905 to 1907. This self-assured man, with his great dynamism, perhaps did more harm than good to his comrades. He made it possible for the police, by means of the informers who followed him, to locate the editorial offices of the illegal Social Democratic publications and to strike at the two largest conspiratorial printing presses working underground—in the literal sense of the word—in the musty cellars of private houses.[27]

Of course, *agents provocateurs* had been planted within the Caucasian Social Democratic organizations earlier. Their reports helped to fill the Okhrana's countrywide system of files, containing data on several thousand revolutionaries.[28] On the basis of the comings and goings of the irresponsible Iosif Dzhugashvili, the authorities gained an even more accurate picture of who formed the Baku and Tiflis leadership of the radical opponents of the tsarist authorities. The local chiefs of the political police carefully examined every step taken by "Comrade Koba", who was becoming increasingly ensnared by the conspiring lifestyle. Eventually they decided to arrest him, probably because Joseph Stalin was keen to unmask informers wherever he turned up: "Provocation reared its head here as well [...]. That's why we could not come up with a response. But now everything is all right," he wrote in the draft of an undated letter to the editors of the emigrant Bolshevik publication *Proletary*,[29] although in those days Stalin would almost get into fights on the street in broad daylight with the informers who followed him.

There are many who do not understand why, during those months, Koba behaved as if wanting to tempt fate. It is most probable that, following the uneventful months spent in exile in Solvychegodsk, too many tasks and too many hard to digest experiences were landed on him in Baku. With false documents and a few rubles in his pocket, without permanent accommodation and surrounded by informers, he attempted to keep a firm hand on the Bolshevik activists in Baku, who coped badly with his difficult nature, and to coordinate the disintegrating Georgian party organizations. He argued with his old, fierce opponents, the Mensheviks and the Socialist Revolutionaries. He started writing articles in Russian, which, at the time, must have been a fairly difficult task for him. At the same time he was trying to live up to the expectations of the Bolhevik émigrés, led by Lenin. However, in the meantime he was secretly further fomenting the polemics between the "foreigners" and the "domestics", especially on the key issue of which group should direct the Russian labor movement. It is no wonder that after a while his nerves began to suffer.

Iosif Dzhugashvili, who at the end of his stay in Baku was like a hunted animal, knew all the informers, who all wore equally ridiculous coats and trousers. On occasion he would warn his acquaintances out loud: "Look, that man works for the police!" He even embarrassed the previously unknown secret agents, who were ordered from Tiflis to watch him.[30] Although he recognized the increasing danger of his position, and although on earlier occasions he had always known when to disappear, he still did not try to escape. It is still not clear why he did not leave Baku in time.

The perplexed authorities used Stalin right up to the last moment as bait. Apparently he was not really taken seriously until as late as 1912—it was only then that they realized that he was coming more and more to the forefront of the countrywide Bolshevik leadership. As a result, the politician in hiding got away with his escape to Caucasia practically unpunished. His illegal activities and network of relationships were an open book to the investigating magistrates. However, they had no proof that "Comrade Koba" had planned the armed robberies that had claimed the lives of innocent people.

Nor did the Baku and Tiflis police know that in early 1910 the idea had arisen that the Bolshevik leadership might elevate Iosif Dzhugashvili to the Central Committee, which had to be permanently renewed due to frequent arrests. Two versions prevailed as to why this did not eventually happen. According to one, Stalin refused the appointment. Bearing in mind how vain he was this is almost inconceivable. One must rather give credence to the second version, according to which the Bolshevik leaders, including Viktor Nogin, a former textile worker— after whom one of the largest downtown squares in Moscow was later named—for some reason were simply unable to find the politician who was hiding underground in Baku.[31]

Nevertheless, by the early spring of 1910 sufficient proof had been collected against Koba in the Okhrana's archives. Gelimbatovsky, a gendarme officer who led the investigation for a while, referring to this proof suggested that he should be deported back to east Siberia, from where he had previously escaped. According to his reasoning Koba, "despite every administrative restriction of his actions, has consistently participated in the activities of the revolutionary parties, in which he always plays a significant role. Furthermore, it should be taken into consideration that he has already escaped twice [...] from exile. He has therefore never entirely completed any of his administrative sentences."[32]

From the authorities' point of view a more serious punishment would have been justified by the fact that the Baku Okhrana, while keeping Iosif Dzhugashvili in custody, came across another secret printing press. In the confiscated documents they discovered the names "Koba" and "Soso". A printing house receipt, dated October 17, 1909, was signed "Koba, Secretary of the [Party] Committee of Bak[u]". It also came to light that Iosif Dzhugashvili under the name of Totomiants hid together in Solvichegodsk with Stefania Petrovskaya, a teacher whose family were Catholic aristocrats and who was in exile. At the inquiry, Stalin denied that he lived with her and had a sexual relationship with her *(v sozhitelstve ne sostoyal).* Petrovskaya, although denying that she was involved in any revolutionary activities in Baku, admitted to an "intimate relationship" with Stalin. This was at the end of March, 1910. On June 29, Iosif Dzhugashvili, who appeared to be a little broken by imprisonment, resorted to a ruse. He humbly made reference to a lung illness and asked the authorities not to be so strict with him. He also asked permission to marry Petrovskaya. The answer was still negative.[33] The head of the Tiflis military district, to whom these files were sent, eventually decided that it was enough for Iosif Dzhugashvili to be deported back to Solvychegodsk. Somewhat incomprehensibly he had the months spent in detention and during the long journey back included in the period of exile already undergone.[34] This is how Stalin became a *vozvrashchenets*, or *obratnik*, that is, an escapee who was forced to stay in the Vologda province until the completion of the sentence he had received earlier.[35]

☆ The local governor in Vologda then sent him to Solvychegodsk again. Arrived on October 29, 1910 in the small town that thus became his enforced home for the second time.[36] In the meantime, the number of his fellow exiles had significantly decreased. Compared to the four to five hundred persons there had been earlier, now only between thirty and forty exiles were living in the uneventful backwater. There were hardly any newcomers, since those who had been newly sentenced were mostly sent to the more remote Siberian settlements. As a result, the authorities were able to pay more careful attention to the remaining few exiles, preventing them from becoming involved in conspiratorial activities.[37] Nevertheless, Mirzafa Bagirov, the notorious falsifier of history, declared that Koba "even then did not break his ties with the Baku proletariat. He sent directives and orders from exile, urging the proletariat of Baku to struggle against tsarism and the bourgeoisie."[38]

There is no evidence for this in the official documents. On the other hand, we do know that the men under Tsivilyov, the Solvychegodsk district police prefect, would, from time to time, burst in on Iosif Dzhugashvili in his rented room.[39] A very detailed record was kept of every house search, although I was unable to find these in the Moscow Stalin archives.[40] The recollections of former landlords of "Comrade Koba", however, do exist. One of them, a Mrs. Kuzakova, described the house searches as being like minor sieges.[41] The police appeared early in the morning, and taking little notice of the cries of the terrified children, kicked in the front door, shouting loudly. A few carefully-edited excerpts from this story appeared in *Pravda* shortly before Stalin's sixtieth birthday, on December 16, 1939. Since by that time the armed men of the NKVD, in their leather coats, had broken into several thousand homes across the huge empire to take away the head of the family, the censors, who were conscious of the unfortunate parallels, omitted a few lines from the original text.

There is no doubt, however, that in Solvychegodsk the exile Koba stood with demonstrative quietness and without expression as the police searched for evidence in the stove, under the mattress, and even in the flower pots. These searches must have been carried out by Tsivilyov and his associates in revenge for the fact that Iosif Dzhugashvili obviously despised them. He was as defiant in the face of the authorities in the godforsaken north Russian settlement as he had been in Tiflis and Baku.

As in the Caucasian period of his life the Bolshevik politician again broke the rules of conspiracy in north Russia. Although he was well aware that as part of the countrywide "black cabinet" there was a censors' office at the local post office,

Unretouched studio photograph taken of the Bolshevik leaders in Baku. First row, from left to right: Mikhail Batiryev ("Comrade Yevgeny"), Stepan Shaumyan, Stepan Yakushev, Alyosha Dzhaparidze, and Vanya Fioletov. Behind them stand Suren Spandaryan and S. D. Vulfson.

in the letters he sent from the small town he informed his acquaintances quite openly that he intended to escape, despite the fact that his period of punishment was about to expire. This, among other things, was the subject of a letter written to Bobrovsky, his former Bolshevik colleague in Baku, on January 22, 1911, which was intercepted by the postal censors two days later. This fascinating letter, which sheds important light on the dictator's biography, was not included in the collected edition of his works since it also contains serious criticism of the Social Democratic politicians in emigration, including Lenin: "We have heard, of course, about the foreign 'tempest in a teacup', and also that blocs have been formed. On one side, Lenin and Plekhanov, and, on the other, the alliance between Trotsky, Martov, and Bogdanov. As far as I know the workers sympathize with the former. However, they think in general that the 'foreigners' should be left to 'stew in their own juice'. […] Those who have the interests of the movement at heart should work, and the rest will take shape by itself. I think it is good that they think in this way. My address is Solvychegodsk, Vologda province. Iosif Dzhugashvili."[42]

These lines reveal that "Comrade Koba", as late as the end of 1912, was regarded as a "conciliatory", or as his contemporaries put it "soft", Leninist. At the same time he respected the main ideologues among the "leftists" who opposed Lenin, whose followers nailed their colors to the mast between 1907 and 1911, one after the other, in Paris, Geneva, and on the island of Capri in the villa of

In his correspondence with people close to Lenin, Stalin often cunningly glorified the "Starik" ('Old Man').

Maksim Gorky. He regarded as talented, sophisticated intellectuals those polilicians who, for a while, belonged to the group around *Vperyod*, distinguished by the names of Aleksandr Bogdanov and Anatoly Lunacharsky. Al though, following the victory of the 1917 October Revolution, he tried to force them into the background politically, according to the old Bolshevik Antonov-Saratovsky, in the depth of his heart he always envied these "leftists" for their theoretical aptitude.

"What is the point of these damned factions distancing us from one another? [...] I think that those siding with Bogdanov are in the wrong, but as far as the needless clashes are concerned, both sides deserve to be quashed," wrote Iosif Dzhugashvili in a letter dated November 5, 1909 to his former mentor Mikha Chakaya, who, in emigration in Geneva, lived under the bynames Gurgen and later Barsov, and who sympathized with Bogdanov's circle. At the end of the letter, written while working underground in Tiflis, Stalin sent his "warmest greetings" to Bogdanov, Lunacharsky, Krasin, and Grigory Aleksinsky—that is, to Lenin's main rivals in the Bolshevik movement at the time.[43] Such a move was regarded as a major sin in the "orthodox Leninist" circles. However, the parties concerned were not aware of it, since, in his letters to Lenin at that time, Stalin always "distanced himself" from Bogdanov's followers.[44]

In around 1910 Iosif Dzhugashvili, while in the depths of his heart, sympathized with the "leftists", he also had excellent relations with an entirely different but no less influential Social Democratic trend, the "rightist", Bolsehvik "Conciliators", the *primirenets*. While Bogdanov's faction was more popular among the emigrants, the "rightists" were supported by a significant section of the Russian-based party organization. This group—unlike Lenin and his followers—showed understanding towards the most moderate Russian Social Democratic groups, including the Mensheviks. "Comrade Koba" probably regarded this group as important—from the point of view of his own career—because, for a while, it was mostly they who controlled the Bolshevik illegal party apparatus in Russia. This is what Trotsky refers to, when pointing out that Stalin, in a letter dated January 22, 1911 in which he complained about the controversy among the emigrant groups, mentions a host of Bolshevik Conciliators in a positive context.[45]

The Bolshevik Conciliators did not form an official faction, and unlike the Bogdanov group did not have a newspaper of their own. Nevertheless, for a while they were represented on the Central Committee of the RSDLP. However, at the national party conference in January 1912 Lenin entirely took over control of the Bolshevik Party, and following this, the voices of the Bolshevik Conciliators were heard much less frequently.

After a time Stalin no longer needed their support either. No matter with whom he sympathized he finally always placed his bets on Lenin, referred to by his followers as "the Old Man", and on his two closest colleagues, Lev Kamenev and Grigory Zinovyev. This is why, at the end of 1910, he was so annoyed by the fact that, following the excitement of his months in Baku, in the uneventful north he was unable to obtain Lenin's secret address in Paris. One of his fellow exiles, Golubev, came to his aid. He advised him to write to Nikolai Yakovlev, who lived in Hamburg. Allegedly, on receiving Stalin's letter the young publicist—who was later, during the Russian Civil War, tortured and executed by the Whites—immediately boarded a train and took the letter in person to the French capital.[46]

Not much later, on New Year's Eve 1910, Stalin defined his credo in a long article, knowing that his words would reach Lenin and Kamenev: "Our most important task is to establish a (Russia-based) central group to coordinate the legal, illegal, and semi-legal activities. First of all we must concentrate on the major centers (St. Petersburg, Moscow, the Urals and the South). It does not matter what we call it: the Russian division of the Central Committee or an auxiliary group working alongside the Central Committee. To create it is as important as air or bread."[47]

With this letter, also copied by the censors, Koba again tried to strengthen his position in the invisible hierarchy of the Bolshevik community led by Lenin. He must have been aware that his proposals would be music to the ears of the recipient. By proposing the creation of a "domestic" "Leninist" Bolshevik center he clearly submitted himself to the "Parisians", comprising mostly the followers of Lenin. Nor did he shy away from some rather boorish flattery: in his New Year's Eve letter he referred to Lenin as a "clever *muzhik*" who "knows what he wants".[48]

From today's perspective the struggles that characterized the internal life of the RSDLP at the time when Stalin was standing at the crossroads are, of course, of little interest. In the early years of the century, however, the disagreement among the various groups and factions was so intense that in their reports even the tsarist political police—who did not normally distinguish among the "rebels"—considered it necessary to analyze the differences between the Russian Social Democratic wings.[49] Abdurakhman Avtorkhanov describes these as follows: "Among the Mensheviks four factions raised their banners. Potresov's faction gathered around the periodical *Nasha Zarya* and stood on the right wing of the RSDLP. The faction formed by Martov, Dan, and Akselrod grouped around the newspaper *Golos Sotsial Demokrata.* Trotsky's group gathered around *Pravda* and supported making peace between the Bolsheviks and Mensheviks. And finally there was Plekhanov's faction, known as the 'pro-party Mensheviks'." According to Avtorkhanov, the Bolsheviks were split into three major factions, "the faction identified by the names of Lenin, Zinovyev, and Kamenev; a second faction identified by the names of Bogdanov, Lunacharsky, Pokrovsky, and Gorky (the *Vperyod* group); and the 'conciliatory' elements, who supported unification with the Mensheviks. [...] As far as the party's three major organizations were concerned the Central Committee's Russian Bureau fell into the hands of the Conciliators. The Central Committee's Foreign Bureau was controlled by the Mensheviks, and the party organ *Sotsial Demokrat* was under the control of the Leninist Bolsheviks."[50] From among these, Koba established the closest relations with the Russian Bureau of the Central Committee. At the same time he was busy corresponding with the informal Bolshevik body directly controlled by Lenin, known as the "Foreign Center", and the Bolshevik editors of *Sotsial Demokrat.*

☆ "Comrade Koba", skilled in intrigue as he was, was therefore in his element. To the wily Georgian's good fortune the "Leninists" knew nothing of the fact that, behind the scenes, he was flirting for years with their rivals.[51] Lenin and his inner circle worked consistently to filter the Conciliators and the "recalcitrants" out of the domestic Bolshevik apparatus, which occasionally gave rise to a whole new set of conflicts. According to Tatyana Vulich, a well-known figure in the Paris Bolshevik emigrant colony, "... In Russia Lenin was, in the literal sense of the word, deified by those who had never seen or heard him. [...] But the more often we met him later in Paris, and the closer we got to him, the more our enthusiasm diminished. Naturally, no one debated his leading role in the party. The majority followed him. They uncritically accepted all his changes of strategy. But there was increasingly strong opposition to him. Often [...] even his most loyal followers did not agree with him, although basically they remained faithful. [...] And Lenin tried to maintain his popularity. He was very

Lenin's encounter with Aleksander Bogdanov (on the right) and other "Leftist" Bolsheviks in Maksim Gorky's summer house on the island of Capri. There was much more at stake than who is winning this chess game. The debate was about who was going to lead the Bolsheviks in the future. After some hesitation, the exiled Iosif Dzhugashvili, who later worked underground in Baku, made his "bet" on Lenin. This choice firmly established him in the Bolshevik movement for the rest of his life.

easily offended. Even the slightest attack against his moral authority angered him."[52]

The suspicious and easily offended Lenin would never have talked so approvingly about Koba's Baku activities in the columns of the Russian workers' press had he realized that his young Georgian follower was politically "fickle". The "Foreign Center", controlled by the Leninists, would never have asked him in early 1911 to be one of their "agents" in Russia, nor would they have nominated him as a member of the Organizing Committee for convening the national party conference.[53] The fact remains, however, that following his New Year's Eve declaration of loyalty, Stalin was even "promoted" twice in Paris in his absence. His new task, requiring a countrywide overview, demanded permanent conspiring traveling. "Comrade Koba" was therefore left with little option but to try to escape once again from Solvychegodsk. We still do not know the exact date, but at the end of February 1911 or in very early March he left his place of exile. This time he did not escape by boat on the river Vychegda, as he had done in the summer of 1909. The district police were keeping him under especially strict surveillance since the local Okhrana had already received a transcript, dated February 16, 1911, from the Vologda provincial police headquarters: "According to our confidential information the political exile Iosif Vissarionovich Dzhugashvili is intending to escape. [...] Please keep him under increased observation and prevent him escaping from police surveillance."[54]

Despite these strict measures Iosif Dzhugashvili boarded a train without permission and, armed with false medical findings, checked into the hospital in Vologda, from where he escaped with the help of a sympathetic doctor by the name of Sammer. From the largely still unpublished sources we learn that "Comrade Koba" spent at least one more week in hiding with acquaintances there.[55] Then he headed in secret to St. Petersburg in an attempt to travel abroad, via Moscow, on a false passport. There, Lenin and his circle would doubtless have supplied the new "agent" with instructions. However, the plan came to nothing.

It is striking how short a time Stalin was able to spend in St. Petersburg at the end of February/early March 1911. It was as if the "doctor of escapology"—as his old acquaintances often called him in the 1920s according to Levon Shaumyan—had got his calculations wrong. It is true that Sergei Alliluyev and another electrician, Zabelin, managed to hide Stalin very craftily.[56] In this respect, therefore, nothing had changed compared to his escape in the summer of 1909, except that he was forced to live on a tighter budget. He could not count on his host in St. Petersburg, since the young worker Zabelin was as poor as a church mouse himself: "Seeing how bleak the interior of my room was, Sergei Alliluyev gave me two chairs and a bed for the comrade in hiding," remembered Zabelin. "One morning, at around ten o'clock, the person in question appeared at my apartment. He moved in and slept there for two or three nights, then disappeared without a sign. I only learned later that the comrade in hiding was J. V. Stalin."[57]

On the basis of his fresh impressions of the capital the Bolshevik politician sent a short report about the mood of the workers in St. Petersburg to the editorial board of *Sotsial Demokrat*.[58] However, for some reason this was not included in his Collected Works in the 1940s.

Apart from this "Comrade Koba" visited all the bookshops in St. Petersburg selling leftist literature and, as was his custom, called on members of the Georgian Bolshevik colony living in the city. However, this did little to cheer him up: "In those days Comrade Stalin was somewhat depressed. He was often pensive," Zabelin told the local historians who interviewed him on September 23, 1937.[59]

The escapee finally gave up his original goal and, via Vologda, returned to Solvychegodsk.[60] In the chronology included at the end of the second volume of Stalin's Collected Works there is no trace of this mysterious interlude.[61] Apparently the dictator, even after long years, regarded the ill-fated trip as a serious failure. Perhaps he was not far wrong. His report on the revolutionary mood of the outer districts of the capital, full of extreme optimism, probably met with the approval of Lenin's circle. However, the foreign trip, indispensable for his further progress in the Bolshevik movement, did not take place since his acquaintances in Vologda and St. Petersburg were unable to collect sufficient money to pay for it.

Such situations were of course fairly common in the lives of underground party workers. "Comrade Koba", however, as was often the case, wanted revenge. One and a half decades after his St. Petersburg interlude he found a scapegoat in the person of a Bolshevik by the name of Aram Ivanyan, who used to live in Vologda. As the all-powerful General Secretary of the party he initiated a disciplinary investigation against Ivanyan. He accused the Armenian politician—who had earlier spent his exile in the town before settling there—of appropriating seventy rubles that had been sent to Stalin. It was claimed that this had happened in early

1911, when Ivanyan was supposed to assist in Stalin's escape. "I heard from Comrade Ivanyan the address to which the money had been posted," wrote the head of the Bolshevik Party during his stay in Tiflis, in the report he passed on to the Central Control Commission on June 7, 1926, which he modestly signed as "Joseph Stalin, party member. Membership number 398543". The report contains the following statement: "Comrade Ivanyan did not hand over the money. He produced a telegram instead, according to which the sum had been sent for my use. In the telegram, however, someone had deleted a few words. By the way, Comrade Ivanyan could come up with no explanation as to where the money had gone. Nor did I get a meaningful answer as to why certain words had been deleted from the telegram. [...] Eventually I managed to get abroad. I met the members of the Central Committee and from the documents I received from them it turned out that they had indeed sent seventy rubles to me in Vologda, to the address mentioned by Ivanyan. It was also proved that the money had not disappeared but had duly arrived where it had been sent."[62]

According to Aram Ivanyan's explanatory letter he had not really known Stalin in Vologda. He was unlucky enough to bump into Stalin by chance in Moscow in 1923, after which a rather extraordinary settling of accounts was set in motion. Ivanyan, the former fellow exile, had earlier been a widely respected person. He was people's commissar for trade in the Armenian Soviet government, before occupying high office in Moscow and in Tiflis. In the early ninety-twenties, he began to be pursued by Lavrenty Beria, then a young functionary in the Georgian OGPU (the Unified State Political Administration, a forerunner of the NKVD). On the basis of Joseph Stalin's report quoted above he was expelled from the party on June 8, 1926 and thus automatically excluded from the *nomenklatura.*

However, it soon turned out that apart from the secretary-general's short letter of complaint no one had any incriminating evidence against him. On April 2, 1927 Ivanyan therefore submitted an appeal to the party's Central Supervisory Committee. At the same time he submitted a letter in which eight former Vologda exiles, without exception long-standing Bolshevik party members, expressed their support for him. They declared that Ivanyan had helped his comrades financially on many occasions. The seventy rubles would have been an insignificant sum to him, since he lived a relatively comfortable life. Nor would he have stooped to embezzlement, since he had high moral standards: "We are certain that Comrade Ivanyan had nothing to do with the misdemeanor or misunderstanding concerning the seventy rubles," the joint letter ends.[63] In parallel with this five prominent members of the Yerevan Bolshevik party leadership, including Yoanisyan, the of the local committee, also gave their backing to their cornered fellow politician. However the waves made by the case did not settle, since Stalin was unable to forget his failures.

Following this second closure of the investigation Ivanyan ended up as a simple council clerk. He was so frustrated by what had happened that many years later, during the period of the Great Terror, he wrote directly to the former "Comrade Koba": "Ten painful years have passed, but I still declare with just as much determination that I had nothing to do with the seventy rubles that were sent to you. I never received the money. Nor did I appropriate it. [...] I am now approaching my fiftieth birthday with this grave accusation associated with me. [...] Please help me clear my name. Please help me obtain my party membership back, too. Your faithful A. Ivanyan."[64]

In response the Soviet dictator had Aram Ivanyan arrested on November 17,

1936. The former "Comrade Koba" had his victim delivered to a detention camp in the neighborhood of Vologda itself. However, this was still not the end of the story. Like Big Brother in Orwell's *Nineteen Eighty-four* Stalin had, in the meantime, made several unpleasant episodes in his earlier life disappear one after the other, including the fact that, in the early spring of 1911, he had returned voluntarily from St. Petersburg to exile in Solvychegodsk. He had Ivanyan, the eyewitness who had spent the prime of his life in fear because of the "seventy-ruble affair", taken to Tiflis at the end of 1937, and, without any court hearing, had him executed. On December 21, Stalin's official birthday, even the unfortunate man's wife was arrested. In her case "the Master" proved more humane. She spent "only" eight years in a Soviet death camp. Interestingly, this was also in the vicinity of Vologda. The case could only be cleared up two decades later because, during an earlier house search, Ivanyan's twelve-year-old son had carefully hidden the thick folder containing his father's personal documents, including copies of all the letters of appeal that proved his innocence.[65]

In the 1920s, during the investigations into the Ivanyan case, the otherwise suspicious party judges did not ask Joseph Stalin whether he had intended the "seventy-ruble affair" as a diversionary tactic. Perhaps his offended vanity, or his bad conscience, had begun to trouble him after so many years. And how could his weeks-long absence from the town without permission go unnoticed by the otherwise vigilant political police in Solvychegodsk? How is it possible that the otherwise persistent informers in Vologda lost him from their view? And why did the police agents, planted in the Bolshevik party organization in St. Petersburg, fail to realize that Koba had arrived in the capital city and had created a network of conspiring connections? Why was no investigation launched into his activities? The police in Solvychegodsk knew almost everything about Stalin's intention to escape, his party building plans,[66] his appointment as a traveling "agent", and even about his frequent correspondence with the secret Bolshevik group in Omsk, Siberia. And finally, why did the party leader later keep these few weeks of his life veiled in such secrecy that he treated an article written at the time as non-existent?

We still have no satisfactory answers to these questions. What is certain is that Stalin resumed his rather humdrum existence on returning to Solvychegodsk. The police prefect Tsivilyov was once again on his heels[67]: on March 18, April 29, and again on May 12, 1911 house searches lasting several hours were carried out in his rented rooms. On all three occasions the police left without finding anything of significance.[68] Despite this the informers still followed the badly dressed, skin-and-bone "Caucasian" wherever he went. (At that time Stalin was referred to by this name in the police reports.) As he approached the end of his period of exile in Solvychegodsk his shortage of money became even more depressing, even though his board was usually taken care of by the Caucasian community in the small town—comprising a few merchants and the exiled Armenian and Georgian salespeople working for them. The cold climate represented a much greater problem for Koba. Since he had no money to replace his worn-out clothes he caught cold several times and even contracted pneumonia: "The thermometer showed minus forty degrees, but Comrade Stalin was walking around in a light coat, a suede hat, and light shoes. Only a *bashlik [a hooded scarf—M. K.]* protected him to some extent from the north wind," noted one of his fellow exiles, Ivan Golubev.[69]

In September 1936, this Bolshevik worker, who was born in the Donetsk Basin, wrote down his very detailed although somewhat embellished recollections, in the spirit of the times, about the months he had spent with the Master of the Kremlin. We learn from these recollections that Stalin gave lectures to the workers who had ended up in Solvychegodsk. Among other things he introduced them to Franz Mehring's *History of the German Social Democratic Party*, which had appeared in three volumes in Russian. Golubev also accompanied Iosif Dzhugashvili to the evening gatherings, during which the exiles, sitting around a huge samovar, feverishly debated and made plans to save the world. When they were tired of politics they recited poems and entertained each other with cheerful stories. Stalin, who as a seminarian had revealed his poetic talents, did not like reciting poetry. He preferred instead to sing in Georgian or Russian when he was not suffering from depression. However, he was even happier when parodying one of the people present at the gathering. One of the usual targets of his jokes was a Menshevik exile by the name of Lezhnev. This handsome, ever-cheerful young man seduced the wife of the prosecutor of Vologda, after which the cuckold husband succeeded in having his rival classified as a dangerous subversive and, as a result, deported to near the Arctic Circle.[70]

We learn much more than what Golubev has to say from the recollections of Aleksandr Shur, a former student in Kharkov, which can also be found in the Moscow Stalin collection. The value of these recollections is enhanced by the fact that the author sent his manuscript to the central Soviet party archives only after the dictator's death, when he had no reason to hope to gain from his action.[71] In the pages of these recollections Stalin appears surprisingly humane. According to Shur, Stalin approached him in a friendly manner on the day he arrived with a consignment of new exiles in Solvychegodsk. He was having problems finding his way around. "The thin, dark-skinned man [...] wore a light black coat and a soft black hat." He introduced himself as "Koba", and immediately found accommodation for Shur with a Polish worker near his own rooms. As the recollections reveal Stalin apparently had unlimited time. When he got tired of reading he would visit his neighbors, and would call on Shur several times a day.[72]

According to his fellow exiles, in Solvychegodsk and Vologda the majority of Koba's library comprised literary works. At that time he also liked reading in Georgian.[73] However, apart from the great Russian realists, the majority of his reading seemed to have a negative impact on him. This is hardly surprising, since he approached literature and art in general, even in the early years of the century, from a utilitarian point of view. In this respect, regardless of their level of erudition, he resembled most Social Democratic politicians who adopted uncritically the simplistic aesthetic views of two nineteenth-century Russian critics, Belinsky and Pisarev: "On one occasion a Bolshevik called Lunin organized a reading in his apartment, so that an exiled *dashnak [an Armenian Socialist—M. K.]* poet called Khatisov could recite his poetry," recalled Golubev. "Iosif Vissarionovich did not like his poems. He even expressed his opinion that a poet or writer cannot entirely lean on his artistic intuition, but must improve himself incessantly. He has to learn a great deal..."[74]

☆ In the meantime Stalin's period of exile came to an end. On June 27, 1911 "Iosif Vissarionovich Dzhugashvili, the peasant from the village of Didi-Lilo in the province and district of Tiflis" could, in many respects, regard himself as a free man. Although he was still not permitted to set foot in the two capitals, Moscow and St. Petersburg, or a number of other provincial seats. In autumn 1910 the military governor of Tiflis had already banned him from the whole of Caucasia. On the day of his release he had to declare his further plans in writing to the district police prefect. The addressee notified the governor in Vologda, as well as the commander of the local police and gendarmerie, that the exile was ready to leave Solvychegodsk on July 6. In fact this happened on the same day. On July 5, the governor of Vologda passed the information on to his colleagues in Baku and Tiflis, as well as to the Okhrana.[75]

In Vologda Joseph Stalin wrote to the governor explaining that he had no money to change residence, therefore for a while he wanted to settle in the town. The local authorities allowed him to do so for two months.[76] Later the permission was renewed, although they were aware that the former exile would take the first opportunity to travel to one of the prohibited cities. The chief of the Vologda police, in a letter to the Moscow division of the Okhrana dated August 21, 1911, reported: "It is very probable that in the near future Dzhugashvili will travel to St. Petersburg or Moscow to meet representatives of the [Bolshevik] organization there." The writer of the letter requested as many compromising facts as possible about Koba, whom he characterized as "very cautious" and "permanently involved in conspiracy", so that a house search could be carried out at his apartment. However, for some reason the Moscow Okhrana did not give its approval.[77]

Iosif Dzhugashvili was keen on giving hypocritical sermons to the under-age Pelageya Onufrieva, while he sent her picture postcards with erotic images. For several decades, the party historians tried in vain to persuade her to donate these postcards to the Stalin collection, until she was eventually willing to surrender. The archivists must have felt embarrassed upon receipt of this postcard because they described the statue on this picture as "a powerful and joyous encounter between a couple."

It seems that Joseph Stalin only wanted to stay in Vologda until he received the money needed for his next move. So as to be able to obtain food and accommodation he received letters of recommendation from "acquaintances of acquaintances" living in the provincial seat. It also proved useful that in the Vologda, as in Solvychegodsk, he could "levy" the local Caucasian community, which stuck together always and everywhere. Thus he was sometimes able to leave Ishemyatov's colonial goods store laden with packages: "He did not need much money to live on," was how one of his acquaintances at the time, Pelageya Onufrieva, characterized Stalin. "He had a great many friends. In those days several food shops were operating in Vologda. The Crimean Tatars and the Georgians were selling fruit. Ishemyatov was a wholesale trader and had many apprentices working in his shop. In the small booths retail traders served their customers themselves. Iosif Vissarionovich, who loved fruit very much, often visited them. I remember that in the row of shops there was a fruit shop called 'Caucasia'. [...] He often called in there and usually left with a bag full of fruit. And then he would offer me some."[78]

Stalin was thus never short of food and could therefore spend his time reading quietly. According to surviving figures, during the approximately four months he spent in the town in two installments, he visited the public library at least seventeen times.[79] However, he never had enough money to patronize the local restaurants. By coincidence, in one of these restaurants the music was provided for a long time by an expelled student with a rather bizarre history. He earned one ruble a day with his mandolin playing, and was delighted when the rather grotesque traders with their big bellies, reminiscent of Ostrovsky's heroes, offered him a liquor or a coffee. By that time the former Socialist Revolutionary, then Bolshevik, youth had already served time as a political prisoner. He was known as Vyacheslav Skryabin.[80] Later, under the name Molotov, he was to become chairman of the Council of People's Commissars (i.e., Prime Minister of the Soviet Union) and a faithful servant of Joseph Stalin. He participated in the internal power struggle in the Kremlin, in the genocide among the Russian, Ukrainian, and Kazakh peasantry, in "conducting" the Great Terror, and in the secret negotiations preceding the pact with Nazi Germany.

In the 1910s, however, Skryabin was not a famous Bolshevik, thus his name does not appear in the records of the Vologda street informers. On the other hand, "Comrade Koba" aroused a great deal of interest among them. They took it in turns to run after him along the dusty streets of Vologda, without taking much trouble to disguise themselves.[81] Their efforts were in vain, however. The otherwise careless Iosif Dzhugashvili was not ensnared. Perhaps this was because most of his time was spent not so much on political as on private affairs.[82] The truth was that he was far from lonely in Solvychegodsk, although until today none of his biographies have mentioned this. The servant Kryukova, however, mentioned above as remembering the exile's reading habits, referred indirectly in her recollections to the fact that for a while Iosif Dzhugashvili was interested in the daughter of his landlady, Maria Bogoslovskaya. Every indication suggests that a stormy relationship could have taken place between the two, who lived under the same roof: "The landlady's daughter was recently divorced and with her three children lived with her mother. [...] She often quarreled with Stalin. They shouted and were almost at each other's throats. During their rows the names of women could be heard."[83]

Once he became the dictator, Stalin did not let any of his acquaintances from Solvychegodsk and Vologda approach him.

"Comrade Koba" even made eyes at Kryukova, then a young girl herself. As an elderly woman, who, under Stalin's Socialism, had carried out hard delivery work better suited to a man, recalled this episode with unconcealed pride: "He liked my dress. Once, after a public holiday, when I returned from the village and went out into the kitchen to the sink, I noticed that Iosif Vissarionovich was watching me from behind the curtain. In those days I had long black hair and I was wearing an attractive dress with a long skirt made of flowered Japanese cloth. Iosif Vissarionovich told me: 'That dress really suits you. In my home in Georgia girls your age wear dresses just like that.'"[84]

During his exile in Solvychegodsk the widowed Iosif Dzhugashvili was therefore seeking adventure mostly in his own environment. From phrases that appear in various recollections it appears that among the exiles there was a tendency for comrades to live with one another "just like that", without being married. Stalin chose to live with a young woman from Saratov by the name of Serafima Khoroshenina. The relationship was not kept a secret and for a while they rented an apartment together. In response to an official question as to whom he shared his apartment with, beside his own name Joseph Stalin wrote in his own hand the name of Khoroshenina. The woman's exile ended earlier than his, however, and although they corresponded later their relationship seems to have been over by the summer of 1911.[85]

After that another woman's name appears in the police files kept on the Bolshevik politician. According to one of the slips found in his biographical file at the Marx-Engels-Lenin Institute, Stalin "established contact with a seventh-grade student at the Tot'ma girl's secondary school."[86] The street informers soon found out that the person in question was Pelageya Onufrieva, barely seventeen years old and therefore underage. The girl was mentioned by the byname "Neat" in their daily reports. A special twist to the story was the fact that she was the girlfriend of Iosif Dzhugashvili's best friend at the time. Judging from her old-fashioned Christian name Pelageya, whom "Comrade Koba" called Polina, or sometimes Polya, probably came from an Orthodox family. She was the partner of Pyotr Chizhikov, a Bolshevik living in Vologda. The girl had traveled to the town without the knowledge of her parents in order to live with Chizhikov only a few weeks before she met Stalin. She had escaped there from the tiny north Russian town of Tot'ma. As she declared proudly decades later, she had no time for old-fashioned customs: "In those days, for instance, one was not supposed to eat on the street. This made me uneasy, but [...] in the neighborhood there was a shady avenue bordered with trees. I went there on several occasions with Stalin, who

often invited me to walk in that direction with him. Once we sat down on a bench and he offered me some fruit: 'Eat some. No one will see you here…'"[87]

Onufrieva's partner, Chizhikov whose exile had also recently ended, is mentioned by the name "Kuznets", that is, "the Blacksmith", in the reports submitted by the informers who were following "the Caucasian".[88] He was generally known as a kind, gentle person. Apparently he was completely dominated by the powerful, aggressive Stalin. Pelageya later told how her partner hated the north Russian climate but was so in love with "Neat" that for a while even after his period of exile was over he did not move back to his home near Rostov-on-Don. He found a job as a salesman in Ishemyatov's colonial goods store, which was an important base for "Comrade Koba" in Vologda. According to the police reports the two Bolshevik politicians also used it as a postal address.[89]

At the same time Chizhikov was in touch with the Bolsheviks in emigration. In the summer of 1911 he was given the task of assisting in the escape of Iosif Dzhugashvili, one of the Russian agents of the Bolshevik "Foreign Center" led by Lenin. According to information that reached the Vologda gendarmerie on August 23, 1911, "Comrade Koba" had mistakenly let slip that he had settled in the town in order to "find out how he could travel further and to obtain conspiracy addresses for this purpose". On September 9, the Vologda gendarmes let the St. Petersburg Okhrana know that "Dzhugashvili, in the near future, will be participating in a meeting of the Central Committee".[90] The information probably referred to the national Bolshevik party conference, which met in January 1912 in Prague.

Iosif Dzhugashvili, who was otherwise usually very keen to escape, was in no hurry to leave Vologda at this time. Despite the prestigious role of "traveling agent" bestowed on him by Lenin he felt happy with Pelageya/Polina, who was playing the role of a precocious *grande dame.* Later, on February 15, 1912, after his sweetheart had returned to Tot'ma to graduate from secondary school, "Comrade Koba" sent letters to her: "Don't write to my old address! […] If you need my new address, you can get it from Petyka *[Chizhikov—M. K.]*. I owe you a kiss in return for the kiss you sent me via Petyka. Let me kiss you now. I am not simply sending a kiss but am *kisssssing* you passionately (it is not worth kissing otherwise)."[91]

As the letter reveals the three members of this small company got along well together. In the evenings they would stroll in downtown Vologda. When the weather turned rainy they would read quietly or play cards in Pyotr Chizhikov's rented room. In the mornings, however, the "troika" would turn into a "two-horse carriage". At around nine or ten o'clock Iosif Dzhugashvili would knock on Polina's door and, while the girl's partner was at work in Ishemyatov's store, would court her: "We were quite happy when we were at home; we would read quietly," remembered Onufrieva.[92]

Thirty years later, when "Comrade Koba" was already the undisputed leader of the Soviet Empire, Polina was living as a simple housewife. She had soon left the teaching profession in 1917, married a mechanic by the name of Fomin, and never worked again. In the early 1930s her father and brothers, classified a *kulak*s, were exiled to Siberia. Her husband was arrested and held for a short time in 1937 as a saboteur. Exactly ten years later he was sentenced to ten years in prison as an "enemy of the people". According to family legend Onufrieva wrote to Stalin when a scholarship was taken away from her son, who was studying at the faculty of railway engineering at the Leningrad University. The directors of the university later overruled their original decision.[93] It is hardly surprising that, according to the records of contemporary researchers, Onufrieva did no voluntary work and was not interested in politics. Nevertheless, even in the 1940s, she was proud to declare that she had once been close to Stalin: "I behaved in all simplicity with him," she said, referring to the fact that in those days it was not decent for young, and particularly underage, girls to appear in public with an older man. This was why they had often hidden in a shady corner of one of the parks in Vologda. In the course of their conversations they also talked about Stalin's past. From Pelageya/Polina's recollections it appears that "Comrade Koba" liked to make jokes, but he also liked to elicit people's sympathy: "He lost his wife at around that time.[94] He told me how much he had loved her and how hard it was for him to lose her. 'I was so overcome with grief', he told me, 'that my comrades took my gun away from me.'[95] He also said, 'I realized how many things in life we fail to appreciate. While my wife was still alive there were times when I didn't return home from work even at night. I told her when I left not to worry about me. But when I got home I would find her sitting there awake; she would wait up for me all night.'"[96]

Pelageya remembered all the details of that "long, hot summer", which in fact lasted scarcely more than a month, during which Stalin told her that his late wife had been an accomplished dressmaker: "He often mentioned the beautiful dresses she had made. Despite being a man, Stalin had good taste. [...] He talked a great deal about the southern landscapes, about how good life was there, how beautiful the gardens were and how attractive the buildings. He would often say to me: 'I know you would love it in the south. Come and see it for yourself. I'll give you a letter of recommendation and you'll be treated as one of the family.'"[97]

The Bolshevik politician would sometimes hypocritically lecture the young girl. Pelageya/Polina once mentioned Mikhail Artsybashev's novel *Sanin*, which appeared in 1907. Filled with erotic scenes, the book had been greeted with widespread controversy. "Comrade Koba" protested angrily: "It is not worth wasting your time on such things. [...] There is no merit in Artsybashev's work. He is vulgar." Meanwhile, at around this time, he sent a postcard of an erotic scene to Pelageya/Polina. *[In Vologda, and perhaps even later during his exile, Stalin collected picture postcards.—M. K.]*

Amidst such emotional storms the date of his long-planned escape eventually arrived. On September 6, 1911 Pyotr Chizhikov met Stalin early in the morning. He gave him his own identity papers, a move that involved great risk for both of them. Chizhikov was later arrested and forced to provide the police with an explanation. He tried to save himself by claiming that his friend had stolen the document from his pocket.[98] Stalin was caught as early as September 9, 1911, having barely had time to set foot in St. Petersburg. He was kept in prison for a long time for traveling to a location from which he had been banned, using someone else's documents. The authorities hoped to break him so that he would make a confession. He was interrogated for the first time on November 12, two months after his arrest. Five days later, as "a threat to the peace of society and to state order", he was exiled for five years, beginning on December 5, 1911.[99]

On the day of his escape the Bolshevik politician had obviously felt that the escape would be trouble-free and that everything would go according to plan. He did not allow Pelageya/Polina to accompany him to the railway station, although they did in fact meet on September 6, 1911. Pelageya asked for a photograph of Koba to remember him by, but he refused to give her one: "I don't give photographs to anyone," he said. "The police have plenty of me as it is."[100] Instead, he gave her a copy of Marxist literary historian Pyotr Kogan's *History of West European Literature*, a deadly boring work, with the following dedication:

"To clever, bad-tempered Polya, from the Oddball Osip." Many years later, when a local historian asked Pelageya Onufrieva what the dedication meant, she gave a rather evasive explanation. She said that the dedication had been prompted by the fact that she had been a sharp-tongued, witty girl.

The same phrase appears on a postcard sent by Iosif Dzhugashvili to Polya on December 24, 1911: "Well, bad-tempered Polya, I am vegetating in Vologda once again, where I embrace your kind and good-natured Petka. We sit at the table and raise our glasses to the health of clever Polya. Drink to the health of your famous Oddball!"[101]

This was written after the escapee had been deported back to Vologda. The local authorities had him sign a declaration that he would not leave the town again. By that time, however, Pelageya Onufrieva had herself left to return home. According to her recollections, at their farewell on September 6, 1911 she had felt that she would never see Stalin again. This was why she had wanted to give him the cross she was wearing round her neck—her most precious possession as an Orthodox Russian. Her "Oddball" would not accept the cross, only the thin chain on which it had been hanging. He promised that he would wear his pocket watch on it.

They continued to correspond for a few years after this, although their letters became increasingly infrequent. According to Pelageya/Polina, Stalin once wrote to her that "you know that I traveled *[to St. Petersburg—M. K.]* to get married, but finally I ended up in prison. However, even now I am not bored. [...] I hope I will be free soon."[102] They were never to meet again.

1 *Dni*, 1928, vol. I, 22, 24.
2 *RGASPI*, fond. 558, op. 4, d. 647. The letter is closed with lofty words: "Comrade Stalin, please accept my kind regards. I wish you lived long and worked on the revolutionary path."
3 Bagirov, 1948, 109.
4 Trotsky, 1990, vol. I, 173.
5 *RGASPI*, fond. 558, op. 4, d. 629.
6 *RGASPI*, fond. 558, op. 4, d. 647.
7 *Voprosi Istorii*, 1992, no. 1, 59.
8 *Istorik Marksist*, 1940, no. 9, 6.
9 *RGASPI*, fond. 157, op. 1, d. 916.
10 In northern Russia Stalin was referred to by the Ukrainian-Russian name Osip, and not by the biblical Iosif.
11 *RGASPI*, fond. 558, op. 4, d. 647.
12 Even though on May 1, 1909, Stalin (as "Soso") sent a message to a Bolshevik named Taker in which he asked him to send money "for the return trip". *RGASPI*, fond. 71, op. 10, d. 406.
13 *RGASPI*, fond. 558, op. 4, d. 647.
14 *Ibid.*
15 *RGASPI*, fond. 71, op. 10, d. 406.
16 *RGASPI*, fond. 558, op. 4, d. 647.
17 *Ibid.*
18 *Ibid.*
19 *Ibid.*
20 Beria, 1952, 191.
21 *Krasny Arkhiv*, 1941, no. 2, 5–6.
22 *Ibid.*, 6–8, 10–11.
23 "We have been unable to identify this person named Koba," complained the agents of Okhrana in the November of 1909. *Ibid.*, 11.
24 *RGASPI*, fond. 558, op. 1, d. 4372.
25 *RGASPI*, fond. 558, op. 4, d. 647.
26 *Krasny Arkhiv*, 1941, no. 2, 12.
27 *Ibid.*, 11.
28 Smith, 1967, 80–103; Spiridovich, 1986, 144–146; *Bolsheviki*, 1990, 7–13.
29 *RGASPI*, fond. 558, op. 1, d. 26.
30 *Krasny Arkhiv*, 1941, no. 2, 12.
31 Trotsky, 1990, vol. I, 175.
32 *Krasny Arkhiv*, 1941, no. 2, 13.

33 Bagirov, 1948, 125. RGASPI, fond 558. op. 4. d. 635. The next day, June 30, 1910, Iosif Dzhugashvili submitted a newer and even more obsequious petition—acting totally against revolutionary ethics—to the authorities, asking them for clemency. This document establishes, in a strange way, that in 1905 *he had already received amnesty once*. Also, he calls Petrovskaya, who would soon disappear from his life forever, his *wife*. Ostrovsky 2002, 330–331.
34 *Istorik Marksist*, 1940, no. 9, 13.
35 One of Stalin's fellow exiles, Golubev used these two phrases to describe Stalin's status. *RGASPI*, fond. 558, op. 4, d. 540.
36 *Krasny Arkhiv*, 1941, no. 2, 14.
37 *RGASPI*, fond. 558, op. 4, d. 647.
38 Bagirov, 1948, 125.
39 *Krasny Arkhiv*, 1941, no. 2, 15.
40 Even though the Master of the Kremlin himself tried to collect all document sources from this period of his life. On March 8, 1927, for example, Ivan Tovstukha, the director of Stalin's secretariat asked Adoratsky, one of the directors of the Central Administration of the Soviet Archives to obtain these documents: "Once you have received them *[from Vologda—M. K.]*, please send them to me for examination or have a copy of them made for me. (We will pay for the copies.)" *RGASPI*, fond. 155, op. 1, d. 37.
41 There is a legend, which is widely believed even today, that Kuzakova's son, Konstantin, who worked in the offices of the Central Committee in the 1940s, was Stalin's illegitimate son as well. The mother herself started to spread the story. But according to the birth records, the boy was born in 1908, before Stalin arrived in the little town. Vasilyeva, 1996, 143–163.
42 *Zarya Vostoka*, 1925, no. 12, 23.
43 *RGASPI*, fond. 558, op. 1, d. 4516. In this letter, which still has not been published fully, there is an interesting reference to "Koba comrade's" plan to travel abroad, and visit Mikha Chakaya.
44 Stalin, 1946, vol. II, 162–166. This did not hold a great importance at that time. Stalin's name, for example, did not even appear in the minutes that were taken at the editorial board meeting of the Bolshevik emigrant publication, *Proletary*. In the foreword attached to a later edition of the minutes, the compilers quoted almost exclusively Stalin. *Protokoli soveshchania*, 1934, vol. V–XIII.
45 Trotsky, 1990, vol. I, 187.
46 *RGASPI*, fond. 558, op. 4, d. 647.
47 Stalin, 1946, vol. II, 209–212. After smaller modifications by the censors, the letter appeared in the complete works of Stalin. Kamenev's name, for example, was left out, even though in the 1937 version, which was published during the Great Terror, it was still in there. *Prazhskaya konferencia*, 1937, 19.
48 Stalin, 1946, vol. II, 209.
49 Spiridovich, 1986, 193–234.
50 Avtorkhanov, 1973, vol. I, 159.
51 Robert Tucker takes it for granted that Koba's letter of January 22, 1911 did reach Lenin. In this letter, Stalin criticized Lenin, who took offense at this. Tucker, 1991, 145. The author grounds this claim on a Soviet biography of Ordzhonikidze. Dubinsky-Mukhadze, 1963, 92–94. This book, however, is a fictitious biography or at most a documentary novel by its genre. There is not a single archival source or credible memoir that could support the "facts" presented by the author.
52 Nicolaevsky, 1965, 134, 12.
53 Only a few sources can be still found on Stalin's "agent" role. *Voprosi Istorii KPSS*, 1963, no. 3, 156. The participants of the Bolshevik conference held in Paris between May 28 and June 4, 1911 nominated him as a member of the Organizing Committee under his old byname, "Ivanovich". *Prazhskaya konferencia*, 1937, 47.
54 *Krasny Arkhiv*, 1941, no. 2, 14.
55 *RGASPI*, fond. 161, op. 1, d. 20.
56 Alliluyeva, 1946, 109.
57 *RGASPI*, fond. 558, op. 4, d. 447.
58 *Sotsial Demokrat*, 1934, no. 16.
59 *RGASPI*, fond. 558, op. 4, d. 447.
60 *RGASPI*, fond. 71, op. 10, d. 20.
61 Stalin, 1946, vol. II, 415.
62 *RGASPI*, fond. 558, op. 1, d. 5097. In a letter written to Kirov, one can learn that Sergo Ordzhonikidze also participated in hunting down Ivanyan: "Stalin remembered this man, and as a consequence, the Transcaucasian Supervisory Committee expelled Iv[anyan] from the party. It turned out that Iv[anyan] is a quite thick-skinned fellow." *Bolshevistkoye rukovodstvo*, 1996, 331.
63 For a publication of the letter—with insignificant modifications—and a discussion of Ivanyan's later fate, see Antonov–Ovseyenko, 1994, 330.
64 *Ibid.*
65 *Ibid.*
66 From the reports of secret agents, on May 18, 1911, the commander of the Vologda gendarmerie learned that "together with other convicts in exile, Dzhugashvili has attempted to bring about a Social Democratic group in the town of Solvychegodsk," and immediately forwarded this

information to Petersburg. Four days after this, one of the chief police officers reported to his superiors that "Dzhugashvili has a significant role among the exiles in Solvychegodsk. He makes his apartment available for meetings among them, and wants to establish a Social Democratic faction from the people present." *Istorik Marksist*, 1940, no. 9, 17–18.

67 In a letter dated March 20, 1991, the head of the Vologda gendarmerie called the governor's attention to watch more carefully an exile named Iosif Dzhugashvili. Already the next day, the governor assigned the Solvychegodsk district authorities with this task. *Ibid.*, 15.

68 *Ibid.*, 16.

69 *RGASPI*, fond. 558, op. 4, d. 540.

70 *Ibid.*

71 After Stalin left Solvychegodsk, he remained in correspondence with Golubev for a while. *RGASPI*, fond. 558, op. 4, d. 150. The Bolshevik politician was still alive in 1936, but his fate after this date is unknown. Shur, on the other hand, was an associate professor at the Kharkov University at the beginning of the 1950s. Despite his "sinful" political past, no one touched him, even though the one-time "Comrade Koba" sent the already quite old former Mensheviks to prison and execution in thousands. Yakovlev, 2000, 398–399.

72 *RGASPI*, fond. 555, op. 4, d. 150.

73 This is the recollection of the then sixteen-year old Kryukova, who worked as a general maid at one of "Comrade Koba's" landlords. Kryukova learned only in 1939 who was their former Georgian tenant. *RGASPI*, fond. 558, op. 4, d. 647.

74 *RGASPI*, fond. 558, op. 4, d. 540.

75 *Istorik Marksist*, 1940, no. 9, 19.

76 *RGASPI*, fond. 71, op. 10, d. 407.

77 *Krasny Arkhiv*, 1941, no. 2, 17–18.

78 *RGASPI*, fond. 558, op. 4, d. 647.

79 *Ibid.*

80 *Sto sorok besed s Molotovim*, 1991, 133.

81 *Krasny Arkhiv*, 1941, no. 2, 15–17.

82 At least this is what one can learn from the plain-speaking memoirs of the Bolshevik contemporaries of the Soviet dictator, which were free of all the frills of Stalin's personality cult. See Zelikson-Bobrovskaya, 1932, 296–304.

83 *RGASPI*, fond. 558, op. 4, d. 647.

84 *Ibid.*

85 *Ibid.*

86 *RGASPI*, fond. 558, op. 4, d. 647.

87 *Ibid.*

88 *Krasny Arkhiv*, 1941, no. 2, 15, 16.

89 *RGASPI*, fond. 558, op. 4, d. 647.

90 *Krasny Arkhiv*, 1941, no. 2, 18–19.

91 *RGASPI*, fond. 558, op. 2, d. 75; see also *Izvestia, CK*, 1989, no. 10, 190.

92 *RGASPI*, fond. 558, op. 4, d. 547.

93 *Ibid.*

94 In fact, in 1907.

95 This is the only document source witnessing that Stalin was armed during his "mail-coach robber" period, most likely he had a handgun with him.

96 *RGASPI*, fond. 558, op. 4, d. 547.

97 *Ibid.*

98 *Krasny Arkhiv*, 1941, no. 2, 21, 22. Cf. *RGASPI*, fond. 558, op. 4, d. 647.

99 *Ibid.*, 22–23.

100 Onufrieva told this story twice. In the second version, Stalin reputedly boasted with these words to her: "I never let anyone take a picture of me. Only in the prison, when they forced me to pose for a picture." *RGASPI*, fond. 558, op. 4, d. 547.

101 *RGASPI*, fond. 558, op. 4, d. 647.

102 *RGASPI*, fond. 558, op. 4, d. 547.

Kliment Voroshilov

July 1926, the Kremlin. Veterans of the Civil War mix with the graduates of the military officer school. Boasting two Orders of the Red Banner on his commander's jacket is Robert Eydeman (x), who later became one of the defendants of the Tukhachevsky Trial. Next to Voroshilov on the right, sits Andrei Bubnov (xx), a Commissar of the Red Army, and later People's Commissar for Culture and Education. Despite his support of Stalin in the early years, he was persecuted during the Great Terror.

Following the Spring of 1940, when Stalin relieved Voroshilov of his duty as Head of the Red Army, and publicly humiliated his old buddy, the marshall's face often reflected his fear.

Marshall Voroshilov and his wife, Yekaterina was fortunate enough to eventually survive the era of the Great Terror—which, in any case, was originally instigated by, among others, Voroshilov himself.

CHAPTER 7
Everyday Life in the Underground Movement

According to former residents of the Kremlin Stalin found it very easy to drop even the most important among his past acquaintances once he no longer had any interest in maintaining a relationship with them. His circle therefore changed rapidly over the years. Nevertheless, before the Bolshevik takeover of October 1917, and even for some time after it, there were various old acquaintances who were always ready to be at his disposal at the drop of a hat and who feature in his story again and again. In autumn 1911, during the short time he spent in St. Petersburg, there were certain people who accompanied him from hiding place to hiding place. These were the same people who, at great personal risk, had hidden him on an earlier illegal visit to St. Petersburg: the two electricians Alliluyev and Zabelin, and his fellow Georgian, the printer Sila Todria. However, they were unable to protect him from the authorities: as soon as "Comrade Koba" arrived, the men of the Okhrana were on his trail. They had even got off the train with him in the capital city. On September 6, 1911 the head of the gendarmes in Vologda had telegraphed St. Petersburg to say that Dzhugashvili, under the surveillance of a street informer by the name of Ilchukov, had departed. The presence of this "escort" was justified by the fact that the former exile was committing a serious offence against the laws then in force. He had been banned from the capital, and furthermore he was traveling with the papers of another exile, Chizhikov. Thus two days later the gendarmes in St. Petersburg inquired via telegram from their colleagues in Vologda whether to arrest Stalin, who was already in hiding in the city. The answer was a definite "no": "Please do not arrest him! Keep him under surveillance. Further details to follow."[1]

As they had done in Baku and Tiflis, the political police were therefore using Iosif Dzhugashvili as bait. In St. Petersburg, in addition to the Vologda informers who knew him personally and who probably regarded this trip to the capital as something of a bonus, various cabdrivers, co-opted by the Okhrana, also followed Koba everywhere. We know from their reports that the escapee, who moved around mostly on foot and who once again behaved rather carelessly, made the "Rossia" boarding house his base. He formally signed in under the name of Chizhikov, thinking that no one would disturb him there.

He was wrong. Already on September 9 a small group of uniformed and civilian armed men was close on his trail and he was arrested on the street. The Okhrana then turned his rented room upside down. However, among the manuscripts they discovered in his bags they found nothing that could have been used against him. He did, however, have some notes that he had made on Marx's *Das Kapital*, a few thematic collections of quotations *(Issues of Political Economy, Notes on Sociology, and Russian History)*, and a German-Russian dictionary, although none of these could be regarded as subversive. The presence of the dictionary led General Klikov, head of the St. Petersburg gendarmerie, to conclude that Dzhugashvili, the notorious escapee, was once again preparing to travel abroad.

House searches were only carried out in Vologda among the acquaintances of "Comrade Koba" on September 21, thus after significant delay. Although no incriminating evidence was found here either, General Klikov still proposed that the Bolshevik detainee should be deported for five years back to Eastern Siberia, from where Iosif Dzhugashvili had escaped in 1904. In response to the Okhrana's proposal the minister of internal affairs closed the case in a somewhat more benevolent manner. Rather than faraway Eastern Siberia or one of the barren northern settlements of the Vologda province, Dzhugashvili was sent to the provincial seat itself, thus was able to live in relatively tolerable circumstances, and his exile was to last for only three years.[2]

The authorities even allowed Koba to travel without an escort to the place of his old/new exile. The historians who preferred to compile the biography of "the Master" exclusively from the more dramatic episodes of his life did not, of course, give much emphasis to this, nor to the fact that, following his release from prison, he lived for several days in the apartment of Sila Todria as if nothing had happened. According to the recollections of Vera Shweitzer, the Bolshevik politician hid for a further ten days with the Todrias.[3] As the police records reveal, he received his travel documents on December 14, 1911 but only registered with the Vologda authorities eleven days later. On New Year's Eve, however, the street informers were obliged to stand in the freezing cold from ten past nine in the morning until 8.40 pm in front of the home of "the Caucasian", at number 27 Zolotushnaya ('Scrofula') Street in Vologda.[4]

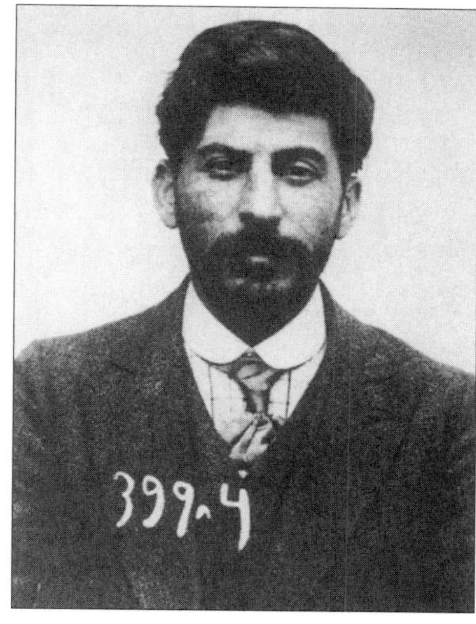

Iosif Dzhugashvili in 1913.

All they found out was that Stalin spent even this holiday sitting at home alone. In Vologda at the very end of 1911 he did not have such good friends as Pelageya Onufrieva or Pyotr Chizhikov. Apparently, Stalin had no intention of making a place for himself in the local community of exiles. He was already concerned mainly with the national question in relation to the Social Democratic movement, despite the fact that in the underground conditions fresh information reached him only after a significant delay. After being arrested in September 1911 in St. Petersburg he could not take part in preparations for the national conference of the RSDLP. Nor was he able to travel to Prague, where the conference was being held. It is not hard to imagine his feelings about this.

The Prague Conference, which began on January 5, 1912 in the Czech Trade Union Center, would have meant more in terms of Stalin's future career than all the other party congresses and conferences combined. Those who turned up for the conference were, almost without exception, Leninist Bolsheviks like himself, apart from two "pro-party" Menshevik delegates, followers of Plekhanov. The fate of these two was later to take a tragic turn. Along with other leaders of the Baku commune Yakov Zevin, with whom Stalin sat together in the Baylovo prison in 1908, known as "Comrade Yan", was shot by rightist SRs on the orders of English officers. The real name of "Comrade Viktor", the other Menshevik delegate, was David Shwartsman. Following the 1917 Bolshevik takeover he was gradually forced into the background and, according to one of the old prisoners in the Gulag, Aleksei Snegov, he had deliberately tried to remain unnoticed during the Great Terror. However, the NKVD agents somehow still managed to find him: because of his Menshevik past he fell into the "execution quota" personally drawn up by Stalin. He was executed following the most summary court proceedings. By that time more than half of the Bolshevik delegates at the Prague party conference had met the same fate. These included Grigory Zinovyev, the first leader of the Comintern; Pyotr Zalutsky, one of the leaders of the party organization in St. Petersburg; Leonid Serebryakov, a secretary of the Central Committee; Aleksandr Dogadov, the moving force behind the Soviet trade union movement; and Aleksandr Voronsky, the famous literary politician, editor in chief of the quality journal *Krasnaya Nov*. They were branded as traitors and spies by Stalin and executed one after the other.

The executions took place despite the fact that it was to these former comrades that Stalin owed his promotion to the upper echelons of the Bolshevik apparatus in January 1912. The conference, which represents an important milestone in his political career, is recorded in the history books as the 6th National Conference of the RSDLP (of the Russian Social Democratic Labor Party, which united several different factions). However, it was not in fact a national conference at all. The delegates from the various regions of the tsarist empire represented mainly those small party cells that had been established by the Bolsheviks. They had been selected chiefly from among the "hard-line Leninists" and had been subject to thorough filtering by Sergo Ordzhonikidze and other "traveling agents" in the previous months. They were doubtless aware of the controversy surrounding the situation from the very moment they arrived in the Czech capital. Even earlier they must have known that some of the party organizations that had selected them to participate in the conference existed only on paper, or at best consisted only of a few Bolshevik militants. They still did not understand why publicly respected veterans from among the large numbers of Russian Social Democrats in emigration had not been included among them, nor why the famous intellectuals of the movement, and even the Latvian and Polish Socialist politicians who mostly sympathized with the Leninists, were not present.

Just before the opening of the conference the "domestic" delegates sent a second lot of invitations to the great figures of "Leftist Bolshevism"—Bogdanov, Lunacharsky, and Aleksinsky—as well as to a host of famous Menshevik politicians including Georgy Plekhanov, the apostle of Russian Marxism. An invitation was even sent to Leon Trotsky, then living in Vienna and editing the publication *Pravda*, to whom Lenin was particularly hostile at the time. They explained the invitations by arguing that the organizers had written to these people anyway, in the course of earlier preparations for the 6th National Party Conference.[5]

Nevertheless, those invited turned down the trip to Prague one after the other. The famous Social Democratic politicians had clearly failed to recognize that by their absence they were merely furthering the dramatically increasing dominance of the Leninists, whom they referred to as "dissidents". Despite this, when Lenin arrived, after some delay, in Prague, he was furious that new invitations had been sent out: "Even if you unite with them, we will declare a split! Open your own conference and we will open ours! We will convene a new conference! Not with you, but against you!" he fumed at the Russian delegates. He threatened them repeatedly, saying that if they opened the gates wide he would immediately leave the conference.[6]

This scared the "domestic" delegates, who had a profound respect for "the Old Man", and they backed down immediately. In the days that followed they faced one defeat after another in the old debate with the "foreigners", which was stirred up once again after the opening of the Conference, despite the fact that in Prague they outnumbered the representatives of the Bolshevik emigration by three to one. At first even Lenin's most loyal "domestic" disciples launched a frontal attack against those based abroad. Sergo Ordzhonikidze spoke with perhaps the greatest vehemence, despite the fact that on other occasions he followed the leader of the party with blind obedience: "Every foreign group is a complete non-entity", he said, in his characteristically straightforward and passionate manner. An equally faithful Leninist, Suren Spandaryan, went as far as proposing the dissolution of the Social Democratic party organizations in emigration: "Whoever wants to work [...] should come to Russia." Nevertheless, Lenin managed to calm his "domestic" followers. He argued above all that the Socialists in emigration were

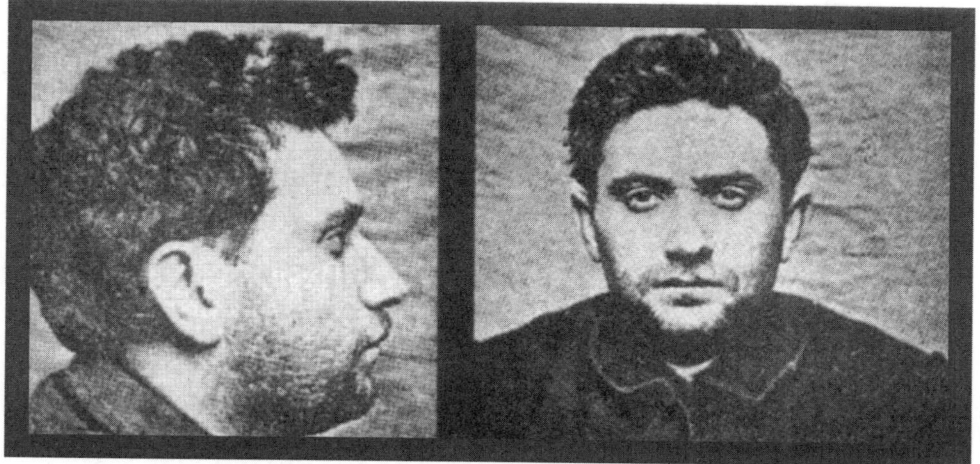

Grigory Zinovyev on a photograph taken by the tsarist police.

"connected by a thousand threads to Russia". The future commissar for health in the first Soviet government, Nikolai Semashko, taking this idea further angrily exclaimed: "You are quite capable of expelling everyone. But by doing so you would destroy the organization which was established to help you."[7]

After a while the debate became calmer. Although those who had gathered in Prague formed only a small group, they were united by the knowledge that they had broken away from all the rival Social Democratic factions and parties and had declared war on the tsarist government from this concentrated defensive formation. The Leninists' long-standing dream seemed to have become reality in the beautiful city of Prague. The delegates, who had spent long years in the same stable as the Mensheviks, the Jewish Bund, and several Bolshevik groups opposing Lenin, finally became a separate body and declared to the world that they regarded as their real allies only those Socialists who accepted the "spirit of Prague" and the primacy of the underground struggle. Another criterion was that everyone should surrender themselves to the new leading bodies elected in the Czech capital—the Central Committee led by Lenin, and the Russian Bureau, which was integrally linked to it.

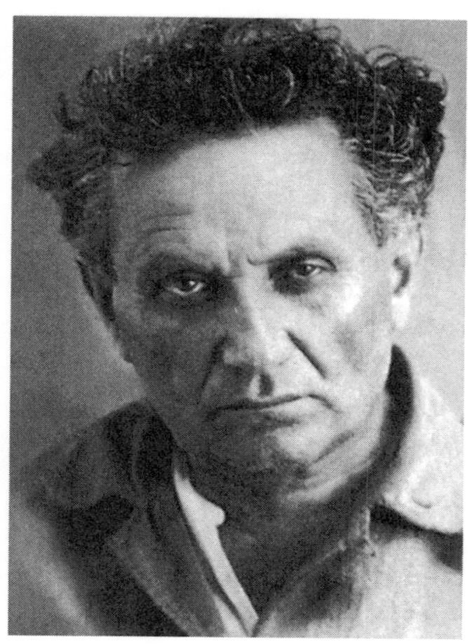

This picture was taken in the Lubyanka prison not long before the execution of the tortured Zinovyev on August 25, 1936.

The organizational decisions taken at the 6th National Party Conference reflected this new situation. The Central Committee was henceforth directed by Lenin and Zinovyev, his alter ego at the time: they set out the work to be done in the organization. However, their third colleague, Lev Kamenev, who was extremely popular among the participants at the conference, was not appointed to the body, which comprised only seven members. It soon became clear that this was merely a tactical move by the triumvirate, who did not want to create the impression that the Bolshevik emigrants had "taken over" the Central Committee. However, as soon as Kamenev had returned to St. Petersburg, having taken advantage of the amnesty declared to celebrate the 300th anniversary of the Romanov dynasty in 1913, he was able to assume control of the Russia-based party organizations as well as the editing of the "Leninist" *Pravda,* even without an official position. The Bolshevik representatives in the State Duma, simple, uneducated workers, who were mostly playing the role of extras alongside Kamenev were not competing with him either.

In 1912, however, the situation was slightly different. The "domestic" Bolshevik manual workers, who had made their voices heard in Prague throughout the conference, delegated Roman Malinovsky, an extremely influential, talented politician, to the newly elected party leadership. When this trade union activist of Polish origin had arrived in the Czech capital, many still had had doubts as to whether he was indeed a faithful Leninist. The rumor spread that at home he had earlier been courted by the Mensheviks. They had promised to turn him into a "Russian Bebel", that is, a high-profile workers' leader.[8] The worker-politician, who had once been a common criminal, had in fact had his trip to Prague paid for by the tsarist political police. He was a shrewd man and had realized that his best chances of moving up in the hierarchy of the movement lay in Lenin's "court".

The other "domestic" delegates were initially unhappy about the aggressive, outspoken Roman Malinovsky. However, attracted by his excellent speeches and the sharpness of mind he demonstrated in his replies, the Lenin–Zinovyev–Kamenev triumvirate took him under their wing. All three of them were tormented throughout their lives by a feeling of inferiority in relation to the "simple people"—a feeling that was extremely common among Russian intellectuals. It was this that decided Malinovsky's fate. The participants at the conference decided to appoint him as a Duma representative and gave him the task of coordinating trade union work. In return for performing these two important tasks he was made a member of the Central Committee.[9]

The shrewd police agent made a pretense of repaying the confidence he had been shown, behaving as if he were a true and loyal Leninist. Ordzhonikidze, Spandaryan, and Goloshchokin, the three other Russia-based party workers who were elected to the Central Committee at the same time, also accepted Lenin's advice on almost every question. Along with Stalin, then in exile in Vologda, and Yelena Stasova ("Comrade Zelma"), who was regarded as the "organizing genius" of the Bolshevik Party, they became members of the Russian Bureau, the most important domestic body of the Central Committee. The seventh member of the Central Committee, Shwartsman, was intended by the Bolshevik party leaders only as a bait to win over the "pro-party" Mensheviks. However, he was soon relegated for not meeting the expectations of the Bolshevik leadership.[10]

Unlike Shwartsman Joseph Stalin was not sidelined, even though he was not present in the Czech capital when the appointments were made. However, it is certainly not the case that the conference was imbued with his spirit, as his court historians later attempted to imply. Nor is it true that in the secret ballot he was unanimously elected by those present as a member of the Central Committee and that he became a kind of president of the Russian Bureau.[11] Nevertheless, Trotsky was wrong in saying that the exiled politician had been elevated to the party leadership by mere accident.[12]

The delegates were able, in theory, to nominate to the Central Committee only those who were present at the conference. Despite this, the co-opting of "Comrade Koba" was an entirely logical move. He had offered his services on several occasions to Lenin and his inner circle. His frequent escapes were regarded as an indication of his courage, and Stalin was able to make his activities in Baku and Tiflis appear in such a way as to win the sympathy of the "Foreign Center". He had also obtained a host of favorable recommendations for himself from Bolshevik veterans. As a result, he had been made a "traveling agent" and then a member of the Prague organizing committee. All these circumstances, whether taken individually or as a whole, enabled Stalin to come dramatically to the forefront. Lenin could indeed already have heard several times how in the Baku and Tiflis organizations there were many who hated his young Georgian follower. In 1911, for example, when "the Old Man" had talks in Paris with the Menshevik Grigory Uratadze, the latter told him a great deal about Stalin, including the fact that the Baku Bolsheviks had once expelled Stalin from the

Leon Trotsky (x), Lev Kamenev (xx), and Grigory Zinovyev (xxx) played important roles in the nascent Russian labor movement at the beginning of the century. This picture was taken in the 1920s when they joined ranks against Stalin. The former Georgian seminarist, who was a much less learned but definitely more cunning man than the three others, by time passing, drove them into the corner.

local party organization. Lenin had reacted in the following way: "This means nothing! This is exactly the kind of person I need!" Uratadze himself remembered being so surprised that he was unable to reply. The Bolshevik leader then poured out a torrent of words at him: "Such expulsions in the underground movement are almost always based on errors, on unverified reports [...], or often on misunderstandings. It is not worth attributing too much significance to such things. If someone is expelled from a group or an organization it does not follow that he must forfeit his party membership. [...] The decision taken by the Baku group, if it was taken at all, must be examined and verified."[13]

On other, similar occasions Lenin was not so lenient. In this case, however, his leniency was doubtless prompted by the great secret that connected him to "Comrade Koba": the series of "expropriations", that is, the Caucasian robberies. Besides Lenin and a few of his trusted followers, only a very small number of Baku and Tiflis Bolsheviks knew the details of these incidents. In shaping Stalin's career in the underground movement, however, the expropriations were decisive. At the end of the 1980s, when I talked to Abdurakhman Avtorkhanov at his home near Munich, my host, using a phrase of Engels' now seldom heard, said that at the Prague conference, as far as the judgment on Stalin was concerned, "quantity became quality". Thus in January 1912 the previously little-known provincial party official was able to become one of the decisive figures in the Bolshevik movement.

He was not the only "domestic" Bolshevik militant to come to the forefront as a result of the Prague conference. The emigrant leadership surrounding Lenin also put their faith in Yakov Sverdlov, Yelena Stasova, Stepan Shaumyan, Mikhail Kalinin, Aleksandr Smirnov (known as "Foma"), and Andrei Bubnov, who, during the revolutionary ebb, gradually came forward from the second line. These previously lesser known "professional revolutionaries" were elected one after the other to the "Prague" Bolshevik leadership. As a result of frequent arrests the members of the leadership, which was unable to hold sessions in Russia, were to change almost entirely in the course of the following year. The members of the new Leninist Central Committee took this into account. It was for this reason that they co-opted Joseph Stalin and Vladimir Belostotsky, a former iron worker who was at that time a clerk employed by the Labor Insurance Fund. Scarcely ten years later Stalin had become the General Secretary of the Bolshevik Party, then the Master of the Soviet Empire. Belostotsky, however, remained a humble clerk, who barely set foot beyond the Urals. He passed away peacefully almost fifty-five years later. He was one of the few who avoided the tragic fate of the former Bolshevik underground activists who fell victim to Stalin.

☆ Sadly, these executed politicians were unable to put their recollections down in writing at the end of their lives. However, even without their authentic memoirs there are plenty of legends concerning this hidden period in the life of the Soviet dictator, who was later to falsify his own biography entirely. According to one such story Joseph Stalin was first of all recommended by Malinovsky, the Okhrana agent, to be a member of the Central Committee in Prague It is even claimed that this probably happened on the orders of the tsarist secret police[14], although there is nothing to prove this. Besides, Malinovsky's position in Prague was not sufficiently strong as to enable him to force the nomination of "Comrade Koba" on the "domestic" delegates. Furthermore, Stalin did not even meet Malinovsky in person until the end of October 1912. Nor is it certain that, prior to this conference, they had even heard of one another.[15] However, over half of the dozen delegates who attended the conference in the Czech capital had already known Iosif Dzhugashvili personally. It can also be proved that at least three of his fellow countrymen supported him. From among the Caucasian group Lev Kamenev, one of the key figures in the Leninist emigration, should be mentioned in first place. The mother of this sympathetic, educated man belonged to an old, Russian noble family and worked as a teacher, and his father was a Jewish engineer. Kamenev grew up in Tiflis and in 1901, thus almost at the same time as Soso Dzhugashvili, began to play a leading role in the local underground Socialist circles. At that time, as a young student, he was commuting between the Georgian capital and Moscow, where he studied law. In 1905, at barely twenty-seven years old, along with his former mentor Mikha Chakaya and Iosif Dzhugashvili, he became a member of the joint Menshevik-Bolshevik committee that coordinated the work of the Social Democrats in the huge Caucasia.[16]

Among his comrades, Lev Kamenev was considered a great theoretician.

In the meantime the young man, who had literary ambitions and who appeared much more mature than his age, was imprisoned and then emigrated. In Paris, then in Cracow, he worked alongside Lenin for the "Foreign Center", the top-secret, informal Bolshevik body. In addition, however, he had many Menshevik friends, since from time to time he adopted a "conciliatory" tone. On the other hand, it was he who put into writing the basic version of Lenin's "party of a new type", the pamphlet called *The Two Parties*.[17]

His wife, Olga Bronstein, Trotsky's younger sister, was the direct opposite of the fundamentally well-meaning Kamenev, who showed kindness to everyone. This ambitious woman dominated her husband and in the company of Kamenev's comrades would give a convincing performance as a faithful Menshevik. However, she did not object to her husband, known under the byname "Comrade Yuly", inviting his old Tiflis Bolshevik and Menshevik acquaintances in Paris to dinner at every possible opportunity. On occasion she even acted as guide to one or other of them through the French capital, jestingly warning them meanwhile not to join the "Leninists" under the influence of her husband and Lenin.[18]

Another possible supporter of the future Master of the Kremlin at the Prague conference may have been Grigory Ordzhonikidze. "Comrade Sergo", who came from a Georgian family of the lesser nobility, was originally an army doctor but worked little in this capacity during his life, which was to end tragically. In the years of the 1905 to 1907 Russian revolution, at barely twenty years old, he organized combat groups and smuggled weapons in Abkhasia and in the vicinity of Tiflis. Later he became an instructor of small guerilla groups in northern Iran before spending time in Russian exile colonies and prisons. "Comrade Sergo" was sentenced to a fairly long period in the Baylovo Prison, infamous for its terrible conditions, in the company of the more erudite and sharp-minded "Comrade Koba". Apparently it was then that the peculiar relationship of dominance and subordination, which was to characterize their friendship until the period of the Great Terror, first developed between them.[19]

In Baylovo, during a fierce debate over the agrarian issue, Stalin witnessed Ordzhonikidze get into a fight with one of their SR cellmates by the name of Ilya Kartsevadze. While "Comrade Koba" obviously enjoyed the scrap he by no means took part in it.[20] In the late 1920s this debate-cum-fight was frequently mentioned in the Russian émigré press. Demyan Bedny, the poet of the party, also referred to it in the December 20, 1929 issue of *Pravda*, which published several articles to mark Stalin's fiftieth birthday. Once, during a Politburo meeting, Kliment Voroshilov passed a small slip of paper to Stalin asking him about the truth behind this story. The General Secretary of the party falsely claimed that the fight had not been initiated by Ordzhonikidze. Nor was it true, according to Stalin, that the SRs, who were a majority in the prison cell, had given Ordzhonikidze a thorough beating: "Sergo was indeed a big hitter, *but not a single SR* dared touch him. Quite the contrary. The SRs were scared and admitted that Sergo had beaten up their spokesman", replied Stalin on February 10, 1928.[21]

Olga Bronstein, Kamenev's first wife and Trotsky's younger sister. In the 1920s she coordinated the Soviet cultural relations and hosted a literary salon. During the Great Terror, she lost her ex-husband and both of her sons. In the summer of 1941, following the orders of Beria, she was executed together with other convicts in the courtyard of the Oryol prison.

This entirely unnecessary lie is further proof that an intention to color the "heroic past" was in fashion in the Kremlin as early as the 1920s. Ordzhonikidze spoke flatteringly of his good friend and mentor in his autobiography, in which he referred to himself in the third person when describing the Prague Party Conference: "Following the conference Ordzhonikidze immediately returned to Russia to set up the Russian Bureau [which was to work under the Central Committee], and traveled to Vologda to see Stalin, who was then in exile there. Stalin was elected at the Prague conference as a member of the Russian Bureau and of the Central Committee. From Vologda, O[rdzhonikidze] traveled with Stalin to Caucasia."[22] This is not accurate. The delegates at the Prague conference did not in fact elect Stalin to membership of any body: the new Central Committee simply "co-opted" him. From Vologda Ordzhonikidze in fact traveled to Baku on his own.

Among those who attended the Prague conference, Suren Spandaryan was also a good friend of Stalin[23], despite the fact that their careers began from very different contexts. Unlike the son of the impecunious shoemaker, the Armenian student, who dropped out of university largely as a result of his laziness, had no financial problems. His father was a rich merchant who lived in Paris and supported his son for years. When "Comrade Timofey"—Spandaryan's underground byname—already a father of two, was forced to hide from the police, his comrades helped him using party funds. The politician spent most of his money on doctors and medicine, since from his youth he had had serious lung problems. He was barely thirty-four when, in 1916, he died in faraway Siberia, in the Turukhansk frontier zone where he had been sent as an exile along with Stalin.

It was for this reason that the Soviet "court historians" later referred to him using strings of superlatives.[24]

However, some of his contemporaries were rather less fond of him. Tatyana Vulich, the Bolshevik activist who, following her husband, later joined the Mensheviks, was in contact with Spandaryan in the Azerbaijani capital for several months in 1908. She remembered that the Armenian, with his comfortable lifestyle, "was Stalin's [...] closest friend and right-hand man. He supported Stalin unreservedly and protected him in everything. Regarding his moral character, he was very close to Stalin although he had one or two characteristics not usually mentioned in connection with Stalin. He was incredibly lazy, a typically sybaritic character [...] and a great womanizer." Zemlyachka,[25] who knew the local Bolshevik community well, once said in Paris that in Baku every child under the age of three bore a suspicious resemblance to Spandaryan.[26]

No matter which of the three Caucasian politicians it was who recommended "Comrade Koba" as a member of the Central Committee, within the strict hierarchy of the Bolshevik community Lenin's prior approval, or at least consent, was required.[27] A letter written by Avel Yenukidze, dated February 13, 1913, supports this. It clearly describes how Stalin's increasing prominence was partly due to the fact that in the early 1910s Lenin had a favorable opinion of the party workers in Baku. Stepan Shaumyan, who came from the Azerbaijani capital, was the recipient of Yenukidze's letter. He must have read these lines with satisfaction: "K[ob]a passed on the words of Il[yi]ch, according to which those in Baku were acting correctly and were the only ones to interpret the "line" properly.[28] He could always rely on them. I was very pleased at these words."[29]

☆ In order to exercise the hard-earned rights that went along with membership of the Central Committee Joseph Stalin, who had recently turned thirty three, had to escape once again from Vologda. Vera Shweitzer, the wife of Suren Spandaryan, recalled how impatiently the exile had awaited news from the Czech capital: "On February 12, 1912 Stalin wrote to me in St. Petersburg from Vologda. [...] He asked if Sergo and Suren had returned from the Prague conference." The picture postcard, signed by Iosif Dzhugashvili simply with the letter "S"[30], was written in the most cryptic language. However, on the basis of their pre-established code the addressee was able to understand every word. In fact, Stalin did not need information from a third party since before long he had received first-hand news of the events in Prague. Sergo Ordzhonikidze, who at that time, thanks to Lenin, was in practice the Russia-based leader of the Bolshevik "Foreign Center", traveled to Vologda after visiting the underground party organizations in Baku and St. Petersburg. According to a letter intercepted by the Kiev police authorities he informed Lenin from there that he had met "Ivanovich", that is, Stalin: "I made a final agreement with him. He is satisfied with the state of affairs", he wrote.[31] They must have talked about the financial allowance, which played a very important role in the life of the "professional" revolutionaries. In Prague, the participants at the conference voted that a significant sum, fifty rubles a month, be paid to "Comrade Koba" as well as to the other members of the Central Committee.[32]

Soon after the departure of "Comrade Sergo" on February 29, 1912, Joseph Stalin disappeared from Vologda. This time he spent only a few days in Moscow and St. Petersburg where once again, now for the third time, he was hidden by Sergei Alliluyev and Sila Todria. He did not even attempt to check in at one of the hotels and thus managed temporarily to mislead the authorities, even though the Vologda police, on the very night of his escape, had began to trail him at two in the morning. They had discovered that the exile had bade farewell to his landlady on the previous night, saying that he would return in a week.

During the period that followed the escapee managed to shake off the street informers several times. In St. Petersburg, for example, he once suddenly stopped a cab. The Okhrana agent who was trailing him also jumped into a cab, but on turning a corner Stalin jumped out and hid behind a pile of snow.[33] After losing his trail both the Vologda gendarmerie and police alerted their colleagues in Baku and Tiflis. They expected Iosif Dzhugashvili to turn up before long in one of the Caucasian cities.[34]

Sergo Ordzhonikidze in 1917, during his exile in Yakutia.

And this is exactly what happened: "Comrade Koba" traveled to Tiflis. There he found the Social Democratic movement in a lamentable state and immediately became involved in building up the party. By that time most of the old Bolshevik party members had moved away from the city, and those who had stayed had turned their backs on politics. However, the enthusiastic conspirator Stalin, even in such a situation, had to be careful that by representing the more radical "spirit of Prague" he did not come into unnecessary conflict with the Georgian Mensheviks. By that time they had taken control of the whole local Social Democratic community and were apparently getting stronger and stronger in Georgia. This picture is supported by the fact that later, following the collapse of the tsarist Empire and the overthrowing of the Kerensky Provisional Government, the Georgian Menshevik leaders radically split from their one-time Bolshevik comrades. From one minute to the next they turned against Lenin's government and declared their own independent state, the government of which enjoyed the support of the overwhelming majority of the population.[35]

In the early 1910s the situation in the former Bolshevik stronghold of Baku was similar in many respects to that in Tiflis. Stalin achieved contradictory results in the "city of black gold" before rapidly departing—probably because he felt that the ground was burning under his feet. In any case, on April 5, 1912 Yelena Stasova, in a letter written in special ink and thus difficult to read today, informed "Comrade Yury", that is, Georgy Pyatakov, the young militant of the Kiev Bolshevik party organization, that "Soso is alive and well. On 30th [March] he traveled to the north." To this letter she attached Stalin's report, written in Baku on the day of his departure. From this it appears that although "Comrade Koba" tried to strike a conciliatory tone with the Baku Mensheviks he was finally unable to shepherd them into the common fold controlled by the Bolsheviks: "I could only get a few men together yesterday", he complained to Stasova. "There is no real organization here (I mean in the local city center), thus I have had to be content with a private meeting attended by the few workers I mentioned. Despite all my efforts I was unable to lure a single Menshevik there. They openly confessed that they were afraid to come to the meeting and appealed to me to stay for a little while [in Baku] until things calmed down. Understand: until the uneasiness caused by news of the latest arrests and provocation had died down. Then a meeting would be possible."[36] The letter is particularly interesting bearing in mind that Stalin, at the time it was written, was composing his pamphlet *For the Party!*, via which he was obviously attempting to create a further rift between the already divided Social Democrats.[37] Once he had become General Secretary of the party these old, fiercely anti-Menshevik, texts appeared one after the other, with his knowledge and consent, in his selected works and subsequently in the second volume of his Collected Works. On the other hand, he tried to conceal from posterity his report, dated March 30, 1912, sent via Stasova to the "Foreign Center" led by Lenin: "It is an insignificant document. There is no point publishing it", he wrote to Major Nikitinsky on October 20, 1939, when the head of the central office supervising all archives, which was part of the NKVD, asked for his consent to publish the document in *Krasny Arkhiv*, which was publishing historical sources.[38] Nevertheless we do know from this archive journal that the Vologda chief of police issued a countrywide warrant against "Comrade Koba" in spring 1912, while he was commuting on his usual route between the two largest cities of Caucasia. On 1 April the head of the Baku Okhrana sent a telegram to the capital, saying that the exile was on his way to St. Petersburg via Moscow, where "he will probably visit the worker Alliluyev, formerly a Tiflis locksmith *[Stalin's future father-in-law was by then an electrician—M. K.]*. His further contacts are unknown", the transcript reads.[39]

It escaped the attention of the political police that Stalin broke his journey for a few hours in Rostov-on-Don, where he managed to talk to Vera Shweitzer: "We met at seven in the evening [...] at the old secondary modern school. Then we sneaked into the railway station and sat in the first-class restaurant," we read in Shweitzer's memoirs, which were drastically cut by the censors in the late 1930s. "This is how we managed to hide from the street informers and tell each other about the state of party affairs. Stalin told me details of Suren's arrest."[40]

The later, much-mentioned "brilliant organizational skills" of Stalin then mostly consisted of such fleeting encounters. The "traveling agents" and Central Committee members, whose movements were directed from a distance by the "Foreign Center" working in emigration, were hunted animals—unless they managed to outsmart the Okhrana agents and bury themselves in the sleepy, everyday life of some Russian town. The secret police found them out sooner or later, wherever they were. When this happened there was only one solution: to move on quickly. In 1912, the most eventful year in his underground life, Joseph Stalin was unable to settle anywhere for long. In March he spent barely three weeks in Baku and Tiflis. In April he spent less than two weeks in St. Petersburg. In September and October, apart from one short break, he was also staying in St. Petersburg. In early April and late October he spent a few days in Moscow. In November and December he worked in St. Petersburg again for almost three weeks. Thus in this year "Comrade Koba", keeping his head well down and ever mindful of the street informers, spent a total of four to four and a half months in one place. In the meantime he was either in prison or forced to eat the bitter bread of the exile. He also traveled abroad. The time in between was only sufficient to allow him to meet fleetingly with local party leaders and activists in various towns and, in the name of the prestigious Lenin, to try and mobilize them. In order to achieve more spectacular results, however, a permanent presence would have been needed.

Thus "Comrade Koba", despite his new rank in the movement, was obliged to continue his all-purpose existence. Fearful of being arrested he could not set foot in any large city with the kind of openness and determination that would have allowed him to undertake meaningful work—for instance in the protection of trade union interests, or the supervision of sick-relief or cultural associations for the workers, which were gaining an increasing role in Russia. Although this was a year of frequent strikes Stalin was not able to organize any significant strike action himself. Only the number of articles he wrote is worth mentioning: in spring 1912 seven short texts by him were published in the Socialist newspaper *Zvezda*.[41] He also wrote the lead article in the first issue of the "Leninist" *Pravda*, which appeared on April 22, 1912.[42]

This output was not much of a commendation, which may have contributed to Stalin's turning to the weapons of the permanently frustrated: ever more frequently he quarreled irritably, found fault with everything, and gave orders to his comrades with unnecessary meticulousness. Understandably he gained little popularity as a result: "Sergo [Ordzhonikidze] and Ivanovich [Stalin] keep giving orders but they say nothing about what is happening around us", complained Yelena Stasova in a letter intercepted by the police on April 12, 1912.[43]

In the meantime, Ordzhonikidze was arrested.[44] The snare began to close in on Joseph Stalin as well after he left Caucasia. On April 5, 1912 "Comrade Koba" met for the last time with "Comrade Sergo" in Moscow. The street informers, who were on the heels of the latter, followed both of them, but after a few hours playing cat-and-mouse they lost sight of Stalin. However, he had little time to enjoy his escape from them. There were so many police agents on the streets of the two capitals that after a chase lasting two and a half weeks Koba, who had lost weight as a result of the permanent state of tension in which he was living, was finally unable to get rid of them. Today we know that the Okhrana agents, who regularly used the help of concierges and cabdrivers, had not picked up the two leading Bolshevik politicians earlier in Moscow since they preferred to wait for the reports of the *agent provocateurs* who were trailing them.[45]

After a while, however, the police realized that Joseph Stalin was no longer useful as bait. There was some truth in this. For instance, on leaving Caucasia at the end of April 1912 he had composed a militant and widely read call in celebration of the First of May. Unlike his other articles, which were written in the dry and didactic style typical of the movement, this was a remarkably lyrical piece: "Nature is awakening from its winter dream. The forests and mountains are turning green. Flowers adorn the meadows and pastures. The sun shines more warmly. We feel in the air the pleasure of new life, and the world is beginning to dance for joy."[46] According to Vera Shweitzer people were passing the First of May leaflet from hand to hand on the outskirts of the two capitals, and copies even reached as far as Tiflis. Later the police confiscated the original manuscript, which was used as the *corpus delicti* during the investigation against the arrested Caucasian Social Democrats. "We found the draft of a leaflet. It was written in black ink on three long pieces of white paper", reads the official report.[47]

Nor, since the Bolshevik movement was swarming with agents provocateurs, could the fact that Stalin had played an important role in editing the first issue of *Pravda* remain a secret for long. "Comrade Koba" had gone too far this time to be allowed to remain at large. He was ambushed on April 22 while staying in the house of Nikolai Poletayev, even though the worker poet, as a Duma representative, enjoyed immunity along with all his guests as long as they remained in his apartment. As soon as the poorly dressed, unshaven Georgian stepped outside, several informers and gendarmes rushed to seize him. At the nearest police station "Iosif Vissarionovich Dzhugashvili [...] declared that he had no permanent dwelling place in the capital city." According to the records no evidence was found against him: in such cases it was not the practice to refer to the reports of planted informers. However, the authorities had the right to keep Stalin in custody because of his previous escapes:[48] the Bolshevik politician had two years and nine months of exile left to complete. Furthermore, by that time the Okhrana's "experts" on the Social Democrats already knew that Iosif Dzhugashvili was a member of the new Central Committee.[49]

In June, during a house search, the Tiflis police got hold of the secret archives of the local Bolshevik organization and of the Russian Bureau of the Central Committee.[50] On the basis of the incriminating documents they had discovered

Stalin could have been tried immediately. However, as on earlier occasions, he inexplicably escaped with a minor punishment, without a trial. Unlike him, Ordzhonikidze, who in the meantime had been traveling around half the country using the papers of an Azerbaijani land laborer, Gasan Novruzogli Guseynov (who had lived near Tiflis but who had died by that time), was sent in chains into solitary confinement in the St. Petersburg dungeon following his trial. This latter politician, who stood on an equal footing with Stalin in the hierarchy of the Bolshevik movement, was soon to become familiar with the *katorga*, or forced-labor camps.[51] "Comrade Koba", on the other hand, who had also commuted using false documents between Caucasia and St. Petersburg, was held in custody for just one and a half months, and in much better conditions. Afterwards he was exiled without *trial* for three years. On July 2 he was sent to Narym, in the province of Tomsk, with relatively few fellow exiles.

☆ In the Vologda transit prison *(peresilnaya tyurma)*, where he had already been on several previous occasions, Iosif Dzhugashvili met Boris Nicolaevsky, who regarded himself as a "conciliatory" Socialist. The later Herodotus of the Menshevik emigration, who became disillusioned with Bolshevism at around this time, had already heard of Stalin in Baku, where, although at different times, both of them had played an important role in local Social Democratic circles. Decades later Nicolaevsky remembered that it was mostly Avel Yenukidze who had told him about Stalin, and that he had made some none too flattering references to his vindictive nature. In the course of their brief encounter in Vologda he was unable to judge whether or not the rumors about his Bolshevik fellow sufferer were true. Stalin was rather more pragmatic. He borrowed his fellow prisoner's blue enamel teacup, which he then took with him when he left.[52]

Following their short conversation in Vologda their paths divided. "Comrade Koba" was taken beyond the Urals, while Nicolaevsky was taken to the White Sea. In the course of our conversations one of his disciples and good friends, the Menshevik historian Boris Sapir, who later emigrated to Holland, described how Nicolaevsky had found his exile hard to bear in the barren north of Russia. He was aware that the authorities were watching him and he was constantly fearful of the spy who had been planted in the exile community. Nevertheless, he remarked that this was nothing compared to what they did to him after the 1917 Bolshevik revolution in Soviet Russia.

Nor was it paradise that greeted Joseph Stalin when, from Vologda prison, he arrived in 1912 in Kolpashovo, near Narym, in northwestern Siberia. The forested and marshy plain, which in the summer swarmed with blood-sucking mosquitoes, required scarcely any guarding when the long winter set in, since it was almost impossible to escape from the snowbound, roadless region. In the summer it was potentially easier, although even then the impassable marshland deterred most escapees. Unless accompanied by a guide with local knowledge it would have been very dangerous to set off on a journey. (The word *narym* means marshland in the Khanty language.[53]) Most escapees, therefore, chose to head towards the European regions of Russia on the heavily controlled river boats, a journey which involved a huge detour. Despite the serious risks many exiles were willing to undertake the journey, desperate to leave behind the stifling atmosphere of the godforsaken, overcrowded Narym colony. In the settlement that comprised one hundred and fifty wooden houses, and in the tiny villages surrounding it, the approximately two thousand political prisoners had nowhere to work. They were left to their own devices all day long and became desperately bored. Those who were better off tried to make their lives more

The elderly Boris Nicolaevsky. This picture was taken in 1965, in Palo Alto, California, where the archives of the Hoover Institute is the home of the huge collection of the "Menshevik Herodotus".

comfortable. From the correspondence of Valerian Kuybyshev, a future key figure in Soviet economic life, we learn that he filled his home with carpets and ordered books from the capital. From other sources we know that the local community of exiles ran an eatery, a butcher's shop, and a colonial goods store in Narym on a cooperative basis.[54] There was a separate fund for political prisoners in need, and for those preparing to escape. We also know that on May First the exiles marched with red flags. These were idyllic circumstances compared to what life in the Narym exile colony was to become under Stalin's rule. At that time it was not in the region of two thousand, but four hundred thousand, forced settlers *(spetsposelenets)*, mostly Russian and Ukrainian *muzhik*s who had been labeled *kulak*s, who lived in the largely uninhabited frontier zone the size of Lithuania and Belorussia combined. The thirty to forty percent death rate was regarded as high, even compared to the terrible conditions in the other Soviet forced settlements.[55]

Stalin's first significant biographer, Boris Souvarine, mentions that in Narym "Comrade Koba" was mostly seen in the company of a jeweler called Shurin, who turned out to be an old *agent provocateur*.[6]

Other acquaintances of Stalin, such as the Bolsheviks exiled to Narym who included Ivan Smirnov, the popular worker who, during the Russian Civil War was known as the "Lenin of Siberia", generally did not write down their memories of Stalin for the simple reason that, in the prime of their lives, almost without exception, they fell victim to the Great Terror.[57] The official biographers of the Master of the Kremlin could therefore rely only on the memories of the few local residents when reconstructing the Narym period of his life. These ridiculously uninteresting and superficial documents were collected in the early 1940s by the member of the Krasnoyarsk party committee responsible for agit-prop, Konstantin Chernenko. The young, provincial *apparatchik* was obviously attempting to emulate the success of the established "Stalin researchers" Beria and Bagirov. Thus, as if he had nothing better to do amidst the bloodshed of the Second World War, he surprised "the Master" with the collection *J. V. Stalin's Exile in Siberia*. The new material published in this volume was the fruit of research carried out by historians who had fled Moscow to Krasnoyarsk and other Siberian cities in order to escape from the German offensive. All they had managed to do was to cobble together at best only a few banal and meaningless pages.[58]

The mind behind the project, Chernenko—who later, in the 1970s, rode to the pinnacle of power in the wake of Leonid Brezhnev—was doubtless hugely disappointed that the volume did not produce the desired effect. I have heard from an elderly researcher of the Marx-Engels-Lenin Institute "the Master" was overcome with anger when the ornate edition that had arrived from faraway Siberia was placed on his table. The furious Stalin allegedly called Krasnoyarsk on the Kremlin's direct line and yelled at Chernenko, whose career, as a result of this incident, suffered a temporary setback.

It is still not clear what made the protagonist of this publication so upset when he learned that the small group of archivists and historians had mapped out his life in Narym by calling on his former neighbors. The minor scandal that surrounded the publication was eventually forgotten, and the records that had been gathered were placed in the Stalin collection of the Moscow Central Party Archive. These included the recollections of the seventy-six-year-old, illiterate Yefrosina Alekseyeva, recorded in 1942: "J. V. Stalin lived for two months in my house. It all began when he arrived at my home and it was no use me saying that we were short of space. He went into the exiles' room, looked around, talked with his comrades, then moved in with the two other exiles. [...] He wore a Russian embroidered, open-necked white shirt, which left his chest exposed. [...] When he set off he said: 'I am leaving my books for the comrades.' My sons Yakov and Agafon took him by boat to the river port. Before his departure he offered us apples and sugar from the parcel he had received. It also contained two bottles of good vodka."[59]

Understandably, not even the Stalinist propaganda machinery was curious about the kind of stories recounted by the housewife Lukerya Tikhomirova, who was exactly twenty-five years old when, at a dance, she had bumped into "the Georgian, who was wearing a double-breasted black coat". The person had introduced himself as Dzhugashvili. Of greater interest to them were descriptions of how he had been preceded by his reputation: "We were expecting a great man", stated with pride the Georgian host that evening, locally known as "the Prince". Tikhomirova recalled that the guests were singing in Russian and Georgian, and were merrily dancing the *lezginka*: "Stalin sat modestly to the side. He drank hardly any alcohol. He played with my two-year-old niece. He sat her on his lap and offered her apples."[60]

It is possible that the exile Stalin was already thinking about escaping at this time. Perhaps this is why he appeared so detached and why he did not react to the young women's flirtatious remarks: "So young, and already smoking a pipe!" According to eyewitnesses he left Kolpashovo in very undramatic style: he simply got on board a small rowing boat before transferring to a larger riverboat.

Yakov Alekseyev, "an illiterate worker employed at the J. V. Stalin Museum," after being asked several times, recalled the moment of farewell as follows: "It was getting dark. My brother and I took him by row-boat to the river harbor. I asked him when he would return. He answered: 'Expect me when you see me.' He was standing there alone on the harbor jetty. We left. [...] A small box of books was left behind. The comrades helped themselves to what was there. My mother scolded them: 'Why are you taking them? He might need those books if he comes back.' But the comrades said that he would not return. Three days later we declared *[to the authorities—M. K.]* that he had gone and had not returned."[61]

Strangely enough nobody stopped Joseph Stalin at any of the river ports during his several-day-long boat trip, even though in Narym and its vicinity every third person was a political exile, watched by several dozen policemen and informers. Apparently the police were not in the habit of knocking on the door of "Comrade Koba's" lodgings several times a day, as they had done earlier in Solvychegodsk and Vologda. The Bolshevik politician was extremely fortunate that it was twenty-four hours before Inspector Titkov informed the district police prefect that Iosif Dzhugashvili, who had rented a flat together with the exiled Mikhail Nadezhdin, had escaped.[62]

"This was his fourth escape," wrote Leon Trotsky in his biography of Stalin.[63] Stalin himself, however, said otherwise in the 1920s, when answering questions addressed to him by the Stockholm correspondent of the first revolutionary news agency, Rosta: "I was arrested seven times. I was sentenced to exile on six occasions (to Irkutsk province, the Narym frontier zone, the Turukhansk frontier zone, etc.). I escaped five times and spent altogether seven years in prison.[64] In 1917 I lived in Russia illegally *[which was not true—M.K.]*, but spent no time abroad (I traveled abroad only occasionally on party business, including London, Berlin, Stockholm, and Cracow)."[65] In the lexicon article written by Stalin's personal secretary Ivan Tovstukha, five escapes are also mentioned. However, the escapes in September 1911 and February 1912 are not treated separately.[66] In the short biographical outline set down by Stalin himself in March 1920 as a participant at a congress of the Ukrainian Communist Party, we read the following: "From 1902 I was arrested eight times (up to 1913). I was sent into exile seven times and escaped six times. [...] From 1910 I was an agent of the Central Committee[67], and from 1912 a member of the Central Committee. [...]"[68] These contradictions are perhaps due to the fact that neither the General Secretary of the party nor his court biographers could decide whether or not to count as a "proper" escape the fact that in February/March 1911 he had traveled to the capital without permission and then, without being arrested, had *voluntarily* returned to Solvychegodsk, the original scene of his exile.

The fact remains that between September 12, 1912 and February 23, 1913 the notorious escapee had lived in freedom. He was the only member of the "Prague" Central Committee, apart from the traitor Roman Malinovsky, to spend time, with longer or shorter breaks, in St. Petersburg. The others—Spandaryan, Ordzhonikidze, and Goloshchokin—were "taken out of play" one after the other. Malinovsky was protected from this fate since the Okhrana were taking the utmost care of him. Besides, from autumn 1912 the "Russian Bebel" enjoyed exemption as a representative of the newly elected State Duma.

On the other hand, the police knew well in advance about Stalin's moves from the reports submitted by Malinovsky and another police agent, Miron Chernomazov, one of the editors of *Pravda*. Living deep in the underground movement Stalin also feared the street informers, who referred to him throughout their reports as "the Caucasian". He was unable to check into a hotel since the receptionists were all cooperating with the authorities. In the evenings, therefore, "Comrade Koba" would invite himself into the Alliluyev family home or to the home of one of his other acquaintances. On occasion he also submerged himself in the nightlife of St. Petersburg, wandering from one pub or teahouse to another. The dawn often found him in some alley or gateway, from where he would peer around cautiously to see whether he had been followed.[69]

1 *Krasny Arkhiv*, 1941, no. 2, 18–19.
2 *Ibid.*, 2–23.
3 *RGASPI*, fond. 17, op. 4, d. 647. It is interesting that in the beginning of the 1920s, Sila Todria, once a close friend of Stalin, became his main enemy among the Bolshevik leadership—and particularly in the Georgian party leadership circles' devastating battle. For a while, Todria was affiliated with the Georgian supporters of Lev Trotsky. Todria's early death was probably the only thing that prevented Stalin from crushing him during the years of the Great Terror. Nesostoyavshysya yubilei. 1992, 127, 129, 131, 139.
4 *Krasny Arkhiv*, 1941, no. 2, 23.
5 Voronsky, 1931, 410.
6 *Ibid.*
7 Avtorkhanov, 1973, vol. I, 20–206. Moreover, in his speech Semashko unquestionably referred to the lack of education among the "domestic" representatives, which makes it impossible for them to engage in debates with Yuly Martov or Leon Trotsky.
8 At the beginning of the twentieth century, almost the complete leadership of the Russian labor movement consisted of intellectuals coming from the bourgeoisie, even the nobility. The events of the 1906–1907 Russian revolution did produce a number of true worker-politician, but in emigration it was again the intellectuals who dominated the labor movement. This is why the attitude of "waiting for Bebel" became fashionable in the Russian Social Democratic movement. On occasion the German worker-politician's 70th birthday, on March 23, 1910, the Baku Committee of the RSDLP issued a leaflet, on which "Comrade Koba" emphasized that "for us, Russian workers, he should be the example. After all, we need the Bebels of the labor movement." Stalin, 1946, vol. II, 208.
9 *Gyelo Provokatora Malinovskogo*, 1992, 13, 49–51, 167. In the election following the long debate, fourteen of sixteen delegates present voted for Malinovsky.
10 Aleksandr Voronsky's novel on the party conference in Prague, which gave a colorful description of what happened in the Bohemian capital, was censored even during the years of *perestroyka*: besides the stylistic changes the editors made on the book, they also left out the positive references to Trotsky, Zinovyev, and Kamenev. Voronsky, 1987, 572–574. The writer was an important participant of the Prague meeting, and in the original version of the book, he cautiously suggested that Lenin basically manipulated the election of the Central Committee members. He induced, even forced the representatives to accept the nomination of Malinovsky. All along, the number one provocateur of Okhrana continuously reported on what happened at the 6th National Party Conference. Years after the conference, Voronsky once asked Lenin why he had trusted Malinovsky so much. The "Old Man" evaded responding to the question in embarrassment. Voronsky, 1931, 420. Ordzhonikidze, however, in his forged memoirs states that Lenin was suspicious of the "Russian Bebel". In his version, it was only the "domestic" delegates who insisted on voting for Malinovsky's membership in the Central Committee. *Gyelo Provokatora Malinovskogo*, 1992, 248–249.
11 This is what the book on the Prague Conference suggests, which does not contain the correspondence of those delegates and guests, who later became victims of the Great Terror. At the same time, the document collection includes several texts written by Stalin, which are not directly related to the history of the party conference. *Prazhskaya Konferentsia*, 1937, 14–19, 47–50. There are other sources that follow this approach, such as Moskalev, 1947, 52; Bagirov, 1948, 130; *Iosif Vissarionovich Stalin*, 1951, 50.
12 Trotsky, 1990, vol. I., 192–193.
13 Uratadze, 1968, 234.
14 Smith, 1967, 246–251.
15 Rozental, 1996, 112–113.
16 *Dyeyateli SSSR*, 1989, 163.
17 Lunacharsky, 1988, 241–242, 259–260.
18 Uratadze, 1968, 226–227.
19 "Comrade Sergo" sometimes did dare to challenge the Master of the Kremlin, but usually failed. Khlevnyuk, 1996, 84, 88, 91–93, 169–186.
20 Avtorkhanov, 1973, vol. I, 192–193.
21 *RGASPI*, fond. 74, op. 2, d. 38.

22 *Dyeyateli SSSR*, 1989, 87.
23 On their earlier underground activities they conducted together, see Smith, 1967, 215; *Soviet Studies*, 1973, no. 3, 374. They met in 1902. *RGASPI*, fond. 161, op. 1, d. 11.
24 Moskalev, 1947, 57–58. One of the distinctive merits that was attributed to Spandaryan is that on January 19, 1912, he assisted Lenin in the secret Leipzig negotiations with the invited "Leninst" delegates of the State Duma and several party representatives from Russia. During this meeting the two Bolshevik politicians aimed to convince the guests that the "Prague line" is the correct one. Once Spandaryan returned home, he gave a number of speeches on the resolutions of the Prague conference in Riga, St. Petersburg, Moscow, Baku, and Tiflis. In March, however, he was arrested.
25 Rozalia Zemlyachka was a popular Bolshevik party leader at the beginning of the century. She was among the few old underground activists who was spared during the Great Terror. What is more, she served in a number of important positions until her death, because for some reason Stalin respected her very much.
26 Nicolaevsky, 1965, 134, 7–9.
27 Rozental, 1996, 110–111.
28 The word "line", as well as the term "central directive" later became important elements in the Orwellian vocabulary of the Soviet *newspeak*. They are the products of the language innovations during the period of underground activities.
29 *RGASPI*, fond. 558, op. 4, d. 211.
30 It seems that at that time "Comrade Koba" started to use his new byname, Stalin, more and more frequently.
31 *RGASPI*, fond. 17, op. 4, d. 647. Due to the screening by the postal censors, Ordzhonikidze's letter reached Lenin with a great delay, who was upset that his "Man in Russia" was silent. "There isn't any news about Ivanovich. What happened to him? Where is he now? How is he? [...] There aren't many useful comrades. Not even in the capital," wrote Lenin on March 15, 1912. In Trotsky's interpretation of these words, this indicated that the party leadership in exile did not know anything about Stalin because the Georgian Bolshevik "worked behind the scenes". Trotsky, 1990, vol. I, 195. This long silence, however, was not unusual among the underground party activists working in Russia. They were simply afraid to be caught because of their correspondence with Paris. To make the situation easier, Stalin agreed with Nadezhda Krupskaya at the beginning of 1912 or 1913 to use Gorky's poem *Oltenian Legend* for coding their correspondence. Among the documents of the Soviet dictator, his handwritten copy of the poem also survived, with Krupskaya's notes on the side: "1912, 1913??" *RGASPI*, fond. 558, op. 1, d. 5167.
32 *Bolsheviki*, 1990, 160.
33 *Istorik Marksist*, 1940, no. 9, 25–26.
34 *Krasny Arkhiv*, 1941, no. 2, 25.
35 Avalov, 1982, 38, 57, 92, 286.
36 *RGASPI*, fond. 558, op. 4, d. 5085.
37 Stalin, 1946, vol. II, 213–218.
38 *RGASPI*, fond. 558, op. 4, d. 3223.
39 *Krasny Arkhiv*, 1941, no. 2, 25.
40 *RGASPI*, fond. 17, op. 4, d. 647.
41 The best received among these articles was the one he wrote on the line-firing massacre against the workers of the Siberian gold mines along the river Lena. Its title "It has started..." referred to the anticipated progression of the Russian revolutionary movement. Stalin, 1946, vol. II, 237–240.
42 Stalin, 1946, vol. II, 248–249.
43 This detail from the letter, which was not quite flattering for the dictator, was marked by a separate slip in the catalogue by the archival assistants of the Stalin collection. See *RGASPI*, fond. 71, op. 10, d. 407.
44 Ordzhonikidze, 1967, 128–129.
45 *Krasny Arkhiv*, 1938, no. 1, 183; *Krasny Arkhiv*, 1941, no. 2, 26.
46 Stalin, 1946, vol. II, 219.
47 *RGASPI*, fond. 17, op. 4, d. 647.
48 *Krasny Arkhiv*, 1941, no. 2, 26.
49 *Bolsheviki*, 1990, 173.
50 *RGASPI*, fond. 161, op. 1, d. 20. Cf. Moskalev, 1947, 71.
51 Ordzhonikidze, 1967, 128–135, 145–148.
52 Kristof, 1972, 23–24.
53 *Istorichesky Zhurnal*, 1940, no. 1, 65.
54 *Narimskaya Khronika*, 1997, 37–38, 78, 123.
55 *Ibid.*, 10–11, 15, 45–46, 53–65, 77, 106–119, 169–181.
56 Souvarine, 1939, 133. The author, who visited, one after the other, Stalins's former emigré acquaintances, did not provide a precise source here. This work, valuable as it was at the time of its publication, first appeared in 1935 in French, and was generally received positively among the Russian socialist refugees. See *Sotsialistichesky Vestnik*, 1935, no. 21, 10, 11–13.

57 The sources that did survive were set aside or falsified by the Soviet censors. Narimskaya Ssilka, 1970, 94–107.
58 Chernenko, 1942, 74–79.
59 *RGASPI*, fond. 558, op. 4, d. 647.
60 *Ibid.*
61 *Ibid.*
62 Chernenko, 1942, 78–79. Four days later the postal censorship intercepted a letter which arrived from the north Russian town of Verkhny Ustya. The writer of the letter, a certain Georgy asked an exile named A. F. Mostayev, who lived in Kolpashovo at that time, "if Iosif Dzhugashvili is with them … or elsewhere." *RGASPI*, fond. 71, op. 10, d. 407.
63 Trotsky, 1990, vol. I, 99.
64 This is quite an exaggeration. Even if we include the time he spent in transit prisons and prison hospitals, the total amounts to less than four years.
65 *RGASPI*, fond. 558, op. 1, d. 4507.
66 *Dyeyateli SSSR*, 1989, 107–110..
67 In fact, from 1911.
68 *RGASPI*, fond. 558, op. 1, d. 1594.
69 Alliluyeva, 1946, 114.

Feliks Dzerzhinsky (x) was not as close to Stalin to Aleksei Rykov (xx), who was the head of the Council of the People's Commissars, the first government after the death of Stalin.

Feliks Dzerzhinsky

Dzerzhinsky (x) and the first leaders of the Soviet political police (the VCHK, GPU, then OGPU). Stalin first sought to utilize their "expertise" in the power struggle against his antagonists, then executed them, one-by- one, save for Dzerzhinsky.

In the January of 1924, Dzerzhinsky (1) led the committee organizing Lenin's funeral. In the first picture one can also see Lashevich (2) and Voroshilov (3). In less than two years, in the midst of a heated political debate, the director of the OGPU died of a heart attack.

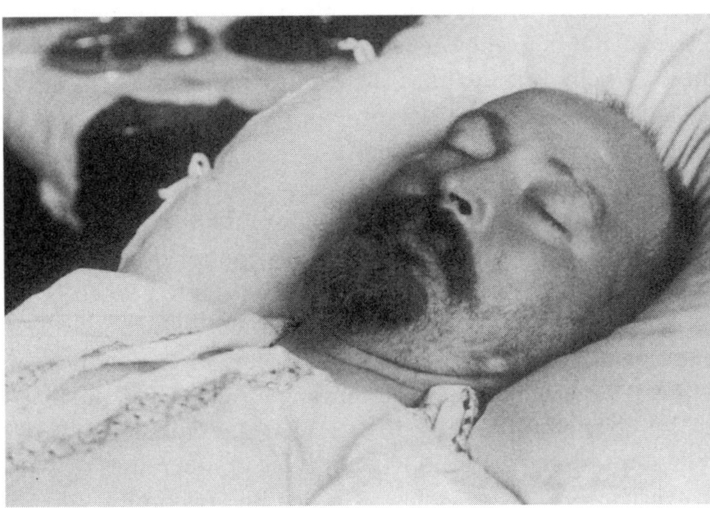

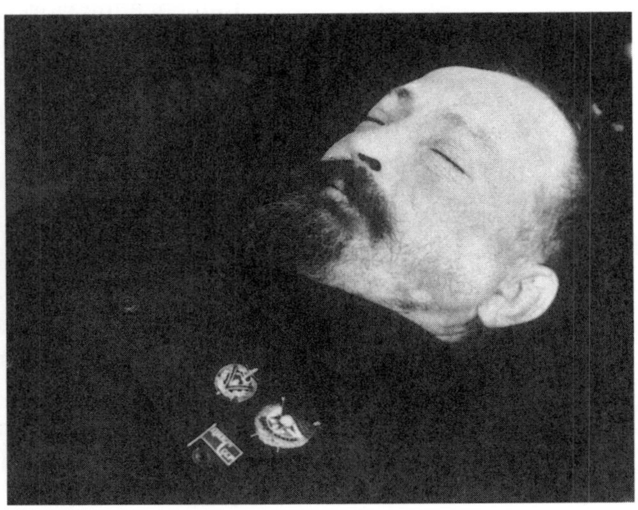

CHAPTER 8
Why Learn Foreign Languages?

After his escape, Joseph Stalin found his hunted existence increasingly hard to bear, thus he would sometimes go "underground" for a few days, disappearing into the apartment of one his wealthy sympathizers. After the opening of the new State Duma, in the evenings he would knock on the doors of the Bolshevik deputies, who enjoyed immunity.[1] "Comrade Koba" was mainly in touch with the Bolshevik workers who had become professional politicians at the end of the election campaign. This was mostly in relation to his work in St. Petersburg, since as soon as he arrived in the capital he joined in the election struggle being waged through the columns of the Bolshevik press.[2] The result of the election, however, was a disappointment to the Bolshevik leadership. Voting took place in several rounds and votes were cast and counted by class and property groups (*curias*), therefore workers and peasants were discriminated against and Lenin's party was able to return only six representatives to the 442-seat Russian Parliament. Nevertheless, with their seven representatives the Menshevik "Liquidators", who in practice had rejected illegal activity, fared little better, despite the fact that their activities were more and more integrated in the work being carried out in the trade unions, workers' sick benefit societies, and cultural associations.

The activity of the Bolsheviks in the Duma was further complicated by the fact that, unlike the unscrupulous but sharp-minded Malinovsky, the other five representatives (Petrovsky, Muralov, Badayev, Samoylov, and Sagov) were uncertain of their movements in parliamentary life. They were, without exception, uneducated manual workers, whose correspondence was carried on in ill-formed, childish handwriting. They were quite unable to make meaningful contributions to the debates conducted in the Tauride Palace where the Duma met. A large advisory committee comprising party intellectuals was therefore set up to help these "simple sons of the people". Before some of the more important interpellations the six representatives even consulted Lenin and Zinovyev abroad. In addition, they received drafts of speeches and statistical data from the emigrants Kamenev and Bukharin.[3]

The Bolshevik "Foreign Center", under the pretext of giving advice, tried to influence the worker representatives in the State Duma, who for their part were only too glad to make use of the help they received. Malinovsky, however, was being controlled by others as well, thus the tone of the ultra-radical speeches that he delivered to the Russian Parliament was set sometimes by Lenin and Zinovyev, and sometimes by the leaders of the Okhrana.

It is strange but the two points of view occasionally coincided. While the Bolshevik "Foreign Center" regarded Malinovsky as the most important figure in Russia in keeping "the spirit of Prague" alive, the tsarist political police were also keen for their agent, under the byname "the Men's Tailor", to spread radical ideas in the Parliament. His speeches scared the government, which now and again loosened the iron grip of tyranny, for instance by forcing the tsar to accept the constitution of October 1905, which included, among other things, the election of a State Duma. Malinovsky's speeches discouraged the Russian government from taking further steps along the road to bourgeois democracy.

By autumn 1912 the avaricious Roman Malinovsky, leading his double life, in many respects had the illegal apparatus of the domestic Bolsheviks in his control. His mentors, both in St. Petersburg and abroad, of course irrespective of each other hoped that alongside his fellow Bolshevik representatives he could generate as many scandals in the State Duma as possible. This would increase the chances of Tsar Nikolai II dissolving the Russian Parliament. Malinovsky, who, due to the tensions inherent in his double life, would eventually escape into alcoholism and lavish spending, achieved the approbation of both the Bolshevik "Foreign Center" and the Okhrana. Sometimes openly, and sometimes as a result of behind-the-scenes intrigue, he stirred up controversy between the Bolshevik and Menshevik wings of the Social Democratic faction, the thirteen members of which had initially sympathized with one another and had generally acted together.[4] The "Russian Bebel" was encouraged to make trouble by Lenin, who was convinced that, following the Prague conference of January 1912, the splitting of the Russian Social Democrats—in contemporary party jargon, the "splitting of the sheaf of wheat"—might take years.[5]

Inessa Armand, the great love of Lenin's life, who was an agent of the Bolshevik "Foreign Center" operating to Russia.

The increasingly prominent worker politician, who not long before had been the favorite of the "Liquidator" Mensheviks, had secretly, it seems, similarly radical views. The other Bolshevik representatives in the Fourth State Duma, however, for a while still resisted the pressure exerted by the "Foreign Center". Since the significant majority of the editorial board and contributors to *Pravda* came from "conciliatory" Bolshevik circles, for many months they sabotaged Lenin's orders, according to which the paper was to launch a campaign against the Liquidators. They even censored the writings of Lenin and Zinovyev, which supported the anti-Liquidator stance. After a while, by way of "punishment", they stopped transferring payment for articles to foreign-based "consistently Leninist" authors, even though they represented the main thrust of the paper. [6] This made Lenin furious. In the autumn of 1912 he tried to bring order among the domestic party workers. Earlier on he had had the people to do this, since before the elections he had given full powers to Inessa Armand and Georgy Safarov,[7] two envoys of the Bolshevik "Foreign Center", whom he sent to St. Petersburg and to whom he had given detailed instructions in Cracow before their mission to Russia. In the middle of September, however, when the two "traveling agents" were finally able to get down to the uniformization of the "domestic" party leadership and the editorial board of *Pravda*, they were both arrested by the Okhrana. Thus a huge space was opened up in the "domestic" illegal apparatus, which, it was planned, would mainly be filled by Joseph Stalin who had escaped from Siberia. Apparently Lenin intended the same role for him as had been assigned at the beginning of the year to Sergo Ordzhonikidze, then in the summer to "Comrade Inessa" and Safarov. They had been ordered to radicalize party work in Russia, thus burning the last bridge between the Bolsheviks and Mensheviks.

Initially "Comrade Koba" was not lacking in enthusiasm: since the Caucasian robberies he had perhaps never put so much energy into illegal work. However, after a few weeks of activity in St. Petersburg news reached Lenin that his number one "agent" was becoming "soft". In the autumn of 1912 "the Old Man" unsuccessfully tried to force Stalin to take a firmer stance against the Bolshevik "Conciliators", basing his authority on his Central Committee membership. However, the old Baku *komitetchik*, or "domestic" party committee militant, was apparently reawaken in Stalin, who opposed the émigrés and thought little of them and their advice. Furthermore, in St. Petersburg he must have found that the majority of Bolshevik workers got along well with the Mensheviks and that he would not be at all popular if he stirred up conflicts between them. Thus, by the end of October, his decisions were less and less influenced by the uncompromising instructions that arrived for him from abroad, sometimes via conspiratorial channels and sometimes through the post in cryptic letters. Lenin, the master of political intrigue, therefore changed tactics. On two occasions, at the end of November 1912 and again in late December, he ordered Joseph Stalin, along with a few other Bolshevik politicians, to attend meetings abroad so that he could put them on the right track.[8]

From the reports of the agents planted in the movement it seems the Okhrana knew of the session of the Central Committee led by Lenin to be held in November in Cracow. The authorities intended to arrest those planning to attend the meeting en route: "Koba Dzhugashvili [...] is in contact with a worker called Badayev, in whose company he intends to travel to meet with Lenin", we read in an official memo. "If those watching him do find him, please do not arrest him immediately. They should rather do so immediately before his departure abroad."[9]

Joseph Stalin, however, suspected that without reliable documents he would not get through the strict border controls. Although he had a passport in the name of a Persian merchant, which fitted his Oriental appearance, he still felt it to be inadequate. Therefore, at the end of October, in the company of Valentina Lobova, whose byname was "Comrade Vera", he traveled from St. Petersburg to Finland to obtain a passport. On the basis of police photographs of her Valentina must have been a very attractive, energetic woman. Her actions were quite typical of the emancipated women in the movement: she rented a hotel room with a man she barely knew and left her one-and-a-half-year-old child at home for several weeks while she traveled abroad. She was exposing herself to serious danger: at the Finland station in St. Petersburg Stalin had to get rid of the street informers, and later they had to dodge the Okhrana agents who had been sent after them to the port of Abo.[10]

The couple in hiding from the authorities chose to travel to the Grand Duchy of Finland since citizens could easily obtain a passport there for a small sum of money. They only had to pay five Finnish marks, that is, one ruble and eighty-five kopecks. An old Bolshevik party member by the name of Aleksandr Shotman had the necessary contacts and he moved quickly, aware that they were following Lenin's orders.[11] Stalin showed little gratitude later. Shotman, a renowned militant in the Russian and Finnish labor movement and someone whom Lenin had greatly loved, fell into one of Stalin's execution quotas at the end of the 1930s. When he was taken away from their home his wife turned to their old friend, Mikhail Kalinin, for help. She wrote how "Stalin must have seen me [in Helsinki, then Helsingfors]. He must remember me from Finland, since in 1912 I helped to organize his journey abroad."[12] However, the unfortunate woman not only failed to help her husband, but landed herself in even deeper trouble by calling attention to her own role. She, too, was taken away before long.

Using the passport he had obtained in Finland Stalin was able to set off to see Lenin in autumn 1912. Hardly any information survives about this trip, which was undertaken in the greatest secrecy—not even the most dedicated researchers into the life of the dictator have been able to find out much about what happened. We know for certain that on November 12 Stalin was already in Cracow: "I arrived after great difficulties", he wrote to the editors of the St. Petersburg Bolshevik journal *Prosveshchenie*, from whom he requested a brief assessment of events following his departure.[13]

In the meantime, on November 12 and 13 Stalin talked from morning to night with Lenin, Zinovyev, and a few "domestic" party workers, including Bolshevik parliamentary representatives. It is strange that the chronology contained in the history of the State Duma's Bolshevik faction does not even mention Stalin's role in Cracow.[14] The chronology in the second volume of Stalin's Collected Works, which the dictator carefully discussed with the compilers, states only that: "Before 10 November J. V. Stalin arrived in Cracow illegally to see V. I. Lenin."[15]

It is also difficult to understand why the twelve-volume chronology of Lenin's life, which appeared in the 1970s in the period of re-Stalinization, makes no mention at all of "Comrade Koba's" first trip to Cracow. The editors of the volume mention only the letter sent by Stalin to Lenin following the meeting. In this letter the politician asked whether he could refer to the opinion of the "domestic" party workers in front of international Socialist bodies.[16]

It is clear that events that took place during the two trips to Poland later became merged in Stalin's memory when he fed his acquaintances with tales of his impressions of Cracow. We learn from the memoirs of his sister-in-law, Anna Alliluyeva, that as the train neared the Russian border he claimed to have reprimanded two fellow travelers for reading to each other aloud from the far-right *Chornaya sotnya* newspaper.[17] According to another of his stories, in the marketplace of a small town on the Russian/Austro-Hungarian border, he made the acquaintance of a poor Polish artisan. Once Stalin had told him he was a Georgian his new well-wisher, who had taken to him immediately, offered to smuggle him across the border. This was extremely useful for "Comrade Koba", who, for reasons of security, had just been forced to tear into pieces the address of the smuggler he had intended to use. Stalin's sister-in-law, or the journalist Nina Bam who edited the memoirs for style, embellished the episode with a rather charming story: "As darkness fell the two men stepped out of the house. On saying farewell at the border Stalin offered some money in return for the man's hospitality and help. But his companion pushed away his hand. 'No!' he said firmly. 'I don't want it! I didn't do it for the money. We, the children of oppressed nations, must help one another!' And with a firm handshake he bade farewell to Stalin: 'A safe journey to you!' I heard this story many years later in Moscow, after the October Revolution. After telling the story Stalin became pensive, as if lost in the past: 'I would like to know', he said slowly, 'where that man is now. What happened to him? What a pity I have forgotten his name and am unable trace him.'"[18]

Perhaps the man in question was still alive when, as part of the secret final clause of the Molotov-Ribbentrop Pact, Red Army troops marched into Galicia in the autumn of 1939. Had he fallen into Stalin's "quota" of Poles, which claimed the lives of more than 150,000 people, he would indeed have appreciated the belated gratitude of the Soviet dictator.[19]

In December 1941, almost thirty years after the conspiratorial journey, at a banquet in the Kremlin attended by Stanisław Kot, the Moscow ambassador of the London-based Polish émigré government, Joseph Stalin described how, on the other side of the border, he had gone into a restaurant in Trzebnia. He had summoned the waiter several times in Russian, and the waiter had ignored him contemptuously as a result. The embarrassed traveler was finally shown mercy by one of the staff who unceremoniously set a bowl of soup in front of him. Stalin then somehow got as far as Cracow on the slow train but for a long time could not find Lenin's apartment. When they finally met his first words were "Give me something to eat! I'm starving. I haven't eaten since yesterday evening." On hearing the story of what had happened in the restaurant his host gave his guest a good ticking off: "How foolish of you, Stalin! [...] Didn't you know the Poles regard Russian as the language of their oppressors?"[20]

The story doubtless belongs to the world of legend. We know today that, in reality, on both the occasions he traveled to Poland Stalin made a huge detour, using his Finnish passport, going via Germany to Cracow.[21] If this is the case, why was he prowling in the bushes on the Russian/Austro-Hungarian border, accompanied by his Polish companion who had turned up to sympathize with the Georgian revolutionary? How did he fail to know the addresses of Lenin and Zinovyev in Cracow, when earlier he had written them down several times? And why would he have insisted on talking in Russian to the contemptuous waiters when he was armed with a bilingual phrase book, *What a Russian Should Know in Germany*, which would have equipped him to order food in German in the restaurant.[22]

What is easier to understand is why he did not mention to Anna Alliluyeva or Stanisław Kot the name of his traveling companion on his trips to meet Lenin. Following the revolution in February 1917, the name of Valentina Lobova would have been poorly received. When the Okhrana archives were opened it turned out that her husband, the journalist Aleksandr Lobov, had been one of the best informers of the tsarist secret police and had only been dismissed by his masters in 1913 after becoming a chronic alcoholic. By that time he had betrayed his comrades one by one and for this, five years later, he was executed by order of the Revolutionary Court. The episode had cast a shadow over his wife as well. The majority of researchers still believe that the woman, who died in 1924 of tuberculosis in St. Petersburg, was innocent.[23] There are some historians, however, who do not exclude the possibility that Valentina Lobova also collaborated with the Russian political police.[24]

In any case it was Valentina Lobova, who at the time enjoyed the full confidence of the "Foreign Center", who fulfilled the role of interpreter during the long foreign journey as Stalin's companion. The Bolshevik politician had absolutely no talent for languages. Over the years he perfected only Russian, although, like the majority of his fellow countrymen, he was incapable of eradicating his strong, characteristic Georgian accent. Perhaps this was partly because he began to learn Russian, the state language of the tsarist empire, relatively late, at the age of eleven. By his thirties Russian had become his second native language, and with neophyte fervor he often sprinkled his conversations with old-fashioned phrases, proverbs, and quotations from the Russian classics.

The German language, which he began to learn at a fairly early age, proved to be a much more difficult task. In the early years of the century German was traditionally the international language of the labor movement, while French was regarded as a sign of belonging to "higher" circles. "Comrade Koba", both in prison and during his periods of exile, studied German expressions diligently but made little progress. Nevertheless, as dictator a whole legendary was created around his knowledge of German. One of his former fellow exiles, Vera Shweitzer, even claimed that during the First World War Stalin had studied the writings of Rosa Luxemburg in the original and had even begun to translate one of her works.[25]

From the letters referred to below we learn that besides German Iosif Dzhugashvili also failed to learn French, although the postcard he sent to France from distant Siberia, from the Turukhansk frontier zone, makes it obvious how hard he tried: "Paris (XIII), M-r Bielynski, 22 rue Maurice-Mayer France. February 27, 1914. Com[rade]! Rumor has it that in Paris there is an association to help

In the Russian police files, there remained very little data on Stalin's journey to Cracow, during which he used a pseudonym and a false passport. During this journey, perhaps he dressed like on this picture taken in 1908, which is originally from the collection of the Ukrainian Gendarmerie, then later thoroughly retouched in the years of the Soviet rule.

Russian exiles, and I believe you are a member of this society. I am therefore writing to ask you, if at all possible, to please send me a French-Russian pocket dictionary and a few issues of some English newspapers. I received your address from an exile by the name of Bograd. If necessary, you can ask about me from Y. Kamenev,[26] to whom I sent my cordial greetings. Iosif Dzhugashvili, exile. My address is: Turukhansk frontier zone, Yenisei province, the village of Kostino."[27] On March 4, 1915 Vera Shweitzer wrote to one of her women friends in St. Petersburg: "Get hold of a copy of the one-ruble Ollendorff course book for home students and send it urgently, C.O.D., to Iosif Dzhugashvili. His address is the same as mine."[28]

In parallel with this Stalin began to learn English as well: "I send warmest greetings to you and V[ladimir] Frey. I am writing to let you know once again that I received your letter. Did you get mine? I am waiting for you to send all the Kostrov books. I ask you once again to send the books by Stirner, Pannekoek, and K[arl] K[autsky].[29] In addition, I would be very grateful if you could send me an English-language (preferably social-science-related) journal", he wrote on May 20, 1914 to Grigory Zinovyev, then living in emigration in Poronin, Galicia. "It doesn't matter whether it's an old or new issue. The important thing is that I read it in English. I'm afraid I will forget everything I've learned if I don't practice the language. For some reason I no longer receive copies of *Pravda.* Do you know anyone who can send me regular copies of the paper? And has [Otto] Bauer[30] answered? Could you send me the addresses of Troyanovsky and Bukharin? I send greetings to your wife and to N[adezhda] K[rupskaya] with a warm handshake. Where is Ro[zen]feld? I am very well."[31]

There is a rather interesting story attached to the English course book. An anarchist exile, Aleksei Ulanovsky, later the New York agent of the NKVD, once borrowed it from Stalin without the owner's knowledge. Nadezhda Ulanovskaya, who later, like her husband, spent years in the Gulag, recalled: "When the sledge delivering my husband went past his [Stalin's] house, Alyosha asked permission from the gendarmes accompanying the sledge to call in on Stalin and take something from him for the long journey, as was customary among exiles. His partner was cooking *pirozhki.* She was rolling the dough on pages torn out of a book by Kant. Alyosha took down Stalin's sheepskin coat from the hook. Then he started to look for something to read in the room. He found only pamphlets dealing with the nationality issue, and the popular English course book. He took it with him."[32]

Without a course book the future Master of the Kremlin had to stop learning English for a while. Following the Bolshevik takeover in October 1917 he could of course have had a language teacher. However, he stuck to the method he had chosen for himself, despite the fact that it led to such disappointing results: "I don't have with me in the *dacha* the Meskovsky course book for home students, which follows the Rosenthal method. Please find it and send it on to me!" he wrote to his wife, Nadezhda Alliluyeva, on September 8, 1930.[33]

By way of a fourth language he tried his hand at Esperanto, which, in the early years of the century, was spreading rapidly among Social Democrats in Russia who used the artificial language in their correspondence with their fellow Social Democrats abroad. "Comrade Koba" was of the opinion that it would soon be the language of the Socialist International.[34] He could have had little idea at the time that, at the very end of the 1920s, and later during the Great Terror, the political police, acting on his personal command, would, in two major waves, round up all the renowned Soviet Esperantists—among them the translators of Stalin's works—and, accusing them of persistently maintaining contacts abroad as well as of being dangerous spies and counterrevolutionaries, would have them eliminated in prisons and the Gulag.

☆ By then Joseph Stalin already knew that he had no need for foreign languages in order to achieve what he wanted. Rather than that he had to learn the "technology of power" from, among others, Lenin and the other leaders of the Bolshevik Party. The dictator was to continue perfecting this knowledge until the end of his life. He learned that sometimes, even with gritted teeth, it was better to give way. This is precisely what happened in the course of his second visit to Cracow in December 1912, when, following a certain amount of resistance, he repeatedly acquiesced to Lenin's demands.

There were at least fifteen people present at the meeting, eight from the Bolshevik emigration and seven representing "domestic" party workers. The decisions accepted by the participants were later published in a pamphlet edited by Lenin, but the original minutes of the speeches still have not been found. Events can be reconstructed largely from the memoirs of Nadezhda Krupskaya, written during Stalin's dictatorship. From the few short, diffident sentences written by the Bolshevik party leader's widow, Leon Trotsky concluded that there had been serious differences of opinion between Stalin and Lenin in terms of the tactics to be followed. The disciple, however, who at the time was more conciliatory than his ultra-radical teacher, finally gave in to "the Old Man" in the interests of his own political career.[35]

Several further indications of this can be mentioned. Almost one and a half years before the Cracow conference, in August 1911, the Bolshevik Mikhail Lashevich, an exile, wrote in a letter intercepted by the postal censors that Koba, then living in Vologda, "corresponds with the Mensheviks". In Lashevich's view he "will not bark at the Liquidators or the Leftist Bolsheviks. If Koba writes in this way, what can be expected from others. This is why they [the Mensheviks] are winning", exclaimed Lashevich, who was an unconditional follower of Leninist orthodoxy.[36] The letter reveals that Stalin, despite his Central Committee membership, resisted Lenin for a while directly before the Prague meeting in January 1912. The discussions at the second meeting in Cracow focused mostly on whether the anti-Menshevik attacks should be eased, or, on the contrary, in accordance with the "spirit of Prague", a new campaign should be launched against the moderate Social Democrats. As Lenin's notes reveal he remained isolated as a result of his ultra-radical stance in Cracow. Of the more influential "domestic" speakers, only Roman Malinovsky supported the "Old Man", posing as the uncompromising Saint-Just. Stalin, however, even on the penultimate day of the meeting on December 31, 1912—although by then it was clear that things would go Lenin's way—still argued that there was no room for an excessively aggressive policy. He made clear the extent of the pressure exerted on the Bolshevik leadership "from below" by the workers, who almost without exception supported the alliance with the Mensheviks.[37]

Also on the agenda at the Cracow conference, which took place in the greatest secrecy, were the wave of strikes sweeping through the tsarist empire, the establishment of illegal Bolshevik institutions, the Bolshevik tactics to be employed in legislation, labor insurance, and the tone of *Pravda*, which Lenin found too conciliatory. Nadezhda Krupskaya, however, dared refer to these issues only with extreme caution in her memoirs, which were published in the early 1930s: "Ilich was very concerned about *Pravda*. So was Stalin. They discussed possible solutions."[38] For "Comrade Koba", however, the story of the Cracow meeting

Between September 1912 and May 1913, Lenin lived in this Cracow house with his family, where Stalin visited him three times.

went beyond such conflicts. The youngest participant was Olga Veyland, a teacher who appeared no more than a teenager. At the very end of 1912 she became part of his life for a short while. Three and a half decades later, shortly before the seventieth birthday of the Master of the Kremlin, she recalled those days in the article "In Austrian Emigration": "The apartment used by the Lenins comprised two small rooms and a kitchen. From the hallway a door opened to the right. It was there that the participants at the meeting held their discussions. [...] On that particular day I sensed a kind of buzz, a special feeling of alertness. Another comrade had arrived from Russia, whom they had been eagerly awaiting. This was Koba, a member of the Central Committee. [...] Vladimir Ilich talked with him at great length."[39]

In the 1960s I myself met Olga Veyland, at the home of the historian Vladimir Turok-Popov in Moscow. Like her, he had spent part of his youth in Vienna. Physically shrunken but mentally completely alert, the old lady was initially slightly uneasy at finding herself in the company of people, friends of the historian's mother-in-law, named Antonova, who had returned from the Gulag. One of them, for instance, instead of introducing himself, asked her sardonically: "Don't you have any interesting stories about your good friend the 'gardener'?"[40] In her confusion Olga Veyland made a few sarcastic remarks about Stalin, perhaps because she recognized how deeply he was hated by those present: "Koba had problems with cleanliness. I washed many of his shirts in Vienna. They were filthy. He never washed his hands before lunch, and when he got up from the table he would belch with satisfaction." However, towards the end of the conversation the elderly woman shyly revealed that in Cracow, and then in Vienna, Stalin had been very fond of her. However, at the time she had been attracted to someone else—"although, to tell the truth, only in a platonic way, to that kind ladies' man, Nikolai Ivanovich." When I asked whom she meant the half dozen people gathered in the small room laughed out loud. Having spent time in the forced-labor camps themselves, these former *lagernik*s knew that the woman was talking about Nikolai Bukharin, who, in the early 1910s, had also lived in the Austrian capital.

His name is not mentioned, however, in the draft of Olga Veyland's memoirs. With respect to Stalin, on the other hand, she described how his speeches at the Cracow conference had had a great impact on her: "Koba did not speak very loudly. He talked in a deliberate, measured manner. He set out his thoughts with indisputable logic. Sometimes he went through to the other room so he could pace up and down while listening to the speeches of the other comrades."[41]

According to her recollections "Comrade Koba", who had arrived in Cracow from St. Petersburg, spent a great deal of time with his host. Following one discussion, which went on long into the night, he did not even return to his lodgings but slept in the kitchen at the Ilich apartment on a blanket on the floor. At the home of Turok-Popov she remembered that in Lenin's presence the Georgian, who otherwise often appeared rather morose, made every effort to avoid grimacing. He was unable to suppress his nervous yawn, however, for which the chairman of the meeting, Grigory Zinovyev, once reprimanded him.

Interestingly, in a letter written to fellow Caucasian Lev Kamenev at the very end of 1912, Stalin cautiously expressed his hope that Lenin would, in the end, give in to him and accept that in the given situation in Russia "it was better to work and to postpone hard politics for a while". Besides, he trusted that he could successfully win over to the Bolsheviks two of the Menshevik representatives in the State Duma. Until then he did not want a serious confrontation either with them, or their colleagues. He wrote that the Bolshevik parliamentary group of six, consisting exclusively of workers, required a leader.[42] He meant himself, of course, but in this respect he was to be disappointed. Lenin, who expended so much energy on "building up" Joseph Stalin, had no intention of giving up his "remote control" of the Bolshevik representatives in the State Duma. The only concession he made to the "domestic" Bolsheviks was that he carefully listened to what they, including "Comrade Koba", had to say, after which everything remained as it had been.

On December 30 or 31 in 1912, despite the vigorous debate, we know for certain that a 180-degree turn was achieved at the Cracow conference. The decision to reprimand the Liquidators and to set the editorial stance of *Pravda* on a more radical track bear the mark of the Bolshevik party leader. In the late evening of December 31, Lenin reported on his victory to the absent Lev Kamenev: "*All* the decisions are being accepted *unanimously*. [...] A huge success!"[43]

Following the initial tension the participants gradually relaxed: "The Bolshevik representatives of the State Duma did not travel home immediately," wrote Olga Veyland in her memoirs. "We decided to go to the theater. But the play was very bad. Vladimir Ilich sat for a while in his seat, then stood up and left with his wife. On New Year's Eve [...] we rented a room in one of the restaurants. Lenin seemed very cheerful. He was joking and laughing. He started singing and even joined in the games we were playing."[44]

1 Samoylov, 1934, 303.
2 Stalin, 1946, vol. II, 250–265.
3 During the years of the Great Terror, it was forbidden to write about this. See *Bolshevistkaya Fraktsia*, 1938, 74–104.
4 Rozental, 1996, 105–106.
5 Aronson, 1986, 24–62.
6 Trotsky, 1990, vol. I, 202–207.
7 The beautiful woman was the great love of Lenin. According to her contemporaries, she was one of the most beautiful women of the age. Vinogradskaya, 1968, 219. On Inessa Armand, see also, Elwood, 1992, 92–95. Safarov, who was very young then, was Nadezhda Krupskaya's relative: the Ulyanovs thus saw him as a kind of "surrogate child".
8 After the National Conference held in Prague, Lenin and Zinovyev moved to Cracow mostly to live closer to the Russian border. Lev Kamenev, on the other hand, stayed in Paris, mostly because he did not have the money to leave. The election campaign exhausted most of the Bolshevik reserves, thus Lenin and Zinovyev was forced to withdraw the earlier allowance from Kamenev, the third member of the "Foreign Center". Lenin, 1999, 113–114.
9 *Krasny Arkhiv*, 1941, no. 2, 28. The Okhrana made mistakes sometimes when it wanted to control Stalin's conspiratory travels. According to another report, for example, the Bolshevik politician visited Lenin in Paris in December 1911. The secret police was convinced that Stalin established contacts with a certain Pyotr Petrovich Shumkin there. *RGASPI*, fond. 71, op. 10, d. 407. However, "Comrade Koba" never went to Paris, and in December 1911, he stayed in Sila Todria's apartment in St. Petersburg, hardly leaving it, before taking off to Vologda Protectorate, to the site of his exile.
10 *Krasny Arkhiv*, 1941, no. 2, 28.
11 Shotman, 1935, 166–176.
12 Tolmachev, 1963, 226.
13 *Istorichesky Arkhiv*, 1960, no. 2, 20. Nadezhda Krupskaya, the director of the underground apparatus of the Bolshevik "Foreign Center", addressed the envelope.
14 *Bolshevistskaya Fraktsia*, 1938, 601.
15 Stalin, 1946, vol. II, 420.
16 *Biograficheskaya Khronika*, 1971, vol. II, 54. The date of the letter signed "K. Stalin, member of the C[entral] C[ommittee]" is December 2, 1912.
17 *Chornie Sotny*, or "Black Hundreds" was a far right, anti-Semitic, pogrom-inciting organization at the turn of the century.
18 Alliluyeva, 1946, 115–117.
19 *Katyń*, 1999, 15–16, 23–26, 29–36.
20 Kot, 1963, XX–XXVI.

21 Smith, 1967, 264–265.
22 The police confiscated the book from Stalin when he was arrested on February 23, 1913. *RGASPI*, fond. 71, op. 10, d. 407.
23 *Delo Provokatora Malinovskogo*, 1992, 277. It is interesting that Malinovsky, who seemingly considered Lobova as a rival, accused her of being an *agent provocateur*. Rozental, 1996, 162.
24 Felshtinsky, 1999, 9.
25 Sweitzer, 1943, 16.
26 At that time, Lev Kamenev often signed his articles as "Yuly" Kamenev.
27 *RGASPI*, fond. 558, op. 1, d. 51. After March 31, 1936, Stalin had a chance to read this postcard again. His former mentor and friend had already spent his ten-year sentence in prison at that time, and he was going to be executed soon. This is probably why the dictator sent back the letter to Sorin, one of the leaders of the Marx–Engels–Lenin Institute, telling him that it is unpublishable.
28 *RGASPI*, fond. 558, op. 4, d. 242.
29 "Frey" was one of Lenin's bynames in the movement, "Kostrov" was Noi Zhordania. Pannekoek was a Dutch socialist.
30 The editorial board of the journal *Proveshchenie* published Stalin's eventually famous article on the "national question" in 1912, in which he vehemently criticized Otto Bauer. A little after the appearance of the text, it was rumored that the famous Austrian Social Democrat intended to reply.
31 *RGASPI*, fond. 558, op. 4, d. 242. Kamenev's name at birth was Rosenfeld.
32 Ulanovskie, 1982, 12.
33 *Iosif Stalin v obyatiakh semyi*, 1993, 31.
34 Avtorkhanov, 1973, vol. I, 194.
35 Trotsky, 1990, vol. I, 307–309.
36 *RGASPI*, fond. 558, op. 4, d. 153.
37 Lenin, 1999, 108–110.
38 Trotsky, 1990, vol. I, 308.
39 *RGASPI*, fond. 558, op. 4, d. 647.
40 This one was one of Stalin's popular mocking name (sadovnik), as he was eager to plant many people.
41 *RGASPI*, fond. 558, op. 4, d. 647.
42 *Bolshevistkoye Rukovodstvo*, 1996, 16.
43 *Biorgaficheskaya Khronika*, 1971, vol. II, 67. According to Yelena Rozmirovich, who was also present at the conference, the documents were immediately duplicated, and it was Valentina Lobova, who handled the machine.
44 *RGASPI*, fond. 558, op. 4, d. 647.

CHAPTER 9
Wanted: A Theoretician

On the first day of the New Year, when the exhausted company slowly dispersed, Lenin and Zinovyev told their Georgian guest that the party's treasury contained sufficient money to enable him to travel to the Austrian capital, where he could study the complex correlation between Marxist theory and the national issue. According to Trotsky, who was skeptical about the theoretical grounding of the future Soviet dictator, this clever move allowed Lenin to keep Stalin from controlling the domestic Bolshevik movement until as late as February 1913. He sent him back to St. Petersburg only once the "Cracow line", following the "Prague line", was deeply enough rooted in Russia.[1]

This was doubtless true. However, Lenin may have had other considerations. At the end of 1912 he added a notebook to his personal archives, which contained his notes on Ukrainian separatism. The title of the notebook—"The National Question II"—reveals that the issue had come to the forefront of his concerns. At around the same time he read the pamphlet written by the Dutchman Pannekoek, "Class Struggle and Nation". In the middle of December Lenin wrote an outraged letter to Kamenev telling him that the Menshevik representatives in the State Duma, along with their Bolshevik colleagues, had declared their stance in favor of "cultural-national autonomy", something he regarded as a fatal error.[2]

The fact that Lenin entrusted "Comrade Koba" with the study of the national question, which was of crucial importance in the multiethnic tsarist empire, can therefore be regarded as a sign of his unconditional confidence. In this context the Vienna mission seems rather to have been a kind of reward. In the Bolshevik "Foreign Center" there was a need for a theoretician, if possible a non-Russian, who was willing to be involved in the mudslinging against the rival Social Democrats in Russia most of whom were non-Russian themselves. Iosif Dzhugashvili appeared to fit the bill, since he had earlier published some shorter texts on the national question, and also because he adopted the "Leninist" viewpoint. In early January 1913 Lenin gave him an individual crash course. During these conversations he made significant improvements to Stalin's almost twenty-page-long study on the national question, the manuscript of which was taken by the author to Vienna to be further amended. At the same time it is still hard to understand why, in his famous letter to Gorky, the Bolshevik party leader misled his addressee by saying that the "wonderful Georgian" who was staying with him had collected together "all the Austrian, etc. material".[3] Lenin knew precisely how lacking Stalin's theoretical grounding was, and that he did not have a reading knowledge of any foreign language.

This, of course, did not present too much of an obstacle to "Comrade Koba". In the second half of January 1913, after he had settled in the Austrian capital, he had the members of the Vienna Bolshevik colony obtain for him copies of the works of Otto Bauer, Karl Renner, and Karl Kautsky on the national question. He had read their more important works at home in Russian translation, and in Vienna he had excerpts from their later writings translated for himself. Armed with this superficial knowledge, of his *Marxism and the National Question* he took issue with Panin, who had translated one of Bauer's works into Russian, for rendering the expression "*das Nationale Eigenart*" not as "national trait", but as "individual national characteristic".[4]

The theoretical conclusions at which Stalin arrived in the Austrian capital were mostly owed to Aleksandr Troyanovsky and his circle of friends. Troyanovsky, a former tsarist artillery officer, was, at the time of the Cracow meeting, an important militant in the Bolshevik movement. For a while he was a member of the Central Committee and of the editorial board of the theoretical journal *Prosveshchenie*, which was partly financed by him. "Comrade Koba" wanted eventually to publish his study in this journal. Troyanovsky, a generous and wealthy man, proved an amenable host. He took Stalin into his home in Schönbrunner Schloss-strasse 30. From October 12, 1912 Troyanovsky had rented this comfortable, three-room apartment with his wife, Yelena Rozmirovich, another underground Bolshevik party worker. Their daughter Galina also lived there, as did Olga Veyland, the girl's governess.[5]

Troyanovsky could have had no suspicion that in the spring of 1945, after Red Army troops had occupied Vienna, the insignificant building would become a place of pilgrimage for the Soviet notables who visited the Austrian capital. Four years later the military commander of the Soviet occupied zone had the local council place a memorial plaque under the window of apartment number 7 to indicate that this was where the great Stalin had lived. The plaque is still there, although in the autumn of 1956 a number of demonstrators, in solidarity with the Hungarian revolution, tried to remove it.

A special twist to the story is that Troyanovsky occupied a prestigious position in the pages of Soviet historiography, while Trotsky, Kamenev, Bukharin, and others who "diverged" from the party line were excommunicated for long decades in their homeland. Troyanovsky could easily have suffered the same fate, since, during the First World War, he accused Lenin of anti-patriotism and openly broke away from Bolshevism. In the years of the Russian Civil War he clearly represented the right wing of the Mensheviks in the leading bodies of his new party. He worked feverishly to overthrow the Bolshevik government and as a result was jailed on two occasions.[6] Unlike several other Menshevik politicians[7] he did not end his life in the Gulag. In the frosty winter of 1921 Stalin unexpectedly stopped to speak to him in downtown Moscow, in Myasnitskaya Street. He embraced him and shouted into his ear: "Tell me, are we friends or enemies after all?"[8]

As befitting a pragmatic politician, over the next weeks Joseph Stalin—in the period of War Communism and faced with a series of peasant revolts—using the mediation of Troyanovsky tried to persuade the Mensheviks, who, like his one-time host in Vienna were undergoing a "crisis of faith", to "lay down their arms". He promised that in return they would be given jobs in Soviet offices, and even in the Bolshevik government. News of the top-secret negotiations eventually leaked out. Thus Stalin's plan, which he had proposed to the Mensheviks probably with Lenin's consent, was never realized. Instead of the large-scale merger to further the new economic policy (*Novaya Ekonomicheskaya Politika*, NEP), only a few influential Menshevik politicians broke away from their party and got jobs.[9]

The former "Comrade Koba" did not blame the mediator Aleksandr Troyanovsky for the failure of the negotiations. He even took him under his wing and gave him a department director position within his own People's Commissariat for Worker-Peasant Supervision. Later on Troyanovsky gave him further help in his career. On July 25, 1923 he merely had to ask in a brief letter to Stalin to be transferred to the People's Commissariat of Foreign Trade and his wish was granted.[10] Only a few years later he became an influential diplomat, and in the 1930s represented the Soviet Union in Washington. Avoiding the official channels he was able to turn directly to Stalin. In 1928, as Tokyo ambassador, he advised the General Secretary of the party to help out Putna, the military attaché, who had got into debt because of his wife's illness. The recipient of the letter, who had proved always willing to bribe his political opponents, came to the aid of the Trotskyite who agreed to give up his views: "Klim! Read Troyanovsky's letter and Putna's request, in which he says he is willing to leave

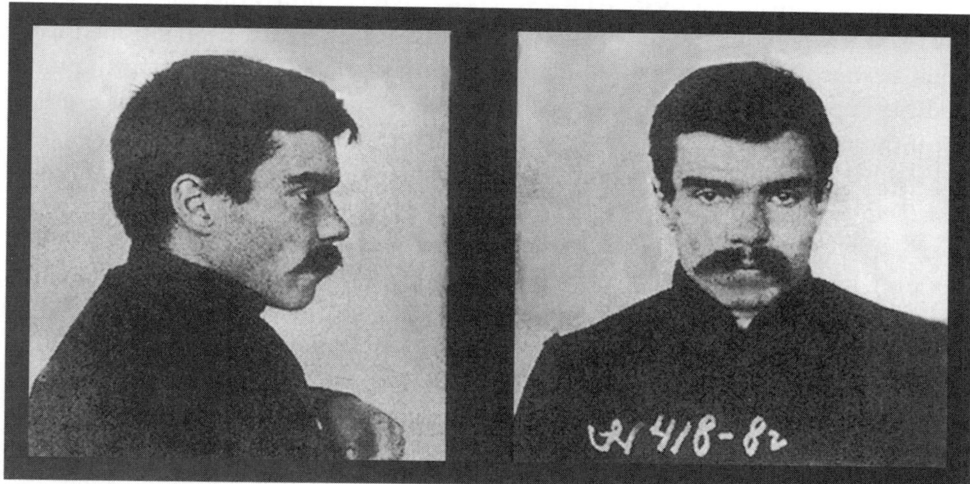

A police file photograph of Aleksandr Troyanovsky. As Stalin's host in Vienna, he was particularly attentive to his guest. However, he disagreed with Stalin on the latter's study written on the relationship between Marxism and the nationality question.

the opposition," he wrote to Voroshilov. "In my opinion: 1. Putna should be told that he can remain as military attaché; 2. His nine-hundred-yen debt should be written off. We should transfer the aid to him in one lump sum; 3. After a while, let's say in half a year's time or more, we can bring him back to the USSR. St[alin]."[11]

This was the kind of influence that a recommendation from Aleksandr Troyanovsky could have. By this time it had long been forgotten that although both he and Yelena Rozmirovich had been kind to Stalin when they first met, they had not taken the "wonderful Georgian" too seriously. In January 1913 the couple had belonged among the advocates of cultural-national autonomy, criticized by Stalin. Thus, behind their guest's back, they tried to persuade Lenin to have Stalin's study, which gained its final form in their apartment in Vienna, published in *Prosveshchenie* only as a polemical treatise. A group of translators also made their mark on the study. On this point several memorable stories have been preserved by Troyanovsky's son Oleg, who knew the family legendary by heart.[12] He knew that his father had paid a Russian student living in Vienna to translate for Stalin as he worked on the article.[13] Bukharin, who was then studying in the Austrian capital, also stood at the Georgian Bolshevik's disposal, which was why the claim later spread that his views were integrated in Stalin's work. Contemporary sources do not support this, however. "Comrade Orlov" (Bukharin's byname in the movement) was perhaps not even particularly interested in the subject of the work in progress: "I'm not an expert on the national question," he revealed to Lenin in a letter written in April 1914.[14] On the other hand, other members of the Bolshevik colony in Vienna were busy studying the issue. "Those few weeks that Comrade Stalin spent with us were devoted entirely to the national question," remembered Olga Veyland. "[Stalin] involved everyone around him in the study. Some analyzed Otto Bauer, others Karl Kautsky.

This was our sole topic of conversation at the time. Little Galochka [...] who loved being in adult company, often complained about it: 'You're always talking about the nations!'"[15]

Like the Troyanovskys, Olga Veyland was later to gain her reward. With the patronage of the Soviet dictator she held several important posts in the party apparatus, and in the 1930s worked for the Comintern. Still, before the outbreak of the Second World War she was pensioned off at the very young age of forty-seven. However, she continued to regard her meeting with Stalin in Vienna as a decisive experience in her life: "Once he called me to his temporary study and asked me to translate a piece from *Neue Zeit*. We sat down together. I was nervous about whether I could translate the text properly, but I soon stopped worrying because Comrade Stalin quietly and patiently helped me to find the most suitable expressions. I was surprised that he knew in advance what was coming up in the text."[16]

Leon Trotsky had entirely different memories about the author of *Marxism and the National Question*: "In 1913 in Vienna, the ancient capital of the Habsburgs, I was sitting at the table beside the samovar in the apartment of Skobelev. My host was the son of a wealthy Baku mill owner. At the time he was attending university and in terms of politics regarded himself as my disciple. A few years later, however, he became my rival as minister *[of labor—M. K.]* in the Provisional Government [in 1917]. In the Austrian capital we were still peacefully sipping fragrant tea side by side. And what else could we have been thinking about but overthrowing tsarism?

"One day, all of a sudden, the door opened without anyone knocking and a man entirely unknown to me appeared. He was a short, thin man. His grayish-brown skin was covered in pockmarks. His stare radiated little benevolence. He held an empty glass in his hand. Perhaps he was not expecting to bump into me at Skobelev's, but I saw nothing in his eyes that could have been regarded as a friendly expression. He uttered a glottal sound, which, giving him the benefit of the doubt, could have been a greeting. He stepped up to the samovar and without a word made himself a glass of tea. Then, as silently as he had come, he left the room. I looked at Skobelev inquiringly. He said: 'That was Dzhugashvili, a fellow Caucasian. He has recently become a member of the Bolshevik Central Committee. He is slowly coming to the fore among them.'"[17]

Elsewhere Trotsky claims that before May 1917, when he returned to Petrograd from his long emigration, he did not know Stalin at all. It is not even certain that Matvei Skobelev witnessed Stalin's stay in Vienna. In his autobiography he states that he traveled to Vienna in 1907 and studied for five years at the local polytechnic while editing Trotsky's paper *Pravda*. In the summer of 1912 he traveled home, and in the autumn, carried on the tide of the Liquidator Mensheviks, became a member of the Fourth State Duma.[18] From then on the tsarist police kept Skobelev under special surveillance: they reported almost every day on where he went and whom he met. Despite this, I found no evidence among the archive documents that in the second half of January or early February 1913 Skobelev had had an apartment in Vienna.

It is likely that in Trotsky's mind, many years after the events, the story was pieced together from fragments of memories connected to different episodes: "This character left a very depressing but entirely unusual impression on me. [...] Or perhaps later events have cast a shadow on our first meeting?" Trotsky himself mused.[19]

☆ But let us return to Joseph Stalin's famous study. Rereading it, it seems incredible that later hundreds of authors hailed the future Master of the Kremlin as a world-famous expert on the national question: "During his stay abroad Stalin wrote his work *Marxism and the National Question*, of which Lenin thought very highly. [...] Before the First World War this work was the most significant expression of Bolshevism as far as the assessment of the national question was concerned," claimed the biographers of the Soviet dictator.[20] The study, which was published under a title borrowed from Otto Bauer and which

As a result of Troyanovsky's mediation in 1928, Stalin seemed willing to forgive Witowt Putna (this picture), for his previous enthusiasm for Trotsky. Ten years later, however, Stalin decided to execute him as one of the defendants in the Tukhachevsky trial. The photograph was taken in the prison.

was a rather unevenly constructed piece, can be regarded as ambitious only compared to other articles by Stalin on the same theme, written in the arcane jargon of the movement. It is unquestionably erroneous to talk about the international impact of the polemical treatise, since it only appeared in foreign translation well after the 1917 Bolshevik takeover.

Although in the depths of his heart "Comrade Koba" yearned for the laurels of the great theoretician, initially even he himself did not think too highly of the study that was finalized in January-February 1913 in fulfillment of Lenin's intentions: "At the moment I am sitting in Vienna and scribbling all kinds of nonsense," he wrote to Roman Malinovsky in a letter dated February 2, 1913.[21] By the 1920s, however, the Soviet dictator had gotten used to the idea that he, and only he, was the undisputed expert on the national question. From an undated note written by the head of Stalin's secretariat, Ivan Tovstukha, it appears that over the years Stalin re-edited the study as much as three times.[22] In the process he slightly changed his concept of the nation. In the mid-1940s in the Soviet capital Milovan Djilas, referring to the study composed in Vienna, asked Stalin what, according to him, was the difference between "people" and "nation". Vyacheslav Molotov, who was present at the interview, interrupted: "'People' and 'nation' are the same." According to Djilas Stalin responded as follows: "No! What a foolish thing to say! They are different. [...] The 'nation' is the product of capitalism with certain peculiarities, while a 'people' is the totality of all workers of a nation. That is, of those workers who share the same language, culture, and customs." As to his study *Marxism and the National Question*, he remarked that "it expresses the concept of Ilich. He edited my work."[23]

If the memory of Milovan Djilas is accurate, then it is possible that by the end of his life Joseph Stalin had modified his earlier definition of the "nation". This read originally: "...a nation is a historically constituted community of people," which "is created on the basis of the spiritual complexion manifested through a common language, common territory, common economic life, and common culture."[24] But even this highly simplistic definition does not seem to be the individual intellectual product of the "Great Theoretician". Without any reference and with minimal changes Stalin had simply lifted this passage from the writings of Karl Kautsky and other "Austromarxists", who, in the early years of the century, were popular among Russian Socialists.[25]

☆ At this time Joseph Stalin was making less and less frequent use of the byname "Koba". He signed the article published in *Prosveshchenie* as "K. Stalin". "From 1919, when he began to write in Russian, he was preoccupied with finding an original but Russian-sounding byname," explained Abdurakhman Avtorkhanov. The Georgian politician used the signatures "K. S." and "K. St." already in 1910. He later tried the bynames "K. Stefin", and "K. Salin", and finally "K. Solin".[26] According to Vera Shweitzer the choice was not made by him alone: "Comrade Stalin wrote a large number of articles for the newspaper *Zvezda*. These texts were often composed in my apartment. [...] The editorial board once changed the signature arbitrarily. The next day, when J. V. Stalin opened *Zvezda*, in which his article had appeared, and saw the signature 'Solin', he smiled. 'I do not like meaningless, borrowed bynames,' he said. The editorial board coined no new versions of his name after this."[27]

During the Cracow and then Vienna interludes in his life, besides the "literary pseudonym" of "K. Stalin" (in which the "K" referred to Koba, which was later changed to Joseph) he used other movement bynames as well. He signed his conspiratory letters sometimes as "Vasily", sometimes as "Vasilyev".[28] These bynames, however, had nothing to do with the name Dzhugashvili, for which Stalin is a mirror translation. *"Dzhuga"* means "steel" in Georgian, which is "*stal*'" in Russian. This may have appealed to him since it resembled the bynames chosen by his two good comrades in the movement, Kamenev and Molotov, which also referred to a firm, hard character. The former comes from the word *"kamen"*, that is, "stone", and the latter from the word *"molot"*, which is Russian for "hammer".

Later, at the peak of his power, many people asked Stalin about the origins of his name. However, only Walter Duranty, his favorite American journalist and the number one popularizer of his cruel system in the West, succeeded in getting him to talk about it during a break in an interview. According to Duranty Stalin "smiled with slight embarrassment and said: 'My comrades gave me this name in 1911 or perhaps in 1910. They thought it suited me. However it happened, it stuck. We old underground activists always used bynames because we had to hide from the tsarist police.'"[29] This answer appeared as part of the one-hour-long interview published in Duranty's newspaper, *The New York Times*, on December 1, 1930. However, before Duranty's interview was published in *Pravda* Stalin checked the Russian translation and pulled out all references to the byname. The Russian title, however, appears in his handwriting on the manuscript of the translation, "A Conversation between Mr. Duranty and Comrade Stalin".

The interviewee also deleted the most flattering description of his appearance: "In the three years since your correspondent last talked with him, Stalin has hardly changed. At most there are a few more streaks of gray in his hair and mustache, and his face has become thinner. His figure, however, in his short, high-buttoned khaki jacket and matching trousers tucked into black boots—he wears no medals—has remained upright and firm, just like his handshake. He himself, however, seems slightly softer and more human," wrote the American columnist in the midst of the "permanent class struggle" that had extinguished the lives of millions in the Soviet Union. "When we first met, your correspondent was particularly surprised by Stalin's deep, expressionless voice. It was as if he were reserving all his power for the colossal tasks ahead of him. On this occasion he was more animated and less reserved."[30] Stalin's rigidity was not only reserved for the foreigner, who was treated with suspicion despite the fact that he served the interests of the Kremlin. From the period of his underground activity, and even from his years as a student, Joseph Stalin was distrustful of *everyone*.

1 Trotsky, 1990, vol. I, 211.
2 *Biograficheskaya Khronika*, 1971, vol. II, 59, 66–67.
3 Lenin, 1965, 162.
4 Stalin, 1946, vol. II, 321.
5 *RGASPI*, fond. 558, op. 4, d. 354.
6 On this period of his life, see Dvinov, 1968, 16, 30–31, 34, 40–41, 43, 53, 55.
7 Broydo, 1987, 163–166; Bogdanova, 1994, 160–170; Popova, 1996, 18–34, 60–61.
8 Oral history interview with Oleg Troyanovsky, the politician's son.
9 Troyanovsky, 1997, 25, 38–39.
10 *RGASPI*, fond. 558, op. 2, d. 152.
11 *RGASPI*, fond. 74, op. 2, d. 38. In the end, almost a decade later in the summer of 1937, Stalin arranged Putna's execution in the Tukhachevsky Trial.
12 My interviewee, the old diplomat, due to his excellent command of English, worked as an interpreter for Stalin in the 1940s, and even escorted him to one of his summer vacations.
13 Troyanovsky, 1997, 25.
14 Kun, 1992, 34–35.
15 *RGASPI*, fond. 558, op. 4, d. 647.
16 *Ibid.*
17 Trotsky, 1991, 46.
18 *Dyeyateli SSSR*, 1998, 46.
19 Trotsky, 1991, vol. I, 46.
20 *Iosif Vissarionovich Stalin*, 1951, 54.
21 Felstinsky, 1999, 10. The author translated Stalin's letter, which was published in English in Edward Ellis Smith's book, back into Russian. Since then I have managed to find the police copy in the Moscow archives. *RGASPI*, fond. 558, op. 1, d. 47. Comparing the two texts, it seems that despite the back-and-forth translation there are only stylistic differences between them, which do not alter the essence. I have to agree with Yury Felstinsky that Stalin ignored the most elementary rules of caution when he sent the letter, as he mentioned in the text, by quite transparent bynames, several Bolshevik politicians, who could have easily gotten into trouble because of this.
22 *RGASPI*, fond. 155, op. 1, d. 77.
23 Djilas, 1992, 112.
24 Stalin, 1946, vol. II, 296.
25 A researcher from Moscow, a certain Semyonov, was among the first who pointed out the "Kautskyan" aspects of Stalin's article. *Narody Azii i Afriki*, 1966, no. 4, 119–121.
26 Avtorkhanov, 1973, vol. I, 199. See also Stalin, 1946, vol. II, 187, 196, 212, 226, 228, 231, 233, 236, 239, 243, 255, 261, 261, 265.
27 *RGASPI*, fond. 17, op. 4, d. 647. The Russian word "sol" means "salt".
28 *RGASPI*, fond. 558, op. 4, d. 647. Cf. *Istorichesky Arkhiv*, 1960, no. 2, 20.
29 *RGASPI*, fond. 558, op. 1, d. 3103.
30 *Ibid.*

Next page:
"Stal" means steel in Russian.
The look on Stalin's face
was always cold as steel when
looking into the camera.

Nikolai Bukharin

Nikolai Bukharin, who felt increasingly isolated, spent his leisure time in locations far away from the Kremlin. In 1934, he climbed the Elbrus Mountains with the alpinist workers of the factory named after Frunze.

July 1926, the funeral of Feliks Dzerzhinsky. Bukharin (1) walks on Stalin's right. To the right of Bukharin, there are Molotov (2), Rykov (3), Kamenev (4), and Tomsky (5). Trotsky (6) and Zinovyev (7) walks in the background. Two years later, the "rightist deviationists", led by Bukharin, Rykov, and Tomsky, start to strongly criticize Joseph Stalin, their earlier ally.

It seemed that after 1930, spending time among women was for Bukharin a way of escaping the political antagonisms. In the north Caucasian resort town of Kislovodsk, he entertained half a dozen of his fellow holiday-makers at the same time.

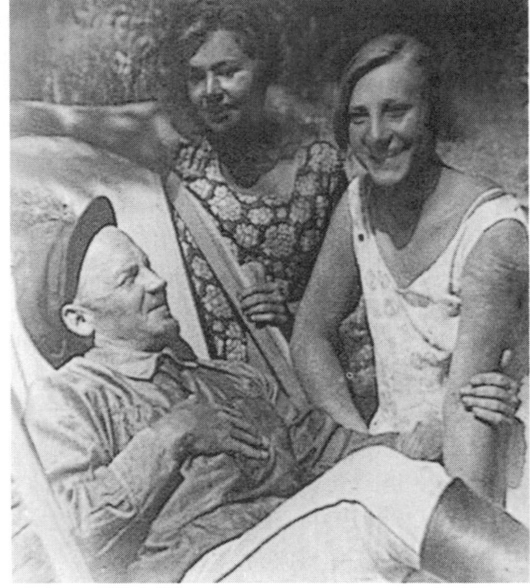

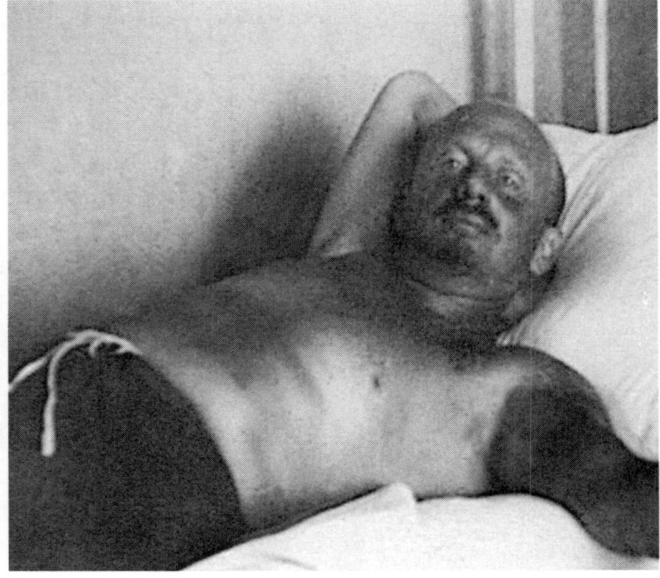

CHAPTER 10
The Last Period in Exile

In February 1913, shortly after Stalin returned to St. Petersburg, the police swooped down on him once again. On February 23 shackles were fastened onto his wrists during a charitable event that he was attending. According to Grigory Petrovsky, it was Malinovsky who had lured Stalin to the gathering, being held to celebrate International Women's Day.[1] The *agent provocateur* had submitted regular reports on "Comrade Koba", who, for his part, had taken a firm stand on behalf of Malinovsky in the face of his detractors. Following Stalin's interlude in Vienna, and while he was in hiding in the Russian capital, he had had to protect Malinovsky because in Menshevik, and even Bolshevik, circles the rumor—which was later to prove true—had begun to spread that Malinovsky was a common informer. As soon as the rumor reached Stalin's ears he paid a visit to Lidia Dan, who was working as a general assistant for the Menshevik representatives of the State Duma. Stalin even went as far as threatening the woman, the wife of the famous Menshevik politician Osip Dan and the younger sister of the real founder of the Menshevik Party, Yuly Martov. He warned her that there would be big trouble if she and her fellow Mensheviks continued to slander Malinovsky.[2] She learned only years later that the Bolshevik politician who had reprimanded her so cruelly—whom the Mensheviks mocked as "scar-faced Vasily" and who had introduced himself to her only as Vasilyev—was none other than Joseph Stalin. A few decades later she was to have first-hand experience of the vindictive nature of the former underground Bolshevik activist. During the Great Terror Stalin almost entirely exterminated the once large Martov-Dan family, whom he especially hated.[3]

Thus while "Comrade Vasilyev" was trying to help his traitor friend, the Bolshevik emigrant leaders seemed to have sensed that their important Russian agent was in trouble. "Why is there no news from Vasily? What's happening to him? We are concerned," wrote Nadezhda Krupskaya in a conspiratorial letter on February 23, 1913. Two days later she warned her correspondents in St. Petersburg that Stalin "needs to be taken care of. It is obvious that his position is uncertain."[4] On the same day, February 25, 1913, Demyan Bedny, the Bolshevik party poet, told the devastating news in a letter to Lenin. However, he added that the "Georgian" was himself at fault for being arrested, since he had not kept to the rules of conspiracy: "The devil may have prompted him, or some idiot invited him to the meeting, but it was certainly impudent of him to go. I didn't even know he was in St. Petersburg. I was shocked when I caught sight of him in the crowd. 'You won't be able to escape from here,' I told him. And he didn't."[5]

It is still not clear why the authorities were in such a hurry to arrest Stalin at the gathering when, on other occasions, they had hesitated for weeks before moving in on him. It is possible that it was simply a preemptive measure on their part. For the leaders of the political police already knew that, following the Cracow meeting and during the Viennese study trip, "Comrade Koba" had played an important role in the illegal Bolshevik apparatus and on the editorial board of *Pravda*. The Okhrana were doubtless annoyed by the fact that the Russian Committee had held a session chaired by "Comrade Andrei", that is, Yakov Sverdlov, in the apartment of Petrovsky, a State Duma representative, at which it had been decided to send Joseph Stalin to the Urals and to entrust him with the creation of an illegal printing press. Sverdlov and Petrovsky were supposed to help him in this. The 150-ruble cost of establishing the printing press was to be met by gold-mine owner Konyukhov, who also owned a cinema in St. Petersburg, on Nevsky Avenue. "He is willing to pay fifty rubles to the party worker who runs the press," we learn from the copy of the police report.[6]

Iosif Dzhugashvili, who was called "Pockmarked Vasily" behind his back, once talked very harshly to Lidia Dan. The woman learned only several years later that she had encountered Stalin. On this picture, Lidia, her husband, the Menshevik party leader Osip Dan.

Instead of the trip to the Urals on illegal party business, Stalin was deported back to Siberia under armed guard, without a court hearing. This period of exile must have been the most tormenting for him. The journey between the Russian capital and Krasnoyarsk took one and a half weeks for Stalin by rail and boat. From there, the Bolshevik exile was jolted and shaken for three weeks in a horse-drawn coach that took him from the provincial seat to Turukhansk, "the capital of exiles". He spent four years in northern Siberia, partly beyond the Arctic Circle, in settlements in which there was no such thing as a library or an outpatient service. The post arrived at best once a month, and if an exile was sent money by his friends, the authorities immediately suspended transfer of the state allowance to which the exiles were entitled.[7]

From the recollections of former political prisoners, we learn of the hardships entailed by their living several days' walk from one another. Almost without exception they found the fact that there was no one with whom they could discuss the questions that occupied their minds extremely hard to bear. Nevertheless, among Stalin's acquaintances many were able to carry out intensive intellectual work even in these miserable conditions. Lev Kamenev, for instance, prepared a slim volume for press which traced, among other things, the history of nineteenth-century Russian political emigration.[8] "Comrade Koba's" other fellow exile, Yakov Sverdlov, who was originally no more educated than Stalin himself and who, in addition, was regarded as a professional party worker who specialized rather in pragmatic questions, educated himself diligently throughout his exile in Turukhansk. By the time he was freed he had already published a number of relatively well written texts in the Siberian press and even in the quality St. Petersburg publication *Vestnik Evropy*.[9]

Unlike them "Comrade Koba", especially towards the end of his exile, be-

"Comrade Koba" tried in vain to ask Grigory Zinovyev to write him while he was in exile. The Bolshevik émigré politician responded only very rarely, and in the end he completely forgot about Dzhugashvili.

came extraordinarily lazy. Not even writing absorbed him. He was, of course, contemplating escape and thus had no intention of settling for long in the village named Miroyegikha, where he spent two weeks, and among the relatively large colony of exiles in the village of Kostino in the Turukhansk frontier zone. According to the unpublished recollections of Kostino inhabitant Kiril Chalkin, which he dictated in 1952, Stalin first rented a tiny room from a peasant by the name of Shadrin. Then, with Yakov Sverdlov, "whom everyone in the village referred to as 'the student' because he wore a black broadcloth coat with shiny buttons," he bought his host's bathhouse. They transformed it and lived in it.[10] According to the old peasant's recollections, before Joseph Stalin arrived in Kostino only one armed guard had watched over the exiles. Later another was ordered to the village, who, morning and evening, would regularly turn up at their lodgings to check on the two "politicals". Utterly bored, Stalin killed time by teaching two of his fellow Georgians, who must have been exiled common criminals, to read and write. According to other sources Stalin came into serious conflict with his fellow exiles while staying in Kostino. On one occasion he took the books of a fellow exile who had moved out of the village. Normally in such cases the whole colony would inherit the books, which were highly prized in the Siberian frontier land. One Bolshevik, Filipp Zakharov, even asked Stalin to share the books with the others. "Comrade Koba", however, treated his fellow exile "as if he were a private who had dared to speak out in the presence of a tsarist general".[11]

His troubles were increased by the fact that he was far from the European part of Russia and even further from the Bolshevik "Foreign Center". Thus he was not able to take advantage of the opportunities offered by his Central Committee membership and his unexpected elevation in the party hierarchy. There is no information to suggest that it occurred to anyone among the Bolshevik leadership at the time to continue working on Stalin's most serious intellectual project until then, *Marxism and the National Question*. Nor do we know whether his mentors in the movement, Lenin and Zinovyev, were thinking about him during his exile as they had done in 1912 and 1913 when the Georgian Bolshevik was living freely in St. Petersburg and abroad. Apparently the Bolshevik "Foreign Center" was only interested in the exile as long as it seemed that he would be able to escape once again. When his escape did not materialize they gradually left him out of their plans. In the meantime the First World War had broken out, which made keeping contact abroad even more difficult.[12]

Joseph Stalin had not expected to be abandoned in this way. During the first month of his exile he had planned to expand his study on the national question, or perhaps to surprise his former hosts in Cracow and Vienna with a new study and thereby retain the "theoretician's laurels" he had gained during his short foreign stay. "As you can see, I am in Turukhansk. Did you receive the letter I sent you on the way here? I am ill. I must get treatment. Send me money. If you need my help, write to me. I will come immediately. Send me the books by Strasser, Pannekoek, and Kautsky.[13] Let me know your address," he wrote to Nadezhda Krupskaya in a letter sent to Zinovyev's Cracow address. He asked for the parcel to be sent to a neutral Kiev address in order to mislead the political police. (In the 1930s Kozlov, head of the department of party history of the Saratov regional party committee, sent Stalin a photocopy of this letter with the following remark: "We presume that you are the writer of the letter." The Soviet dictator, who by that time disliked being reminded that he had once sought the sympathy of Zinovyev and other influential Bolshevik emigrants, ordered the document to be filed away without any further remark. Like his Siberian letters referred to below, it was not included in his Collected Works.)[14]

"Comrade Koba" asked questions of other members of the "Foreign Center" similar to those that we read in his letter to Krupskaya. Until the outbreak of the First World War he apparently carried on a one-sided correspondence with them on several occasions: "I am sending a picture postcard. It will be better this way," he wrote from Kostino on December 7, 1913 to Zinovyev.[15] "I received your letter dated November 9 [1913], but not the books by Krautsky and others. This is a serious problem. Here I have got hold of Kostrov's[16] pamphlet written in Georgian. I would like to write something based on this, giving a piece of my mind to the others as well. I ask you once again to send the books. Besides, I have been informed that I have a parcel from Tiflis. I think it contains books. Perhaps these are the very books. I am very glad (of course!) that your affairs are progressing well at home.[17] But it couldn't have been otherwise. [...] I have had a terrible cough since the weather turned colder. I have absolutely no money. I am in debt. No one lends me money. Things are really bad. I have seen A[ndrei] [Yakov Sverdlov]. He has settled in quite well. The important thing is that he is healthy. Like K[oba] St[alin], he is here with nothing to do. [...] I shake your hand."[18]

Letters referring to his dreams of escape reached their addressee, then living in Galicia, only after long delay. Nor was Grigory Zinovyev in any hurry to reply. The requested books were not sent to Stalin by him, Lenin, or Krupskaya, although in the Russian workers' press the old debate on the national question was rekindled from time to time. Stalin sensed that his opinions were no longer of much importance to his comrades. He tried to do something about this, knowing that in the company of the Khanty and Yakut hunters and drunkard tsarist gendarmes he would soon lose any reputation as a theoretician that he had acquired. He bombarded Zinovyev with further letters: "Austria, Krakau, Ulica Lubomirskiego 35. An Herrn Radomislski. Österreich. Why are you silent, my dear friend? A certain "N." has written to me in your name, but I'll be damned if I know who it is. I have not received a letter from you for three months. What can I do...? Some recent news is that Stalin has sent a massively long article to *Prosveshchenie*," continues the letter, in which the author praises his own work referring to himself in the third person. "The title is 'On Cultural National Autonomy'. It seems rather good. He hopes to be well paid for it. This would save him from having to beg money from everyone. I think his expectations are well founded. Besides, in the article he criticizes Kostrov's Georgian-language pamphlet. The author echoes the main views of the supporters of autonomy. Well, I shake your hand. I send greetings to my acquaintances as well. January 11 [1914]."[19]

Nevertheless, the correspondence between the faraway Turukhansk frontier zone and Cracow became no more frequent even after this. Lenin and Zinovyev were preoccupied with managing the daily affairs of the domestic Bolshevik movement and of emigration. The third member of the triumvirate, Lev Kamenev, taking advantage of the general amnesty declared to mark the three-hundredth anniversary of the Romanov dynasty, moved home and took over the editorship of *Pravda*. But neither did he inundate his old Tiflis acquaintance with letters. Stalin, however, living in the godforsaken village in a bathhouse transformed into lodgings, could not afford to be offended. He therefore chose the tactic of repeating his questions again and again *ad nauseam*. He also took care to express his humble gratitude on the rare occasions that his correspondents answered him.

The faraway Kureyka was the site of Stalin's last period in exile. At that time, it had only a dozen or so houses, but it was not a flourishing town in the 1930s either, when this picture was taken.

There were times, however, when his frustration got the better of him. At the end of 1913 he took issue with Zinovyev over a sum of money he considered as owing to him in payment for articles written earlier on the national question: "In your letter dated September 9 you wrote that you would send my money in small installments. I would appreciate it if this could happen as soon as possible, no matter how small the installments. [...] I say this because at the moment I am in desperate need of money. I would get by somehow if I were not tormented by illness, which demands treatment (that is, money) and which makes me lose my temper and patience. In other words, I am waiting. As soon as I receive the German books I will complete the article and will send it in a rewritten form." On a copy of the letter Stalin has later added the sardonic remark: "Comrade Orakhelashvili! Send back to the Marx–Engels–Lenin Institute this insignificant letter that I jotted down in 1913 in the village of Kostino in the Turukhansk frontier zone."[20]

☆ However, soon something was to happen to Stalin that would make him weep for his days in Kostino, in spite of all the problems he had faced there. In the first half of March 1914 the local authorities deported him, along with Sverdlov, to the Kureyka police district near the Arctic Ocean. This region, which in wintertime was entirely cut off from the civilized world, surrounded by endless snowfields, and where temperatures dropped to minus fifty degrees, had a worse reputation among the political exiles than any of the forced-labor camps *(katorga)*. In the spring life was made almost unbearable by the mosquitoes. The slow and complacent life of the local authorities was shaken abruptly by the appearance of the newcomers, which enhanced their vigilance.

On May 12, long after the two exiles had left Kostino under armed escort, the chief of the local police informed the governor that "the center of the Russian Social Democratic Labor Party led by Lenin has convened a party congress" in

Vienna, during council of the Second International planned for August. Before the congress illegal regional conferences were to be arranged throughout the tsarist empire after "several renowned party workers have visited the local party organizations". Among those mentioned by the informers were Suren Spandaryan, Yakov Sverdlov, and Iosif Dzhugashvili. The chief of police, who held the rank of colonel, nevertheless assured the governor that he had taken measures to prevent the mentioned individuals from escaping.[21]

The three Bolshevik exiles were naturally aware that their every step was being watched closely. From near the Arctic Ocean they did not have much hope of escaping anyway. In Kureyka, which consisted of ten, or according to other sources eight, wooden houses, living conditions were so wretched that in the winter months Joseph Stalin could only venture out to the outside latrine with a loaded rifle because he was afraid of the tundra wolves that were extremely aggressive during their mating season. Little wonder that after a few months the son of sunny Georgia became something of a snarling lone wolf himself. In this respect there is a huge gap between his "pre-Kureyka" and his "Kureyka" period. Not even the Soviet dictator's avid biographers could obtain proof that the enforced isolation had had a beneficial effect on Stalin, although, after the Second World War, they asked the dictator's fellow exiles about this.[22] On April 10, 1950 the staff at the Stalin archives invited the two former worker representatives of the State Duma, Petrovsky and Muranov, for a meeting that lasted several hours. Earlier they had carried out an in-depth interview with the baker and confectioner Ivanov, who was exiled to Siberia at the same time as Stalin. An old Bolshevik party member, Pozner, had participated in both meetings. In response to a remark made by Pozner ('...according to one version Comrade Stalin was working for one of the Siberian periodicals'), Ivanov gave a very evasive answer: "It wasn't a periodical, but the newspaper *Sibirskaya Zhizn'*. Many exiles wrote for this newspaper, perhaps Comrade Stalin was one of them. I know for certain that Sverdlov did."[23]

Within a few months of their arrival in godforsaken Kureyka, Stalin clashed with Sverdlov, with whom he had already been in conflict in Kostino. "In the new place it was much harder to settle in," complained Sverdlov to his wife in his letter dated March 1914. "It was bad enough that I didn't have a room to myself. There were two of us sharing. Dzhugashvili the Georgian lived with me. He was an acquaintance whom I had met during my previous exile *[in Narym, in the summer of 1912—M. K.]*. He is not a bad chap, but in everyday life he is too much of an individualist."[24] Two months later, on May 27, 1914, Sverdlov made another complaint about his fellow exile: "We know each other too well. In exile and in prison one is laid bare before the other and every little thing becomes apparent. The worst thing is that it is these 'small things' that dominate a relationship. There is little chance to show one's better side. I have moved apart from my comrade and we seldom see one another."[25]

By that time they were indeed living separately, although only a few houses from one another. Stalin rented a room with the Perepigin family. The furniture there was extremely basic, comprising a wooden bed, a small desk, and a bedside table. In the other room lived the seven Perepigin brothers and sisters, four boys and three girls, who were to lose their parents at an early age. According to eyewitnesses the future Soviet dictator lived in wretched conditions. The floor was filthy, being covered by the soot that poured out of the stove. Since the owners of the house could not afford glass, they either boarded up the cracks in the broken windows or stuffed them with newspapers. When Stalin was cold he would tear a book apart and push the cover into the finger-wide cracks. He spent the long evenings in the dim light of a kerosene lamp.[26]

From the rather limited sources it is hard to reconstruct the relationship that existed between the exile and the local inhabitants. Sometimes he would give them medicine and on other occasions hunted and fished with them. "My mother, Darya Alekseyevna, baked bread for him. Lunch was prepared by Comrade Stalin himself," recalled Arseny Ivanov, a *kolkhoz* peasant, to a member of the Igarka party committee. "Sometimes he would have tea with my mother, and on such occasions they would talk. My father did not take part in the conversations because he was deaf. [...] When I[osif] V[issarionovich] left Kureyka, he gave my mother a signed photograph and two coats, one grayish autumn coat and a brown one. The photograph was taken away by someone from the Turukhansk NKVD *[then the OGPU—M. K.]*, who left a receipt for it. The coats eventually wore out."[27]

The recollections of another villager, Anfisa Taraseyeva, have also survived. She was able to spend a longer time with the exile since Stalin lived with her for a short while before moving in with Sverdlov. Taraseyeva remembered that her tenant "read a lot and lived a self-sufficient life. He went fishing and hunting. [...] He had a local friend, Martin Petyerin, who went with him."[28]

Even in the early 1950s Lidia Perepigina remembered this local man clearly, although she had only been about fourteen at the time when she first met Stalin: "Stalin went fishing with him. Peterin was a Khanty," she recalled. She also said that initially, even in winter, Stalin had worn a light black-collared overcoat. Later a woman by the name of Matriona Saltakova had made him a warm hat lined with rabbit fur, and some knitted gloves and socks.[29]

"In his leisure time Stalin liked to go to evening dances," recalled Lidia, unaware that such things should not be said about the Master of the Kremlin. "He could be merry as well. He liked to dance and sing. He particularly liked the song that began 'I am guarding the gold, the gold'. He often called to see people and took part in birthday dinners. He also drank," she added.[30]

The landlady must have kept quiet about the fact that one of their visits together to a neighbor had had an unwelcome consequence: she was made pregnant by her tenant and as a result her brothers were said to have called Stalin to account. However, the story later reached the Alliluyev family: "My aunts told me that during one of his periods of exile in Siberia he [Stalin] lived together with a local peasant woman and that their son now lives there somewhere, poorly educated and preferring anonymity," wrote Svetlana Alliluyeva at the beginning of her life in emigration in America.[31] In the 1960s Jiři Hanzelka and Miroslav Zikmund, the two famous Czech world travelers, also found evidence of this incident in Siberia. Some of their travelogues appeared in the Czech press at the time of the Prague Spring.[32]

Despite the scandal Stalin remained in Kureyka throughout his exile. He obviously did not even attempt to get away from the settlement, as Sverdlov did, and move to the larger village of Monastirskoye, several hundred kilometers away, where several of his old acquaintances were living in exile, even though this would have been feasible. Sverdlov had bombarded Kibirov, the local chief of police from Ossetia, with petition after petition, until the morose official had given in and allowed him to move away. Stuck in Kureyka, strangely enough Stalin's only friend remained a guard by the name of Mikhail Merzlyakov. He had replaced the previous guard, who had treated both Sverdlov and Stalin with great cruelty. The guard had knocked on their door several times a day, and even during the night, and had harassed them to such an extent that, due to the string of complaints about him, the chief of police had replaced him with Merzlyakov.[33]

From then on Merzlyakov alone guarded Iosif Dzhugashvili, who had a reputation as a notorious escapee. In 1936 the former tsarist gendarme recounted his recollections of the one-time exile to the director of the Krasnoyarsk Museum. He signed a copy of the conversation and posted it to Stalin. From the still unpublished manuscript we learn that he was rather a servant than a guard to the exile. He allowed his charge to go off on a two-week fishing trip, and always tried to be at the disposal of the exile who was so much poorer than he was himself.[34] He stated that he had never prevented "Comrade Koba" from visiting a former cellmate called Odintsov, who lived thirty-seven kilometers from Kureyka.[35]

Several times a year they visited Monastirskoye together: "Stalin met political exiles there, but I don't know who," remembered Merzlyakov. "He also bought food. We spent a long time in the village, sometimes five or seven days. I had no idea where he was during this time, who he was seeing, or where he lived. I[osif] V[issarionovich] eventually always returned to the police station himself to say that we could go back. In the summer we went to Monastirskoye by boat. On the way there the boat was pulled by dogs and on the way back we rowed ourselves. In the winter we went on horseback. Stalin always smoked a pipe. He smoked a short, curved pipe. He filled it with simple *makhorka* or light tobacco. [...] In the winter he wore boots, and for the journey he had fur-lined footwear made of reindeer skin that he had been given by the local inhabitants."[36]

From these recollections, which frequently digress into insignificant details, it unexpectedly turns out that the Soviet dictator was grateful to the gendarme even years later. In 1929, when Merzlyakov faced expulsion from the *kolkhoz* because of his past, he turned to Stalin for help. Stalin openly defended him. He wrote to the village soviet that although the gendarme had not been his friend he had not been hostile to him, either: "...Mikh[ail] Merzlyakov carried out the task he was given by the chief of police according to the book, but without the usual police zeal. He was not spying on me. He did not make my life a misery. He did not bully me. He tolerated my frequent disappearances. He criticized his superiors on several occasions for their many orders and prescriptions. I regard it as my duty to confirm this to you."[37]

☆ Merzlyakov would sometimes set off on Stalin's request and travel by sledge to a neighboring settlement where the post arriving for the exiles was held. "Comrade Koba" awaited the return of his guard with undisguised impatience. From his letters we learn that in those days he frequently wondered why the St. Petersburg Bolshevik newspaper editors failed to publish the texts he wrote in Siberia, even though, according to Anna Alliluyeva, one of these texts, which was fittingly on the national question, even reached Lenin abroad.[38] We can only speculate as to what made everyone reject these manuscripts. The periodical *Prosveshchenie*, which Stalin targeted, was mainly edited by Bolshevik publicists who, like him, were loyal followers of Lenin. Furthermore, the name of the future Bolshevik government's people's commissar for nationalities was included among the permanent staff listed on the inside cover of *Prosveshchenie*. The editors were thus going against the principle of solidarity with the exiles by not publishing his texts, even though the author was spending his exile in difficult financial circumstances in Siberia. However, within the very small circle to which his earlier pamphlet, *Marxism and the National Question*, had been addressed the new manuscript sent from Siberia probably received more criticism than praise, and this was the real reason why it was not published. David Ryazanov, the best

Grigory Petrovsky (x) the people's commissar for internal affairs in Lenin's first government, sitting in front of Kliment Voroshilov.

Russian expert on the heritage of Marx and Engels, referred disparagingly to this text by Stalin in a letter dated as early as September 1913. He asked Aleksandr Troyanovsky, his fellow emigrant in Vienna, whether *Prosveshchenie* indeed wanted to launch a debate based on this study by "a certain Stalin".[39]

It is far from certain that such news reached Stalin in the Turukhansk frontier zone. However, he became increasingly morose as a result of his rejection by the editors of the periodical. We can only imagine how he would have reacted had he learned that it took only two years' absence for Lenin and Zinovyev to forget his real name...[40]

Furthermore, first in the village of Kostino and then in Kureyka, Stalin permanently suspected that his fellow exile Yakov Sverdlov was beginning to "overtake" him in terms of his relationship with the "Foreign Center". From autumn 1913 the easily offended "Comrade Koba" began to wonder whether Lenin and his circle in fact wanted to rescue "Comrade Andrei" rather than him from exile in Siberia. In reality, however, at the Bolshevik Party's last pre-war Central Committee meeting held in Poronin, Galicia, no one made any distinction between the two exiled politicians. The plan was to rescue *both of them*.[41]

This news reached Stalin only after long delay and with great inaccuracy. In his nervous state the brooding exile therefore unburdened himself to two of the worker representatives of the State Duma, Grigory Petrovsky and Roman Malinovsky. The two letters written to them are full of transparent conspiratorial terms, which allowed the Okhrana to decode the message with no difficulty.

One of the letters, signed "Vasily" and dated March 20, 1914, arrived at its destination, after something of a detour, from Yeniseysk province: "Com[rade] Petrovsky. Please give this to Roman.[42] I am only troubling you since I do not kno his address." The letter, with its uptight expressions and constant whining, continues: "About five months ago someone in Piter recommended that I move back there.[43] [...] He[44] wrote to me that if I agreed there would be money for the journey. I answered four months ago but have received nothing since then. Could you clear up this misunderstanding? Three months ago Kostya[45] sent me a picture postcard. He wrote: 'My brother! Until I have sold the horse you can ask for one hundred rubles.'[46] I did not understand this message at all, nor did I ever see the one hundred rubles. Meanwhile, Comrade Andrei[47] received this amount at another address. I think this money belongs to him. Only to him. However, I have received no letter from Kostya ever since."

The complaints still did not end: "I have not received anything from my sister Nadya[48]. It has been four months. I am the victim of a whole series of misunderstandings, probably because there was talk that I would be moving back to work in Pityer.[49] However, none of this has happened. Kosta's choice has fallen on someone else, that is, on Andrei, to whom they sent the one hundred rubles. Am I right, my brother? My friend, please give me a *straight and frank answer*. Please do not respond with silence as you did before. You know my address. I need a clear answer because a lot may depend on it and I appreciate straight talking. [...]"[50]

Once Stalin realized that his correspondents in Poronino, Lenin, Krupskaya, and Zinovyev, were taking little care of him and that Roman Malinovsky was behaving as if they were no longer good friends[51], he turned to Grigory Petrovsky once again. His second letter is very kind, and in places almost humble. At the very beginning he hints at the fact that Petrovsky is his last resort. He heaps praise on the increasingly dynamic actions being undertaken by the St. Petersburg workers, on *Pravda*, and on the Bolshevik faction in the State Duma, before

After 1917, Petrovsky was very proud of his worker background and his huge, rough hands. But once he became the leader of the Soviet Ukraine, he lived in a palace, surrounded by rare plants.

cruelly attacking the Mensheviks: "I read Martov's article on the opposition. He tries to whitewash the Liquidators and in the meantime blackens you as a Bolshevik. I swear by all that is sacred that in the whole Socialist press there is no juggler of words to match Martov."[52]

After this Stalin finally came to the point: his problem was that his articles had not been published. However, in the meantime he had sent "a lengthy article to *Prosveshchenie* on cultural-national autonomy". "Comrade Koba" suggested a host of other possible themes in his letter to Petrovsky. He offered a lengthy article for publication in *Pravda* in "about five installments", under the title "The Foundations of Marxism". Then, constantly referring to himself in the third person, he mentioned further topics: "He will be ready with an article called "The National Question" (for *Prosveshchenie*) and, should the demand arise, will send *Pravda* a popular article on the national question, which will be readily accessible by the workers. Just write and order it..."[53] Finally, between the lines, he referred to how offended he was that the foreign Bolshevik leadership had not organized his rescue: "New winds are blowing here these days. The new governor has moved me to the far north and has had the money that arrived in my name confiscated (a total of sixty rubles). That's how we live here, my friend. It turns out that someone had spread a rumor that I would not be staying for the whole of my exile.[54] What nonsense! I swear, and I'll be damned if I don't keep my word, that this will not happen. I will remain an exile until my sentence ends (in 1917). At times I have considered escaping but now I have finally rejected this idea. Entirely. There are many reasons for this, and if you are interested I will write them to you in detail."[55]

On August 17, 1937 this confidential letter was sent back to "the Master" by Grigory Petrovsky, with the following comment: "Comrade Stalin! Comrade Poskryobishev[56] has ordered me to turn in all my documents and notes related to the Central Committee. While going through my papers, I found your letter and I regard it as my duty to return it to you."[57]

Petrovsky was a worker-representative in the State Duma in tsarist time, the people's commissar for internal affairs in the first Soviet government led by Lenin, and then, in the 1930s, for a short while a candidate member of the Politburo. Nevertheless the tone of his covering letter is nervous: the fact that he had been asked to turn in his documents reveals that his position had become uncertain. Although one of Ukraine's largest industrial centers, Dnepropetrovsk, was still named after him, he was waiting day by day for the NKVD to knock on his door with his arrest warrant.[58] By that time nemesis had already struck his children, to whom Stalin, many years earlier, had sent "kisses" in a letter written to their father: his son Pyotr, who was a famous newspaper editor and one of the disciples of Bukharin, had been imprisoned and then executed, like Petrovsky's son-in-law Zager. The other son of the elderly politician, Vladimir, a division commander in the Red Army, had been expelled from the party following the Tukhachevsky trial and then for a short while had been arrested and placed under police surveillance. At the beginning of the Second World War, along with several other Red Army commanders of a similarly tragic fate, he was sent to the front, where he lost his life under suspicious circumstances. Grigory Petrovsky felt that he might be the next, and could be grateful that Samoylov, a former member of the State Duma's Bolshevik faction and director of the Moscow Revolutionary Museum, took him on as a kind of caretaker. Sometimes young researchers would inquire from the gray-haired, permanently nervous "Uncle Grigory" what it had been like in the 1910s when he was kindling the revolutionary flame at Stalin's side. Petrovsky would give a very cautious answer. He could only breathe freely after the dictator's death and was among the first to recommend the rehabilitation of the tormented and executed old Bolshevik party members.[59]

Some historians and contemporaries idealized Petrovsky because in the years of the Great Terror he unexpectedly found himself outside the leading Stalinist circles. However, Brezhkov, Stalin's interpreter, who lived in Kiev in the nineteen-thirties, presented an entirely different picture of Petrovsky: "This old revolutionary, who had spent several years in tsarist prisons[60] [...], did not mind moving into a house which looked like a Scottish castle. It was built of gray granite slabs and the entrance was surrounded by huge marble columns. Ukrainian notables *[similar to Petrovsky—M. K.]* used to be driven in Buicks and Lincolns. Stalin used these "bourgeois" luxuries to corrupt old Bolshevik party members. Some of them may have initially felt uncomfortable because of this lifestyle, but soon they realized that Stalin did not tolerate any difference in opinion, and that he would sarcastically retort that they were seeking cheap popularity by democratic "window-dressing". It was an important principle in the Stalinist regime that the stately homes and the servants attending to them were provided for the "red barons" only as long as they were in favor with the Master. Stalin could at any moment take all this away with reference to their disobedience, alleged or true crimes. Generally, he also took their lives."[61]

The aged Petrovsky produced the old, tarnished photographs only when, after Stalin's death, the possibility of rehabilitation was discussed. The pictures were taken when the Bolshevik representatives of the State Duma, along with Lev Kamenev, the head of the domestic party organization, had been exiled to the Turukhansk frontier zone on a charge of conspiracy against the war. The photographs show him in the village of Monastirskoye in the company of other exiles, including Joseph Stalin who was visiting them. As recently as the late 1980s these photographs could only be published in the Soviet Union after "the enemies of the people" had been carefully edited out.[62]

But this is a later story. In February 1917, after the overthrow of the tsarist system, Stalin set off with Kamenev, who was later executed on his orders, from the Turukhansk frontier zone to European Russia. In those days he still respected his later victim. Sources made available to researchers only recently show the last weeks of his life in exile in an entirely new light. Along with his fellow exiles the authorities intended to draft him to serve in one of the remote Siberian garrisons. He was to escape this fate as a result of his physical defects. Later, however, he was furious with his sister-in-law Anna Alliluyeva for writing that he had been given an exemption because of his deformed left hand.[63]

On the orders of the Drafting Commission the exiles were forced to travel to Krasnoyarsk, which in comparison to the snow covered town of Kureyka seemed a metropolis. On this journey a strange, almost carnival-like atmosphere prevailed. The procession, comprising decorated sledges, passed through twenty-four settlements of various sizes and stopped off at each one. Stalin traveled in the company of eight other exiles, one of them Boris Ivanov. The memoirs of the Petrograd confectioner have survived. In the first of the two versions he answered questions asked on December 29, 1940. He described how the authorities had dressed them up for the journey: "We were given a Siberian *sakun*, that is, a fur coat, a reindeer *bokari*, or boots, and gloves and hat also made of reindeer skin. Only one person traveled in each sledge *[in a semi-recumbent position—M. K.]* in a kind of cradle made of linen."[64] The other exiles, including Sverdlov, who, as a Jew, had not been drafted "as a punishment", said farewell to the procession in the village of Monastirskoye.

In the late 1950s Boris Ivanov wrote down his recollections once again. In this second version there are no sections praising the Soviet dictator. However, he does mention that Yakov Sverdlov and Filipp Goloshchokin, who were also members of the Central Committee, suggested to Stalin that they should make peace and forget their former differences of opinion. "Comrade Koba", however, morosely refused.[65] Apparently he had already mentally turned his back on the unsuccessful Kureyka period of his life.

The procession then set off. The chief of police Kibirov, who was benevolent towards Stalin, sent advanced notice to all the settlements that they should provide the travelers "...with beds, (plump) feather pillows, milk, meat, and fish". "In some places we stayed for a few days. In Verkhnye-Imbatskoye, in the middle of the Turukhansk frontier zone, for instance, we spent almost a week," remembered Boris Ivanov. The reason that his recollections were never published was that they were too frank: "We did not feel like traveling on as we were exhausted by the journey. But why would we have been in any hurry to be drafted? 'There will be plenty of time for the Germans to make mincemeat of us!' the exiles would say. And Stalin also thought we had no reason to hurry."[66] The conscripts "had a party on two or three nights" in the settlements they passed through. On such occasions "Comrade Koba" would lead the singing. On other occasions he would tell stories.

The guards soon realized that at this pace they would only reach home after a long delay and they became increasingly morose. They sent a telegram to Kibirov informing him that the exiles did not want to travel on. According to Ivanov, "Kibirov answered that he would send Cossacks after us. But we telegraphed back: 'We are ready for your Cossacks.' Stalin also took part in word-

David King, the distinguished English researcher of Stalin's times, gave the title "Siberian Summer" to this set of three pictures. In 1915, more than two years before the Bolshevik takeover, Joseph Stalin (1) participated in a meeting held in the village of Monastirskoye together with some of his fellows in exile. This is when this crinkled group picture was taken. In the row standing in the back, there is Suren Spandaryan (2), Lev Kamenev (3), Grigory Petrovsky (4), Yakov Sverdlov (5), and Filipp Goloshchokin (6). In front of them sits Fyodor Samoylov (7), Vera Shweitzer, Spandaryan's wife (8), Aleksei Badayev (9), and Nikolai Shagov (10). The little child squatting in front of the group is Sverdlov's son, Andrei, who became a merciless torturer of the NKVD in the 1930s.

ing the telegram." Needless to say the exiles had little to lose since they were several hundred kilometers from the place of their departure, Monastirskoye.[67]

Eventually the column of sledges arrived in Krasnoyarsk, where the Drafting Committee classified Iosif Dzhugashvili as *untauglich* for service. Fortunately for him, however, he did not have to return to Kureyka for the short time that was left of his period of exile. He spent some time in Krasnoyarsk, the capital of the region, then moved to Achinsk, one of the smaller settlements near the city. A local clerk, himself a former exile, remembered that the future Soviet dictator was forever smoking a pipe. The most striking feature in his "pockmarked face" was his low forehead "above which there was a thick shock of uncombed hair. His mustache was stained from his pipe. His small, dark brown, almost black eyes peered morosely from under his bushy eyebrows." The writer of these recollections, Baykalov, who was later forced to emigrate, was obviously a keen observer: he recognized that Stalin, who sometimes had to search for the right word and who spoke with a heavy Caucasian accent, was by no means a "leader of the pack" among his fellow exiles. He would sometimes give way if Lev Kamenev, at times sardonically, interrupted what he was saying.[68]

As to the Achinsk period of Stalin's life we also know that he was first hosted by Vera Shweitzer, the widow of his recently deceased friend Spandaryan. He then rented a room from a "petty bourgeois", Pavel Chernavsky. "When he entered our house," remembered Valentina, the host's daughter, "we noticed his linen-lined black and beige coat, which had no fur collar. His jacket and trousers were dark, too. He wore a Russian shirt, also dark, the collar of which buttoned at the side with white buttons. I saw him in the town on two occasions. I noticed that when walking I[osif] V[issarionovich] put his left hand in his pocket and with his right held the lapel of his jacket."[69]

After the Second World War the staff at the Achinsk Stalin Museum interviewed some further eyewitnesses. One old worker, Pyotr Kozlov, only remembered that the future Master of the Kremlin once "stepped out of the house without his coat and hat".[70] Thus he had had a clear view of his "unshaven face", as well as his clothes—a gray shirt and black trousers.[71] A librarian by the name of Aleksandra Pomerantseva, herself a Bolshevik party member, lived in

The next, doctored version of the photograph was most likely made before the period of the Great Terror. Only Lev Kamenev is missing from among these comrades in exile.

the same house as Stalin. In an interview on April 10, 1950 she described how the Achinsk Bolshevik colony was taken by surprise at the news of the overthrow of tsarism: "It happened on a market day and it occurred to me that the peasants would leave the market without knowing anything about what had happened. So I hurried there and told them we no longer had a tsar. His rule had been overthrown. On my way I met Comrade Stalin. He recognized the excitement on my face and asked me where I was going in such a hurry."[72] On hearing the answer, the exiled politician aggreed with the woman's intentions, but did not himself talk at the hastily convened gathering in the town. He did not even sit in the presidium, but was hiding in the crowd.

From this version, which was published in 1939 in the album dedicated to Joseph Stalin's sixtieth birthday, another five persons are missing. At least four of them were victims of the purges in the mid-thirties.

1 Before 1917, the celebrations of the International Women's Day followed the schedule of the Western European, not the Orthodox Christian calendar.
2 Dan, 1987, 101–104.
3 Popova, 1996, 18–59.
4 Moskalev, 1947, 136.
5 Rozental, 1996, 107.
6 *RGASPI*, fond. 558, op. 4, d. 208.
7 *Komsomolskaya Pravda*, December 21, 1929.
8 Kamenev, 1916, 18–83, 93–106.
9 Sverdlov, 1957, vol. I, 46–53, 131–136.
10 *RGASPI*, fond. 558, op. 4, d. 662.
11 Smerch, 1989, 49–50.
12 This is what all of the exiles living in Siberia and northern Russia complained about in their letters.
13 The writer of the letter most likely referred to J. Strasser's book, *Der Arbeiter und die Nation* (Reichenberg, 1912), and A. Pannekoek's work, *Klassenkampf und Nation* (Reichenberg, 1912).
14 *RGASPI*, fond. 558, op. 1, d. 48.
15 This is a reference to the practice of the postal censors, who inspected closed envelopes more carefully than open postcards.
16 Noi Zhordania's byname.
17 Labor movement in Russia did in fact strengthen during the months preceding the First World War, which is what the writer of the letter referred to.
18 *RGASPI*, fond. 558, op. 1, d. 49. Mamia Orakhelashvili, the deputy director of the Marx–Engels–Lenin Institute at the time, sent the letter to Stalin on April 28, 1933, but the Soviet dictator did not approve of its publication.
19 Again, he referred to Noi Zhordania's pamphlet. *RGASPI*, fond. 558, op. 1, d. 5168.
20 *Bolshevistskoye Rukovodstvo*, 1996, 17–18.
21 *RGASPI*, fond. 554, op. 4, d. 662.
22 *Ibid.*
23 *Ibid.*
24 Sverdlov, 1957, vol. I, 268.
25 *Ibid.*, 276–277. For details see Ostrovsky 2002, 399-403.
26 *RGASPI*, fond. 558, op. 4, d. 662.
27 *Ibid.*
28 *Ibid.*
29 *Ibid.*
30 *Ibid.*
31 Alliluyeva, 1969, 330.
32 *Politichesky Dnevnyik*, 1975, vol. II, 476. Stalin's long period of living in Kureyka also has some "blank spots". According to some sources, he made a failed attempt to escape. Ostrovsky 2002, 415-420.
33 *RGASPI*, fond. 558, op. 4, d. 662. The name of the gendarme was I. Laletin. During one of the conflicts, he took the blunt sabre *(saska)* and supposedly wounded Stalin in the neck.
34 *Ibid.*
35 *Ibid.*
36 *Ibid.*
37 *Ibid.*
38 Alliluyeva, 1946, 118.
39 *RGASPI*, fond. 30, op. 1, d. 8.
40 Tucker, 1990, 150.
41 *Bolsheviki*, 1990, 204.
42 That is, to Malinovsky.
43 That is, that he escaped.
44 Roman Malinovsky.
45 Again, Malinovsky.
46 For the expenses of the escape.
47 Yakov Sverdlov.
48 Nadezhda Krupskaya.
49 That is, that he would escape and go back to St. Petersburg.
50 *RGASPI*, fond. 558, op. 1, d. 52.
51 On May 8, 1914, Malinovsky gave back his mandate in the State Duma, and soon left the country, because he was afraid that his activities would be exposed. It is interesting that in the following months Stalin did not react at all to the scandalous news appearing in the press.
52 *RGASPI*, fond. 558, op. 1, d. 5394.
53 *Ibid.*
54 Meaning that he would eventually escape.
55 *RGASPI*, fond. 558, op. 1, d. 5394.
56 Personal secretary of the dictator, as well as director of the dictator's secretariat.
57 *RGASPI*, fond. 558, op. 1, d. 5394.

58 Nekrasov, 1995, 51–56.
59 *RGASPI*, fond. 482, op. 1, d. 18.
60 Evidently the author meant the years Stalin spent mostly in exile.
61 Berezhkov, 1998, 262–263.
62 King, 1997, 29–30.
63 Alliluyeva, 1946, 167.
64 *RGASPI*, fond. 554, op. 4, d. 662.
65 Olga Shatunovskaya made it possible for me to take notes from this manuscript in the mid-1980's in Moscow.
66 *RGASPI*, fond. 554, op. 4, d. 662.
67 *Ibid.*
68 *Vozrozhdenie*, 1950, no. 3–4, 118.
69 *RGASPI*, fond. 554, op. 4, d. 662.
70 Which is quite extraordinary in temperatures of minus 35–40 Celsius.
71 *RGASPI*, fond. 554, op. 4, d. 662.
72 *Ibid.*

The eldelry Stalin and his "family": Kaganovich (1), Malenkov (2), Zhdanov (3), Vasya (4), Svetlana (5) and the ever-present bodyguards.

Next page: Stalin, Kaganovich, Voroshilov, and Yezhov walking in the courtyard of the Kremlin.

PART II

THE "MASTER'S" FRIENDS AND ENEMIES

"Stalin is the most distinguished mediocrity in our party."

LEON TROTSKY

"When he died in 1953 he left a monster whose own death throes are not yet over, more than a generation later… He combined patience with outburst of capricious rage. He combined a certain heavy ordinariness with the ability to force through quite extraordinary social and political changes. And his inner drives, or demons, never rested."

ROBERT CONQUEST

CHAPTER 11
Kira Alliluyeva

For many decades the inaccessibility of sealed archives was regularly blamed for the fact that we knew surprisingly little—and therefore made our judgments on the basis of stereotypes and ideological assumptions—about the twentieth century, an era which produced an unprecedented number of bloody dictatorships. Despite the changed situation today, it is interesting to observe that, worldwide, few researchers have chosen to undertake the study of unpublished documents relating to the rule of Joseph Stalin, which have finally come into the public domain. Historians of the Soviet era, who had become used to having to wait for the publication, following a traditional and strictly conventional order, of only one important source at a time—and surely the realm of Clio could hold few greater pleasures for them than such eagerly awaited "discoveries"!—now seem bewildered at the new mass of documents, amounting to hundreds of thousands of pages, that substantially affect the judgment to be passed on an entire era. As a result of almost three decades of eager "rummaging" through the archives, as well as lengthy conversations with surviving contemporaries in various countries throughout the world, I myself believe that this point in time represents the very last opportunity we have for an examination of the Stalinist model in a fundamentally new light.

As the years were passing, relaxation became increasingly important in Stalin's life.

I was prompted to write my book *Nikolai Bukharin. His Friends and Enemies* by the importance of a number of unpublished documents that I felt cried out to be more widely publicized. The book was written in Russian and published in Moscow soon after the collapse of the Soviet Empire.[1] However, as I completed the final version, I came to regard as more and more important those elements in the work for which I did not have any written source. It became clear that during Stalin's reign and later—even in those decades that were witnessing the triumph of the written word—perhaps the most important decisions with respect to the essence of the Soviet system were made orally and in the greatest secrecy in the presence of just two or three persons in the Kremlin. Thus, in parallel with the publication of as yet unpublished sources I had more and more frequent recourse to the application of the methods of *oral history*.[2] I visited the surviving leaders of the Stalinist system one by one, as well as the dictator's secretaries, his advisors and interpreters, the one-time residents of the Kremlin and their children and grandchildren, and famous artists who had been closely linked to the political elite. Some were proud to describe the terrible acts they had committed; others—mostly those who, from the pinnacle of power, had been plunged directly into the deepest hell of the penal system and who had suffered for years in prisons and the Gulag—were less willing to idealize the past.

Almost without exception the eyewitnesses of this bloody era resembled one another in the initial caution, perhaps even suspicion, they showed when answering my questions. At the beginning of our conversation one of them "tested" me on my knowledge of the bible of the era, the Bolshevik Party's *Kratky Kurs*. Others took me for a Western spy a kind of "intellectual James Bond". "How do I know that you're not a wolf in sheep's clothing?" asked a frowning Yury Zhdanov, the son of the Soviet cultural "pope" and Stalin's son-in-law. Yet in spite of all his suspicions he finally agreed to travel twice from Rostov-on-Don, to Moscow to meet me—as he put it, to present his own version of the

Soviet decades to the "Western reading public". In some cases my interlocutors were only willing to talk to me *because* I came from "over there". As strange as it may sound, even today these people are more afraid of *each other* and of the return of the loved and hated, dreaded but still idealized, Soviet system, than of foreign visitors. A clear indication of this is the fact that in the early spring of 1996—when Russia seemed on the verge of a neo-Communist restoration—several elderly Soviet politicians went back on their promise to talk to me about their past. However, those who were willing to talk would sometimes, after one or two hours of beating about the bush, become astonishingly open. In reconstructing various fragments of memories they regarded and accepted me as a contemporary and readily showed their annoyance if I failed to "remember" certain tiny details of everyday Soviet life between the 1920s and 1940s. The act of recalling the past almost always broke through even the most tightly closed floodgates, and conversations would range almost without limit. These elderly people, who, in talking to me, were recalling and putting things into words often for the first time, even for themselves, would, as the conversation proceeded, generally agree to carry on with their stories in front of a tape recorder or video camera.

For the historian who has become used to relying on written sources this type of "investigation" represents an entirely new task that requires a great deal of patience and discipline. One often pays for the "results"—listening to the especially gruesome stories that follow cynical attempts at self-justification—with sleepless nights. It is no easy task to witness the present misery of victims of the Soviet Regime who have been both physically and mentally broken, alongside the carefree lives of corpulent and complacent former executioners. On the other hand, such conversations provide a primary historical source which it would be impossible to reconstruct from the archives, and which in fact explains several apparently inexplicable or unknown aspects of Soviet—and to a great extent post-war East European—history.

Following in-depth interviews lasting several hours, my elderly interlocutors generally allowed me to record on video their invaluable collections of photographs and historical documents, and before saying goodbye often "recommended" me by telephone to other important witnesses of the era. This was how I was able to capture for posterity, in the form of approximately fifty video recordings and as many tape-recorded interviews, a wealth of details, even the apparently insignificant, that help to place the flood of newly released written resources into a historical and logical context.[3]

The majority of the recordings were made in Moscow between 1989 and 1998, literally at the eleventh hour. Many of my interviewees have since died, among them Dmitry Sukhanov who "selected" Beria, the man regarded as the chief hangman of the Stalinist era—in other words, in the late 1930s it had been Sukhanov, along with his boss Malenkov, who had placed Beria's personal file on Stalin's desk. After a great deal of encouragement on my part Aleksandr Shelepin, one of the most controversial heads of the KGB *(Komitet Gosudarstvennoi Bezopasnosti*, the "Committee for State Security"), eventually revealed some important secrets for the first and last time before a foreign historian. I was also received by Yelizaveta Tukhachevskaya, the intelligent and charming sister of the executed marshall, who revealed some interesting facts about her family background, which in many respects had determined the rather controversial historical role of her brother.[3]

I received similar help from another woman with whom, between 1997 and

1998, I had several lengthy conversations about the atrocities committed by the dictator and the secrets of the Stalin family. Kira Alliluyeva is today the oldest surviving member of the once numerous Alliluyev–Svanidze–Redens family, which was decimated by Stalin. Now about eighty years old, this actress, with her apparently permanent cheerful disposition, can truly be said to have lived through hell. Her frequent, nervous laughter revealed just how painful it was for her to relive the past and to recall the era during which Joseph Stalin—or, as she still referred to him, "my dear relative"—had victimized many of her nearest and dearest, like some Moloch demanding sacrifices. During the troubled years of the great purges prior to the Second World War, Kira Alliluyeva managed to retain a fundamentally balanced personality. The proximity of the Kremlin provided her with a protective shield. Not even the first arrests that took place around her troubled her accustomed lifestyle. Even today she declares almost cheerfully: "It was no more unusual for someone to be taken away from our circle than for a person to be awarded the Order of Lenin or to be promoted from regimental to division commander."

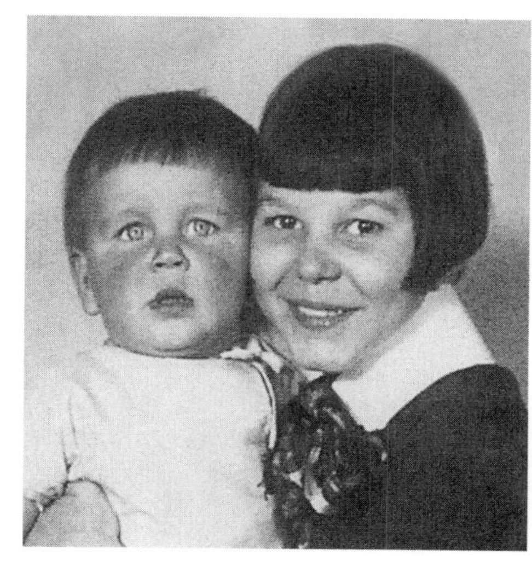

The children of the Alliluyev family considered Kira their "adopted mother".

The outbreak of the "Great Patriotic War" was the real turning point in her life. In the summer of 1941 Hitler's troops were approaching the heart of the Soviet Union with terrifying speed. A young woman at the time, she escaped with her family into the hinterlands, and as a self-conscious Soviet citizen she temporarily left drama school and went to work in a factory. It was then that she became aware of just how many of her fellow citizens had been cold and hungry during the "good old days" of peace. Before that, her parents and her acquaintances, who belonged to the highest echelons of the elite, had never talked to her about such things. She confessed to me that, apart from a few exceptions, she had never come into contact with average Soviet citizens and the kind of physical hardships they suffered, living as she had until then in the privileged environment of the Kremlin, in the Berlin villas that were home to the high-ranking officials of the Soviet colony in Germany, and in the "House on the Embankment", the monstrous gray building made famous by the novel of Yury Trifonov,[4] from where she was taken, in early 1949, by men from the political police.

Prior to this, Joseph Stalin had already struck at several members of his own family. Kira's aunt (Nadezhda Alliluyeva, Stalin's second wife), and her father (Pavel Alliluyev) died in suspicious circumstances. The elder brother of Stalin's first wife, Keto (Alyosha Svanidze), and his wife Maria Korona, along with the "Master's" (Stalin's code name during the Second World War) sister-in-law (Mariko Svanidze), all of whom the Master of the Kremlin had known and respected for several decades, suffered years of cruel torture in Lubyanka Prison before being executed. During the Great Terror the same fate befell Stanisław Redens, who had played an important role in the apparatus of the NKVD *(Narodny Kommissariat Vnutrennikh Del, the "People's Commissariat for Internal Affairs")*, and who was the husband of Stalin's other sister-in-law, Anna Alliluyeva. Ten years later Anna and her best friend Yevgenia Alliluyeva—Kira's mother—were also imprisoned on a charge of "suspected spying and terrorism". Following several months of interrogation the special jury sentenced them to long-term detention, like their mostly Jewish acquaintances who had also been arrested. It later became clear that the lives of the two women had only been spared in order for them to be "available" when the huge anti-Semitic show trial took place in Moscow. Stalin suspected members of the Alliluyev family, Kira among them, of having, over many years, passed information about his private life to the "Zionists", who in turn had passed the information to the hated and feared Western secret services.

For Yevgenia, Kira's mother, the price of having formally assumed the name Alliluyev—a name which rang well in the Bolshevik movement—was poor health and the disintegration of her second marriage. Her aunt, Anna, who had always suffered from nervous problems, went mad while being held in solitary confinement in the Vladimir Prison. Compared with this, Kira, who was twenty-eight at the time of her arrest and just starting out on her career as an actress, survived the investigation relatively easily. From the outset, the intention must have been to give her a minor role in the bloody farce to which her "dear relative" had destined the Alliluyev family.

Furthermore, because she was so afraid of being beaten she proved to be a "co-operative" detainee. She signed whatever confessions against herself and others the interrogating officers placed in front of her: "I spent six months in solitary confinement. Sometimes I was forced into a tall, coffin-shaped cupboard and made to stay there. It should hardly be surprising that after that I agreed to sign all their lies, almost without reading them. I think my confessions were immediately forwarded to Stalin, who must have decided what to do with me at the end of the interrogations. But what else could I have done? Even physically strong men like Tukhachevsky and Blyukher, two Soviet marshals, confessed to anything that was expected of them. Besides, I was certain at first that I would be executed and I was only concentrating on not being tortured too severely beforehand," Kira recounted grimly during one of the breaks in our conversation, recorded on video in Moscow.

On another occasion she remarked that her life had only been spared because she did not appeal to the dictator for mercy: "Stalin did everything contrariwise. Had I begged for my life, he would certainly have had me killed. The men from the Ministry of State Security kept encouraging me: 'Write to him! You're a relative of his after all.' But I said it would be too awkward. Deep down I thought I would be worse off if I did."[5]

Perhaps this was indeed the reason why Kira Alliluyeva was sentenced "only" to five years' exile in the provinces. However, on being released from prison she did not have sufficient money to buy a train ticket to the small town of Shuya to which she had been banished. She therefore had to spend several more days in prison until financial help arrived from members of her family. In Shuya it was some time before she had anywhere to sleep: she spent her nights in a barn, using a large wooden trough that she found there as a bed. She considered herself lucky to find a post as a teacher in a school for backward children: "Why did you antagonize your relative?" the local police wanted to know. Kira, however, always managed to give an evasive answer.

Nevertheless, she was aware that her every step was being watched. This explains why she did not dare to travel to Moscow in secret to say farewell to her dying maternal grandmother. Nor did she know where her mother and her Aunt Anna were being held in prison. She was not able to gain any advantage from the Alliluyev name. She is naturally a very sociable person even today, thus it was extremely hard for her to bear when old acquaintances looked straight past her when they met on the street. Her first husband left her during the first years of her exile, and when, after Stalin's death, she was permitted to move back to Moscow, the management at her old workplace, the reputable "Small Theatre", did not dare to take her back since she was a relative of Stalin. Under threat of further punishment she was obliged to keep silent until the late

"Stalin caused trouble for everyone captivated by him."

The 1930s, immediately before the Great Terror. Yevgenia Alliluyeva (x) and Kira (xx) still look happy; they would have never thought that their "dear relative" would once put them in prison out of revenge.

1980s about what had really happened to the Alliluyev family. As she put it a the end of the video recording session, she had been "scorched" and "battered" by her proximity to her tyrannical relative.

As an elderly woman she still lives in obvious poverty on the outskirts of Moscow, in a tiny panel apartment. Besides her memories, only a few old photographs link her to the "House on the Embankment". When she was forced to move she was not allowed to take her furniture with her, since, to her surprise, she was told that the cupboards and chairs were the property of the Treasury. We had initially intended to talk about her years in prison and about the atmosphere of the 1940s. However, she first recalled the more peaceful years of her childhood.

☆ *K. A.:* I was born in Novgorod in 1920. My mother, to whom I have felt closest throughout my life, was Yevgenia Zemlyanichina. She met my father when she was nineteen, a red-cheeked Russian beauty, although at nineteen her appearance was that of a mature woman. On one occasion she went to a fortune-teller, who told her: "You will move up in the world very soon, my dear, but the higher you get the further you will fall." My mother did not believe her, although *[sighs]* things like that often do turn out to be true. But why should my mother have believed that such dangers lay ahead when, in 1918 *[sarcastically]*, at the dawn of a new era, she had fallen in love with a young soldier in the Red Army, Pavel Alli-

luyev. Since my mother's immediate circle comprised entirely religious people—not to mention my Orthodox pope grandfather—only a church wedding was possible. Otherwise, my mother could not have been very devout: following the victory of the Bolshevik revolution she had the icons removed from the wall of the telegraph office where she was working, along with the portrait of Tsar Nikolai II.
M. K.: Then why did she insist on a church wedding?
K. A.: *[Shrugs.]* I don't know. She must have been emancipated, since she got pregnant before the wedding. On the other hand, it would have been very shameful for her, with her background, if Pavel Alliluyev had not married her. So she had to get married *at any price*... My Red Army soldier father was so much in love with her that he agreed to a church wedding. He must have thought that nobody would ever find out. However, my mother was visited by my paternal aunt, Anna Alliluyeva. She discovered the great crime my parents had committed, and gossiped about it to half the Kremlin. Even Lenin found out that my father *[laughter]* had come under "clerical influence". Stalin also learned about it. But there was no great scandal!

I think I must have been three years old when I was taken to Moscow. My parents were already living there.[6] My paternal grandmother, Olga Alliluyeva, frequently recalled the story of my first meeting with Stalin: "You were hiding in one of the rooms and Iosif Vissarionovich called loudly: 'Kirka!'. You ran to him as fast as you could and he told you 'You have a hole in your head.' This scene was repeated some time later. 'Kirka!' called Stalin. Since he had a kind voice you forgot that he had offended you and you ran to him on your tiny legs that were bowed with rickets. But again you were told 'You have a hole in your head.'"

Indeed, *my dear relative* was always keen to mock others and I was probably not cross with him. I have never stayed angry with people for long, and still don't bear grudges.
M. K.: But after what happened to your family you must feel bitterness towards your "dear relative".
K. A.: *[Laughs, then looks grave and makes a gesture of dismissal.]* Why would I be bitter? It all happened a long time ago. Everything fades with time.
M. K.: Did you often see Stalin in the first half of the 1920s when your family lived in the Kremlin?
K. A.: Very often. Our family lived in the same house as he did, a four-storey building, which in tsarist times was called the Kremlin's "officers' wing". We also knew it by this name. This building was the home of Krupskaya [the wife of Lenin]; Lenin was dead by that time.[7] Stalin also lived there, as did many other Georgians. I recently asked the daughter of Ordzhonikidze, Eteria whether they had lived in the same house, but she told me they hadn't. I remember all the Georgians from my childhood clearly, because they were very kind people. Only Stalin appeared cheerless, although he pretended to be kind if he had to. He could even be charming if he felt it necessary. I vaguely remember that once, when I was fighting with his son Vaska, he stood between us and tried to separate us.
M. K.: Are you sure it was him?
K. A.: Of course. Even at that time Joseph Stalin was the ultimate authority in the family. Everyone sought his favor. Even my father, Pavel Alliluyev, who was a very proud man otherwise. He only beat me once in my life, and that was because of Stalin. It happened when my younger brother Sasha made a loud neighing noise behind our father's back in the billiards room at the summer resort. My father thought it was me and that I risked waking Stalin who was sleeping in one of the neighboring rooms. In a fit of anger he broke the cue

across my back. Then he began to cry because he had never hit me before. Nor did he ever hit me again. You can see how Stalin brought trouble to everyone who came into his sphere. And to us, the Alliluyev family.

1 Miklós Kun: *Bukharin: Jego druzya i vragi. (Nikolai Bukharin. His Friends and Enemies)* Moscow: Izdatelstvo Respublika, 1992.
2 My first book of such kind is Miklós Kun: *Prágai tavasz, prágai ősz: 1968 fehér foltjai.* Budapest: Akadémiai, 1998. English version: *Prague Spring, Prague Autumn: Blank Spots of 1968.* Budapest: Akadémiai, 1999.
3 Based on these interviews, I made a series of documentary films suh *A KGB alkonya (The Twilight of the KGB). On the Ruins of the Empire,* another series I made, has been on Hungarian TV for tree years.
4 This building with a terrible exterior was designed by the architect Boris Yofan and according to Yevgenia Drabkina, the old Bolshevik party member who Stalin personally supervised the plan. As the memoir of one of the residents of the "House on the Embankment" reveals, the building was originally intended to open as a hotel for cadres and important foreign guests (Aroseva-Maksimova 1999, 21). Populating the building was not an easy process, though. The edifice burnt down at the beginning—this was considered the work of the enemy, thus the manager of the construction—which employed hundreds of engineers and workers—was arrested and executed. The building complex was finally completed in 1931. The press immediately named it *Dom pravitelstva*, or government building, and the contemporary public mockingly called it *Titanic* and *DOPR* (for *Dom predvaritelnogo zakluchenyia*, or prison for pretrial detention). This vast eleven-story house accommodated more than 500 comfortable apartments for the Soviet elite. Over the years, six Politburo members, sixty-three commissars (ministers), ninety-four deputy commissars (deputy ministers), nineteen marshals and admirals, and numerous high-ranked military and interior ministry officers, as well as veteran party members lived in it. And to save a longer trip for the residents, there was a restaurant and a walk-in unit that belonged to the Kreml hospital in the building complex, as well as a "government drugstore" filled up with Western medications, and a movie theater, fittingly named *Udarnik*, or "ace worker". The majority of the residents were killed during the years of the Great Terror. The family members of the victims then had to move out of the apartment house—with rare exceptions. Korsunov-Terehova, 1995, 16–26, 35–36, 49–50, 69–70, 79–101, 107–109, 129–130, 227–228, 229–270, 281–282, 297–298, 329–330.
5 Alliluyeva, 1992, 214.
6 Elsewhere, Kira Alliluyeva remembers that she was only 18 months old when she was taken to Moscow. Alliluyeva, 1992, 193.
7 When Kira's parents moved in the Kremlin, Lenin was still alive. He lived in the Kremlin until the spring of 1922, during the autumn, and also at the beginning of 1923. "Once he shook the hand of my mother, who was so proud of this that for a while she did not wash her hands," recalled the elderly actress with a hearty laugh. "Maybe it is only a family legend, but I also heard from my parents that Lenin always found time to look around in the kitchen to see if there is milk left for his favorite cat. Later I myself very often saw this fat tabby in the courtyard. Everyone fed and pampered 'Lenin's cat'."

CHAPTER 12
The Alliluyev Grandparents

M. K.: You must have been about seven years old when your father was transferred abroad. By that time the Wehrmacht had established a close and multifaceted military relationship—although in many respects a secret one—with the Soviet Union. Apparently Pavel Alliluyev played a key role in the secret arms trade, despite the fact that at the beginning of his German mission he spoke very little German.
K. A.: Why would he have needed to be fluent when he had colleagues around to act as interpreters? He had a whole staff of people working for him. I helped him as well at first. I used to interpret for him in hotels and shops. I learned German very quickly and my father sometimes even took me with him on his journeys to the countryside. We lived for five years in Germany, from 1927. First in Düsseldorf, then in Berlin. So I only came into contact with Stalin again when, after the suicide of his wife—my aunt Nadezhda—he lifted us into his immediate circle. We lived for a while in the Zubalovo resort village with him. Moving there for the summer was a particularly memorable experience for me. Not so much because of Stalin, but because I was able to meet my grandparents, who from then on played an increasingly important role in my life.
☆ The spacious, closely built resort houses, which were used the year round, were for decades the scene of many vital decisions concerning the Soviet state, although we know little about the place even today. The houses all bore traces of their former owners, the Armenian Zubalov brothers, who owned oil refiner-

The Alliluyev couple often had quarrels, but in the eyes of their children the mother and the father were exemplary parents.

ies in Batumi and Baku, and who were descended from one of the wealthiest families in Caucasia. During the Civil War the brothers fled abroad. It was then that three members of the Bolshevik political elite, whose previous life in the Bolshevik movement had also been linked with Baku—Joseph Stalin, Anastas Mikoyan, and Klim Voroshilov—moved into these houses near Moscow with their families.[1] Stalin's *dacha* was Zubalovo-4. Levon Karakhan (Karakhanyan), the deputy commissar for foreign affairs; Adolf Warski, who was one of the leaders of the Polish Communist Party; the family of the late Feliks Dzerzhinsky; and Ian Gamarnik, the head of the political staff of the Red Army, also had houses in the Odintsivo district resort village, located between the Usovo railway station and the hamlet of Kalchuga.[2] In the "Stalin villa", a two-storey house surrounded by armed guards and a high fence, three or four families sometimes lived at the same time, while their staff stayed in the small houses nearby.

The wall giving onto the garden in the downstairs hall was mostly glass, since the doctors had prescribed regular sunshine for one of the Zubalov brothers, who was suffering from tuberculosis. This room was transformed by Sergei Alliluyev, Stalin's father-in-law, into a carpentry workshop. There was a small movie projection room in the house, as well a pianola, which Stalin sometimes tried to play. Another of his favorite pastimes was shooting with a double-barreled shotgun at crows, which were common in the area.[3] Leon Trotsky also describes how, in Stalin's *dacha*, "in one of the rooms there is a projection screen, and in another a pianola—an expensive player piano to satisfy the musical needs of the host. It seems that Stalin is not able to get by without the arts. He spends his recreation hours bent over the player piano, admiring the melodies of *Aida*. In music, as in politics, he likes the obedient machine. In the meantime Soviet composers follow to the letter the instructions of the dictator, who owns two pianolas."[4]

The house was rebuilt based on the ideas, and even the sketches, of Nadezhda Alliluyeva, not long before she committed suicide; even the color of the wooden paneling was her choice. In the early 1930s part of the garden was converted to provide space for sporting activities, and before the war a large, white *yurta* was erected in the courtyard. In the winter Stalin's guests played billiards or dominoes in one of the downstairs rooms.[5] However, Zubalovo-4 was only one of the *dacha*s—or country villas—used by Stalin.[6] It was much more modest than the Lipki resort, which was also refurbished using plans drawn up by Nadezhda Alliluyeva. According to a diary entry by Maria Korona there was "a wonderful English-style park there; it featured an enormous lake in front of the house, with a bridge across it, and a waterfall dividing it into two large pools. It was full of fish and crabs."[7]

Other resorts near Moscow were also at the disposal of the Soviet dictator and his circle. Following the death of Nadezhda Alliluyeva her relatives initially tried to live in Zubalovo, Lipki, or one of the other *dacha*s near Moscow, in order to be near Stalin. However, they soon realized that this did not always please their "dear relative". Thus in early 1935, contrary to Caucasian tradition, even Sergei Alliluyev, the patriarch of the large family, found it necessary to appeal to his son-in-law for permission: "Dear Joseph! I am very ill. I am depressed and miserable about my…arteriosclerosis. I need some peace and quiet. Please allow me to live in Zubalovo. With a firm handshake and greetings: Sergei." Stalin's answer reveals that, barely two years after the mysterious death of his wife, he did not dare, or did not want, to expel the Alliluyev family—and especially its head—from the Zubalovo paradise: "Sergei! What a terrible man you are! Why are you asking for my approval when you have every right to move to Zubalovo and live there without permission? Go and stay there for as long as you like. J[oseph] Stalin. January 26, 1935."[8] (Interestingly, before the Alliluyev family moved into Zubalovo-4, Sergei Alliluyev had obtained a place in a health resort for himself and the family of his son Pavel, not through his son-in-law but through Mikhail Kalinin: "My dear comrade, Mikhail Ivanovich!" he wrote on May 12, 1932 to his old friend from "Caucasian days", who, in the meantime, had become the formal head of the country. "Please be kind enough not to turn down the request of an old man. I am turning to you for the following reason: my son Pavel has recently returned from spending five years in Germany. This is the first time I have seen his children, my German-born grandsons, on Soviet soil. They are desperately in need of fresh air. That is why I am turning to you. [...] I would like to be given the use of a few rooms in the Arkhangelskoye resort. I would pay all expenses and require no board. I could spend the summer with my little grandsons in the open air, near the forest and among the wild flowers. Where the countryside is so beautiful. You will have my undying gratitude for this. With Com[munist] greetings: Sergei Alliluyev.)"[9]

According to documents left by Alliluyev the life of the ill-fated head of the family continued to be eventful after 1917. During the Civil War he was sometimes to be found in the Crimea, which was controlled by the Whites, and sometimes in Georgia. In the early 1920s he settled in Petrograd, where he was elected as a member of the body that controlled the nationalized electrical power plants. Sergei Alliluyev, who appeared much older than his age, was frequently in poor health. According to one source, in the summer of 1924 he spent over a month in the sanatorium named after Trotsky, which was reserved for privileged patients. In 1925 he spent two months resting in Caucasian health resorts.

In those years the former underground Bolshevik activist frequently went to Moscow on official business, and on such occasions he would pay a visit to his children who lived in the city. Nevertheless, he moved to the capital only after his retirement. In spite of being one of Lenin's favorites and the father-in-law of Stalin, in the Soviet era Sergei Alliluyev was assigned no special, confidential tasks: between 1924 and 1928 he controlled the electric cable network in Leningrad.[10] (In the 1910s he had fulfilled the same task in the Viborg district of the city.) However, he never became a Soviet representative, nor a member of any party body. After October 1928, when he suddenly gave in his notice to his superiors, there was much controversy even concerning the amount of his old-age pension. ☆

M. K.: I have heard from many people that the real cohesive power in the Alliluyev family—its "leaven", to use the phrase of Doctor László Pollacsek, the famous ear, nose, and throat specialist and Stalin's Hungarian doctor—was Sergei Alliluyev. And you were his favorite grandchild.

K. A.: [Nods emotionally.] That's quite true. My mother, who was quite strict with us, often scolded my grandfather for spoiling me. But he always told her: "When Kira grows up she will do the cleaning and ironing, but until then let the little darling play and enjoy herself." Many of the former residents of the Kremlin and the "House on the Embankment" must have told you what a warm-hearted man my grandfather was. But he could also be as hard as stone. *[Whispers.]* Just like his daughter Nadezhda. He couldn't stand seeing the weak being picked on. He sometimes even reprimanded Stalin for this—although I personally never witnessed him doing so. My grandfather was a fascinating, adventuresome man, just like his Gypsy ancestors must have been. In his youth

"Olga Alliluyeva is said to have wrapped many men around her finger in her youth."

he had often got into fights. If he was working for someone, for instance, and recognized that the boss was mistreating his employees, he would beat him up. Whenever this happened he would be fired, of course. But my grandfather was proud of his skills as a worker and of how much he earned, under the old regime, in the electric power plants. It meant he was able to give all four of his children an education, despite the fact that in those days the fees in secondary schools and universities were extremely high.

M. K.: It is certainly interesting that under the rule of Tsar Nikolai II, whom he hated so much, Sergei Alliluyev, the locksmith turned electrician, was able to rent a *dacha* near Petrograd in the summers for his family. In the summer of 1917, when he was hiding Lenin in his home, he fired his *housekeeper* to prevent the news from getting out—which tells us that, as a skilled worker with many children, he could afford to have a housekeeper in the first place. Under your "dear relative", skilled workers were never as well off as that. Apart from the celebrated Stakhanovites.

K. A.: [Giggles.] That's all quite true! As an old man he would sometimes mention that in the "tsarist hell" skilled workers were much better paid than in the world of *pyatiletka*s, or five-year plans. But he always added: "Man does not live by bread alone!" I think he was among the first to join the Bolsheviks in Caucasia. At the beginning of the Soviet era this was regarded as a major virtue. Until Stalin got out the list of old underground party members and began to "gather them in". My grandfather, however, survived. He was, after all, still the father of "poor Nadya". Besides, everyone knew that in the summer of 1917 he had hidden Lenin.[11]

☆ On this point Kira Alliluyeva proved herself rather too naive: in the time of the Great Terror a former conspiratorial relationship with Lenin represented a serious danger for old party members. Joseph Stalin began hunting down former underground Bolsheviks who, in the summer of 1917, had given shelter to Lenin—then in hiding from the authorities of the Provisional Government on a charge of betraying the country—and to the Soviet dictator's later chief rival, Grigory Zinovyev. In the era of show trials and mass genocide the Master of the Kremlin ordered the execution of Kayurov, the leader of the workers in the Viborg district, who had also hidden Lenin. Kayurov's sons were also executed. He had Yemelyanov, the owner of the mythologized "Razliv hay barn", imprisoned, and his two sons executed. He began to pursue Ajno Rahja, one of the founders of the Finnish Communist Party, even though he had helped Lenin escape from his hiding place, the "Razliv hay barn", into Finland. All these people were good acquaintances of Sergei Alliluyev. Stalin even struck at Lenin's friends from his youth, who by that time were very old. The elderly electrical engineer Ivan Radchenko, who had joined the Russian Social Democratic movement in 1897, was dragged from his apartment in Moscow on the fortieth anniversary of his party membership. In February 1938 he was sentenced to twenty-five years in "strict isolation". This characteristic Soviet-era euphemism usually meant the death penalty. The prisoner was an old benefactor of the Alliluyev family: before 1917 he had provided work for Sergei Alliluyev on several occasions in the electrical plants under his control. He had sent Alliluyev's daughters Anna and Nadezhda on regular vacations and had helped in their education. Little wonder that on March 15, 1943 Alisa, the wife of Radchenko, claiming that the veteran engineer had been sentenced "as a result of the interference of domestic and foreign fascists", turned to Stalin's father-in-law to ask whether her husband was still alive. "He was suffering so much physically from the cold and morally from being unable to do anything—and in particular from the fact that he did not understand what had happened to him ('If only I knew why I was arrested')—that for him, and now for me, too, death would be the best way out."[12]

Among the documents left by the Master of the Kremlin is an article by Sergei Alliluyev, which appeared in the 1923/6 issue of *Krasnaya Letopis*, a party historical periodical published in Leningrad: "How Comrade Lenin and Comrade Zinovyev Hid in July 1917. (Excerpts from a memoir)." Written on the article is a brief message from Stalin to his wife: "Tat'ka! Read your father's work. S[talin]."[13]

Sergei Alliluyev was later forced to falsify the past in his memoirs. Since this was obviously something he found difficult to do he occasionally restricted himself to providing only lists of who met whom, and where, among the militants of the Bolshevik movement during the years of underground activity. Thus he avoided the kind of elaborate eulogistic clichés that were compulsory at the time.[14] However, apart from this self-censorship he had ambitions as a writer and a boundless desire to communicate. This did him little good in terms of the quality of his recollections, which first appeared in newspaper and periodical articles, and after the war in book form, with a commendatory foreword by Mikhail Kalinin. Furthermore, like most semi-erudite people, he was fond of "theorizing", thus his texts were substantially rewritten by the editors of the various publications in which they appeared.[15] His old acquaintance Maksim Gorky advised him in a letter written in September 1934: "I have read your manuscript. In your recollections about Ilich [Lenin] it seems to me that there are too many reflections and too few facts. [...] Nevertheless, I strongly advise you to continue writing. If you consider it necessary I would be glad to read and correct the manuscript."[16] ☆

M. K.: In the early 1930s which of the better-known politicians belonged among Sergei Alliluyev's circle of friends?

K. A.: [Frowning.] One was Gorky, who always encouraged my grandfather to write his memoirs. Another was Kalinin. My grandfather knew him already from the early years of the century in Tiflis. A third was Kirov, with whom he shared even his most secret thoughts.[17] My grandfather was less familiar with the younger politicians—but don't forget that my grandfather was born in 1866, soon after the liberation of the Russian serfs. He belonged to another generation.

M. K.: Svetlana Alliluyeva, Stalin's daughter, wrote the following about her grandfather's funeral: "He lay in his coffin like an Indian holy man—there was something attractive about his fine, withered features, his arched nose, his white mustache and beard. The bier was placed in the Museum of the Revolution, and many people made their pilgrimage there, especially from among the old Bolsheviks. Litvin-Sedoy, an elderly revolutionary, spoke at the graveside. At the time I didn't fully understand what he said, but I have remembered his words ever since and grasp their true meaning only now *[in the early 1960s—M. K.]*: 'We, the members of the older generation of Marxist idealists...'"[18]

K. A.: Unfortunately I was in Sochi at the time. I went there to rest, hoping to find my grandfather alive on my return. But he died of stomach cancer. Years earlier he had been beaten by tsarist gendarmes in prison. He had been knocked to the ground and kicked in the stomach by men with heavy boots. Perhaps that was the reason why this horrible disease attacked him later. At the end of his life he was in such pain that he could not eat. He died of starvation. But by then not even on his deathbed did he truly make peace with my grandmother.

☆ Apparently, at the time of the Great Terror, Sergei Alliluyev deeply condemned Joseph Stalin. However, despite his reservations he still chose to be submissive before his tyrant son-in-law, who had brought so much suffering to his family. Among his papers can be found drafts of letters that reflect this fact: "My dear Joseph! Accept the heartfelt and warm good wishes of an old man on being decorated with the well-deserved Order of Victory. At the same time I congratulate you from the bottom of my heart for being awarded the highest military rank and becoming the supreme leader of the Soviet Union."[19]

In his will the old Bolshevik party member left his archives, and all his possessions, to his daughter Anna. Like many others, during our meeting in Moscow Tatyana, the daughter of Stalin's secretary Ivan Tovstukha, recalled that if a person near to Stalin or another member of the party leadership died, the political police would try to get hold of their documents immediately. This did not happen in the case of Stalin's father-in-law. In a letter dated 7 September 1945 Anna officially asked Vyacheslav Molotov that from then on she be paid the money due to her father, and that she be exempt from paying inheritance tax.[20] Shortly after this she forwarded to Stalin a letter that her father had written to the Master of the Kremlin before his death. The letter revealed how anxious the old Alliluyev was about the fact that the appearance of his book was being constantly delayed. In her covering letter Stalin's sister-in-law, Anna, mentioned that she had also written her own memoirs. "Both books are with Comrade Zhdanov. [...] Since my father was very concerned about this matter, I have made up my mind to turn to you."[21] Apparently the letter found the addressee in a good mood, since he gave permission for the two memoirs—which later caused an enormous stir—to be published in book form.[22]

Almost two years later, on April 18, 1947, Anna Alliluyeva turned to "dear Joseph" once again in the name of her deceased father. From this bitter letter it appears that Stalin had displayed pettiness towards his "model Bolshevik" father-in-law, as well as the female members of the Alliluyev family. It was on his orders that the NKVD authorities had turned the family's large home in the "House on the Embankment" into communal apartments.[23] Being the descendant of poor serfs the former electrical fitter had lived comfortably in the artificially created communal apartment house, since compared to the average poverty-stricken Soviet citizen, he still lived reasonably well. Stalin, however—who dealt personally with assigning the apartments in the "House on the Embankment"—took care to make the lives of his relatives hell.

Anna knew this only too well. She turned to Stalin in writing since, by that time, she had given up asking to be received by him in person. "Life goes on and with it appear new problems to burden one," she exclaimed. Although she sensed only too clearly that the elderly dictator had "dropped" those relatives who had previously belonged to his court, she was determined to help her family get rid of their unwelcome co-tenants. "Even during my father's lifetime people were moved into our apartment," she wrote. "Since then a total of six families lived in the apartment. My father and I asked Comrades Molotov, Kalinin, and Mikoyan to rid us of them. This never happened. We were told that it was on your orders that strangers be moved into my father's apartment. (It measures ninety square meters, forty square meters of which are occupied by co-tenants.) Although the apartment was assigned by Comrade Beria to my father in perpetuity back in 1938 after he wrote to you about it several times, we have not been able to have a home of our own for the last six years, which caused my father, and all of us, a great deal of bitterness. Joseph, I ask you, if

Stalin's cronies were particularly afraid of Olga Alliluyeva. After getting divorced from her husband in their old age, Stalin decided to let her stay in her not too large Kremlin apartment. In this picture Olga Alliluyeva sits between her daughter, Anna and her grandson, Vasily.

it was indeed on your orders, allow me to have to myself the apartment in which my father used to live."[24]

The sender apparently had little confidence in a favorable decision from her omnipotent brother-in-law, thus at the end of her letter she appealed in the name of her mother, Olga Alliluyeva, who was respected by Stalin until the end of his life: "...my mother has grown much weaker. She is suffering from cardiac seizures and would like to see her son-in-law as soon as possible." Thus Anna attempted to be received by Stalin using her mother's high standing with him. However, the dictator refused to receive his sister-in-law. Subsequently, by way of punishment, he even distanced himself from his mother-in-law, of whom we know very little. Today, there is hardly anyone left from among the former residents of the Kremlin or their immediate families who knew Olga Alliluyeva. In the early 1920s she seemed a strong-willed, attractive woman. She often boasted of her German and Georgian ancestors, and spoke Russian with an accent until the end of her life.[25] She was proud of her wealthy family, who had only agreed to her marriage with the impoverished Sergei Alliluyev after the bridegroom seduced her and eloped with her. Olga was less than fourteen at the time!

According to family legend, however, the romance did not last for long. In the course of their long marriage Sergei and Olga quarreled constantly. In their old age they divorced officially—something that was not unusual among the former underground Bolsheviks who had got into power. According to the memories of contemporaries such as Yelizaveta Drabkina, Olga would often exclaim to her husband in the presence of others: "You gypsy! Why don't you go back to your ragged relations in their camp? My ancestors were wealthy German settlers, not like yours!" In addition, she found it hard to put up with her husband's militant atheism. Olga must originally have been a God-fearing soul.[26] Her religious inclinations were only increased by the blows of fate delivered against her family by Stalin, who was one year her senior. Following the early and tragic death of her daughter Nadezhda and her son Pavel she was broken both physically and mentally. Nor could she come to terms with the fact that one of her sons-in-law, Joseph Stalin, had had the other, Stanisław Redens, the husband of her daughter Anna, executed. Little wonder that she referred to the Soviet political police as the *Gestapo*.[27]

Despite this the old woman, who had a reputation for being sharp tongued, apparently enjoyed a relatively stable position until the end of her life. The Soviet dictator's entourage feared her like the plague. After her divorce it was Stalin who decided that she should be allowed to remain in their not very spacious apartment in the Kremlin. Nor did she have to put up with co-tenants, like her former husband, Sergei Alliluyev. She received a comfortable old-age pension and was able to stay at Sosni, the sanatorium used by the Soviet elite near Moscow. She had use of the cars in the party garage, and when she had heart problems could reach the doctor at the Kremlin hospital by telephone. Thus, until the end of her life, she retained her status as "Stalin's mother-in-law". ☆

K. A.: My grandparents were very different from one another. My grandfather Sergei was a family-oriented man, while Olga Alliluyeva is said to have wrapped many men around her finger in her youth. Svetlana also refers to this in her book.[28] They say that grandmother even had an affair with Stalin, but I don't believe it. It is a true, however, that Stalin had the greatest respect for Olga Alliluyeva. He even wrote a letter to her from exile in Siberia.[29] Later, as a sign of his unconditional trust, Joseph Stalin allowed my grandmother to stay in the Kremlin even after the war. She often told us that after 1945 Stalin scarcely spent any time in his old home, preferring to live in his *dacha* in Kuntsevo, near Moscow.

M. K.: But what made Stalin change so much?

K. A.: It seems that solitude became more important to him than anything else. Whenever he was not partying with members of the Politburo, that is. There was one aspect in which my grandparents resembled one another: they were incapable of petitioning great men. They could have achieved anything, even from Lenin, who loved the Alliluyevs so much. But they turned to him only on one or two occasions. Nor did they make use of Mikhail Kalinin or other friends of the family when they needed help.

☆ In fact, this is not the truth. In March 1920, during the Civil War, at the request of Olga Alliluyeva, Lenin saw to it that the Red soldier, signalman Pavel Alliluyev, was withdrawn from the front and sent to a sanatorium. The sickly young man was then reassigned to service in the hinterland, in the pleasant climate of Caucasia.[30] Olga Alliluyeva bombarded others with similar requests, including Avel Yenukidze, who was "responsible" for the welfare of the Bolshevik leaders.

As revealed in an undated letter, filled with spelling mistakes, written to the nominal head of Soviet-Russian state Kalinin—probably in December 1920—the Alliluyev family was not always as tight-knit as their descendants liked to claim. For instance, it never occurred to Olga that, faced with financial difficulties, she should make use of the help of her son-in-law, Stalin. Although her daughter Nadezhda was already living in the Kremlin, she did not answer Olga Alliluyeva's letters. Nor to her other daughter, Anna, who also lived near the "pot of gold" and who, like her younger sister, was for a while secretary to Stalin, then Lenin.

At the time of writing her letter to Kalinin, Olga was the librarian of the half-completed power plant in Shatura, near Petrograd. Apparently she was on the verge of starvation. At the time, however, because of the Civil War and War Communism, the majority of the population—with the exception of the members of the Bolshevik elite in power—was also starving and impoverished. Stalin's mother-in-law was prompted to write her letter on recognizing that former underground party activists like her husband, who, along with members of their families, had become part of the *nomenklatura*, had enjoyed numerous privileges almost from the very first.

Having known Mikhail Kalinin well for twenty years, Olga was in a position to challenge him about such privileges in all frankness. All the more so, since the "all-Soviet *starosta [a village elder in tsarist Russia—Trans.]*",[31] who had once been an impoverished land laborer, then a mechanic, already had a reputation in the early 1920s as a man who loved good living. He had actress lovers—including Tatyana Bach, the corpulent operetta prima donna—and in the years of the Civil War sought the company of Shalyapin and other celebrities. He was also fond of money: financial motives had often determined his decisions even before the Bolshevik takeover. In the late summer of 1917, for instance, when the leadership of his party appointed him as head of the Petrograd city duma, he hesitated a great deal as to whether to accept the honor, since at the time he was earning a good salary as a skilled worker at the Ayvaz machine plant.

Olga Alliluyeva therefore had every reason to hope that she would obtain a monthly allowance—or, as she called it, a "stipend"—from Kalinin, who as a private individual was good-hearted and rarely denied the requests of his old friends. Another appeal from Olga provides a good illustration of the state of public affairs at the time. She asked the "*muzhik* head of state" to send her, by official courier, a large quantity of salt, which, in the countryside, could be bartered for basic foodstuffs at a good "exchange rate": "Take into account how wretched my budget is. It is barely enough for mere survival, especially with the present high prices. Money can buy nothing. One can only barter, but people will only give things in exchange for salt. If I had salt I could stay afloat for a while. I want to know how I can get hold of some. I'll come to the point: tell me frankly if you can get some for me via Avel [Yenukidze]. Just for me. You may well ask why I am not turning directly to Avel. I am very cross with him. He is behaving coldly towards me, obviously because he has become a commissar. [...] My two sons are at the front. My health has deteriorated. My daughters are living their own lives and I might as well be dead for all they care. They never write a single line to me. They have forgotten everything [I have done for them], but God forgive them, they cannot understand since they are young. [...] I wait in hope. Do not destroy my faith in comradely relationships and in you."[32]

1 Alliluyeva, 1981, 24–26, 29. According to Sergei Alliluyev, the Subalov family did support the revolutionary movement financially
2 Mikoyan, 1999, 283.
3 Even during his Black Sea vacations, Stalin was eager to shoot at empty wine bottles with his handgun. Buber-Neumann, 1995, 177.
4 Trotsky, 1991, 56.
5 Alliluyev, 1995, 115–121.
6 The leaders of the Stalinist times always complained about their serious—or rather, imagined—illnesses. Yet, in the meantime, they wrote a lot about how many different sports they were doing and how luxuriously they were spending their vacation. "With Molotov, we ride horses, play tennis, go bowling and boating, shoot at targets, in a word, we have a great rest here," boasted Anastas Mikoyan to his wife, Ashen, in his letter of June 8, 1928. Mikoyan, 1999, 292.
7 *Iosif Stalin v obyatiakh semyi*, 1993, 179.
8 *RGASPI*, fond. 668, op. 1, d. 15.
9 *RGASPI*, fond. 78, op. 1, d. 430.
10 *RGASPI*, fond. 668, op. 1, d. 15 and 16.
11 *RGASPI*, fond. 668, op. 1, d. 15.
12 *RGASPI*, fond. 668, op. 1, d. 15.
13 *RGASPI*, fond. 668, op. 1, d. 3460. "Tat'ka" was the nickname of Stalin's second wife, Nadezhda. It appears frequently in the correspondence between them.
14 An example for this is his long letter he wrote, as a response to the request of the researchers of the Leningrad Institute for Party History, on his five encounters with Stalin (in July 1909, twice in February 1911, in early September 1911, and in early autumn 1912). Alliluyev, 1946, 81–83.
15 This is what happened, for example, with his article published in *Proletarskaya Revolutsia*, 1937, no. 8.

16 *RGASPI*, fond. 668, op. 1, d. 15.

17 The insider Mikhail Roslyakov, a close associate of Kirov and a good acquaintance of the Alliluyevs, also confirms this. See Roslyakov, 1991, 115–119.

18 Alliluyeva, 1981, 39.

19 *RGASPI*, fond. 668, op. 1, d. 15.

20 *Ibid.*

21 *RGASPI*, fond. 668, op. 1, d. 14.

22 Before the Second World War, Stalin had already agreed once that the memoirs of Sergei Alliuyev and Anna Alliluyeva be published in a journal series form.

23 *Ibid.*

24 *RGASPI*, fond. 668, op. 1, d. 15.

25 "My grandmother was born as the ninth child in the family. Although she received the ancient Russian name Olga, she spoke German at home, and Georgian in public. [...] She remembered her German very well, and often sang the *Stille Nacht* to me." Alliluyeva, 1988, 251–252.

26 Alliluyeva, 1981, 40.

27 *Vremya i My*, 1999, no. 142, 183.

28 "...my grandmother often fell in love with men. On occasion she had an affair with a Polish, then a Hungarian or Bulgarian, she even had a romance with a Turkish man. She liked the Southern types, and she sometimes huffed: 'Russian men are all bumpkins.' The children already came to terms with this when they went to secondary school. The affairs sooner or later ended, and family life went along its normal course." Alliluyeva, 1981, 39–47.

29 Alliluyeva, 1946, 117–118.

30 *The Trotsky Papers*, 1971, vol. II, 128.

31 It was Leon Trotsky who first coined this widely used phrase for Kalinin. In the spring of 1919, after the death of Yakov Sverdlov, Trotsky the head of the Red Army worked hard to persuade the Soviet party leadership to appoint the only *muzhik* or peasant member of this elite to the chairmanship of the Central Executive Committee. Trotsky, 1991, 239.

32 *RGASPI*, fond. 78, op. 1, d. 458.

The Hours of Relaxation

After the Civil War, Stalin regularly retreated for several weeks to one of his lavish villas along the Black Sea coast or to one of the mountain resorts in the Caucasus. In the photograph Stalin goes hunting together with Voroshilov (x). The company is led by Yevdokimov, a high-ranking militia officer.

During the excursions, which often involved hunting tours, the bespectacled Lavrenty Beria, the first secretary of the Caucasian party organization, was Stalin's cicerone. The future "chief executioner" of the Soviet Union wore an ax on his side. A lower-rank official collects firewood for a camp-fire.

This picture was taken in the mid-1930s. The relaxed company (from the left, Yegorov, Voroshilov, Stalin, Tukhachevsky, and Lakoba) looks at Vlasik, an amateur photographer and one of the commanders of the government guard. During the Great Terror, two marshals of the Red Army, Yegorov and Tukhachevsky were executed on Stalin's orders, while the ruler of Abkhazia, Nestor Lakoba were poisoned by Beria. The third marshal, Voroshilov, who was always senvious of the successes of his comrades, was willing to commit anything to save his own life. The second picture shows him (X) and Stalin collecting pebbles, while the indispensable guards are watching them.

CHAPTER 13
Nadezhda Alliluyeva

The fact that the letters of Olga Alliluyeva have remained untouched among the documents in the party archives is something of a miracle, since the addressees of similar petitions and documents often burned whatever "did not fit" the image they had created for themselves. No doubt Joseph Stalin was motivated by similar considerations when he "sifted" through his files from time to time. He only retained a hand-picked selection of his correspondence with his wife Nadezhda. I have not come across a single message written during their periods of estrangement among the unpublished writings of the dictator.

After the unexpected death of Nadezhda Alliluyeva the fact that something must have been wrong with their marriage soon became known. There was nothing surprising about this, since dozens of people had regularly witnessed their rows and heard the obscenities that Stalin yelled at her when he was angry.[1] Tokayev, an officer of the engineer corps, who met Nadezhda Alliluyeva at the Moscow Technical Academy shortly before her death, also noticed her broken condition.[2] It also transpired that the dictator sometimes punished his wife by not speaking to her. Boris Bazhanov, a member of Stalin's secretariat who fled abroad at the end of the 1920s, recalled: "Nadya repeatedly told me with a sigh: 'He's been silent for three days now. He speaks to no one, he does not respond when someone addresses him. He is a particularly difficult person.'"[3]

However, Nadezhda Alliluyeva was not an easy character either. Like in Stalin's case, her family background weighed heavily upon her. From the very beginning the son of the violent, alcoholic Vissarion Dzhugashvili and Nadezhda who had weak nerves made an "odd match". She was the daughter of the hypersexual Olga Fedorenko (Alliluyeva), many of whose relatives suffered from schizophrenia. Nadezhda was the weaker partner in the marriage, but still sometimes returned her husband's blows with violence. Sometimes she would lose her temper and move out of the Kremlin for weeks. "A woman of very strong character. She is like flint. The Master is very rough with her, but even he is afraid of her sometimes. Especially when the smile disappears from her face," this is what Károly Pauker, Stalin's confidant and one of the commanders of his bodyguards, said once to László Pollacsek, a leading doctor in the Kremlin hospital.[4]

Pauker's words were also quoted by his good friend Aleksandr Orlov, a former representative of the NKVD in Spain: "There was a party at the Paukers' some three days after Nadezhda Alliluyeva's death. At a certain moment the conversation turned to her. Someone said that her death was a pity and that she had died too early: 'Stalin's wife did not take advantage of her high position. She was a modest and simple woman.' 'Was she, indeed?' Pauker retorted sarcastically. 'You can't have known her very well if you say that. She was extremely hot tempered. You should have seen how red in the face she got on one occasion. She yelled at [Stalin]: Who do you think you are?! You're a butcher! You are torturing your own son, tormenting your wife...and you have tortured the whole of your nation to death.'"[5]

The author of the memoirs continues: "I heard about similar confrontations between Alliluyeva and Stalin. In summer 1931, for instance, one day before the couple were to leave for a holiday in the Caucasus, Stalin took offense at something and screamed obscenities at his wife. Nadezhda Alliluyeva spent the following day preparing for the journey. Stalin finally appeared. They had lunch and afterwards the bodyguards took the small suitcase and the attaché case [his luggage] down to the car. The rest of the things had been taken in advance to Stalin's private train. Alliluyeva picked up her round hat-box and made a gesture towards her suitcase. But Stalin unexpectedly said: 'You're not coming with me! You're staying here!' And he got into the car beside Pauker and drove off. Alliluyeva was left standing there, dumbfounded, with her hat-box in her hand."[6]

This picture was taken by Bukharin's distant relative, the famous Moscow photographer, Paolo-Svishchov. Nadezhda Alliluyeva was an unsociable, sensitive, and depressed woman.

It appears from various comments scattered throughout the memoirs that the marriage of Joseph Stalin and his wife had in effect come to an end by the late 1920s. This partly explains why Nadezhda Alliluyeva became a regular student at the Industrial Academy. Stalin personally congratulated the institution that bore his name on the day the first batch of students started work after graduation. Using somewhat garbled metaphors, the dictator expressed his hope that the graduates "will play the role of the first arrow" fired by the Bolshevik power "towards the camp of our enemies, against recent production standards and technical backwardness."[7] But this was not why Nadezhda Alliluyeva became a student. She was obviously not fulfilled with the upbringing of their two children, nor was she interested merely in ordering the nurses and nannies about. She began studying in order to escape her solitude: "You say you are bored. You know, dear, things are just the same everywhere," she wrote to Maria Korona, a friend living in Berlin. "I have literally nothing in common with anybody in Moscow. It's strange, but I haven't made any good friends after all these years. I suppose it's a question of character. Oddly enough, I feel drawn to people who have stayed outside the party, at least as far as women are concerned. This is doubtless because they are more simple. I am very sorry to have tied myself down with yet more family bonds."

The last sentence refers to the fact that she was about to give birth to her daughter Svetlana. In the same letter Stalin's wife describes in detail how dispirited she had been made by secretarial—"errand"—work. She also recommends Maria Korona that she got some kind of vocational training in Germany, since this would set her on the road to independence.[8] On other occasions, however, Nadezhda clearly enjoyed being Stalin's "eyes and ears" in Moscow during her husband's absence, even if she informed him mainly about changes in the cityscape and steered clear of political intrigue and the gossip that circulated round and about the Kremlin.[9] However, on many occasions people attempted to gain admittance to Stalin or to obtain something from him with her help. Nadezhda Alliluyeva would tactfully escape from such situations. The same thing happened when Klavdia Sverdlova, the wife of the Bolshevik leader Yakov Sverdlov who died in 1919, tried to obtain Stalin's permission to write a short biography of him for schoolchildren. "I'm sorry to respond belatedly, but even now I cannot give a definite answer," she wrote on September 16, 1932, not long before her death. "I have asked that your letter be sent to him and I have inquired about his answer. But Iosif Vissarionovich is a very busy man. I have reminded him two or three times of your request, but he has not yet given a definite answer. He hasn't had time."[10]

Sometimes, however, Nadezhda Alliluyeva gave in to the pressure. In a letter dated June 13, 1931, which was among the papers left behind by the leader of the Central Executive Committee Mikhail Kalinin, Stalin's wife took up the defense of a woman who was a total stranger to her. In the letter she asked Kalinin—to whom she had already mentioned the matter once on the way home from an evening at the theater—to restore the citizen's rights of the woman in question.[11] Otherwise, the petitioner would join the ranks of the *lishentsi*, that is, those deprived of the majority of their citizen's rights, and who were therefore at risk of being unable to make a living. This large group of people comprised officials of the old regime, aristocrats, intellectuals with higher education, as well as rich peasants.[12]

Nadezhda Alliluyeva probably only thought of getting professional training once she could leave little Svetlana in someone else's care. This was when she began studying chemistry at the Industrial Academy, an institution with aims more modest than its glamorous name: it had been created to provide crash courses for "red directors" and party workers with no secondary education. The most interesting figure among the new acquaintances that Nadezhda Alliluyeva made at the academy was a semi-literate party worker, whose letters written at that time were filled with terrible spelling errors. The young man's name was Nikita Khrushchev. He was the party secretary of his grade and owed his vertiginous career to Nadezhda Alliluyeva in many respects: it was she who called Stalin's attention to him. In the memoirs that Khrushchev dictated into a tape-recorder after his retirement—which were unfortunately almost totally rewritten in the course of transcription—he spoke of his patroness with great warmth. "I was very sorry when she died. The October holidays [November 7] were just underway [...]. The parade was marching past. I was watching it by the Lenin Mausoleum with a group of party activists. Alliluyeva was standing next to me and we were chatting. It was chilly, and Stalin was standing there in his military jacket on the parapet of the mausoleum. He was always wearing that jacket in those days. It wasn't buttoned up and the wind blew it open. There was a strong wind. Alliluyeva glanced at him and said: 'Just look, my husband hasn't put a scarf on. He'll catch cold and be ill.' Those words suggested such intimacy! They did not fit the image that had been created about the leader. [...] Well, I felt genuinely sorry for Alliluyeva. She was a good soul. While she was studying at the Industrial Academy [...] she was elected party steward. She often came to me to discuss the wording [of the party meeting decisions]. I was always very careful about how I put things on those occasions. I was aware that she would go home and pass on to Stalin the information I gave her. [...] And she was so modest in her private life! She never used any means of transport apart from the tram to get to the academy. She mixed with people. And she never pushed herself into the foreground, never played the big man's wife."[13]

An important document from this period is the diary of the "red professor" Aleksandr Solovyov. The following passage is part of the entry he made on December 14, 1931: "I took part in the Moscow city party committee meeting, at which we were given instructions. [...] Khrushchev's speech was confused and chaotic. It's incomprehensible how he got to that position, obtuse and narrow-minded as he is." The theme reappears in the entry for January 28, 1932: "I am, like many others, astonished at Khrushchev's rapid rise. He did very badly in his studies at the Technical Academy. But he has won the sympathy of his classmate, *[Nadezhda—M. K.]*. Last year [...] he was nominated as General Secretary of the district, then he was transferred to the Moscow party committee. He is now the second secretary below Kaganovich. He is an incredibly obtuse man. And a frightful bootlicker."[14] Khrushchev is depicted in similar terms in Anastas Mikoyan's memoirs, even though the latter was his good friend and ally for years: "Khrushchev made a career for himself in Moscow literally within a couple of years. As for how and why—it was because almost everybody else had been put in prison in the meantime. Besides, Khrushchev had Alliluyeva as his patron. They met at the Industrial Academy where Khrushchev was active in fighting against the opposition. It was then that he became secretary of the district party committee. He finally got onto the Central Committee over others' dead bodies, as it were."[15]

☆ But let us return to the events leading up to Nadezhda's tragic death. The years she had spent at the Industrial Academy—there were only a few weeks left before her graduation[16]—had brought about a revolutionary change in her ideological opinions. Among her contemporaries, news spread that Alliluyeva had kept hearing stories from the students from the provinces that hundreds of thousands of people were starving in Ukraine, that the cream of the technical intelligentsia was in prison, and that *apparatchik*s classified as "deviant"—among them the followers of Nikolai Bukharin, of whom Stalin's wife had always had a high opinion—were being dismissed and exiled. It is probably not far from the truth to suppose, along with Stalin's daughter, that the originally private conflicts that existed between the Master of the Kremlin and Nadezhda Alliluyeva were aggravated over the years by the emerging differences in political opinions. She recalled that her mother "left behind a letter written to my father. She must have written it on the night *[of her suicide—K. M.]*. Of course I never saw it; it was no doubt destroyed immediately. But I heard of its existence from people who had seen it with their own eyes. It was a terrible letter, full of reproaches and accusations. It wasn't merely a private letter, it was partly also a political document. After my father had read it he must have thought that my mother had only seemed to be on his side but in reality had shared the views of the opposition. My father was deeply shaken, and he was furious with my mother."[17]

Besides their private differences, a number of well-informed contemporaries also trace the tragedy back to the political confrontation between Nadezhda and Stalin. One such contemporary was the Soviet *chargé d'affaires* in Athens, who fled to the West during the years of the Great Terror. Aleksandr Barmin saw Nadezhda Alliluyeva in Red Square the day before her death. In contrast to Khrushchev's later memoirs he remembered her looking pale and tired.[18] Similar information reached Leon Trotsky, then living in emigration. However, he presented events as being mostly a "political protest", which was an exaggeration: "At a time of radical collectivization, of mass executions, and with famine ravaging the villages, during which Stalin was living in an almost complete political vacuum, Alliluyeva—probably influenced by her father—spoke up for a change in agrarian policy. Her mother, who had close connections with the provinces, continuously told her horror stories about life in the countryside. [...] Once, at a meeting at Voroshilov's [...] home, Alliluyeva dared to contradict Stalin, who answered her with an obscenity. She went home and committed suicide."[19]

It is interesting to consider Irina Gogua's (who worked in the Kremlin at that time) opinion about Nadezhda's death. Irina had known her well since childhood: "Nadezhda was very pretty, with proportional features. But her beauty was only noticed after her death. There was nothing striking about her. In Iosif's presence she seemed plain; it was obvious that she was tense." According to this eyewitness,[20] Stalin did not go home after that scandalous evening, but instead went to see Lyolya Treshtsalina., a pretty woman with no scruples who worked at the protocol department of the Kremlin. In the meantime, at half past one in the morning, Voroshilov visited Yenukidze "and said that he had not liked the look on Nadya's face at all when she left. Avel answered that they should visit [them] the following morning. 'I'll pop in on the way to work.' The children's

**Stalin's wife was not so fortunate as to live a simple, happy life at home. Her husband's "enemies", however, were able to create microcosms of love and affection around themselves, up until the Great Terror terminated their happy lives.
This picture shows Christian Rakovsky with his wife and daughter. For a while, he was head of the Soviet-Ukrainian government, then worked as a diplomat in France. Later on he was sent to exile together with his family. Eventually, he was executed in the summer of 1941, in the courtyard of the Oryol prison.**

nanny said that when Nadezhda arrived home she had woken the children and burst into tears. Then she said she was going to bed and gave instructions not to be woken up before eight in the morning. Nobody heard the shot. When we went into her room she was already dead."[21]

However, this is only one side of the story. In letters that came to light a few years ago it appears that up to the end of the 1920s the Soviet dictator was deeply attached—albeit in his own "Asiatic" way—to his wife, who was twenty-three years younger than him. Initially he had also been sexually attracted to her, even if it is likely that this attraction did not last very long. Lidia Shatunovskaya, who chronicled the fall of the Alliluyev family, came to the following conclusion on this subject: "I believe, as far as her intimate life was concerned, Nadezhda was very unsatisfied. It is very difficult to discuss this question since, with respect to sexual life, the deception and hypocrisy of Soviet society [...] was certainly comparable to Victorian England. Nevertheless, according to Yevgenia Alliluyeva's cautious remarks it appears that, in spite of Stalin's Caucasian origins, his sexual potency was extremely low. And this caused much suffering to the young and fiery Nadezhda."[22] However, the fact remains that Nadezhda Alliluyeva was for a while attracted to her husband; she was even made jealous by him.[23] It is perhaps for this reason that she was unable to make the decision to break off with him after their frequent rows.

However, on the night of November 8, 1932 Nadezhda Alliluyeva finally ended her relationship with Stalin. Most—complementary—sources would seem to prove that she killed herself with her small pistol. The official version, which even members of the Alliluyev family helped to spread for a long time, was that she died of a perforated appendix and/or of heart failure. Even her best friends believed this at first. Among these women were Alisa Radchenko, who had been a confidante of Stalin's wife since she was a young girl. It was to her, for instance, that Nadezhda had confessed that she wanted to obtain an engineering degree mainly in order to alleviate her inferiority complex. In Radchenko's unpublished diary, from which we have already cited extracts concerning her husband's life in a prison, we read the following: "On her last visit she declared that she had decided, 'now that she was old', to start serious studies, and that she would go to university. 'You know, I am in a delicate situation', Nadezhda said. 'To be honest, my knowledge, experience, and talents would only allow me to apply for the most modest of jobs as a secretary. On the other hand, because of my husband's position—or so I have heard from the women of the Kremlin—this wouldn't be at all suitable for me, so I feel uncomfortable. I have therefore decided to apply myself to my studies in order to prepare myself for a job with real responsibilities.' [...] We never met again after that, we only talked from time to time on the phone. Nadya was totally absorbed by her classes and her exams. Family duties and social work also took her attention. No wonder she exhausted herself. Her sister told me that her relatives begged her to have the operation as soon as possible—she had been diagnosed as having appendicitis. She only waved her hand and said: 'After the exams'... But the treacherous sickness did not wait until the end of her exams."[24]

It is almost certain that this form of escape from her life had already occurred to Nadezhda Alliluyeva. According to the available documents and memoirs she was often sick. The Moscow doctors were unable to alleviate her severe headaches. She even traveled to Berlin under a false name to be examined there, as did many members of the Soviet elite. However, the reason for her suicide was certainly not the fear of illness—whether brain tumor or early menopause. According to most people she was pushed towards the fatal gesture by Stalin's repeated cruelty. I personally heard of a number of similar incidents from surviving members of the old Bolshevik set. Celina Budzińska, a former Polish party worker who survived the Soviet camps, told me repeatedly during our conversations in Budapest during the 1960s and in Warsaw during the 1970s how she had witnessed in the apartment of Stanisław Unslicht (also Polish), one of the leaders of the OGPU, how Stalin had shouted at his wife when she arrived for dinner somewhat late and wearing a low-cut dress that revealed her cleavage: "Where have you been? Why are you dressed like a whore? Should I maybe tell Stanislavsky or Nemirovich-Danchenko that you want the role of the *Dame aux camélias* at the Art Theater?"

Over the years scenes of jealousy increased on both sides. Stalin sarcastically called to account Mikoyan, who was considered a perfect gentleman in those circles, and Bukharin, who was very popular among women simply because of his kindness, for having courted his wife. This was extremely humiliating for Nadezhda, especially since—following the principle of "a woman's shame is a man's glory"—Joseph Stalin was indulging in casual affairs in an increasingly open way. Their final, spectacular row, which took place in the Kremlin apartment of their mutual good friend Klim Voroshilov, began precisely for that reason. According to a number of witnesses Stalin had been flirting with the fickle wife of Yegorov, the future marshal. Later several versions of this incident circulated in Moscow. Aleksandr Yakovlev, the ideologist of perestroika described how Mikoyan in his old days recalled the events. He mistakenly said that the incident occurred in Gorky's *dacha:* "we were sitting there, talking and joking. Tukhachevsky had brought along a famous actress wearing a low-cut dress. Stalin made small pellets of bread and threw these at the 'bare surfaces' of the lady. Alliluyeva obviously was not pleased. She said something, but Stalin retorted crudely. Then Voroshilov raised his glass to the woman, surely to ease the tension. However, Stalin failed to raise his goblet and went on staring at the actress. Alliluyeva threw her glass to the floor and started towards the door.

Karl Radek, who was a brilliant journalist and spoke half a dozen languages, decided to cooperate withthe NKVD at the end of the 1920s. Yet, he was sentenced to many years of prison in 1937, and later was secretly executed. Four years before his imprisonment, he looks like a happy man in the company of American guests at a Moscow reception.

Someone tried to stop her, but Stalin simply said: 'Let her go'."[25] This was at least as humiliating for Nadezhda as the fact that, in the course of a conversation, he had shouted at her: "Hey, you! Are you listening to me?" and had thrown a piece of bread at her. Several eyewitnesses remembered this incident. Nadezhda had retorted: "I'm not 'Hey, you!' to you. You know my name!" She had then left the apartment and had walked for one and a half or two hours in the park outside the walls of the Kremlin with her friend Polina Zhemchuzhina, the wife of Molotov.[26]

Almost all the witnesses who describe the fatal row side with Nadezhda.[27] Molotov, however, who was present when the incident took place, found fault with Nadezhda: in his opinion Stalin's wife was "already something of a psychopath at that time. She left the gathering with my wife. They took a walk inside the Kremlin walls *[according to another version they walked in the park just outside the Kremlin—M. K.]* and she complained to my wife: 'I don't like this, I don't like that.' [...] And why did Stalin flirt with *[Yegorov's wife—M. K.]?* It is quite simple: Stalin had drunk a little too much, he made some jokes, and it had an effect on his wife."[28]

From this point on the recollections of the witnesses and the memories of their relatives and acquaintances diverge. Some of them—who had only heard the story—say that the furious Stalin got into his car and drove to one of his summer residences (possibly Zubalovo) and was thus not at home at the time of the fatal shot. According to Anna Larina, Bukharin's widow: "N[ikolai] I[vanovich] was also standing by Nadezhda Sergeyevna's coffin. Stalin found it necessary to go up to him and tell him that he had gone to his *dacha* after the gathering and had only been informed by telephone the following morning." However, Nikolai Bukharin did not exclude the possibility that Stalin had killed Nadezhda, who had secretly sympathized with his—Bukharin's—peasant policy.[29] According to the other version, Joseph Stalin was at home throughout that night.[30]

There are two different interpretations of the tragic incident. According to some, Stalin locked himself in his room, leaving his helpless and hysterical wife on her own. Before committing suicide she left a letter full of accusations con-

These pictures were taken in the Moscow streets shortly before Nadezhda Alliluyeva was shot dead. The photographer was a Moscow correspondent of the AP at the time, who acted like a paparazzo and followed the woman everywhere. David King claims that these are the last photographs of Nadezhda Alliluyeva.

cerning their private life and political issues.[31] According to others, the Master of the Kremlin went into his wife's room—the couple had been sleeping in separate bedrooms for some time. They started shouting at each other, then came to blows, and Stalin fired the pistol that his wife always kept within reach. According to this version Nadezhda's death was not suicide, but murder.[32]

The next day the Soviet leaders started damage control to lessen Stalin's responsibility. For instance, in the morning of November 9, 1932 Aleksandr Arosev visited Molotov, who had been his classmate in Kazan', he directed the guest to his wife Polina Zhemchuzhina. She told Arosev: "Yesterday we had dinner with comrades at the Voroshilovs. Stalin's wife Alliluyeva was very lively and, as always, very kind. Later, it must have been one or two in the morning, she left with Stalin and Kalinin. She went home, while Stalin and Kalinin decided to take a car ride through Moscow. It was late when Stalin arrived home, around three in the morning. He looked in on his wife and found her sleeping in her room. At eight o'clock in the morning the servant wanted to wake Alliluyeva, who did not move. Then she pulled off the blanket and found her dead. One of her hands was thrown aside, the other holding a small gun in the fist. The barrel of the gun was directed to her heart. The servant immediately phoned Yenukidze, who called Molotov and Voroshilov. Then all of them went into Stalin's room to wake him."[33]

We will probably never know the truth. One thing is certain, however: the references to appendicitis and/or heart failure were meant to deceive the Soviet population. In any case Joseph Stalin, who was known for his self-possession, was so insecure in the following days that he issued one contradictory directive after the other. He first gave orders as to how the members of the *nomenklatura* were to be informed of Nadezhda Alliluyeva's death. According to Khrushchev's memoirs, he had Kaganovich, the head of the Moscow party organization "call together the district party secretaries of Moscow. There he *[Kaganovich—M. K.]* informed them that Nadezhda Sergeyevna had departed this life with tragic suddenness. Even at the time I wondered how it could have happened. I had spoken to her just a few days earlier. She had been so beautiful and had appeared to be blooming. And I felt genuinely sorry for her. But all kinds of things happen, and people go… One or two days later Kaganovich called us together—the same people—once again and stated: 'I am speaking on Stalin's orders. He has instructed me to tell you that Alliluyeva did not die [of an illness] but instead, she killed herself.' That was it. Nobody told us the reason, of course. She had killed herself, that was all. Then she was buried. […] You could see on Stalin's face how much he mourned her."[34]

☆ Indeed, despite his inherent cruelty Joseph Stalin must have felt responsible. Nevertheless, he was sometimes filled with hatred at the thought of his deceased wife. As a man who had grown up in an eastern culture it was his deepest conviction, held until the end of his life, that with her suicide Nadezhda had humiliated him, her husband, in the eyes of his relatives, his friends, and his court.

The diary entries written by Maria Korona suggest that the man who became a widower in his fifty-fifth year knew very well that with Nadezhda's death a very important stage of his life had come to an end. In keeping with Georgian tradition he continued to raise his glass to his wife on family occasions. However, he also continued to say that his wife "had made his life a misery".[35] On other occasions he would argue, as if trying to explain to those around him: "I have no time for myself. I did not look after my wife either."[36] According to Molotov he was always apologizing: "I was a bad husband. I did not have time to take her to the movies."[37] As for Svetlana, who up until her sixteenth birthday believed that her mother had died of acute appendicitis, this is how she recalled the reaction of her father to the death of her mother: "Later, as an adult, I was told how shaken my father was by what had happened. He was shocked because he did not understand why [his wife] had done this to him. Why had she stabbed him in the back in this way?"[38]

Rumor reached the ears of the widower "blackened" by his sorrow—this expression was used by Levon Shaumyan—that many people severely blamed him for the early and tragic death of his wife. At the same time Stalin received many official and personal letters of condolence. Lenin's widow, Krupskaya, added some political elements to her letter. She hinted subtly that the last years of her husband's life had been darkened by the intense personal conflict that had existed between him and Stalin.[39] *Pravda* did not at first publish her words along with the rest of the letters of condolence. The letter was eventually published one week later, and was made quite conspicuous by being printed in italics. Alisa Radchenko, an old friend of Lenin's widow, wrote the following in her diary on December 11, 1932: Krupskaya "[...] was very upset that the paper had published her confidential letter of condolence to Stalin." However, the diary writer did not understand her indignation: "What did she expect? And why did she write the letter in such a confidential tone?"[40]

The Soviet ambassador to the Swedish capital, Ms. Kollontai, who in character and culture stood worlds apart from Stalin, still reacted with deep sympathy to the news of Nadezhda's death. The human tone of the letter stands in sharp contrast with the rest of her letters to Stalin, in which she was clearly currying his favor: "Dear Iosif Vissarionovich! At times of deep and severe sorrow, feelings should not be written down. Nevertheless, I must tell you that I am thinking of you with warm friendship in these difficult days for you. A great many of your comrades and good friends share your sorrow and hold you in their thoughts. Everyone knows that some beings are as tender and delicate as flowers. She [Nadezhda Alliluyeva] was one of them. Those who knew her will treasure the beauties of her soul in their memories. I shake your hand warmly! Please remember that the Cause has need of you. Take care of yourself! With communist greetings: A[leksandra]. November 17, 1932."[41]

The extent to which Stalin changed after the death of his wife struck not only his most intimate circle: there were also outsiders who noticed it. Ms. Kollontai wrote in her diary on July 28, 1933: "I went back inside the Hall. Stalin and Voroshilov were standing there. Stalin has lost a lot of weight in the past year and his hair has become quite gray. His expression was very grave."[42]

It is striking to see how quickly news spread at that time. According to Aleksandr Solovyev, the students at the Industrial Academy "talk a lot about it, and try to guess what happened. Some say that she was shot by Comrade Stalin. He was sitting in his office alone well after midnight, looking through his papers. He heard a noise at the door, behind his back; he grabbed his pistol and fired. He killed her immediately. He had become very suspicious, he constantly believed that someone was going to kill him. Others claim that the couple was divided by deep political differences. Alliluyeva accused Stalin of being cruel to the opposition. She said that he was too ruthless in his elimination of the *kulak*s. Comrade Stalin shot her during a row. Still others say that the accident happened during a family dispute. Alliluyeva was standing up for her father, an old supporter of Lenin, and for her sister [Anna]. She accused her husband of persecuting them in a merciless and inadmissible way, simply because they did not agree with him. Comrade Stalin could not bear such criticism. And so he fired the shot." These rumors were immediately passed on by informers to the Central Committee of the Bolshevik Party. There the necessary phone calls were made to put an end to all such gossip. The students at the Industrial Academy were summoned by members of the party committee and ordered to study rather than indulge in such guessing games.[43]

In addition to this flood of gossip, the blow that had struck the Master of the Kremlin was made even worse by the fact that, apart from all that had bound the

The deceased Nadezhda Alliluyeva lying on the catafalque, ornamented by white flowers brought from Georgia.

couple together—their physical and mental attraction, their common home, their two children, Vasya and Svetlana—there was also their *common past in the movement.* Back in the 1910s, when Iosif Dzhugashvili was in exile in Siberia, it was the teenage Nadya, who, in her round, schoolgirl handwriting, had addressed the food parcels sent to him by his comrades and her parents. "Send my regards to the girls!" Stalin had had Nadya and her sister Anna in mind when he wrote these words from the godforsaken village of Kureyka, where he had been ordered to live until the end of his exile. In the same letter he complained to the Alliluyev family about "the incredible dreariness of nature in this damned region."[44]

In early spring 1917 the newly liberated prisoner hurried to St. Petersburg: the Alliluyev family was the first to be visited by him. According to Anna Alliluyeva, he spent his first night in their home. The next day he traveled downtown by train with Anna, Nadezhda, and one of the Alliluyev boys. "'Where are you going?' Stalin asked us. We answered that we wanted to find an apartment downtown. That we were fed up with having to travel all the time on this chugging steam train. 'Look then, and look well!' Comrade Stalin replied. 'But don't forget about me! Find a room for me, too.' We finally succeeded in renting an apartment at Rozhdestvenskaya Street 10. We set aside one of the rooms for Iosif Vissarionovich. This apartment later acquired a significant place in history. Lenin hid there, and Stalin lived there."[45]

The dictator's sister-in-law, Anna Alliluyeva, probably under pressure from the censors, felt obliged to write in her memoirs that Stalin had been very happy during the summer of 1917. Others, among them Irina Gogua, remembered him as being perpetually in a dark mood.[46] However, despite the intensification of historical events Stalin spent more and more time in the company of the two schoolgirls. He later told Vladimir Antonov-Saratovsky (the judge in the first showtrials) about these old times, while traveling in his railway carriage during one of his tours of inspection. He described how, after a few weeks' hesitation, he had made a conscious decision not court the nineteen-year-old, "somewhat pedantic and tiresomely talkative" Anna, but rather Nadya, who was just sixteen

This picture of Nadezhda Alliluyeva is published for the first time. Imitating Pushkin's Tatyana, the Alliluyev girls put the photographs of their relatives and friends into their albums. The adolescent Nadezhda looked perhaps like this, when in the summer or early fall of 1917 she fell in love with her future husband, Joseph Stalin.

but who "was mature for her age in her thinking," who "stood with both feet on the ground," and who "understood him better".[47]

After the Bolshevik takeover on October 25 (November 7), 1917 Stalin—who had only recently been persecuted—became the people's comissar for nationalities in the first Soviet government, and his future wife became his secretary. In the spring of the following year Stalin succeeded in convincing the girl to accompany him to the front, together with her brother Fyodor. In the town of Tsaritsyn (which later bore the name "Stalingrad" for decades), situated on the Volga, Joseph Stalin and Nadezhda were already living together as a couple. Later the young woman worked for a while in Stalin's secretariat in the Kremlin.[48] However, she saw her husband only very rarely, since he was visiting the fronts during the Civil War. Then things changed again. Nadezhda became Lenin's stenographer, typist, and filing clerk. "Lenin liked my sister Nadya, who started working in his secretariat after my departure from Moscow. She was a cryptographer clerk and ran errands for Lenin and Stalin. She deciphered the secret documents that Stalin sent Lenin from the front. She even worked at night," remembered Anna Alliluyeva.[49]

The writer of the memoirs says nothing about how difficult it had been for Nadezhda to get this very prestigious job. According to the regulations in force during the first years of Bolshevik power, husband and wife were not to work in the same place. Lidia Foteva, the head of Lenin's secretariat, tried to convince her superior to make an exception in Nadezhda's case. However, her first attempt was unsuccessful: "We mustn't contravene the decrees! Such a proposal in itself is enough to send you before the tribunal," was how Lenin reprimanded his favorite secretary.[50] These severe words were not followed by action: Lenin obviously did not want to hurt Stalin's feelings. After a while he agreed that the decree should "not concern" his new colleague.[51] Moreover, when Nadezhda—along with her brother Pavel—was implicated during the 1921 "party purge" and stood under threat of expulsion from the party because she had been denounced by her colleagues, Lenin intervened once again. Referring to the political merits of the Alliluyev family, he requested in writing that the decision be revoked.[52]

At first Nadezhda did a "second shift" of housework after her working hours, since a large army of domestics only began working for the Stalin household after 1923. Only two years earlier the atmosphere in the Kremlin had still been rather patriarchal. Nadezhda sometimes had to hunt for more food for Stalin, who suffered from poor health, because she had been unable to ration their reserves. "Last month's allowance consisted of fifteen chickens (they were Stalin's exclusive ration), fifteen pounds of potatoes and a slab of cheese. [...] We have already used up ten chickens and there are still fifteen days left. Since Stalin is on a diet he can only eat chicken," Nadezhda wrote to Mikhail Kalinin, with a request that he raise her husband's allowance to twenty chickens.[53]

It seems that initially married life brought more happiness than suffering to Nadezhda. She sometimes accompanied her husband on his tours in the provinces. This is proved by one of Joseph Stalin's unpublished telegrams: "Moscow. The Kremlin. To Nadezhda Alliluyeva. Go to Zina's *[the wife of Sergo Ordzhonikidze—M. K.]* in Tiflis. After a few days travel to Sochi. I will be there soon. Reply to Tiflis, to the Ordzhonikidzes. Stalin." The laconic, official-sounding reply was sent to Stalin's train, number 2206: "Travelling directly in the direction of Tuapse-Sochi, Thursday at 12:30 on train number 7. Stopping at Tiflis difficult. Alliluyeva."[54]

Yekaterina Voroshilova, who depicted the years under Stalin in an idyllic light throughout her diaries, also remembered that the dictator sometimes took Nadezhda Alliluyeva with him on holiday to Sochi: "I remember how proficient Iosif Vissarionovich was at playing *gorodki*, a real virtuoso! As for Nadezhda Sergeyevna, she played tennis. I also remember the picnics around Sochi. That was when N[adezhda] S[ergeyevna] was still alive. Iosif Vissarionovich loved taking breaks outdoors. We would travel by car and stop by a river. We would make a fire, grill *shashlik*, and sing songs. We joked a lot. What great times they were; we got along with one another in such a simple, friendly, frank, and comrade-like way. But with time our relationships became so ambiguous that I almost cringe with pain at the memory."[55]

☆ We do not know when it was that Stalin's wife realized her husband was not the romantic hero she had believed he was, but the fact is that her death caused great waves. If only because many subordinates thought him perfectly capable of killing her. The Soviet authorities were well aware of the political overtones that the news of Nadezhda's death would carry. Even many years after the tragedy they would immediately start an investigation if someone dared to bring up the subject.[56] For many years, from the mid-1930s onwards, the agents of the NKVD spread the news that Joseph Stalin often visited his wife's grave in the Novodevich cemetery. They described how he repeatedly pushed back and forth the black cast-iron rose that lay on the large stone cube on the pedestal of the beautiful, snow-white marble statue. In reality, however, it was the director and party secretary of the cemetery who took care of the grave. In addition, before the war an armed guard watched over the statue. ✰

M. K.: Kira, we know almost nothing of your aunt Nadezhda Alliluyeva's trip to Berlin. Some say she was genuinely seriously ill, while others maintain that she was simply escaping from home.

K. A.: There is some truth in both versions. You know, we lived in Berlin for a long time, until 1932. My middle brother Sergei, who is now a renowned physicist, a doctor of science, was born in the German capital. After he was born my mother complained that her breasts were very painful when she fed him. A doctor examined her and established, to his great surprise, that the Bolshevik baby born on his ward had teeth.

Anna visited my parents when we were living in Düsseldorf. I was already eight years old and remember her visit well. But I have only vague memories of my aunt Nadezhda's visit to Berlin, even though we often talked about it later in our family. As far as I know she was originally going to Karlsbad to cure her inflammation of the colon. She was tormented by this illness, like everybody who had suffered from under-nourishment during the Civil War. However, it occurred to her during the journey that it would be a good idea to be examined by the doctors in Berlin. She had been suffering from terrible headaches for years. She had such severe migraine attacks that she thought she was going mad. In Berlin she was examined by a German psychiatrist who, as far as I know, suspected that she had a brain tumor. He openly admitted that it was a difficult case. Besides *[quietly]* he did not know who his patient was. Nadezhda went to see him under a false name. I heard from my mother that the professor told her to rest as much as possible and interrupt her studies for a while. But she didn't follow his advice, and the tragedy happened shortly after we moved back home.

M. K.: I have heard that Stalin blamed your father, Pavel, for Nadezhda's suicide. He reproached your father the fact that she had killed herself with the small woman's pistol that she had been given by him.

K. A.: Well, there was more to the story than that. Nadezhda had had a pistol before. My father only swapped with her. He asked his sister to give him her enormous blunderbuss and he gave her a small woman's pistol instead. According to my mother Stalin was not on bad terms with Pavel Alliluyev. But yes, he did once remark: "That was a really nice gift!"

✰ However, Kira Alliluyeva was wrong. Stalin—particularly in his old age, when he was tormented by crises of paranoia—attributed a demonic signification to Pavel Alliluyev's gift.[57] When he heard that Sergo Beria, the son of the head of the NKVD, had offered the teenager Svetlana a small German pistol, he summoned the young man to the Kremlin and reprimanded him severely: "Have you any idea what happened in our family with a weapon like that? No?! Svetlana's mother was once in a bad mood and killed herself."[58] Molotov, later remembered that in his presence "Stalin lifted the gun with which his wife killed herself and said: 'This is a small toy gun, it is fired only once a year.'"[59] ✰

M. K.: It is also possible that in front of other people Stalin blamed your father by making him responsible for what happened, but that he behaved differently when he was with members of the Alliluyev family.

K. A.: That's very possible. You know, Georgian people never say things straight. I still believe that above all Stalin was furious with Nadezhda. Because she had dared to do this. To him! Because she had put him in such a delicate situation! For the outside world must have realized after Nadezhda's death that there had been serious problems in their relationship.

M. K.: Did Stalin have a jealous nature?

K. A.: That's putting it mildly! He was possessive not only with Nadezhda, but also with Svetlana, his daughter. He made endless remarks about her skirt being too short. He said her knees were showing. Svetlana was hardly more than ten at the time! On other occasions he said nothing, just kept up a sullen silence. He was really very possessive about the female members of his family.

M. K.: I know from former residents in the Kremlin that he often spoke to his wife using obscenities.

K. A.: [Dispiritedly] It's true that he was an ill-mannered, uncouth man. Extremely so.

M. K.: What did Anna Alliluyeva, your other aunt, tell you about this relationship? Was it a love match?

K. A.: I think it was. I have heard that Nadya was one year old when they first met. In fact my aunt fell into a river and Stalin, who was visiting the Alliluyevs, saved her. But this is probably only a family legend.[60] The fact remains—and I have heard this from many people, among them my aunt Anna—that Iosif Vissarionovich Dzhugashvili was often the topic of conversation in our family at the turn of the century. They wondered about where he was spending his years of exile, or about when he was coming back and how he was doing. Then one day Stalin turned up in St. Petersburg. He was traveling secretly, with a false passport. He had to hide and he found refuge with my grandparents. He probably first met Nadezhda then, between 1911 and 1912. Then in summer 1917, when Kerensky's policemen began pursuing the Bolshevik leaders, he hid again in the apartment of his old Caucasian friend Sergei Alliluyev. Lenin also hid at my grandparents' for a while. And slowly... *[searches for the right expression...]*

M. K.: Slowly Stalin, who was more than twenty years older than her, fell in love with her... And then they became lovers.

K. A.: Mein Gott! But that's the right way to put it. They spent the summer of 1917 shut up together in one apartment. They were sometimes alone with each other. Nadya saw the romantic revolutionary in Joseph. Of course she fell in love with him!

✰ It may have happened in the autumn after all. According to the diary entries recorded by Alisa Radchenko, a good friend of the Alliluyev family, Nadya unexpectedly turned up in their *datcha* on the outskirts of the Russian capital and told them, referring to the situation in St. Petersburg where Civil War was raging, that her parents considered it dangerous for her to stay in their apartment. She spent two months with them, then went back to St. Petersburg for the beginning of the school year.[61] ✰

M. K.: But Stalin, with his sullen and difficult moods, his deformed hand, his yellowed teeth, his pockmarked skin and foul manners couldn't have appeared very attractive in the eyes of a teenager! What was so romantic about him?

On holiday without Stalin. This is the only photograph that shows Nadezhda Alliluyeva (x) relaxed and cheerful. Avel Yenukidze, her godfather, whittles a piece of twig on the right. He would be the first to see the shot woman and to tell Stalin the shocking news, who in turn would have the unpleasant witness executed. In the middle of the picture there is the Orakhelashvili family. The parents would perish during the years of the Great Terror; their daughter, Ketevan—who was going to be Yakov Dzhugashvili's fiancee for a while—would spend many years in the Gulag.

K. A.: Are you quite sure that's what he was like? When my mother first saw Stalin in Moscow she found him quite attractive. "A thin man, strong and energetic," she told me. "He has an incredible shock of hair and shining eyes." This accursed man, who later sent all of us to prison, at first immensely appealed to my mother.[62]

M. K.: But how did your grandfather Sergei, the head of the Alliluyev family, react, when he saw a man almost forty years old courting his underage daughter?

K. A.: I don't think he knew about it. In the summer of 1917, when Joseph and Nadya, as you put it, became lovers, or at least when their relationship was moving in *that* direction, the whole family loved and respected Stalin. That was why she was allowed to travel with him to the front in Tsaritsyn. Officially they were only married in 1919. But the paper counted for little at the time.

My grandparents told me that Stalin had probably already had a taste of my aunt's difficult character at the Tsaritsyn front. She wouldn't address him informally, she answered him back, and even put him in his place when he behaved callously. Stalin, with his eastern nature, would not put up with that kind of behavior very readily.

M. K.: In 1932, when your parents came back from Berlin, you spent the summer vacations with them at the Black Sea. Was Nadezhda also there?

K. A.: No. She was still alive but she wasn't with us. But Stalin was on holiday nearby. That is, in principle, since he was constantly disturbed by his colleagues even during his holidays.

M. K.: By whom, for instance?
K. A.: I remember Kirov and Ordzhonikidze. Voroshilov also used the sports ground at our summer residence. And Budenny, with his gigantic mustache. They were cheerful and played *gorodki.* Nobody would have thought that Joseph's private life would soon be shattered into pieces.

You know, that shot proved fatal for all the members of the Alliluyev family. And Stalin was only furious with Nadezhda at first. "You have left me like some kind of enemy," he hissed in fury on the day of her burial. He just about kicked the coffin in his temper. Then our turn came, too. But only one after the other, in an orderly way.
M. K.: They say Stalin spoke very crudely to his wife at that gathering held in Voroshilov's apartment to mark the anniversary of the Seventh of November. There are various versions of what exactly happened there that day.
K. A.: I heard about it from my mother and from Anna Alliluyeva only many years later, of course, when they were freed from solitary confinement in the Vladimir Prison. This might be of interest to you, since after the war they were the people who knew most about Stalin's private life. By then everybody else, Avel Yenukidze included, had been executed. Well, they told me the story that is known today. That Stalin had been rude to Nadya, that he had flirted with another woman. That she ran away. Then it happened…
M. K.: Did you see Stalin in the days following the burial?
K. A.: Of course. There are no words to describe how low he looked. He was unable to sleep. My father, my mother, and the members of the Svanidze family stayed up near him all night. They were afraid he would harm himself. You have doubtless been told that he had stopped seeing the Alliluyev family. But that was not the case: it was then that he invited us to live with him in Zubalovo. Vasya and Svetlana were with him for the whole summer. And all the nannies. I was already at school then and could only spend the weekends at Stalin's *dacha.*
M. K.: And didn't Stalin, who was sullen by nature and then mourning his wife, mind the noise the children made?
K. A.: He didn't at first. He really liked my brother Sasha, for instance. I remember he often caught hold of him and swung him high over his head. He took him along when he went out walking, or sat him on his lap and rocked him: "What a beautiful little boy you are!" he said to him. "Just like a little mushroom." But then he usually grew tired of the game and shooed Sasha away, talking to him as if he were an adult: "Listen, leave me alone now! I have to work with my comrades." My brother cried, saying he would only go away if he got some chocolate. Stalin then *took the necessary measures* and Sasha left him alone.

But he was different with his own children. On more than one occasion he rebuked them harshly in front of us. *[She shrugs with open arms.]* As if out of duty. But only Vasily and Svetlana. He never took any notice of the older boy, Yasha. When Yasha once attempted suicide he mocked him. He reveled in ridiculing his eldest son. He used to say: "So you can't even fire a pistol properly!"

He didn't give Yakov money, either. The boy was genuinely desperately poor. He sometimes asked my mother: "Zhenya, can you give me a ruble?" My mother would have given him more, since she liked the poor boy. But he refused gravely: "I won't be able to give it back if I get more."
M. K.: Was Stalin such a stingy father? Or did he deliberately let his son from his first marriage, whose mother had also died young but from natural causes, live in such poverty?
K. A.: He didn't like Yakov. But at the same time he had no idea about the price

of things or about how people lived: "A twenty kopeck coin was enough for us back then, but Svetlana is pestering me for money all the time," he complained to my mother. As usual Mama contradicted him: "Joseph, you don't know the price of things nowadays..."

But let's get back to Zubalovo! After a while we realized—I believe my father noticed it first—that our presence had become a burden to Stalin. The summer residence was large enough for all of us, but our lives had a very different rhythm from his. Our "dear relative" used to stay up late into the night. Sometimes until dawn. Then he slept until noon. As for us, we were all early risers. So one day we moved to Mikoyan's *dacha*. There were many children in their family but they welcomed us warmly. So we spent our summers in one of the annexes of their summer residence.

Oh, I almost forgot! According to my mother, in around 1937, at the time of the mass arrests, Stalin started going on about Nadya, criticizing her over and over again in front of my mother. He said her suicide had put an end to the prestige *he* had enjoyed among his comrades. And what a scandal her suicide had been. That was what upset him most. Not that poor Nadya had died so young. That's awful, isn't it?

1 Shatunovskaya, 1982, 188; Orlov, 1983, 301.
2 Tokayev, 1955, 160–161. The Ossetian Grigory Tokayev had a key role in the Soviet rocket industry. During his trip to Germany in 1947, he went over to the British side. His English language books on the lawlessness of the Stalinist era are full of factual details, but sometimes his statements are on the verge of fiction.
3 Bazhanov, 1983, 154.
4 During the 1960s and 1970s, I made several interviews with Doctor Pollacsek in Budapest. I heard from him for the first time that at the end of the 1930s, the Soviet dictator ordered the execution of Pauker, despite of the dog-like faithfulness he had showed to Stalin.
5 Orlov, 1983, 303–304.
6 *Ibid.*
7 Tucker, 1997, 42.
8 *Iosif Stalin v obyatiakh semyi,* 1993, 154.
9 *Ibid,* 25–27, 31, 34–36, 38.
10 *RGASPI,* fond. 668, op. 1, d. 15.
11 *RGASPI,* fond. 78, op. 1, d. 43.
12 *Lishenie izbiratyelnikh prav,* 1998, 22–50.
13 Khrushchev, 1997, 21–23.
14 *Nyeizvestnaya Rossia,* 1993, vol. IV, 170–171. Sometimes the reader has the feeling that the diary is in part antedated, especially at the entries that give an a *posteriori* evaluation of the leading Soviet political figures. Still, it is undoubtedly an invaluable document, due to the precise details that reveal the *Zeitgeist* of the time.
15 Mikoyan, 1999, 614. His colleagues were fair when they wrote about him later that he was a semiliterate person.
16 *RGASPI,* fond. 668, op. 1, d. 15.
17 Alliluyeva, 1981, 107–108.
18 Barmine, 1945, 63.
19 Trotsky, 1985, vol. II, 212.
20 This woman was usually accurate in recounting the "secret history" of the Kremlin, being Avel Yenukidze's immediate colleague and also, rumor has it, his lover.
21 *Druzhba Narodov,* 1997, no. 5, 83.
22 Shatunovskaya, 1982, 190.
23 *Iosif Stalin v obyatiakh semyi,* 1993, 22, 29–35.
24 *RGASPI,* fond. 558, op. 4, d. 666.
25 Yakovlev, 2000, 139.
26 Alliluyeva, 1981, 103.
27 Shatunovskaya, 1982, 196–197.
28 *Sto sorok besed s Molotovim,* 1991, 250.
29 Larina, 1989, 122.
30 This is the version, for example, what Levon Shaumyan heard from his fatherly friend, Avel Yenukidze.
31 *Sto sorok besed s Molotovim,* 1991, 251; Alliluyeva, 1992, 201.

32 Shatunovskaya, 1982, 197–200, 202–220. This is what the wife of one of the best known militant leaders of the Comintern suggests in her memoir. Kuusinen, 1974, 91–92.
33 Aroseva-Maksimova, 1999, 79.
34 Khrushchev, 1997, 21.
35 *Iosif Stalin v obyatiakh semyi*, 1993, 177.
36 *Ibid.*, 181.
37 *Sto sorok besed s Molotovim*, 1991, 251.
38 Alliluyeva, 1981, 107.
39 Vasilyeva, 1995, 173–174.
40 *RGASPI*, fond. 558, op. 4, d. 666.
41 *RGASPI*, fond. 134, op. 1, d. 351.
42 *RGASPI*, fond. 134, op. 3, d. 35.
43 *Nyeizvestnaya Rossia*, 1993, vol. IV, 172.
44 Alliluyeva, 1946, 118.
45 *RGASPI*, fond. 558, op. 1, d. 5568.
46 *Druzhba Narodov*, 1997, no. 4, 78.
47 Personal communication with Vladimir Antonov-Saratovsky.
48 *RGASPI*, fond. 558, op. 1, d. 4508; *RGASPI*, fond. 558, op. 1, d. 5586.
49 *RGASPI*, fond. 558, op. 1, d. 5568.
50 *Biograficheskaya Khronika*, 1975, vol. IX, 573–574.
51 *Biograficheskaya Khronika*, 1976, vol. X, 6.
52 *Biograficheskaya Khronika*, 1982, vol. XII, 59–60. At the time Nadezhda Alliluyeva still worked as a cryptographer. *RGASPI*, fond. 5, op. 1, d. 1250.
53 *RGASPI*, fond. 78, op. 1, d. 46.
54 *RGASPI*, fond. 558, op. 1, d. 3265.
55 *RGASPI*, fond. 74, op. 1, d. 439.
56 Shatunovskaya, 1982, 186–187, 204–206; Adamova-Slyozberg, 1989, 19.
57 Alliluyeva, 1981, 108.
58 Beria, 1994, 48.
59 *Sto sorok besed s Molotovim*, 1991, 251.
60 It was in fact much later that Iosif Dzhugashvili became acquainted with the Alliluyev family.
61 *RGASPI*, fond. 558, op. 4, d. 666.
62 Molotov also was of the opinion that "Stalin was a handsome man. Women must have liked him because he was successful with them." *Sto sorok besed s Molotovim*, 1991, 251. Molotov also recalled that Stalin had once cut him out with a woman named Marusya. *Ibid.*, 240.

The Rulers in Oriental Dress

On the left, Stalin hugs Mamlakat Nakhangova, the little girl who was among the cotton harvesters. No one dared to say the truth openly: child labor was widespread in the Soviet republics and autonomous territories of Middle Asia, just like under the tsarist regime. The leaders of the party visited Middle Asia quite often in order to accelerate cotton production, which was strategically important: the Soviet Empire perpetually prepared for war, and accumulated a huge reserve of pyroxylin or gun-cotton, which was made of cotton.

These pictures, taken in 1935 at the reception celebrating and decorating the best Tajik and Turkmen kolkhoz peasants, were on the covers of Soviet magazines, and became well-known throughout the world. On the right are Kaganovich and Mikoyan, dressed in delicately ornamented Oriental dresses.

Joseph Stalin dressed in a Buryat folk costume, in 1936. He seems to enjoy wearing a knout on his side.

Stalin and Voroshilov enjoy the company of Turkmen and Uzbek women.

CHAPTER 14
Competition for the Widowed Stalin

For a few months after the death of his wife Joseph Stalin was no longer keen to allow his relatives into the Kremlin. Among those family members received at the Zubalovo *dacha*, several women were in competition to control the upbringing of the orphans and thus to get into a closer relationship than their rivals with "poor Joseph". Of the members of the Alliluyev–Svanidze–Redens clan, the two Svanidze girls, Sashiko and Mariko, the sisters of the dictator's first wife, were hoping to be favored by the widowed Stalin. According to her diary Maria Korona, the wife of Alyosha Svanidze, was in love with him. Anna Alliluyeva and Yevgenia Alliluyeva, and even at one time Polina Molotova, the wife of the Head of the Soviet Government, also believed that they might become indispensable to Stalin. ☆

M. K.: Why didn't Stalin get married again following the suicide of his second wife? At fifty-something he was still not too old. In Caucasia it was quite customary to "rekindle the fire when the flame died out". After all, there were those two small children left without a mother.

K. A.: As far as I know, he immediately began to look for a wife for himself once he been made a widower. But he didn't find anyone suitable. He thought the children were too old for him to be able to marry just *anyone.* There were people to take care of their upbringing and education: there were many nurses, governesses, and teachers to look after Vasya and Svetlana. There were the guards as well.

M. K.: Before the war it was rumored among members of the Soviet political elite that Joseph Stalin occasionally invited actresses for secret rendezvous—singers from the Bolshoi and film stars. The names Valeria Barsova, a soprano at the Bolshoi, and her colleague Natalya Shpiller were mentioned most often.

K. A.: I heard many such stories. But as my poor mother would say, *there was more smoke than fire.* I know this particular milieu well, since I started out in life as an actress. That's why I can easily imagine that a famous actress or film star, simply for the sake of her career, might have responded to Stalin's advances. But I don't think these were romantic rendezvous. "My dear relative" simply sent a car for them and they met with him in the Kremlin. In complete secrecy.

But could Valeria Barsova really have been the one he chose? She wasn't young. At the time Nadezhda died she was perhaps over forty.[1] And she wasn't that pretty. Vera Davidova, on the other hand, the mezzo-soprano at the Bolshoi Theater, was beautiful both on and off stage, even without her make-up. Imagine, she's still alive! She has moved to Tbilisi to be with her son. Not long ago she said on television that Stalin had once asked her to be his "housekeeper". But, as she said, she turned him down because she loved her husband.

As for the equally beautiful Natasha Shpiller, I heard some time in the mid-1950s that Stalin was in love with her and courted her passionately. And *[laughing]* she also claimed to have turned him down. She "chased him from the trough", as they say in theater circles… Believe that if you want to… Besides, "my dear relative" was the world's most selfish and most aggressive man and wouldn't have been at all slowed down by the women's refusals. Wicked as he

was, he even set the women against one another. In the presence of several dozen people![2]

As yet, virtually no research has been carried out into the relationship between the rulers of the Kremlin and the world of the arts. Not without significance for the history of twentieth-century Russian art is the fact that the major financial decisions affecting the world-famous Bolshoi Theater were, in the 1930s, approved by the people's comissar for defense, Klim Voroshilov, who had only completed two elementary classes at school. The future marshal, along with Stalin, even influenced the repertoire and generally had the final say in the allocation of important roles, awards, and bonuses.[3] The artists themselves, and especially the attractive actresses, who were inundated with honors and financial rewards and who were the idolized favorites of millions, in the meantime were forced to undertake several humiliating tasks at private functions in the Kremlin, where they entertained the leaders of the country.

The Soviet notables preferred to arrive for such gatherings on their own, in the hope that they would leave accompanied by one of the elegant ladies who had performed for them. "None of us ever saw members of the Politburo bring their wives along," recalled violinist Yury Yelagin, who chose to emigrate following the Second World War. This cultural chronicler of the era described how the Soviet leaders treated the actresses in just the same way as the rich Russian boyars had treated the unfortunate members of the playhouses in the eighteenth century. "They often had them telephoned in the middle of the night and told to get ready immediately. Was it a request or an order? In any case, after a few

After the death of his wife, Stalin frequently demonstrated in public how "good a father" he was. From the left, Vasily, Stalin's younger son, Andrei Zhdanov, the little Svetlana, and Stalin. A bit farther to the right, Yakov Dzhugashvili, Stalin's son from his first marriage.

minutes a large, curtained car, bearing the Kremlin number plate, arrived to pick up the famous ballerina or singer, who only had time to get dressed hastily, grab an overcoat, and powder her sleepy face."

An outraged Natalya Shpiller told Yelagin how she had had to perform at four in the morning at a private concert in front of half the Politburo: "Some of them were so drunk they could barely move or talk." Others were yelling out and boasting of their virility. The prima donna had been woken up in the middle of the night to sing them a few Russian folk songs: "It was dawn when she was taken home."

We also learn from Yelagin's memoirs how the dictator himself behaved in the company of artists who had been ordered to entertain him: "At the receptions held in the Great Kremlin Palace Stalin often joined the actors and actresses and chatted with them. They would greet each other and usually exchanged insignificant commonplaces. Sometimes, however, a more significant conversation took place. At the beginning of 1941 Stalin's exchange with Davidova, the mezzo-soprano at the Bolshoi Theater, had a great influence on the Moscow art world." According to the writer of the memoirs, on New Year's Eve well after midnight Stalin approached Vera Davidova with his "slightly uneven" gait: "The tall, handsome woman was wearing a low-cut silver dress with rings and a necklace of precious stones, and around her shoulders was a fine silver fox fur." According to Yelagin there was a striking contrast between the elegant woman and the Great Leader, who, despite the festive gathering, was wearing a shabby jacket and smoking a pipe. Stalin reprimanded the diva harshly: "'Why have you dressed in such a provocative way? What good is all this?' he asked, pointing with his pipe at the singer's necklace and bracelets. 'Don't you realize how tasteless your dress is? You should behave more modestly. Spend less time thinking about your clothes. And more time thinking about how to perfect yourself. Take her as an example,' said Stalin, pointing to his favorite, Natalya Shpiller. [...] She was a real beauty. A real Anna Karenina: tall, slim, with proportional features. [...] But she was dressed with ostentatious modesty. She always wore dark, high-necked dresses. She wore no jewelry and hardly any make-up. 'Look. She doesn't spend as much time thinking about her clothes as you do. She is always thinking about her art,' continued Stalin. 'And look how successful she is! And how well she sings...'"[4]

According to Galina Vishnevskaya, the world-famous Russian actress, Stalin's impromptu "art criticism" had a profoundly negative impact on the humiliated Vera Davidova for several years afterwards.[5] The dictator followed the careers of several famous ballerinas of the Bolshoi with similar interest. ✩

M. K.: I heard from Maria Semyonova, perhaps the most beautiful dancer of her day—she is still alive and not long ago, at the age of ninety, was working as a dance teacher in Tokyo—that there was scarcely any member of the Politburo who did not support the dancers of the Bolshoi Theater out of sheer "love of the arts".

K. A.: [Outraged] Is that what Maria Semyonova said? She was the very person who, rumor had it, had had a relationship with Stalin. And even with Voroshilov. Her husband was Levon Karakhan, the deputy people's comissar for foreign affairs and later ambassador to Ankara, who was imprisoned in 1937. He was executed. And imagine, Maria Semyonova, his wife, wasn't harmed at all for some reason. She continued to parade herself at the Kremlin receptions just as she always had done.

✩ Lidia Shatunovskaya, who was kept well informed via the Alliluyev family and who heard about the private lives of the Soviet leaders from the other residents of the "House on the Embankment", assumed that "Stalin cheated on his wife from time to time. Half the city gossiped about one such affair, his relationship with a ballerina called Semyonova, who later became the wife of Karakhan, the famous Soviet diplomat. Yevgenia Alliluyeva told me that the gossip was true."[6] Perhaps it was her *rejected admirers* who spread the rumor about the ballerina, who today still has great dignity. Some of those admirers made no secret of how enthusiastic they were about her. When Klim Voroshilov learned that Semyonova was preparing to travel abroad, he immediately sounded the alarm. On April 10, 1933 he wrote anxiously to the other "patron" of the Bolshoi Theater, Avel Yenukidze: "I am most definitely against allowing her to travel to Paris. The Messerers *[the famous solo dancer of the Bolshoi and his younger sister—M. K.]*, in whose case no permission should ever have been granted for the sister's journey, are at the moment in Paris being greeted with huge acclaim, mostly generated by White Guardist newspapers and circles.[7] They are being courted with such determination that there is every danger they won't return to Moscow. If Semyonova appears in Paris or any other European capital she will certainly outdo the Messerers, as well as all the other dancers, whether ours or theirs. There would be such fuss and attention surrounding Semyonova that it will quite dazzle her. This has happened to others, so how much more to a naive little girl like her. Why should we cause ourselves unnecessary trouble? You believe she will return. But what makes you so sure? At one time I was certain that Shalyapin would return. I even bet a bottle of cognac with the late Mikhail Frunze. And I lost. It is quite conceivable that Semyonova will not return. And this is sufficient reason to oppose her journey."[8] But this was still not the end of the story. The anxious people's comissar for defense asked the same question of Lazar Kaganovich, head of the Moscow party committee, at a committee meeting. He slipped a piece of paper into his hand on which was written the following: "Semyonova requests permission to travel abroad for a short time. What do you think? Shall we let her go? Won't she escape?" Kaganovich apparently knew that Maria Semyonova had been to the Kremlin to see the dictator and that Stalin had approved the Paris trip. He thus answered Voroshilov rather mysteriously: "I think she will not escape. She is a very proper person and it makes little sense for her to escape. She is not tempted by money, the high life, etc. L[azar] K[aganovich]. P. S. When we meet I will fill you in on the details."[9] ☆

The celebrated young ballerina, Marina Semyonova never made a secret out of her deep religiosity. She was not willing to join the Bolshevik Party, but still survived the Great Terror. Her husband, however, the famous diplomat Levon Karakhan, was executed as "an enemy of the people".

M. K.: We have come up with a whole list of women who are supposed to have had an affair with Stalin. But we shouldn't leave out Alla Tarasova, the blonde-haired tragic actress, even though she usually attended the Kremlin banquets accompanied by her husband, Ivan Moskvin, an outstanding Chekhov actor. Stalin was always excessively attentive to him: Moskvin was the only person whom he showed to his seat and he always carefully helped the actor on with his coat when he escorted his guests to the door.

K. A.: [Laughs.] I can imagine that "my dear relative" was indeed interested in Alla Tarasova at one time. He was quite a snob, and in the rave reviews she received he may have read how outstanding Tarasova was in the role of Anna Karenina in the wonderful performance by the Art Theater. However, according to my mother—who in 1937 met real Russian princesses and countesses in France—Tarasova would have been better suited in the role of the buxom wife of a rich merchant in an Ostrovsky play. But she was a nice, blonde doll. And Stalin, like most Georgians, preferred blondes. It is no coincidence that before the war in Russia the flaxen-haired Marina Ladinina and the platinum-blonde Lyubova Orlova were the greatest movie idols.[10] Or sex symbols, as they say nowadays.

M. K.: It is also said that Stalin was delighted when someone asked Vera Davidova, Alla Tarasova, or one of his other favorite actresses to dance in his presence. But he himself never danced at the receptions held in the Kremlin. He only watched…
K. A.: After Nadezhda's death it's true, he didn't dance. He just stood at the edge of the dance floor, like a teenager. My father and mother always received invitations to these *[searches for the proper expression]* private dance evenings. I can imagine how bored everyone must have been there. But they couldn't tell Stalin that.
☆ The dance parties started to become fashionable at the end of the 1920s in the Kremlin and in the *dachas* around Moscow, when the Soviet upper leadership began to feel secure in its position. In her diary, written in the mid-1950s, Yekaterina Voroshilova, who retained fond memories of the era, made special mention of them: "The hospitality of I[osif] V[issarionovich], as well as the singing and dancing, have stayed in my memory. Yes, yes, the dancing. Everyone danced just the way they wanted to. S[ergei] M[ironovich] Kirov and V[yacheslav] M[ikhailovich] Molotov danced a Russian handkerchief dance with their partners. A[nastas] I[vanovich] Mikoyan hovered around Nadezhda Sergeyevna [Alliluyeva] and asked her to dance the *lezginka* with him. Mikoyan danced very quickly and with great energy. He held himself straight and looked much taller and thinner while dancing. Nadezhda Sergeyevna was timid and shy, just as she always was. She covered her face with her hand and when her turn came in this most attractive and sophisticated dance she could hardly escape from the fervent A[nastas] I[vanovich]. Kliment Yefremovich [Voroshilov] danced the *khopak*. Then he asked one of the ladies to dance the polka with him; he was particularly good at it."[11]

After the death of Nadezhda Alliluyeva Stalin banished dance from his life for a while. Then a change took place and before the war he would sometimes organize small dance parties, even at home. "We finished dinner at one in the morning," Maria Korona noted in her diary on December 3, 1934. "We had a great time. Our host *[Stalin—M. K.]* produced a gramophone and records. He wound up the gramophone himself and, as on other occasions, he put on the records he felt like listening to. We danced, and he ordered the men to ask the ladies to dance and to 'spin them around'. Then the Caucasians sang slow songs in many harmonies. Our host then joined in with his high little tenor voice."[12]

Exactly one year later the dance party held for Stalin's birthday was repeated. The diary writer gives an equally enthusiastic account of it: "They sang Abkhazian and Ukrainian songs, old student songs, and toasts. Postishev *[the Ukrainian Bolshevik leader who would be executed before long—M. K.]* was in high spirits. He was dancing the Russian national dance together with Molotov. […] After dinner everyone went through to the large room, the study. J[oseph] wound up the gramophone and the Russian dancing began. After that Anastas Ivanovich Mikoyan danced the *lezginka*. He danced quite wildly and sometimes lost the rhythm. Then, as usual, the foxtrot began. We started dancing as well. We asked J[oseph] to join in, but he said that since the death of Nadya he no longer danced. He put on the same record as he had done the year before. This was the foxtrot he liked best and he didn't want to hear a different one. Well, there are some things he insists on."[13]

It is hard to believe that the dreaded Stalin, in his "better moments", actually undertook the role of a "disc-jockey" at these small gatherings. "When we visited him in his *dacha* in the south *[on the Black Sea coast—M. K.]* he himself wound the gramophone. Some of the records were labbeled: 'Good', 'Excellent'. These were the ones he selected. He played many records, mostly Georgian folk songs. He explained to us that Georgian men sing on their way to the market," noted Belyakov, the famous pilot who was involved in polar exploration, after one of these gatherings. His recollections describe how the dictator not only became sentimental as a "disc-jockey", but sometimes worked himself into an emotional state. Referring to one Russian folk song with a tragic ending he remarked: "There is terror and foreboding at the heart of this song."[14]

The members of the Soviet elite were aware of this habit of the Master of the Kremlin. According to Aleksandr Barmin, *chargé d'affaires* at the Soviet embassy in Athens, at state receptions held by the dictator for the "Stakhanovists, the heroes of labor, or for polar-researching aviators, he adopts a pose of calculated simplicity. He behaves towards everyone, especially towards those from the countryside, as a good friend. And when he receives guests in his home he selects the records, which he plays himself. He never dances but urges others to do so. He encourages his guests not to feel uneasy. He even finds partners for some of the young men."[15] ☆

K. A.: Stalin often watched my mother as well when she was dancing. It was mostly Stanisław Redens, Anna Alliluyeva's husband, who asked her to dance, on the orders of Iosif Vissarionovich. They made a wonderful couple. Interestingly the Master loved it when they danced the foxtrot, so much criticized by the Soviet press. Who would have believed of him that he loved this "decadent Western dance"? He even applauded my mother and her partner. Sometimes he would congratulate the other couples as well. But he was far from pleased when any of the women, excited by the dance or by the champagne, tried to be intimate with him in front of the others. He also immediately stopped any of the men who tried to fraternize with him, even Valery Chkalov.

M. K.: But he was the most famous test pilot of the era, and Stalin's number one favorite.

K. A.: He still stopped him once in the presence of my parents. Once, when he was drunk, Chkalov dared to say something to him like: "Come on, Comrade Stalin. Have a drink with me!" But Stalin shrugged off the over-familiar hand that the pilot had laid on his shoulder and immediately made a show of turning his back on the man they called "Stalin's hawk". Besides, I haven't got that high an opinion of Chkalov. I regard him as a common scoundrel. He's one of those people who really puts your back up, but of course he was a very brave man. Once he flew his enormous plane under the bridge near our house. The wing of the plane almost touched the water. The whole of Moscow was raving about Chkalov's stunt. But not me. There were people on the bridge at the time. There could have been a terrible accident![16]

M. K.: Your story about Stalin loitering at the edge of the dance floor suggests that perhaps what he needed above all was not a lover but a "first lady". It must have been particularly uncomfortable for him during the war to appear as the head of state unescorted at official receptions. It is no coincidence that he summoned Svetlana to act as hostess when Churchill visited him at home in the Kremlin.

K. A.: But my mother believed that Stalin clearly exploited the fact that he had been left alone. With his eastern, Georgian background he could, in his own words, have four or five concubines. I don't think, of course, after all the late nights, that he had sufficient energy left for "that". *[Shrugs dismissively.]* Not after he had been planning who would be taken away that day by the police. But seriously, "my dear relative" was above all a careerist who was quite satisfied when he was able to remove someone from his path. First the Trotskyites, then Zinovyev and Kamenev, then Kirov, and later Bukharin. And many others besides. He was very keen…

M. K.: …to send as many political opponents to their deaths as possible.

K. A.: [Contemptuously.] For him this was a substitute for arousal. Like everything else he did, it was done out of vanity. To an extreme.

1 The gifted and celebrated actress of the time, Valeria Vladimirova (Barsova is her stage name) was indeed born in 1892.

2 Svetlana Alliluyeva had been on the same opinion before she started to whitewash his father in the early 1980s: "My father felt liberated after my mother passed away, as she had always been an impediment at home." Alliluyeva, 1970, 330.

3 Gromov, 1998, 64–70, 138–146.

4 Yelagin, 1988, 58–59, 358–366.

5 Vishnyevskaya, 1993, 122.

6 Shatunovskaya, 1982, 190.

7 On December 5, 1933, Avel Yenukidze, who supported the Messerers, asked Voroshilov to let the two dancers of the Bolshoi Theater go abroad for a performance tour of "no more than two months". The people's comissar for defense replied angrily, "Comrade Yenukidze! As long as the theater season lasts, I am against permitting any performance tours abroad. Voroshilov. December 5, 1933." *RGASPI*, fond. 74, op. 1, d. 394.

8 *Sovietskoye Rukovodstvo*, 1999, 232–233.

9 *RGASPI*, fond. 74, op. 2, d. 42.

10 It seems that Stalin did not cease to favor Orlova after the war. Once he recommended the star of the "Soviet Hollywood" to the attention of Sergei Eisenstein. *Vlasti i khudozhestvennaya intyelligetsia*, 1999, 616.

11 *RGASPI*, fond. 74, op. 1, d. 439.

12 *Iosif Stalin v obyatiakh semyi*, 1993, 169–170.

13 *Ibid.*, 189.

14 *RGASPI*, fond. 558, op. 4, d. 648.

15 Barmin, 1997, 305.

16 Upon examining the recently declassified archival documents, Chkalov's daughter came to the apparently logical conclusion that in the course of the Great Terror, her father was persecuted by the agents of NKVD following a direct order from Stalin's circles, and especially from Beria, despite the dictator's openly enthusiastic support of the test pilot. Chkalova, 1999, 37–61.

Lazar Kaganovich

Lazar Kaganovich, the merciless coordinator of the forced resettlement of the Ukrainian peasants and Kuban' Kozaks, who was responsible for the death of thousands of railroad workers, engineers, and party workers, nevertheless lived an exemplary family life.
According to his contemporaries, Kaganovich affectionately loved his wife, Maria, the well-known trade union activist, his daughter, and his adopted son.

In his rare leisure time, Kaganovich enjoyed riding horses. He was eager to cite the ironic dictum from Isaak Babel's *Twilight:* "When a Jew jumps on a horse, he ceases to exist as a Jew."

CHAPTER 15
All the Soviet World is a Stage

"I went home with Pasternak, both of us drunken with joy," writes Kornei Chukovsky, the popular storyteller, in his diary on April 22, 1936. The two famous non-party writers had been so affected because, at a Komsomol meeting, they had seen, with the other guests of honor, from the sixth of seventh row, that is close-up, Joseph Stalin: "There he stood, a little tired, pondering, but grandly. You could feel that he had got used to radiating great power. At the same time a sort of female gentleness dominated his whole personality. I looked back and saw only loving, tender, enchanted laughing faces. What we saw caused us all great happiness. Simply to see it. [...] We watched his every move with devotion. I would never have thought that I could feel such things. The chamber clapped, he took out his pocket watch and with a wide smile showed it to the audience. The whole room started to whisper: 'Look, there's his watch, the watch! He showed his watch!' Even at the coat check we were still talking about his watch. On the way home Pasternak spoke enthusiastically all along. Just as I did."[1]

These ecstatic sentences were put to paper by a rationally thinking Russian intellectual who in the 1910s was even a follower of the cadet party,[2] which occupied a center right position in Russian political life. According to his contemporaries and family members, Chukovsky never made a secret of the fact that he loathed the Social Democrats and the Bolsheviks even more. It is true that in the stormy autumn of 1917, after Lenin's government had come to power, the writer—who was a compromise-seeking type, unlike most of his colleagues—did not wish to turn his back on the Soviet authorities.[3] But with the passing of the years he became increasingly disillusioned with the rulers of the Kremlin. Primarily with Joseph Stalin whom he called "deformed gardener" in my presence in the 1960s. By this expression he not only meant that the Soviet dictator literally liked gardening, but also that he was keen on "planting"—that is, imprisoning people.

Kornei Chukovsky, who was otherwise very cautious and constantly feared house searches, mentioned in his diary several times in very condescending terms the intellectual circle which flocked to Stalin, of which he too was part.[4] Once he smuggled a letter secretly out to Finland in which he tried to dissuade his father's good friend Ilya Repin, who was living in his *dacha* near the Finnish-Soviet border, to let the Kremlin to lure him back home. In 1969, not long before his death, he told me that "it would have been painful to see for many of us if the greatest Russian painter of our time returned home and thus legitimized Stalin's rule." Perhaps Chukovsky's letter did take part in Repin's decision that he eventually stayed in Finland— even though not only homesickness, but also financial difficulties made him often ponder that he should return home.[5] From what we know today, the painter was afraid to make peace with the Soviet leadership openly primarily because of the news he received of the terrors of agricultural collectivization. His very sick daughter Tatyana, who was a teacher, was forced to eke out an existence with her family on a small plot near Vitebsk (Lunarcharsky, the famous Soviet politician, noted this in an outraged letter to Voroshilov). She was nearly deported to Siberia with other similar *kulaks*. Even the

After the premiere of the drama *Lyubov Yarovaya*, the author, Konstantin Trenov (1) hosted Gorky (2), Stalin, and Molotov (3) in the reception hall of the Moscow Artist Theater.

clothes she was wearing were put on the list of personal items to be confiscated. When she refused to transport wood on a horse and cart saying that she was too ill, she was imprisoned for a short time.[6]

So Kornei Chukovsky had reason to warn Ilya Repin to stay away from this terrible world. He was pleased that the NKVD could not finally lay their hands on the great Russian painter. But they did seize his possessions: in 1940 during the Soviet-Finnish war Repin's old home was seized. Among his papers the zealous young agents found the above-mentioned letter from Chukovsky, for which, in the time of the Great Terror, he would have deserved "the second degree of social defense", that is, ten-fifteen years of "isolation". But luckily for the writer Stalin was in a more peaceful mood by then and Chukovsky was one of the country's most popular men, a storyteller to millions. This also contributed his avoiding arrest—although in the succeeding years he was condemned by *Pravda* several times.[7]

Knowing all this it is then strange that Kornei Chukovsky and Boris Pasternak, the other sovereign writer of the period and perhaps its greatest poet, who was soon to write *Doktor Zhivago*, were so much affected by the madness surrounding the "Red Tsar." And just at the time of the show trials, collectivization that killed millions of peasants, and the persecution and liquidation of intellectuals branded as the "rotten petit bourgeois." Furthermore, in Pasternak's case this does not seem to be a transitional phenomenon. A short time before the scene described by Chukovsky, on December 5, 1935, Pasternak sent a peculiar, mystical-sounding letter to Stalin. He turned to him "allowing for the secret relationship that binds You and I." In a devoted, respectful way he thanked the ruler of the Kremlin that he did not name him, but Mayakovsky, the greatest poet of the Soviet age. He added that many Soviet writers "under western influence" had exaggerated his, that is Pasternak's significance. And even before Stalin had created the Mayakovsky cult which was so fearsome for his contemporaries: "I can now breathe freely and live modestly, and continue my work in peace. Without unexpected turns and in the secrecy without which life is worth nothing. In the name of this secrecy, I am your warmly affectionate, loyal B[oris] Pasternak"—so ends this almost childishly cunning letter.[8]

Chukovsky, who lived to a great old age, at the end of Stalin's rule, like in our conversation during the 1960s, already used the expression "herd instinct mixed with paranoia" in describing the psychological state among Soviet people. But at the time of the Komsomol congress, perhaps even he himself was unable to understand the invisible link that connected the two European, cultured, sensitive intellectuals to the cunning and cruel Georgian *kinto*.[9] Their behavior was not exceptional, although during the Great Terror both of them had come to oppose the terrible Stalinist system. Unlike the two of them, there were others who were unable, or did not wish, to rid themselves from the "mysterious enchantment" they felt in the dictator's presence, even later. Yevgeny Gabrilovich, for example, a well-known scriptwriter of the period, admits himself that the Soviet authorities bowled him over. On approaching his ninetieth year he started to tell how after his compromise with the Stalinist system he felt he was locked in invisible locks. That is why he hated the cultural people's comissars who always heaped him with praise: "I got a host of government awards for my bowing and scraping, and perhaps my hard work, I even received the Stalin Prize, thus I belonged to the elite," he sighed at the end of our nine-hour conversation in Moscow. This is when he explained the great weight of the phrase *ordyenonosets* during Stalin's rule—in this case it means intellectual who received government awards. It did not protect you against the persecution of the political police but awards of a certain level—generally the Red Banner Order of Work, Order of Lenin, and Hero of the Soviet Union, and the Stalin Prize—meant that you automatically entered the nomenclature.[10]

It was not as if Gabrilovich and many of his contemporaries were politically blind all along. His eyes were opened by the agricultural collectivization that sacrificed the lives of millions, as well as by the trial of Mikhail Tukhachevsky, whom he respected until the end of his life, and the decimation of the Red Army. But at the same time, as a writer of popular melodramatic scripts about Lenin and the Bolshevik movement, he always tried to stay close to the fire. One of his most memorable recollections was when at the beginning of the 1930s he personally met Stalin at Gorky's flat. At the moment he noticed the Master of the Kremlin, he recalls, he felt as if his whole being were permeated with a peculiar warmth. During our conversation, the man who was the same age as the twentieth century leant forward and said "it was as if invisible but strong hands had grasped me and lifted me." He had to really concentrate in order to hear the General Secretary of the party who spoke very softly and articulately so that people would really pay attention to what he said. At the end of his long monologue Stalin, for the first time, called the writers at the service of the system "the engineers of human souls". "After his speech we stood around," wrote Yevgeny Gabrilovich of the same meeting elsewhere. "I clearly felt that I am standing next to the man on whom the destiny of the entire world depends. Of course, you may now think that I was a simpleton, but I remember very well that it is how I felt then. It is true, however, that I was amazed at how small he was. And that his face was pockmarked and that his body smelt unwashed."[11]

Maksim Gorky (x), the author of *Mother* and *Klim Samgin*, was on very good terms with the leaders of the OGPU, the Soviet political police.

☆ In the mid-1930s the Soviet dictator had an even greater success with the speech he gave to pre-selected "simple people." For such occasions Stalin spent days preparing. He always spoke about the concrete problems that interested the "ordinary people" to an audience of *kolkhoz* peasants, who were bussed in to Moscow from the provinces and paraded before him in colorful national costumes, as well as to Stakhanovists, army officers' wives, award winning scientists and artists, or to the builders of the Moscow metro, who received great publicity during the mid 1930s. Sometimes he spoke slang and even crude language. For example on May 4, 1935 at the opening of the first section, the inner circle, of the pompous Moscow metro named after Lazar Kaganovich, he said when speaking about which workers would receive prizes: "So what will happen to the other comrades?...As we see you from the presidency not everyone has the same mug." His words were received with great applause. Seeing how much the not exactly cultured audience loved this sort of vulgar talk, Stalin continued: "[We see that] some of you are pleased *[because they had been decorated—M. K.]*. While others are puzzled, *[as if they were saying—M. K.]* 'what's this, have the scoundrels left us out?!'" The next day's issue of *Pravda*, of course, did not include this part of the speech in the edited version.[12]

The radio often broadcast these speeches live, playing an important role in creating Stalin's "good tsar" legend. But during the Great Terror the tyrant, who was terrified of terrorist acts, went less frequently on these "walks among the people." He only spoke before much smaller audiences at the meetings of the Central Committee the composition of which, due to the purges, had almost completely changed, or to a few dozen reliable intellectuals. But even these rare appearances were well-rehearsed shows of spontaneity. He continued to think that these speeches were very important. Sometimes he even received representatives of the "progressive western world," who, since the beginning of the 1930s, had been competing fiercely to see who would actually get to see Stalin.[13]

At the beginning the Kremlin ruler had a hard time winning over the Soviet people themselves. Many of the peasants and Cossacks forced into the *kolkhoz* cooperatives, those deprived of citizenship *(lishentsi)*, and the various peoples living in far-away provinces hated him earnestly. People on the Gulag felt the same, including those convicted for ordinary, non-political crimes, who called him the "Mustache" and the "Cannibal". Indeed at the beginning many of the members of the party apparatus, who had been held in a tight fist since the October 1917 revolution, did not like the "Master" either. In the second half of the 1920s *samizdats* condemning Stalin were still circulating among party members. One of the first examples was Vagarshak Ter-Vaganyan's meticulous analysis of the emerging Stalin cult, which the official theoretical periodical *Pod Znamenem Marksizma* was not willing to publish so it was issued by the author himself.[14]

But with the passing of time the effect of brainwashing, the information vacuum and mass psychosis became ever greater. In addition, Stalin and his circle managed to purge the new generation of any respect for traditional values. The Master of the Kremlin, through the rhetoric he had learned in the Tiflis Theological Seminary, enriched with redundant elements and well-edited sentences and quotes properly suited to the occasion, enchanted the new generations who had grown up without values. As Stalin, who spoke with a strong Georgian accent, could not address the citizens of his empire in his mother tongue, he copied out old phrases and folk sayings from the famous *Dal* Russian dictionary to counterweight this problem. He was also fond of quoting Marxist classics and Lenin. He generally knew these citations by heart but even so had them typed out by his secretaries from the worn copies in his great library. Later Stalin increasingly made up his own phrases. Most of these are difficult to understand today: "Lenin was a golden eagle!" he said, for example, with great affection. Even today one can feel the threat beneath his oft quoted announcements: "Which extreme is more dangerous, the right wing or the left wing? Well, the one which we are fighting against at this minute." Even more frequently heard was the wisdom that "everything depends on the cadres."

The spread of such banalities obviously was helped by the fact that Stalin's speeches were quoted again and again on the yellowing pages of factory and district papers. But often they were published and distributed verbatim, too.[15] A good few readers were nevertheless shocked by their nonsense, such as when Stalin, according to Georgian custom, raised his glass to the long dead Lenin's *health*.[16] However, one was not permitted to notice such things in the totalitarian Soviet system. Just as nobody dared interrupt his speeches which were like theater performances. One contemporary remarked that Stalin's speeches were like the *peoples' radio* blaring from the public buildings in Soviet towns from dawn to late at night: "However awful it was to hear, one couldn't argue with him."[17]

☆ After his fiftieth year Stalin increasingly talked about himself in company and indeed before the public in the third person. Sometimes with a sly smile he would slowly start listing his own virtues. At other times he would suddenly raise his glass and, mimicking paternal affection, toast one of the *kolkhoz* leaders or pilots researching the poles (known as *Stalin's falcons* in the terminology of the time). The pilot Vladimir Kokkinaki, who was brought to the fore by Stalinist propaganda in the 1930s, noted down the Kremlin ruler's message to them, the little cogs in the great wheel. Vasily Molokov, another brave researcher pilot, was held up as an example: "he is one of the modest and simple heroes who avoid fuss. That is why I drink to Comrade Molokov not only because he is a hero but also because he is a modest simple man. And he does not ask for the stars."[18]

But a scandal broke out around Molokov, the holder of the Hero of the Soviet Union award. One of the employees at *Izvestia* mixed up the letters in an article

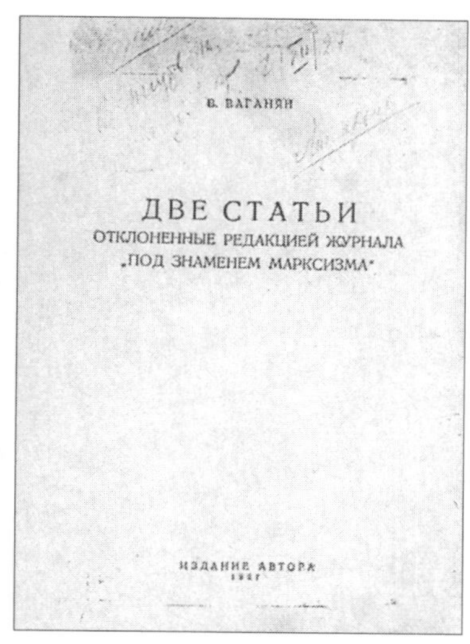

Vagarshak Ter-Vaganyan little before his execution. His persecution by Stalin was to a large extent due to the fact that his book, published as a samizdat by Armenian Bolsheviks, mercilessly criticized the Stalinist practice of falsifying history.

and instead of writing Molotov, the Head of the Council of the People's Commissariat , he wrote Molokov. Nikolai Bukharin, the editor of the paper, whose every move was being watched, was forced to make a humiliating apology: "Dear Vyacheslav Mikhailovich! I ask your forgiveness for the annoying, inexcusable blunder. [...] I have officially sent my explanatory report to comrade Stetsky[19] to the cultural and propaganda section [of the party headquarters]. We have dismissed the comrade who drafted the material. [...] You know there was a great deal of work [...] and the TASS material only came in at four in the morning. That is why it took a terribly long time to lay out the pages again. In addition the editorial secretary and my deputy were ill and in bed. This of course is not an excuse. We have punished those responsible. But this has been very, very unpleasant for me anyway. So please accept my personal apologies as well as the official ones. Your Bukharin." In the corner of the letter the offended Molotov's notes can be read: "This has nothing to do with it."[20]

This story demonstrates that in the Stalinist system the career of a "simple cog"—in this case the responsible editor that day—could be broken because of such a tiny mistake. We know of numerous tragic cases where journalists, proofreaders, and printers were sent to prison or concentration camp or even death row because of similar "counter-revolutionary" spelling mistakes.

☆ So this message of Joseph Stalin's to the "simple cogs in the wheel" to be patient and modest, so that they won't encounter any problems, was by no means accidental in his speeches. They should be content living in peace in the shadow of their beloved leader. The signs are that the Great Teacher of the Peoples' was preoccupied with this notion throughout his life. But he disguised it as usual, making this toast in the Kremlin at a reception to celebrate the victory over Nazi Germany: "I would like to make a toast to all those who are not of high rank or occupy envious posts. A toast to those who are thought of as 'small cogs', but without whom we aren't worth a pin, if I can express myself crudely, no matter that we are marshals, front and army commanders. There are many of them, we're talking about tens of millions. Modest people. Nobody writes about them, they have no rank, but we rely on them as a building does on its foundations."[21]

The Soviet dictator usually demonstrated modesty at such gatherings, especially if there were foreigners present. Nearly all the western guests noticed his puritan dress. Just as the cogs in the wheel they had no idea that Stalin wore fine silk shirts under his simple gray or white military jacket which was known by everyone in the Soviet Union as "semi-military dress." Before the war, the entire Soviet leadership wore the same out of mere docility, apart from Molotov, Kalinin, and Beria.

Under the cover of seeming Puritanism Joseph Stalin had luxury tastes. In food as well. Several near Moscow, Georgian, and Crimean state farms were exclusively maintained for growing, as one would say today, *organic food* for the Kremlin. In addition, during the feasts that lasted until dawn Stalin often simply pulled the tablecloth towards himself if he wanted another plate. The plates, groaning with food, fell on a heap on the floor which he then had taken out and cleaned up by the waiters. This of course meant that the dining services which had come from the tsar's court were smashed to smithereens. "He was a cynical and unpleasant man," said Valentin Berezhkov, who had been Stalin's English interpreter during the Second World War, to me about these scenes. "Although the others were no different either. My bosses had fresh fruit sent up to them from the Caucasus or Central Asia several times a week even during the most difficult and risky times for the Red Army, such as during the Moscow and Stalingrad battles."

Berezhkov mentions other interesting secret stories from the Kremlin in his memoirs. He says, for example, that in the summer of 1942 Dekanozov, the deputy people's comissar for foreign affair, traveled to Stockholm where, with the help of mediators, he conducted negotiations in the greatest secrecy with delegates from the Third Reich about leaving the war. From Stalin's former interpreter, we also know that in the first phase of the Battle of Stalingrad and during the Germans' successful invasion of the northern Caucasus, when it was clear that the Normandy landings would not yet take place, Stalin, who was afraid of the situation worsening, wanted to go to India with Molotov and set up an émigré Soviet government there. Berezhkov also recorded a cynical dialogue between the "Great Teacher of the international proletariat" and the influental English Labor party politician. "Once in the toilet—the interpreter sometimes even had to accompany his boss there too—Bewin standing next to Stalin told the following joke: 'This is the one place in the capitalist world where the worker can rightfully take the means of production in his own hand'. Stalin slyly smiled and continued the joke: 'The same can be said for the Socialist society.'"[22]

☆ It is not always easy to unravel Stalin's sentences after so much time. At first reading it is not clear what the dictator was getting at in his dedication on the cover of an album produced by three famous Soviet cartoonists, Kupryanov, Krilov, and Solokov who published under the joint name of Kukriniksy: "To Comrade Kirov, the great strategist. J[oseph] St[alin]." And underneath it: "To my dear friend S. M. Kirov, leader, Voroshilov, leader."[23] These lines were written in the summer of 1934 a few months before Kirov's murder. The Soviet dictator had for a good few years seen himself as the Bolshevik Party's *only* strategist. His dedication probably is sarcastic at the Leningrad party secretary's expense. He could not forgive the fact that at the Bolshevik Party's 17th Congress, which has entered history as the *Congress of the Victorious*, many more people voted for Kirov at the election of the Central Committee members than for him. But from Voroshilov's dedication it seems that the military people's comissar had not noticed that his fellow Sergei Kirov was in great trouble.[24]

The players in the drama of Soviet life do not seem to have repeated the fight of good and evil, say of Sarastro and Monostratos. "In the camp I realized how

Mikhail Bulgakov, the famous Russian writer and his wife, Yelena. Her diary from the period of the Great Terror is full of notes similar to this one: "The news is Litovsky has been arrested. It is too good to be true!"

much I had made people suffer during the Civil War," I heard from Viktor Urasov, a former tailor who in the "Leninist heroic period" was a low ranking functionary in the political police in Siberia. As a result of struggles within the Bolshevik Party, he also found himself behind barbed wire at the end of the 1920s. He was of the opinion that—as it becomes clear primarily from the correspondence of the exiled or imprisoned Bolshevik elite, and from the sources that are extant in the Palo Alto, Boston, and Amsterdam collections that contain the Trotsky bequest—the later that Stalin swooped down on someone, the greater the probability that that person was already twisted psychologically. Those who clung to the good life and thought that they were firmly entrenched in power generally behaved strangely and irrationally as time went by. It is not otherwise possible to explain why during the Great Terror, when he was expecting arrest any time, Levon Karakhan—one of the famous leaders of Soviet foreign policy and Ambassador to Ankara, many of whose friends had fallen from favor and gone to prison by that time—asked Voroshilov on December 31, 1936 to help him transfer to the NKVD's "international section" where as an assistant to Yezhov he would work in the struggle against the "enemies of the people."[25]

The extremely valuable diary entries of Yelena Bulgakova, third wife of the great Russian writer, show that the "typical non-party" intellectuals were also characterized by this collective psychosis. This extraordinarily cultured woman was very distant from the machinery of the Stalinist terror, yet her entries demonstrate that the totalitarian system was capable of distorting the way of thinking not only of the hedonist, although disciplined party member Karakhan, but that of Bulgakov's *The Master and Margarita* too. Indeed it becomes clear from the documents that this pretty woman, who can be seen as *Homo Sovieticus*, could also make a malicious man out of her husband in the years of the Great

Vladimir Kirson, Stalin's favorite drama writer, in prison.

Terror. Although at other times Mikhail Bulgakov sympathized with the victims, especially if they were friends, even intervening on their behalf as in the case of the period's famous playwright, the exiled Nikolai Erdman. It shows more than a little courage that Bulgakov wrote a letter with several others to the authorities requesting Erdman be allowed back to Moscow.[26]

But the couple was unashamedly overjoyed when the NKVD swept down on Bulgakov's former censors and critics. Although creative artists always and everywhere are susceptible to jealously and envy, it must be said that this was not typical of the Russian intellectuals in the nineteenth and early twentieth centuries. But Bulgakov's malicious delight at others' misfortune cannot in itself be explained by the fact that most of the acquaintances behind bars were dogmatic proletarian writers, editors, and theater critics of Stalin's court. All were passionate opponents of the great writer and had for years tried to prevent his works from being staged or published. The much attacked, deeply humiliated Bulgakov took this very badly and could never forgive them. In two of his great prose works, *The Theater Novel* and *The Master and Margarita*, he tried to express this feeling. At the same time, unlike many of his fellow writers who were politically written off, he had no financial problems despite his difficulties. The NVKD agents who circled him made his life unpleasant, yet the authorities allowed him to regularly meet foreign diplomats, in this he was a rare exception. In exchange, Bulgakov made a series of compromises with the authorities. At the end of the 1930s, he even contemplated making his peace with the system he had despised since the Civil War. It was then that he wrote *Batum*, a play about Stalin's youth.[27]

The hesitant idea of striking a deal with Stalin came to Bulgakov precisely during the time of the Great Terror. In 1937 the writer and especially his wife, for whom that year had left a "bitter taste in her mouth,"[28] made a horribly sarcastic statement about the tragedy of their former enemies. That is why the woman's diary is proof of their servility to the Soviet dictator. In contrast, she had no good word for those who were arrested: "they say that there is trouble around Kirson and Afinogenov. [...] Have they really faced their nemesis?" she asked on April 20, 1937. On August 16 she noted, "Ardov said they have arrested Bukhov. I always loathed that man."[29]

Of these two famous playwrights, Kirson was really arrested and executed, while Afinogenov, who waited everyday for the political police to come knocking at his door, was "only" expelled from the party and his nerves shot to pieces by the constant uncertainty. His situation was further worsened by the fact that he was held to be a western spy in Stalin's court by virtue of his American wife. But in the end he was not touched, he died at the beginning of the war during a German air raid on Moscow.[30] Four days after receiving news of Afinogenov's fall, Bulgakova maliciously commented on the fate of one of those responsible for the Central Committee's propaganda section: "[...] they say that Angarov has been arrested. M[ikhail] A[leksandrovich] [Bulgakov] remarked that Angarov has done terrible damages by his [plays] *Ivan Vasilyevich* and *Minin*."[31] And about a theater critic who worked from 1932 until 1937, she wrote that "the news is Litovsky has been arrested. It is too good to be true."[32] In the meantime the diarist notes several times, (as if to justify herself) that the arrested person "practiced self-criticism" and sometimes that "they confessed their crimes."

Today it is still hard to judge how much these "confessions" were believed at the time. We probably have a lot more to learn from the mostly unpublished diaries, submissions, and private letters of the Stalin period. But it is obvious that in the Soviet era even the best of friends were capable of reporting each other for careerist reasons and then increasingly out of sheer terror. One of the earliest examples is Klim Voroshilov's undermining of his old friend Semyon Budenny. When at the beginning of April 1923 Voroshilov was informed that the agricultural portfolio was to be given to the great mustachioed Budenny, who could hardly read and write, he wrote a letter full of political insinuation to Stalin: "Budenny [...] is too much of a peasant, extraordinarily popular and cunning," he informed him. And to make things completely clear he added his good friend might, in a difficult situation, turn into a popular leader and could even revolt against Soviet power.[33]

Yet despite this opinion Voroshilov spoke about Budenny with great enthusiasm publicly for years. Voroshilov often said how well they understood each other in the years of the Civil War, he and the commander of the First Cavalry, whose people's comissar he was appointed. He even praised this military man—who was uncultivated and awkward despite the courses he attended—when at the turn of the 1920s and 1930s and then in the second half of the 1930s storm clouds gathered over the Red Army's commanding officers. However, Stalin, who feared a military putsch, knew very well why he entrusted the key Moscow military sector to Budenny during the Great Terror. By doing so he had ensured that the "red cavalier" turned marshal would support him in destroying his former Civil War military comrades. In that period Budenny fell morally in his private life as well: he did not do anything when at the Master's orders the NKVD had watched his young opera singer wife, Olga, for long months, then arrested and sent her to the Gulag.[34]

Even in those terrible days this was rare. If politicians or military officers were arrested, they usually confessed everything sooner or later so that no harm would come to their families. But sometimes men brought to their knees denied their parents, reported their spouses and even their children. The letter which Alexander Shcherbakov, the secretary of the Soviet Writers' Alliance, sent to Shteyn during the wave of arrests that followed the Kirov murder on February 9, 1935 is typical of this. Vilgelm Shteyn was one of the most influential agents of the NKVD. Shcherbakov wrote to him that "I feel it my duty to report the following facts: Today, on February 9 Uglanov[35] came into my office and said the following: he has a nineteen-year-old daughter, I believe she is called Lyuda. When Uglanov returned from Siberia he saw that his daughter had changed. She was expelled from the workers' faculty[36] and left her place of work. Along with other young girls (the mother of one of them is a cleaner at the Central Committee), she takes part in drinking bouts organized by a literary historian called Kish. Uglanov said he does not like his daughter's behavior. He is worried about her not only as a father but also as a party member. The thing is worrying because in Leningrad a depraved section of youth has openly stepped onto the path of terrorism. That is why the fate of his daughter and other girls worries him, by giving themselves to drink they could go even further. It is possible that Uglanov is well-intentioned but is also possible that this is an exercise in deception as he feels guilty. It would be good to sort out this affair."[37]

People who had gone mad from terror sometimes even rushed ahead and reported themselves. They believed that they would be treated better in prison and would at least be free from the unbearable feeling of uncertainty that preceded arrest. This might have been the motive of the daughter of Inessa Armand—Lenin's great love and an old member of the Bolshevik Party, who died in 1920—who on January 26, 1937 wrote a letter to the party committee of her workplace, the Marx–Engels–Lenin Institute. In it she confessed to personally knowing Nikolai Bukharin, his first wife, Nadezhda and his sister-in-law Sofia.

In the atmosphere of the overwhelming hysteria around spying incidents, it was surprising that Aleksandr Afinogenov was not arrested, even though he had an American wife. But he lost his job and party membership. Every night they sat in front of the fire-place, waiting for the men of the NKVD to take them away.

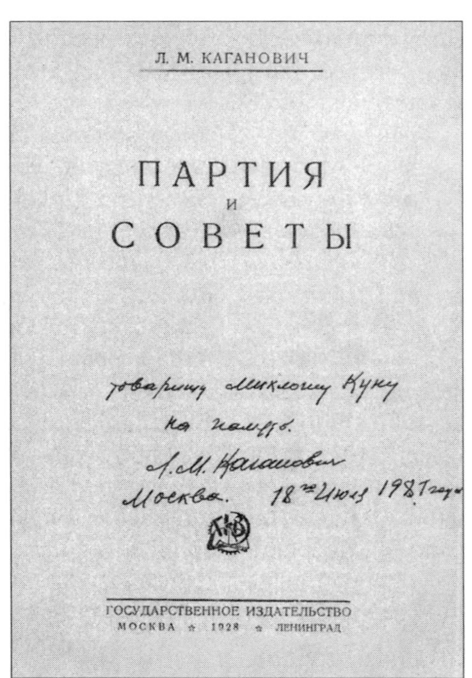

Despite all my hopes, I was unable to learn anything interesting from Lazar Kaganovich, the great survivor, about the Stalin era.

In 1933 she received a large package from them which contained Bukharin's letters. According to Armand the Bukharin family entrusted her with the papers because they were afraid of house searches. She felt it was important to take them and know what was in them. And if necessary to pass them on "to where it should be", that is to the political police. When she read the letters she saw that they were not counter-revolutionary documents. But later she was sorry that she had done nothing about them: "Now I know," she writes, "that I committed a serious crime against the party when I did not inform the party organization about these events. It showed lack of vigilance."[38]

It is highly unlikely that she avoided arrest because of this letter—despite the fact that her husband, the veteran German communist Hugo Eberlein, had already been declared "enemy of the people". At the same time, neither her workplace party organization nor the directorate of the Institute appreciated her *reporting herself*. By May 9, 1937 a report put together by Armand's chiefs was sitting on Yakov Agranov's desk, who was Interior Commissar Yezhov's deputy. It said that the woman had taken part in 1920–1922 in Trotskyist oppositional activities, and in 1928, when she lived in Germany, she had shown "tolerant behavior" towards the right wing of the German Communist Party for exactly three months.[39]

A typical example of the "period of cannibalism"—this is how the Chechen Kremlinologist Abdurahman Avtorkhanov, who went through the NKVD torture chambers, referred to the years of the Great Terror—was the behavior of Ivan Bulat. Like many of his fellows, the former manual worker became a "universal cadre" after the change in October 1917. In the 1920s he was given mainly administrative tasks in the central party apparatus. Over the following decade he was first the secretary of the iron workers' trade union and then an independent party secretary for the transport people's comissariat. Then he directed the Moldavian Autonomous Soviet Republic's party organization in Tiraspol. Although he had no law degree, he became the deputy people's comissar for justice in the government of the Soviet-Russian Federation and then president of the Supreme Court.[40] In this capacity he wrote a long letter to Stalin and Molotov on November 22, 1935. "After the Kirov murder the number of counter-revolutionary agitation cases has grown significantly," he writes. "For example in the first quarter of this year we had to deal with 882 cases in the special college[41] alone. In the second quarter we investigated 1340 cases, while in the third quarter the number reached 1673. Most of the accused in these cases were sentenced to imprisonment."[42]

But soon Bulat himself got into trouble. At the end of July 1937 the NKVD seized Dmitry Lebed. The agile deputy president of the government of the Soviet-Russian Federation had been a good friend of Bulat's for decades. The unfortunate chief judge, who had hundreds of innocent people on his conscience, took up his pen and as a last resort turned to Stalin. On August 4, 1937 he sent a copy of his letter to the three secretaries of the Central Committee, Kaganovich, Andreyev, and Yezhov, who were traveling around the country during the Great Terror directing the arrests of the nomenclature. In his letter signed with a trembling hand he informed them that he was completely innocent, that he had never heard any sort of hostile statement from Lebed, who had anyway avoided him for the last couple of months. Once he started his confessions, the Ivan Bulat also admitted that in 1937 his own brother was arrested in Leningrad as an "enemy of the people." He stated that from that time on he had been in agony, especially after they had arrested his best friend Lebed: "[...]

I must admit that I was blind, as I did not help unmask Lebed to the party." Then he said that the acts of the "enemies of the people" "must be revenged without mercy and relentlessly, including physical liquidation. I have denied and excommunicated my brother, who became an enemy of the people and brought shame on our family in which there are five Communists. In the same way I deny and excommunicate Lebed, who is an enemy of the people. I assure you, dear Comrade Stalin that I will conduct a relentless, merciless struggle against the enemies of the people in future. I am doing it right now in my daily work as a judge. Any aggressive act against the party and you personally will be met with the most decisive Bolshevik resistance, as far as I am concerned."[43]

This servile letter written on company paper and signed "party member since 1912" did not move the Master. Stalin's secretariat had received too many similar letters over this period, one that was dangerous for the old Bolshevik guard. The pleaders occasionally even harmed themselves and their relatives by taking such steps. The wife of Rudolf Peterson, the arrested commandant of the Kremlin, for example rang Stalin on his direct line and complained that her son Igor had been thrown out of the Zhukovsky Air Force Officer Academy. The Soviet dictator soothed her saying that the boy cannot be responsible for his father's actions. Let him continue studying, he said. A few days later, however, the political police swooped on the Peterson family for the second time.[44]

Only a few of the suspected old party members managed to escape by writing similar Bulat-type *mea culpa* letters. Among them was Klavdia Nikolayeva, one of the leaders of the Bolshevik women's movement. Even though she must have been really "suspect" because, according to the NKVD agents, in the mid-1920s she had played an important role in the "Leningrad opposition" represented by Zinovyev, Kamenev, and Nadezhda Krupskaya, who criticized the party's directive. But she, as it becomes clear from the letter she wrote on September 3, 1936 to Nikolai Yezhov, managed to go over to Stalin's side just in time. After a few years of hard work "she crawled back" to the top by running down her old colleagues.[45]

On the eve of the Great Terror the masculine looking, energetic Nikolayeva controlled the party organization of the Ivanovo-Voznesensk region famous for its textile industry, in her post as second secretary. To her misfortune, she was accused of letting one of her colleagues, who was arrested in the meantime, engage in "Trotskyist intrigues." Nikolayeva denied the accusations but did admit in the above-mentioned letter that she felt guilty: "I am very upset that I did not show proper Bolshevik vigilance. I allowed the asp viper to deceive me. And the party too. [...] Yet I have given my whole life to the party of Lenin and Stalin. I always moved along with our party, never missing a step. The party has brought me up since my young days. I have marched alongside the Central Committee of the Russian Communist (Bolshevik) Party, alongside Comrade Stalin. And I will do so in the future too [...] I was not the last to unmask the followers of Trotsky and Zinovyev. The whole party organization knows this. [...] At the same time I feel responsible before our party, its Central Committee and Comrade Stalin. It hurts, what has happened. It hurts a great deal."[46]

The case of Nikolayeva, who almost committed suicide because of the attacks on her, was not finally decided on by Yezhov but by Stalin. We still do not know today why but he stopped the drive against her. He also let a few dozen old party members stay alive, as if they were historical monuments. The Nikolayeva case was just one of the successive scenes which Stalin played out over the years. The younger and younger actors of this theater company changed in a rapid turnover, and the stage set was altered many times. Only Joseph Stalin remained unchanged on the stage, he who was both protagonist and director of the play.[47]

☆ The only changes that took place in the last years of his life was that the Soviet dictator became increasingly morose and anti-social. He withdrew more and more. Since the Great Terror he continually reduced the number of people who could see him. From 1946 onwards he spent long months in his luxurious Black Sea villas. Once when he needed a small operation the young female surgeon asked to operate—whose every move was watched by the bodyguards who stood around the operating table—had to slice into his purulent leg from behind a curtain, so she could not see on whom she was operating. She only later found out that it was Stalin.[48] From the beginning of the 1950s, he had started to fear doctors too: he was afraid they would make a bid for his life. This fear was at its height when he most needed medical help. From the mid-1940s onwards he had little strokes which had become increasingly frequent. The old man afflicted with high blood pressure and unstable nerves, looked a lot older than his years. He projected his fear of death onto his doctors. So the doctors' trial cooked up in 1953 was a type of rebellion on his part against people he had earlier admired, who were, however, not capable of prolonging his life—and the majority of whom happened to be Jewish.

This strange hatred had no serious precedents except for the drive that he made against Nadezhda Alliluyeva's doctors. While his wife lived, he had in general behaved decently, if not always sweetly, with their doctors. He always made sure that whenever he went on holiday, an experienced medical staff from the Kremlin Hospital traveled with him.[49] In September 1923, for example, he sent a telegram from the spa of Yessentuky in the Caucasus to Molotov and Rudzutak, two secretaries of the Central Committee. "Tell Semashko *[the people's commissar for health—M. K.]*," he wrote, "that because of my illness, and at my request, Doctor Aleksandrov will remain in Yessentuky for another three weeks. I need the permission of the health people's comissariat for this."[50] It seems that the cure worked on the general-secretary. Otherwise the following short text, which was worth a fortune in the Soviet Union which was struggling with unemployment, would not have been written: "For the information of the Soviet and party organizations. I testify that the bearer of this paper, Maria Generalova, employee of the Yessentuky spa is loyal to the Soviet Republic and deserves all confidence. J. Stalin. September 15 [1923]. I agree: Voroshilov."[51]

1 Chukovsky, 1995, 145.
2 The party supported the establishment of a constitutional democracy.
3 *Russky Berlin*, 1983, 27–44.
4 Chukovsky, 1995, 38–39, 56, 214, 235–237.
5 Sources on his friendship with Chukovsky and avoiding his returning home are published in *Sovietskie Arkhivi*, 1989, no. 3, 89–90; *Sovietskie Arkhivi*, 1991, no3, 65–73.; *Zvedzda*, 1994, no. 8, 152–178.
6 *RGASPI,* fond. 74, op. 1, d. 297.
7 *Pamyaty,* 1980, no. 3, 311–325.
8 *Vlast i khudozhestvennaya intelligentsia*, 1999, 275.
9 This Georgian word entered the Soviet dictator 's biography primarily due to Trotsky's followers. A synonym for an uninhibited, semi-cultivated, unreliable, slightly comical, and yet at the same time boastful man.
10 The list of awards, including the Stalin Prize, was prepared by the appropriate NKVD chief officers and party center *chinovniks,* then Stalin personally approved it. *Vlast i khudozhestvennaya intelligentsia,* 1999, 374–377; 413–414.
11 Korzhikhina, 1997, 286.
12 Gromov, 1998, 179; cf. Stalin, 1967, vol. XIV, 67–68.
13 Taylor, 1990, 168–171, 179.
14 Ter-Vaganyan, 1927, 12–23.

15 Stalin, 1951, vol. XIII, 29–43, 51-80, 236–256; Stalin, 1967, vol. XIV, 47–51, 53–55, 56–65, 67–70, 74–78, 19–102, 102–113, 113–116, 133–135, 184–189, 253–256, 275–279.
16 Stalin, 1967, vol. XIV, 278. At other times, he called Lenin "our father and teacher" just as the servile Soviet press called him. *Ibid.*, 114.
17 Sitz, 1991, 209. The Moscow historian at the beginning of the 1930s smuggled his historical diary out to Paris, in which—perhaps the first one to do so—he calls the Soviet dictator *duce*.
18 *RGASPI,* fond. 558, op. 4, d. 648.
19 Bukharin's former favorite pupil and right hand man who in 1929 went over to Stalin. As a reward he became leader of the cultural and propaganda section of the party headquarters. During the Great Terror, however, he was also executed.
20 *RGASPI,* fond. 82,. op. 2, d. 1442.
21 Stalin, 1967, vol. XV, 206.
22 Berezhkov, 1998, 324. This story was told the memoir writer by Pavlov, Berezhkov's former interpreter colleague in 1954, after Stalin's death.
23 *RGASPI,* fond. 558, op. 1, d. 4679.
24 On the surface, however, it seemed different, as if Kirov became closer to Stalin before his tragic death. Knight, 1993, 158–159.
25 *Sovietskoye Rukovodstvo*, 1999, 360–361.
26 *Vlast i khudozhestvennaya intelligentsia*, 1999, 387.
27 Gereben, 1998, 94–102.
28 Bulgakova, 1990, 180.
29 *Ibid.*,140, 160.
30 Disturbing documents about the Kirson–Afinogenov case are published in *Vlast i khudozhestvennaya intelligentsia*, 1999, 359–363, 368–370, 373–374.
31 Bulgakova, 1990, 160.
32 *Ibid.*, 166.
33 *Voyennie Arkhivi Rossii*, 1993, 408–409.
34 Vasilyeva, 1995, 209–212, 219–222. Budenny, who was called "Soviet Murat" by his bootlickers, who followed him everywhere, was an immoral person even earlier. In the mid-1920s during a family row he shot his first wife, the Nadezhda, who was of Cossak origini the head. His contemporaries, among them Tatyana Litvinova, daughter of the people's comissar for foreign affairs, said that at the intervention of Stalin and Voroshilov the criminal investigation against him was dropped.
35 Nikolai Uglanov was originally a locksmith, then shop assistant. Already by the 1920s he had entered the party leadership. With Stalin's support he scrambled to the top. In 1928 he was the leader of the Moscow party organization. However, he was then already regarded as a supporter of the Bukharin–Rykov–Tomsky "right leaning" group and was dismissed and then exiled to Siberia in the 1930s.
36 Rabochy Fakultet, a high-school level evening school for young workers.
37 *RGASPI,* fond. 88, op. 1, d. 578.
38 *RGASPI,* fond. 71, op. 3, d. 105.
39 *Ibid.*
40 *Stalinskoye Politbyuro*, 1995, 266.
41 A body established to speed up the trials of political cases.
42 *Sovietskoye Rukovodstvo*, 1999, 316
43 *RGASPI,* fond. 81, op. 3, d. 417.
44 Galagan-Trifonova, 1995, 242–243.
45 *Stalinskoye Politbyuro*, 1994, 296.
46 *RGASPI,* fond. 83, op. 1, d. 35
47 Antonov-Ovseyenko, 1995, 7–11, 13–19.
48 Moshentseva, 1998, 6–7.
49 *Golosa Istorii*, 1992, vol. II, 119–128.
50 *RGASPI,* fond. 558, op. 1, d. 2547.
51 *RGASPI,* fond. 558. op. 1. d. 2548.

Fading Group Pictures

The members of the Bolshevik leadership enjoyed posing in front of the camera. In the 1920s, and even at the beginning of the 1930s, Stalin was still eager to mix with ordinary party workers. In the first picture, the general secretary sits next to Sergei Kirov (x) wearing brightly polished boots.

The next photograph shows, besides Stalin, Molotov (1), Kaganovich (2), Voroshilov (3), Kalinin (4), Ordzhonikidze (5), and Kuybishev (6).

This picture, just like many others, was taken in a rotating manner. Joseph Stalin and the leather jacketed Kalinin (x)is surrounded by the doctors of a thermal bath and the members of the guard corps. The nurses, cooks, and the spa guests themselves changed places between the photo shots. Eventually the local photographer was the beneficiary of the event: the participants of the group could order copies of the picture from him.

CHAPTER 16
Aleksei Tolstoy, the Soviet Count

From this letter of recommendation it seems that at the beginning of his career, Stalin was often kind and helpful to people. He sometimes recommended people for party membership—even "little cogs" like an insignificant *apparatchik* called Anna Rudneva. The following undated note was addressed by Stalin to the party base organization to which the workers in the Soviet government apparatus belonged : "I recommend that Comrade Anna Rudneva be accepted into the party as a completely reliable comrade who is loyal to the working class."[1]

In those years the party general-secretary was glad to hand out recommendations and certificates while traveling round the country. According to the extant documents in the archive on August 23, 1921, he also intervened on behalf of a little known member of the public: "To the Kabard district party committee. At the request of Comrade Kirochkin, I testify that he, namely Mikhail Panteleyevich Kirochkin worked with me in 1907 in the Baku Bolshevik Party organization. The old Bolshevik Party members in party circles there knew Comrade Kirochkin. J. Stalin, member of the Russian Communist (Bolshevik) Party Central Committee."[2]

Later people like Kirochkin could not get anywhere near Stalin. The increasingly inwardly turning dictator locked himself away in his study which was fitted with a complicated system of locks. If he did step out of his circle of ten-twelve direct colleagues who surrounded him like a phalanx, then he mostly spent his time with famous actors, painters and composers. The former inhabitants of the Kremlin and the "House on the Embankment" recall that after Maksim Gorky's death (1936) during the Great Terror he greatly admired Aleksei Tolstoy, author of *Golgotha* and *Peter the First.*

When he was drunk, this knowledgeable but spineless and cynical writer, who deep in his heart loathed the Bolsheviks all his life, called himself the "Soviet Count". At the beginning of the 1920s, he returned from his voluntary exile in France and then Germany and immediately began to hawk his talent. He played an important role in the political police's and Soviet authorities' drive to destroy Russian émigrés in the west through his numerous declarations and his novel *Black Gold*, which is more like a pamphlet. In his verbose publications he cynically painted a false picture of Soviet reality. It is true that those who commissioned these texts were no less cynical, such as Nikolai Bukharin, editor-in-chief of *Izvestia.* He once sent this letter to Aleksei Tolstoy: "To Worker-Peasant Count Tolstoy. Dear Aleksei Nikolayevich, as you are "a bit of a trickster", to put in mildly, you must be feeling a pang of conscience. This is to urge you to write a short 150-line text for *Izvestia.* A sketch of the " knight of the work", of anyone, peasant or worker. It does not matter if it is not a real person just a generalized type. Please do not take this article anywhere else but bring it to me. Your N. Bukharin. P.S. Deadline is October 28 [probably 1935][3]."

Albeit he was always pleased to undertake such well paid requests, according to informers' reports Aleksei Tolstoy made skeptical declarations about the long-term viability of a Soviet Socialist regime, even at the height of his influence.[4] But this did not stop him from being a propagandist of the system in his articles, or from striving to convince influential intellectuals in the West that Stalin's country was the proletarian paradise. He never missed an opportunity when abroad to try and persuade the Russian opponents to the Soviet regime, who had emigrated during the Civil War, to return home. In 1937 at the height of the show trials and arrests it was not a little due to him that Aleksandr Kuprin decided to return home. One of the greatest Russian writers at the beginning of the century, Kuprin had been an outright critic of the Soviet authorities in the Paris

The writer with his wife, Lyudmila. "Without her help, I could not have fulfilled the task alloted to me."

Russian press. However, he became incapacitated and mentally deranged before his return home.[5]

When Aleksei Tolstoy became a deputy in the Supreme Soviet in reward for his services, he frequently besieged the rulers of the Kremlin with letters full of political ideas. At the turn of 1936–37 for example he several times suggested to Stalin and then to Molotov that they should entrust him with directing Soviet propaganda in the West—primarily in France which was then hosting the World Fair. He wrote that the French "love sensation, and are gullible, as people living without a purpose usually are," therefore it matters what sort of information they receive about the Soviet Union.[6] The over-zealous writer also interfered in cultural policies more than once. In November 1936 he tried to get the future Soviet cultural pope, Andrei Zhdanov, to allow the Leningrad Opera to put on stage Smetana's opera *Sold Bride*. If the premier does not take place "it will be disadvantageous for us in Prague from every aspect," he writes.[7]

Stalin and those of his colleagues who knew Tolstoy's works gave the "Soviet Count" jobs that were partly confidential, top security, and intelligence tasks. Before going on his long trips abroad the writer regularly discussed his work with the then head of the NKVD Genrikh Yagoda, and later during the Great Terror with Nikolai Yezhov, who apart from directing the Commissariat for Interior Affairs also controlled the civil and military intelligence. The world-famous writer wrote openly about his role as a propaganda agent *(agent vliania)* in an undated letter: "Deeply respected Nikolai Ivanovich, I am turning once more to you because of my Spanish mission. I request the same as I did this spring when I went to London to the Congress for the Friends of Peace and the Soviet Union: please let my wife Lyudmila Ilynichna Tolstoya travel with me. Firstly, because of my heart condition it would be careless of me to go alone. Secondly, which is

The Stores
Wallington
Near Baldock
Herts.
England

2.7.37

Dear Comrade,

I am sorry not to have answered earlier your letter dated May 31st, but I have only just got back from Spain and my letters have been kept for me here, rather luckily, as otherwise some of them might have been lost. I am sending separately a copy of "The Road to Wigan Pier." I hope parts of it may interest you. I ought to tell you that parts of the second half deal with subjects that may seem rather trivial outside England. I was preoccupied with them at the time of writing, but my experiences in Spain have made me reconsider many of my opinions.

I have still not quite recovered from the wound I got in Spain, but when I am up to writing again I will try and write something for you, as you suggested in your earlier letter. I would like to be frank with you, however, and therefore I must tell you that in Spain I was serving in the militia of the P.O.U.M., which, as you know doubt know, has been bitterly denounced by the Communist Party and was recently suppressed by the Government; also that after what I have seen I am more in agreement with the policy of the P.O.U.M. than with that of of the Communist Party. I tell you this because it may be that your paper would not care to have contributions from a P.O.U.M. member, and I do not wish to introduce myself to you under false pretences.

The above is my permanent address.

Yours fraternally

George Orwell

In 1937 Aleksei Tolstoy attempted to take control of the foreign relations of the Soviet Writers' Union. This organization had been for long a "branch office" of the NKVD. When George Orwell, returning from the battlefields of the Spanish Civil War, wrote his Moscow fellow writers in a letter that he did not agree fully with the official Communist policies, the officials of the Writers' Union responded harshly.

more important, Lyudmila Ilynichna's secretarial, assistant, and interpreting work is indispensable to me. Without her help I could not have fulfilled the task allotted me at the Brussels congress and the Paris meetings at which I had to make contact with French writers."[8]

The favorite writer of those in power, however, did not always recognize the limits to which he could go. After Gorky's death he tried twice to seize hold of the Soviet Writers' Union. In order to do so he sent material to the Party leadership containing compromising details of the then head of the Union, Aleksandr Fadeyev's alcoholism and arrogant behavior.[9] But the "*chinovnik*s of culture" wrapped the knuckles on Tolstoy and put a stop to it. They often found him difficult to bear. In the autumn of 1937 Tolstoy even gave advice to Stalin in a long letter reporting *Pravda* and *Izvestia* colleagues for not being vigilant enough. The two condemned papers had not published one of his articles attacking the persons accused in the show trial, "which was only published by *Literaturnaya Gazeta.*" Tolstoy hoped that if his articles appeared in the central papers then the foreign presses would take them too. He told Stalin that in the West, primarily due to bad propaganda, "they received news of the first trial *[against Zinovyev and Kamenev in 1936—M. K.]* with amazement and disbelief. They observed only the second one—against Pyatakov, Radek, and Sokolnikov—with trust, while our friends saw it with relief."[10]

"If my articles are not published for their length, or because they do not suit the paper's style then I must protest," complained Tolstoy. "This causes serious damage. The editors often do not understand that ideas have to be planted in people's minds. Banalities are brushed aside. During the Pyatakov trial a female journalist came to me in order that I sign an outraged declaration. She laid before me seven typed versions from which I might have chosen. She explained that this makes things easier: people are busy so it is easier for them merely to sign a ready-made text. These mistakes upset me, dear Iosif Vissarionovich, that's why I took up my pen to write to you."[11]

Naturally the celebrated writer had a fat dossier in the NKVD files. So they were completely aware that Aleksei Tolstoy in his circle of old friends disparaged the Soviet system. But they also knew that despite this, he could be handled easily as he was greedy for money and corruptible. In the letters he sent abroad he often boasted how well he lived in this country of "workers and peasants". "I have managed to assemble an art collection on a European scale of which I am very proud," he noted to an émigré friend in January 1927.[12]

"At that time he lived in grand style with servants and held huge receptions," recalled Yury Yelagin, an excellent chronicler of Moscow's literary-artistic life. "He had an old servant, who had worked for his parents [...] before the revolution. He addressed his master as 'Your Excellency' in the old way. [...] When one of the famous party leaders went to see Aleksei Tolstoy the old butler humbly informed him that his excellency deigned to attend the city party committee meeting."[13]

After a while Tolstoy's relations with the party leadership and primarily with Stalin were motivated not only by his careerism and money grasping but also by a strong ideological element. The court writer, who had been a great Russian nationalist in his youth, noticed at the end of the 1920s, much earlier than many of his contemporaries, that the world revolutionary slogans of the old Bolshevik Party members were just hot air. In the second half of the 1930s, paralleling Stalin's rise to total power, these slogans were increasingly exchanged for ones professing imperial supremacy. Seeing these changes which really were close to his heart Aleksei Tolstoy surprised the Master with his novel *Peter the First* and his series of plays about *Tsar Ivan IV (The Terrible)*. In the latter work he used his historical sources in such a cunning way that the terrible ruler who decimated his boyars and terrified his subjects, reminded the reader of Joseph Stalin who also destroyed the people around him and harbored similarly megalomanic plans of conquest. Although Ivan IV fought chiefly against Poland and Sweden, the dramatic scenes written in the midst of the Soviet-German war suggest that even in the sixteenth century Russians had to defend themselves against the "tyrannical German aggressors."[14]

However, the first part of the drama, which was planned as trilogy, was beset by problems. Aleksandr Shcherbakov, the over-zealous cultural politician, managed to prevent its being awarded the Stalin Prize, or indeed being shown at all in any of the country's bigger theatres.[15] The desperate writer wrote a lying but vociferous letter and sent it as an attachment to the typed manuscript to Stalin. In the draft of his letter, which was much longer than the final version, he states that he turned to this important theme in October 1941. "I wrote it during the most difficult times [...], in order to use Russian cultural history as a weapon."[16] But in reality he had started writing the text in February 1939 and even got paid for a libretto about Ivan the Terrible in the meantime.

"Sixteenth century Russia had fallen behind Europe in the sphere of material culture," we can read in the uncorrected version of his letter to Stalin. "Houses were built of wood, there were no windows, the roads were inferior, they had not discovered printing, most of the population could not read or write. Commerce

В Иностранный Отдел НКВД

Редакция журнала "Интернациональная Литература" получила из Англии письмо от писателя Д. Оруэлла, которое в переводе Вам направляю к сведению, в связи с тем, что из ответа этого писателя выявилась его принадлежность к троцкистской организации "ПОУМ".

They sent the outline of the reply (which is published here for the first time) to the counter-intelligence department of the NKVD for approval.

Yenukidze, Stalin, and Gorky at the Kremlin Wall.

in the cities was hardly developed. It was an agrarian country and this determined our backwardness in material culture. Michelangelo would have had a hard time in the Moscow Rus." This introduction was just the jumping board for his further imperialist-nationalist discourse, which later appeared in Sergei Eisenstein's film *Ivan the Terrible* and even seeped into Stalin's view of history: "But spiritual culture developed very forcefully and in a unique way in Moscow. In the sixteenth century it characterized only us, Russians to grasp the idea of a Russian state, to endeavor boundless, immense tasks, to seek and represent the Good in social transformation, and the force of integrity. The most typical Russian figure in this period was Ivan the Terrible. He was a real renaissance man. But he created a renaissance which is unique to us."[17]

When he wrote these lines, the German military machine had just started to assemble itself after the defeat it suffered at the gates of Moscow. Hitler regrouped his forces in order to move them towards the slopes of the Caucasus and Stalingrad. Tolstoy certainly knew that in this serious situation the running down of the Germans was like balm to Stalin's soul: "The terrible tsar embodies our national character. From him, from these sources spring the streams of Russian literature and its wide rivers. In contrast what can the Germans show for themselves in the sixteenth century? (And in the following centuries?) Martin Luther, the typical *petit bourgeois*? Everything great, or maybe huge in the Germans can be traced back to the Romans. Later the Germans came under Russian cultural influence."[18]

From the writer's letters it becomes clear that on orders from above he rewrote his plays about Ivan the Terrible: "I have edited both texts both in terms of style and content. I have marked the main changes and expansions and the new scenes in pencil,"[19] he writes. This makes clear that Stalin was not only a careful reader of the two plays but also their critic and censor too.

☆ The Soviet dictator had in any case acted as a censor throughout his rule; from the beginning of the 1920s he had found it hard to tolerate if anyone doubted his capabilities or judged him on anything. At the height of his power he got extremely angry if an author employed the obligatory epithets *(epithethon ornantis)* of the dictator for other persons. After having waved the flag of Russian patriotism—which anyway differentiated him from most of the Bolshevik politicians of the "heroic age" known for their internationalism—he did not allow the adjective "patriot" to be used even for Lenin. For example, in a great tome about the founder of the Soviet state he crossed out the phrase "Leninist patriotism" with the following sarcastic comment: "What, was Lenin a *patriot* too, and Suvorov and Peter the Great as well? Is there no difference between them?"[20]

Isaak Babel's prison photograph. The writer of *Red Cavalry* and *Tales of Odessa* was executed in 1940.

When the ruler of the Kremlin discovered the otherwise bad writer, Fyodor Panfyorov's novel *Bruski*,[21] which enthusiastically praised the carving up of villages as well as the Soviet dictator 's plan to liquidate party opponents, he wrote to Molotov that his new favorite must be puffed: "Vyacheslav! You must read Panfyorov's *Bruski*. It is a wonderful book. Today's contradictions in village life, the class struggle, the artisans' *artels*[22], and the remnants of the old world, all appear in it. All this is described by the writer observantly. I suggest: 1. We make *Pravda*, *Komsomolkaya Pravda*, and *Bednota*[23] publish two-three articles about the contents of *Bruski*, in popular form. These articles shouldn't be artistic-review rubbish; 2. Make *Krestyanskaya Gazeta*[24] publish *Bruski* in installments; 3. Commission Shvedchikov[25] to make a film of the novel; 4. Commission the Moscow State Proletars' Theater company, perhaps Kirson[26] personally, to dramatize it, if the writer does not want or cannot adapt the novel for the stage; 5. Accept Panfyorov into the Central Committee's circle and give him all support. *Bruski* is good because it is an objective work. It does not have the sentimental features that typify Gladkov's[27] stories about the peasant communes. It is excellent that the novel reflects a contemporary and sound feeling towards the new developments in village life. It is true that it does not provide the most typical examples of class struggle and the *kolkhoz* movement. Real life produces much more plastic and expressive stories. But this is not a big problem. It does, however, depict the new, the most everyday, the most elementary. It could influence the widest mass of peasants, especially the village communists. Well enough for now. J[oseph] Stalin. August 9, 1928."[28]

The Soviet dictator, who before the Second World War spent a lot of time nurturing his relations with writers and artists, sometimes capriciously "dropped" his favorites. At the beginning of the 1930s, for example, the news spread through Moscow that Sergei Eisenstein, who was then shooting in the US and Mexico, "had chosen the free world". Stalin did not check whether the news was true, although he could easily have done so, but started to mock the director of *Battleship Potemkin.* He even pretended that he couldn't remember his name properly. The story started when "the American writer Sinclair wrote a letter to Khalatov[29] and then to Kalinin, in which he requested them to support a project he had started with Aysenstend (!)," wrote Stalin in an undated letter to Kaganovich. "This person is our famous director who has escaped from the Soviet Union. A Trotskyist or even worse. This Aysenstend certainly wants to trick us with Sinclair's help. In other words a dirty affair. I suggest: a.) Postpone the decision until I arrive *[from his holiday at the Black Sea—M. K.]*; b.) Recommend Khalatov and Kalinin that thei did not reply to Sinclair until the question has been decided in the Central Committee."[30]

Stalin touched on the same theme in an instruction written to the members of the Politburo. The confidential text was taken to Kaganovich by one of the government couriers on June 4, 1932: "Keep an eye on Eisenstein, this conniving sneak, who with the help of Gorky, Kirson, and some Komsomolists, wants to be the Soviet Union's *chief cameraman [sic]* by hook or by crook. If he reaches his goal due to the indecisiveness of the cultural and propaganda section of the party headquarters, his victory will mean that every present and future deserter will think that they will be rewarded."[31]

It seems that the party general-secretary was more preoccupied with cultural political questions during his months spent hidden away in his *dacha* than in the Kremlin where he was weighed down with everyday affairs. From a letter written on June 7, 1932 to his then confidant Kaganovich, it seems he also reserved the right to make decisions in aesthetic issues: "*Novy Mir* is publishing Sholokhov's novel *Podnyataya Tselina (Virgin Soil Upturned)*. An interesting little piece. It seems Sholokhov has thoroughly studied agricultural collectivization in the Don region. I believe he has great artistic talent. In addition he is a very conscientious artist: he writes about that which he knows. In contrast to 'our' feverish Babel who always writes about that which he knows nothing. Like for example the *Red Cavalry*."[32]

☆ The Kremlin ruler's attention was not only drawn to literary questions but to small scandal which he often followed with sick curiosity, like the scandal concerning the provision of the party holiday resort near Moscow. "July 5, 1923. To Comrade Sapronov, secretary of the Central Executive Committee. To Comrade Yenukidze, secretary of the Central Executive Committee. Copy. To Comrade Ksenofontov, head of the economic section of the Central Committee. We have learned that Comrade Metelev has slowed down funds to the Central Committee's Maryino holiday resort. As those spending their holidays there have not been receiving the necessary provisions they are fleeing the resorts. Please look into all the means at your disposal in order that the rightful demands of Maryino and its leaders can be fulfilled. In the case of further delays I will be forced to demand that Comrade Metelev be dismissed from all his posts and give the case to the Central Supervisory Committee. J[oseph] Stalin. CC secretary."[33]

As the years went by the "Master" increasingly expected everyone to do his bidding and to worship his personal cult ever more fervently. In December 1939, the celebration of his sixtieth birthday lasted for weeks. By then twenty-five big cities and smaller settlements bore his name: including Stalingrad, Stalino on the far away Kamchatka peninsula, Stalinobad, the capital of Tadjikistan, Staliniri, the seat of the Southern Ossetian autonomous region, as well as the Soviet Union's highest peak of 7,495 meters. Today we still do not know

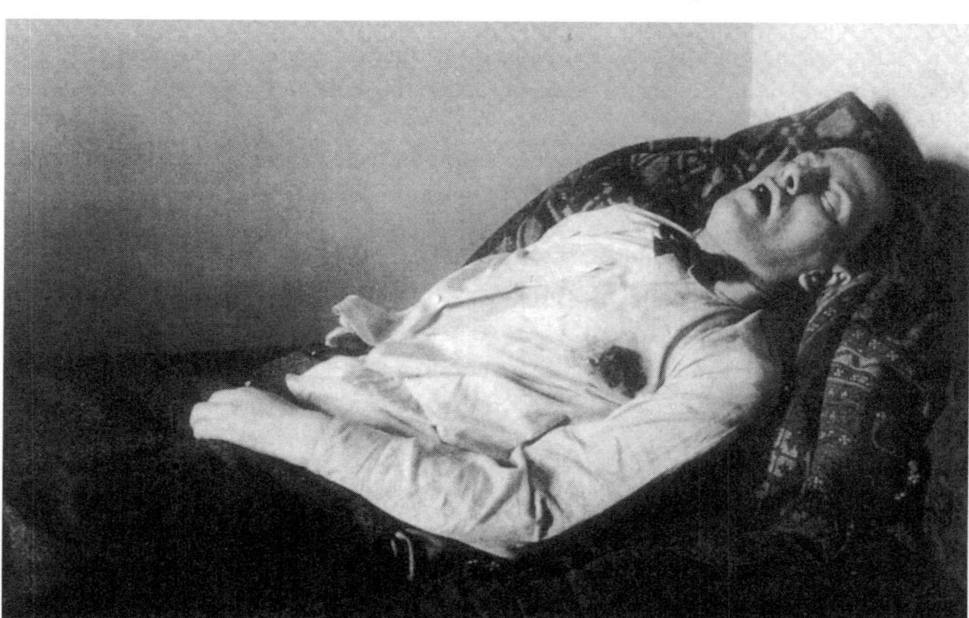

Eventually, Stalin was willing to get over Mayakovsky's futurist roots and later his suicide, which had been qualified as "petit-bourgeois conformism" by the hypocritical Bolshevik commentators.

why despite "the demands of the great masses", he did not agree to re-christen Moscow *Stalinodar* (meaning Stalin's gift) at the beginning of 1938.[34] During that period the Bolshevik Party leadership, the Kremlin personnel, the government guard, and finally the middle and lower ranks in the nomenclature addressed him only in the third person. Sometimes he was referred to using terms such as *Instantsia [Forum]*. This latter expression was used already in the Soviet *Newspeak* of the 1920s, before the era of total dictatorship. But at that time it referred to a group, the members of the Politburo: "if the Forum orders me to commit hara-kiri then I will do so," writes on September 27, 1929 the foreign affairs people's commissar Georgy Chicherin who was undergoing a cure in Germany and shied away from returning home.[35] In the following decade this name—in a concrete context—just referred to Stalin, even after the dictator's death: "For nearly eight years we informed the Forum about the counter-intelligence activities of SMERSH and the State Security Ministry," admits Colonel Broverman, one of the Soviet political police's chief officers with most blood on his hands, during a trial held in the period of "thaw".[36]

In a certain sense this depersonalization contributed to Joseph Stalin's suspecting everybody around him. During Second World War he listed one of his oldest and dearest friends, Klim Voroshilov, among his potential traitors. It is true that the marshal, who had been a locksmith, played a pitiful role in the command of the front in August 1941, as the defender of besieged Leningrad. Stalin then sent a special committee headed by Molotov and Malenkov to the city in order to find out who was responsible for the series of Soviet defeats. In those dark days the ruler of the Kremlin also started to suspect another of his loyal arms bearers, the General Secretary of the Leningrad party organization, Andrei Zhdanov[37] . Going over both their heads he sent a hysterical telegram to Molotov on August 8, 1941[38]: "I have just been informed that the enemy has taken Tosno. If this goes on like that, Leningrad may be surrendered in an idiotic, stupid way. All Leningrad divisions may be taken prisoners of war. What are [Markian] Popov[39] and Voroshilov doing? They have not even informed me what they want to do to avert this danger. They are preoccupied with finding a way to retreat. They think this is their duty. Where does this passivity, this typical peasant fatalism come from? What sort of men are they? They are worth nothing. There are now a lot of KV tanks[40], planes, and Katyusha rockets in Leningrad. Why did they not deploy them on the Lyuban'–Tosno front? What can an infantry regiment do against German tanks without these weapons? Why don't they use the great Leningrad technical facilities? Don't you think someone wants deliberately to let the Germans in at this decisive part of the front? What sort of man is Popov? What does Voroshilov do exactly? And how can his aid to Leningrad be described?

I am writing about this because I am very worried about the Leningrad command's, for me incomprehensible, delay. I think you should come to Moscow on the 29th [of August]. Please do not delay the journey!"[41]

In his letter Stalin targeted the man who he had trusted more than anyone else for two decades and with whom he shared his most jealously guarded secrets. During the famine in the days of the Civil War, he even entrusted Voroshilov with rounding up provisions for him. Such men were known as *meshochnik*s [peddlers] at that time, when food transportation across administrative borders was strictly forbidden and severely punished. But Stalin always felt that he was free to do anything: "Well, buddy, I think that on August 10, I will go to Rostov and from there to Moscow," he wrote to Voroshilov on June 27, 1921. "It would be good to meet, discuss what is going on in the south east. If possible get ten *pud*[42] of bread for me. If you can't then never mind. With firm handshake. Regards to Budenny and Bubnov. Your Stalin."[43] One might wonder if he remembered then that in 1918, at the Tsaritsyn front, Stalin had had several people executed for possessing and peddling with a similar amount of grain.

1 *RGASPI,* fond. 558. op. 1. d. 2325.
2 *RGASPI,* fond. 558. op. 1, d. 2211.
3 *RGASPI,* fond. 269, op. 1, d. 56.
4 *Vlast i khudozhestvennaya intelligentsia*, 1999, 497.
5 On the circumstances of the writer's return, see *Minuvsheye,* 1988, no5, 353–359.
6 *RGASPI,* fond. 269, op. 1, d. 1.
7 *RGASPI,* fond. 269. op. 1. d. 10
8 *RGASPI,* fond. 269, op. 1, d. 14.
9 Babichenko, 1994, 67.
10 *RGASPI,* fond. 269, op. 1, d. 2.
11 *Ibid.*
12 *Russky Berlin,* 1983, 121.
13 Yelagin, 1988, 132.
14 *RGASPI,* fond. 269, op. 1, d. 4.
15 *Vlast i khudozhestvennaya intelligentsia*, 1999, 478, 486–487, 500–501.
16 *RGASPI,* fond. 269, op. 1, d. 4.
17 *Ibid.*
18 *Ibid.*
19 *Ibid.*
20 *RGASPI,* fond. 558, op. 1, d. 5166.
21 The four volumes of the novel were written between 1928 and 1937.
22 A type of cooperative.
23 A daily paper for poor peasants, published during the times of agricultural collectivization.
24 A daily paper for a wider audience of village people, which published much expert advice.
25 The functionary who ran the Soviet film industry at the end of the 1920s.
26 One of the Soviet dictator's favorite playwrights who was subsequently executed during the Great Terror.
27 Fyodor Gladkov started his career writing about village themes in the pre-Revolutionary era. He was the author of the 'first proletarian great novel', *Cement.*
28 *RGASPI,* fond. 82, op. 2, d. 1420. In the second half of the 1920s, Stalin became somewhat disillusioned with Panfyorov. L. *Vlast i khudozhestvennaya intelligentsia,* 1999, 453.
29 The Armenian Artyom (Arthashes) Khalatov between 1932 and 1935 was a member of the Collegium of the Transport Commissariat . Then in 1937, until his arrest, he organized the "invention movement". He was a famous cultural politician of the time. For a few years he supervised state-owned publishing.
30 *RGASPI,* fond. 81, op. 3, d. 100.
31 *RGASPI,* fond. 81, op. 3, d. 99.
32 *Ibid.*
33 *RGASPI,* fond. 558, op. 1, d. 2539.
34 Starkov, 1995, 89–91.
35 *RGASPI,* fond. 558, op. 2, d. 48.
36 Stolyarov, 1997, 196.
37 Salisbury, 1969, 388–404.
38 The fact that the dictator sent the telegram to Aleksei Kuznetsov, the second secretary of the Leningrad party, with the instruction that he give it to Molotov and not to Zhdanov, says a lot.
39 Then Voroshilov's general deputy, one of the most talented military leaders in the Second World War. He directed several fronts during the war. But Stalin did not like him and this is why he was only made a general and not a marshal.
40 Heavy tanks made in the Kirov (formerly Putilov) factory, which were named after Klim Voroshilov.
41 *RGASPI,* fond. 82, op. 2, d. 1421.
42 One *pud* = 16 kilograms.
43 *Voyennie Arkhivi Rossii*, 1993, no. 1, 405.

CHAPTER 17
Expulsion from Paradise

The building of the Kremlin was finally completed in the seventeenth century. It was constructed according to the plans made by medieval Italian architects. According to Lev Razgon, the chronicler of the Stalinist period, the building complex with its airy, lacy walls was "until 1936 just like a provincial town."[1] The writer, who was a prisoner in the Gulag for many years, mentions 1936 because it was by then that most of the old inhabitants were moved out of the Kremlin. In the "House on the Embankment" or in the center of Moscow, luxury apartments were converted for the politicians who had used to live next to Joseph Stalin because he wanted to get them out of the way. "Even so this was a bad move for all of us. We thought that the 'House on the Embankment' was a terrible, gloomy, dirty gray building," recalled Natalya Rykova, daughter of the head of the Council of People's Commissars, first post-Lenin Soviet government, during our conversation in Moscow. "They officially built it so that the comrades could move out of the two best Moscow hotels, the National and the Metropol. But in reality we were moved into a communal house so that it would be easier to keep an eye on us."

Lidia Shatunovskaya writes in a similar vein about the "House on the Embankment". According to her the staff, deployed by the NKVD headquarters at Lubyanka, kept an eye on the inhabitants: "If a guest came they had to give

The early 1930s, the Kremlin from the Manezh Square. The castle district of Moscow at this time still looked "like a provincial town".

Natalia Sedova, Trotsky's wife, was willing to confront any challenge. More than fifteen years after her husband's assassination, she called on the people of the Soviet Union to rise up against the heirs of Stalin. However, her call, which was aired by the Russian-language American radio station Liberation, did not have an effect on the people.

their names to the concierge and announce whom they had come to see. The concierge then called up the resident in question and respectfully announced that this or that comrade would like to see them. The guest could call the lift only after receiving an affirmative reply. This procedure allowed the concierge to give regular and exact information to the commandant's office and through them to the state security authorities, about who came in and for how long and also noted and reported who, when, and for how long left the house. They also observed the relationships between the residents, and who made friends with whom. They gathered information about our private lives in different ways, for example, through servants' gossip. We lived in a bell jar, being constantly watched by the state security services. But all this was done under the guise of great deference, so even those who knew what was going on, thought it a normal, natural procedure."[2]

It was even easier to observe the residents of the Kremlin. They did not like the ordeal[3] that surrounded living there, but found it even more difficult when they faced "expulsion from Paradise". Of the privileges gained after the 1917 takeover by the new Soviet ruling elite, Kremlin apartments were probably the most treasured. Those who managed to obtain such an apartment, later started to petition for its renovation, or tried to exchange it for an even better one. Among them was Joseph Stalin who, from the very beginning, allowed himself more freedoms than anyone else. Trotsky, who was his chief rival then, recalled:

VOL. XLVI. № 15.718. TUSDAY, JULY 10, 1956. ВТОРНИК, 10

Н. И. Седова, вдова Троцкого, призывает к свержению сталинской олигархии

Призыв к населению Сов. Союза радио - станции « Освобождение

Говорит Наталия Ивановна Седова, вдова Льва Давидовича Троцкого из города Мексико. Я обращаюсь к рабочим и крестьянам и главным образом

в течение десятков лет ни один из них, этих коллективных вождей, не осмелился из-за страха за собственную жизнь открыто выступить с

этой, поистине, чудови ткани лжи. Лжи бюрокр против Троцкого, Зинов Каменева и сотен других позиционеров. Они не о

"In 1919 I accidentally noticed that in the cooperative shop of the Council of People's Commissars Caucasus wines were being sold. I suggested they be removed as at that time the sale of alcohol was forbidden. 'What would happen if news got to the front that they are carousing in the Kremlin?' I said to Lenin. 'That would make a very bad impression.' Stalin was present at our conversation. 'But what will happen to us Caucasians?' he interrupted angrily. 'How can we live without wine?!' I capitulated without resisting further."[4]

Trotsky also wrote about the conflict between his wife Natalya Sedova and Lenin, which emerged around the planned reconstruction work in the Kremlin. The scandal began when Stalin started to complain bitterly that he was sleeping badly because of the continual noise. That is why he sought a new flat in the autumn of 1921. One of the Belenky brothers, who directed Lenin's bodyguard, Abram or Grigory advised him to put up a few walls in one of the most splendid palaces of the Kremlin, in fact in its banqueting hall, and to choose from one

Karl Radek in his youth. After returning from his exile in Siberia, he wanted to return to the ranks of the ruling elite.

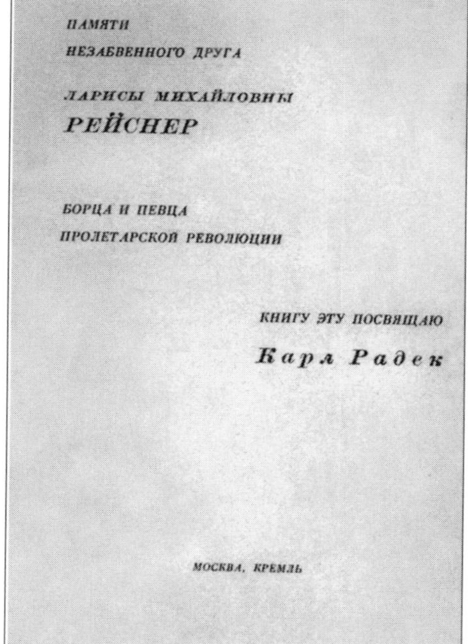

ПАМЯТИ
НЕЗАБВЕННОГО ДРУГА

ЛАРИСЫ МИХАЙЛОВНЫ
РЕЙСНЕР

БОРЦА И ПЕВЦА
ПРОЛЕТАРСКОЙ РЕВОЛЮЦИИ

КНИГУ ЭТУ ПОСВЯЩАЮ
Карл Радек

МОСКВА, КРЕМЛЬ

of the new flats created in this way. "My wife, who had for nine years seen to the supervision of the museums and historical sites, protested at this as the palace was a historical monument," recalled Trotsky. "At this Lenin wrote a long letter to her persuading her that the more valuable furniture could be taken out and guards placed before the chambers. But that on the other hand Stalin needed an apartment in which he could sleep in peace. Young comrades were to move into his present flat who would not be disturbed by anything, even gunfire in their sleep, etc."[5]

But Natalya Sedova did not intend to leave it at that. In turn, Leonid Serebryakov,[6] who was always well-intentioned, gave Stalin his own flat in order to stop the argument. Despite this sacrifice, Trotsky notes, seventeen years later Stalin executed his self-sacrificing neighbor.[7] Serebryakov was sentenced to death actually earlier, at the beginning of 1937, as one of the defendants in the Pyatakov–Radek–Serebryakov trial. In reality the fate of this man, who was close to Stalin for a while, is still linked to one of the unknown and enigmatic episodes in the struggle for power in Kremlin. In the first months of 1926 he mediated between the Trotsky-led opposition on the one hand, and Stalin and his then allies Rykov and Bukharin, on the other. Leon Trotsky, who saw himself as a balancing factor, believed that he could get back into power politics along with his followers if he compromised with one of the two big factions in the Bolshevik leadership, either with the followers of the "central line" or with the "Leningraders." In order to do so he was even willing to meet Stalin, whom he loathed, in secret, before coming to a deal with Zinovyev and his colleagues. According to an unpublished, undated letter from Rykov, Serebryakov also took part in this conspiratorial meeting.[8] It was only natural that as a consequence, later on the life of this unpleasant witness would not be worth a *kopeck* in the eyes of the Master of the Kremlin.

Trotsky only put this story about the insomniac dictator, who cared for no one else's peace, to paper in September 1939: by then his memory was not entirely clear. In reality Joseph Stalin did not have his eye on the Kremlin palace's banqueting hall but directly on part of the Oruzheynaya Palace, the huge chambers of the former tsar's treasury which is today a museum. Trotsky, however, was right when he recalled that Natalya Sedova refused Lenin's request, despite the fact that she looked up to him almost as if he were a demigod.

I could not find the Lenin letter Trotsky referred to neither in the Soviet nor the western archives. Nevertheless, I did find Sedova's unpublished, hard-to-read reply not long ago in Moscow. This document bears witness to the fact that her tough stance forced Stalin, who later killed her husband and children, to withdraw. She wrote to Lenin: "Dear Vladimir Ilych, I am not at all angry. But you, forgive me for saying this, are too lenient. Naturally Comrade Stalin must have a quiet flat. That we are obliged to find. But he is a living man and not an exhibit in a museum. He himself is not willing to live in a museum. He does not want to be fobbed off with a residence that Comrade Zinovyev refused last year. Comrade Stalin would like to get Comrades Flakserman's and Malkov's flat. [...] Anyway the Treasury is very cold, Vladimir Ilych. Only a single room can be heated, where the treasures to be sent to the mint are being selected. [If Stalin moves in,] this work would come to a standstill."[9]

The twenty-year-old Flakserman worked alongside Lunacharsky who ran the Commissariat for Culture, while seaman Malkov was the commandant of the Kremlin. He made history when he himself executed Fanya Kaplan, who was charged with the August 30th 1918 attempt on Lenin's life, in the Kremlin courtyard with a revolver; he then burnt her body in a rusty iron barrel. Later Malkov was expelled from the Kremlin for chronic alcoholism. During the Great Terror both men mentioned in the Sedova letter were sent to the Gulag but they survived. Malkov, once freed, published his memoirs about his years with Lenin; the text was prepared for publication—and falsified—by Yakov Sverdlov's son Andrei. The educated Flakserman, however, chose to remain in the background throughout. He did live to see the time of *perestroyka* and made several telling statements about the innocent millions who died in Soviet death camps.

But that is the end of the story; back at the beginning of the 1920s the tug-of-war in the Kremlin was around the four small rooms of Flakserman and Malkov, which Stalin maintained would not be suitable for him. It was then that Leonid Serebryakov ran to his aid. Finally, it was his home that became known as Stalin's flat. Its description appears in most of the biographies of the Soviet dictator. The main source of this description is Boris Bazhanov, who, as Stalin's secretary for a while, regularly visited the dictator in the flat: "Stalin lives in the Kremlin in a simply furnished flat in which the palace servants used to live."[10]

But the Master of the Kremlin wished for greater comfort. So in August 1925 construction workers converted his home to a two-storey apartment, in accordance with Nadezhda Alliluyeva's tastes. As a result another conflict arose, pitting the neighboring Soviet political leaders against each other. Klim Voroshilov—then commander of the Moscow military sector—reproached Avel Yenukidze, who was in charge of the refurbishment, that he wasn't working to Stalin's orders: "... if I remember correctly the kitchen was to be on the upper floor," he writes in an angry letter. "This has angered Koba and N[adezhda] Alliluyeva. If the flat is not done properly it will have to be immediately changed [...] Koba is willing to live in the present palace for several months (he emphasized this in our conversation), as long as they do the refurbishment properly and make good all the mistakes. The worst of it is that the kitchen is downstairs." Yenukidze made a note on the letter: "I have done everything you asked." Five days later he reported in writing to Voroshilov that he had taken the General Secretary's message as an order.[11]

Stalin later changed flats twice in the Kremlin, with great fuss on each occasion. In November 1926, when Sergo Ordzhonikidze moved to Moscow from Rostov with his wife Zinayda and their adopted daughter Eteria, they lived with Stalin to begin with: "After a while a flat was prepared for Ordzhonikidze [in the Kremlin]," recalls Zinayda Ordzhonikidze. "We were getting ready to move out of Stalin's house. But he said, 'I see that you Sergo and Zina like my home. Is that so?' 'Yes,' replied Sergo. 'Then you all live here and I will move.' And so it was."[12]

After his wife's mysterious death Stalin unexpectedly offered Bukharin, who not long before had been his political opponent, to swap flats. Bukharin had only moved into the Kremlin a little before and therefore he had not yet received a properly luxurious and comfortable flat. But the walls of the flat that he got from Stalin seemed to radiate fear, especially during the Great Terror. Anna Larina said that Nikolai Bukharin not long before his arrest had said bitterly: "...unlucky Nada [Alliluyeva] perished in this flat. And my life is to come to an end here, too."[13]

☆ It is strange that even in the mid-1930s, Stalin often personally took care of distributing flats for members of the nomenclature, and decided even over their holidays. Dmitry Milyutin, an old party member, turned to him on February 26, 1934 when he got into trouble: "Dear Comrade Stalin! Yesterday while I was at work, the wing of the Mamontovka Santarorium in which I stayed with my daughter, who suffers from tuberculosis, burned down. We were spending our prescribed Sanatorium stay there. Now I turn to you for help. I have little strength and without your personal help and categorical orders, I will not last long in this world if I have to see to the rapid rebuilding of the wing. Nearly all our worldly possessions fell prey to the fire. I ask you once again to help us. With communist regards: Dm[itriy] Petr[ovich] Milyutin." The dictator helped the old, troubled and seemingly disordered comrade that very day. As he wrote on his request: "To Comrade Yenukidze. J. St[alin]."[14] And the job was as good as done.

But scarcely three years later Dmitry Milyutin had no need of a cure in sanatoriums. On Stalin's orders he was seized by an NKVD commando and taken from the rapidly rebuilt wing.

The bitter rows over the allotting of flats, refurbishment and people being moved out, was typical of the lives of the Soviet political elite. "Comrades Voroshilov and Shkiryatov!" was how on April 15, 1931 Avel Yenukidze addressed officially his old friends, the all-powerful military people's commissar and one of the leaders of the Bolshevik Party's Central Supervisory Committee. Yenukidze, apart from his numerous other duties, also organized the distribution of the flats for the leaders. "Krestinsky, Sverdlova, Osinsky, and Stuchka have sought me out. They categorically requested (pleaded) that I did not move them out. What should I do? This is very difficult. Everybody is very persistent. Especially Krasikov and Vinokurov."[15] All the people mentioned in the letter were "old Kremlin inhabitants."

Between 1919 and 1921 Nikolai Krestinsky led the secretariat of the Central Committee of the Bolshevik Party. At the end of the Civil War he joined Leon Trotsky in the raging factional struggle, and that is why he was "demoted" to people's commissar for finance. But instead of being repentant he was drawn to the party opposition and as further punishment was sent as Ambassador to

Berlin. Then in 1928 he spectacularly broke with his Trotskyist past and was allowed home. At the beginning of the 1930s he became deputy people's commissar for foreign affairs. Klavdia Sverdlova, who is also mentioned, was the widow of the Bolshevik leader Yakov Sverdlov who died in 1919. After the death of her husband, who was celebrated as one of the founders of the Soviet system, she worked in the Central Committee apparatus. Valeryan Osinsky (Obolensky), an expert economist, was the people's commissar for agriculture in the 1920s, and then a talented diplomat. At the end of that decade he was head of the Soviet Statistics Office.

The Latvian Pyotr Stuchka was a lawyer, legal historian, and a drafter of laws. In 1918–1919 he was head of the short-lived Red Latvian government and then president of the Soviet-Russian Supreme Court. From the mid-1920s onwards he was head of the Central Supervisory Committee of the Comintern, and at the same time directed the publishing of the Great Soviet Encyclopedia. One of his best friends was Pyotr Krasikov, veteran of the Russian Social Democratic movement, who after the Bolshevik rise to power was given an important job in the Ministry of Justice, and then, during the persecutions, right up until 1938 was deputy president of the Soviet Supreme Court. Aleksandr Vinokurov was also an old Bolshevik Party member who, due to his medical degree, dealt with welfare issues in Lenin's first Soviet government. But as professional expertise did not always play an important role in the selection of cadres, Vinokurov was appointed president of the Soviet Supreme Court after Stuchka was dismissed in 1924. Later the doctor turned lawyer was the hard-line leader of the so-called Eighth Department supervising the Bolshevik state's church policies, but this great collector of church treasures was then slightly marginalized because by 1938 he was running only a nation-wide health information service.

Almost all the politicians listed above came to tragic ends. Krestinsky was executed in 1938. He was the only accused in the Bukharin trial who publicly withdrew the confessions tortured out of him. Klavdia Sverdlova lived to be an old lady and was able to publish her memoirs about her husband and her age. Her son Andrei became a NKVD officer at the Lubyanka: he interrogated a string of his arrested friends with whom he had been brought up in the Kremlin. At the end of the 1930s the young Sverdlov even worked for Beria's secretariat but in 1951, when an anti-Semitic campaign swept through the Soviet Union, he himself was in prison for a while.[16] He was rehabilitated after Stalin's death. Then he became a party historian and continued informing as he had done since his teenage years. Obolensky, however, who was a former neighbor of the Sverdlovs, was severely tortured, forced to act as a witness at the Bukharin trial, then—just like his son who was accused of terrorism—he was executed. Even more stunning is Stuchka's case. He died in 1932 "in his bed," but was then denounced *post mortem* as "tending to the right wing" and as an "enemy of the people." The "Old Man" Krasikov, who tried to open Stalin's eyes during the Great Terror was, according to his adopted daughter's memoirs, poisoned in a sanatorium on orders from the dictator.[17] And finally there are the still unclear circumstances of his best friend, Aleksandr Vinokurov's death. The earlier official date of 1944 does not tally with the facts. But we do know that the politician became suspect, and from the second half of the 1930s was watched by the NKVD very closely.[18]

Among the members of the post-1917 political elite, those requested to be allowed to stay in the Kremlin who were increasingly being marginalized of the Soviet leadership. Like other Bolshevik notables, they argued that in 1918 they had moved into the Kremlin with Lenin, and with his permission. Because of this, they contended, the apartments there were *rightfully theirs* until the end of their lives. Interestingly, at the very beginning of the 1930s, this argument had some influence on the former second rank politicians replacing the protagonists of the "heroic age", whom they demonstratively looked down on. "I believe if not everybody, then some of them could be moved. The time has come. The House *[on the Embankment —M. K.]* is ready. Help us, A[vel] S[afronovich]," wrote Matvei Shkiryatov, who was otherwise not at all sentimental, to Yenukidze.[19]

☆ The Damocles sword of the humiliating order to move out of the Kremlin was already hanging over the heads of those who opposed the Bolshevik Party's centrist tendencies by the second half of the 1920s. Leon Trotsky was among the first of the Kremlin inhabitants to be told to leave in the autumn of 1927. The same happened to Lev Kamenev later. By the beginning of the 1930s almost all of Trotsky's and Zinovyev's former followers found themselves outside the Kremlin walls; including those who, in one of the most used jargons of the time, were willing to *lay down their arms before the party*.

Occasionally an opposition politician "gone astray" would indeed "lay down his arms before the party" and would return to Moscow. None of these were, however, allowed to move back into the Kremlin, although they were kindling nostalgic memories about the days they had lived there. Karl Radek could take especially badly that he was pushed out of power. Maybe it was this injustice that prompted him to write *Moscow, Kremlin* as the place of publication of his book published in 1933, although he had no longer been residing there.[20]

On November 30, 1930 even a Politburo decision was made on the changes in the Kremlin. Among other things it stated: "c)...we insist that Comrade Stalin does not walk about the city on foot; d) The Central Committee's secret section must move from Staraya Square into the Kremlin as quickly as possi-

According to the writer Lev Razgon, the House on the Embankment purgatory for the designated victims of the Kremlin, before reaching the deepest corners of hell, the torture cells of the Lubyanka prison and eventual execution.

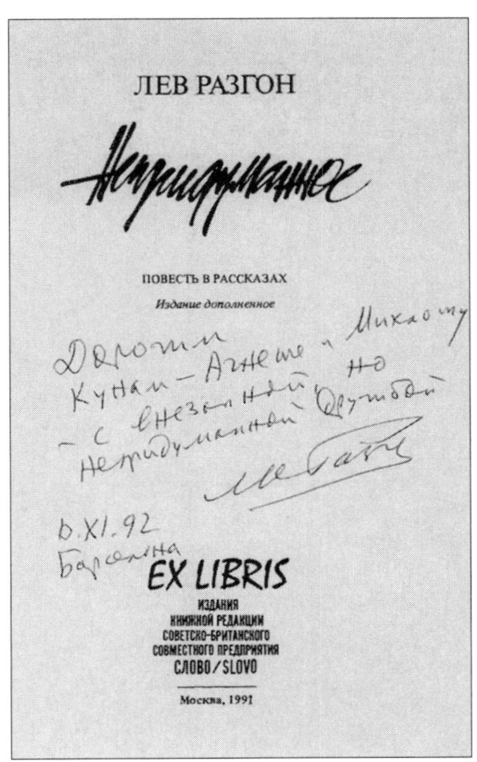

ЛЕВ РАЗГОН

Непридуманное

ПОВЕСТЬ В РАССКАЗАХ

Издание дополненное

6.XI.92

EX LIBRIS

ИЗДАНИЯ
КНИЖНОЙ РЕДАКЦИИ
СОВЕТСКО-БРИТАНСКОГО
СОВМЕСТНОГО ПРЕДПРИЯТИЯ
СЛОВО/SLOVO

Москва, 1991

ble; e) We entrust Comrade Voroshilov with speeding up the sweeping out of the Kremlin the unreliable inhabitants now living there."[21] Later on those who had fallen into disfavor, and the veterans of the Bolshevik Party living there, were kicked out. In the middle of the decade, the commandant of the Kremlin put this leading question to the former leaders of the "right wing tendency": "How many vans do you need from the Kremlin garage for the moving out?"

The new Soviet aristocracy—most of whom had come to power from fairly "low" beginnings and liked to brag with their beggarly serf and worker ancestors—had been spoiled over the years. Kremlin residents could use an excellent restaurant where they could also invite their friends and relatives. In addition they could regularly order the best provisions from the exclusive distributors—known as *sklad* (store) or *baza* (base).

They did not even have to pay for their apartments. And could avail themselves of a staff most of whom had been inherited from the time before the revolution. For example in Leon Trotsky's home lunch was served on a dinner service with the tsar's monogram by an old butler who had learnt his profession in the court of Nikolai II, and strangely enough was genuinely attached to the "Red nobles." Trotsky's little sister Olga, wife of Lev Kamenev, created a literary salon in her home, which was held in tandem with great dinners. The best known writers and artists did not go only for spiritual nourishment when they made their pilgrimage to her home. "The Kamenevs have the best home cooking in Moscow," they joked as they wandered home, well-fed, in the early hours of the morning. While all around them shivering, hungry, unemployed people queued before employment offices of the Soviet capital.[22]

The more puritan and modest members of the "new class" of course stuck out like sore thumbs. "Stopani, the head of the old Bolshevik Party members community, once came round," recalled Lidia Shatunovskaya. "He sat for a while and then bitterly spat out why he had come. 'My friend, Pyotr Ananyevich! You have put us all in a difficult situation. Especially Avel Yenukidze, at whose request I am now here.' 'What's your problem with me?' asked Krasikov, amazed. 'You are the only one who pays for provisions from the Kremlin warehouse.' 'Why, what do you do with the bills?' 'We put them in the paper bin,' replied the leader of the old party members.'"[23]

Many members of the new Soviet ruling elite devoted themselves from the beginning to their passion for collecting. On April 8, 1937 a house search was held in the apartment of ex-NKVD chief and people's commissar for communications, Genrikh Yagoda. The following were seized: 22,927 rubles in cash, 1,229 bottles of wine, several dozen fur coats, 22 suits, more than one hundred bolts of English textiles, countless animal furs, three swan skins, leopard skins, 70 pairs of silk knickers, 9 cameras, a Zeiss projector, a dinner service of more than 1,000 pieces, 3,904 pornographic pictures, 11 pornographic films and 115 condoms were seized.[24] The latter are all the more striking because one of Yagoda's chief preoccupations from the early 1920s was safe-guarding public morals. He fought zealously for not letting foxtrot type western music, "erotic" dances, and doubtful "pub songs" infect the minds of Soviet subjects.[25]

And this was just the tip of the iceberg. It is clear from the texts that had been unpublished for a long time that the NKVD spent 605,000 rubles annually on merely maintaining Yagoda's two country houses, his *dacha*, which was equipped with medical and nursing staff like a sanatorium, and his two Moscow apartments. And if we also count his array of servants, his guard, and gardeners then at the very least the Soviet people contributed annually one million one hundred and forty five thousand rubles to the funds of the populous Yagoda family. Yagoda spent an additional hundred and forty thousand rubles annually on "supporting" his relatives. The ghastly interior people's commissar also "sponsored" Timosa, Gorky's daughter-in-law, for years as his lover.[26]

Further millions of rubles were given to well-known politicians, writers and famous beauties. At the behest of Yagoda, the financial section of the NKVD often used its "secret funds" for such purposes. The furniture for the two celebrated communist playwrights Kirson and Afinogenov, for example, was made in the prisoners' workshop at the Butirki prison. But this "red aid" was not always paid out to "insiders". The period's greatest painter of religious themes, Korin was favored by Yagoda for his pictures of onion-domed churches, thus the painter did not need to spend a lot keeping up his central Moscow villa and huge studio. Even his most insignificant bills were handled by the NKVD's financial section. The furniture in the villa was also made by the master carpenters imprisoned at Butirki to designs by the painter himself. All this extraordinary spending at a time when the average salary in Moscow was in the range of two hundred and twenty to two hundred and sixty rubles.[27]

As time went by, other exclusive restaurants and provisions stores were opened on the Kremlin model in the provinces as well as in Moscow. It was not only the party apparatus who had these privileges. In the second half of the 1930s, NKVD employees generally fared better than the Bolshevik political elite who lived under constant suspicion, and the retired members of the old, underground Bolshevik Party. Members of the political police, for example, could shop in top secret stores, where for next to nothing they could buy valuables seized by the customs authorities and from the "enemies of the people." However the Kremlin residents enjoyed other advantages not open to NKVD officials. They had everything under one roof: medical care, sports facilities, repair shops and not least the wonderful park along the castle walls.

From the Kremlin garage cars could be ordered by those authorized to use such a car for themselves and their families. It was a bizarre episode of the Soviet elite's history that while Voroshilov was entrusted to make decisions about the refurbishment of the Kremlin and its environs—as the superior of Avel Yenukidze, the Kremlin garage was the preserve of one of the party's ideologists, Yemelian Yaroslavsky. The big mustached, old Bolshevik was one of Stalin's most ardent followers. He must have been an all-rounder, too, if one takes into account that he ran the country-wide atheist propaganda network, as well as editing *Pravda* until the dictator put his own secretary, Lev Mekhlis, on his back. Yaroslavsky was also one of the main exponents when it came to Marxist history as well. But the veteran, who referred to himself in the third person and regarded himself a great scholar, was not at all put out that most of his time was spent sorting out the problems of the Kremlin garage. "Klim, you ruin the garage business, moreover, without any reason," he wrote with great pleasure to Voroshilov. "It is in vain that you protest against us throwing out unreliable old cars! And that we will order a few new *[Rolls]*-Royces, including one which we have long promised you. For five years no new cars will need to be bought by the garage. I am not willing to let Stalin and others to be driven around in Packards. Don't be stubborn, Klim!"[28]

But the Master of the Kremlin had got used to the black Packard. According to Aleksandr Yakovlev, designer of Yak vehicles, a few of these were bought from the US before the Second World War: "They were armor-plated with thick, green bullet-proof windows. When Stalin traveled round the city or in the countryside he was always accompanied by two cars with his body guards in them."[29]

According to contemporaries, in the early 1920s, Stalin frequently strolled in the downtown area of Moscow. Later, however, he preferred to be driven, mainly along the big boulevards flanked by armed guards and secret agents.[30] After the Second World War for a time Stalin kept on using the old Packard. In 1947, however, when the dictator—allegedly on vacation—traveled through the countryside, the Moscow–Kharkov distance proved to be hardly manageable with the old car. It was then that, as recalled by general Vlasik, Stalin decided for the Russian-made luxury car ZIS-110.[31]

Cars played an even greater role in Stalin's life when he spent one and half hours commuting each morning and evening. As he got older he spent less and less time in his Kremlin apartment. His chauffeurs, however, were not considered important staff: their "social prestige" was much lower than that of his bodyguards or than Svetlana's nanny. Because of this we know almost nothing about his drivers. I only accidentally found out that in the autumn of 1917 when Stalin was promoted to people's commissar for nationalities affairs—he "inherited" Mikhail Kuzmin who had formerly been a car washer in the tsarist court's garage and then a van driver. During the Provisional Government he was the personal chauffeur of Nekrasov, the transport minister. In the spring of 1918, when the "car base" of the Bolshevik government moved to Moscow, Kuzmin also left Petrograd. And at the same time he changed bosses: he entered the service of Lunacharsky, the people's commissar for culture and education.[32] Stalin soon after went to Tsaritsyn. He was appointed "people's commissar with extraordinary powers" and ordered a chauffeur from the general staff garage there. Nearly ten years later this man asked for documentation of this post from the dictator—at that time he still made such gestures: "I certify that Comrade M. I. Kachurin served as a chauffeur in Tsaritsyn. He served members of the Revolutionary Military Council, including me among others. Comrade Kachurin is trustworthy. Joseph Stalin. February 16, 1927."[33]

The Kremlin inhabitants, who were political leaders of the upper and sometimes middle rank, could, from time to time, also rely on financial support from a special, secret fund. In the Soviet Union such "black bursars" operated in numerous important enterprises and institutes at the time. "Two or three times a year I turned to Avel [Yenukidze], when in difficulties, for financial support as I was only living off my regular salary. I had no way of earning extra money from literary activity or other work," wrote Mikhail Tomsky in a letter to his old colleague Mikhail Kalinin.[34] The writer here refers to the "party maximum" which, in the name of enforced equalization from the early 1920s, put Bolshevik Party members at a slight disadvantage. The decree declared that party members could not earn more than a set sum. After the currency reform in the 1920s this was set at 225 and then at 250 rubles. The people's commissars' and the deputies' wages were then set at a maximum of 500 rubles, which was two and a half times as much as the pay of a skilled worker or foreman, but did not necessarily reach the wages of a non-party chief engineer or well-known scientist. These measures, in principle, would keep careerists out of the party ranks. But at Stalin's orders the upper limit to party salaries was canceled on February 8, 1932. Four years later a secret decree was passed signed by Molotov and Stalin, in which the regional and district-level party and state employees' wages were increased significantly. The upper and middle ranking leaders had anyway enjoyed many privileges before this too; among other things they got furnished apartments and

СТАИН Е. К., влад. маг. Международная ул., 23, при маг.
СТАКЛИНСКИЙ Ив. Вас., торг. Петровский бул., 21, кв. 39.
СТАЛБОТЬЯН А. А., преп. Страстная пл., Путинковский п., 5, кв. 5. (Центр. техн. им. К. Маркса).
СТАЛИДЗАН Донат Павл. 3-й Самотечный п., 4, кв. 3. (Мосстрой).
СТАЛИН Иос. Виссар. Кремль. (Чл. През. ВЦИК, Генер. секр. ЦК РКП и Чл. През. ИККИ).
— Пав. Ив. Чистые пруды, Телеграфный п., 7, кв. 4. (Госселькож).
СТАЛИНСКИЙ С. П., арт. Долгоруковская, Чухинский туп., 4, кв. 3. (Опера бывш. Зимина).
СТАЛКИНД Сам. Ефр. Кропоткинская ул., Еропкинский п., 11, кв. 2.

In *All Moscow*, a directory published in 1925, there were actually two Stalins: Iosif Vissarionovich, resident of the Kremlin, member of the Central Executive Committee, General Secretary, and member of the Executive Committee of the Comintern; and Pavel Ivanovich, resident of Tyelegrafny Lane, and employee of a state leather trading company.

In the 1930s it was almost impossible to enter the Kremlin because the security was so tight. Molotov (1), Kaganovich (2), Mikoyan (3), Kalinin (4), Yezhov (5), Shkiryatov (6) and Khruschev (7) were, of course, exceptions: the young NKVD officers moved away out of their way to let them in.

dachas for free. In the hard years they shopped in the exclusive network of secret shops and stores. They got special medical treatment and received regular provisions (so called *paiok*) that were enough to feed big families.

But as a result of setting an upper limit to party salaries, members of the Soviet nomenclature could not, until the start of the 1930s, get hold of big sums of money. If they wanted cash, they took second jobs, gave open lectures or wrote articles. Apart from this, there were the occasional payments mentioned in the Tomsky letter, which Stalin made regular after the war, ordering the handing out of certain "lined envelopes" among leading party workers, directors of companies, and generals.[35]

All this was done in the greatest secrecy and many details of this are unclear to this day. All we know is that the envelopes either contained many times over the lucky person's monthly wages or at other times—less frequently—just a fraction of them.[36] The high ranking Soviet leaders who received these secret donations "by favor of Comrade Stalin" included the former people's commissar for the oil industry Nikolai Baybakov, the one-time head of the Komsomol Aleksandr Shelepin, and Dmitry Sukhanov, who for years ran Malenkov's secretariat. During our conversations in Moscow they often said contradictory things about this system. But on one thing they agreed, they paid no tax or party dues out of this money. We only know little about all this because the lucky envelope holders usually rushed to pay the money into secret bank accounts so their families would not find out about the "surplus." But even the still living members of the "peacetime" Soviet nomenclature did not willingly tell of how on the First of May and the Seventh of November they also received luxury gifts, along with the envelopes, from a secret fund—always presented as the same "by favor of Comrade Stalin". Members of this chosen caste received gold watches, cameras, hunting rifles, and sometimes even cars. Their "better halves", to use a favorite expression of Stalin's, were also given precious rings, gold watches, or Meissen dinner services. The objects were for a long time usually of German origin, and came from the Soviet army's trophy collecting units. This secret system of bribes was only stopped by Stalin's successors after his death and then only gradually, a cessation which enraged the party apparatus.[37]

Tomsky found the above-mentioned letter very hard to write as it was well-known that this formerly influential trade union *apparatchik*—who had been demoted to economic adviser in 1929 and then to book publisher and who also had to move out of the Kremlin—was a very conceited person. A failed politician, who was small and looked more like a Tatar than a Russian, had to lay aside his pride: "As I am now moving out of the Kremlin I have to reckon on unforeseen costs. I do not know to whom I should turn—perhaps to you? [...] I would like to ask your advice. I myself often give money to my colleagues from the secrets funds I handle. But of course it is not right for me to use them for myself."[38]

But one of the chief characteristics of the Stalin period was that the leaders, after a while, did not dare embrace their ill-favored fellows. So Mikhail Kalinin did not reply to Tomsky, although as a former machinist he had entered the proletarian state's elite from the great Russian workers' movement along with his old engraver friend, and this fact had linked them for a long time. It was a miracle that he did not tear up Tomsky's letter but had it filed. However, others were offended by the Soviet president's seeming indifference. During the Great Terror his old acquaintances from time to time came to see Kalinin at his office in the center of Moscow and asked him why he did not help them. Then the president of the Supreme Soviet Presidency would first of all quickly check that no one was listening at the door, and then whispering, gesticulating, sometimes in sign language, explain that he *had a knife at his throat*. Nevertheless, when the guests left, he would sigh, sometimes even with tears in his eyes, and sign the next long list of those to be arrested. One of his best friends, Vladimir Antonov-Saratovsky, said in my presence at the Sosni sanatorium near Moscow that he now regrets reproaching Kalinin for his indifference to the "old ones" in their difficulties: "I am sorry I called him heartless and reproached him. As I was no different. At the end of the 1920s, as a judge with power over life and death, I could have done something for a few imprisoned bourgeois friends from my youth and faced no serious consequences. But by then I had grown cowardly just like most of my circle."

He also said that he himself had simulated gastric ulcer in 1938, escaping to the Kremlin hospital to avoid arrest: "For two or three days I sprinkled ground glass into my morning porridge instead of salt or sugar. I soon started to bleed and I was rushed by ambulance to the party hospital. Stalin was immediately informed that I was dying. He then told Yezhov to leave me alone. I survived but from that time on had continual stomach bleeding. I withdrew from public life and said goodbye to most of the privileges. But I made one mistake: when Stalin won the Patriotic War I wrote a heartfelt letter to him. It seems he was furious that I was still polluting the air, only a few streets from the Kremlin. He asked a common acquaintance, Rozalia Zemlyachka *[one of the founders of the Bolshevik Party—M. K.]*, whom he respected till the end of his life, to call me. He sent me this message: "You have deceived me, Comrade Antonov-Saratovsky." Zemlyachka did not understand the message but I knew exactly what he was referring to. I lost masses of weight [from fear] but finally the Master showed mercy on me once more."

This sounds like a chapter of some absurd novel. The other protagonist of the story Mikhail Kalinin did not fare better either. He did not try to prevent his wife, Yekaterina, being arrested at Stalin's orders. Her original Estonian name was Johanna Lerberg and she had worked as a weaver at the beginning of the century. But by the time she was arrested, she was a Soviet Supreme court judge, a mother of five. After that she spent eight years in various "socialist" prisons and death camps.[39] In fact, prior to her arrest she had been separated from her sensual, actress-chasing husband for a long time. As a response in the late 1920s, she moved away from Moscow and ran a state farm in the distant Altay region, to which she returned several times later. Soon after she moved to Moscow she was put in prison. Stalin's motive was not only to manipulate Kalinin. The Master of the Kremlin hated "the wife of the *starosta,*" as she was called by her cell mates, because she had been a good friend of Nadezhda Alliluyeva.[40] In addition, at the end of the 1930s, Kalinin's wife, her friends, and other similar embittered old party members, dared to criticize Stalin's policies. Information on them gathered by informers and operative officers eventually found its way onto the dictator's desk. And he acted immediately.

1 Razgon, 1991, 12.
2 Shatunovskaya, 1992, 69.
3 This kind of ordeal took tragicomic forms at the beginning of the 1950s. See Mikoyan, 1998, 106–114.
4 Trotsky, 1991, 54.
5 *Ibid.*, 54–55.
6 The famous party politician started his career as a worker. He was already one of the secretaries of the Central Committee in 1919 and 1920, and for a short time the holder of the Transport portfolio.
7 Trotsky, 54–55.
8 *RGASPI,* fond. 669, op. 1, d. 5.
9 *RGASPI,* fond. 5, op. 1, 1417. In 1921 Sedova came into similar conflict with her own husband, Trotsky who was supervising the appropriation of church treasures. *Politbyuro i Tserkov,* 1997, vol. I, 57–60. Sedova lived a very long life. After her husband's death she appeared to have distanced herself from her husband's revolutionary past, although she never gave voice to this in public. Interestingly, in 1956 she did not at all take Khrushchev's "secret address" to the 20th Congress of the Soviet Communist Party seriously. Moreover, through the Russian language broadcast of the american Liberation Radio (later Radio Liberty), she responded to it by calling the Soviet people to rise up against "Stalin's heirs'. *Novoye Russkoye Slovo,* June 10, 1956.
10 Bazhanov, 1983, 153.
11 *RGASPI,* fond. 74, op. 2, d. 41.
12 Mikoyan, 1999, 331.
13 Larina, 1989, 241.
14 *RGASPI,* fond. 667, op. 1, d. 16.
15 *RGASPI,* fond. 74, op. 2, d. 41.
16 *Istochnik,* 1995, no. 3, 126–170.
17 Shatunovskaya, 1982, 221–227.
18 From personal communication with Aleksei Snegov.
19 *RGASPI,* fond. 74, op. 2, d. 41.
20 Radek, 1933, 5. In the second edition, the title no longer included the word Kremlin.
21 *RGASPI,* fond. 17, op. 162, d. 9.
22 From personal communication with the old Bolshevik Party member, Polina Vinogradskaya, who for a while was wife of Yevgeny Preobrazhensky, the renowned economic politician.
23 Shatunovskaya, 1982, 39–43.
24 Yagoda, 1997, 89–93. This very important document source was published in only two hundred copies for restricted distribution only.
25 *Ibid.*, 313–318.
26 According to one apparently reliable version, Yagoda, in a fit of jealousy, killed the woman's husband, Maksim Peshkov.
27 Yagoda, 1997, 440–445.
28 *RGASPI,* fond. 74, op. 2, d. 45.
29 Yakovlev, 1974, 472.
30 Valentinov, 1971, 252–253.
31 Loginov, 2000, 106–108.
32 *RGASPI* fond. 558, op. 4, d. 554.
33 *RGASPI* fond. 558, op. 1, d. 5304
34 *Sovietskoye Rukovodstvo* 1999, 306.
35 Voslensky, 1990, 294. At the same time there were also companies where the employees did not receive wages for a great length of time. Romanovsky, 1995, 92–93.
36 Voslensky, 1990, 294, 342–343.
37 Aleksandr Yakovlev, the main ideologist of perestroyka, who belonged to the lower ranking nomenclature after the Second World War—he was leader of a regional party committee—states in his memoirs that following his appointment his living standards significantly improved. Apart from

his 1500 ruble wages, he received a further tax free 3000 in a separate envelope *(paket)*. Yakovlev, 2000, 54.

38 *Sovietskoye Rukovodstvo*, 1999, 306.

39 A fellow prisoner in the camp described her life with telling details. Razgon, 1991, 51–58. As a young woman, she had taken part in the 1905–1907 Revolution and then was maid to Stalin's future love, Tatyana Slovatinskaya, for a while. It is there where she met Mikhail Kalinin. *Istorichesky Arkhiv*, 2000, no. 6, 212. It has turned out only recently that Kalinin wrote a letter on June 8, 1944 to Stalin before undergoing a serious operation: "Comrade Stalin I look calmly into our country's future, the future of the Soviet people. I only wish that you will preserve your strength for as long as possible. The success of the Soviet State relies on this. I turn to you with two personal questions: show mercy to Yekaterina Ivanovna and disburse my older sister *[with pension—M. K.]* to whom I have entrusted the two boys who are orphans. *[The Kalinin family's adopted children—M. K.]*. I send my last greetings from my heart: M. Kalinin." The old politician eventually survived the operation but Stalin for another two years failed to pardon Yekaterina Lerberg. *Istorichesky Arkhiv*, 2000, no. 6, 213.

40 From personal communication with Yelizaveta Drabkina and Lili Cséri, a Hugarian woman who spent years in Soviet prisons. The latter wrote in rich detail on the prison cell in which Kalinin's wife spent her sentence. See Cséri, 1989, 72–86. Because of her trials and tribulations, she did not dare to write down the name of the Soviet leader's wife. She wrote the manuscript at the beginning of the 1960s, in which "the wife of the *starosta*" is presented as her cell mate, who was always very clumsy washing herself at the public bath, for which one of her mates called her "unfortunate animal". *Ibid.*, 82.

Stalin and other high-ranking functionaries watching the Tushino air display

The Cars of the Kremlin

The members of the Bolshevik elite, who had emerged from the lower strata of the tarist society, seized the best automobiles of the country almost immediately after the military takeover in October 1917. The confiscated cars were used at first by high-ranking functionaries, but later their family members were also allowed to drive them.

This picture shows Stalin (x) and his wife, Nadezhda Alliluyeva, as they leave the Kremlin complex in their favorite Packard automobile.

Joseph Stalin embarks upon yet another hunting trip.

CHAPTER 18
Polina Zhemchuzhina

Today there are hardly any surviving eyewitnesses of the Stalin era, which has sunk like Atlantis. Lev Razgon, one of the last chroniclers of this vanishing world, died in 1999. His memoirs, published in the early 1990s, are all the more valuable since for a while, as a result of his marriage, he was a member of the Soviet "new class" and thus had many acquaintances living in the Kremlin. He describes how "...like the residents of a small town [...], they liked to know all about one another's private lives: who was sleeping with Demyan Bedny [...] or how merrily Avel Yenukidze spent his nights. [...] They also discussed the fact that Koba (Joseph Stalin) had also recently joined in the merriment organized by Avel."[1]

The Demyan Bedny mentioned in the memoirs *[bedny in Russian means "poor"—M. K.]* was practically the only person in the Kremlin to represent the "creative intelligentsia". His original name was Yefim Pridvorov, but the political/literary byname that he had chosen for himself remained with him until the end of his life. The plump poet with his egg-shaped head and bulging eyes, who worked mainly in the genre of "political fable"—a genre particularly popular in Russia since Ivan Krilov—came from very low social ranks. One of his chief traits was an unhealthy exhibitionism, displayed in the fact that he chose to "air his family's dirty laundry" in his official autobiography, in which he indulged in descriptions of the everyday life of his prostitute mother.[2] Even some of his comrades, including Trotsky, were irritated by the cruel political fables that he published before the war in the columns of *Pravda*, on the pretext of attacking the "oppressive" classes. Although Bedny sometimes made an effort to scale the heights of poetry, he always ran out of breath.

One particular episode can be seen as characteristic of the writer's morbidity. While walking in the Kremlin he saw Fanya Kaplan, who had made an attempt

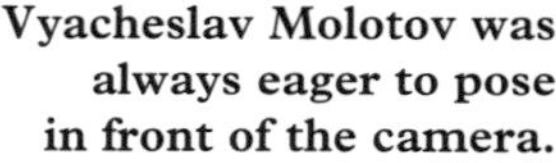

Vyacheslav Molotov was always eager to pose in front of the camera.

on Lenin's life, being led to the scene of her execution by Commandant Malkov and some of his colleagues. "Poor Demyan" watched the woman's death agony and then how she was "cremated" in a huge cast-iron barrel.[3] From several slips of his tongue, the writer appears to have been an anti-Semite, which he had to hide initially. But as soon as Stalin came into power, "poor Demyan" could give voice to his views. On November 28, 1927 Kornei Chukovsky wrote in his diary: "I visited Bedny [...] he told me about Trotsky, how he quarreled with Zinovyev, and that the opposition in general has nothing to hope for. 'Do you realize that the opposition consists exclusively of Jews? And to make things worse, they are all *[former—M. K.]* emigrants. Trotsky has said that if anything happens, he will go abroad. We, genuine Russians, however have nowhere to go. This is our country, our spiritual home'."[4]

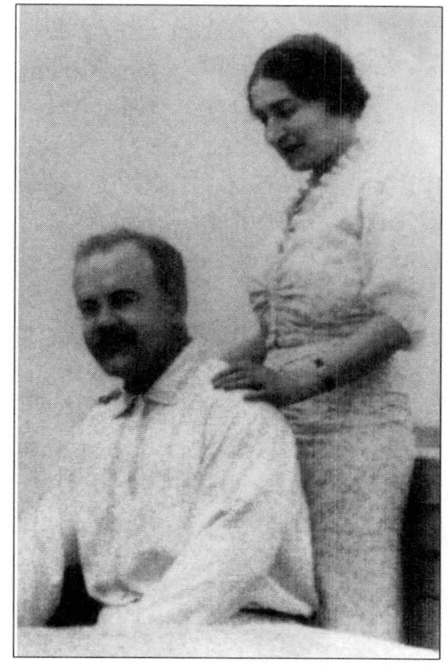

Molotov and his wife Polina.

Following October 1917, as the "court poet" of the ruling Bolshevik Party, Demyan Bedny was able to command huge sums of money for his primitive verses. His high income enabled him to collect one of the most precious private libraries in Moscow, which, at the end of his life, comprised more than thirty thousand volumes.[5] This passion for book collecting was the cause of the first serious conflict with his good friend Joseph Stalin. The Soviet dictator, who read a great deal although not in a systematic manner, often borrowed books from Bedniy, who lived nearby. However, he did not always return the much-treasured library items to their owner. When the beautifully bound books with their *ex libris* inscriptions were eventually returned after several requests, they usually bore the greasy marks of the General Secretary's fingers, yellowed from pipe tobacco.[6] On occasion, instead of using a paper knife, Stalin would even tear the uncut pages with his finger.

Demyan Bedny complained about this to several people. These complaints eventually reached Stalin's ears and made him extremely angry. In Moscow, in the early 1970s, I heard from the elderly son of "Poor Demyan", who was the spit and image of his father, that the furious dictator had then taken action to remove the Bedny family from their apartment in the Kremlin. He had had enough of the "gossipy Demyan", he said, thus "he withdrew his support from the rhymester". He also turned others against the disgraced poet: "I have not read his poem, and I don't even feel like doing so," he wrote to Lazar Kaganovich on September 29, 1931, having learned that Demyan Bedny was regularly popularizing Soviet foreign policy in rhyme in *Izvestia*. "I am certain there is no point wasting time on his poetry. What an odd character he is: he tries to be political merely by hobnobbing with the political elite. He is quite impudent enough [...] to have come out with a huge amount of nonsense. First of all the editorial board of *Izvestia*, then Demyan and Litvinov *[the people's commissar for foreign affairs—M. K.]* should be called to account for this. What is there to prevent us from making them answerable, after all? Well, then. All the best, J[oseph] Stalin."[7]

From the late 1920s there were also other conflicts between Stalin and his "court poet". The Russified non-Russian Stalin used the rhetoric of Great Russian imperial policy more and more often. Along with his sudden personal antipathy, this explains why he was increasingly annoyed by Demyan Bedny's frequent mockery of Russian *oblomovshchina*, that is, "the Oblomov habit", laziness.[8]

Like other Kremlin residents who had been forced to leave, the hedonist Bedniy, for whom proximity to "the Master" was a symbol of status, found it hard to cope with this episode in his life, even though earlier, as a kind of test, he himself had offered to Avel Yenukidze to move out of the Kremlin: "Dear

Comrade! I am writing to inform you of my decision to bid farewell to the Kremlin," he wrote on December 16, 1927. "I should have done this a long time ago. Both reason and emotion tell me it is what I should do. There is no place for me here. And I don't want to wait until others call my attention to the fact."[9]

As a result of such self-deprecating whining Demyan Bedny was perhaps the only resident of the Kremlin who managed to postpone—in his case for as long as five years—his expulsion from paradise, despite the angry threats of Stalin. In November 1932, however, Rudolf Peterson, the commandant of the Moscow "Castle district", showed the poet his new apartment, the side wing of a small, neglected townhouse in downtown Moscow. The resourceful Demyan, even at this point, tried to avoid the unavoidable. He pulled from his pocket Joseph Stalin's earlier *letter of exemption*, according to which his library and study were to remain undivided. But not even this helped. Following his expulsion from the Kremlin he faced a whole sea of troubles. In 1929 the party leadership was still looking after "Poor Demyan". As the result of a Politburo decision passed on July 8, fifteen hundred dollars were transferred to the otherwise rich poet to enable him to travel abroad for medical treatment. The only condition was that his wife could not go with him.[10] One year later the secretariat of the Central Committee reprimanded *Pravda* and *Izvestia* for publishing the poet's "feuilletons", which "abused the feelings of the Russian people by mocking their laziness and ponderousness". The offended Demyan protested on December 8, 1930 in an indignant letter to Stalin, in which he referred to his eighteen volumes of published work. Four days later, in a lengthy letter, the dictator "cut down to size" his neighbor in the Kremlin. He charged him with "libeling the Soviet Union, the past and the present of the country".[11]

The poet's situation continued to worsen. Following renewed fierce attacks in the press, inspired—no doubt—by Stalin, Demyan Bedny was unexpectedly expelled from the party. From then on the once loud-mouthed and unscrupulous man almost shrank and cowered like a scared rabbit: in the meantime the editor of the State Publishing House, Mikhail Prezent, had been imprisoned. He was one of the confidants of Yenukidze, who had been declared in the meantime "an enemy of the people." Prezent had often visited "Poor Demyan", and on returning home in the evening had written down the stories he had heard from the poet about the residents of the Kremlin. It is significant that his confiscated diary ended up in Stalin's private archive.[12] It is hardly surprising that after this the Master of the Kremlin spoke only in negative terms of Bedniy's fables. He concluded that the "modern-day Dante", as he sarcastically referred to the poet, had in fact been thinking of the Soviet system while criticizing Nazi Germany.[13]

In the meantime the NKVD's "body technicians" had beaten out of Stetsky, the Central Committee member responsible for *agitprop*, the fact that in the early 1930s Demyan Bedny had been cruelly dismissive of Stalin and Molotov but had praised Rykov and Bukharin. The informers reported that he was still heaping abuse on the Master of the Kremlin: "Stalin is a terrible man [...]. Every significant leader surrounds himself with his most outstanding fellow warriors, and look what Stalin has done to his! He has got rid of everyone. None of them are alive today. [...] Such things have only ever happened in the days of Ivan the Terrible."[14] On September 9, 1938 this report landed on Stalin's desk, but the poet was not arrested for some reason.

Towards the end of the war Demyan Bedny was a wreck of a human being, who inundated his former comrades with whining pleas for help. On February 7, 1945, not long before his death, he turned to Vyacheslav Molotov: "My dear old

The diligent and obedient bureaucrat, Vyacheslav Molotov was Stalin's number one ally since the beginning of the 1920s. The two politicians formed a great pair: Molotov was more tenacious and industrious, while Stalin was more diplomatic, yet aggressive.

friend! I turn to you in an apparently insignificant affair, but which is of crucial importance to me. The year before last I fell ill, and since then my health has deteriorated completely. I am beginning to resemble the late Olminsky *[a veteran of Bolshevik journalism—M. K.]*, who, by the end of his life, could only shuffle his way through the Kremlin. I am practically unable to walk. That's why I don't go out anywhere. But there is one place I have to go more often than I would like: the outpatients' department of the Kremlin hospital. Despite the relatively short distance (I live near the Moscow City Soviet building) I am simply unable to get there." The poet asked the first deputy of the Soviet Prime Minister and the influential people's commissar of foreign affairs, if he could occasionally request a car from the Kremlin's fleet. He closed his letter "with heartfelt greetings (from a sick heart)". The otherwise not quite sentimental Molotov came immediately to his aid.[15]

☆ The misfortunes of "Poor Demyan" may be construed as typical, though not particularly dramatic compared to the fates of those millions who were dying in exile colonies, in the Gulag, or in execution tunnels under the prisons. In the late 1930s this whole process was governed by a special system of quotas: Joseph Stalin and the members of the Politburo decided personally the number of executions that were to take place in the various regions, big cities, and concentration camps, according to monthly or quarterly breakdowns. The local authorities often made "Stakhanovist offers" to increase the number of arrests and executions.[16]

The dictator continuously "sieved" through the people in his own environment. In the years of the Great Terror one of his main problems with the ever-decreasing number of Kremlin residents was the fact that they invited guests in from outside the red-brick castle walls. For security reasons he ordered that at larger gatherings, including children's parties, NKVD agents disguised as guests or staff were to supervise the proceedings and submit a written report about what had taken place.[17] It is hardly surprising that the powerful members of the Soviet political elite became terrified and stopped seeing other people. Perhaps it was only Polina Zhemchuzhina[18], the wife of the head of the government, Molotov, and for a while favored by Stalin,[19] who allowed herself some murmurings of discontent, since the Kremlin gates were closed in front of her large circle of friends. She was famous for her almost royal household and for her magnificent clothes, and she was offended at being denied the admiring and envious glances of her guests.

"You know, formerly the Molotov family would give huge receptions for large numbers of guests in the Kremlin. And this was something Polina enjoyed," I was told by Natalya Rykova when we met in Moscow. "This imposing, vivacious, black-eyed woman adored wearing attractive, glittering dresses. I once visited their apartment, and on both floors the wardrobes were crammed with clothes and furs." The daughter of Aleksei Rykov, head of the Soviet government following Lenin, who as a young woman taught Russian language and literature at the police academy to people with a poor peasant background, was astonished to hear from Polina that she had furnished her dining room on the basis of a scene from *Anna Karenina*. "Do you remember when Levin visited his fiancée and noticed that behind the enormous table there were dressers laden with all kinds of food?[20] This is exactly what I found in the Molotov apartment," continued Rykova. "In the dining room, on the dresser, plates had been set out in three tiers. They were filled with all kinds of delicacies, which during the Soviet system no one ever saw altogether in one place like that. There was fish, game, and meat, all prepared in the most delicious ways. Not to mention caviar and rare fish from the Caspian Sea. There were beautifully decorated fruit baskets that outdid one another in their splendor, and steaming tea everywhere."

Polina, coming from a small town in Belarus, was the great love in Molotov's life. However, his brothers did not like the "Jewess from the province". True, she did not care about their attitude. As the years went by, she increasingly wanted to rule. According to her contemporaries, she was physically predestined for such a role: "She had bright green eyes, and a figure as if emerging from the pages of the Bible. She wore her red hair with a golden shine in a high knot. Her voice was deep. At home she commanded everyone including her husband. She smoked a lot and had an excellent wardrobe."[21]

Perhaps this was why Polina Zhemchuzhina found it so hard to radically reduce the number of her guests under pressure from the dictator. "I remember how the otherwise phlegmatic Vyacheslav Molotov, the typical henpecked husband, sometime in the summer of 1937, perhaps a few days after the execution of Tukhachevsky and his colleagues, made a scene in my presence that sounded like a lovers' tiff. He demanded to know why she, as one of the leaders of Soviet light industry, was visited in the Kremlin by 'inexperienced and greenhorn' male subordinates," recalled Dr. László Pollacsek, the family doctor and confidant of the members of the Soviet leadership. "This man, wearing his pince-nez, was livid with anger and stammered even more than usual that day. It was obvious that he had not brought up the subject at that moment by coincidence. I just didn't understand why he had brought it up in front of me. From something he said I sensed that he was acting as a result of pressure from Stalin, who had suddenly turned into guardian of morals."

"In response to this lengthy reprimand the hot-blooded and proud Polina made a huge scene herself," the former head of the Kremlin hospital's ear, nose, and throat department carried on. "And since Molotov, unusually for him, refused to back down, she ran out of the room and slammed the door behind her. Early the following day she unexpectedly visited me in the Kremlin hospital. She complained that her husband, for security reasons, had for a while forbidden her to walk and shop in downtown Moscow unless accompanied either by body-

Pavel Dibenko, who became a high ranking commander of the Red Army from an ordinary sailor during the tsarist times, and his wife, Aleksandra Kollontai, who was sixteen years older and had been born into a distinguished, noble family. The beautiful woman was a leader of the Bolshevik women's movement, and a propagator of free love. She introduced Molotov to Polina Zhemchuzhina, who deeply respected and loved Ms Kollontai until her death.

guards or by their good friend German Tikhomirnov, who was the only one to remain from among their old acquaintances."

"Eventually there was only Tikhomirnov left to pay court to me," wept Molotov's wife, who in the 1920s had been one of the most highly emancipated participants in the Soviet women's movement. "Perhaps my husband and Iosif Vissarionovich—who apparently no longer likes me, or why would he have set up all these prohibitions?—believe that German cannot compromise me, because he has known Molotov from the days of the underground movement?"

This was in fact true. The two Tikhomirnov brothers were closer to Vyacheslav Molotov than his own brothers. From recently disclosed secret police reports we learn that Viktor, the elder brother, along with Molotov, who at the time was using his original name, Skryabin, sympathized for a short while with the SRs. In the autumn of 1906, along with several fellow students from the Tatar capital Kazan', they had founded the Non-Party Revolutionary Circle. Despite the name of the group Tikhomirnov and Skryabin regarded themselves as Social Democrats, even Bolsheviks. Later on both of them were arrested. On the basis of the verdict passed by the tsarist court, Vyacheslav Skryabin was exiled to the north Russian city of Vologda, where, for a while, he earned his living as a restaurant musician.[22]

The life of Molotov's best friend, Viktor Tikhomirnov, was somewhat more conventional. He received a huge inheritance from his father, who died in 1911, but, as he told his friends, the money was "burning" his hands. He visited Lenin in emigration and offered to use the huge amount that had unexpectedly come to him to publish a legal leftist daily in the Russian capital. His generous gesture greatly contributed to the fact that soon afterwards the Bolshevik *Pravda*[23] was published in St. Petersburg and from then on appeared regularly.

With the outbreak of the First World War, the Bolshevik papers, which were mostly published using Tikhomirnov's money, were banned one after the other. In response the two "defeatists" founded the anti-war group known as the Alliance of Bolsheviks of 1915 in Petrograd. This might have contributed to the fact that following the February 1917 revolution, and especially the October Bolshevik takeover, Molotov, who had a reputation as a good organizer, suddenly took a huge step upwards in the hierarchy of the Bolshevik movement: first Zinovyev and Lenin, then Stalin, pushed him to the fore. In 1921 this untiring man, who always had to keep his nervous tension suppressed, became director of the secretariat of the Central Committee.[24]

Only a few people were aware of the mental and physical difficulties of the reserved Molotov. Lenin was one of them. With the help of Nikolai Semashko, the people's commissar for health, and a number of famous German doctors who traveled to Moscow expressly for this reason, in May 1922 he had a survey carried out to assess the extent to which the Bolshevik elite had been "exhausted" by the years of the Civil War and War Communism. Those politicians who were found to be in the worst state were sent to hospitals in Switzerland and Germany. Some were sent immediately to nearby Latvia for treatment, while others were "forced to rest" in the best sanatoriums on the Crimean Peninsula and in the Caucasus. Among them was Stalin, who had frequently been ill over the years, who tired easily, and who, in the previous year, had undergone a major operation. Despite this, on the list of those examined the only comment made about him read: "Healthy. Has overburdened himself," followed by the recommendation: "Short rest. Improved nourishment." Molotov's diagnosis was rather more serious: "Nervousness and related atony of the digestive system." The doctors recommended fresh air and a vegetarian diet. However, his name is not included on the list of those who had to be sent to a sanatorium immediately.[25]

Allegedly, Lenin was even considering for a while assigning to Molotov or Stalin the post of chief secretary to the Central Committee, a post given official recognition in 1922. He naively believed that this would be his own "super-secretariat" and would take the majority of organizational work off his shoulders.[26]

☆ In terms of his career in the Bolshevik movement, Viktor Tikhomirnov was left well behind by his friend. During the Civil War he stayed mostly in Kazan', in his homeland, and as a member of the steering committee of the People's Commissariat for Internal Affairs he was involved in pacifying those villages that were rebelling against the Soviet system. On one such trip in 1919, during the devastating Spanish Influenza epidemic, he contracted the flu and died. Unable to accept the loss of his best friend, Molotov then took under his wing the younger Tikhomirnov brother whom he loved as a son. He placed the shy and timid young man in his own secretariat. German, however, who had ambitions as a scientist, never became a good bureaucrat. His boss, Molotov, who was well-known for his pedantic nature, often reproached him for this.[27]

It is still not quite clear exactly when German Tikhomirnov joined Molotov's secretariat. From a note written in red ink it appears that he was already working there on October 26, 1922: "The Council of People's Commissars, to Comrade Miroshnikov. The Secretariat of the Central Committee of the Russian Communist (Bolshevik) Party requests that you provide with an entry pass to the building of the Council of People's Commissars the colleagues of the Central

When little Svetlana was growing up her parents did not want her to be bored. For this reason, her mother took one of Vyacheslav Molotov's nephew and their housemaid's daughter into their house, thereby separating them from their parents.

Committee secretaries, Com. Tikhomirnov, Com. Kanner, and Com. Tovstukha. J. Stalin, secretary of the Central Committee of the Russian Communist (Bolshevik) Party."[28]

Two years later the Soviet party leadership entrusted the younger Tikhomirnov brother with the curatorship of the secret archives of the Bolshevik Party. On November 14, 1924, for example, he traveled to Leningrad with the following order: "Comrade Tikhomirnov, the bearer of these lines, as a member of the committee collecting documents relevant to the history of the RC(b)P for the archives of the Central Committee, is traveling to Leningrad. During the time of his [...] mission he will study these materials (originals or copies, as agreed) in the city archives. In addition, he will be visiting certain comrades. J. Stalin, secretary of the Central Committee, S. Kanatchikov, chairman of the Committee."[29]

However, one of Tikhomirnov's foreign missions is still shrouded in mystery. Along with several others he accompanied Nikolai Bukharin on his famous trip to Paris in the spring of 1936. As became clear later, the journey was in many respects a provocation. Stalin, who was thinking "in perspective", was preparing for the showdown with his failed rival, Bukharin. Perhaps by that time the script of the large-scale show trial had already taken shape in his mind. It was therefore useful to him for Bukharin, the editor of *Izvestia,* who was still popular in Russia, to compromise himself by meeting Western politicians and Russian Menshevik emigrants in Paris. German Tikhomirnov, who took part in Bukharin's talks, was busy trying to collect as many "compromising" facts about the selected victim as possible. In the meantime, his enthusiasm for research had not deserted him. The original intention of the Soviet delegation that traveled to Paris was to purchase from the leaders of the Socialist International and the German Social Democrats in emigration the part of the Marx and Engels legacy that had been taken out of Nazi Germany.[30] During the talks Boris Nicolaevsky, the historian and professional archivist of the Russian Menshevik movement, played the role of intermediary. After a time Tikhomirnov managed to get access to the documents looked after by Nicolaevsky. Then, with Nicolaevsky 's tacit approval, he "lifted" one of Stalin's letters from the collection: "While looking through the Koltsov archive[31] I accidentally came across a picture postcard written by Comrade Stalin on April 27, 1914 to Balinski *[in reality Bielynski—M. K.]*, asking him to send an English and a French dictionary.[32] I simply pocketed the postcard and Nicolaevsky made no great protest," he reported in the confidential account of his trip written for Stalin and Molotov.[33] In a short note about the "expropriation" he boasted enthusiastically to Meshkovsky, a colleague in Moscow, about how he had come across this treasure: "I am sending you the picture postcard written by Stalin. Guard it with your life. [...] Recently I have been searching through the archives of the GSDP [German Social Democratic Party] and that of the Russian Mensheviks. I have got so much into the confidence of Nicolaevsky that he is even willing to make relatively large sacrifices for me. I found this picture postcard among the various papers in the Koltsov legacy. I rather cheekily took it at once. I said to Nicolaevsky: 'I found it. You would never have found it and so it would have been lost.' He agreed with my argument. I pocketed the postcard and it would have been awkward for him to demand it back from me afterwards. He [Nicolaevsky] was somewhat put out and said: 'Don't tell anyone about this.' I promised him I wouldn't. You should also bear that in mind. Send the picture postcard and the photograph to Stalin with a covering letter. You should include the fact that I found it in the archive of a Menshevik and that I cheekily pocketed it before Nicolaevsky even had a chance to read it."[34]

The widowed Stalin and Polina Zhemchuzhina, who always spoke enthusiastically about him.

☆ Today the name of German Tikhomirnov, good friend of Zhemchuzhina, has been completely forgotten. At the time, however, he was occasionally involved in carrying out important and confidential political tasks. In 1938, for example, in the years of the Great Terror, Tikhomirnov was appointed director of the Soviet pavilion at the New York World's Fair. Strangely enough, his regular presence in the company of Molotov's wife was regarded as a "party task". Later, at Stalin's suggestion, he was officially "appointed" as an escort for Polina Zhemchuzhina. According to László Pollacsek the Soviet "first lady" sulked for a long time about this. At around the same time she was forced to break off several other friendships, mainly with her male colleagues, that were genuinely important to her. Nevertheless, in spite of his interference in her private life she did not dare, or perhaps did not want, to come into conflict with Stalin, whom she revered as a demigod. Even at the height of the Soviet anti-Semitic campaign, having been imprisoned as a "Zionist saboteur", she blamed her husband's jealous rivals, and Beria in particular, for her ill fortune. It did not even occur to her to blame her imprisonment on Joseph Stalin, who was in fact responsible for her suffering.[35]

Several other rumors circulated about Zhemchuzhina, which was useful to Stalin in his efforts to keep the woman, and especially her husband, under his control. On August 10, 1939 the Politburo concluded, probably at his suggestion, that the woman "forges relationships without discrimination." Thus "many hostile, spying elements have turned up in her circle..." According to these hypocrites, Polina thus unwittingly "facilitated their spying activities". The influential body therefore decided to have "all the material related to Comrade Zhemchuzhina" examined. Their decision, worded in the characteristically wooden language of the apparatus, contained another rather vague sentence: "Comrade

Zhemchuzhina must be dismissed from the position of people's commissar for the fishing industry. The decision must be executed taking into account the principle of gradualism." Another two weeks later the Politburo—whose meetings were usually chaired by Molotov!—discussed the case again. On this occasion it came to the conclusion that certain "enemies of the people", who by that time were enjoying the hospitality of the NKVD, had intentionally blackened the woman's name in their confessions.[36]

Nevertheless, the wording of the original decision, in which it was stated that "she had forged relationships indiscriminately", remained valid. Zhemchuzhina was therefore removed from the leadership of the people's commissariat, as had been suggested. The three secretaries of the Central Committee—Andrei Andreyev, Georgy Malenkov, and Andrei Zhdanov—held a special session to find a place for the woman, who eventually returned to her old working place on the steering committee of the people's commissariat for the light industry.[37]

This hounding of the emancipated woman, which was directed from the wings by Stalin, served at the same time to exert control over Molotov. This claim is supported by the fact that the former tobacco-factory worker—whom the previously powerful Bolshevik veterans referred to sarcastically as an "ambitious Carmen", but whom many Soviet Jews, who knew very little about the hidden inner life of the Kremlin, called admiringly *"our Yiddische Mamele"*—after further disciplinary proceedings was deprived of her candidate membership of the Central Committee in February 1941.[38] It was due to sheer coincidence that Zhemchuzhina escaped arrest in those days. Despite this, during the Great Terror she was strongly linked to the Master of the Kremlin both psychologically and ideologically, as was her husband, who was singled out as the main victim of the post-war showdowns. Svetlana Alliluyeva, who was a frequent visitor at the couple's home, made some interesting remarks about this in her book *Only One Year*. She met the Molotov couple in the early 1960s, during the months of the Chinese Cultural Revolution. Molotov himself "spoke little, as usual. He was just an onlooker. Earlier he had always made a show of agreeing with my father. Now he nodded at every word his wife said. Polina was full of energy. [...] She [unlike Molotov] had not been expelled from the party. She therefore attended the meetings of the party branch organization in the same chocolate factory in which she had once worked as a young woman. The family sat around the table and Polina said to me: 'Your father was a genius. He annihilated the "fifth column" in our country. When the war broke out the party and the people remained united. Today, however, there is no revolutionary spirit. Opportunism is the rule everywhere. Have you seen what the Italian Communists are doing? It is shameful! They frighten everyone by saying that war will break out. We can only trust China. It is only there that the spirit of revolution prevails.' Molotov nodded his agreement. Their daughter and son-in-law remained silent and kept their eyes down. They looked fixedly at their plates. This was another generation. They were embarrassed. Their parents reminded them of dinosaurs frozen in a glacier."[39]

1 Razgon, 1991, 12.
2 *Dyelateli SSSR*, 1989, 401–403.
3 Tucker, 1997, 42.
4 Chukovsky, 1997, 427.
5 Smirnov-Sokolsky, 1959, 88–92.
6 *Minuvseye*, 1992, no. 7, 95.
7 *RGASPI*, fond. 81, op. 3, d. 99. For more on the contrasts between Stalin and Demyan Bedny, see Gronsky, 155.

8 Tucker, 1997, 42.
9 *RGASPI*, fond. 667, op. 1, d. 16.
10 *RGASPI*, fond. 17, op. 162, d. 7.
11 *Vlast i khudozhestvennaya intelligentsia,* 1999, 131–137.
12 Gronsky, 1991, 155; Skoryatin, 1998, 223.
13 Maksimenkov, 1997, 194–195.
14 *Vlast i khudozhestvennaya intelligentsia,* 1999, 415–416.
15 *RGASPI*, fond. 82, op. 2, d. 1441.
16 Bukovsky, 1996, 76–78.
17 This is what an emigrant Soviet journalist reported on in his important novel that made him famous. See Solovyev, 1963–64, 316.
18 Her original name was Perl Karpovskaya. She created the movement byname, Zhemchuzhina from the mirror translation of her original given name (*perl* and *zhemchuzhina* both mean "pearl").
19 Khrushchev, 1997, 75.
20 A couple years earlier in the same flat the guest could see not the expensive furniture transported there from the former palaces of the aristocracy, but fashionable, modern, Western tables and chairs. "I had an interesting visit with to the Molotovs in the Kremlin," noted Aleksandra Kollontai in her diary at the beginning of 1934. "Zhemchuzhina was a subordinate of mine at the women worker's department of the party. And I met Molotov at the same place, when Vyacheslav Mikhailovich came to see us representing the Organizational Bureau of the Central Committee. I liked their apartment very much, it was completely modern, with only a few pieces of furniture. I admit that it felt a bit cold because it is furnished not according to their own design. Nevertheless, it radiates a healthy rationalism. The hosts bear in mind the constraints of hygiene, and seek to make the chores of cleaning easier. *RGASPI*, fond. 134, op. 3, d. 21.
21 Aroseva-Maksimova, 1999, 30.
22 *Sto sorok besed s Molotovim*, 1991, 133.
23 *Dyelateli SSSR*, 1989, 553–556.
24 *Ibid.*, 556.
25 *RGASPI*, fond. 5, op. 1, d. 1417.
26 From personal communication with Ivan Vrachev.
27 Bazhanov, 1983, 23.
28 *RGASPI*, fond. 558, op. 1, d. 5359.
29 *RGASPI*, fond. 558, op. 1, d. 2526.
30 These unsuccessful negotiations were in essence a continuation of an earlier series of talks. Tikhomirnov and a noted Soviet diplomat, Aleksandr Arosev, had proposed to Stalin, perhaps already in 1935, to order the allocation of a larger sum to the Soviet Embassy in Paris. The Master of the Kremlin, however, chose his words of reply carefully: "Yes, sure, we may allocate the money, but we need to know first what we purchase as archival material. We cannot buy a pig in a poke. Let us get from them the list of archived materials with a brief description of the contents of the documents. Then we can send the 50,000 rubles. July 15 *[probably 1935—M. K.]*. Stalin." *RGASPI*, fond. 71, op. 3, d. 51.
31 Most of the documents today can be found at the Hoover Institute, as an important part of these special bequest named after Nicolaevsky.
32 See page 148 in this book.
33 *RGASPI*, fond. 71, op. 3, d. 186/4.
34 *Ibid.*
35 On this part of her life, see Gereben, 2000, 291–292, 400–407, 475, 497.
36 *Stalinskoye Politbyuro*, 1995, 171.
37 *Ibid.*, 172
38 *Soviet narodnikh komissarov*, 1999, 262.
39 Alliluyeva, 1971, 353.

Vyacheslav Molotov

Reading newspapers was not a truly relaxing exercise for Molotov. On the pages of the papers he could see *kulaks* to be resettled, neighboring states to be occupied, or political enemies to be arrested.

Stalin did not hide the fact that he was considering Molotov as his successor. At the banquet celebrating the victory over Nazi Germany, he lifted his glass to give a personal toast only to the health of "our Vyacheslav." Thus he managed to make all other party leaders hate Molotov (1). This picture shows Kalinin (2) decorating Molotov with yet another medal, while Andreyev (3), Zhdanov (4), and Svernik (5) look at them enviously.

CHAPTER 19
Anastas Mikoyan

From the mid-1920s members of the Bolshevik leadership were increasingly sacrificing their personal friendships to their fierce struggles against one another. Initially, of course, their years as students together, the time they had spent at the same workbench, the conversations they had had while in prison, and their common experiences at the front still counted for something in these relationships: "Dear Klimenty! Thank you for your letter, and thanks to Shkiryatov for his greetings. You know, it felt just as good as when—do you remember?—one received a letter from a friend during exile," wrote Avel Yenukidze on September 16, 1925 to Klim Voroshilov.[1]

Eventually, however, the old ties that had been forged within the movement loosened. The time came when, in the minds of those living in the Kremlin or the House on the Embankment, belonging to the *same platform* became the one and only criterion for friendship. In this respect it was probably the rather small circle around the reserved Leon Trotsky that saw the fewest changes. He was visited mostly by his old followers: former Social Democrat—but by no means always former "orthodox" Bolshevik—fellow emigrants, and, in the years of the Civil War, the military commanders and people's commissars who came into the circle of the Red Army leader. On the other hand, a significant number of old illegal Bolshevik Party members with an "impeccable past"—especially in Leningrad—lined up behind the two main ideologues of the "Leningrad opposition", Grigory Zinovyev and Lev Kamenev. Through Nadezhda Krupskaya, who was close to them personally, the two men inherited a kind of aura from Lenin, who died in January 1924 and who was buried with grand ceremony. The inner core of this originally very large group—like Trotsky's—was also formed by onetime fellow emigrants.[2]

Although in the early spring of 1926 the followers of Zinovyev and Trotsky merged, certain reservations remained between the members of the two allied groups. At the end of the 1920s the same marked politicization characterized the friendly relations of Nikolai Bukharin, Aleksei Rykov, and Mikhail Tomsky, who were regarded as "right-wing" by their opponents. The factional struggles that had taken place in the middle of the decade had decisively determined their relationships with Trotsky and Zinovyev, their fiercest opponents. In those days the "right-wing troika", as they were mockingly referred to by their rivals, for a while met frequently with Joseph Stalin and Vyacheslav Molotov. However, this situation ended abruptly in the space of few weeks in early 1928. From then on Bukharin, Rykov, and Tomsky, who were near neighbors in the Kremlin, were able to rely only on one another. Among the members of the party leadership living in the Kremlin these three allies apparently made joint excursions at the weekends, exchanged books, and would sometimes drink together. On occasion Bukharin and Tomsky, like thoughtless adolescents who had spent their pocket money more quickly than they should, would turn to the thriftier Rykov for a loan. He was willing to help out every now and then by sending a *chervonets*.[3]

Around the three leaders of the "right-wing deviationists" there had already formed smaller, independent concentric circles of friends. At the time of the break from Stalin's central party directive Nikolai Bukharin, for example—"the favorite of the party"—was mostly defended by a phalanx of his former disciples. The "showcase proletarian" Mikhail Tomsky was usually surrounded by former workers in the large industries, who had become independent national trade union functionaries in their forties. The Soviet prime minister, Aleksei Rykov, who was more family oriented than the other two, least according to his daughter Natalya would usually spend his time at home with his family after

This picture shows the members of several overlapping friendship circles. From the left: Konstantin Ukhanov (1), the head of the Moscow Soviet, Joseph Stalin, Karl Bauman (2), the head of the Moscow party organization, Mikhail Tomsky (3), Mikhail Kalinin (4), Lazar Kaganovich (5), Anastas Mikoyan (6), and Vyacheslav Molotov (7). Ukhanov, Bauman, and Tomsky did not survive the Great Terror. The little boy in the middle is Artom Sergeyev, who grew up in Stalin's family and later became a stately general of the Soviet Army. In the left corner, is the little Vasya Stalin.

work. However, even at his home, plates would be laid at the table for half a dozen or so guests, especially his colleagues. In the meantime, those *apparatchik*s who had never stood politically close to Trotsky, Zinovyev, or the three imposing right-wing figures—who were working way above them—were looking to find a place for themselves. Sooner or later these *apparatchik*s ended up in the vicinity of Stalin. The herding of the first "Stalinists" into the same stable began as early as around the end of Lenin's rule. The process was largely initiated by the two most important confidants of the future dictator at the time, Vyacheslav Molotov and Lazar Kaganovich. Both men dealt mainly with cadre issues in the Bolshevik Party center, something which would be of enormous help to Stalin, as General Secretary, in creating a huge *inventory of personnel data*. This enabled him increasingly to put his own men into key positions, even in the remotest provinces of the country.[4]

Up until the early 1930s there were some exceptions to the way these relationships were formed. At this time contacts among residents in the Kremlin were still determined by common cultural interests or similar educational background. In the correspondence of Klim Voroshilov, who proudly referred to himself as an "excellent locksmith", we find traces of a certain "worker's arrogance". He liked to mock the despised intelligentsia, especially when writing to his old friend, the leader of the Soviet trade unions, Mikhail Tomsky: "What times we live in, Misha! Today, writers and their like are happy to be regarded as workers," he remarked smugly in a letter dated May 5, 1927, to which Tomsky replied in a similar vein.[5] The correspondence between the two men focused mainly on their shared hunting experiences: at a time when the queues were lengthening in front of the labor exchanges in the big Soviet cities, in the most beautiful forests of the "proletarian" empire dozens of beaters were driving game for the two "genuine proletarians" Tomsky and Voroshilov. The country's leading politicians were busy discussing national problems during one session of the Politburo while the two great friends, who had both scaled the peaks of power from very humble beginnings, entertained one another with such notes as the following: "Misha! Where do you want to go? Are you just hunting bears, or are there some wolves around there, too? I find it really hard to shoot bears. They are such nice creatures, much nicer than those animals that are more like us in nature. V[oroshilov]." On the back of the slip of paper we find the self-satisfied answer of his good friend: "There are bears there, but there are lynx, too. M[ikhail] T[omsky]."[6] These stories usually had even more tawdry endings. Following hunting expeditions and excursions to the countryside the residents of the Kremlin often surprised one another with splendid gifts: "I am moved. Both your thoughtfulness and the boar are truly wonderful. Warmest thanks. I am curious as to how much the boar weighed, since the skin alone weighs more than thirty pounds. Thank you again. G[enrikh] Y[agoda]," wrote the infamous NKVD boss to Voroshilov. On another small slip of paper he expressed his gratitude to the "Red Marshal" as if they were both the noble owners of Russian country mansions: "I received the horse. It is not just a horse but a full-blooded thoroughbred. With my warmest thanks. G[enrikh] Y[agoda]."[7]

It was Voroshilov's habit to ask Nikolai Yezhov, the head of the NKVD, by writing on a small piece of paper to arrest as many high-ranking officials as possible.

The members of the elite Soviet leadership of course referred to the important affairs of the country in their private letters. In 1928 a number of non-party engineers and clerks—including German citizens—were arrested in the coal-mining center of Shakhty, near Rostov-on-Don, and in several nearby mining towns. After undergoing beatings and psychological torture many of them confessed to being "saboteurs", "industrial spies", and "counter-revolutionary agitators".[8] Initially almost every one of the "Shakhty saboteurs" faced the death penalty. However, a fierce struggle for power was taking place in the upper echelons of the Bolshevik Party at the time, and this divided the Politburo even with respect to the Shakhty affair. It is extremely hard to believe that Nikolai Bukharin, Aleksei Rykov, and Mikhail Tomsky, who were apparently far more "liberal" on the peasant issue, stood up for the death penalty, while Stalin, who had invented the whole showcase, along with his followers, proved more pragmatic and eventually made the sentence more lenient.[9]

In the proceedings phase of the "Shakhty affair" Klim Voroshilov, one of the future executioners during the Great Terror, somewhat surprisingly smelt a rat in connection with the "case of the mining engineers": "Misha! Tell me frankly. Won't we get into the shit if we hold an open trial in the case of the mining engineers? Perhaps the local authorities have exaggerated the affair. Perhaps [...] the men of the OGPU?" The Politburo had entrusted Tomsky, along with other functionaries, with the investigation of the case, thus he answered Voroshilov with assurance: "I see no such danger in the Shakhty case, or in the case of the mining engineers in general, since everything is quite clear. The protagonists have revealed everything. In my opinion *[besides the non-party engineers—M. K.]* it would be good to arrest about half a dozen Communists as well. M[ikhail] T[omsky]. March 20, 1928."[10]

As the "situation intensified" this circle of people created, and came close to perfecting, its own Orwellian language. Among the favorite phrases of the masters of the Kremlin was the apparently innocent word *razgurzit'* (to unload something), which meant "to deport", or even "to execute": "...we have drawn up the unloading plan for Kronstadt. And measures by which we can guarantee the unloading. I have made a transcript on this matter for the Council of Work and

Defense. Please give your support when I put this into motion," wrote Andrei Zhdanov on May 7, 1935.[11] It is no coincidence that Zhdanov, who, following the Kirov murder, had come to the fore of the Leningrad party organization, turned for support to Klim Voroshilov. By that time the quota-based wave of arrests and executions sweeping through the city on the bank of the Neva had reached the fortress of Kronstadt. The Leningrad NKVD functionaries thus had to coordinate their acts of terror with the people's commissar for defense.

On other occasions Voroshilov made decisions on the fate of his subordinates, wording them cryptically in calligraphic handwriting on small slips of paper: "Memo. Nikolai Ivanovich, please take an interest in the [Leningrad] artillery corps and inform me of your valuable opinion in respect to this case," he wrote to Yezhov, the NKVD chief, on December 17, 1937. Yezhov was also a secretary of the Central Committee and occupied the key post of chairman of the Central Supervisory Committee during the Great Terror. The expression "take an interest in" was in this case a synonym for "arrest". Another *terminus technicus* was "take in", which also meant "arrest immediately": "N[ikolai] I[vanovich]! Nikolayev inquired whether Uritsky[12] should be arrested. When can you take him in? You have already managed to take in Slavin and Bazenkov. It would be good if you could take in Todorsky, too. Is this feasible? K[liment] V[oroshilov]."[13]

☆ In addition to several dozen fellow party leaders, in his *technology of power* Stalin initially relied mainly on his fairly small secretariat. Among those carrying out the highly confidential tasks only one genuine old underground Bolshevik was working in this restricted, tight-knit community: Ivan Tovstukha. This multilingual, well-read music lover—a former political emigrant—had begun working with the future dictator by sheer coincidence.[14] He was looking for a job when a friend from his youth, the deputy people's commissar for nationalities Stanisław Pestkovsky, recommended him to his boss, Joseph Stalin. Subsequently the pedantic Tovstukha organized the meetings of the people's commissar for nationalities, then of the General Secretary of the party, for years. Sometimes he worked as a speech writer and supervised the filing of confidential documents. However, the gaunt and reserved man had returned from his exile in Siberia with serious lung and heart problems, and was therefore often off work for months at a time. In addition, he was clearly unhappy at having become a "pen-pushing bureaucrat". Eventually he got Stalin to agree that he could spend the majority of his time on party historical research.[15] This involved, among other things, the collecting and ongoing censorship of documents on Stalin's life.[16] Tovstukha, who was far more erudite than his colleagues—and especially most of the colleagues of his boss, the members of the Politburo—was tormented by an incomprehensible inferiority complex. The proximity of the dictator generated a strange melancholy in him.[17] This perhaps explains why he finally decided not to undertake the writing of Joseph Stalin's biography.[18]

The three leaders of the General Secretary's secretariat began their careers in the movement in Jewish revolutionary parties working separately from the Russian Social Democratic organizations. Yakov Brezanovsky[19] and Georgy Kanner[20] came from the Bund, while Lev Mekhlis was an activist in the Jewish Social Democratic Party before joining the Bolshevik Party.[21] The organizational structure and operation of Stalin's secretariat and the *secret department* of the Central Committee closely linked to it, where these three former Jewish Socialist politicians worked, requires further intensive study.[22] Some further assistants who served the General Secretary—Grishin, Graskin, Makarova, Sergeyev (the minutes taker of the Politburo), and Boris Bazhanov—apparently played a smaller role in the dictator's circle in the early 1920s than the "group of five" made up of Brezanovsky, Tovstukha, Nazaretyan, Kanner, and Mekhlis. After a while, however, both Brezanovsky and Nazaretyan left the secretariat, and in the late 1920s Kanner declared that he intended to return to his studies. The offended Tovstukha, who had been left to shoulder a huge burden alone, threatened to resign, although the General Secretary did not take his threat seriously: "Ha, ha, ha! What a cockerel! J. Sta[lin]," he scribbled on the edge of the note from Tovstukha.[23]

Even today, when discussing Stalin's all-powerful secretariat, even the most learned researchers in this area strangely mention Tovstukha and Poskryobishev as the most important "aides" who took part in the practice of the "technology of power". However, this was not the case. It was Yakov Brezanovsky, for instance—who came from the ghettoes in the settlement zones *(tsenta osedloty)* allocated to the Jews during tsarism and who was ten years younger than his boss—who accompanied Stalin on visits to the fronts during the Civil War. In the summer of 1920, during the months of the Russo-Polish War, he became the secretary of the most important body of the southwestern front, the Revolutionary Military Council.[24] By the middle of the decade he was managing the economic affairs of the entire Bolshevik Party center. In the meantime, together with Ivan Tovstukha, he directed the top-secret department of the Central Committee reporting directly to Stalin. After graduating as an architectural engineer from the Industrial Academy—where he attended some of the lectures with fellow student Nadezhda Alliluyeva—he was appointed as secretary of the Moscow City Council. After this he again managed the economic affairs of the Central Committee. However, for reasons that are still unclear his apparently straightforward career ran aground in February 1936 when he was demoted to the rank of cadre officer in the people's commissariat of the Food Industry. In December the next year, on the orders of his former patron, Joseph Stalin, who had earlier supported him in his career, he was taken by the political police and, after a brief interrogation, was executed.[25]

His fate was shared by another man who was party to all Stalin's secrets, Grigory Kanner. His biography reads like a carbon copy of the career of Brezanovsky, who was ten years his senior: breaking out of the ghetto, service at the front during the Russian Civil War, hard work in Stalin's secretariat and other top-secret departments of the Central Committee, then diligent study at the Industrial Academy, after which he became a renowned economic expert. Then the black-haired, young-looking *apparatchik* was arrested. Despite the common milestones in their lives Brezanovsky was remembered by his acquaintances, among them László Pollacsek, as a fundamentally well-meaning, slightly narrow-minded official, who became prematurely complacent. By contrast, everyone was in awe of the sharp-witted Kanner—who was reputed to have a brilliant mind and who, on account of the spectacular successes he achieved on the heavy-industry "fronts", was awarded the Order of Lenin in 1935—since he was regarded as a man of ruthless ambition who was quite prepared to walk over others on his way to the top. The rumor spread that in the spring of 1937 Stalin got rid of him mainly because the unscrupulous young man—on the orders of the General Secretary of the party—had become involved in a series of political murders during the years of the clashes between the different factions within the party.[26]

Of all the dictator's secretaries it was Lev Mekhlis who took the most active role in running the mechanism of tyranny. It is no coincidence that, as a reward, it was he who went the furthest. The many positions that he held in various periods of his life included the editorship of *Pravda* and leadership of the political directorate of the Red Army. He then became deputy head of the Soviet government and at the same time the people's commissar for state supervision. His position as editor of the central party organ, the *Pravda*, provided several advantages for Mekhlis.[27] At the conference of the Communist Academy, held on November 27 and 28, 1935, in which only a select group of the leadership took part, he was awarded the degree of Doctor of Science without having to defend his thesis. Soon afterwards the institution was dissolved, but the politician was able to retain the prestigious-sounding title until the end of his life.[28]

Still, Stalin's favorite assistant was an uneducated, basically ignorant person. On August 6, 1933 the diplomat Aleksandr Arosev wrote in his diary: "Crimea Mukholatka. Late in the evening we went to the observatory. We watched the moon. It turned out that Mekhlis is just as stupid as almost all cultural workers nowadays. He wanted to know where the moon is getting its light from. He was amazed when he got the expert reply. He was also surprised when he learned that the moon has no atmosphere and therefore is not surrounded by clouds. When the (wonderfully patient) professor explained that there is no water on the moon he found this extraordinary."[29]

Stalin must have been aware of the lack of mental abilities of his assistant. Nevertheless, he made Mekhlis Central Committee member in 1937. Whatever mistakes this man made, he was only mildly rebuked. Stalin's patronage only came to an end following the war, when Mekhlis suffered a stroke and became paralyzed down one side of his body. With the words "this is not a hospital!" Stalin refused his former secretary permission to take part as a guest in 1952 at the 19th Congress of the CPSU. Nevertheless, on the last day of the congress he unexpectedly ordered that, in recognition of his former services, Mekhlis should be elected to the Central Committee.[30] Thus the anti-Semitic Stalin, even in the midst of the "anti-cosmopolitan campaign", was not troubled by Mekhlis's Jewish origins. In selecting his colleagues in the beginning he had other criteria in mind: he demanded decisive action against his opponents, an exceptional capacity for hard work, and, above all, blind obedience. Bazhanov once witnessed one of Stalin's cruel anti-Semitic outbursts and afterwards asked Mekhlis for his opinion. Mekhlis evaded the uncomfortable question, saying: "I am a Communist, not a Jew." According to the author of the memoir "this was a convenient stance. It made it possible for Mekhlis to remain a faithful and obedient Stalinist until the end of his life."[31]

Outside his official relationships the Master of the Kremlin ostentatiously kept a certain distance between himself and all the members of his secretariat. Nevertheless he would come to their assistance if they were in trouble, thereby tightening the chains of obligation that bound them. One pertinent letter reads as follows: "June 19, 1923. To Comrade Kakhiani, secretary of the Georgian Communist Party Central Committee. Please make sure that Comrade Y. Makarova, a responsible and valuable colleague at the Central Committee, is placed in the best and most suitable conditions. We hope that these conditions will enable her to make the proper progress in the lengthy medical treatment she is about to undergo. J. Stalin, secretary of the Central Committee."[32] The following undated telegram from Stalin is also relevant: "The Crimea, Suuk-su village. To Brezanovsky. Please let me know immediately about Kanner. How can his position be improved? Does he need to be taken anywhere? Does he need money? Shouldn't we have him and Makarova taken to Mukholatka or to Suuk-su? I await your reply. J. Stalin."[33] On another occasion, on July 17, 1925, the

Anastas Mikoyan (x) in the company of friends…

General Secretary, who was taking a holiday in Sochi, sent a coded telegram, marked "strictly confidential", to Rykov and Molotov, on Mekhlis: "I am asking both of you to send Mekhlis to Mukholatka *[a government resort—M. K.]* or to another good sanatorium. Ignore any protest from Mekhlis. He doesn't listen to me, but he must listen to you. I await your response *[to the telegram—M. K.]*. Stalin."[34] As a result of such gestures all his secretaries, including Boris Dvinsky and Aleksandr Poskryobishev, who were appointed later to the service of the General Secretary,[35] behaved with ostentatious servility towards him.

☆ Among the members of the secretariat it was only the Armenian Amayak Nazaretyan—who had earlier played an important role in the Tiflis Bolshevik political elite—who was initially able to feel that the General Secretary regarded him not only as a subordinate but also as a friend. Stalin usually asked Nazaretyan to forward his letters, marked "secret", to Lenin.[36] It was also Amayak Nazaretyan who delivered Stalin's more important letters in early 1923 in the course of his exchanges with Leon Trotsky.[37] According to Bazhanov, who proved to be an accurate observer, the Armenian party worker was "a very cultured, clever, well-meaning and well-balanced man. […] There were only three men who were on informal terms with Stalin: Voroshilov, Ordzhonikidze, and Nazaretyan. All three of them called him by his old byname "Koba". I had the impression that Stalin was increasingly annoyed by the fact that his secretary addressed him informally. He was aiming at the role of tyrant of the Empire and this interlude was becoming unpleasant for him. He eventually got rid of Nazaretyan, and not in a very sophisticated way. […] In 1937 he had him shot in the head."[38]

The ill-fated Nazaretyan was a Caucasian, a fellow countryman of the dictator. Until paranoia got the better of Stalin—that is, until the beginning of the 1930s—this represented a *very serious advantage* at the top of the Soviet machinery of power, since the private, friendly relationships of the General Secretary were mostly created on a "geographical" basis. Sipping wine in the company of fellow Caucasians, with their distinctive humor and their common dislike of Moscow in the wintertime, he enjoyed recalling memorable stories from their common past. Inside the Kremlin he tried to recreate conditions reminiscent of leisurely siestas in the midday heat of Tiflis or Baku with his fellow villagers. On hearing about the "Caucasian get-togethers" Avel Yenukidze would drop into

...and fierce Caucasian warriors.

Stalin's office with a huge food hamper, from which he produced Georgian wines and tangerines.

On such occasions the company would choose a *tamada*, or master of ceremonies, and would sometimes sing Caucasian songs until dawn. They often danced the *lezginka* or other dances for men. Although the assembled politicians would humbly embrace their host almost entirely in the interests of their careers, when they went on their way in the morning they had the genuine feeling of having breathed the unique air of the Caucasian mountains. Up until the early 1930s two key figures in the Stalinist leadership, Molotov and Kaganovich, were conspicuous by their absence from these Caucasian sprees. However, it was inconceivable that Sergo Ordzhonikidze, despite his occasional disagreements with Stalin, would be omitted from the list of those invited.[39]

From the correspondence of residents of the Kremlin and the recollections of contemporaries we learn that the "Caucasian circle" organized around Stalin had a number of offshoots.[40] Although there were certain rivalries among members of the small cliques that created loose alliances with one another, they basically held together. In the 1920s the "Caucasians"—Georgians, Armenians, and Russians working in the southern area of the country in Rostov-on-Don, Baku, or Tiflis—began to take over the Moscow party center and the more important people's commissariats. Then, in the years of the Great Terror, through Lavrenty Beria, they also filled the NKVD. It is no coincidence that at the session of the Central Committee of the Bolshevik Party, held in June 1926 three young "Caucasians" were elected as candidate members of the Politburo: Ordzhonikidze, Kirov, and Mikoyan.[41] For a while the leaven of this community was Anastas Mikoyan, the popular *tamada* of the "Caucasian gatherings".[42]

Like Klimenty (otherwise referred to as Kliment or Klim) Voroshilov, Mikoyan dropped the old-fashioned version of his name soon after joining the Bosheviks. In the Tiflis Seminary, where his impoverished carpenter father had sent him to study, he had been known as "Anastasy". None of his then official biographies, however, makes mention of this. The shrewd Armenian was an expert in misleading people. Even today those who did not know him personally believe that Mikoyan was a kind, well-meaning man throughout his life. In part of the relevant literature he is portrayed as helping those in trouble whenever he could in the course of the bloody purges throughout the Soviet era. It is also claimed

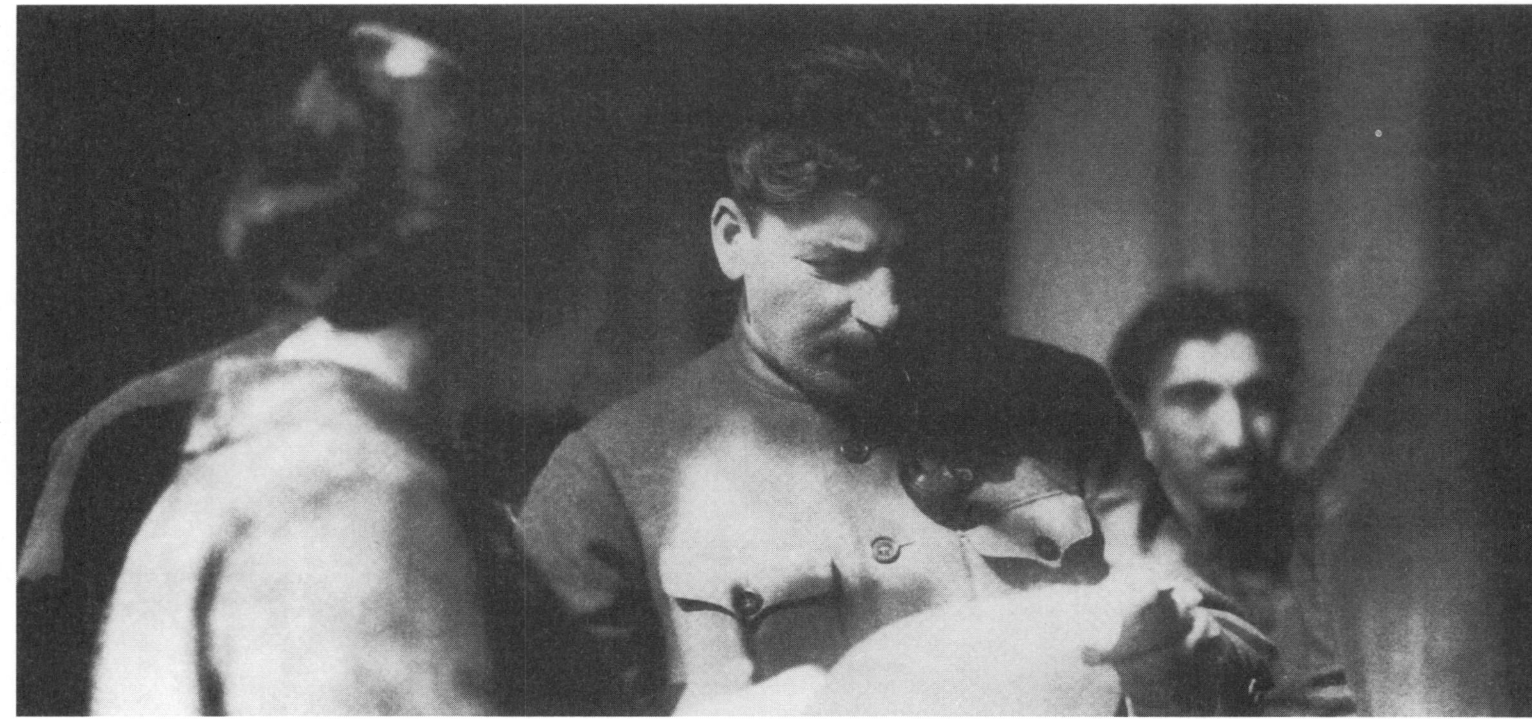

Stalin smoking a pipe among the members of his "Caucasian clan". Anastas Mikoyan belonged to this circle.

that he went even further in the revision of Stalinism than Nikita Khrushchev, whose "secret speech" exposed Stalin. This is partly supported by archival sources recently declassified.[43] But it is only part of the truth. Nevertheless, I have found out that it was exactly Anastas Mikoyan, who forwarded Olga Shatunovskaya's letter to the members of the Presidium of the CSPU Central Committee, in which she made Stalin responsible for Kirov's death. It is evident from the—still unpublished—letter that its author has been encouraged by Mikoyan. The envelope bears in his handwriting: "to N. S. Khrushchev. *Strictly confidential.*"[44]

Later, in the years of the "détente", Anastas Mikoyan indeed made provision for the survivors who were returning from the prison camps and for their families. From among Stalin's immediate colleagues he was perhaps the most distraught by his conscience because of the friends of his who had been killed. He was also tormented by the memory that in the summer of 1937, along with Georgy Malenkov, the rising star in the party leadership, he had instigated a bloodbath in Armenia despite being an Armenian himself. He can also be held responsible for the arrests of several of his subordinates.

Less well known is the fact that Mikoyan, until the end of his life, was strongly bound to the past that he had lived through with the other masters of the Kremlin. He was even able to forgive many things to Beria with whom he formed an ad hoc alliance against Zhdanov in the mid-1940s, during the power struggle for Stalin's post.[45] In July 1953, when positions were being redistributed in the upper echelons of power, the idea of the coup-like removal of the chief executioner Lavrenty Beria came up. However, it was primarily Mikoyan who opposed the plan.[46] His immediate colleagues, who had suffered so much at his hands, wrote of him: "He had learned a great deal from his loved and hated patron—he was both hypocritical and callous, he was an expert in duplicity, and was cruel to his subordinates. And, for the sake of his career, he was ready to sacrifice any of them."[47]

But it did not take much for him, too, to become one of the last victims of the

Master of the Kremlin. Not long before his death, Stalin was already preparing to get rid of him, since by that time the Master of the Kremlin had been taken over completely by persecution mania and for some reason had come into conflict with Anastas Mikoyan.[48] Earlier, however, he had regularly relied on his friend for over two decades. He appreciated the fact that the lenient Armenian imitated him even outwardly: "When we met privately I continued to be on informal terms with Stalin," remembered Mikoyan. "In general only a very small circle of people addressed him informally: Ordzhonikidze and Kalinin, somewhat later Molotov and Voroshilov, then Kirov, Bukharin, and Kamenev."[49] From letters written by Stalin that have recently been made available to researchers it appears that Mikoyan was a target of the dictator's mockery more often than anyone else. On several occasions, however, in front of other people, he assured the Armenian politician—who, like him, spoke Russian with a heavy accent—of his sympathy, just as he did the other pillar of the Caucasian circle, Sergo Ordzhonikidze. He even took care of him in his own way. In June 1933, when Anastas Mikoyan traveled to the countryside on an official tour of inspection and, despite the Central Committee's ban, made the journey by plane, Stalin succeeded in getting the party to take disciplinary action against him by highlighting above all the fact that the airplane he had used had crashed only the following day.[50]

The dictator's reaction at the same time moved and embittered Mikoyan, who wrote the following in his undated letter to Klim Voroshilov: "I learned yesterday from Sergo that the pilot died. I would like to talk to you and request that the disciplinary action be withdrawn. The airplane trip took place by chance. I had completely forgotten the decision of the Central Committee forbidding it. In future I will not fly, I will not use other means of transport, and I will not even walk if the Central Committee forbids it. But I don't want to suffer the punishment I have been given. A[nastas] Mikoyan." His addressee responded with friendly teasing: "So, if you won't fly, won't use other means of transport, and won't even walk, are you going to go crawling around on all fours? This is a provocative attitude, which also merits disciplinary action! V[oroshilov]." The slip of paper found its way to Stalin, who merely noted in the margin: "Very true!"[51]

On the other hand, Anastas Mikoyan was one of the few people who for years spent their holidays not far from Stalin. The two families, who lived very near one another in Zubalovo, met regularly until the tragic death of Nadezhda Alliluyeva, and even afterwards for a while. "In 1934 Stalin was so fond of me that in the evenings we would sit together for hours. On such occasions he heaped advice on me," we read in Mikoyan's memoirs. "Once he suggested that I sleep at his *dacha*. Naturally, I stayed. I called my wife to say that I was at Stalin's place. This was the first night *[since they had moved to Moscow—M. K.]* I had not spent at home. My wife was not at all pleased. Then a few days passed and Stalin again came up with the idea. I called my wife again to tell her I would not be coming home. When it happened a third time I saw that my wife did not know whether to believe me. (She said nothing openly, but I saw it in her eyes.) However, she had no way of knowing whether I was really with Stalin or not. [...] When Stalin suggested that I sleep at his *dacha* again I said that my wife worried when I wasn't at home. And then he stopped asking me.

"After me it was often Svanidze, his first wife's brother, who stayed over at his *dacha*. Apparently Stalin was bored on his own. After Svanidze's death there was no one left to stay at the *dacha*, and Stalin didn't invite anyone. [...] He shut himself in his bedroom by himself. It seems that his persecution mania had got the better of him because of the way he got rid of people. And he was scared."[52]

Even later, immediately before the purges started, the cunning Armenian did not lose his place among Stalin's inner circle of friends, by that time, consisted almost exclusively of the members and candidate members of the Politburo. From the early 1930s it was mainly Molotov, Kaganovich, Voroshilov, Yenukidze, and Ordzhonikidze who belonged to this group, while Kirov, Skiryatov, and Kuybishev were somewhat on the periphery. After a time, however, Mikoyan, too had to struggle to stay afloat: "He is not suited to being at the head of the Ukrainian party organization. Not even to directing the people's commissariat for provision. He is no more than a weak agitator, who, besides, is not even a good organizer." This was how Stalin dismissively characterized him in an undated letter, probably written during the summer of 1932 while on holiday at the Black Sea coast, to his deputy in Moscow, Lazar Kaganovich.[53]

Those less well informed, however, still believed that Anastas Mikoyan was a key figure in Soviet economic policy. In the summer of 1932 Ms. Kollontay, the Soviet ambassador to Stockholm, visited him for supply in his *dacha* near Moscow. From her diary we learn that she nearly fell in love with him, having found him to be such a "visionary politician": "A hot July evening. A table was laid for us on the east-facing terrace. [...] He appeared handsome, lean, and dynamic. As if it were not two in the morning. As if he did not have a whole working day behind him. He is currently concerned with the building of the canal connecting the White Sea with the Baltic Sea *[the work was carried out by prisoners in the Gulag, for as long as they survived—M. K.]*. The Bolsheviks are turning the dream of Peter the Great into reality, he tells me. He is less preoccupied with the poor harvest in the Ukraine than with the shortage of raw materials and parts needed to put the massive industrialization plans into practice."[54]

"Poor harvest" was one of the euphemisms frequently employed among the nomenklatura of the time. It was a Soviet neologism, like "isolator"—a place of solitary confinement for political convicts; "education by labor"—working prisoners to their death in the Gulag; "the highest level of social defense"—execution; and "body mechanic"—none other than an NKVD employee who specialized in torture.[55] Anastas Mikoyan, who was responsible for the food supply to the Soviet population, frequently used the phrases similar to the Orwellian Newspeak, such as "temporary supply problems", a synonym for the artificially generated famine in Ukraine. His guest, Aleksandra Kollontay, must have known—if only from the dramatic reports in the foreign press—that the tragedy was affecting whole districts and provinces, while in the meantime the mass deportation to Siberia of Ukrainian peasants and Cossacks from Kuban' who refused to become members of *kolkhozy* continued. In the meantime Soviet grain was being exported at a forced rate, well under world market prices—in the West this action was referred to as "Russian dumping". The armed police and the soldiers of the Red Army were ordered not to allow the emaciated, starving Soviet population to flee to areas where there was some food left in the shops and markets. In response, Stalin's unhappy subjects occasionally resorted to armed resistance. The hunger riots—which swept through Ukraine first, then Kazakhstan, then northern Caucasia—were bloodily suppressed by heavily armed "peace-keeping forces", which massively outnumbered the rioters.[56] Perhaps Ms. Kollontay noted this fact in her diary, in the censored version, however, a typed copy of which was sent by her in the early 1950s to Stalin's secretariat, we read only about Mikoyan's cynical boasting.

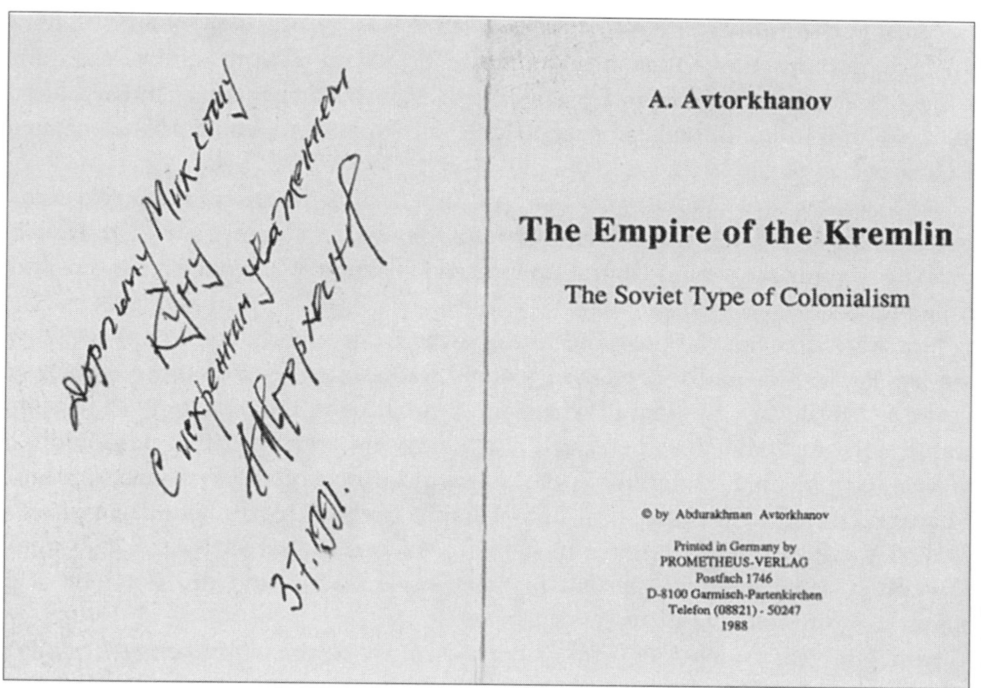

A. Avtorkhanov

The Empire of the Kremlin

The Soviet Type of Colonialism

© by Abdurakhman Avtorkhanov

Printed in Germany by
PROMETHEUS-VERLAG
Postfach 1746
D-8100 Garmisch-Partenkirchen
Telefon (08821) - 50247
1988

Abdurakhman Avtorkhanov, a Chechen party worker who later became a famous Kremlinologist researcher in exile in Western Europe, knew the Stalinist power plays perhaps the best. At the beginning of the 1930s, he almost drifted to the fringes of the Caucasian power center in Moscow.

Other contemporaries were aware of how hypocritical the Armenian politician could be. "No one is more capable than he of finding his way in a given situation, and of adapting himself," we read in the draft version of the memoirs of Marshal Georgy Zhukhov.[57]

According to archive material recently made available to researchers, the picture is somewhat more complex. Following the Civil War Mikoyan, despite his inherent careerism, was willing to be content with a less prestigious position, far from the "hubbub" of Moscow. He felt comfortable in the role of one of the Kremlin's most important provincial governors. From Rostov-on-Don he had control over a part of southern Russia, the steppes of Kuban', and the north Caucasian mountains. However, at the age of only thirty-one he was ordered to Moscow to be appointed people's commissar for external and internal trade, replacing Lev Kamenev who had been exiled as ambassador to Rome for being a "deviationist". Having learned of this plan, Mikoyan, in a letter dated June 4, 1926, desperately protested to Vyacheslav Molotov, the secretary responsible for cadre affairs in the Central Committee: "Dear Vyacheslav Mikhailovich! I cannot keep secret how outraged I am that you have selected me as a candidate member of the Politburo. In my opinion you have made a great mistake. The future will show how right I am. And as to the idea that I should become people's commissar for external and internal trade, there is no sense even talking about it.

I am not willing to submit to any such decision taken by the Politburo or the [Central Committee] plenum. My whole being revolts against this proposal. My motives are as follows:

1. I am not ready to fulfill this extremely difficult position; it involves the need for intrigue, and I'm not even capable of it.

2. I have never dealt with economic work. I am not even particularly attracted to it and am therefore certain to fail.

3. You are unwittingly driving me quite mad with such proposals. If I knew that this was for the benefit of the party I would sacrifice myself. But in the given situation you are destroying the cause as well as me.

Thus, at the moment I have no wish to leave Rostov[-on-Don]. I am still useful here, perhaps even indispensable. However, if you want to remove me I am willing to accept it. If you do, I would like to work in the provinces in Russia, or in the Comintern, initially abroad. But I am unable to contemplate leaving Caucasia before the congress."[58]

To Stalin he wrote as follows: "I am not suited to the position of people's commissar of external and internal trade. Generally speaking I am not suited to being a people's commissar at all. I cannot undertake a task that is beyond my powers and capabilities..."[59]

Nor was Mikoyan the only one to shy away from such honors. In the 1920s, among the friends and followers of Joseph Stalin, others were no more keen to move to Moscow or Leningrad where they would be in the proximity of the unstable and unpredictable dictator. "...it has been suggested that I should be placed to work in Leningrad. Today I was informed of the firm decision and I naturally rejected the proposal out of hand. Sergo [Ordzhonikidze] was also against the idea," reads a letter to his wife written by Sergei Kirov, who until December 1925 led the Azerbaijani party organization and did not have the slightest desire to leave Baku.[60]

Almost a year later—following Mikoyan's move to the capital city—Ordzhonikidze was transferred from the control of the party organizations of the three Transcaucasian republics to Rostov-on-Don, where he was appointed secretary of the northern Caucasian borderland. The sensitive Sergo, who was just as hot-tempered as his two "Caucasian" friends Kirov and Mikoyan, was "spitting fire" as a result. Molotov, who had been responsible for the transfer, tried to calm him: "...I hope that in the near future you will be moving to Moscow," he wrote to him kindly.[61]

One of the reasons behind the transfer was that Stalin, who never took much interest in the private plans of his vassals, had calculated that with the help of the "Caucasians" it would be easier for him to pacify the permanently renitent Moscow and Leningrad. This calculation proved largely correct. However, as was made clear in the letter quoted above, the fortunate/unfortunate nominee Mikoyan did not settle quietly in the capital city. In a long letter addressed to the General Secretary on June 26, 1930—in order to preempt any difficulties—he asked to be relieved of his post. He requested two months' holiday and suggested that on his return he work as the head of one of the remote major state investment projects. Stalin, who from time to time was himself dissatisfied with Mikoyan,[62] hesitated for a while. Then, ignoring the fact that Aleksei Rykov was officially prime minister at the time, he and Molotov took the decision to divide the people's commissariat of external and internal trade in November 1930. The external trade portfolio was given to the erudite, multilingual Arkady Rozenholts. The new people's commissariat for provisions (that is, internal trade) was given to Mikoyan. This commissariat managed the supervision of internal trade and the direction of the food industry. Mikoyan, however, still did not feel at ease in this role. In October 1934 he was once more considering departure. However, the Politburo again rejected his resignation.[63]

It is hard to understand why, in the early 1930s, storm clouds occasionally gathered over the head of Anastas Mikoyan, who was no more dull than his colleagues but who was, in fact, even more shrewd.[64] "I remember in 1933 he was slandered in his own people's commissariat *[by members of the party committee—M. K.]* because he did not take part in party work at all," I was told scornfully in 1998 by the late Dmitry Sukhanov, who for years was head of Malenkov's secretariat and who, even at the age of over ninety, impressed people with his phenomenal memory. According to him Mikoyan was famous for always being able to slip out of the grip of the dictator's iron hand. "The rascal was able to walk through Red Square on a rainy day without an umbrella without getting wet," continued Sukhanov, laughing. "He just sneaked between the raindrops."

From an informal letter written to Lazar Kaganovich, dated before September 17, 1936, we get a clear idea of how consciously Mikoyan was positioning himself in the storm that swept so many others away. Knowing that the permanently restructured friendships in the Kremlin were rooted primarily in the power relations in the highest echelons, he sent messages via his addressee exclusively to those people whom he knew to be faithful followers of Stalin. He also suspected that, via NKVD channels, copies of his letters would reach "the Master", who took great pleasure in watching the mutual relationships among his colleagues. "Dear Lazar! I am writing to you from Chicago. [...] I have visited many food factories, stores, shops, and restaurants. There is something for us to learn everywhere. [...] I am convinced how useful my trip to America has been. How well this was foreseen by our brilliant leader, who recommended that I travel to America to study the food industry here and then plant the experience in Soviet soil! [...] Please forgive me for this hasty, scarcely legible, and long-winded letter. I will tell you everything when I return. I send warmest greetings to all my comrades. Please give my special greetings to Sergo [Ordzhonikidze], Molotov, Voroshilov, Andreyev, Chubar, Zhdanov, Khrushchev, and Yakovlev. Don't forget to write in your next letter to him that I send my warmest greetings to Our Master. How good that we have so quickly got rid of the Trotskyite gang of Zinovyev and Kamenev," continued Mikoyan, demonstrating exultation. The two "deviationists", who had been sentenced to death in Moscow, had in fact once been the political idols of the author of the letter. "And how just is the verdict! How true is the great cause of Lenin and Stalin! What a pity Trotsky has got away for the time being without sharing the fate of this gang of criminals!"[65]

The letter's postscript highlights another interesting fact. Emigrants from Tsarist Russia, in this case, members of the Armenian *Dashnak* community, sometimes contemplated attempts against famous Soviet politicians traveling abroad. Were they really preparing to kill Mikoyan? Or is the letter written to Kaganovich only an expression of the paranoia that had taken over the residents of the Kremlin? "The internal comrades here *[probably the Soviet secret agents working in the United States—M. K.]* were right when they warned me that the Dashnaks are preparing an attempt on my life. Yesterday in Chicago I received a letter from Navasardian, which he posted on 8 September in New York. It was addressed to our embassy in Washington in my name. In the letter he urges me to receive him, of course not on private business. It turns out that I know him. I met him about twenty years ago. Even then he was a real villain."[66]

It has only recently come to light how unexpectedly this American journey of Anastas Mikoyan came about in the early autumn of 1936. He was preparing to travel on holiday to the Crimean with his wife and five sons when Stalin mentioned to him, in the presence of Molotov and Voroshilov: "Why shouldn't you go to the United States instead of the Crimean? You can have a rest but, most importantly, you should study the results achieved by the United States in the food industry." This is how it happened that the five Mikoyan boys, accompanied by their governess, traveled to the Crimean, while the politician and his wife Ashkhen went overseas. They were accompanied by a small group comprising mostly engineers and NKVD officers. At the last moment, after the "team" had assembled, Stalin ordered his confidant Vasily Burgman to accompany Mikoyan. Burgman was a Caucasian German, who over the next few weeks acted as interpreter at the confidential talks. On their return he was probably requested to make a detailed report of the trip, in the course of which Mikoyan and his entourage covered more than twelve thousand miles by rail and car.[67]

Another interesting episode in connection with Mikoyan's American trip is his meeting an American "capitalist" by the name of Cohn, who was a distant relation of Polina Zhemchuzhina, in Molotov's *dacha* shortly before the journey. Soon also Stalin appeared in the *dacha*. Mikoyan recalls that Stalin took him aside in the garden and gave him the following instruction: "This Cohn is a capitalist. You should meet him in America. He will help us to start a political dialogue with Roosevelt." When in America Mikoyan found out that although Cohn owned six gas stations, he was far from being an influential capitalist. Henry Ford, however, volunteered to set up a meeting between Mikoyan and Roosevelt. Troyanovsky, Soviet Ambassador in Washington, reported this to Stalin, who failed to reply.[68] This strange story shows what a dilettante Stalin was at the time regardy foreign affairs.

1 *RGASPI*, fond. 74, op. 2, d. 41.
2 At the beginning of the 1990s, during my interviews in Moscow I heard many stories on this from the last Trotskyist alive, Ivan Vrachev, a former editor of the underground journal *Byulleten' Oppozitsii*.
3 "Dear Aleksei! I send 10 *chervonyets [ten rubles, originally ten golden rubles—M. K.]* with this letter. Thank you. I apologize for the delay. I had to rake it together kopeck by kopeck. Your Bukharin," reads the undated letter sent to Rykov by the editor-in-chief of *Pravda*. *RGASPI*, fond. 669, op. 1, d. 30.
4 Avtorkhanov, 1959, 344–345, 349–350.
5 *RGASPI*, fond. 74, op. 2, d. 45.
6 *Ibid.*
7 *Ibid.*
8 *Ekonomicheskaya kontr-revolutsia*, 1928, 105–159.
9 Kun, 1992, 254.
10 *RGASPI*, fond. 74, op. 2, d. 45.
11 *RGASPI*, fond. 74, op. 2, d. 41.
12 For a while he was the head of the Soviet military intelligence agency, the GRU.
13 The name Slavin may have referred to the political officer directing the political work of the whole Red Army or to the people's commissar of a division. It seems that Voroshilov's note mentioned the latter person, as Bazenkov was the commander of the 98th Division, and both of them were executed. From among the listed names, only Army Corps Commander Todorsky survived. After he spent many years in the Gulag, he worked hard for the legal rehabilitation of his comrades. He was the first to put together a detailed chart with the names of high-ranking military commanders who were persecuted by Stalin and Voroshilov. In the spring of 1955, upon the request of Marshal Zhukov, Todorsky was promoted to the rank of lieutenant general. *Reabilitatsia*, 2000, vol. I, 214.
14 Tovstukha's fellow exile, Yelena Nechayeva wrote the most suggestive account on the early years of the politician's life and career. *RGASPI*, fond. 555, op. 1, d. 108.
15 *RGASPI*, fond. 82, op. 2, d. 1426.
16 *RGASPI*, fond. 81, op. 3, d. 255.
17 *RGASPI*, fond. 155, op. 1, d. 85.
18 Conversations in Moscow with Tatyana Tovstukha.
19 *RGASPI*, fond. 17, op. 100, d. 123651.
20 *RGASPI*, fond. 17, op. 100, d. 85705.
21 *RGASPI*, fond. 386, op. 1, d. 1.
22 The first attempts to study this area were made by a Siberian researcher. See Pavlova, 1993, 44–53, 133–137, 144–147.
23 *RGASPI*, fond. 558, op. 1, d. 5227.
24 *RGASPI*, fond. 558, op. 4, d. 321.
25 *RGASPI*, fond. 17, op. 100, d. 123651.
26 Bazhanov, the only assistant at Stalin's secretariat who later turned against the Soviet regime, mentions a number of such cases in Bazhanov, 1983, 53–59, 141, 152.
27 Rubtsov, 1999, 72–82.

28 *RGASPI*, fond. 386, op. 1, d. 6; *RGASPI*, fond. 81, op. 3, d. 100.
29 Aroseva-Maksimova, 1999, 48.
30 Ortenberg, 1995, 184.
31 Bazhanov, 1983, 82.
32 *RGASPI*, fond. 558, op. 1, d. 5096.
33 *RGASPI*, fond. 558, op. 1, d. 2592.
34 *RGASPI*, fond. 558, op. 1, d. 5040.
35 His feared boss eventually made the agriculture specialist Dvinsky the General Secretary of the Rostov-on-Don party organization, and even later minister for procurement. Time passing, Poskryobishev became such an important *chinovnik* for Stalin that even the members of the Politburo were afraid of him.
36 *RGASPI*, fond. 5, op. 2, d. 275.
37 *RGASPI*, fond. 5, op. 2, d. 276; *RGASPI*, fond. 5, op. 2, d. 277; *RGASPI*, fond. 5, op. 2, d. 278.
38 Bazhanov, 1983, 53.
39 From personal communication with Levon Shaumyan.
40 Avtorkhanov, 1976, 141–144.
41 Mikoyan, 1999, 129.
42 From personal communication with Levon Shaumyan and Aleksei Snegov.
43 Reabilitatsia, 2000, 255–257, 275, 296, 308–309.
44 APRF, fond. 3, op. 24, d. 446. I thank Aleksandr Yakovlev for his kind permission to read this letter.
45 From personal communication with Yury Zhdanov. According to the son of the Soviet "Culture Pope", his father sarcastically called *gruppa*, or group the small circle of allies, consisting of Beria, Malenkov, Mikoyan, and partly Khrushchev, who formed an alliance with each other against Zhdanov.
46 Beria, 1991, 273–275.
47 Korolyov, 1995, 128–129; Menshikov, 1996, 95–104, 109, 116–119.
48 Pikhoya, 1998, 69, 77.
49 Mikoyan, 1999, 352. The recently published memoir is a very important inventory of facts and stories from the Stalinist period. Nevertheless, it seems that the parts in the book that denounce "the personality cult" of Stalin bear the marks of "skillful editorial updating" to the time of publication—like in the case of Khrushchev's memoirs.
50 *Stalinskoye Politbyuro*, 1995, 41.
51 *RGASPI*, fond. 74, op. 2, d. 42.
52 Mikoyan, 1999, 356.
53 *RGASPI*, fond. 81, op. 3, d. 99. Concerning the unpublished correspondence betveen Stalin and Kaganovich, for the Hungarian edition of this book, I relied on only archival sources. Since then, much of this correspondence was made available in Moscow. Stalin i Kaganovich 2001.
54 *RGASPI*, fond. 134, op. 3, d. 18.
55 Fesenko, 1955, 31, 45–50; Boykov, 1957, vol. I, 116; *Stalinskoye Politbyuro*, 1995, 61. On this terrible distortion of Russian language, see Selishchev, 1928, 102–132.
56 Kollektivizatsia, 1997, 43–69, 95–485; Osokina, 1993, 44–63; Slavko, 1995, 27–71, 131–139, 151–171.
57 *Istorichesky Arkhiv*, 1999, no. 3, 63.
58 *RGASPI*, fond. 82, op. 2, d. 1423.
59 Mikoyan, 1999, 273.
60 *Bolshevistkoye Rukovodstvo*, 1996, 314.
61 *Ibid.*, 336–337.
62 One evidence for this is Stalin's letter of August 23, 1928, to Molotov. *RGASPI*, fond. 82, op. 2, d. 1420.
63 Khlevnyuk, 1996, 81–83.
64 Especially since for a long time, and despite all his reservations, it was still Mikoyan whom Stalin regarded as his main adviser in any questions related to grain production. Pribitkov, 1995, 78–82, 87–90, 108–110.
65 *Sovietskoye Rukovodstvo*, 1999, 346–349.
66 *Ibid.*
67 Mikoyan, 1999, 300–315. Burgman was the nephew of Karolina Til, the governess of little Svetlana.
68 Berezhkov, 1998, 276–277.

Secretaries in All Shapes and Sizes

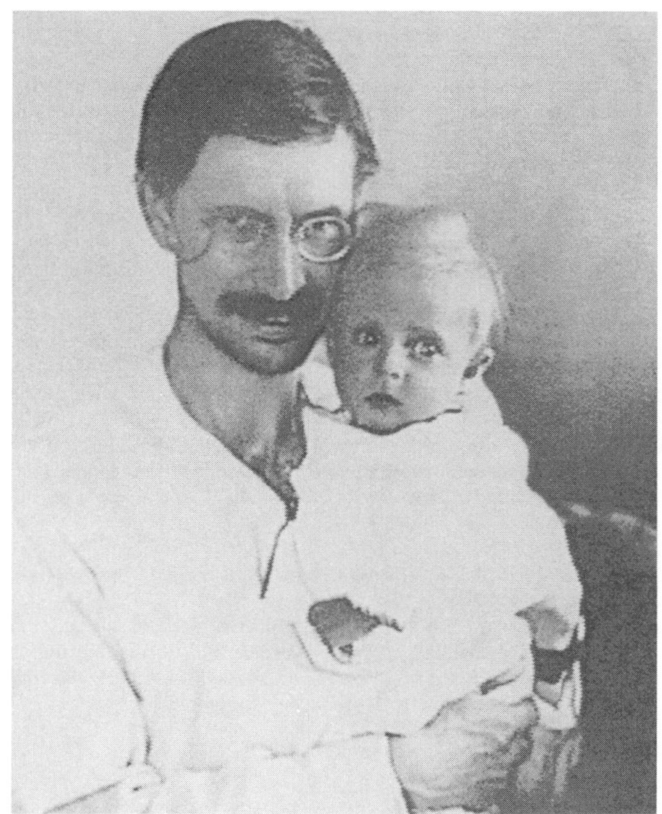

Ivan Tovstukha, the secretary of the Soviet dictator, in his adolescent years.

1923. The Stalin secretariat became increasingly omnipotent. The members of the secretariat: Kanner, Sergeyev (X), and Tovstukha on the right.

1931. The erudite party historian Ivan Tovstukha with his son, Tolya in his arms. The little child died while still young. His father also died prematurely: or one may say “in time” before the crescendo of the Great Terror. His boss, Stalin, nevertheless sent his wife to prison.

This picture was taken most likely on the day of the Orthodox Easter in 1924. Tovstukha’s daughter, Tatyana, told me that the members of the secretariat disappeared from their offices as a joke, leaving behind their boss, which made Stalin very angry.

1924. Kanner (1), Tovstukha (2), and Nazaretyan (3) with the office clerks working at the Stalin secretariat.

Behind Stalin's back, one of his favorite secretaries, Boris Dvinsky, who became Minister for Procurement after the end of the Great Patriotic War.

Lev Mekhlis, here imitating Napoleon and Stalin at once, became a deputy head of the government at the peak of his career.

CHAPTER 20
Avel Yenukidze

Avel Yenukidze.

There is nothing surprising in the fact that Anastas Mikoyan, who successfully managed to stabilize his position in the upper echelons of power, in a letter revealing his survival techniques did not even mention the name of Avel Yenukidze, who had nevertheless been one of his best friends not much earlier. The reason for this was that Yenukidze, who for long years was secretary of the Executive Committee of the Soviets of the USSR and in charge of the administration of the Kremlin, had been expelled from the party on account of his "political deviationism and dissolute lifestyle" by a decision of the Central Committee plenum held between June 5 and 7, 1935. At the same time he was stripped of all the positions he had held, including his Central Committee membership, which he had only exercised since early 1934. It was primarily the neophytes in the Stalin leadership who played a leading role in the persecution of Yenukidze, who not long before had been right at the forefront. According to Nikita Khrushchev, the veteran Bolshevik had acted as lawyer of the enemies of the working class. Andrei Zhdanov put it somewhat more harshly when he said of Yenukidze that he became a disgusting petty bourgeois, an excessive, overweight lord with Menshevik leanings, and lost his Communist façade in the meantime.[1]

The politician, who not much earlier had been regarded as omnipotent—especially in the eyes of the art world—thus suffered a massive fall in the eyes of his acquaintances. Even those who had formerly used a very humble tone in addressing him—as the largely unpublished correspondence of Yenukidze reveals—quickly forgot that they had ever known him. The great figures of the era, including the two outstanding stage directors Konstantin Stanislavsky and Vsevolod Meyerhold, had at one time inundated this multifaceted member of the Stalinist leadership with almost subservient letters: "Deeply respected Avel Safronovich! Thanks to your benevolent help, I have received from Moscow the 1,800 dollars, with which I can pay my most pressing debts. In the time agreed I will be in Moscow again, so that in the summer heat I can get back into the familiar rut and prepare for the theater season. Allow me to express my deep gratitude to you once again for treating me so kindly and considerately. With cordial greetings, your indebted follower K[onstantin] Stanislavsky," wrote the chief director of the Moscow Art Theater from Paris on June 6, 1934.[2]

A day later Stanislavsky explained in detail to "the deeply respected and dear Avel Safronovich" how grateful he was to be released temporarily from the grip of debt. He hinted at how good it would be if, before every one of his journeys abroad, he could be given 1,800 or 2,000 dollars. Then he explained that he would like to settle his foreign debts by publishing abroad a book by the title *An Actor Prepares*: "I think I will remain able to work for a while. I can do something for theater and for our art. [...] And this is all thanks to you. I will forever keep this gratitude in my memory and in my heart for the enormous help you have given me. In sincere admiration, your ever-faithful K[onstantin] Stanislavsky."[3]

The prominent Soviet artists were not so resolute in formulating their views. They pretended to consider Yenukidze "someone from their circles", a pillar of the literary and theatrical parlors. Such an attitude is shown by the letter of

Zinayda Raikh. She was the wife of Sergei Yesenin, one of the greatest Russian poets of the twentieth century, then of Vsevolod Meyerhold, the prominent theatrical director. She sent her letter to Yenukidze through a messenger on January 31, 1935, not much before his downfall: "Dear Avel Safranovich! *The Queen of Spades* envisaged by Meyerhold was finally staged by him in Leningrad. We would like to celebrate his success, since the play is adored by the audience. [...] At 10 o'clock p.m., on 1st February, a few people will be present at our house. Of your friends, the Karakhans and the Eliavas will be invited, of our friends, the Petrovskys (from Vienna) and Mr. and Mrs. Baltrusaitis. There won't be other guests. By 10 o'clock p.m., the session of the Congress[4] will be over, so no pretext will be left for you to refuse my invitation. You have to come by all means. Vs[evolod] Em[ilevich] sends his greetings and so do I. I wish you good health. Your Zinayda Raikh-Meyerhold.[5]

☆ Following the June 1935 plenum of the Central Committee, Avel Yenukidze lived for a while as a semi-exile in Abkhazia, where he carried out the formal task of directing the local resorts. Then, he vegetated in Kharkov, managing a smaller transport company.[6] In 1937, the repeatedly disgraced politician was ordered to Moscow where he was taken in chains by prison transport—commonly referred to as the "black crow"—to the Lubyanka Prison. There, by means of torture, they extracted from him the information that, along with other members of his "counter-revolutionary group"—including Levon Karakhan, the former Soviet ambassador to Ankara, and the Latvian Bolshevik Rudolf Peterson, who for a long time had been the commandant of the Kremlin—he had carried out subversive work against the Soviet power. Then in October 1937, during a closed trial all three of them were subsequently sentenced to death by firing squad and executed. The Soviet press gave the briefest of accounts of the whole affair.[7]

We now know exactly when it was that the fate of this jovial Georgian, who was kind to everyone, took a downhill turn. Up until the early 1930s Yenukidze could regard himself as blessed by fortune. He was the godfather of Stalin's second wife, Nadezhda Alliluyeva, the confidant of many old party members, and the best friend of Sergo Ordzhonikidze and Anastas Mikoyan, Stalin's two Caucasian "arms bearers". Then everything changed. The beginning of the Yenukidze affair coincided with the radical change of direction in the upper echelons of power in the early spring of 1935, for which Stalin had been waiting ever since the day of the Kirov murder. To counterbalance the witnesses of the "heroic Leninist age", the future important figures of the Great Terror now came to the fore in the Soviet party and state leadership, including Andrei Zhdanov, Nikolai Yezhov, Andrei Andreyev, Andrei Vishinsky, and Nikita Khrushchev. It is particularly interesting to note that, even as these new figures emerged, Stalin still did not get rid of Kalinin, Molotov, Kaganovich, Voroshilov, Ordzhonikidze, Mikoyan, and Yagoda, the members of the former leadership.

With the Politburo decree passed on March 3, 1935 the Master of the Kremlin sent a clear message to his old and tested vassals: if he deemed it appropriate he would not hesitate to sweep aside the former underground Bolshevik Party members, who, like Yenukidze, were otherwise loyal to him. In order to make the charge against Yenukidze credible, "Comrade Avel" was implicated in the most elaborate of cases. Inspired by Joseph Stalin, two consecutive Politburo decrees passed in March 1935 stated that, due to Yenukidze's permissive cadre policies, there were bourgeois elements working in the Kremlin's library and offices. According to the document, based on the reports of the highly imaginative secret agents, some of these elements were preparing an attempt against Stalin's life.

The lie was propagated in the lengthy, unpublished pamphlet *From Faction to Open Counterrevolution*, written between autumn 1935 and spring 1936, in an attempt to justify the first showcase trials, by Nikolai Yezhov, a secretary of the Central Committee, who dealt with the charges against Yenukidze. The diminutive politician, who, on the dictator's orders, supervised and eventually directly controlled the work of the NKVD, stated in the pamphlet that after a while Lev Kamenev's brother had taken over the leadership of the "counter-revolutionary conspiratorial group" comprising librarians, including aristocratic women.[8] According to him the "uncovered enemies" had hoped to be able to sneak into Stalin's apartment. "Kamenev counted primarily on this group. Since he [had formerly] lived in the Kremlin as well, he was familiar with what went on there. He therefore concluded that this was the easiest way to achieve the goal that had been set. The members of the group planned [...] that with the help of Yenukidze, the former secretary of the Central Executive Committee, and of his closest colleagues they would be able to get into the apartment of Comrade Stalin. [...] And if he [Stalin] let the librarians in, then the terrorists would have an opportunity to carry out the monstrous plan. Comrade Stalin, however, firmly rejected their 'services'. This was the only reason that the evil plan failed."[9]

According to Genrikh Yagoda, then in charge of NKVD, Joseph Stalin himself initiated the investigation against the librarians, code-named as "Coil" in the files of the political police.[10]

The list of suspects then became longer and longer.[11] Following the Politburo resolution of March 3, and the even more harshly termed resolution of March 27, a showcase trial was held in the Soviet capital, amidst the strictest security measures, against the Kremlin employees who had been accused of terrorism, their relatives, and their acquaintances. The main defendant was Lev Kamenev, who, as the "instigator" of the Kirov murder, had been serving a five-year prison sentence since January 1935. In the course of this trial he was sentenced to a further ten years. Avel Yenukidze, however, who, in the meantime, was severely criticized in the columns of *Pravda*, was not charged at this time. Even so, the name of this public figure, who had spent more time than most of the others in

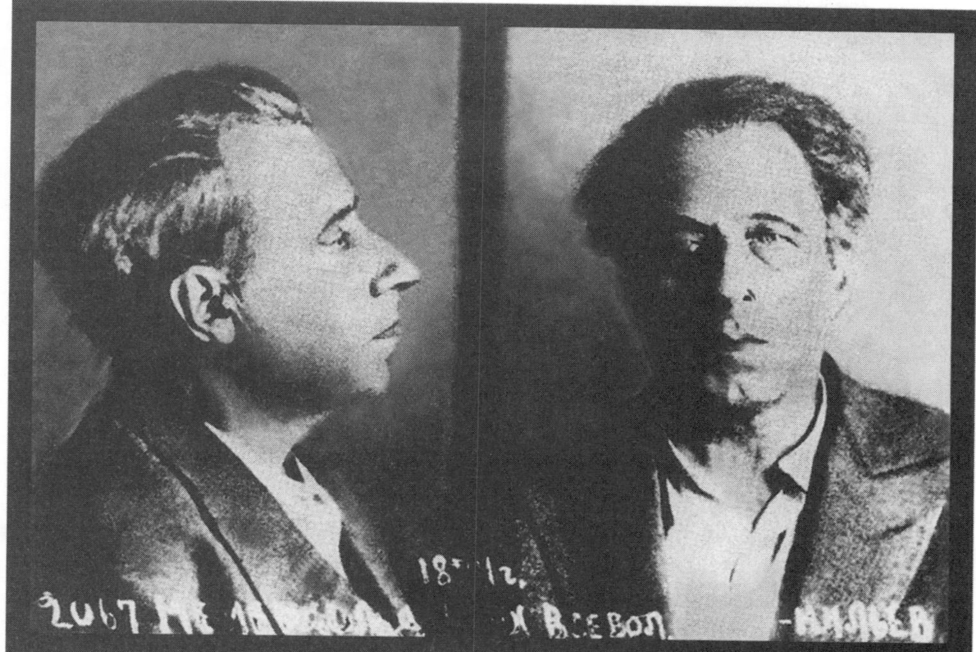

Vsevolod Meyerhold, one of the greatest experimental theater directors of the twentieth century, was Yenukidze's close acquaintance. The artist was executed on February 2, 1940, following several months of torture. His wife, Zinayda Raikh was stabbed to death by NKVD agents who pretended to be burglars, shortly after Meyerhold had been arrested. This criminalized world was not suitable any more for Avel Yenukidze, who had earlier been a servile supporter of the "Master".

the limelight, was mentioned several times during the investigations. His friends knew only too well that his arrest was only a matter of time. Thus—with the exception of Sergo Ordzhonikidze—they avoided him like the plague.[12]

As to the depravity of Avel Yenukidze, who was criticized for his "dissolute lifestyle", the Politburo decree of March 3, 1935 contains several factual elements. The reserved and easily embarrassed man, whose ostentatious debauchery was perhaps a compensation for his original shyness, did indeed abuse his position on several occasions by luring women who depended on him into his bed by the dozen. Among his papers a few private letters hinting at this have survived. In one of them, the parents of a novice ballerina express their gratitude at length in the name of their daughter who was then touring abroad. One renowned singer, who apparently had first-hand experience of the "casting couch", expressed her humble thanks to her "dear Avel Safronovich" for his help.[13] Yenukidze's frequent "affairs", however, did not come to light only in 1935: the entire Soviet party leadership, including Stalin and his circle who enjoyed partying with Yenukidze, could have known about a lot of things from the very beginning.[14]

In her very important diary Maria Korona, the wife of Alyosha Svanidze, Stalin's brother-in-law, recounts in detail the scandalous private life of the formerly influential politician. She was most outraged about the fact that Avel Yenukidze—who had been one of her husband's best friends since tsarist times—eventually tried to seduce mainly underage girls. She expressed her anger to Joseph Stalin on June 8, 1935, not long after the Politburo council on the Yenukidze case. "Since Avel had occupied such an [important] position since the Revolution, he had a huge influence on our lives for seventeen years. But he was a dissolute man! And a lecher! He tried to corrupt everything around him.

Lev Kamenev with his daughter-in-law, the actress Galina Kravchenko, shortly before his arrest. Kamenev was made the leader of the trumped up "Kremlin conspiracy" by the NKVD.

This picture shows Kamenev shortly before his execution. In the course of a year and a half, he was brought to trial three times.

He took delight in acting as a pander. He set members of the same family against one another. He seduced teenage girls."[15]

On the other hand, Leon Trotsky attributed Yenukidze's spectacular fall to Stalin's forthcoming change of political course and his persecution complex. In his essay "Outside the Kremlin Walls", which takes the form of a patchwork of memories, written in January 1938 for his emigrant journal *Byulletyn' Oppozitsii*, he stated: "Yenukidze was politically second rate, a man without personal ambitions, whose great talent was his ability to adapt to the given circumstances. [...] The biblical Avel was younger than Cain. Yenukidze, by contrast, was two years older than Stalin.[16] [...] The Kremlin's service personnel, who appreciated in Yenukidze his simplicity, kindness, and fairness, related to Stalin extremely badly."

During the factional struggles in the 1920s Trotsky seldom mentioned the name of Yenukidze, and when he did do so it was generally disparagingly. In emigration, however, he recalled what had happened in the Kremlin somewhat differently: "In order to further restrict Yenukidze's movements, Stalin made him a member of the Central Supervisory Committee. He became a member of this body, which was supposed to guard the morals of party members. Did Stalin foresee that Yenukidze would one day be called to account for his contravention of these very principles? Stalin never bothered about such anomalies. It is sufficient to remember that Rudzutak, an old Bolshevik Party member who was arrested on similar charges, was president of the Central Supervisory Committee for years. That is, the highest-ranking guardian of Soviet and party morals."

During his last years in Moscow Leon Trotsky, who had nodded his farewell to the sentenced Yenukidze, learned—according to his favorite phrase, via invisible "capillaries"—that his chief enemy Joseph Stalin owned a secret private archive in which he kept compromising documents on all the Soviet leadership. "In 1929, when Stalin openly broke away from the right-wing members of the Politburo, Bukharin, Rykov, and Tomsky, he could only force Kalinin and Voroshilov to support him by threats to expose their immorality."[17]

This is all true. However, Trotsky could not have known that, in parallel with this, the Master of the Kremlin was desperately trying to get rid of anyone who knew anything about his conflicts with his second wife, which had eventually led to her tragic death. On November 9, 1932, early in the morning, it was Avel

Yenukidze who first learned from little Svetlana's governess that Nadezhda Alliluyeva had taken her own life. The staff only dared alert Stalin afterwards.[18] In the days following the tragedy it was also Yenukidze, along with members of the Alliluyev–Redens–Svanidze clan and Molotov's wife Polina Zhemchuzhina, who kept vigil beside the broken Stalin to prevent him from harming himself. It is typical that, without exception, these sympathetic family members and friends eventually ended up in prison or before the firing squad.[19]

Yenukidze was to be first in line. Joseph Stalin struck at the pockmarked man, who like him had once been a seminarian in Tiflis, quite unexpectedly. A letter written on June 25, 1933, not so long before the showdown, reveals how Stalin pretended to be on confidential and friendly terms with the gray-haired Georgian, who had heart problems and regularly traveled to Germany for treatment: "Hello Avel! I received your letter. I didn't answer before because nothing was said in it about your health. The picture only became clear with the arrival of Rudzutak. It turns out that you do not have arteriosclerosis as the Moscow doctors said, but cardiac insufficiency due to a hypertrophy of fat. But this is not that dangerous: you must get rid of the fat and you will be healthy. Please try to stick to the diet! Get more exercise and you will be quite well. We are extending your vacation by a month. The rest is up to you.

"Things aren't going badly here. We have boosted agriculture and speeded up the production of coal. Now we want to crank up railroad transportation. In the south the harvest has already begun. In Ukraine and north Caucasia there is certain to be a good yield. And this is the most important thing. For the moment the outlook is good in other regions as well. I am in good health. I send you my greetings! Yours, Stalin."[20]

Once Yenukidze had returned from his treatment in Germany, Stalin entrusted him, along with Nikolai Bukharin and Karl Radek, with feeling out informally from German diplomats working in the Soviet capital—that is, Ambassador

Avel Yenukidze (X), who started out as a seminarist in Tiflis, and Mikhail Kalinin (XX), who had been a locksmith before 1917, learned over the course of the years how to negotiate self-confidently with the foreign guests of the Kremlin.

von Dirksen and Counsellor von Twardowski—if there was a way of improving Soviet-German relations following the Nazi takeover. According to the German ambassador Avel Yenukidze, the "high-minded, blue-eyed Georgian with his wonderful mane of hair, who obviously had German sympathies," following Hitler's rise to power, made a distinction between the "state-building" and the "propagandistic" gestures of the Nazi Empire. It is probable that, at the proposal of his patron, he attempted to persuade the German diplomats to make moves towards a rapprochement between the two states.[21]

☆ The correspondence of Avel Yenukidze reveals precisely how, for a long time, he was used by "the Master" in his manipulation of his main vassals: "M[ikhail] Ivan[ovich], Stalin would like to talk to you," he wrote diplomatically to his superior Kalinin, the formal head of the Soviet state. "His plans are as follows: 1. On the tenth anniversary of the birth of the USSR *[December 30, 1932—M. K.]* we should hold a festive convention in the Bolshoi Theater. We should invite the participants of the plenum of the Central Committee; 2. He thinks it is not expedient to declare an amnesty; 3. We can also mark this day by transferring some money to the auton[omous] and allied national republics for cultural and educational work. Please talk to him yourself about these issues. December 10, 1932. A[vel] Y[enukidze]. In fact, we have already begun drawing up a plan for the festive convention and for the transferring of the money."[22]

Besides Stalin, who manipulated the friend of his youth like a puppet, Klim Voroshilov was also on friendly terms with Yenukidze. Their relationship, too, dated back to the first years of the century when they were courting the same Jewish SR seamstress, Golda Gorbman, who came from Mardarovka, near Odessa. The three young people spent their exile in the province of Arkhangelsk. The vivacious, black-eyed Golda first became involved with Yenukidze. The handsome Georgian, however, after seducing her and making her pregnant, failed to accept the consequences of their relationship. The unhappy woman contemplated suicide. She suffered a miscarriage and was told by the local doctor that she would be unable to have another child. It was Voroshilov who was there for the abandoned Golda. A few years later he married her—now with the new name of Yekaterina—in an Orthodox Church ceremony.[23] As the years passed their regular correspondence reveals that the Voroshilov couple forgave the "womanizer Avel". For his part, he never failed to send his affectionate greetings to Yekaterina and to the couple's adopted son Petya, whenever he wrote to Voroshilov.[24]

Later in Moscow they met almost every day. Besides the memories of their years in the underground movement Yenukidze and Voroshilov were linked by a wide range of cultural political tasks: the supervision, as censors, of the Moscow Bolshoi Theater, the Art Theater, the Vakhtangov Theater and the Russian film industry. They both took care of the Frunze children, Tanya and Timur[25], who were orphaned at an early age and who spent their teenage years in the Voroshilov household. Despite this, after a time, they maintained a strict distance in their relationship, resulting from their different political positions. In the early years of the century Avel Yenukidze had been regarded as a much more famous Bolshevik militant. However, in the invisible hierarchy of the movement Klim Voroshilov, who in the late autumn of 1917 became, for a short while, head of the revolutionary militia at Petrograd, seemed to have caught up with his former fellow exile who, at the time, was working in the military soviet of the capital city. Then things changed once again. In the mid-1920s Voroshilov was given two key positions one after the other. Following the mysterious death of Mikhail

On a page of the album *Ten Years of Uzbekistan,* which was published in 1934, one can see Yenukidze (X), who was in daily contact with the representatives of the nationality regions, next to Molotov, the head of the Soviet government. A year after this book was published, the Uzbek language version came out without the figure of Avel Yenukidze.

The painter Aleksandr Rodchenko, the greatest Soviet photographic artist of his time, retouched the picture—and in the new Russian edition, which was found by David King in the Rodchenko bequest, he dropped black ink on the face of Yenukidze and the other disfavored comrades.

Frunze he was appointed to the people's commissariat for defense, and not much later became a member of the supreme body of the party state, the Politburo. From then on—although very tactfully—he gave orders *ex officio* to Yenukidze. After a few years he became used to just having to snap his fingers for "my friend Avel" to stand at his disposal in all practical questions.[26]

Reading the yellowed letters of these members of the Soviet leadership it would be easy to believe that this group of old acquaintances formed one large community. They apparently behaved like members of a family who were interested in one another's everyday concerns. "Yan [Rudzutak] is still resting, but he feels quite well," wrote Voroshilov to Yenukidze. "On the 24th [of June, 1933] I was with him at K[oba]'s *dacha*. Yan gave us a detailed account of everything [...] and told us about you. K[oba] listened carefully and questioned Yan in detail about your life abroad and the treatment you were receiving. This Koba is a wonderful man! It is inconceivable how he manages to unite the enormous brains of a proletarian strategist, the huge will of a statesman and a revolutionary, and the soul of an unaffected, good comrade who takes care of everyone. He remembers even the tiniest things in connection with people whom he knows, loves, and appreciates. It is good that we have such a Koba."[27] Scarcely a month later, on August 30, 1933, Avel Yenukidze got down to penning a similar "love letter", amounting to a declaration of political loyalty and written on the occasion of Joseph Stalin's summer tour that took in the river Volga and the south Russian cities: "I was very happy that you were with Soso. Firstly, I was sure that while you walked together you would see many pleasurable and delightful sights. Secondly, that you would come across faults, errors, and unsolved problems that you would be able to deal with on the spot. I came to this same conclusion in relation to your journey in the eastern regions of the USSR, and also when, with Soso and Kirov,[28] you visited the north. In this case, however, you were traveling through locations (towns and villages) which you and Soso conquered with bare chests from our enemies *[during the Civil War—M. K.]*."[29]

In the meantime the omnipotent Soviet dictator was working on how he could get rid of the "faithful Avel" as soon as possible. However, the chosen victim was incapable of believing this. He had no real inkling of what was awaiting him when, as a result of the Politburo decision of March 3, 1935, he was ordered to take over control of the local Central Executive Committee, the nominal body of power of the three Transcaucasian Soviet republics. At first sight it did not appear to be a particularly harsh punishment. Yenukidze, like other *apparatchiks* who were dismissed at around that time, also hoped that he would get away with a party disciplinary hearing. He did not think it impossible that the wrath of Koba would fade and that he would then be given another position in Moscow, if possible somewhere in the theater world so dear to his heart. "Dear Kliment Yefremovich! I wrote to the Central Committee and the Central Executive Committee [of the Soviets], informing them as to how many bodies I had been a member of. However, I received no reply," he complained to Voroshilov on March 17, 1935. "I myself would love to remain a member of the theater committees, the Pushkin Committee *[which was founded in 1935 to prepare for the memorial events around the one-hundredth anniversary of the great Russian poet's death—M. K.]*, of the Red Cross, and other social-cultural bodies. But I am writing this for your eyes only."[30]

A few days later Yenukidze realized that if he was removed from the Kremlin he would soon have to leave the Soviet capital as well. He did his best to avoid this. In a letter dated March 22, 1935 he asked Voroshilov and Ordzhonikidze, those nearest him, to try to represent his interests before "the Master". As a sign of his "penitence" he humbly informed his friends that he entirely agreed with the new decision of the Politburo, dated March 21, which severely condemned him for a second time. "I would have liked to write directly to S[talin], or to visit him. But I didn't have the strength, I am so devastated by this. [...] You—and S[talin] even more—must really understand that following the Politburo's letter and the just charges against me, I am unable to travel to Tiflis to work. I am willing to take the lowest position on the orders of the Central Committee, as long as it is not in Transcaucasia.[31] These are not words of false shame and pride. I am simply incapable, mentally and physically, of becoming the president of the local

According to Dmitry Likhachev, who spent his sentence on the prison island of Solovki, Stalin differed from his predecessors only in degree: under his rule, the terror started by Lenin and Trotsky only intensified and the number of victims reached the millions.

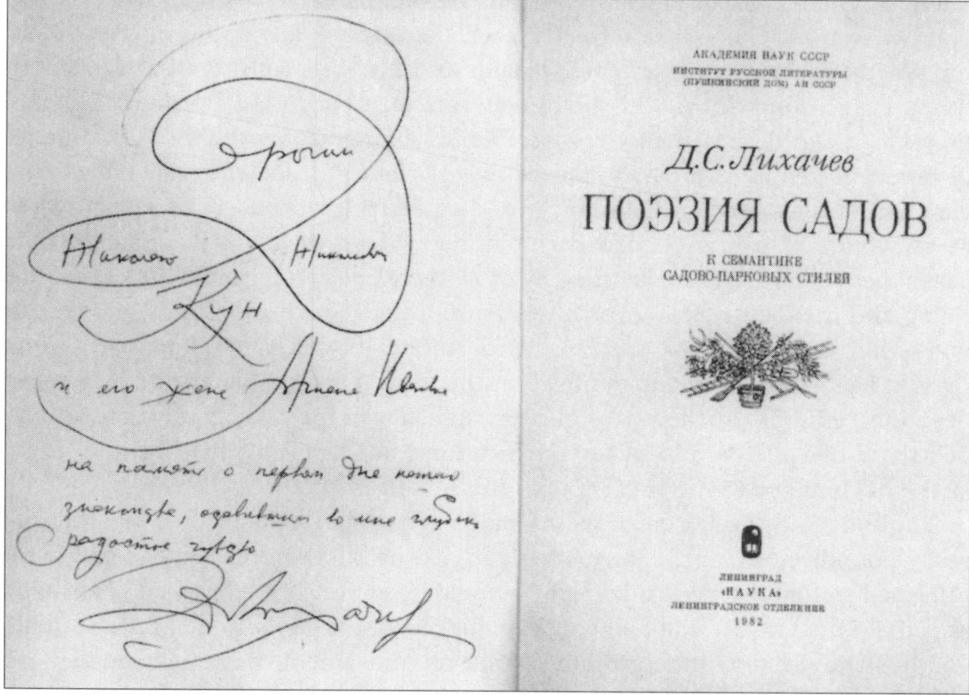

Дорогим
Николаю Николаевичу
Кун
и его жене Арине Ивановне
на память о первом дне нашего
знакомства, оставившем во мне глубокое
радостное чувство
Д. Лихачев

АКАДЕМИЯ НАУК СССР
ИНСТИТУТ РУССКОЙ ЛИТЕРАТУРЫ
(ПУШКИНСКИЙ ДОМ) АН СССР

Д.С. Лихачев

ПОЭЗИЯ САДОВ

К СЕМАНТИКЕ
САДОВО-ПАРКОВЫХ СТИЛЕЙ

ЛЕНИНГРАД
«НАУКА»
ЛЕНИНГРАДСКОЕ ОТДЕЛЕНИЕ
1982

Central Executive Committee. […] In the name of our old friendship and as comrades I beg you to help fulfill my request. Yours as ever, A[bel] Yenukidze."[32]

However, the craven coward Voroshilov did nothing for Yenukidze, and with this the correspondence between the two men came to an end. The people's commissar for defense, who maneuvered much more successfully in power intrigues than on the battlefield, understood that the dictator had *forever* written off his fellow countryman. On September 8, 1935 Stalin wrote of Yenukidze with complete contempt to Lazar Kaganovich: "I have attached [...] the NKVD reports on the 'Yenukidze group', which consists exclusively of 'old Bolsheviks', old farts, to use Lenin's phrase. Yenukidze is a stranger to us. It makes me wonder why Sergo [Ordzhonikidze] is still on friendly terms with him. That is all for now. Greetings, J. Stalin."[33]

In the meantime, Genrikh Yagoda, one of the chief initiators of the Great Terror, was sent to the "internal" prison of Lubyanka. In his totally absurd "confessions" worded in advance by the interrogating officers, Yenukidze's name was frequently mentioned.[34] Later, during the Great Trial held in March 1938 (Bukharin and Rykov being the two main defendants), Yagoda was forced to repeat his slanders. Up to the last minute, the authorities feared that, due to his weak nerves, the ex-boss of NKVD would refuse to make a confession at this show-trial in accordance with what had been beaten out of him during his interrogation. Therefore, his old confidant, Vladimir Kirson, the playwright, who was also arrested, in the meantime and who was executed soon after performing his task, was planted in his cell. Kirson, not much earlier Stalin's favorite author, wrote a short report on this meeting to his detainers. This piece of writing is presumably the most horrible example of the denunciations of this era, also a typical document. It reveals how much a humiliated human being debased himself in the Soviet totalitarian dictatorship which was just as inhuman as the Nazi regime. It also makes clear why Yagoda undertook the role of the star witness in this purge trial. The leaders of the political police initially intended a similar role for Avel Yenukidze, as well.[35] However, finally, the Yenukidze case was separately handled as a closed trial.

It has not been known so far whether Yenukidze felt any pangs of conscience for strictly following the orders of Stalin and his associates. But whatever the frame of his mind during this time, he was a member of the Bolshevik generation which can be made fully responsible for extinguishing the lives of millions of innocent people. This was pointed out by Dmitry Likhachev—the academician and famous literary historian, who died recently at the age of 93 and who, in his youth, also himself had been imprisoned on the Solovki prison island. Later, he worked at the construction of *Belomorkanal*, the canal connecting the Baltic and the White Seas, a project costing hundreds of thousands of lives. In one of his last writings, he tried to dispel "the myth which, for some mysterious reason, has persisted in our minds, that the most merciless period of repression began in 1936–37. I believe that one day statistics of the revengeful persecutions will show that the wave of arrests, executions, and banishments began as early as the beginning of 1918, before the official start of the 'Red Terror'."[36]

The endgame of the Yenukidze case is clear proof that Stalin's revenge was literally boundless: since his bachelor friend had no children his brother had to be punished so that the Yenukidze family would be entirely exterminated. This happened despite the fact that Semyon Yenukidze—also a good friend of Stalin in his youth—who in the underground Bolshevik movement was nicknamed "the black", and also "Cain" to distinguish him from the red-haired Avel, had always tried to keep a low profile when his brother was mentioned. The masters of the Kremlin regarded him as a sound economic expert and in particular as a reliable cadre. Thus for years he directed the State Mint, under the joint control of the people's commissariat for finance and the NKVD. The members of the Central Committee—an ever-decreasing number due to Stalin's purges—passed a decree on June 15, 1937: he would be dismissed and a certain Semyonov, the director of *Pravda*'s printing house, would take over his post. Joseph Stalin, however, did not find simple dismissal sufficient: "I would find appropriate the dismissal and arrest of Yenukidze. Semyonov should replace him," he wrote casually on the document placed in front of him.[37] And there was no arguing with this.

1 Conquest, 1974, 175–176.
2 *RGASPI*, fond. 667, op. 1, d. 16.
3 *Ibid.*
4 The meeting of the Central Executive Committee, the titular Soviet parliament.
5 *RGASPI*, fond. 667, op. 1, d. 16. Salva Eliava was a noted Georgian politician working in the Soviet capital. Petrovsky was a Soviet diplomat and intelligence agent living in Vienna. Baltrusaitis was a famous symbolist writer, who wrote originally in Russian at the turn of the century, and in the first half of the 1930s he was a cultural attaché of Lithuania in Moscow.
6 *Reabilitatsia*, 2000, vol. I, 428.
7 *Pravda*, December 19, 1937.
8 The residents of the Kremlin owned enormous libraries, as they were entitled to receive copies of every published book and journal. These people were mostly uneducated, thus unable to find their way in the piles of books. It is interesting that most political leaders were able to obtain "enemy literature" as well. Stalin, for example, regularly received fourteen different White emigré journals. *RGASPI*, fond. 71, op. 3, d. 14. At first, his library managed by Shushanika Manucharyants, Lenin's former personal librarian. She communicated with Stalin in writing, asking about how to expand the stock of books and what kinds of shelves she should order. *RGASPI*, fond. 558, op. 1, d. 2723. On March 8, 1926, the Master of the Kremlin even dedicated his book *Questions of Leninism* to her. *RGASPI*, fond. 558, op. 1, d. 2764. Before soon, however, the librarian herself was very rarely allowed to enter Stalin's library hall. "He did not let anyone near his books, and maintained the library himself," recalled Kirov's sister-in-law, Sofia Markus, who once even hinted to Stalin that refined people always get a librarian "to put the books on the shelves in the correct order." But it seems that the idea did not work with the Soviet dictator. After a librarian came, "Comrade Stalin did not find any books without looking first in the catalogues. So he reordered his books according to his will." *RGASPI*, fond. 558, op. 4, d. 649.
9 *RGASPI*, fond. 671, op. 1, d. 274.
10 Yagoda, 1997, 189–190.
11 From among the more than one hundred defendants, twenty-six was executed immediately after the sentences were read, including Kamenev's brother and his wife, who was a librarian in the Kremlin. *Ibid.*, 427–428.
12 At the same time the Soviet leaders made an ideology out of their cowardice. Hearing about the Yenukidze case, Nikolai Bukharin made the remark "the bureaucracy is depraving". See Larina, 1989, 94.
13 *RGASPI*, fond. 667, op. 1, d. 16.
14 *RGASPI*, fond. 667, op. 1, d. 17.
15 *Iosif Stalin v obyatiakh semyi*, 1993, 182.
16 In fact, only one year older.
17 Trotsky, 1991, 233, 237, 241, 242.
18 Alliluyeva, 1981, 104.
19 See pages 217 and 422 in this book.
20 *Sovietstkoye Rukovodstvo*, 1999, 240–241.
21 Dirksen, 1952, 118.
22 *Sovietstkoye Rukovodstvo*, 1999, 196.
23 Vasilyeva, 1995, 190–191. I heard the same from Polina Vinogradskaya, who knew Yekaterina Voroshilova well.
24 *RGASPI*, fond. 74, op. 2, d. 41.
25 *RGASPI*, fond. 74, op. 2, d. 153; see also Galagan-Trifonova, 1995, 5–11.
26 *RGASPI*, fond. 74, op. 2, d. 41.
27 *Sovietstkoye Rukovodstvo*, 1999, 241–242.
28 Among other things, they visited the work projects on the Gulag archipelago.
29 *Sovietstkoye Rukovodstvo*, 1999, 252.
30 *Ibid.*, 304.
31 At the time, the three Soviet republics, Azerbaijan, Armenia, and Georgia formed an alliance within the Soviet Union, under the name Transcaucasian Federation.
32 *Sovietstkoye Rukovodstvo*, 1999, 305.
33 *RGASPI*, fond. 81, op. 3, d. 100.
34 Yagoda, 1997, 169–179, 181, 189–190, 197, 214.
35 From personal communication with Viktor Ilyin, a former high-ranking officer of NKVD. He recalled many details from the first phase of the Bukharin trial, as he himself was also present at the arrest of the politician. Later Ilyin was imprisoned, too, and spent many years in solitary confinement.
36 Likhachev, 1997, 11.
37 *RGASPI*, fond. 17, op. 163, d. 1157. Before soon, Semyon Yenukidze's wife was also arrested.

Journey through the Gulag

Stalin and Voroshilov inspect the work of the Gulag prisoners, the recently opened section of the Moscow-Volga Canal.

Idyllic picture on a small sloop, off the coast of Abkhazia. Sitting at the table, from the left: Vasya, Stalin's son, Lakoba, Kalinin, Beria, Svetlana, the General Secretary's daughter, and, at the end, Stalin himself.
The sailors and bodyguards watch respectfully.

CHAPTER 21
A Correspondance Discovered

On November 9, 1932, on the morning after the tragic death of his wife, Joseph Stalin did not have the strength to tell his half-orphaned children that from then on he would raise them on his own. He sent six-year-old Svetlana and eleven-year-old Vasya to the distant village of Sokolovka, and left the unpleasant task to one of the closest friends of the family, Klim Voroshilov. "Towards the end of the day Kliment Yefrimovich [Voroshilov] visited us. He took us out for a walk. He tried to play a game with us but he was crying all the time," was how Stalin's daughter recalled that terrible day decades later.[1]

In the mid-1930s the childless Voroshilov couple would sometimes have little Svetlana and Vasya for days at a time. There were always several "foster children" around in their home. These friends of their son Petya, whom they had officially adopted during the Civil War, would sometimes stay for months with them in the Kremlin. Following the early death of Mikhail Frunze and his wife, Klim Voroshilov became one of the official guardians of Timur and Tanya, the orphans of the people's commissar for defense, and from 1931 the two children lived in the Voroshilov household.[2]

The affectionate marshal later took care of his grandchildren, and even of the children living around him. On the other hand, in a letter written on March 19,

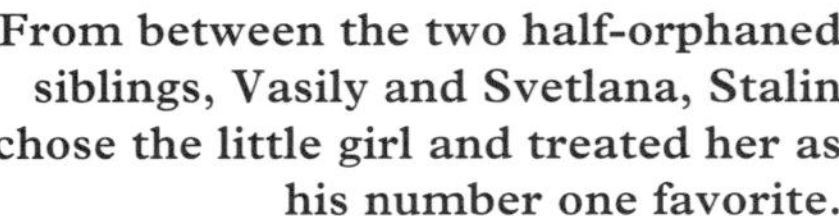

From between the two half-orphaned siblings, Vasily and Svetlana, Stalin chose the little girl and treated her as his number one favorite.

1935 to Stalin, Molotov, and Kalinin, it was he who recommended the execution of a nine-year-old(!) boy, who had stabbed and wounded the thirteen-year-old son of the deputy public prosecutor of Moscow.[3] According to Soviet customary law at the time, minors could be executed "only" from the age of twelve. However, the ruling was regularly ignored by NKVD officers (especially in the the Gulag). From 1937 onwards, the people's commissar for internal affairs, Yezhov himself took charge of the "struggle" against the children of the "people's enemies".[4]

Even years later the graying marshal, who was particularly devastated by the fact that the fatal quarrel between Stalin and Nadezhda Alliluyeva had taken place in his apartment, would burst into tears whenever his mission to Sokolovka was mentioned. After the death of "the Master", he could be seen to wipe tears from his eyes on the rare occasions that he encountered one of Stalin's children. "I have known you since the day you were born. I even looked after you. [...] We were neighbors in Tsaritsyn. Stalin lived with your mother, his fiancée at the time, and I lived with Yekaterina Davidovna and Petya,"[5] he told Vasily Stalin on April 9, 1960, soon after Vasiliy's release from solitary confinement in the Vladimir Prison. Voroshilov had been ordered by the Soviet party leadership to have an in-depth talk with Vasily, whose breath reeked of alcohol. Voroshilov reminded him that there were permanent complaints about his constant drunkenness, scandalous behavior, and even his "political aberrance". "You have been in prison because you deserved it," he told the graying Vasily, whom he had once dandled on his knees. "Now that you've been released, just watch what you do. Behave yourself! Look at your younger sister. Svetlana lives just as she ought. Nobody writes petitions about her *[to the party leadership and the KGB—M. K.]*. She loves you. But your behavior is dreadful. If you pull yourself together and be strong you have a chance of improving yourself." At this point the marshal, by then an elderly man, "let slip" something in a way that can scarcely be regarded as accidental: "Bear in mind that there may well be agents provocateurs among those whose company you keep. People sent here by our enemies." He regarded this as so important that he repeated it at the end of the conversation that had been somewhat embarrassing for both parties. "Don't talk to such people! You might give something away in your drunkenness. They will embellish it and exaggerate what you have said. And you will be in serious trouble once again."[6]

By that time, of course, the mixture of tender attention and terror that had surrounded the children of Joseph Stalin, the common orphans of the Bolshevik elite, immediately following their mother's death in November 1932, was a thing of the past. No one suspected then that Svetlana would one day be forced to reject the name Stalina, nor that her brother still wearing the mourning-band would shout drunkenly, in the summer of 1953, "You bastards, you killed my father!"—which resulted in his being sentenced to solitary confinement. Following detention in the prison in Vladimir, under the byname Vasily Pavlovich Vasilyev he was to pace the very same corridors in which, on the orders of his much-feared father, two of his aunts—Anna, who went mad in prison, and the broken Yevgenia—had earlier walked day by day without hope. (According to one version Vasily Stalin chose his own byname: the name Pavlovich could have been inspired by his uncle, Pavel Alliluyev. At the same time, the common name Vasilyev had occasionally been used by the Soviet dictator during the Second World War. In tsarist times "Comrade Vasily" had been one of Iosif Dzhugashvili's bynames, although not one that he had used frequently.)

But to return to the late autumn of 1932: the residents of the Kremlin did everything they could to spread as widely as possible the idea that the widowed

Stalin was a "model parent", who devoted much of his free time to the upbringing of his children.

In reality, nothing could have been more alien to the character of the dictator, a man who enjoyed playing with much higher stakes. Nevertheless, it seems he was aware of the valuable role of "simple human gestures" in increasing his popularity, which had been shattered by the suicide of his wife. It was perhaps for this reason that Stalin had a photograph of his children published in a wide-circulation children's journal. "Hello, mistress of the house! How are you?" he wrote playfully to his daughter in an undated letter. "I am sending you a copy of *Pionerskaya Pravda.* Treasure it. There is a photograph of you and Vasya inside. Write to me more often: your little secretary *[Joseph Stalin himself—M. K.]* will soon not know what to do if he doesn't receive your daily orders and commands." The letter, written in blue pencil, ends as follows: "When will you be in Sochi? Your daddy, the little secretary of Setanka *[Svetlana's pet name—M. K.]*, the mistress of the house, J. Stalin."[7]

The dictator also used the columns of *Pionerskaya Pravda* to send "messages", but not with such a playful tone. In early 1937, when he had had his former good friend and ally Nikolai Bukharin imprisoned, he informed him via Voroshilov that if he accepted a lead role in the forthcoming show trial his relatives would not be harmed.[8] In order to drive home the message he had a reporter from *Pionerskaya Pravda* write an article about the school class in which Svetlana Gurvich, Bukharin's daughter by his second marriage, was a pupil. But Stalin did not keep his word on this occasion, either. Bukharin suffered such mental torture in prison that he underwent a complete personality change: he inundated the Master of the Kremlin with "love letters". Even so, the dictator's revenge still reached almost every member of the family of *Bukharchik*, as Stalin had earlier nicknamed him. Bukharin's crippled wife Nadezhda Lukina going about on crutches and affected by severe heart disease, from whom he had been separated for many years, was executed.[9] One of Bukharin's brothers, Vladimir, and the politician's third wife, Anna Larina, were sent to a prison camp. At the end of the 1940s this same fate awaited his second wife, Esfiry Gurvich, and eventually her daughter Svetlana, who was once the playmate of the other little Svetlana in Zubalovo.

Almost no one knew about this. Following the death of his wife, the private life of the Master of the Kremlin remained hidden. With the partial opening of the former Soviet party archives, historians dealing with Stalin's career began to look for the "playful correspondence" conducted between the tyrant and his daughter up until the outbreak of the Second World War. For a long time it seemed that the many notes had been lost for good, except for only a dozen and a half notes, which Svetlana Alliluyeva published in her autobiography *Twenty Letters to a Friend*—and even those in abridged versions.[10]

A few years ago, however, I came across the photocopies of sixty, so far unpublished, letters and notes in Moscow.[11] Most of them were the "daily orders" issued by the young Svetlana to her father. The little girl addressed her letters "To my Secretary Number 1", and sometimes "To my little secretary-of-sorts", or "To my little secretary". Members of the Politburo—Molotov, Zhdanov, Voroshilov, and others—were also referred to as "secretaries", and numbers were added to their names in the order in which they figured in her life. These numbers are a curious reflection of the places they occupied in her father's "court".

Stalin, who had invented the correspondence game, always answered in writing, without delay, to every piece of "official correspondence", initially written

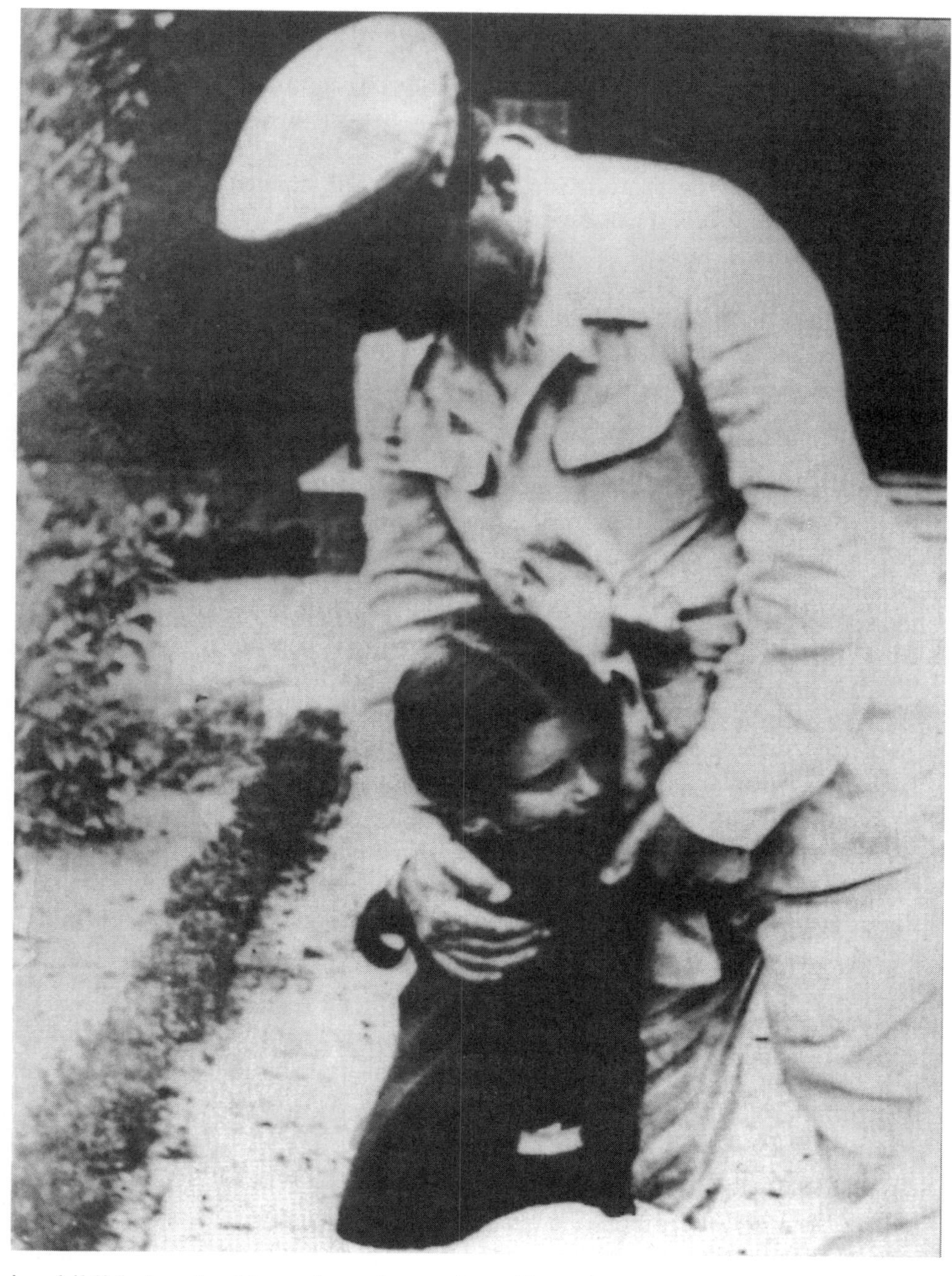

The little Svetlana hugs her "little secretary".

in childish handwriting, then almost in calligraphy, and with a five-hand star stamped at the bottom of the page. "Svetlana is constantly fidgeting about near her father, and he caresses his daughter, kisses her, admires her, feeds her from his plate, and chooses her the tastiest morsels," noted a moved Maria Korona in her diary. "The little girl, in her 'Order Number 4', asked her father to let her spend her holiday (the 6th, 7th, and 8th), in Lipki. He has a resort house here. It was Nadyusha [Nadezhda Alliluyeva] who chose the place, although the building was only finished after her death."[12] I discovered this very "daily order" among the copies, although with a different number: "Daily Order Number 7: November 3, [19]34. I order you to allow me to travel to Lipki on the evening of the 5th, and to spend the 6th, 7th, and 8th there. Setanka, the mistress of the house." At the end of the note comes the inevitable reply in red pencil: "I obey. Setanka's little secretary. St[alin]."[13]

A few days later, on November 6, 1934, Maria Korona returned in her diary to the subject of this correspondence, which had begun after the death of Nadezhda Alliluyeva: "During dinner there was a big commotion. Svetlana wrote an order to her father: 'I order you to allow me to go to the theater or to a movie with you.' She signed it 'Setanka, the mistress of the house'. Then she addressed it: 'To my 1rst *[sic]* Secretary, Comrade Stalin.' She handed the note to Iosif, who merely said: 'Well, what else can I do? I obey.' They played like that for a year. So, Svetlana is lady of the house here. She has secretaries, the '1st Secretary' is daddy, then come Kaganovich, Molotov, Ordzhonikidze, Kirov, and the others. [...] Svetlana writes daily orders, Iosif signs them, and then they are pinned with drawing pins to the wall next to the telephone [...]. Nor does daddy ever deny his daughter's requests."[14]

This was indeed the case. On June 15, 1934, Joseph Stalin wrote to his daughter: "Hello Setanochka! I received your letter. I see that you have still not forgotten your daddy. That makes me very happy. I am well, but it's quite boring here without you. Your daily orders do not arrive, so your little secretary is bored. I am sending you some postcards. Have a look at them. Perhaps you will like them. All your secretaries send their greetings. Please do not forget them. And send us as many orders as possible! Kisses to my beautiful mistress of the house. Your good father."[15]

The Master of the Kremlin sometimes referred to himself in the third person when writing to his daughter. In a letter dated April 8, 1936, written in purple ink, he was clearly poking fun at the Politburo sessions: "Greetings and humble reverences to Svetlana, the mistress of the House, from her little secretary, Comrade Stalin. Comrade Mistress of the House! Your little secretaries received your letter and we discussed its contents to our great satisfaction. Your letter enabled us to find our way in some complicated international and domestic political questions. Write to us often, Comrade Mistress of the House! We positively demand it. I am in good health (Vasya too), but you are greatly missed. It is too bad that the mistress of the House is not with me. Warm kisses to you, my little sparrow, my great joy. Your father, J. Stalin."[16]

Evidently, Stalin sometimes ran out of ideas as to what to write to his daughter; then he simply gave some rather long-winded answers showing feigned respect. "July 2, 1938. Hello, my little sparrow! I received both your letters. I didn't answer the first one because it contained no order to do so. At first I thought I would answer anyway, but then I abandoned the idea. I realized that you had given no order, therefore I had no right to answer. In your other letter, however, there is an order for an immediate answer. Since I dare not displease you, my little sparrow, I have decided to answer. You asked me how I am and whether I am well. I'm not doing badly and am quite well. It's a little boring here, but what can be done? One has to accept things as they are. Is there good fishing there *[in Mukhalatka, a government resort on the coast of the Black Sea—M. K.]*? If there is a good catch, my little sparrow, send me a few dozen sculpin. Well then, best wishes to you, my little sparrow! I send my very warmest kisses. Your little secretary, Stalin, the poor peasant."[17]

During the summer holiday, the little princess almost daily corresponded with her "subordinates". Once, she sent an autographed photograph to Károly Pauker, regarded as her "surrogate father", as if the bodyguard had been a public figure. (Incidentally, the photograph was of a cat.) She kept urging her "little secretary" not to worry about her. For instance, it is evident from her undated letter from Zheleznovodsk in the northern Caucasus, that her escorts had en-

The main protagonist of the playful correspondence between the father and his "mistress of the house" was not the little Svetlana but Stalin himself.

sured for her the same comfort she had been used to in Moscow. "I like Zheleznovodsk. I do feel fine here, I am not bored. I have two girl-friends. We are playing, walking around and learning German together. Besides the German lessons, I also attend music lessons. I am playing the piano almost all day.[18]

In front of the other "secretaries" of the "little mistress of the house" the much-feared Stalin for a long time tried to create the impression that he danced to his daughter's tune.[19] In 1936, he took her to spend their holiday together in Gagri, at the coast of the Black Sea. When had to leave, he left behind his car with driver and bodyguard at her disposal.[20] Whenever one of his bodyguards brought him one of her "urgent daily orders" Stalin would put everything else aside and, with a wry smile, would immediately pen a humble answer, which he occasionally discussed in detail with the leaders of the country. In imitation of the bureaucratic style of official correspondence he would sometimes even make them sign the notes, in which he referred to his addressee as "my little sparrow", "my little fly", "my little mistress of the house", or "the meaning of my life". In order to write to his daughter, the General Secretary of the party would even, on occasion, set aside the thick "albums" brought to him, usually late in the afternoon, by Nikolai Yezhov, the head of the NKVD, who needed Stalin to sign the list of those to be liquidated. Photographs of these people were attached to their brief, typed biographies, by way of reminder. Stalin, his immediate colleagues, and his provincial governors eventually did little more than flick through all the names on the long lists. The procedure gave rise to another "indirect" euphemism: a decision made in "album order" (in Russian, '*v albomnom poryadke*'), i.e. "according to a list", meant a decision to execute, just like the phrase "the highest level of social defense", which also referred to execution.[21]

There were, however, days when Stalin was in a bad mood. On such occasions he would slap his daughter's face with the back of his hand, although this did not happen as frequently as he hit his son Vasya.[22] According to László Pollacsek, the ear, nose, and throat specialist who treated the Stalin family, the Master of the Kremlin once broke the teenage Vasya's nose. Together with the traumatologist he had the task of treating the child's face. The boy was apparently ashamed of the episode and told the doctors that he had accidentally walked into a chest of drawers at home. Károly Pauker, however, who took the child to the Kremlin hospital, whispered the truth to his fellow countryman in Hungarian, in the presence of the others. Unlike Vasya, Svetlana maintained a deep silence in her memoirs about the slaps she had received at her father's hand. She was far more keen to recall the kindness of "her little secretary" during the weekends they spent together in the Zubalovo *dacha*. Her father's friendliness touched her all the more, since it was in such contrast with her mother's coldness.[23]

Levon Shaumyan who was befriended with the dictator's family, told me on several occasions, during our meetings in Moscow, how he had the impression that Stalin was competing with his dead wife for his daughter's affections. It was as if he wanted to prove to the little Svetlana that he, the good father, was far better than his dead wife, Nadezhda. "I didn't understand this," said Shaumyan. "Then on one occasion Varo Dzhaparidze, that beautiful woman whose husband, along with my father, was executed by the SR Detachment in 1918 at the command of the English, and whose daughter Lyusya, like my younger brother and I, was regarded as one of Stalin's "foster children", well, she warned me: 'The whole family is sheer pathology. Don't visit them so often in the Kremlin! You're better off knowing as little as possible about them!'"[24]

Svetlana, "who looked like her grandmother, Comrade Stalin's mother, was of a slightly withdrawn and reserved nature," Nikolai Vlasik, one of Stalin's favorite bodyguards, recalled.[25] He must have, however, referred to her childhood.

☆ According to the recollections of the Alliluyev family, in the 1930s the Master of the Kremlin was occasionally bored by Svetlana and tried to get her out of his way. Even so, the family was still surprised by the fact that, during the war, the loving relationship between father and daughter deteriorated. But Stalin had been offended and jealous of her even before this. Svetlana was only thirteen when, during a holiday in Georgia, in the company of her bodyguards, she had visited the picturesque Lake Ritsa with a boy. The incident was immediately reported to Stalin, who was consumed with jealousy. "I have learned that you have been to Lake Ritsa, and not alone but with a male escort. Well, fancy that! What am I to say? Lake Ritsa is a lovely place, especially when one has a cavalier, my little sparrow...," he wrote in a letter sent by courier on June 8, 1938.[26] That the incident was blown up into a real "case" is proved by the fact that a year later, when Svetlana visited the same place again—accompanied by her brother Vasily, who was visiting a nearby game farm—she was obliged to give an account of her visit to her father: "This time I was there without a 'cavalier'."[27]

According to former residents of the Kremlin, in the summer of 1940 Joseph Stalin then "froze out" Sergo, Beria's handsome son, to whom Svetlana had been attracted for a long time. The disappointed youngster then began to court Marfa Peshkova, the granddaughter of Gorky, whom he eventually married. The stubborn Svetlana, unable to accept defeat, tried in response to undermine the relationship between her best childhood friend and Sergo. Before the marriage she visited Lavrenty Beria's wife Nina and told her that her future daughter-in-law had inherited a serious lung disease from her grandfather, Maksim Gorky. At the same time Svetlana alarmed Yekaterina Peshkova, Marfa's grandmother, who, as a Red Cross representative, had helped many Soviet political prisoners over a long period of time and who enjoyed great public respect, by saying that the members of Beria's family were, without exception, a bad lot. However, these below-the-belt blows did not achieve the desired result.[28]

As the little girl matured into a young woman such conflicts became a permanent feature in her life. The first major scandal arose when Svetlana fell in love with a scriptwriter, Aleksei Kapler, who was many years her senior. Stalin began to behave offensively towards his daughter. At the end of his life he even used obscenities to "his one and only Setalochka" in front of his court. The breaking point in their relationship came with the appearance in the girl's life of her first suitor, "the dissolute filmmaker", who wanted to claim her innocence and, even worse, to control her. Stalin did everything to undermine the woman in Svetlana: "Take a look at yourself!" he shouted at her. "Who could possibly want you?"[29]

The Master of the Kremlin gave this signed photograph of Svetlana to Aleksandr Belyakov, the pilot exploring the Arctic.

"Perhaps he was irritated by the fact that I did not look like my mother. For a long time I was a sporty youngster and he felt the lack of something in my appearance. Then my inner self began to irritate him," wrote Svetlana, referring mysteriously to the Freudian roots of the conflict with her father. However, she immediately added: "But I have grown up, and the childhood games and pleasures that so amused my father have been left behind in the distant past."[30]

The Soviet dictator's daughter indeed changed dramatically during her teenage years. The gangling Svetlana, who had gone on playing with her dolls for years, who had spoken with affected childishness, and who had ruled over an army of bodyguards and governesses, had become, by the age of twenty-one, a seriously neurotic, jealous young woman, who resembled her father in his youth. She was driven by a relentless need to prove herself, which stemmed from the inferiority complex that she had inherited from her mother. In addition, like Nadezhda Alliluyeva, the former "little mistress of the house" suffered from alternating bouts of depression and euphoria. Early in her life she displayed signs of hypersexuality, inherited from her maternal grandmother, which, as a teenager, she was only able to repress with great effort, just like the manic need to keep changing place, which had been a lifelong characteristic of her maternal grandfather. In addition to her unbalanced parents, the anomalies she experienced around Stalin and the shocking scenes she witnessed in the Kremlin, in the "House on the Embankment", and at the government resorts, all left their mark on her. I heard this, among others, from Ivan Gronsky, the former editor in chief of *Izvestia.* The former confidant of Stalin himself had suffered the pains of hell. Then, due to his old friend, Molotov, he was rehabilitated. After more than one and a half decades spent in prisons and prison camps, he became Svetlana's colleague in the Gorky Institute of World Literature in the second half of the 1950s. "Today, with L. A. Shatunovskaya, I visited Svetlana Stalina's aunt," he recorded in his diary. "Shatunovskaya, as well as Yevgenia Aleksandrovna [Alliluyeva], complained that Svetlana is not interested in working. She would like to leave the Institute of World Literature and in general does not behave as she should. We talked a lot about the fact that, by temperament, she greatly resembles her grandmother *[Olga Alliluyeva, who, as a young woman, was widely known as a man-eater—M. K.]*. This will bring her a great deal of trouble."[31]

At the same time Svetlana was smarter, and in her own way more erudite, than her two brothers, as well as more self-sufficient. Following the death of Stalin, however, she faced one traumatic experience after another. This was what prompted her decision, in the early 1960s, to unburden her soul by telling the world the tragic story of the Alliluyev–Svanidze–Redens family, and above all that of her own mother, who had been destroyed by Stalin. However, as soon as she took up her pen the fear that had been drummed into her since her early childhood, and the hypocrisy that had become second nature to her through her proximity to her father, got the better of her. Even so her books, which at certain points broke through the earlier complete embargo on information, created huge waves in the West. However, in the middle of the 1980s, in the context of a curious collaboration with the Soviet political police, she publicly denied these books, claiming that they had been worded mostly by CIA experts rather than her.[32]

It is also notable that, following her escape in 1967 via India, Joseph Stalin's daughter wandered restlessly from city to city, then country to country, joining one religious sect after the other. Today, when the once talkative, red-pigtailed little Svetlana is asked to talk about her father and the olden days, the vacant old woman, who spends most of her time simply staring into space, or at best playing solitaire, crosses herself, then yells that the intruder is a son of Satan. On other occasions, like some heroine in an absurd drama, she asks for writing paper and an envelope so that she can write to her "little secretary", who has been dead since March 1953.

Doubtless she does not remember that it is more than half a century since the Master of the Kremlin had last written teasingly to her, on June 4, 1948. By then Svetlana had divorced her first husband—who, according to the pathologically anti-Semitic Stalin, had been commended by the "Zionists"—and had traveled to the Black Sea, to one of her father's empty residences, to comfort herself. She received the following short letter while she was there: "Hello, little mistress! I received your letter. Vorontsovka *[the word Voroshilovka is crossed out—M. K.]* is a very good place. You have done the right thing to go there. I recommend you return to Moscow no later than August 10. If you come any later you won't find me here. I am sending you money in two small envelopes. Please come back by the 10th, then we can travel to the south. Kisses from your daddy."[33]

☆ Svetlana Alliluyeva perhaps never understood that the main protagonist in the playful correspondence was not in fact Svetlana, the little mistress, but Joseph Stalin himself. By means of the letters he was making it clear to his circle that he, the first man of the country, the *General Secretary,*[34] on whom the lives and deaths of millions, the "sifting" of social classes, and the deportations of entire nations depended, felt so secure in his position that, like the clowns of the Russian Middle Ages, he could even afford to play the part of the humble "little secretary". Like an experienced theater director[35] he created a play, comprising a series of repeated scenes, in which he only had to adopt a costume when *he* felt like it.

Increasingly aware of how bizarre the "daily orders" were, Svetlana asked her father if they could cut down on the "official correspondence" and be content with just one exchange of letters during the six-day week.[36] However, even as a child she had realized that this game provided her with a special status in the Kremlin. "In return" for the demonstrative love of Joseph Stalin, the young girl, who grew up among competing family members, favorites, teachers, and bodyguards, had to prove that she was worthy of her privileged position. Being a proud and determined child with a good memory, unlike her two academically rather poor brothers and the other spoilt cadre children, she tried to excel in her studies. At the age of nine she wrote to Stalin: "You know, my dear daddy, I want to be top of the class this year as well. I will always get 'A's or perhaps 'B's, but I will never get a 'C'..."[37]

From what she wrote it seems that the Kremlin's "little princess" was interested in political questions, and even reveled in politics. On one occasion, on 29 June, for example, she wrote: "Daily Order Number 3. I order you to show me what happens in the Central Committee! Strictly confidential. By special courier. Stalina, the mistress of the house." The playful answer written on the back of the note, as so often in this correspondence, read: "I obey. J. Stalin, Setanka's

Stalin on holiday in Abkhazia with his two children, making a boat trip.

secretary."[38] As the years passed father and daughter appeared in public increasingly frequently. "To Secretary Number 1, Comrade Stalin. Daily Order Number 4. March 19, 1934. I order you to come with me to the Bolshoi Theater, to a performance of *Carmen*."[39] On May 4, in a letter full of spelling mistakes, the little girl ordered her father to take her on a boat trip on the *Clara Zetkin* steamer on the river Volga.[40] A "Daily Order Number 4" to the "Secretary Number 1, Comrade Stalin", is dated May 20, 1937: "I order you to give me permission to go with you and Comrade Molotov to the theater. Setanka, the mistress of the house."[41]

Before Stalin finally destroyed his wife's family in the late 1930s, he was delighted that his daughter helped keep up the appearance that his family relationships were important to him, even after the death of Nadezhda Alliluyeva. "Hello, Setanka! Thank you for your presents," begins an undated letter, sent by government courier to his daughter, who was spending her holiday at the

Black Sea coast. "Thank you for the Daily Order as well. I see you have not forgotten your father. When Vasya and his tutor come to Moscow you should stay in Sochi and wait for me. Is that all right with you? So then, kisses from your father."[42]

The playful tone he used with his daughter was sometimes used by Stalin in official letters addressed to his colleagues, which otherwise dealt with serious issues. "I propose to put an immediate stop to *Prozhektor*, a *completely useless publication*," he wrote with reference to the popular illustrated weekly in a letter to Lazar Kaganovich, the second secretary of the Central Committee, who deputized for him during his vacation. "The paper thus saved should be given to *Ogonok*, which is far superior. It would be worth enhancing it. Assign a different job to Vasilyevsky *[the editor in chief of* Prozhektor*—M. K.]*. He has proved to be a narrow-minded and useless man. Greetings! J. Stalin." In the postscript he abruptly changes tone: "Svetlana, the mistress of the house, will be in Moscow on August 7. She demands that I allow her to go to Moscow *[from the Black Sea coast—M. K.]* to supervise her secretaries' work. J. Stalin."[43]

It obviously flattered the dictator that his youngest child was concerned about his health, and it gave him pleasure to pin the related "Daily Orders" on his study wall: "December 1, 1938. To Comrade J. Stalin, Secretary Number 1. Daily Order Number 5. I order you to wear a winter coat as of today!"[44] When Stalin did not obey, Svetlana warned him again on December 13: "Papa!!! My Daily Order to wear a coat is still *valid*. It is your duty to obey. Setanka, your mistress of the house." The answer was written in red pencil: "I obey. J. Stalin, the little secretary."[45]

The playful letters between father and daughter sometimes reveal things that we do not know from other sources. We learn how, amongst themselves, the Bolshevik leaders cynically mocked the propaganda campaign, in which they forced tens of millions of citizens throughout the empire to attend seminars on Marxist theory and Bolshevik Party history, in order to study the hagiographic biographies of Lenin and Stalin. The Soviet leaders pretended to "examine" Svetlana on party history, and they kept a record that was "attested" by the little girl, their "boss", with her childish signature. "*Question*: How did Lenin help the workers to create a new life? *Answer*: Lenin convened illegal meetings, then wrote letters to the workers during his exile. He wrote these in milk *[for secrecy—M. K.]*, and he explained in these letters how the new life should be constructed. Setanka, the mistress of the house. *The answer is considered to merit a distinction*: L[azar] Kaganovich, M[ikhail] Kalinin, J[oseph] Stalin."[46]

The permanent praise heaped on her kept the little girl in a constant state of euphoria. She regarded as her greatest reward an invitation to a film projection from her "little secretary" and her other "secretaries". Such screenings often took place, since movies were the highest intellectual pastime of these men, who, almost without exception, lacked erudition, or even education.[47] Two separate cinemas were built for the nomenklatura living in the Kremlin and the "House on the Embankment" so that they would not have far to go. The members of the Soviet political elite, in their official capacity, regarded the art of film as an important asset in *agitprop*. They themselves, however, liked to watch not only stereotyped Soviet films on Stakhanovites, or heroic epics on the Civil War; they preferred Western comedies in color. In the second half of the 1930s these "home-screened movies" took place in something of a family atmosphere: before the war sometimes even the wives of the party leaders participated. Later, however, Stalin put an end to this pleasant atmosphere and the projections in the Kremlin often took place amid great tension. The audience—generally made up of four or five, and at most ten to fifteen, comrades—watched jealously to see whom Joseph Stalin, who sat in a comfortable leather chair, would invite to sit next to him. On several occasions Stalin angrily had the screening halted, even if he was the only one who was not enjoying the film.[48]

More often, following the inevitable cinema newsreel, Stalin, in a sentimental mood, would want to go on watching the shallow Hollywood tales until dawn. The members of the Politburo had to remain with him throughout the night. During the lengthy screenings the politicians would repeat his wisecracks out loud with respectful admiration, and would sometimes even imitate his gestures and tone of voice. The dictator enjoyed this extremely, and in order to confuse them would sometimes discuss what was happening on screen with Beria in Georgian during the projection.[49]

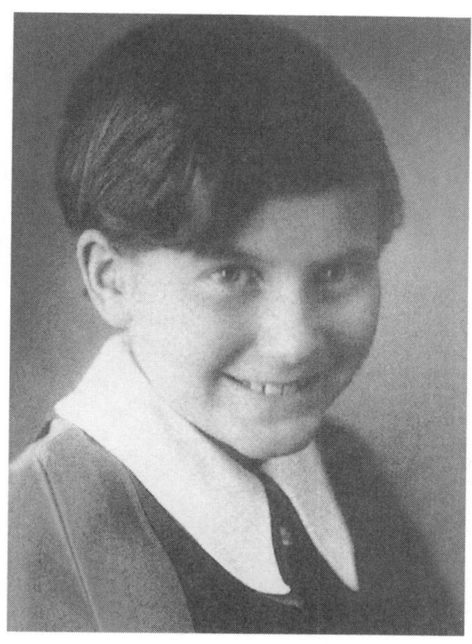

The red-haired "little princess"

These private film evenings continued regularly even during the Second World War Stalin wasted a huge amount of time on his hackneyed old favorites. But then a new theme appeared: at a time when the Red Army was facing serious defeat the dictator—mixing dream with reality—sent for Soviet films on an optimistic note. In the Arbatskaya underground station, which had been transformed into the GHQ bunker, in the company of politicians and high-ranking officers who had been summoned to make up the audience, he watched such pre-war films as *When War Breaks Out Tomorrow*. In the film the enemy army, reminiscent of the Germans, employs poison gas. In the foreign country, however, the Red Army crushes the cowardly retreating enemy soldiers, who are stymied by the pro-Soviet workers' revolt that breaks out behind the front.[50]

Stalin even offered foreign statesmen, including Churchill and De Gaulle, the chance to watch Soviet films with him during their visits to Moscow. In the middle of the Second World War he sent Roosevelt the comic film *Volga-Volga*, based on situational and character comedy, in which his favorite actress, Lyubov Orlova, played the leading role. The American president and his colleagues dutifully watched the dull comedy with the help of a simultaneous interpreter, then spent a great deal of time trying to figure out the possible hidden message.[51]

The Soviet dictator's passion for the cinema declined somewhat only in the last years of his rule. By that time he knew by heart the American Westerns and the output of Goebbels' film industry. These latter were obtained from the eastern zone of occupied Germany exclusively for Stalin and his circle. Stalin enjoyed them immensely, since they were very reminiscent of Soviet socialist realist films. At the same time, however, the Master of the Kremlin did not have a particularly high opinion of the first Italian neo-realist films or of French and English film dramas. From the late 1940s, as a result of his increasing nationalism, he had almost exclusively Soviet historical films screened for himself. He even contemplated how he could have re-cut, or re-made by another director, such classics as *Peter the First* or *Ivan the Terrible*. He ordered members of the party leadership to join him, on a rotating basis, in the work of film selection—increasingly as a substitute for real activity.[52]

At the time of the correspondence between the "little secretary" and the "mistress of the house", these projections took place in a very different way. At the end of the 1930s the screenings put on exclusively for Svetlana on the orders of the "Red Tsar" were organized by Ivan Bolshakov, the Kremlin's chief projectionist, who had the rank of minister. He had formerly controlled the economic affairs of the apparatus of the head of the Soviet government.[53] Prior to him, the important position of projectionist had been occupied by Semyon Dukelsky, widely regarded as rather a dull man, whose background was in the political police. Before him, until the beginning of the Great Terror, the position was held by the old Bolshevik Party member Boris Shumyatsky, who had been promoted to it from being a respected expert on China and Mongolia.[54]

Joseph Stalin's daughter, however, did not give them orders directly but told her father when, in her opinion, it was time for a projection to take place: "December 11, 1935. To Secretary Number 1, Comrade J[oseph] Stalin. Daily Order Number 1. I order you to allow me to go to the cinema. Setanka, the mistress of the house."[55]

The stubborn girl sometimes demanded a screening *immediately*. On such occasions the reels—always at the last moment—were delivered from the film directorate in downtown Moscow in huge metal boxes. "April 8, 1935. To Secretary Number 1, Comrade Stalin. Strictly confidential! Daily Order Number 10. I order you to allow me to go to the cinema immediately. The stamp of J. Stalin. The signature of the secretary. Setanka, the mistress of the house." The response, written in blue pencil, is legible at the bottom of the note: "You can go to the cinema, Comrade Mistress of the House. This is the answer from your little secretary, J. Sta[lin]."[56] The wording of the messages between father and daughter barely changed over the years: "To Secretary Number 1, Comrade J. Stalin. October 31, 1935. Daily Order Number 1. I order you to allow me to go to the cinema with you. Setanka, the mistress of the house. [...] The signature of the secretary." "I obey, my mistress of the house. The little secretary of Setanka *[the words 'the poor peasant' were crossed out—M. K.]*. Stalin."[57]

On other occasions the little girl organized joint visits to the Kremlin's projection room. "To Secretary Number 1, Comrade Stalin. I order you to go to the cinema today with Comrades Molotov, Kaganovich, and Zhdanov, and with Vaska and me. (The compulsory visit to the cinema is valid for today.) Setanka, the mistress of the house," read the "Daily Order Number 3", dated May 20, 1937.[58]

☆ The playful correspondence became increasingly frequent in the course of 1937. In the Kremlin, comedies were projected much more frequently than earlier, despite the fact that this year, according to the man of letters Razumnik Ivanov, a long-time resident of the Soviet prisons and exile colonies, surpassed, in terms of its horrors, all the other bloody years of the Soviet era: "In 1937 the terror reached heights that we had not experienced even during War Communism. Arrests took place not by tens or by hundreds, but by tens and hundreds of thousands. There was no home, family, or acquaintance who did not mourn relatives who had fallen victim to the harsh and senseless terror. It seemed that the Bolshevik counter-revolution was attempting to equal the French dictatorship of 1793. Equal? Rather to outdo... The number of dead under Robespierre's Terror seems a child's misdemeanor compared to the victims of Stalin's and Yezhov's massacres. The people's terror reached to the skies. Fear and dread reigned in every home."[59]

During these months the political police attempted to keep Stalin's daughter hermetically sealed from the outside world. She attended an elite school in downtown Moscow, traveling there by car accompanied by bodyguards.[60] Her classmates were exclusively "cadre children", but she was not even permitted to play with them during breaks, nor could she walk over to the school canteen. She had to sit in a little booth reserved for her unless the old NKVD officer, disguised as a childminder, took pity on her and allowed the "little princess" to spend some time with her friends.[61]

Otherwise, the Master of the Kremlin strictly forbade his daughter to receive petitions for mercy from the relatives of those arrested, or other letters, or even to talk to the children of politicians who had been declared "enemies of the people". According to Svetlana, her father used to ask her: "'Why do you meet people whose parent have been punished?' He must have been informed like that. Often, on his orders, the headmaster put these children into parallel classes."[62] It occurred only once in 1940, during the transitory "thaw" that Stalin, requested by his daughter, gave orders to release Salvitsky, father of Svetlana's friend from prison.[63]

The Buryat Gelya Markizova could have been a living symbol of the happiness of Soviet children, had Stalin not declared her father a Japanese spy and not executed him during the Great Terror.

In the course of our Moscow conversations Svetlana's former friends told me that it sometimes still occurred to the "little mistress of the house", whose eyes were usually shut to the anomalies of the outside world, to ask what their neighbors had done when she saw them being forced to move out of the Kremlin one after the other. News of the executions of almost the politicians she knew personally reached her from the "House on the Embankment". In the better case women were sent to the Gulag and their children to orphanages. The young girl, however, surrounded by an army of servants, had other things to occupy her mind. Besides her school studies she had private lessons with the best tutors in the city and watched films almost every evening in the company of her "little secretary".

Around 1937 the behavior of the other "secretaries" who pampered the child also radiated calm, benevolence, and friendliness. The dictator's occasionally changing colleagues, who supported his policy of terror without comment—and this was generally the key to staying alive—were quick to learn the technique of survival, acting amongst themselves as if nothing special were happening around them. "Life has become more pleasant, life has become more cheerful. And if we live more cheerfully then our work progresses more rapidly"—"the Master's" latest words of wisdom were quoted everywhere.

In such an atmosphere why would Stalin's daughter not appear cheerful? "February 5, 1939. 1. To Stalin. 2. To Voroshilov. 3. To Zhdanov. 4. To Molotov. 5. To Kaganovich. 6. To Khrushchev. Daily Order Number 8," wrote the thirteen-year-old Svetlana. "I am traveling to Zubalovo. I am leaving you on your own. Hold onto your bellies with an iron hand! Setanka, the mistress of the house. Stamp here." At the end of the note appear the following brief answers: "I obey. Stalin, the poor peasant. L. Kaganovich. The obedient Voroshilov. The diligent escapee Ukrainian: N. Khrushchev. V. Molotov."[64]

On two occasions the "PR experts", who changed rapidly during the years of the purges, illustrated—and on both occasions very dramatically—how Joseph Stalin was the father of *all* the children of the country. They made a brief film of him in the company of a little Turkmenian girl, Mamlakat, who was made a Stakhanovite for picking cotton so quickly. Then a series of photographs, still famous today, were issued throughout the country. The show the Master of the Kremlin picking up and embracing Gelya Markizova, the sweet little daughter of the people's commissar for agriculture in the Buryat-Mongol Autonomous Province. Yerbanov, the "Buryat Stalin", who was "governor" of the faraway province, stands next to them smiling. Thousands of statues and paintings were produced based on this photograph.[65]

Yerbanov, however—even though he had been diligently fulfilling the arrest and execution quotas set by Stalin for the Buryat Autonomous Province—himself became a victim of the purges after having been declared Japanese spy and "pan-Mongolian" nationalist.[66] Gelya's father, Ardan Markizov was also executed, and her mother, Dominika, was knocked down by a car in suspicious circumstances. The little girl herself was taken to Kazakhstan, far from her homeland. The photograph, however, could not be wasted! The "enemies of the people" were therefore edited out of the picture, which, from then on, showed only Stalin and Gelya, symbolizing the symbiosis of the Leader and the happy children. (As for the little girl, the disinformation department of the NKVD spread the idea that she was one and the same child as Mamlakat.)[67]

In the meantime the "best friend of all Soviet children" continued his playful correspondence with Setanka. "Greetings to my little mistress of the house, my little sparrow! I received both your letters. The mistress of the house deserves to be thanked for them! It is nice that you do not forget your father. I see you do not know, my little mistress, whether or not to travel to Sochi. You must decide! You can go whenever you want. You can either not go at all, or spend the entire summer in the Crimean. It is entirely up to you. It will be just as you choose. You ask how I'm doing. Quite well. Hoping for even better times. Well, goodbye, my little fly. I send you the very warmest kisses. Your daddy, J. Stalin."[68]

1 Alliluyeva, 1981, 106.
2 Topolyansky, 1996, 160.
3 *Stalinskoye Politbyuro*, 1995, 144.
4 Yakovlev, 2000, 392–394.
5 Pyotr Voroshilov, the future military engineer general, is remembered by all of his childhood acquaintances as a kind and righteous kid, unlike the other, spoiled children of the cadre elite. Natalya Rykova told me in an interview that at the end of the 1920s, at Stalin's orders, the adolescent Pyotr was imprisoned for a while, together with other children of certain Soviet leaders—on charges of "oppositional behavior". With this move, Stalin sent a clear message to his best friend and ally, the people's commissar for defense, Klim Voroshilov that his life is in the dictator's hands. Moreover, Pyotr's name was mentioned in the documents of the infamous OGPU, later as well. In the November of 1933, the people's commissar for defense, Klim Voroshilov received a letter from the Lubyanka that his son spent his time drinking, joy-riding, and dancing together with the children of other Soviet leaders. The report mentions a nineteen-year old young woman, who said that conspirators of "catholic" and "noble" origin could thus obtain information that allowed them to plot an assassination of Stalin and Voroshilov. Needless to say, the "tracked-down secret society" did not in fact exist. Yagoda, 1997, 369–372.
6 *Iosif Stalin v obyatiakh semyi*, 1993, 137, 141, 143.
7 *RGASPI*, fond. 558, op. 3, d. 5125.
8 From personal communication with Viktor Ilyin, a former high-ranking officer of the NKVD.
9 Borin, 1991, 96–117.
10 Alliluyeva, 1981, 141–144. We do not know even today where the original pieces of the collection can be found.
11 *RGASPI*, fond. 558, op. 1, d. 5104–d. 5165. The documents were filed at the former Soviet party archives on April 5, 1954, with the note "From S. Y. Stalina, through the Central Committee of the CPSU" written on it.
12 *Iosif Stalin v obyatiakh semyi*, 1993, 158.
13 *RGASPI*, fond. 558, op. 1, d. 5135.
14 *Iosif Stalin v obyatiakh semyi*, 1993, 161–162.
15 Irina Gogua recalls this with almost exactly the same words: "Stalin was devastated. The only human being who could console him was Svetlana. When the little girl hug his father's soft boots, Iosif Vissarionovich always calmed down. But Vaska always made him angry." *Druzhba Narodov*, 1997, no. 5, 83.
16 *RGASPI*, fond. 558, op. 1, d. 5113.
17 *RGASPI*, fond. 558, op. 1, d. 5115.
18 *RGASPI*, fond. 558, op. 11, d. 1552.
19 Stalin sometimes acted as if he were under his daughter's thumb. With a mischievous smile he would say that he has to ask for permission from his daughter if he wanted to smoke. Aroseva-Maksimova, 1999, 30.
20 Mikoyan, 1998, 33.
21 *Repressii Protiv Polyakov*, 1997, 30.
22 Razgon, 1991, 12.
23 Alliluyeva, 1981, 92–93.

24 In the 1960s Levon Shaumyan worked at an encyclopedia publishing firm, his career running on a kind of "side track". He frequently told his audiences that he had been an ardent Stalinist in his youth. The times of the Great Terror, however, caused him a lot of painful thoughts, thus he condemned the Stalinist system at every given opportunity. Together with Anastas Mikoyan, he tried to work for the rehabilitation of many old political prisoner party members on a number of occasions. "In the years of completing kolkhozization, upon the advice of Lazar Kaganovich, I co-authored a little pamphlet to prove that it was right to forcefully resettle a whole Cossack village in the Kuban' area because its residents were not willing to join the collective," he told me during our last meeting. "This trash was published in huge numbers of copies. Now I feel ashamed that I was one of the pen-pushers hailing the terror that killed millions. Once I write my memoirs, although this is not the time yet to do so, I will perhaps set at least something right from what I did," he explained with tears in his eyes. His premature death, however, prevented him from completing this plan.
25 Loginov, 2000, 97.
26 Alliluyeva, 1981, 143.
27 *Iosif Stalin v obyatiakh semyi*, 1993, 66.
28 Vasilyeva, 1996, 258, 260–261.
29 Alliluyeva, 1981, 170.
30 *Ibid.*, 147.
31 Gronsky, 1991, 198.
32 After she left her homeland again, she claimed that her words she had said at the Moscow press conference were misinterpreted by the APN correspondents. Alliluyeva, 1991, 50–51.
33 *RGASPI*, fond. 558, op. 1, d. 5121.
34 Stalin was appointed to this position in the spring of 1922. It seems that Lenin knew well why he wanted to establish this "institution" within the Bolshevik Party. As the *de facto* leader of the party and head of government, he wanted someone to direct his own *super-secretariat*. The position of General Secretary gained importance during Lenin's illness, and especially after his death. Following the 17th Congress (the 'Congress of the Victorious') held in 1934, this denomination, strangely enough, did not appear in the official party documents any more. But it was not decent to talk about this. Thus in the Soviet Union, as well as abroad, Stalin was still referred to as "General Secretary", up until the moment of his death.
35 This peculiar feature of the dictator's character was first analyzed by Antonov-Ovseyenko, 1996, 3–4, 7–38, 48–82, 232.
36 Alliluyeva, 1981, 144. The idea of *shestidnevka*, or six-day week, came up in the mind of a Hungarian communist engineer and economist, Gyula Hevesi, who lived in exile in Moscow. In his telling of the story, the Soviet authorities originally intended to leave out Sunday, the seventh day of the week, in the midst of the anti-religious campaign, so that the working people could not attend church services and the "outdated family ties" could loosen up. The Soviet government, the Council of Comissars, first introduced the six-day week as an experiment, during the period between May 25 and November 27, 1930. The successive workdays were named after the numbers one to five. The sixth day, as the contemporary press wrote, "in rebelling against the church calendar" was the day of rest. The rest day following the five workdays was a different day at each institution or factory. Thus the workweek became shorter, and tens of thousands of unemployed workers could go back to work. At the beginning, productivity figures also soared spectacularly. But because of the differences between the structure of the workweek at different places, transportation of goods and materials started to be disorganized, office work began to slow down. And no one liked it that the family could not rest together on Sundays. A variation of *shestidnevka* was *neprerivka*, meaning *continuous workweek*, which was introduced in the factories already on August 22, 1929, following the decision of the Politburo. Larin, 1929, 5–32; cf. Osokina, 1998, 75. Due to the smoldering popular dissension, the Soviet government eventually reinstated the traditional workweek, the one from Monday to Saturday.
37 *Iosif Stalin v obyatiakh semyi*, 1993, 52–53.
38 *RGASPI*, fond. 558, op. 1, d. 5132.
39 *RGASPI*, fond. 558, op. 1, d. 5127.
40 *RGASPI*, fond. 558, op. 1, d. 5129.
41 *RGASPI*, fond. 558, op. 1, d. 5147.
42 *RGASPI*, fond. 81, op. 3, d. 100.
43 *RGASPI*, fond. 558, op. 1, d. 5104.
44 *RGASPI*, fond. 558, op. 1, d. 5159.
45 *RGASPI*, fond. 558, op. 1, d. 5155.
46 *RGASPI*, fond. 558, op. 1, d. 5143.
47 Despite its role in deciding over the life and deeds of the Soviet Union, between the beginning of 1930 and the spring of 1941, the Politburo did not have a member who had a university degree.
48 Maryamov, 1992, 8–13, 94–95.
49 Antonov-Ovseyenko, 1995, 162–163.
50 Djilas, 1989, 95–96. The memoir writer recalls that at the end of the film, Stalin noted calmly: "The story is not far from what really happened, except there was no poison gas and the German proletariat did not revolt."

51 Originally, Stalin and his daughter saw *Volga-Volga* together with Zhdanov, the chief ideologist of the Communist Party and Svetlana's "No. 3. Secretary", on December 22, 1938, as part of celebrating the dictator's birthday. *RGASPI*, fond. 558, op. 1, d. 5158.

52 Maryamov, 1992, 94, 111–114.

53 Stalin, who always feared that he would be assassinated, with rare exceptions, did not let interpreters work at the screening of Western films. Thus Bolshakov, who did not speak any language but had an excellent ability to memorize, learned all dialogues by heart. And when he happened to forget the translation, he would rather improvise than remain silent.

54 Antonov-Ovseyenko, 1995, 162–180. Shumyatsky was executed during the Great Terror. Dukelsky, the "versatile interior officer", however, became people's commissar for the navy fleet, and later deputy minister for justice. Bolshakov died early of heart failure, as a result of all that stress he suffered during the screenings.

55 *RGASPI*, fond. 558, op. 1, d. 5137. Stalin's daughter made a similar "order" on November 8, 1934, October 31, 1935, September 21, October 7, and December 14, 1937.

56 *RGASPI*, fond. 558, op. 1, d. 5140.

57 *RGASPI*, fond. 558, op. 1, d. 5142.

58 *RGASPI*, fond. 558, op. 1, d. 5146.

59 Ivanov-Razumnik, 1953, 13.

60 Holmes, 1999, 3, 12, 38, 58, 72, 141, 165–168.

61 Her first childhood love was also thwarted by the opposition of the "supervisors". The young adolescent Svetlana read Maupassant already at the age of eleven, just like her boyfriend Misha, who was her classmate. During the classes they wrote "I love you" notes on blotting paper. And if very rarely they had the opportunity, they kissed. The love letters, however, reached the desk of the school principal. Misha was expelled from the school, and it was also because by that time his parents and aunt had been imprisoned. "The friendship came to an end, and we met only once for a short time during the war," recalled Svetlana in her book. Alliluyeva, 1970, 6.

62 Alliluyeva, 1970, 132.

63 *Ibid.*, 131.

64 *RGASPI*, fond. 558, op. 1, d. 5160.

65 King, 1997, 152–153.

66 *Reabilitatsia*, 2000, vol. I, 207–208.

67 *Pamyat'*, 1978, vol. I, 344–345. Gelya's real name was Engelsina. *Izvestia*, February 8, 1995.

68 *RGASPI*, fond. 558, op. 1, d. 5114.

Stalin and his number one military advisor, Shaposhnikov, who had already been a colonel in the tsar's army.

CHAPTER 22
The Threat of War

From the above correspondence, most of which is published for the first time in the present volume, we sense that Svetlana saw her father not only as the Great Leader of the world's proletariat, but as a fairy-tale ruler from the *Arabian Nights.* To her he was a kind of miraculous Bolshevik Harun al-Rashid, who, on June 13, 1937, amidst the bloodiest purges, in order to impress his "mistress of the house" unexpectedly promised her that she could travel to the Black Sea by special train. "To Secretary Number 1, Comrade J. Stalin. Confidential! Daily Order Number 7. I order you to come to Sochi as soon as possible. Place stamp here." Then comes the casual answer in Stalin's handwriting, as if it were a question not of a long, exhausting journey but of an excursion to Zubalovo, just outside Moscow. "I obey. The little secretary of Setanka, mistress of the house. J. Stalin."[1]

Perhaps it is no coincidence—at least this is what the childhood friends of Svetlana recall—that at the time one of Stalin's daughter's favorite poems was Aleksandr Pushkin's tale *The Fisherman and the Fish.* In her early teens the girl would recite the long poem about the incredible fortunes of the simple fisherman several times a day. Whenever she reached the point when the greedy *muzhik* suddenly finds himself back in his old ramshackle hut instead of at the palace, her voice always trembled. She felt huge sympathy for the unlucky character. However, the subconscious fear of the "little princess", who had been born into power, could not have lasted for long, otherwise she would hardly have demanded with such self-assurance on August 8, 1937, the day of the traditional Tushino Air Show, in her "Secret Daily Order Number 13/a", that her father order the projection of the film *Peter the First.*[2]

In a note written on a piece of lined paper torn from a school exercise book, bearing a hammer and sickle stamp and marked "Strictly Confidential", the young girl also ordered her father, "Secretary Number 1", and Andrei Zhdanov, "Secretary Number 3", the leader of the Leningrad regional party organization: "No later than next holiday, that is, on December 24 [1938], in Moscow and the Moscow area, and even in Leningrad and the Leningrad area, the snow must fall. In Moscow, at the same time, the temperature must rise." The addressee, Zhdanov, the future dreaded executioner of the Soviet Empire's intelligentsia, sent a humble answer which echoes Stalin's tone: "Everything will be sorted out exactly as you wish. The little secretary of Comrade Mistress of the House, Zhdanov."[3]

Among the photographed copies are notes in which Joseph Stalin mentions dinners that took place among restricted circles, which were, at the same time, working dinners and drinking-bouts. In those days, in the court of the Soviet dictator, it was hard to distinguish between official Politburo meetings and the informal events that followed them—the get-togethers among "the Five" and "the Six", and the dinners which originally started as a "political club". According to Anastas Mikoyan it the Stalin who used the term "political club" of these drinking-bouts, which made the lives of those around him so wretched.[4] (Should someone from the immediate party leadership—such as Andreyev, or later Voroshilov, and finally Molotov and Mikoyan—not receive an invitation to the "club", it was a sure sign that they had fallen out of favor.)

At the get-togethers, which usually lasted until the early hours, the Master of the Kremlin found his greatest amusement in snapping his fingers, at which sign the drunken members of the Politburo—as in the slapstick comedies of Laurel and Hardy—would put a tomato or a piece of cake on the chair of Poskryobishev, the leader of Stalin's secretariat, or Anastas Mikoyan, who tolerated such tasteless jokes with better grace than the others. We learned from the families and colleagues of those present that the guests sometimes urinated unnoticed under the table onto each other's shoes and trousers, or stirred salt instead of sugar into the tea of a neighbor while he wasn't looking. They sprinkled the soup of the elderly and short-sighted Mikhail Kalinin with virgin tobacco, and the formal head of the Soviet state suffered it with the same obedience as the younger leading politicians, whose readiness to be involved in such stupidities was prompted by both fear and careerism. In his memoirs Milovan Djilas draws a vivid picture of these dinners, although Stalin's colleagues usually held themselves back in front of foreigners.[5] In addition, the researcher who analyzed the depraved scenes—reminiscent of the practical jokes of rather backward teenagers—found evidence of many other perversions that took place at these feasts. He also described how Stalin, who only indulged in such wild behavior in male company, would order the Soviet leaders to ask one another to dance a polka or waltz.[6]

Svetlana Stalina pretended for a long time that she found nothing distasteful in her father's all-night partying. She warned her "little secretary" and other "secretaries" only seldom and very cautiously—for instance in her letter dated December 15, 1938—not to take such revelries to extremes. "Hello, darling daddy! (I am writing from far away.) I apologize for not waiting up for you. I couldn't wait, since I had to go to bed early. Otherwise I don't get a proper sleep. My orders are as follows: 1. Have a proper lunch! 2. You can also drink (only don't take it to extremes). Of course, I know that *my* secretaries would never do such things. 3. You can go to the cinema or any other place (I leave it up to you). Warm kisses to my daddy. The mistress of the House."

In his reply, written in blue pencil and sent in the names of the statesmen who took part in the gatherings, Stalin reassured the writer of the letter in the following way: "I obey. J. Stalin, the little secretary." The people's commissar for defense, in his role as surrogate father, also responded to the warning in respectful tones: "We will drink to your health, our dear mistress, but naturally we won't go to extremes. Secretary Number 2, Klim Voroshilov."[7]

Nevertheless, in the mornings, when she knocked at her father's study, the little girl would often find that Joseph Stalin was nowhere to be seen and was not even out of bed. When this happened, Svetlana would "call him to account": "My dear little secretary! Why have you recently been coming home so late? [...] Never mind, I wouldn't like to make my respected secretaries miserable with my strictness. Eat as much as you like. You can drink, too. I only ask you not to put vegetables or other food on the chairs in the hope that someone will sit on it. It will damage the chairs. As well as the secretaries' clothes. So, I remain your Setanka. The mistress of the house. And I send my very warmest kisses to my daddy."

At the end of the letter the dictator added, in scrawling handwriting that clearly suggests he was drunk at the time: "We obey. Kisses to my little sparrow. Your little secretary, Stalin."[8]

This light-hearted piece of correspondence was dated March 13, 1941. The masters of the Kremlin were thus indulging in their revels barely three months before the outbreak of the German-Soviet war, when Hitler's powerful war machine was already poised to attack the borders of the Soviet Union. The German General Staff, which by that time had invaded half of Europe, did not make much of a secret of who its next victim would be. Adolf Hitler, who was preparing for Operation Barbarossa, based on a *Blitzkrieg*, talked disparagingly to his close associates about the Red Army, which had indeed performed miserably in the Soviet-Finnish War. He even presented Joseph Stalin—probably for psychological reasons—with one of the most up-to-date German warplanes, suggesting how unafraid he was that the Soviet engineers would have sufficient time to copy the creations of their German colleagues.[9] As part of these tactics of fear a German fighter plane "lost its way" in Soviet airspace in May 1941. The pilot of the Junkers-52 got as far as Moscow unharmed, and in order to increase panic he circled the Kremlin for a long while before landing on the grass of the Dynamo Stadium. The Soviet press made no mention of these sinister events.[10]

As a result of the pressure being exerted on him by Hitler, Stalin nearly developed a severe nervous illness. In the greatest secrecy, and somewhat clumsily—in parallel with his earlier policy of "give and take"—he made up his mind to carry out a "preemptive strike", that is, to make preparations for an offensive. From the summer of 1940 Stalin was apparently well aware that the leaders of Nazi Germany were less and less friendly and were ostentatiously ignoring his recent territorial claims. Half a year prior to the German-Soviet war it was no longer a matter of any importance to Adolf Hitler to have Stalin join the Berlin–Rome–Tokyo Axis at war with the Western democracies. Quite the contrary! The Führer obviously regarded the Soviet Union as easy prey. Expecting a rapid endgame he sent the select battalions of the Wehrmacht to the rivers Vistula and Bug, where the officers of the two countries, following the invasion of Poland, ceremoniously greeted one another before the newsreel cameras.[11]

The Soviet dictator, who was being forced more and more obviously onto the defensive, still inexplicably insisted, until the very day of the Nazi aggression, on June 22, 1941, on keeping to the trade agreements that had followed the signing of the Molotov–Ribbentrop Pact dividing the majority of the European continent and coordinating the war industrial plans of the two allied powers. He kept to these agreements even when, as a result of the precise information gathered by Soviet intelligence, he was finally given a realistic insight into the true extent of the approaching danger.[12] In response to Hitler's moves the Master of the Kremlin cautiously had dusted down an earlier plan for a preemptive Western campaign, which had been worked out in the early 1930s by Mikhail Tukhachevsky and his officers, who were later to be executed alongside him. However, in front of a significant audience Stalin mentioned only once—at a reception held for the graduate students of the Military Academy that took place in the Kremlin in May 1941—or rather hinted that the Soviet Union's future enemy was Nazi Germany.[13]

In the festive speech and the various toasts made by the Soviet dictator at this reception we can clearly observe an increasing atmosphere of alarm in the Kremlin. Yet at the same time, strangely enough, in the months before the war this was scarcely reflected in the lifestyle of the upper echelons of the Soviet leadership, the "secretaries" of little Svetlana. On the threshold of the most extensive and bloodiest military clash of the twentieth century the strongly "counter-selected" group, which to some extent was molded together during the Great Terror, spent the majority of its leisure time on the same obscure pseudo-activities. It was as if they were trying to convince themselves that they were not in fact sitting on a barrel of gunpowder. Following the nights of revelries in the Kremlin apartment of Joseph Stalin—who in the meantime had been appointed head of the government—or in one of his *dachas,* these people staggered late into their offices, exhausted, unshaven, and suffering from headaches and stomachaches. They closed their doors and lay down on their couches to sleep as soon as they could. In the meantime, the most important members of the General Staff, army engineers, factory directors, and even foreign diplomats were kept waiting for hours in the corridors. These officials as well as the diplomatic couriers and intelligence officers who came at top speed with news of the looming German aggression, had no idea that their bosses were not in fact exhausted by the stresses of their work. For the masters of the Kremlin there was no stopping or escape: faithful to the choreography of the revelries, which barely changed in the course of the years, they dutifully spent long hours every day at tables laden with rich meats, fine Georgian wines, and bottles of vodka. In the intermissions between drinking bouts—fearing the wandering gaze of Stalin, who had been suffering from insomnia for years—they mimed devoted attention while Semyon Budenny, the Red Cossack[14] with the enormous mustache, played the accordion and sang Civil War military songs. Then Andrei Zhdanov, who in this circle was reputed to be an outstanding musician, sat down at the piano to play popular film music and Russian folk songs by ear, without a score. Klim Voroshilov, who had the most pleasant singing voice in the rowdy company—"our choirmaster", as he was referred to affectionately at the time by Stalin—occasionally created an improvised choir from the members of the Politburo.[15]

According to the unwritten rules that governed these gatherings, by the end of the "cultural program" the participants became almost bestial. But even in their alcoholic stupor they were careful what they said in the presence of their dreaded master. Nikita Khrushchev, who was quite willing to play the role of "court jester", later told how the stifling atmosphere of the approaching war was felt more and more depressingly, and how the dictator's obscenity increased in proportion to it. With the help of Lavrenty Beria Stalin attempted to get his most faithful followers drunk, in the hope that they would spill out something in his presence that he could use to keep them further under his thumb and blackmail them. Apparently Khrushchev was offended even decades later by the ugly behavior of Joseph Stalin: "The phone rang almost every evening: 'Come on, let's dine together!' Those dinners were terrible! Stalin threw tomatoes at those present—for instance during the war when we were living in the bunker. I witnessed this myself. Whenever we approached him concerning military issues, following our reports he always invited us to his bunker. Then a dinner would begin, which often ended with him throwing fruit and vegetables. He sometimes fired them against the ceiling or walls. He would use his hands, or sometimes a fork or a spoon."[16]

On such occasions "Secretary Number 1" would drag Svetlana out of bed and force her to entertain his "secretaries", who were lolling about in an alcoholic stupor. The "mistress of the house" protested desperately: "Please don't wake me up!" she wrote to her father on September 11, 1940.[17] Stalin, however, proved merciless, even though earlier he had been particularly gentle with the little girl. As the years passed, he became increasingly rough with her, occasionally snarling at her: "Go and dance with them at once!" At the end of the 1940s this "loving daddy" even dragged the young woman Svetlana by her hair into the company of the drunken men, who were lurching around hanging onto each other.

Later, after the war, Stalin would not even care to undress after such evening sprees, he just fell onto his bed. But he could not sleep; he was constantly keeping an eye on the curtains, fearing that an "assassin" was hiding there. In his fear, he even refrained from pulling off his boots.[18]

1 *RGASPI*, fond. 558, op. 1, d. 5149. Stalin eventually did not make this trip.
2 *RGASPI*, fond. 558, op. 1, d. 5150.
3 *RGASPI*, fond. 558, op. 1, d. 5157.
4 Mikoyan, 1999, 353.
5 Djilas, 70–72, 95–100, 138–139, 147–148.
6 Rancour-Laferrière, 1996, 157–159. On more than one occasion, Stalin had the same peculiar idea to propose for the guests of the dance parties held at the Kremlin. See also page 227 of this book.
7 *RGASPI*, fond. 558, op. 1, d. 5162.
8 *RGASPI*, fond. 558, op. 1, d. 5164.
9 Saragin, 1971, 90–91.
10 *Voyenno-Istorichesky Zhurnal*, 1990, no. 6, 45–46.
11 Bezimentsky, 2000, 442.
12 *Sekreti Gitlera na stole u Stalina*, 1995, 3–17, 23–179. The earlier simplifying views, which explained Stalin's "submissive" politics with the lack of sufficient information on the looming danger, are persuasively disproved by the vast volumes of still unpublished documents that have recently emerged from the former Soviet archives. *1941 god*, vols. I–II, 1998.
13 *1941 god*, vol. II, 158–162.
14 It is an ironic twist of fate that the model Cossack Budenny was not in fact a Cossack. His family belonged to the category *inogorodnie*, that is those who had migrated to the land of the Cossacks.
15 *RGASPI*, fond. 74, op. 1, d. 439.
16 Khrushchev, 1997, 232. Even during the first part of the war, Stalin ordered Khrushchev to travel to Moscow and report to him, and—although there would have been a greater need for the politician's presence in the war-torn Ukraine—he kept him in the capital without any specific reason. Khrushchev believed that Stalin did this because he was afraid to stay alone with his thoughts. *Ibid.*, 92–93.
17 *RGASPI*, fond. 558, op. 1, d. 5163.
18 Shepilov, 2001, 68.

This was how on September 28, 1939, Stalin and Ribbentrop divided Poland.

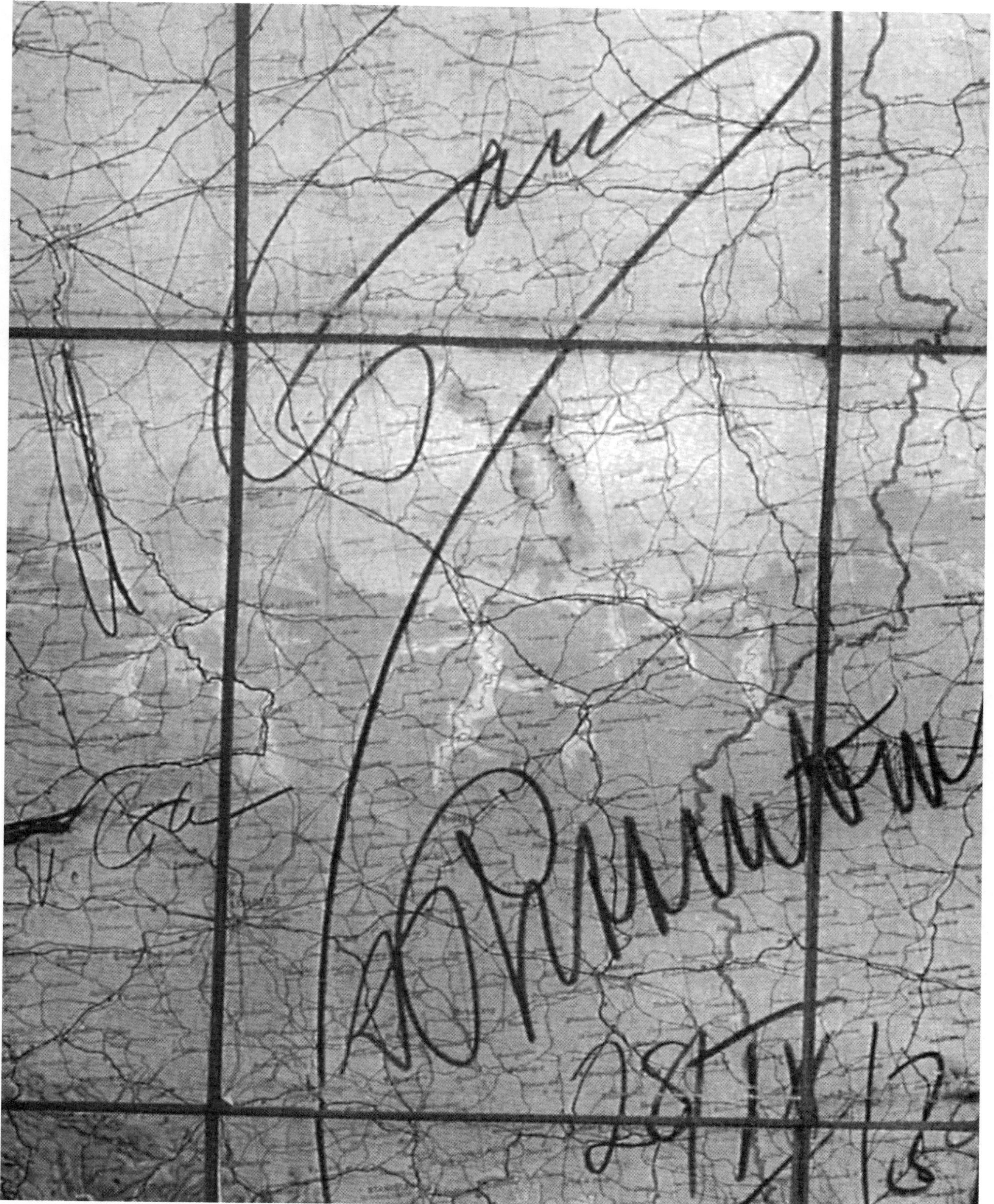

The Molotov–Ribbentrop Pact

The negotiations were held under a Lenin picture. This room was also the site where Joseph Stalin made his famous toast, in which he praised the Führer as the beloved leader of the German people. The friendly handshakes sealed the fate of Poland and the three Baltic republics. They made it possible for Hitler to concentrate on the western theater of war, and for the Kremlin to pose territorial claims against Finland and Romania.

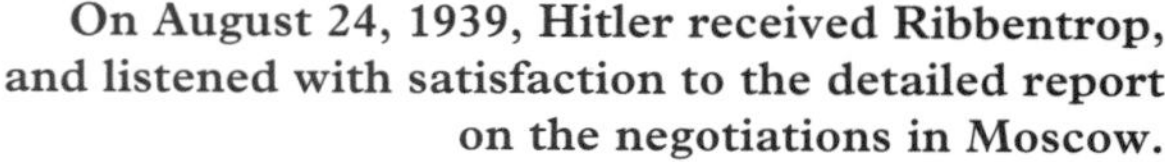

On August 24, 1939, Hitler received Ribbentrop, and listened with satisfaction to the detailed report on the negotiations in Moscow.

By the autumn of 1940, the Soviet-German relationship had significantly deteriorated. Hitler, who was winning battle after battle, started to leave Stalin out of his politics of expansion. As a response, Joseph Stalin sent his confidant Vyacheslav Molotov, the Head of the Council of People's Commissars to Berlin, to find out more about Hitler's plans.

Molotov was given a cordial reception in Berlin. He was escorted by Vladimir Dekanozov (x), a deputy people's commissar for foreign affairs and an insider of the political police, whom Stalin intended to nominate as the new ambassador to Berlin.

The self-confident smile concealed great insecurity. In the breaks between negotiation rounds, Molotov sent encrypted telegram messages to Stalin, asking him what to do next.

Although he conducted thorough negotiations with Ribbentrop (1), Himmler (2), and Göring (3), Molotov was unable to realize the Soviet plans to repartition South-East Europe and the Near-East.

CHAPTER 23
Yakov Dzhugashvili

Besides the Freudian jealousy caused by the appearance of suitors around Svetlana, the breakdown in the relationship between Stalin and his "mistress of the house" could be a result of the girl's discomfort at being in the company of drunken men. Another contributing factor, if only in part, was the "change of place" that came about in the first period of the Soviet-German war between the teenage Svetlana—who was becoming increasingly alien in the eyes of Stalin—and her brother Vasily, who walked with increasing self-assurance in the corridors of the Kremlin in his air force officer's uniform. On the rare occasions when the Soviet dictator wished to remember his old family ties, he had his youngest son "at hand". Svetlana, however, from the beginning of the war until summer 1942, was living in Kuybishev. The Soviet diplomatic representations and important offices had been evacuated to this city on the Volga to escape the German attack against the Soviet capital. The Soviet government had partly also moved its seat there. The soldiers of the construction battalion had rapidly built a huge, deep bunker for Stalin, connected by a complex system of tunnels to the bank of the river Volga and a number of public buildings. In the end, however, the Master of the Kremlin did not leave Moscow, and until the late spring of 1942 Svetlana received only brief messages from her busy father, with whom the playful correspondence had finally came to an end. Nor did the two parties find much pleasure in their reunion. After the teenager, who continued to behave as a "little princess", had visited her relatives near the Urals on a private plane and had returned to the Soviet capital, she must have realized that her father no longer behaved towards her in the same way. However, the real break only came when the girl became involved in a passionate love affair with the much older scriptwriter Aleksei Kapler. The man was introduced to her by Vasily Stalin at the Zubalovo *dacha* in October 1942.[1]

Stalin soon learned about it and clearly felt badly cheated. Compared to this action of his "little sparrow", whom he had so recently adored, the scandals of the notorious Vasily counted for nothing. From the end of July 1941 the handsome air force officer, who was tacitly promoted as the "heir to the throne" in the dictator's court, was further "valorized" by the news arriving from the front: Yakov Dzhugashvili, Stalin's elder son, had fallen into German hands in the first weeks of the war.

The Master of the Kremlin had long ago "written off" Yakov, his first-born son. He did not even permit him to adopt the name Stalin. Thus, in official papers he was always referred to as Dzhugashvili. Whenever Stalin looked at Yakov he was probably reminded of the few happy months spent with the mother of his first-born, his first wife, during their brief marriage.

We still know very little about how "Comrade Koba" and Yekaterina (Keto) Svanidze first met. According to one version the professional revolutionary fell in love with his future wife when, while in hiding in 1906, he was taken in by one of his old friends Misho Monaselidze, who happened to be the husband of Sashiko, one of the Svanidze girls. However, Olga Sokhadze, the cousin of Stalin's first wife, remembered in the mid-1930s that "Comrade Soso" had taken refuge with Keto's parents, the Svanidzes.[2] If this was really the case then events

Yakov, the first-born son of the Soviet dictator, could never bear his father's name chosen in the Bolshevik movement. His character also differed from Stalin's ...

...and he was more like his mother, Yekaterina (Keto) Svanidze, who had died young.

were to be repeated in exactly the same way a decade later, when, in the Alliluyevs' apartment in St. Petersburg, love blossomed between Nadezhda, the daughter of the hosts, and the escapee Stalin who was staying with them.

No matter how they met it was not long before the young couple decided to get married. In terms of social hierarchy they were very close to each other. Yekaterina Svanidze's father was a railway worker and owned some land. Thus the girl benefited little from the fact that she had noble origins, being a descendent of a prince on her mother's side. In turn-of-the-century Georgia she was regarded as emancipated, since she tried to escape from poverty by her own resources: following the example of her elder sister Sashiko she became a seamstress in the little sewing workshop of the Svanidze family.[3]

Apparently, "movement" motives also played a part in the budding relationship between Iosif Dzhugashvili and his future wife. "My dear compatriot! I have so far been unable to write to you because I have been so busy," we read in a letter from Stalin, written on a slip of paper without date or address, and filled with mysterious allusions. "I hope this doesn't make you cross. I am feeling fine. The news from here promises nothing good. But there's no use dwelling on it. It is enough to stay alive, and the rest will take care of itself. I greet you all. Perhaps I will find Alyosha *[Svanidze—M. K.]* and will set him on the 'wrong path'. Unless this would make Yekaterina Semyonovna *[Keto—M. K.]* unhappy. Your friend: Soso."[4]

The young couple were married on July 16, 1906. Misho Monaselidze had to find a Georgian Orthodox priest on whom they could depend, since at that time the future Soviet dictator was staying in Georgia with a false passport, under the name Geliashvili. Eventually the choice fell on Kita Tkhinvaleli, the priest of the Davidovo church. Although he knew that Stalin's documents were false he still married the young couple, since he had once attended the same classes as the bridegroom at the Tiflis Seminary.[5] According to contemporaries the marriage, which was initially happy, eventually brought troubles as well as pleasure to Keto Svanidze, who, for conspiratorial reasons, retained her maiden name. Despite this precaution she was arrested on November 13, 1906. She was forced to spend two and a half months in detention under remand since, in a house search carried out in a Moscow apartment, the police had confiscated a letter in which her name appeared: "Freylinskaya Street. To the seamstress Svanidze. Look for Soso! [that is, Iosif Dzhugashvili.]" She was pregnant at the time: her son Yakov was born on March 18, 1907. Interestingly, he was only taken to be christened in 1908 by Keto's mother, Sapora.[6]

According to Levon Shaumyan, who spent a great deal of time in the company of the young Stalin's acquaintances, including Mikha Chakaya, it was rumored that following the marriage tensions arose between the new husband and the Svanidze family. Perhaps this was why Stalin moved with his family to Baku in the summer of 1907. However, according to Sashiko Svanidze Stalin returned the critically ill Yekaterina to the Georgian capital three months later.[7] Within just three weeks she had died of acute tuberculosis, combined with pneumonia of both lungs. It is not clear why Stalin left his wife alone in the days before her death: according to one version he moved back to Baku. According to Misho Monaselidze, however, it was Soso himself who closed his wife's eyes.[8]

As we can learn from eyewitnesses Iosif Dzhugashvili almost collapsed after his wife's death. However, the funeral of little Yakov's mother ended almost farcically: the grieving husband was obviously afraid that the secret police who attended the funeral would arrest him. Without even waiting for the end of the ceremony he suddenly ran off and jumped over the fence.[9]

From then on he rarely visited his old home and seldom saw his son Yakov. For a while the child was brought up by Keke, Stalin's mother, then by Aleksandra (Sashiko), and Maria (Maro), his late wife's sisters. All three were sorry for the orphan. At the same time, it was striking that no one ever took a special interest in Yakov Dzhugashvili throughout his life, not even after the outbreak of the Soviet-German war when, on July 16, 1941, he was captured by the Germans near Vitebsk. He shared the fate of several hundred thousand Soviet youths. Yet among the residents of the Kremlin and the "House on the Embankment" the rumor still spread that Stalin, in a first fit of anger, blamed Yakov for "surrendering like a coward" to the enemy. The Nazi German propaganda machine immediately showered the Soviet trenches with leaflets. These stated that, with the exception of "commissars and Jews", they promised good treatment to those Red soldiers and commanders who surrendered unarmed. Several leaflets featured a photograph of Yakov Dzhugashvili, smiling at the Wehrmacht officers surrounding him. Printed on the back of one of the propaganda publications was a copy of a letter he had written to his father. It had been extracted from him by the Germans immediately after his capture, and via diplomatic channels had been forwarded to its addressee: "Dear Father! I have been taken prisoner. I am in good health. I will soon be sent to a camp for officers in Germany. I am being treated well. I wish you good health! Greetings to everyone. Yasha."

Artyom Sergeyev, who had grown up with Stalin's children, brought the news on Yakov Dzhugashvili's capture.

According to the recollections of Wilfried Strick-Strickfeldt, a German military intelligence officer and former Baltic German merchant, the Nazi propaganda leaflets that were printed in huge numbers in the early days of the war had originally mentioned party and Komsomol members among those to be shot. Strik-Strikfeldt regards it as a personal achievement to have persuaded the members of Marshal von Bock's staff against the idea.[10] It is hard to tell how much of this is true. It seems entirely credible, however, that Strick-Strickfeldt once met Stalin's elder son in the building of the General Staff at German front headquarters: "Major Yakov Dzhugashvili[11] had an intelligent face with typical Georgian features. He gave the impression of being a quiet and reliable person. [...] He told me that his father had said farewell to him on the phone before he left for the front. He attributed the incredible poverty of the Russian people under Soviet rule to the fact that the army needed to be armed. Since the October revolution, he argued, the Soviet Union had been surrounded by technically advanced and well-armed imperialist countries.

'You Germans have attacked us too soon' he said. 'That's why we appear so poor and badly armed. But the time will come when we will not spend the fruit of our labor on arms, but on improving the living standards of the Soviet peoples. [...] You treat us in an off-hand manner, as if we were aborigines from some island in the Pacific Ocean. But I have experienced nothing since I was taken prisoner that would make me look up to you. True, I have met many kind people here. But the NKVD, too, show benevolence when they want to achieve their goals!"[12]

☆ There are still many contradictory legends in circulation about the death of Yakov Dzhugashvili, as there are about all the important events in his life. General Artom Sergeyev, who is inclined to idealize his former guardian, Stalin, and his circle, recalled: "The Germans surrounded Yakov's battery. The order was given to retreat. But Yakov did not obey the order. I tried to persuade him [...] but Yakov answered: 'I am the son of Stalin and I do not permit the battery to retreat.'"[13] From many other sources, including the confession the prisoner made in front of the officers of the Abwehr, the German military intelligence, it appears rather that the retreating Yakov Dzhugashvili was handed over to the

It is not clear how far Yakov Dzhugashvili went in cooperating with the Abwehr officers who questioned him. It is also bizarre that his confession was full of anti-Semitic remarks considering that his wife was Jewish.

Germans by his father's unhappy subjects, the Russian *muzhik*s, who hated the *kolkhoz* system and the Soviet power in general. In the first hours of capture the panic-stricken young man got rid of his officer's insignia and hid among the masses of POWs. Unfortunately for him he was recognized by one of his former comrades who immediately turned him in. Soon afterwards the unshaven artillery officer, who was unable to accept the catastrophic collapse of the Red Army, was interrogated by the Abwehr's most highly trained Russian experts. All his words were carefully written down, although only part of these documents have been made public. In any case, from the records of the first interrogations we can conclude that Yakov Dzhugashvili did not abase himself in front of the Germans.[14]

After a while, however, the cornered artillery officer inevitably became more open. He had a very bad opinion of his own division, and even about other units of the Red Army, which had been insufficiently prepared for the war. He told his captors that the Red commanders behaved improperly in peacetime and often even during combat. He added that the rich peasants, the *kulak*s, who had formerly been "the protectors of tsarism and the bourgeoisie", dominated the Soviet system. According to him even some of the manual workers felt the same, although their children were "being raised in a very different spirit. They mostly turned their backs on such parents."

With respect to England, the new military ally of the Soviet Union, Yakov, who was thinking in Soviet clichés, considered that "this country has never helped anyone". As he explained to the German officers, apart from his own country there was only one major empire in Europe, and that was Germany: "The whole of Europe would be worth nothing without her," he said. "What significance do states such as Hungary, Finland, etc. have? What kind of countries are they at all? Germany is the one that matters."[15]

The contemporary reader may well be surprised that Stalin's elder son fed the Nazi reconnaissance and counterintelligence corps—mostly German emigrants from the Baltic States who spoke excellent Russian—with anti-Semitic remarks: "...the Jews and the Gypsies resemble one another in that they do not like to work. For them, trading is the most important thing. Some Jews living in our country say that their situation would be better in Germany, where trading is permitted. We don't mind if they beat us, they say, as long as they allow us to stand behind a counter. [...] In other words, the Jews in our country do not want to, and cannot, work. They trade, or aspire to careers in engineering, but they do not want to be workers, technicians, or peasant laborers. That's why no one in our country respects the Jews." His childhood years in Georgia, then the time he spent in Moscow and Leningrad, by no means explain Yakov's anti-Gypsy and anti-Jewish sentiments. Even though his last wife, Yulia Meltser, with whom he lived quite happily, came from a religious Jewish family from Odessa. Nevertheless Yakov repeated: "I don't know if you have heard that in the Soviet Union there is a territory by the name of Birobidzhan. It is an autonomous province on the border between Manchuria and the Soviet Union, but there is not a single Jew living there any more. Its population today consists exclusively of Russians since they [the Jews] cannot work, and do not want to."[16]

When answering questions about his family it turned out just how loose his ties were with his father. He gave the year of the death of his stepmother, Nadezhda Alliluyeva, as 1934 rather than 1932, nor could he say exactly how old his younger brother Vasily was. Although he remembered that his younger brother had wanted to be an air force officer it did not occur to him that, by that time, Vasya had been serving for more than two and a half years in the Soviet air force. He answered these questions relatively quietly. However, when asked whether his father's new wife was not Jewish, and whether by chance she was not called Roza Kaganovich, he became very distressed.[17]

Rumors about the supposed marriage of Stalin and the non-existent Roza Kaganovich were mostly spread in Western anti-Semitic circles following the death of Nadezhda Alliluyeva. "I had only one sister, but she died in 1924," protested Lazar Kaganovich when he was questioned about this. A niece of his, by the name of Roza, the daughter of his elder brother, had lived for a long time in Rostov-on-Don and moved to Moscow only after the war with her husband and son.[18]

☆ Over the next months the German secret services could obtain little new information from Stalin's elder son, who was temporarily guarded in a villa in Berlin. Joseph Goebbels and his colleagues initially hoped, however, that they could make a puppet of him and involve him in the Russian-language radio propaganda broadcasts. When their plan failed, Yakov Dzhugashvili, whose nerves by that time had obviously deteriorated, was taken on the orders of Himmler to the Sachsenhausen concentration camp, after spending time in several temporary officers' camps. The special Division A of the secret camp comprised just three barracks, surrounded by a low stone wall and an electric barbed wire fence. It was here that Stalin's elder son was shot dead, late in the evening of April 14, 1943, in circumstances that to this day remain unclear. According to one widespread version the prisoner unexpectedly started to walk out of the camp and deliberately, or accidentally, touched the barbed wire fence. Then one of the guards shot at him. It is conceivable that he committed suicide: he had had suicidal tendencies since his youth. Whatever the case, he was finding it hard to cope with the pressures exerted on him by visitors arriving from Berlin with cameras and tape-recorders. He even got into a fight with his English fellow prisoners, who treated him disparagingly and on several occasions hurt him physically. Apparently, he had been involved in one such confrontation on the day he was killed.[19]

Yakov Dzhugashvilis's fiancée, the beautiful Ketevan Orakhelashvili, the daughter of the well-known Georgian politician, fell in love with Yevgeny Mikeladze, the conductor of the Tiflis Opera, and eventually married him. Stalin persecuted both during the Great Terror.

The news of the capture of his elder son probably only reached Joseph Stalin after a significant delay. In any case, as early as late summer 1941 the supposition arose in the paranoid brain of the Soviet dictator that *someone had betrayed Yakov*. He became suspicious of his daughter-in-law Yulia Meltser, although at the time Yakov was captured the woman was living several hundred kilometers from the front. The paranoid Stalin gave orders that Yulia should be imprisoned, thus finally breaking up the once large family that had surrounded him. The Master of the Kremlin was never again willing to meet with his relatives: he kept track only of his son Vasily and—whenever he was not angry with her for changing her partners too often—his daughter Svetlana.[20]

The two younger Stalin children reacted in different ways to the tragedy that had befallen their brother. The otherwise unfeeling, sly Svetlana proved in this instance humane. She took in her niece, the little Galina, who, following the arrest of her mother, had remained alone. She begged her father on several occasions to free Yakov's wife, and when her sister-in-law was finally released from prison she took her under her wing.[21] Her elder brother—who was only his half-brother—meant so much to Svetlana that after defecting from the country she wrote in her application for American citizenship: "Although Yakov was much older than me, he was a very good friend of mine, much better than Vasily, my own brother."[22] Vasily, on the other hand, made little secret of the fact that he could not be bothered about the fate of his captured brother. Their old rivalry must have contributed to this. According to Levon Shaumyan, "on the rare occasions when they met they snarled at each other, like the wolves in the *Jungle Book*. They were always quarreling and sneering at each other cruelly. Stalin sometimes had to shout at them."

The same conclusion can be reached from the memoirs of Svetlana Alliluyeva: "Following my mother's death something happened in Zubalovo that had never happened before: bickering between relatives became a daily routine. Uncle Fedya, who sometimes stayed there, antagonized my brother Yasha. He had also settled in Zubalovo with his wife. Yasha quarreled with Vasily. The two brothers were so different that there was no single issue on which they agreed... Yasha's wife was permanently at odds with my grandfather and grandmother, who also nagged at each other. On top of this, the wife of my uncle Pavlusha *[Yevgenia Alliluyeva—M. K.]*, who became a widow in 1938, made acid remarks that eventually turned everyone against everyone else. And we, the young children, whispered among ourselves. We sometimes sided with one, sometimes with the other, although we had no idea what the disputes were really about. Only my nanny, the great peacemaker, was able to preserve good relations with everyone. Diplomatic missions were down to her, and these somewhat improved the situation."[23]

There are hardly any written traces of these permanent family rivalries. The correspondence of Stalin's first-born son has still not been published. Far fewer recollections have survived about Yakov Dzhugashvili than about Vasily or Svetlana. The most telling portrait was drawn by Boris Bazhanov, a former member of Stalin's secretariat: "Yakov, Stalin's son from his first marriage, also lived in the General Secretary's apartment. Everyone called him Yashka. This extremely reserved, silent, and secretive young man was four years younger than me. He gave the impression of being a miserable, humiliated person. There was one trait of his that I found astonishing—what might be called a nervous deafness. Since he was always sunk in his own, secret, inner conflicts he did not even hear when someone turned to him to say something. But later on he would still react to what they had said. [...] Stalin did not like the boy, and persecuted him in every possible way. Yashka wanted to study, but he forced him to be factory worker. The son hated his father secretly and profoundly. He always tried to remain unnoticed..."[24] An illustration of this situation is the fact that Yakov applied to university only in 1930, at the age of twenty-three.

Yevgeny Mikeladze

Nevertheless, he tried to break away from his father's environment earlier than this. As a first step he began living with the daughter of an Orthodox priest, Zoya Gunina. The outraged Stalin, however, refused to accept the young woman, who had formerly been a classmate of Yakov. As a result of the permanent conflicts the deeply hurt young man attempted suicide. The tyrant father never forgave him for this: "Tell Yashka that he has behaved like a hooligan and a blackmailer, and I will not have, and cannot have, anything to do with him in the future. He can live wherever he wants and with whomever he chooses," he wrote to Nadezhda Alliluyeva on April 9, 1928.[25] Mikoyan, the good friend of the family, is mistaken when he claims that Stalin was angry with his son because he intended to marry a Jewish girl.[26]

According to him it was for this reason that Yakov had attempted suicide. The bullet pierced his lung but missed his heart. This prompted the dictator to make the sarcastic remark: "You couldn't even do this properly."[27]

Yakov Dzhugashvili was treated in the Kremlin hospital for three months following the attempted suicide. After this he moved with his wife to Leningrad, where, after completing a course, he found a job as an electrician. In the meantime Zoya gave birth to a daughter, but the baby died of a childhood disease at the age of eight months. In 1929 the couple separated and Yakov, as a prodigal son, turned up at his father's apartment. After great effort he was eventually admitted to the circle around Stalin, although he was not allowed to move back into his old room. Afterwards, the rumor circulated in the Kremlin and in the "House on the Embankment" for a long time that Yakov, who had strong Georgian roots—up to the age of fifteen he had spoken hardly any Russian—would marry Ketevan, the daughter of Mamia Orakhelashvili, one of the famous representatives of the Georgian political elite. However, their deep friendship never went as far as marriage because the shy Yakov was too slow in proposing to the girl. Ketusya Orakhelashvili grew tired of waiting and suddenly married Mikheladze, the young conductor of the Tiflis opera. Later Stalin, who, probably for political reasons, had earlier criticized the choice, mocked his son in the presence of the whole family: "If Yasha lives with me *[in the Kremlin—M. K.]*, not only Ketusya but even her mother will divorce her husband."[28]

In the Great Terror fate struck at the Orakhelashvili family as well. Mamia, the head of the family, was executed. His wife, after suffering various tortures, was killed in her prison cell. Their son-in-law, who in the meantime had become a famous conductor, was also sentenced to death. As for the beautiful Ketevan, she was to know the deepest circles of hell in Stalin's never-ending empire of labor camps.[29]

According to the recollections of Levon Shaumyan, Yakov Dzhugashvili had suffered agonies of jealousy when, while escorting Ketevan on the streets of Moscow, someone had made eyes at his sweetheart. It was as if no one else existed for him except this girl. In reaction to their break-up he started womanizing. He longed to start a family, but for a long time he was unable to find the right person. Then, on a trip to the countryside, he made the acquaintance of the accountant Olga Golisheva. He persuaded her to live with him in Moscow. However, the young couple parted soon after their son Yevgeny had been born because Yakov, in the meantime, had fallen desperately in love with Yulia Meltser, who was four years his senior. In conventional fashion he "rescued" the beautiful Odessa dancer from her husband, an NKVD functionary.[30]

Yulia, who fancied herself in the role of a *femme fatale*, must have been tempted to gain entry into Stalin's court by means of her marriage. However, it soon became apparent that her husband was ignored by his father, who gave him no support at all in making a living. After great hardship Yakov had obtained a technical qualification, but this had brought him only the most menial of jobs: "Between 1936 and 1937 I was a chimney-sweep engineer at the electric power plant of a factory named after Stalin," he wrote in his autobiography.[31] In peacetime the evening classes at the Artillery Academy, which he attended on his father's orders before the war, did not offer any special prospects. However, when war broke out Yakov's path led directly to the front. His father did not even say farewell to him in person. He only phoned him, giving a bombastic piece of advice: "Go and fight!"[32]

Yakov Dzhugashvili, who had suffered from his insignificance in the Kremlin, was certainly valuable in the eyes of his captors once behind the barbed wire. Stalin received the first, apparently authentic, news of his son via North Africa. In December 1943 William Taylor, one of the leaders of British military intelligence, forwarded the testimony of a French refugee, who had reached Casablanca, to Bogomolov, the Soviet ambassador to the French Resistance in Algiers and then to the North African headquarters of the Allied Forces. According to the self-declared eyewitness the Germans had earmarked the role of "Soviet Quisling"[33] for "Artillery Captain Stalin",[34] but he had resisted the attempt. According to him the prisoner was held for a while in the Oflag 10 C concentration camp: "He was put in a small, glassed-off room at the end of the barracks. Three guards guarded him day and night. He was not allowed to leave the room, but POW officers were allowed to visit him. They first had to write their names in a book so that the Germans knew the identity of his visitors."[35]

According to the eyewitness "Captain Stalin" was highly respected in the camp. "He received no packages from the Red Cross and accepted none of the food offered to him by the other prisoners, since other Russian prisoners of war did not receive these additional parcels *[that complemented the daily rations—M. K.]*." All this was pure fabrication, just like the statement that Yakov spoke fluent English and French. Also in contradiction to other sources is the statement that "Yakov made no secret of the fact that he supports his father's policies." Later, according to the testimony, Stalin's son was delivered to an unknown destina-

Family idyll shortly before the war broke out. This picture shows Yakov Dzhugashvili and his wife, Yulia Meltser with one of the new cars of the Kremlin garage.

tion in June 1943, since "the Germans discovered a tunnel leading from his room. As a punishment the residents of the camp were not allowed to collect letters and parcels for ten days."[36]

The letter about "the son of Comrade Stalin" was translated into Russian by Bogomolov's wife: "Not a single outside person saw these documents," reported the ambassador to Molotov, the people's commissar of foreign affairs.[37]

In the meantime certain information also reached the Kremlin via the channels of Soviet military intelligence. The confidants of Joseph Stalin for a while considered sending a commando, into the heart of Germany and snatching Yakov from the hands of his captors. First a group comprising veterans of the Spanish Civil War, then another Soviet commando were ready to free him, however, the move finally failed. Despite the news blackout, many moving stories emerged following the war about the sufferings of Stalin's elder son. Like pretender tsars and tsareviches, men claiming to be Dzhugashvili appeared in the barracks of POW camps, among emigrants, and even on the territory of the Soviet Union.[38]

1 Alliluyeva, 1981, 163.
2 This is what, among other authors, Elisabedashvili wrote, who counts as one of the more trustworthy sources. *RGASPI*, fond. 558, op. 4, d. 651.
3 *Iz glubini vremyon*, 1997, no. 7, 193–195.

4 *RGASPI*, fond. 558, op. 1, d. 5095.
5 *RGASPI*, fond. 558, op. 4, d. 651.
6 Torchinov-Leontyuk, 2000, 421.
7 *RGASPI*, fond. 558, op. 4, d. 651.
8 *Ibid.* The news about the death of Stalin's wife—in which she was called by the name Yekaterina Svanidze-Dzhugashvili—appeared in three successive issues of the daily *Tskaro* (Spring) on November 22, 23, and 24 in 1907. According to the family legend, however, Stalin's first wife died of typhoid. *Druzhba Narodov*, 1993, no. 6, 184.
9 Trotsky, 1985, vol. I, 129–130.
10 Strik-Strikfeldt, 1975, 10–12.
11 The author was incorrect here in citing the military rank. Yakov was only a lieutenant at the time.
12 *Ibid.*, 28–29.
13 Mikoyan, 1999, 362. For more information see Torchinov-Leontyuk 2000, 190–191.
14 *Iosif Stalin v obyatiakh semyi*, 1993, 70–72, 88–89. Meanwhile, the Soviet authorities behaved as if there was no connection between Stalin's elder son and the German leaflets with the "compromising" photograps and facsimile documents that were published after he was imprisoned. The *Krasnaya zvezda* paper on August 15, 1941, praised Yakov Dzhugashvili for his heroic behavior in the Vitebsk battle. In the same issue, they repoted that the lieutenant was decorated with the order of the Martial Red Banner. It is interesting that in 1977, in the utmost secrecy, the Soviet government awarded Yakov Dzhugashvili posthumously witrh the order of the Patriotic War, first degree *(Orden Otechestvennoi voyni i stepeni).* The family was not allowed to have the award at time, howerer.
15 *Ibid.*, 80.
16 *Ibid.*, 81.
17 *Ibid.*, 77–80.
18 Chuyev, 1992, 49–50.
19 In the extensive literature discussing this event, there are divergent interpretations of the same sources. *Iosif Stalin v obyatiakh semyi*, 1993, 69–89, 92–93, 96–100.
20 *Druzhba Narodov*, 1993, no. 6, 178.
21 *Ibid.*, 177–178.
22 Alliluyeva, 1970, 174.
23 Alliluyeva, 1981, 140.
24 Bazhanov, 1983, 156–157.
25 *Iosif Stalin v obyatiakh semyi*, 1993, 22.
26 Actually this happened much later.
27 Mikoyan, 1999, 361.
28 *Iosif Stalin v obyatiakh semyi*, 1993, 171. Marianna Orakhelashvili directed Georgian cultural politics for a while.
29 Antonov-Ovseyenko, 1995, 192.
30 *Druzhba Narodov*, 1993, no. 6, 175.
31 *Iosif Stalin v obyatiakh semyi*, 1993, 83.
32 Vasilyeva, 1996, 92, 95.
33 The Norwegian politician, Vidkun Quisling, collaborated with the occupying German forces during the Second World War.
34 Again, the indication of military rank is incorrect here.
35 *RGASPI*, fond. 82, op. 2, d. 1441.
36 *Ibid.*
37 *Ibid.*
38 *Druzhba Narodov*, 1993, no. 6, 185–186.

CHAPTER 24
"Red Vaska"

Vaska, the "little rascal"

While the life of Yakov Dzhugashvili ended in circumstances that are still unclear, in the court of the Soviet dictator a real "tsarevich" was emerging. Stalin's younger son referred to himself proudly as "Red Vaska" from his teenage years.[1] He was born before his parents' marriage had deteriorated, and perhaps this is why he was the favorite of Nadezhda Alliluyeva. Svetlana, however, was conceived during one of the armistices between the bitter quarrels and mutual recriminations, and this left its mark in her relationship with her mother.[2]

As soon as she was able to Nadezhda Alliluyeva entrusted her daughter to the care of nannies and governesses. However, she apparently remained close to Vasily, even when the boy reached school age and was getting wilder. But she did not over-pamper him. For Nadezhda, who had formerly devoted the majority of her time to her husband, this period coincided with her attempts at emancipation. In addition, she was tormented by permanent headaches and by an early menopause. Above all, she wanted to study. At around this time, besides the burden of the neglected and unloved Svetlana, she also began to feel encumbered by the presence of the permanently untidy Vasya, who would throw his toys around shouting inarticulately and making animal noises. Nadezhda Alliluyeva once had her son placed in the boarding nursery in the Kremlin so that she could go on a long journey with Stalin. To stop Vasya from getting bored in the absence of his parents they found him a kind of surrogate brother in the person of Artom Sergeyev, the son of an old party member who had died in an accident. This was a fairly cruel solution, since the chosen little boy was thus only able to see his mother at the weekends.[3]

The two children were raised together until the end of the 1930s. They were like fire and water. During my conversation with the elderly General Sergeyev in 1997 it was hard to understand what connection there could have been between the gentle, lazy, kindly half-orphan—or, as he was called by those around him, Tomik, or Tom[4] for short—with the tall, dynamic, rough-mannered "Red Vaska".

In the course of our meeting in Moscow Eteria Ordzhonikidze, who had also spent her childhood in the Kremlin, shuddered as she recalled "the mischief that the insufferable little devil was capable of". Stalin's younger son once stole his father's hunting rifle and began shooting with it. On other occasions he fired snowballs at the Kremlin staff. Following one of his escapades Joseph Stalin, as was quite typical, gave Vaska a good hiding, then dragged him to Sergo Ordzhonikidze. He asked the Georgian politician, who was then his main confidant, to take the "wicked scoundrel" into his household.

Despite his privileged position the younger son of the dictator suffered a great deal as a result of not receiving at home even a fraction of the love that he experienced in the families of Mikoyan, Ordzhonikidze, and Voroshilov. Following the tragic death of his mother his relationship with his father was not made any easier by the playful correspondence that gave such pleasure to his little sister Svetlana. Initially Joseph Stalin would occasionally greet his younger son in messages written on small scraps of paper. Later, however, along with Yakov, he often completely disregarded Vasily: "I am sending you pomegranates. In the next few days there'll be tangerines. Eat and be cheerful. [...] I am sending noth-

The adolescent Vasily in the foreground of the picture. On the bench are his friends, Styopa Mikoyan, the chubby Tom Sergeyev, and Volodya Mikoyan.

ing to Vasya because he is not studying properly," he wrote to his favorite "little sparrow" on October 8, 1935.[5] Ten days later Stalin complained to his "mistress of the house" that Vaska was creating permanent trouble.[6] Aware of such tensions, on the rare occasions that Svetlana actually mentioned Vaska she referred to him merely as her last secretary, or "Secretary Number 10."[7]

Only few letters written by "Red Vaska" can be found among the documents available. There were much more rudimentary than the little slips of paper written by his sister, Svetlana, although he was the elder. In a letter of September 26 (otherwise undated) the boy asked his father's permission to play football. Apparently, the guard watching over him made this dependable on Stalin's permission. "Please, let me know if I can play or not. I will follow your instructions."[8]

Another of his undated letter, mailed during his holiday, abounds in spelling mistakes. They were carefully corrected by Stalin in pencil. "Well, we have been staying in Sochi for two days. I got sunburn. Sveta is not allowed, however, to sunbathe and so she must stay at home."[9] It is also to be noted that "Red Vaska" did not dare to sneak on the "little princess" to his father. The girl, however, preferred to do so: "Daddy, after Vaska had gotten your letter *[a scolding one as a result of the girl's complaints—M. K.]*, he calmed down," she wrote to her "little secretary" on September 15, 1933.[10]

Perhaps as a consequence, the deeply hurt teenager often had tantrums. After a family trip on the Moscow metro, he "threw himself onto the bed" and sobbed hysterically.[11] It is understandable that after a time, he was looking for a *surrogate father* for himself. The first candidates were inevitably Stalin's bodyguards: "Dear Comrade Pauker! I am well. I have stopped fighting with Tom. I am eating well and plentifully. If you are not too busy you should come to visit us!" he wrote to his father's Hungarian bodyguard in mid-June 1934. "Comrade Pauker! Please send me a bottle of ink for my fountain pen. I greet you, Vasya." The high-ranking NKVD officer, whose years in Moscow are largely shrouded in obscurity, took immediate action. In response the grateful Vasya wrote another note and sent it by government courier to his new patron: "I received your letter and the ink, Comrade Pauker. [...] As far as I know Comrade Yefimov also forwarded my request for a shotgun, but I haven't received one. Perhaps you have forgotten about it? If possible, send one. Vasya."[12]

The rumor spread that Károly Pauker, who was initially a simple bodyguard and Stalin's barber, had been catapulted from this lowly position to being the leader of the NKVD's special department.[13] The former residents of the "House on the Embankment" remember him as a handsome gallant and a music-loving hedonist. "He ordered cars of the latest brand for Politburo members from abroad," recalled Aleksandr Orlov, one of Pauker's best friends during the Great Terror. "He also arranged for thoroughbred dogs, vintage wines and radio sets, to be imported. For the wives he ordered dresses, silk cloth, perfumes and other trifles from Paris, while for the children, expensive toys. After a time, Pauker became a kind of Santa Claus with the difference that the gifts were distributed all year long.[14] In the time of the Great Terror, however, Pauker soon became "a suspicious foreigner", then a "terrorist" with designs on Stalin's life. He was arrested and executed in August 1937.[15] Unlike him, Sergei Yefimov, who preferred to stay in the background, peacefully retired as a much-decorated general soon after the burial of the beloved Master. He retired not entirely of his own free will but as a result of the nagging of his one-time colleagues, who, in the name of the struggle against the "cult of personality", had suddenly become turncoats.[16] According to the former residents of the Kremlin Yefimov, Stalin's faithful bodyguard, who, in the early 1930s, had become the caretaker of the Zubalovo-4 resort with the support of Nadezhda Alliluyeva, gave the impression of being a complacent, paternalistic, elderly man, even in his thirties. The two younger Stalin children were always hanging around him.

Perhaps this was why the dictator entrusted him with the upbringing of "Red Vaska" after the suicide of his wife. Yefimov regularly discussed the carrying out of this difficult task with the third main bodyguard of the Kremlin, Nikolai Vlasik. "Stalin's faithful dog", as he was referred to by everyone in the "House on the Embankment" also pampered the half-orphan Vaska. Once the boy became a teenager he was one of his main confidants, a kind of "mental dustbin", and later a drinking companion.[17] "A few days ago K[arolina] V[asilyevna] *[governess to the two smaller Stalin children—M. K.]* found ten rubles in the boy's pocket. When asked where the money had come from Vasya answered that it was none of her business. Then he said that he had sold the stamp collection he had been given as a gift," we read in Yefimov's letter to Vlasik, written on September 22, 1935. "On September 19, he wrote his name on a piece of paper and at the end added: 'Vasya St...' (he wrote this in full), 'born March 1921, died 1935'. K[arolina] V[asilyevna] told me this the next day. I did not see the piece of paper personally since she had destroyed it. But I have a bad feeling about it. Is he thinking of something? I am on good terms with Vaska, but sometimes he is unpredictable. Tom *[Sergeyev—M. K.]* lives with him in the Kremlin. They spend all their time together. On days off the children go to Zubalovo. Otherwise Vasya thinks of himself as an adult and demands that his, often fairly stupid, wishes are fulfilled. We clash over these from time to time, but with persuasion and rational argument the disagreements are soon resolved."[18]

As the example illustrates Stalin's entourage did not have much pedagogical sense. The guardians from the internal affairs department were somewhat in awe of the unpredictable, unstable Vaska. Perhaps tormented by the ghost of his mother he often threatened to commit suicide. The main bodyguards were very much afraid of this and tended to indulge Stalin's younger son in everything. Later on they gave him drinks and accompanied him to the riding hall, which the "tsarevich" visited under the name of Volkov.[19] They even encouraged him to take lovers—anything to prevent him from making great scenes every day, news of which might reach the Master. The young tyrant obviously enjoyed the fact that he could give orders to those in his father's court; without exception high-ranking NKVD officers, of whom the residents of the Kremlin and of the "House on the Embankment" were terrified. Following the arrest of Vasily Stalin—as his letter, written to the presidency of the CPSU makes clear—he realized in his prison cell only years later, at the age of thirty-four, how mistaken he had been in the path he had chosen as a teenager. But he also blamed others for this—his guardians from the internal affairs department, who had formed his company before the war, and, indirectly, Joseph Stalin himself: "I was left without a mother at a young age. And there was no way for me to be brought up under my father's everyday supervision. All my life has been spent among adults, among guards. Nor were they particularly moral, or even considerate. This was to leave a deep mark on the whole of my private life and character. I began to drink and smoke at an early age."[20]

☆ The choice of wording reveals that smoking, for some reason, was regarded as an unpardonable sin in Stalin's circle, even though the dictator himself, as a teenager, had liked to chew and smoke tobacco. As an exile he had always used cheap virgin tobacco, and once in power he was seen everywhere with his familiar pipe. Nevertheless, he often reprimanded his colleagues if they smoked in his presence. Whenever he caught his children, especially Yakov, smoking, he gave them a severe beating. According to the memoirs of Leon Trotsky: "…we often found the young boy, who, until the age of ten, had been raised in Tiflis by his relatives and then brought to the Kremlin, in the room of our two sons. He preferred to stay with us than with his father. I came across a note about this written by my wife: 'Yasha is about twelve years old,[21] a very gentle little boy with a dark complexion. His black eyes, which sparkle with gold, are very attractive. He is thin, almost miniature. I have heard that he resembles his mother, who died of pneumonia. His behavior and manners are very gentle. Yasha told Seryozha *[the Trotskys' younger son—M. K.]*, with whom he is very good friends, that his father tells him off severely and beats him if he smokes. But, as he said, he can't get him off cigarettes by beating him. Seryozha said that Yasha had spent the night in the corridor with the guard. Stalin had thrown the child out of the apartment because he had smelt tobacco on him. Once I found Yasha in the boys' room with a cigarette in his hand. He smiled nervously. 'Carry on,' I said to him, to put him at ease. 'My father is completely insane!' said Yakov with determination. 'He himself smokes but he stops me.'"[22]

In his draft, *Joseph Stalin, A Character Study*, which is virtually a psychiatric case study, Trotsky recalls another, similar scene: "Bukharin told me this, probably around 1924, when he was moving closer to Stalin but was still on friendly terms with me. 'I have just come from Koba […]. Do you know what he did? He took his one-year-old son [Vasya] from his cot, filled his mouth with pipe smoke, and blew it in the little boy's face… 'What kind of nonsense is that?' I interrupted. 'I swear to God that's what happened! On my honor!' answered Bukharin rapidly, with his characteristic childishness. 'The little boy choked and cried, and meanwhile Stalin was roaring with laughter: 'No problem! It'll only make him stronger…' He imitated Stalin's Georgian accent. 'But that's barbaric!' 'It's obvious you don't understand Koba. You know, he is so unusual and original…'"[23]

In the middle of the photograph is the suddenly serious "Red Vaska" in a military school uniform.

Finally, in his unfinished draft *Stalin*, Leon Trotsky traced "Koba's" senseless cruelty and conflicts with his sons, almost on a Freudian basis, to the dictator's own childhood: "The Dzhugashvili family existed on the borderline of provincial artisanship and utter poverty. Their roots reached back to the rural Middle Ages. They lived in a world of traditional destitution and traditional superstition. When the boy became a professional revolutionary he did not continue the family tradition but broke away from it. However, the rejected tradition—in the form of primitive cultural habits—continued to infiltrate his nervous system and consciousness, even following his break away. His emotions remained cruel and his horizons narrow. The disparagement of women and the despotic treatment of children left their mark on Stalin's whole life."[24]

A similar story is revealed by the confession of Stalin's younger son, "Red Vaska", quoted above: "Although I was a talented child, at secondary school I only picked up my course books just before the exams, thus I was never anything more than a mediocre student. I wanted to be an artilleryman, so I applied to the Number One Artillery School in Moscow. My father, however, decided that it was no good if both his sons served in the artillery. *[Yakov, who already had an engineering degree, had also just applied to the school—M. K.]* Thus I ended up attending the Air Force Officers' Training School. I obtained excellent results and received the rank of lieutenant. From that day on my conversations with my father were no longer father-son conversations. When we met we restricted our talk to military air power."[25]

The diary entry for November 17, 1935, written by the wife of Stalin's brother-in-law, Maria Korona, apparently also addresses the same theme: "J[oseph] gave Vaska two months to mend his ways. He threatened to throw him out of his home and take in three talented boys in his place. Nyura cried bitterly, and there were even tears in the eyes of Pavel *[Anna Alliluyeva and Pavel Alliluyev—M. K.]*. Not even they believe that Vasya can change in two months. That's why they think Stalin will carry out his threat. His father thinks that Vasily is talented and is capable of pulling himself together. Naturally the boy needs cutting down to size. He has become extremely cocky, being the son of a great man. He behaves

After finishing military officer school, Vasily Stalin regularly reported on the high-ranking officers of the Soviet Air Force to his father.

badly towards those around him. Her father regards Svetlana as less talented, but he sees her as dutiful. He considers both of them as cold creatures, not really attached to anyone, who have forgotten their mother unforgivably quickly. According to him the children are unbalanced. He knows them down to the last detail, and he's right about everything. What an analytical mind! What a psychologist!"[26] However, some days later, on December 4, 1935 she found out that Stalin's younger son had once again escaped his father's scorn. "Vasya has already been forgiven. He visited his father. He seems to have improved his marks. I am extremely pleased. Vasya is a very resourceful boy, he is smart, too—he can even trick his father. He can make us believe that he is straightforward and sincere, although he is not."[27]

But this is only one side of the story. The truth is that the Master of the Kremlin, who before the Second World War was so proud of the progress of little Svetlana, was never particularly interested about Vasily 's studies. The scandal only exploded when the history teacher Martishin wrote a letter of complaint to him about the teenager, who was falling behind in his studies and constantly playing truant. In his reply, dated June 8, 1938, Stalin made it clear that the teaching staff of "Special School Number Two", which was run for the elite, were dealing with a "spoilt youngster of mediocre talents".[28] According to him Vasya was "a little scoundrel (a Scythian type!). He does not always tell the truth. He likes to blackmail his weak superiors and is sometimes insolent. He doesn't have a very strong will, or, more exactly, he lacks focus. Perhaps the only reason this impudent boy has not destroyed himself is because in our country there are still pedagogues who will stand no nonsense from the wayward young master. I advise you to make stricter demands on Vasily. Do not be afraid when the scoundrel pretends to blackmail you by threatening to commit suicide. In this respect you can count on me. Unfortunately I do not have the time devote to sorting Vasily out, but I promise to take him by the scruff of the neck from time to time."[29]

The "wild Scythian" Vasily had by that time got so out of control that he could not be allowed to appear in front of the school graduation board. In the midst of the great scandal Martishin, who, however cautiously, had listed the boy's wicked deeds, was removed to another school. In his reply the pedagogue still wrote emotionally to Stalin that his message had been "an unforgettable experience", being "a model of the directness and simplicity characteristic of genius."[30]

Lavrenty Beria, the Georgian party secretary who had been ordered to the Soviet capital and appointed to head the NKVD, then became the next tutor of "Red Vaska". Apparently he took to heart the warnings of the fired pedagogue. Once Vasily had turned seventeen he advised that the high-school failure, who had since risen to the rank of trainee officer, should no longer be accompanied at all times by armed guards. Nevertheless, on Beria's orders he was surrounded by secret agents, and later by informers disguised as adjutants, wherever he went: "He did not live with us in the barracks, but in the headquarters. Whenever he entered the garage he would take a swig from his hip flask before getting on his motorcycle. Once he almost had a serious accident. His leg was dislocated and he ended up in the military hospital, from where he was sent to the garrison of our flying squad. A telegram arrived about him, the text of which I still remember word for word: 'Trainee Officer Stalin should be treated exactly as everyone else. J. Stalin'," recalled one of the fellow trainees of the "tsarevich".[31]

In another extant letter, dated November 13, 1939, Vasily Stalin solemnly wrote to his father that he would be a different person in the air force. He was not even willing to travel home from his air base in the Crimean until he had passed his last exams.[32] This promise was again in vain even though, according to some of his former fellow cadets, Vasily could have been an excellent air force pilot. If he had not drunk so much. This was the opinion of, among others, Stepan Mikoyan, one of the most renowned Soviet test pilots, who, as a retired general in Moscow, told me at length about his youth in the Kremlin with "Red Vaska".

Before the war, the rumor circulated in Soviet elite circles that Stalin's younger son took delight in shouting cruelly at the "ordinary" trainee officers in order to humiliate them. At the same time he would beat up those who tried to fraternize with him and flatter him. There is little wonder that he was deeply hated by many of his superiors and inferiors. They knew very well that, by inclination, the young man was only too happy to be the "eyes and ears" of his father in the air force. As soon as he could he passed compromising information to the Soviet dictator about the most famous and most celebrated of "Stalin's hawks". His written and oral information played a very important—even if not decisive—role in the ignominious pursuit that Iosif Stalin conducted before and after the Second World War, in two major waves, against the high-ranking commanders of the Soviet air force.[33]

1 This is how, for a long time, he signed also his letters to his father. Sukhomlinov, 2001, 27–29.

2 Alliluyeva, 1981, 27, 92–93.

3 Mikoyan, 1988, 206.

4 "Tomik" is an abbreviation of *tozhestvo marksizma i kommunizma*, or "the victory of Marxism and Communism". This is another one of the strange neologisms of the time.

5 *RGASPI,* fond. 558, op. 1, d. 5111.

6 *RGASPI,* fond. 558, op. 1, d. 5112.

7 *RGASPI,* fond. 558, op. 1, d. 5131.

8 *RGASPI,* fond. 558, op. 11, d. 1552.

9 *Ibid.*

10 *Ibid.*

11 Sukhomlinov, 2001, 26.

12 *Iosif Stalin v obyatiakh semyi,* 1993, 48.

13 In reality, he made a very long journey before arriving at this position. In the Civil War, he fought in Central Asia. He was twice awarded the Military Order of Red Banner. Petrov-Skorkin, 1999, 335. According to one of Orlov's suggestions, Stalin felt "more than brotherly love" in his relationship with the handsome Károly Pauker. Orlov, 1983, 323, 334–335. This suggestion is not supported by another source.

14 Orlov, 1983, 325.
15 A year after this, when Yezhov was about to resign from his position of people's commissar for internal affairs, he made a comment on the "conspirator" Pauker and his "dirty band". Bryuhanov-Shoshkov, 1998, 127. It seems that Pauker was a Yagoda associate. The arrested former NKVD chief, Yagoda at least, spoke well about him during his interrogation: "He was the closest to me. He was very loyal." Yagoda, 1997, 129–130. It is telling that the Russian authorities are not willing to rehabilitate Pauker officially, nor many other former Yagoda associates.
16 Alliluyeva, 1981, 120–121.
17 Contrary to popular belief, the first time Vlasik personally met Stalin was not during the Civil War, at the Tsaritsyn front, but in 1927. That is when he became one of Stalin's bodyguards. Loginov, 2000, 94–95.
18 *Iosif Stalin v obyatiakh semyi*, 1993, 53–54.
19 Galagan-Trifonova, 1995, 22.
20 *Iosif Stalin v obyatiakh semyi*, 1993, 126.
21 In fact, he was older than 12 then.
22 Trotsky, 1988, 67–68.
23 Trotsky, 1991, 56–57.
24 *Ibid.*, 57.
25 *Iosif Stalin v obyatiakh semyi*, 1993, 126.
26 *Ibid.*, 183–184.
27 *Ibid.*, 185.
28 Originally, the school was intended to be a boarding school in which orphans from the countryside would mix with the children of the elite. This experiment to eliminate class differences did not work out. The "special school" became a typical cadre training center. Cf. Holmes, 1999, 7–13, 19–21, 44–52.
29 *Iosif Stalin v obyatiakh semyi*, 1993, 54–55.
30 *Ibid.*, 57–58.
31 Vasilyeva, 1996, 118–119.
32 *Iosif Stalin v obyatiakh semyi*, 1993, 126.
33 *Iosif Stalin v obyatiakh semyi*, 1993, 121–122, 134; Smirnov, 1997, 208–218; Pikhoya, 1998, 45–47.

As the Generalissimo of the Soviet Army, Stalin was eager to deepen his knowledge of military and foreign politics. This picture shows him inspecting a tank near the Kremlin, most likely in 1943.

The Generalissimo

During their negotiations in Moscow in October 1944, Winston Churchill and Joseph Stalin wore military uniforms most of the time, but sometimes they dressed and chatted more casually.

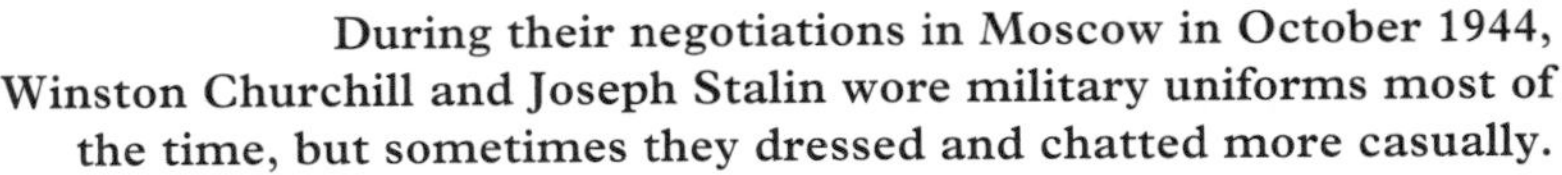

Joseph Stalin in the company of Field Marshal Montgomery, the great British hero of the Second World War.

CHAPTER 25
The Young General in Prison

For a long time the kind of breathtaking careers enjoyed by Napoleon's marshals was dreamed of by Vasily Stalin for himself: the lieutenant, who had merely been stumbling his way through the training bases and hinterland garrisons, was transferred to the front in August 1941 and was given a series of special promotions. Prior to this the intelligence directorate of the Red Army General Staff had inquired in a letter to the cadre department of the party's Central Committee whether his father approved of the transfer. For conspiratorial reasons, in the document that decided the fate of the young officer, Vasily Stalin was referred to as V. I. Ivanov.[1]

After receiving this permission everyone at the air bases near the front made exceptions for the young man. His commanders allowed him to fly missions only on rare occasions, and whenever this happened a whole formation would accompany him. According to a report written on July 4, 1945, Vasily Stalin "during the Great Patriotic War, took part in combat missions on a total of twenty-nine occasions and in the course of these missions shot down two enemy planes."[2]

Even these embellished figures are not particularly impressive. Furthermore, Colonel-General Rudenko, the commander of the Sixteenth Air Division, did not mention the fact that Vasily Stalin became notorious among his fellows for using obscenities in front of pilots older than himself. On one occasion he even slapped the people's commissar of the unit in the face with a pair of leather gloves because he had warned him not to smoke while sitting on the airplane wing. Also, during an argument, he once pulled out a gun in front of his fellow officers and shot into the air. Near the end of the war the "tsarevich" even took the liberty to send a thin, wounded old horse away from the front on a special airplane, because he felt sorry for it. Yevgeny Savitsky, the later air marshal—who, following the defeat of Hitler, was the commander of one of the air corps stationed in the Soviet occupation zone and for a while Vasily's immediate superior—remembered how arrogantly the young officer had behaved when introducing himself: "He arrived accompanied by four bodyguards and an adjutant."[3]

Stalin's younger son sometimes gave the impression of being a brave man, especially if he went on duty the worse for drink. However, in spring 1942 he accepted without hesitation the order of his superiors, who were somewhat afraid of him, that instead of further service at the front he should travel to Moscow and should join the work of the supervisory committee working under the General Staff, who, among other things, had the task of exploring the conditions in the air force.

This should have involved frequent inspection trips. Vasily, however, did not like to leave the capital of the warring country, although he did take the opportunity to fly over to Kuybishev to visit his sister Svetlana and her friends. When he was sent to study at the Air Force Academy, after a while his teenage "truant syndrome" appeared once again: he had little inclination to study. He preferred to give parties for his circle, which comprised actors, journalists, convalescing flight officers, and pretty women in particular, in his father's *dacha* in Zubalovo or in the "House on the Embankment". Among his large circle of acquaintances there was much talk about how, in the late summer of 1942, he seduced Nina

General Vasya, the youngest high-ranking officer of the Red Army, seemed to emulate his father's marshals in collecting medals.

Orlova, the wife of the famous cameraman Roman Karmen, and how the stern father had sent the country's procurator general after his younger son and his beautiful lover. Then, on April 4, 1943, he was involved in a much more serious accident. Vasily, who by the age of twenty-two had risen from lieutenant to colonel in the course of barely one and a half years, dropped explosives into the river Moscow while fishing with a few fellow officers and was wounded in the resulting blast. According to the records of the director of the Kremlin hospital the patient's face and left leg were badly injured in the accident.[4] A flight engineer died at the scene of the explosion.[5]

Joseph Stalin was forced to react. In a special daily order he reprimanded his son and demoted him from his position as a regimental commander. Apparently, however, not even he took the strict punishment seriously. He was much more distressed by the first love affairs of his daughter Svetlana than the serious consequences of Vasily's "manly" behavior, even though his son had disgraced himself on several occasions. Barely one and a half years later the "Soviet generalissimo" rehabilitated his younger son by promoting him to the rank of commander of an air division.[6] In the next few months, however, this division—despite the huge losses it sustained—destroyed only twenty-nine German airplanes over Berlin in the course of the battle against the Luftwaffe. Rather than a reprimand Colonel Vasily Stalin received a commendation: his father promoted him to the rank of general. Thus at only twenty-four years of age he became the youngest major-general in the Red Army. According to the official reports of his superiors he was "a very easily tired and nervous" man, although he was twice decorated with the Order of the Red Banner, as well as with the Order of Aleksandr Nevsky and the Order of Suvarov, usually awarded to commanders at the front and less often to field commanders.[7] Despite being showered with decorations he remained impossible to get along with. "In 1946 he was serving in Germany. He occupied a two-storey villa. His children lived with him—a boy and a girl. He was guarded by border guards in green berets. The border guards delivered his food on two donkeys. He was well-known for his lack of mercy. He was greatly feared in the army, but the German population was especially terrified of him. At the same time he took care of the families of officers," was how Yevgeny Savitsky, his commander, remembered Stalin's son.[8]

In 1951 a brochure entitled *Data on the Participation of Major-General V. Stalin in the Great Patriotic War* was complied in Georgia by the scholars of the Georgian Academy of Sciences.[9]

The collection of medals further increased when the dictator transferred his son to Moscow. Vasily had feasted and pilfered his way through half of Germany, and his photograph, despite a new series of scandals, had appeared in the popular illustrated journal *Ogonek*. On this photograph a smiling Major-General Stalin sits in the cockpit of an airplane. The father, in an unexpected outburst of affection—earlier perhaps repressed?—rewarded the good-for-nothing air force officer with a seat in the Supreme Soviet and membership of the Central Committee. Abdurakhman Avtorkhanov, who understood Soviet court intrigue better than any other analyst, recognized that the Master of the Kremlin was following in the footsteps of the Russian tsars when, on June 18, 1948, he entrusted his own son with command of the air force of the Moscow Military District. This had a coded meaning: it was as if Joseph Stalin, who, by the end of his life, suspected a conspiracy in every corner, was promoting the twenty-seven-year-old Vasily as one of his main bodyguards.[10] Nevertheless, in March 1952—according to another version in July that year—he "dropped" his son once again. Having appeared in front of him during an inspection parade staggering drunk, Vasily was removed from his position. Some see behind this action the hand of Beria, who was preparing for the removal of the dictator. Others attribute it to the increasingly serious alcoholism of the young general.[11]

In any case Joseph Stalin forgave his son too much. He had not even been disturbed by the fact that the private life of "Red Vaska" was as scandalous as his military career. His marriage in 1941 to a blonde beauty by the name of Galina Burdonskaya, who came from a reliable NKVD family, soon ran aground. At the end of the war Vasily chased the woman away, keeping both their children.[12] His next wife, the voluptuous Nonna Timoshenko, the daughter of a marshal who had formerly been a mounted Cossack, beat and starved the children like a wicked fairy-tale stepmother. However, fate was to strike down this handsome woman, who spent her days in speculative trading and casual affairs. The two children that she bore to Vasily Stalin both became chronic alcoholics and died early: her son Vasily at the age of twenty-three, and her daughter Svetlana, who underwent psychiatric treatment, at the age of thirty-eight.[13]

Vasiliy's cruelty, blended with sensuousness, was unlimited. "General Stalin, almost every day got drunk, failed to go to work and skipped not a single woman"—his adjutant Polyansky confessed against him. "He has had so many affairs that if someone asked me how many, I could not answer the question".[14]

From among his many women, his last great love before his arrest, Kapitolina Vasilyeva, proved to be the most faithful. The former swimming champion, who is still alive today, is able to speak for hours about her "dear Vasenka". She still regards as one of the greatest experiences of her life her two-week holiday in the autumn of 1950, in the government villa near the Caucasian Lake Ritsa, in the company of Joseph Stalin. Afterwards, as a sign of his friendship, the Soviet dictator sent her by courier an envelope containing ten thousand rubles.

Kapitolina is still unable to accept how much her partner suffered when, following the death of Stalin, he was demoted to the rank of private, then imprisoned.[15] Vasily himself tempted his fate in various ways. For a long time he wore a black armband in mourning for his father. This was how he appeared when summoned by Nikita Khrushchev. When the issue was raised as to where he should serve in the future he sarcastically answered that he was "willing to take the seat of Bulganin, the minister of defense".[16]

The interrogation of "Red Vaska", whose hair turned rapidly gray in prison, was initially conducted by Lieutenant-General Vlodzimirsky in Lubyanka Prison. He was Beria's favorite investigation officer. The drunken and cowardly prisoner, whose personality had by that time already disintegrated, needed little persuasion to sign the confessions placed in front of him. The main investigator—who not much later, in December 1953, faced the firing squad himself—proved to be a good psychologist. For several hours he read to Stalin's son from the testimonies against him written by his former wife, partner, adjutants, and doctor. Along with him, namely, two other brigadier generals, one colonel, four lieutenants-colonel and one major, Vasily's driver and his barber were put to prison mainly charged with fraud. However, they were all released in 1953 and 1954.[17]

Finally the cornered prisoner confessed embezzling and wasting vast sums of money over the years. For instance, from the enormous amounts that had been transferred for the development of the air force of the Moscow military district he once stole three million rubles. In Soviet society, where the impoverished population was starving and cold after the war, this was an incredibly large sum. But it was not enough for Vasily. He admitted that soon afterwards he embezzled another five million rubles.[18]

Stalin's younger son defended himself by arguing that the money was "pruned" from his budget as a commander, and particularly from the budget of the Soviet ministry of defense, were not used only for high living but that he had also supported several top athletes. Even admitting that he was not the only benefiting of the several hundred thousands, moreover millions embezzled and that the Soviet machinery of justice, having hardly changed after the Soviet dictator's death, may have gone too far, still the facts revealed by the investigation documents cannot be questioned. These show how "General Vasya" had used

The high security prison of Vladimir, and the prisoner named Vasilyev, Stalin's younger son.

treasury money to pay for a whole army of gamekeepers and beaters, cooks, and governesses for his children, as well as to finance countless casual lovers. Not to mention the state-of-the-art sports facilities, the huge airplane hangars transformed into warehouses, luxury cars for his own use, and about a dozen motorcycles which he had delivered from the eastern zone of Germany by special airplane to Moscow. Besides these "trophies" he had had luxury items purchased for foreign currency in Western capitals for his family and his large entourage. According to the documents, if anyone made a tentative comment about this, Vasily Stalin would answer that he was carrying out his father's wishes. Apparently, this was mostly the case. Marshal Khrulyov, who was responsible for the economic affairs and the entire logistics of the Soviet army, remembered that in 1949 Stalin's son had involved his own father and Nikolai Bulganin, the minister of defense, in an entirely irregular building racket near Moscow, which ran up huge expenses for the treasury, and especially the army, and created opportunities for a whole series of abuses.[19]

In the circle of his childhood friends and family the "tsarevich" would often say that no one would dare to stop him as long as his father was alive. "And what will happen afterwards?" he asked rhetorically. "Well, the future does not hold much good for me. I must hurry before they liquidate me," he added darkly. It was probably for this reason that he devoured life's pleasures at such a rate. He even had a direct telephone line installed in the garden outhouse of his *dacha*, which resembled the mansion of a rich nineteenth-century Russian landlord. He had the beautiful forest surrounding the resort fenced off and had a concrete dam erected on the nearby river so that he would have better fishing. He was not in the least troubled by the fact that, as a result, half the people in the village were forced to resettle.[20]

Besides his heedless wastefulness Vasily sometimes proved to be petty, or even pathologically mean. In this respect he also resembled his sister Svetlana. During one summer, on the pretext of prudence, he had his acquaintances sell the fruits and vegetables grown in his estate-sized garden at the nearby *kolkhoz* market. The money, which was only a fraction of the hundred thousands that had been transferred to the air force of the Moscow military district and then used for his own purposes, was of course pocketed by him. However, in doing so, he was only following the example of the marshals and ministers of his father. In the last phase of the Second World War a part of the Soviet military and political elite—including the victors of Berlin, Georgy Zhukhov and Ivan Konev—engaged in extensive pillaging in the eastern part of Germany and the other invaded countries. Nor did they stop the "great robbery" even after the capitulation of the Nazi leadership.[21] However, no one called the victors to account until such plundering became politically suspicious in the eyes of Joseph Stalin. "Red Vaska" was unable to understand until the end of his life why he was the one accused of profiteering and embezzling. Indeed, it is ironic that the investigation, carried out from the autumn of 1953 into the appropriation of large sums of money, should have been coordinated by Ivan Serov, who he himself was one of the chief plunderers in the Soviet army.[22]

☆ The days of Vasily Stalin were spent amidst doubts, self-questioning, and nervous fits in the dreaded Lefortovo Prison run by the political police, then in the Central Prison in Vladimir. This was the name, in tsarist times, of the special institution that served as a place of detention for enemies of the Soviet system and for those, like Stalin's son, who had "lost their way". According to contemporaries this latter category of detainees enjoyed several privileges.[23] "Red Vaska", however, had become a nervous wreck and would bang his head against the wall and the iron-plated door in order to attract the attention of his captors. We know from a confidential letter written to Stalin in December 1950 by the director of the Kremlin hospital's that, besides delirium tremens, Vasily suffered from epilepsy.[24] The Soviet leaders, who had known the boy from his schooldays, were informed of this. It is hard to decide whether Stalin's heirs were genuinely tormented by their consciences as a result. These men, who, without exception, were the creations of the Soviet dictator, kept the son of their benefactor in solitary confinement, under the name Vasily Pavlovich Vasilyev. The members of the "collective party leadership" made this decision unanimously even though, from the spring of 1953, they quarreled with one another constantly on every other issue. The "aberrant" Vasily Stalin was therefore condemned to an iron-barred dungeon, just like the disobedient descendants of former Russian tsars had been in Russian history.

"Three of four cells away from me a certain Vasilyev was being held," remembered Pavel Sudoplatov, one of the most infamous figures of the Soviet political police, who had been imprisoned with other members of Beria's former circle in the Vladimir Prison. "In reality he was Stalin's son Vasily, who even in the prison made scene after scene. Once, when his wife, the daughter of Marshal Timoshenko, visited him, he got into a fight with her. He demanded that she turn immediately to Khrushchev and Voroshilov and request his release."[25] From time to time Vasily Stalin himself did the same. In the same year as his arrest, on November 28, 1953, he wrote humbly to Malenkov, his father's heir in the position of prime minister: "Dear Georgy Maksimilianovich! I am not able, either morally or physically, to endure my recent isolation. Please receive me for an audience so that I can explain. This would mean that I could convince you in person, and not with the help of intermediaries, of the sincerity of my repentance and my guilty conscience. I beg you not to deny my request! Yours, V[asily]

Stalin."[26] A few months later he took up his pen again and turned to his former "surrogate father", Klim Voroshilov, in his capacity as head of the Supreme Soviet: "Petition. Since my health has seriously deteriorated I request to be allowed to see my sister. V[asily] Stalin, January 20, 1954."[27] Finally, after many such petitions, the prisoner achieved certain concessions from his captors. Although "Red Vaska" was not released, his father's former apprentices took action to ensure that he would receive special treatment. Many of the old Vladimir prisoners remember the extent to which exceptions were made for him by the local representatives of the KGB, not to mention the prison commander, who idolized the Kremlin's late Master. Vladimir Menshagin, the former mayor of Smolensk who, during WWII, had collaborated with the Germans, left a detailed memoir on tape about the sufferings he underwent in prison. He noted what the guards had said: the tyrant's son was kept in a spacious cell that had been transformed from the former prison chapel, where, from time to time, his wife or partner visited him: "...they spent three of four days with him in the cell, then [...] they sent various parcels for him. There were no restrictions on them."[28]

Then, at last, the day of freedom arrived for Stalin's prodigal son. Following the execution of Beria, Vasily occasionally tried to bargain with the existing masters of the Kremlin: from his cell he sent messages to those politicians who, at the time, seemed to be winning in the wrestling match that was going on for Stalin's scepter. In his "moments of clarity" he "suddenly remembered" incriminating information, first about Lavrenty Beria, then about Nikolai Bulganin and Georgy Malenkov. Finally Khrushchev and his circle appeared to grant some concessions. On January 5, 1960 KGB boss Aleksandr Shelepin and prosecutor general Roman Rudenko, referring to the prisoner's serious illness, proposed that he should be given a "partial amnesty". In parallel with this they had the Moscow soviet assign a three-room apartment to him, and he was given a one-off sum of thirty thousand rubles. (At the time this represented an enormous sum.) His valuables, which had been confiscated during the house search, were returned to him, and a large pension was also granted.[29] There is no doubt that the Soviet leadership did not treat any of the surviving victims of Stalin's rule with such generosity.

Vasily, however, even after his release, piled scandal upon scandal. In a drunken state he criticized his father's "ungrateful stooges", and once, in the middle of Moscow, he crashed his car into that of a foreign diplomat. He was temporarily imprisoned again for this, in Lefortovo.[30] Then in April 1961 he was exiled to Kazan', accompanied by a nurse from the KGB who had been promoted to the rank of "wife". To prevent him from drinking to excess his special three-hundred-ruble general's pension was halved.[31] Meanwhile all his documents were made over into the name of Dzhugashvili, without his knowledge. He responded in a cautious but sentimental letter. However, he could not bear the old name of the family for long.[32] On March 19, 1962, "Red Vaska" Stalin died in suspicious circumstances in one of the hospitals of the Tatar capital. The members of his family, who even now suspect murder, had still not been shown the post-mortem report.[33]

☆ When the news of his death reached Moscow, the KGB's disinformation department began to spread the idea that Stalin's younger son had never been entirely sane. There is some truth in this. According to the unpublished diary entries of one of his mother's friends, Alisa Radchenko, those around the boy soon realized that "something was wrong with him": "In spring 1923 I visited Nadya [Nadezhda Alliluyeva] with my son, at the *dacha* where she was on holi-

Svetlana (on the right) and her sister-in-law, Galina Burdonskaya, who was Vasily's wife in the early 1940s.

day with her three-year-old son Vasyatka. We were shocked, and she herself was worried, by how restless and hyperactive the little boy was. He was running up and down non-stop without a word in the long, dark room, like some kind of whirlwind or a *tachanka*[34] from the Civil War. [...] At the end of summer 1927 Nadezhda invited me and my son to her apartment in Moscow, which was in a small white house that stood at the Kremlin's Trinity Gate. She had invited me specifically to observe the behavior of Vasyatka, who by then was already seven years old. She asked me whether his vivaciousness and hyperactivity were normal. At the same time she wanted to boast about two-year-old Svetlana, who was the direct opposite of the little boy: she seemed to be an unusually balanced, quiet child."[35] According to Kira Alliluyeva, who remembered all three of the "Master's" children very well, no one was truly normal in that aberrant family. ☆

M. K.: Apparently, you don't have many good memories of Vasily.

K. A.: Even as a small child he behaved like an impudent little devil. And when he grew up he turned completely bad. *[Very angry.]* He talked back insolently to adults. He drank. He was a womanizer. Not like a *[sighs]* romantic youth, but like a depraved and debauched character.

M. K.: Was he like his father?

K. A.: Yes, in this respect too. During the war he drank like a fish. My mother, and especially my aunt, Anna Alliluyeva, scolded him repeatedly because of it. But he just replied arrogantly and after a while he began to hate my aunt. He started to turn Stalin against her, and against the other members of the Alliluyev family.[36]

M. K.: He didn't like you either?

K. A.: For some reason he liked me better than other members of the family. Perhaps because in his childhood I often beat him up *[she illustrates with gestures]*. We were almost the same age, but I proved the stronger. At least when we were fighting. Then in 1942 I was fated to meet him again regularly. The drama school where I was studying had just returned to Moscow after being evacuated. I lived at home in the "House on the Embankment", and Vaska lived in my aunt Anna's empty flat on a different staircase in the same building. He always invited me whenever he was having company. They were mostly actors and air force officers who came to see him. But these evenings were always respectable and orderly when I was present. *[Sarcastically]* Like in the most decent of families.

M. K.: Who were Vasily Stalin's guests?

K. A.: I remember Mark Bernes, the famous singer and movie actor. I sang duets with him and accompanied him on the piano. At the time Vasya was still on good terms with the writer Konstantin Simonov and his wife, Valentina Serova, the blonde bombshell. During the war Simonov had dedicated his volume of poetry *With You and Without You* to her. Everyone was desperate to get hold of it, since at the front and in the back lands people were fed up with political verses. But in the Politburo one of the guardians of morals—rumor had it it was Molotov—put the little volume on Stalin's desk. It was common knowl-

Svetlana with her first husband, Grigory Morozov, whom she eventually had to divorce on Stalin's orders.

Svetlana Stalina with her son, Iosif.

edge that Stalin hated love poetry. "My dear relative" flicked through it and said: "It would have been quite enough to print only two copies of this book. One for the author, the other for the addressee." The next day half of Moscow was talking about this "aphorism". As if it were a great revelation. *[She shrugs.]*

M. K.: It is interesting that Vasily's actor acquaintances wrote nothing about him. We don't even know for sure whose company he regularly kept.

K. A.: Who else do I remember? Gelovani also appeared regularly at the "House on the Embankment". He was a famous Georgian actor who played "my dear relative" in several films. Later, after Stalin's death, he was unable to play any other role. You see, this man brought trouble to everyone who had any contact with him. They say that Lepeshinskaya, the famous ballerina, also went to my aunt's apartment, which Vasya had transformed into a lovers' nest. Rumor even linked the young Maya Plisetskaya with my good-for-nothing cousin. But I never saw them together.[37]

M. K.: Were these parties, which are mentioned by Svetlana in her book, "only" dance parties?[38]

Andrei Zhdanov, the main Soviet cultural ideologue.

Yury Zhdanov today, in his Moscow home.

K. A.: Perhaps I was naive, but I only learned from others how these "musical evenings" ended, well after midnight… I went home much earlier. Vasya didn't try to persuade me to stay. He was afraid that his affairs would become common knowledge, or perhaps that I would talk about him to my mother or my aunt Anya, and his dear father would get to hear about them.

M. K.: A few things still got out.

K. A.: Once there was a huge scandal when Vasily seduced Nina, the beautiful wife of Roman Karmen, the most celebrated Soviet cameraman of the day. He barricaded himself in the Zubalovo *dacha* with her. Roman Karmen, who was reputed to be something of a daredevil, behaved pathetically. As my poor grandfather would say, he was like a beaten dog. First he told everyone what had happened to him. Then, in a letter written in shaky handwriting, he begged Stalin to return his beloved wife to him. Finally the prosecutor general himself went out to Zubalovo-4… *[She laughs long and heartily.]* The shocked Vaska was so scared that he himself ushered the woman out of the house. He was charged with "hooliganism" and was punished with fifteen days' detention. But he remained the *Liebling*. In the meantime the little goody-goody Svetlana fell out of her father's favor. She didn't take into account how jealous "daddy" was going to be when he learned that his daughter was seeing Aleksei Kapler. The scriptwriter of the Lenin films was a kind of *[looks for the word]* Western type. And Svetlana yearned for him like a female cat in the early spring for the experienced, self-assured tom… It was Vaska, the great man of intrigue, who let everyone know how Stalin had characterized the relationship using this simile—even though it was Vaska himself who had introduced her to the great charmer Kapler. Of course, I did not see it myself, but I heard from others that "my dear relative" was fuming. Perhaps he was afraid that "that filmmaker", despite his old connections with internal affairs circles, would talk. That he would talk about Svetlana. About the other residents of the Kremlin. Stalin was also unhappy about the fact that Lyusa Kapler, as he was commonly called, belonged to a Jewish family. Nor did he approve of the large age difference between him and Svetlana. It did not occur to him that he himself could have been poor Nadya's father.

M. K.: Do you put the blame entirely on Stalin for the series of scandals that resulted in Kapler's ending up in a prison camp?
K. A.: Look, Svetlana made the mistake of going against her father. But only once. But you know, according to my family experiences a relationship with Stalin was like walking through a minefield. You only have to step on a mine once. End of story!

I heard several times, and in many versions, how the jealous father came down on the loving couple. He searched his daughter's bedroom himself. He saw to it personally that Kapler was sent to one of the distant labor camps of the Gulag. The once adored Svetlana lost her former special status in the family overnight. She was inconsolable for a long time because her father—as she told my mother—"had trodden into the mud" her first great love. At the same time she concluded from the scandal that she was already an adult woman. Not long after the Kapler affair she decided it would be better to get married. But she got it wrong again. Someone whispered in Stalin's ear that Grisha Morozov, her new husband, was an incurable careerist. And besides, he was Jewish. For Svetlana there was no way back. After a while even divorcing Grisha achieved nothing, since she could never move back to her own apartment in the Kremlin near her father. She had ceased to be "the little mistress of the house" forever.
M. K.: But she didn't have to leave Zubalovo-4?
K. A.: No, not there. Not until she married Yury Zhdanov. He didn't come from a Jewish family *[sarcastically]* but he was a great scientist and the world's ugliest man. He was like a sparrow. His arms and legs were like four tiny sticks. Between the two marriages Svetlana lived very near to us in the "House on the Embankment". In those days we met her frequently, as we did in the late 1930s. Stalin's daughter cried in the courtyard, in front of everyone, when my aunt Anna, whom she respected as her mother, was taken away by the police before the war.
☆ Svetlana's one-time friends state that her marriage to Grigory Morozov—his original name was Moroz—deteriorated because she was disappointed in him. Anastas Mikoyan, however, explains the divorce mostly as resulting from political reasons: "In those days Stalin had very strong anti-Jewish feelings. He had Morozov's father, a simple, ordinary man, arrested, and told us that he was an American spy. And that, by means of his son's marriage, he had been given the task of getting into Stalin's favor and forwarding all the information *[that he gathered as a result—M. K.]* to the Americans.[39] Afterwards Stalin handed his daughter an ultimatum: either she divorce him, or her husband would be arrested. Svetlana agreed and the divorce went ahead."[40]

According to Mikoyan it was eventually him who found a job for Grigory Morozov. In the meantime, he himself unwittingly almost became a relative of Stalin. One day the "Master" told Mikoyan about one of his conversations with his daughter. "After mentioning to Svetlana that it would be appropriate for her to marry again, she responded by saying that she would either marry Stepan Mikoyan or Beria's son, Sergo.[41] 'I told her she would not be the wife of either of them but must marry Zhdanov's son.' I was very pleased that Stalin had given this advice to his daughter. If her choice had fallen on my son he would have permanently interfered in the life of our family. Beria also said how good it was that Stalin's daughter had not married his son. 'That would have been disastrous', he commented."[42]

The marriage between the "little sparrow" and her new husband soon deteriorated. "As far as Yury Andreyevich Zhdanov is concerned we decided, even before the New Year, that we would separate for good," wrote Svetlana to her father on February 10, 1952. "This is an entirely logical consequence of the fact that for half a year we have been neither wife nor husband, but God knows what. Yury clearly proved—not by words but by what he did—that I am not the love of his life and that he does not need me. And after he told me for the second time that I should leave my daughter with him *[Katya, who had been born in the meantime—M. K.]* I had had enough of this dry professor, this heartless bookworm. Let him bury himself in books! In my experience he needs neither a family nor his daughter. He has many relatives instead.

In other words, I am not at all sorry that we have divorced. I am only sorry that I wasted so much emotion on this iceberg."[43]

According to the most recently available resources and oral history records, the image of the former "little sparrow" as a vulnerable, apolitical young woman seems to collapse, despite the fact that in emigration in the West she spread this view of herself for years. In her book *Only One Year*, she blamed her father for getting Solomon Mikhoels, the world-famed Jewish actor (she alleged that she ear-witnessed a relevant conversation) done away with. After this, she maintains, she avoided meeting her father, who similarly was not keen to meet her.[44] However, this was not what in fact happened. Svetlana did her best to restore herself in his father's graces. One of her arguments was her motherhood. "Dear Daddy! Just look at your grandson, Osip and me as well in the role of a mother"—she wrote to Stalin also sending two photos with the following note: "I made the snapshot of the boy myself."[45] Another time she sent him an autographed copy of the periodical *Molodoy Bolshevik*, which published her article "Removing Conflicts and Abolishing Differences between Village and Town in the Soviet Union".[46] After deciding to separate from her second husband Yury Zhdanov—who had adopted Svetlana's son Iosif, born to Grigory Morozov—she decided to make a career in ideology. She was not satisfied with the fact that, having completed her studies at the department of history at Lomonosov University in 1949, she had remained in the department of Marxism-Leninism as a junior researcher. "I would like to continue my scientific work on the ideological aspect of literature and on the party's literary policy," she wrote on October 1, 1951 to Mikhail Suslov, the relevant secretary on the Central Committee. She asked to be admitted as a junior researcher to the department of literary history and theory at the Academy of Social Sciences, working alongside the party's Central Committee. Four days later two members of the party apparatus, Stepanov and Yefgrafov, to whom Suslov had given a pre-signed letter, set down the decision of the secretariat of the Central Committee. On March 5 the Academy—ignoring such formalities as an entrance examination—reacted positively "to the request of Comrade S[vetlana] I[osifovna] Stalina".[47] After the death of her father, it was absolutely impossible for the young woman to be involved in any political activity. Therefore, she once again became preoccupied with the ups and downs of her stormy private life.

1 *Iosif Stalin v obyatiakh semyi*, 1993, 89.
2 *Ibid.*, 94.
3 Vasilyeva, 1996, 124.
4 *Iosif Stalin v obyatiakh semyi*, 1993, 91.
5 Smirnov, 1997, 216.
6 The contemporary Stalinist-leaning biographers of the "tsarevich" argue, without providing proof, that Vasily rightfully deserved promotion as he had developed his military corps into a model division. See e.g. Gribanov, 1999, 171–202.
7 *Iosif Stalin v obyatiakh semyi*, 1993, 94.
8 Vasilyeva, 1996, 125.
9 Suhomlinov, 2001, 311.
10 Avtorkhanov, 1981, 201–213.

11 Vasilyeva, 1996, 132–133.
12 By that time, the unfortunate Galina had already felt humiliated because her husband openly cheated on her, and had already started to drink.
13 *Vremya i mi*, 1999, no. 142, 184. See also Alliluyev, 1995, 60.
14 Suhomlinov, 2001, 194–195. Although the author, who published the court records, was himself a lawyer, he played an important role in the recent campaign for Vasily Stalin's rehabilitation that had been launched by old Stalinist military officers. The infernal stories attributed to the "Red Vaska" are cited at length only in his book, which is rich in sources and references. Yet, he claims that these stories were made up by the subsequent rulers of the Kremlin. But if only a fraction of these charges is true, then one can say that an amoral beast had grown up in the Kremlin. (The investigation revealed that Vasily lived together with the sisters of one of his wives, and forced them to sleep with him, etc.) Svetlana, his own sister, wrote about him: "He beat each of his wives, so wildly as the *muzhik*s do in the countryside. He was able to hit his aide-de-camp, his chauffeur, his subordinates, even a policeman on the street—all this was overlooked. Then all this became evidence against him." Alliluyeva, 1970, 317.
15 Tarkhova, 1998, 79–89, 92.
16 Mikoyan, 1998, 117.
17 Suhomlinov, 2001, 308–309.
18 *Iosif Stalin v obyatiakh semyi*, 1993, 105–120.
19 Kumanyev, 1999, 363–367.
20 *Iosif Stalin v obyatiakh semyi*, 1993, 113–114. At the farm that belonged to the resort, many months after Vasily's arrest there were still armed guards watching the horses, the cattle, the pigs, and the flock of sheep. Suhomlinov, 2001, 304–305.
21 Knisevsky, 1994, 115–134, Pihoya, 1998, 47–56.
22 *Voyennie Arkhivi Rossii*, 1993, vol. I, 184–190.
23 Menshagin, 1988, 95–105.
24 *Iosif Stalin v obyatiakh semyi*, 1993, 102.
25 Sudoplatov, 1997, 629.
26 *RGASPI*, fond. 82, op. 2, d. 1460.
27 *Ibid.*
28 Menshagin, 1988, 99.
29 *Iosif Stalin v obyatiakh semyi*, 1993, 136–137.
30 His aunt, Anna Alliluyeva frequently visited him at this prison. The convict once asked her to bring some hair tonic, and once he opened the bottle, he drank it up, and got wasted immediately. Suhomlinov, 2001, 267–268.
31 *Ibid.*, 144–145.
32 Suhomlinov, 2001, 272–273.
33 Tarkhova, 1998, 103–106.
34 It was a machine gun stand, made from a transformed peasant cart, which was disguised as an appliance of peasant work during the period in between battles.
35 *RGASPI*, fond. 558, op. 4, d. 666. The diary keeper is mistaken here: in fact, Vasily was born in 1921, Svetlana in 1926.
36 Shatunovskaya has similar recollections. See Shatunovskaya, 1982, 250–251.
37 Sulamif Messerer, the famous ballet dancer of the Bolshoi Theater, was one of Yulia Meltser's best friends. *Druzhba Narodov*, 1993, no. 6, 179. It is not unlikely that Maya Plisetskaya, who was a niece of the Messerer siblings, turned up at the "House on the Embankment", in the vicinity of Vasily Stalin for exactly this reason. The spouse of the latter, Kapitolina Vasilyeva remembers her visits very well. Girbanov, 1999, 253.
38 Alliluyeva, 1981, 160.
39 The old Morozov did not work for the American intelligence, of course. But his past was far from spotless. He spent some time in prison in the 1920s for black market activities and embezzlement. It seems that he had seen a lucrative business opportunity in his son's marriage with Stalin's daughter. Kostirchenko, 1994, 88.
40 Mikoyan, 1999, 362.
41 This affair is an evidence for Svetlana's fickle morality, as both young men were already married and fathers. Moreover, the two wives had been Svetlana's best friends when they were adolescents.
42 Mikoyan, 1999, 363.
43 *Iosif Stalin v obyatiakh semyi*, 1993, 103.
44 Alliluyeva, 1970, 133–135.
45 *RGASPI*, fond. 558, op. 11, d. 553.
46 *RGASPI*, fond. 558, op. 11, d. 1556.
47 *RGASPI*, fond. 17, op. 119, d. 582.

CHAPTER 26
Anna Alliluyeva

"Nyura! *[A shortening of Anna—M. K.]* Please make sure that the request by the comrades from the Industrial Academy is taken care of. You will find Nadya's notes and notebooks in the cupboard. Speak to Andreyev's wife[1]—it is possible she can help you. J[oseph] Stalin." This undated, official-sounding letter was probably written around the end of 1932, or the beginning of 1933.[2] The addressee, Anna Alliluyeva, played a very important part in the life of Zubalovo-4 after the funeral of Nadezhda, her younger sister. She saw to the upbringing of Vasya and Svetlana.

But this unique monopoly did not last long. The people around Stalin were jealous of her. Even certain members of the Politburo, their wives, and indeed high ranking officers in the guard besieged the Master of the Kremlin with various child-rearing notions.[3]

Besides, Anna Alliluyeva's very sweet nature was not capable of handling the swarm of people in the buildings of Zubalovo-4. Hardly a year and a half after Stalin's wife's tragic death even the servants did not take her seriously. "Nadya brought the children up very strictly," noted Maria Korona in her diary. "But everything changed after her death. It is only *[natural—M. K.]* that many servants surround such a great man of his age as J[oseph]. It is in their interest to bring the children up in a special way so that they too could enjoy the benefits of such status."[4]

At the beginning of the 1960s I had occasion to meet Anna Alliluyeva in Moscow. She looked much older than her age, and her looks were fairly neglected. At the beginning she answered the simplest questions sporadically with the wheeze of an asthmatic. But when it came to chronicling the forgotten past she became quite animated. She spoke with great affection about the musical salons in Moscow between the wars, as if they were islands of peace in which famous artists met musical government officials and party workers. "Even leaders of the NKVD appeared at those evenings, my husband included, whose voice was praised by professional singers," she proudly announced. "I remember we were often with a colleague called Olsky who went from being a high ranking interior official to a catering professional."[5] She recalled that the Moscow music salons were often frequented by Marshal Mikhail Tukhachevsky—a good friend of Shostakovitch's and a lover of the violin—as well as Ivan Tovstukha, leader of Stalin's secretariat, and Károly Pauker, the chief Hungarian bodyguard of the Master.

During our conversation Anna Alliluyeva suddenly changed the subject. She said how much she liked and still likes "Bukharchik." That is, Nikolai Bukharin, whom Khrushchev—the first man of the Soviet party at the time—"is still not willing to rehabilitate." Although according to her, "he deserves it," because on December 21, 1924, at the end of Lenin's death agony in Gorky "he closed Ilych's eyes."[6]

At this point Anna Alliluyeva rapidly collected her things and left. As the door closed behind her my hostess Rita Kirson—widow of Vladimir Kirson the Soviet playwright who was for a long while favored by Stalin and then executed for "Trotskyist leanings"—noted that, "There is no more humane person than

Nyura in the world for overlooking the mistakes, indeed the sins of others. Even before the war she was a typical Russian lovable fool *[chudachka—M. K.]*, a five year-old child could have taken her in."

Yury Dombrovsky, the famous writer who had his share of suffering, had a completely different impression of Stalin's sister-in-law when he met her during the time of the Great Terror. This portrayer of the life in the Soviet prison and lager world met her during his exile in Alma-Ata in the office of the local museum's director, who was an old Bolshevik Party member and his boss. She returned his greeting in a swift, condescending way. The reason for Alliluyeva's striking self-confidence was that her husband, the Pole Stanisław Redens, had been appointed interior people's commissar for Kazakhstan at the beginning of 1938, said Dombrovsky. At that time they did not yet know that this type of "kicked upstairs" position was a sure sign of approaching arrest in Stalin's circle.[7]

Anna Alliluyeva, Nadezhda's sister and best friend.

When at the beginning of the 1970s I met Dombrovsky in Moscow, the writer, who recalls her sarcastically in his masterpiece *The Faculty of Superfluous Things,* added that Anna Alliluyeva acted the spoiled "dreamy grand dame." It was common knowledge in the Kazakh capital that Stalin's sister-in-law dominated her husband's large bodyguard. At the same time pretending that she didn't know that Redens had arrived at his new post with a complete harem.[8] "If Anna Alliluyeva was such a good-hearted woman," said Dombrovsky gesticulating furiously, "then why did she allow her husband to so enthusiastically serve so many murderers from Dzerzhinsky to Yezhov without so much as a word? And why did he take part, during the arrests, in the liquidation of his old comrades, many of whom were, like him, Polish communists?!"

But Celina Budzińska, a former Muscovite émigré Pole and her Polish husband, whom she had met in one of the Soviet death camps, did not agree with this. I spoke to them a few times at the beginning of the 1970s in Warsaw about "the horrors of the old times" as they put it. Budzińska knew the famously polite Stanisław Redens well. Redens kissed women's hands and used the polite form of address with his official employees, which was unusual in the Soviet hierarchy. Although she did not like her influential compatriot, she took Anna Alliluyeva's side. "You cannot accuse her of her husband's crimes," she said. "This fine noble lady was never a careerist. She withdrew behind the family defenses, and she could hardly have known what was happening in the NKVD offices: about torture, druggings, and mental agonies. This was proved in the first half of 1937 when a storm blew through the Muscovite Polish colony. Most of the orders for arrest were signed by Stasik Redens, chief of the NKVD in the Moscow district and a great bosom friend of my first husband's. A few of us women flew to Anna Alliluyeva asking for help. She did not believe it. She said she could do nothing but showed none of us the door either. She just sat there hunched up and wept. When it came to say goodbye she gave us all the money she had on her. There are sometimes a few like this among those related to leading politicians. Although by that time the conceited functionaries, who twenty years after the Bolsheviks took power still called themselves *professional revolutionaries,* had changed utterly."

☆ Anna Alliluyeva acted so humane perhaps because similarly to Fyodor, Nadezhda's other brother she had done secretarial work for the " big bosses." From her unpublished manuscript entitled *At Lenin's Secretariat* we learn that at the beginning of 1918 she worked in the Central Executive Committee apparatus of the soviets. Thanks to her parents' merits in the Movement she was given permission to travel with Bolshevik notables when the Soviet government, the Council of People's Commissar finally moved from Petersburg to Moscow in several trains. "Comrade Stalin appeared saying he would help us," recalls Anna Alliluyeva. "He sought us out late at night [...] and invited us to breakfast in Vladimir Ilych's wagon. [...] We were reluctant but Comrade Stalin came over a second time. 'Why are you hiding?' he scolded us and forced us to go with him."[9]

Not long afterwards, at the beginning of 1919, Anna Alliulyeva met the then twenty-seven year old Stanisław Redens, who was secretary to Feliks Dzerzhinsky, head of the Soviet political police. She fell in love with the famously womanizing, already married man and told him of her feelings. After struggling a bit, Redens finally decided on her side. From that time on the happy young woman put herself completely at the disposal of the dashing interior official. She went everywhere with her husband wherever his work called him. She accompanied him to Tiflis, the city of her childhood (there she came to hate Lavrenty Beria, Redens' rival of the time[10]). Then she followed him to Minsk where he was the Belorussian representative of the OGPU from March 1931 to June 1932. In November 1932, during the time of the forceful collectivization of agriculture and the famine which was artificially induced from Moscow, the Redens couple were in Kharkov, the then capital of the Ukraine. It was there that they heard of Nadezhda's death.

In the late summer of 1932, the Soviet dictator was apparently dissatisfied with the leadership of the Ukrainian party and state security force, even though they had carried out purges affecting several million citizens with incredible cruelty. Joseph Stalin, who was undergoing a cure on the shores of the Black Sea, wrote angrily on August 11, 1932 to Lazar Kaganovich, who was standing in for him in Moscow, saying that he was not pleased with the zeal of the Ukrainian governors. He mentions Redens several times in his objections: "For us the Ukraine is the most important now. But things are going badly there. They say in two governing bodies (I believe the ones in Kiev and Dnepropetrovsk) nearly 50 district party committees stood out *against* the cereal-harvest plan. And that they see the indicators as *unrealistic.* According to the news the situation in the other districts is not much better either. What sort of thing is this? This is slowly not a party but a parliament. Instead of Kosior *[the General Secretary of the Ukrainian party apparatus—M. K.] directing* the districts, he always maneuvers between the central committee directives and the demands of the districts. He has maneuvered so long he will burn out. Lenin was right when he said that you cannot be a real Bolshevik leader if you do not have enough courage to go against the current in time. We also fare badly in the areas of Soviet work. Chubar *[the head of the Ukranian government—M. K.]* is not a real leader. Things are also going badly in the GPU *[Gosudarsvennoye Politicheskoye Upravlenie, State Political Supreme Command—M. K.].* Redens is not suited to the fight against counter-revolution in such a very important republic as the Ukraine. If we do not reverse the Ukrainian tendencies then we could lose the Ukraine. Take note that Piłsudski is not sleeping, his network of agents in the Ukraine is much stronger than Redens or Kosior think. Also note that in the Ukrainian Communist Party (five hundred thousand members, ha-ha!) rotten elements, unconscious Petlura[11] followers, and Piłsudski's immediate agents are not lacking. As the situation worsens these elements will not delay in opening a front within (and outside of) the party and *against* the party. The worst of it is that the Ukrainian leadership does not see the danger, this cannot go on. We need to: a) remove Kosior from the Ukraine and replace him with you *[with Kaganovich—M. K.]*, leaving you in your post as Soviet Communist (Bolshevik) party secretary; b) *then* transfer Balitsky to the

Ukraine as head of the GPU [...] and make Redens Balitsky's Ukrainian deputy."[12]

Stanisław Redens.

Contrary to this slyly framed opinion from Stalin, who even in his circle of confidantes was deliberately enigmatic, there were lower ranking party leaders who were open about the fact the Soviet elite did not dare to mention publicly: the famine. Khatayevich, one of the secretaries of the Central Committee of the Ukranian Communist Party, for example, argued cynically: "a bitter trial of strength is going on between our power and the peasantry. Famine had to result in order to show them *[the Ukrainian peasantry—M. K.]* who is the master of the house. The famine took the lives of several million people. But by today at least the *kolkhoz* system had put down roots. We have won this battle."[13]

In this terrible situation Anna Alliluyeva immediately set off for Moscow at the news of her sister's suicide. She returned to Kharkov briefly only for her personal belongings. In February 1933 Redens—probably at Stalin's request—was transferred officially to the capital. He became the area leader of the NKVD in Moscow. This rank in the political police's intricate hierarchy was equal to the post of deputy people's commissar. It seemed that his influence was growing influence when in 1934 he was elected member of the Central Supervisory Committee at the Bolshevik Party's 17th Congress. From a later confession that an NKVD Orenburg area chief made in the cellars of the political police, we learn that in July 1937 a banquet took place in Redens' summer residence during which the chief of the NKVD, Yezhov urged his employees from numerous towns all over the country, who had been summoned there, to execute as many people as they could, and in the cruelest way possible, regardless of their positions. As Redens' guest, Yezhov, the "bloody dwarf" made a speech drunkenly, "Now what are you afraid of? All power is in our hands. We can execute who we want, and show clemency to whom we wish. You the area chiefs *[NKVD—M. K.]* just sit there and shake before every useless area party secretary. You must know how to work! Understand that we are—everything!" When asked whether they should inform the local prosecutors about the arrests to avoid further complications, Yezhov laughingly announced that the prosecutors were members of the *troikas*, the three-person summary justice courts which since 1934 had also overseen political cases among others. They will sign the orders for arrest when the person concerned is already sitting in jail.[14]

Nikolai Yezhov's greatest form of relaxation during the time of the Great Terror—he was seriously afflicted with tuberculosis[15]—was to drink vodka with his own people. He used to call on Stalin's relations too. So at this point the social weight that Stanisław Redens enjoyed again becomes clear. Apart from the inevitable political involvement of the Alliuyeva-Redens couple in such conversations, Yezhov's "policy-making speech" on what became the Great Terror could take place in their *dacha* because it was well known that little Svetlana spent some of her time with the Redens family in the mid- 1930s. It was also known that the head of the family was a guest at Zubalovo-4 every weekend because of his wife. At that time the "black crow" could swoop at any time on the other party leaders and NKVD officers. But the arrest of the Redens couple was *unimaginable* at the beginning, according to Dr László Pollacsek who was also their doctor. This is why it makes sense that the Redens case became such an important issue in the year of Khrushchev's "détente". On May 7, 1954, at a conference in Leningrad, Nikita Khrushchev claimed—evidently to obscure the truth—that Beria once got Redens drunk, "who became unconscious and Beria threw him out to the street. Then Beria himself called the police, who found the drunken Redens on the street, and realized he was the Georgian People's Commissar for internal affairs. *[This detail is evidently wrong, as Redens was the chief of the Georgian OGPU at the end of the 1920's—M. K.]* I can only repeat myself: Beria was a terrible man. He managed to arrange Redens' [...] banishment. I do not know if he is alive at all."[16] At the meeting of the Presidium of the CPSU on December 30, 1955, it was Lazar Kaganovich's turn to come up with something new. He said that Redens accused the chekists *[by then called NKVD—M. K.]* of murdering Kirov.[17]

☆ "Auntie Anna, Uncle Pavlusha *[Pavel Alliluyev—M. K.]*, grandpa, and others send their love," wrote Stalin in an undated, unpublished letter to his daughter who was on holiday by the Black Sea, probably before 1935.[18] Svetlana remembered her aunt and her husband with affection years later,[19] although she never mentioned that after a while the dictator and his court found Anna Alliuyeva unpleasant, as her talkative nature meant that she was capable of criticizing anyone at any time. She also spoke too much, which offended Stalin, as shown in a letter to Voroshilov: "Klim! Yesterday, when we were in front of other people, primarily my sister-in-law (who's a gabbling woman) and the doctors (they might let it out), I didn't want to say the exact date of our journey. But now I must say that I have decided to leave tomorrow, Saturday. There is no need to spread this around. We two are just too big to fall because of our own carelessness *[to the alleged terrorists, of whom Stalin was inordinately afraid throughout his life—M. K.]*. I will order Yusis[20] to shunt into the station unexpectedly and link up the wagon *[to the government train—M. K.]* without saying who will travel. So I am traveling tomorrow at two o'clock. Yusis will prepare everything with the *chekists*. St[alin]."[21]

But Stanisław Redens, Anna Alliluyeva's husband, was beyond all suspicion up until the time of the Great Terror. Perhaps that explains the "proud Pole's" enthusiastic letter about his brother-in-law that he mailed to Sergo Ordzhonikidze at the beginning of October 1927: "Koba had me summoned," he wrote. "It is wonderful how he looks after you. He decides personally what your needs are. You know I would never have thought he could be so gentle. I left him completely enchanted..."[22]

It is probable that his genuine respect and subordination diminished over time. When, during the years of the Great Terror, Redens was transferred to Alma-Ata and appointed chief of the NKVD in Kazakhstan, he carefully pointed out that he did not appreciate the liquidation of the old comrades—in which, of course, he had taken part to the end. "I felt instinctively that although Redens did carry out Stalin's and Yezhov's orders, he did not work with complete devotion," we can read in the memoir of one of his deputies, Mikhail Sreyder. In his book, which gives an *inside* glimpse into the crimes of the Soviet political police, indeed those of the whole system, he shows that the Polish *chekist*, while in the Kazakh capital, "permitted only moderate torture. On one occasion he burst out, 'well, nearly all the Central Committee secretaries of the Soviet republics are in prison. Yet many of them were excellent Communists. Certainly no one can touch such bastards as Beria. Or Kaganovich and Khrushchev and other bootlickers either'."

From the same Sreyder memoir it becomes clear that Redens, in the months before his arrest, knew what was coming to him. From time to time he complained to his deputy: "After all, I am a people's commissar [...], a member of the Central Supervisory Committee [...] and a delegate to the Supreme Soviet. And yet I am incapable of turning against this dirty maelstrom. Moscow puts permanent pressure on me, continually urges me *[to increase the number of arrests*

This picture was taken in the vine arbor of a government resort: Anna Alliluyeva and Zinayda Ordzhonikidze, sitting on the back of a lion.

in accord with the central quota—M. K.]. I feel that it will end soon with my arrest and execution." Then he quietly explained to Sreyder that most of the terror against "enemies of the people" was the work of Joseph Stalin. "He cannot bear any sort of opposition," he said, but was quick to point out that he would never rebel against his brother-in-law—nor indeed against the Yezhov type executors. "Before the revolution we all struggled against the tsarist tyranny. But if we now started to fight with Yezhov and people with even greater power than him *[that is with Stalin—M. K.]* then that would be like stabbing the party in the back."[23]

Before soon, he proved right. On November 20, 1938 things came to a head between Joseph Stalin and Anna Alliluyeva after Redens was arrested in Alma-Ata and then taken to the Soviet capital. Rumors went that Nikolai Yezhov, the NKVD chief, doubted the loyalty of the Polish *chekist*. And Yezhov's deputy and subsequent successor Lavrenty Beria, who had been trying to blacken his former Tiflis boss, made no secret of his joy that Redens had reached his nemesis. Of course, neither he nor Yezhov would have dared to touch Stalin's brother-in-

The executioners of the Great Terror, who eventually became victims of the system themselves. Nikolai Yezhov (x) is in the lower right corner.

law—let alone approve his death penalty—if the Master himself had not ordered to do so. But the Master of the Kremlin was not satisfied with simply imprisoning his brother-in-law, he also wanted Anna Alliluyeva to reject her husband, while he was detained under remand. Beria tried to make the woman break from him by saying that they had never officially married.[24] But Anna, who was completely crushed and incessantly weeping, was not willing to let her husband down. At this Stalin—who for a time believed that Anna was "a fool" whose good-heartedness "was a greater sin than infamy"—simply banned her from the Kremlin.[25]

It is not surprising that the dictator distanced himself from his old environment. His wide family circle tried to do everything to please, even to flatter him, but they were simply not able to see him as a god. Unlike what a well-known Ukrainian soprano, Donets did, for example. She wrote in a note, "I sang while I was still sick. The doctors tried to convince me not to. [...] I was in a very bad state physically. In such a state it is very difficult to even utter a word. But then Comrade Stalin appeared and some sort of strange hot wave went through my body. And whether you believe it or not, I was instantly cured. The next moment I didn't feel ill at all."[26] Yorin, another Ukranian artist who performed that day at the Moscow Bolshoi Theatre, was a witness to this unbelievable moment. He speaks as if he himself was also *enlightened*: "It happened in the middle of the first act. The government box was over the orchestra. [...] At the beginning it was empty. Then suddenly I felt a fork of lightning strike the orchestra. The violins became harder, more forceful, the musicians' faces became grave. At the same time I glimpsed Comrade Stalin in the government box surrounded by members of the Politburo and the government."[27]

After her husband's arrest, Anna Alliluyeva was incapable of such a performance and so her many years of friendship with Stalin came to a complete end. Although it is also true that, as her youngest son Vladimir remembered, in the spring of 1941 the dictator unexpectedly spent half a day at Zubalovo-4 in the company of Molotov, and then it seemed as if he had made his peace with the Alliluyev family. And after the outbreak of the war he asked Anna to take herself and some of her family to the countryside far away from the front.[28] But other sources do not support the claim that Stalin really made peace with his sister-in law. It is a fact, however, that he kept her under surveillance until the end.

It speaks volumes that whatever problems the Alliluyev family had, besides the Kremlin administration, it was the people's commissariat for state security or interior that was responsible for dealing with them. "I report that I have carried out the orders. We went to Merkulov *[Chief of the interior portfolio Beria's first deputy—M. K.]* with the old man [Sergei] and his daughter Anna Sergeyevna. We solved a few problems. [...] The old man thanks you for helping him and sends his regards," wrote Colonel Lyetsky to Marshall Voroshilov to the front.[29]

☆ Then came 1943. At the orders of the Soviet dictator, Leonid, Anna Alliluyeva's oldest, but still under-age son was taken to the NKVD's central Lubyanka prison on charges of conspiracy. I heard numerous details of this strange story from Sergo Mikoyan, one of his companions, at the end of which the two boys were transported to Tadjikstan where he lived as an "administrative exile."

The Kremlin ruler's drive against the teenage children of the elite was provoked by the tragic love story of two secondary school students—a Soviet Romeo and Juliet. The lovers, Volodya Sakhurin, son of the people's commissar responsible for airplane manufacture, and Nina Umanskaya had to part as the girl's father was appointed ambassador abroad. When the time for farewells arrived Volodya invited Nina onto the bridge near the "House on the Embankment". As he did not want to suffer parting he shot first the girl and then himself with a German-made pistol he got from his school friend Vano Mikoyan. The tragedy caused a storm in the "House on the Embankment". I have tried to piece together this story for years. I managed to speak to a series of witnesses including Sergo Mikoyan, who went to prison as a result of this affair, and I sought out Tatyana Litvinova, the daughter of the former Soviet people's commissar for foreign affairs, and then the Soviet Ambassador to Washington. This Russian painter, who has been living in England for years, went to the spot soon after the bloody drama took place. Yet everyone remembers the events differently. It is still not clear whether any of Sakhurin's friends knew what he was about to do.

But one thing is sure: the senseless destruction of the young couple was used by Stalin for a political showdown. While the Second World War raged the generals and colonels of the Soviet state security system—instead of hunting down German spies and traitors—turned night into day interrogating eight Moscow secondary school students in the inner dungeons of Lubyanka. The dictator who was directing the investigations from behind the scenes used it to put a stop to coeducation in Soviet schools.

Volodya Sakhurin's diary, which he supposedly wrote soon before his death and is still marked "top secret" in the Moscow archives, reveals that he was a fan not only of the Master of the Kremlin but also of Adolf Hitler. In the thick notebook he hid in Anna Alliluyeva's flat he enthusiastically cited long quotes from Hitler's *Mein Kampf* and wrote that after Stalin's death he would be the "Soviet Führer'. Long in advance he assembled the list of the government to be: most of the ministerial portfolios were intended for his schoolmates in the Kremlin or

House on the Embankment. Among them were Anastas Mikoyan's two sons Sergo and Vano, the sons of Mikoyan's secretary Barabanov, and of General Khmelnitsky, Marshall Voroshilov's *aide de camp*. Also the teenage son of the age's most famous Soviet surgeon, Professor Bakulev. Most unfortunately for Leonid Alliluyev, the murderer/self-murderer was his best friend.

Sakhurin's friends still today, more than half a century afterwards, remain staunchly silent on whether they knew about his "Führer" government plans. It is certain however that none of them intended to do away with or oust their favored Stalin. But the Master of the Kremlin—who got hold of the diary from Volodya Sakhurin's mother—*saw potential terrorists* in these pimpled youths. "To prison with them!" he screamed. When I spoke to one of them, Sergo Mikoyan, who had been able to break away from the Stalinist ideology, he said that they had treated them like real adult political prisoners in Lubyanka. They placed "stoolies" next to them in the cells and tried to get them to denounce each other during the interrogations. Finally they squeezed false confessions out of them. The protagonists in this sometimes surreal but ultimately tragic story suffered a life-long trauma from their time in prison. After they were released from detention, some of them were sent into internal exile and others to the front as a punishment.

Joseph Stalin visibly enjoyed holding their parents in the palm of his hand who remained silent out of fear and terror. The Mikoyan couple, for example, lived next door to the dictator in the Kremlin, thus often ran into him but they did not dare to ask for mercy for their children. Mikoyan's wife became ill when Sergo was finally sentenced to a year's administrative exile in Central Asia.[30]

Unlike the other parents, Anna Alliluyeva acted decisively, and besieged the authorities with requests. For example, in her letter addressed to the "Special Council Adjunct to the Interior Ministry" and personally to "Comrade Minister Kruglov", she writes: "Dear Comrade Kruglov. In July 1943, my eleven year-old son Leonid Redens-Alliluyev was arrested in the eight student case of School No. 175. This concerns the following: V. and S. Mikoyan, A. Khmelnitsky, L. Barabanov, P. Bakulev, A. Gammer, and Kirpichnikov. (The suicide case of Vladimir Sakhurin.) Please review the case in the Special Council."[31]

After this her every step was watched even more closely by the Soviet political police. Even more so after Svetlana, the dictator's daughter, following the war moved into the House on the Embankment where the rest of the Alliluyev family lived. Svetlana had left her husband and, as in her childhood, spent a lot of time with her relatives to whom it seems she was very attached.[32] This visibly irritated Stalin. Just as the fact that after Anna Alliluyeva published her memoir, she started to attend writer-reader meetings and had a great success at them. Looking at her memoir today, the pages seem to hardly differ from the contemporary party histories that were stuffed with lies. Yet people lined up to buy it as at least they could find something out about the youth, private life, and habits of the Olympian Stalin. Especially because until the end of his life, Stalin appeared in public only twice a year—on May 1 and November 7—on the parapet of Lenin's tomb on the Red Square.

This successful book was in fact a collective work. Numerous censors went through it numerous times taking out the "unsuitable" bits. An old friend, the journalist Nina Bam helped her with the manuscript, primarily with the dialogues. She could not guess at that time that as an "accomplice" she would soon find herself in prison, too. In the meantime, the leaders of the Soviet Alliance of Writers, who had much experience when it came to judging the way the politi-

"Look, there are three of us sitting in this photo: my father, Anna Alliluyeva and me. You can see how much I am attached to my aunt."

cal wind was blowing, thought that the upper leadership supported the work. Otherwise they would never have attempted to make Anna Alliluyeva a member of the organization. "I did not push myself into the writers' set," she wrote bitterly to Stalin. "When Comrade Fadeyev *[President of the Soviet Writers' Union—M. K.]* congratulated me on my membership, I laughed and said, 'but what kind of writer am I, and why is it necessary?' Comrade Fadeyev then said that it was necessary. So I thought, all right then, so be it..."[33]

But of the charges against her for the publication of the memoir was not the gravest. An exact picture of the long list of objections can be seen in an anti-Alliluyeva article in *Pravda*. Pyotr Fedoseyev, the writer of the denouncing article, an influential ideologist in the Soviet party apparatus, accused the memoir of falsifying history, of fawning on party leaders, of playing for cheap popularity, and of greed. The author, along with her quick-witted contemporaries, knew that Stalin was behind the denouncement. The worst passages in the article—as in the case of other *Pravda* denouncements—were probably added to the original version—which was written for him—by the dictator himself.[34]

The wisest thing Anna could have done was to remain silent and withdraw. Instead she threw herself into a counter-attack. She replied not to Fedoseyev but directly to Stalin. A typed unsigned version of this letter still exists in the Alliluyev family letter box as well as two shorter—written on June 1 and 6, 1947—versions. In these letters, which can be seen as criticism rather than explanation in the given 'code system', Anna asked her brother-in-law to defend her from these "unjust slanders." "I never fawned *[on Stalin or on other Bolshevik leaders—M. K.]*. Me and my father did not start to write because of ourselves."[35]

Following this argument which is not entirely true, she went on to give details of how the book came about and who revised it. It turns out that Fedoseyev himself was one of the censors, but he did not say a word about the "grave political mistakes" in the book after finishing his job. According to Anna Alliluyeva, upon reading certain chapters in the book, several veteran Bolshevik politicians, including Mikhail Kalinin, clearly encouraged her to go on with it. Indeed, and this is the high point in the letter, one of the Soviet party's highest leaders, Georgy Malenkov even told the author that Stalin himself had agreed to publication. Despite this, fumed Anna Alliluyeva, *Pravda* attacked the memoir. In the meantime the mass publication of the book in Leningrad was stopped.[36]

"Whatever steps you take, I will be very grateful to you," closes the second version of the letter which is at once protesting and pleading for intercession. In the third, really harassed, version Anna puts her case even more strongly: "With this letter I would like merely to point out the order of events [...] I will add that despite these ordeals I do not regret publishing the memoir. [...] The members of our family, myself included, were always loyal to the best traditions of our country and ancestors. The money necessary for publishing the book just came and went. There are people whom our family saved from death. This is not self-adulation but the bare truth which is easy to ascertain. I feel it important to say these few things."[37]

Ten years after the crescendo of the Great Terror, Joseph Stalin was not used to receiving such untempered reproaches from the widow of an executed politician. His reaction was clear: not only did he not review his decision but burned with new revenge against the family of his dead wife. First he imprisoned Yevgenia Alliluyeva, the widow of his brother-in-law Pavel who had died under suspicious circumstances. Then he did the same to Anna Alliuyeva, the author of the memoir he found so inopportune. ✩

M. K.: On the old photograph you showed me the huge difference between Yevgenia and Anna Alliluyeva is apparent. Your mother and aunt must have been two completely different worlds. But their fates were surprisingly similar in the second half of the thirties.

K. A.: They did not look like each other at all. When Anna first went to Novgorod my mother was struck at how small and fragile she was. I heard from both of them that my mother, who was 175 cm (5,8″) tall, was all strength and muscle, once she even seized Anna, lifted her up and then gently put her down again: "What a charming little thing, just like a miniature!"

M. K.: When you were very little your Aunt Anna looked after you. Other people gladly entrusted their children to her care. Did she really have a gift with children?

K. A.: Look, there are three of us sitting in this photo: my father, Anna Alliluyeva and me. You can see how much I am attached to my aunt. Perhaps because she let us do a lot. She left everything to the children. At that time I liked that a lot. But now, in retrospect *[she waves her hand sadly]* I have realized that she didn't understand child rearing at all. She thought the softer she was the better we would love her. That's why her youngest boy Volodya was such a cheeky boy. Although it's true that Leonid, the bigger one, was well brought up.

But Aunt Anna never let me do any housework. I remember once when I was already a teenager my mother sent me into the next room for a chair. Anna said, "Stay here Kiroshka! here's your father. Pavel will bring it." At this my mother retorted: "What are you teaching the child?" But my aunt was unrepentant: "Leave her, she is still little! Such a fragile creature..."

M. K.: And Stanisław Redens, Anna Alliluyeva's husband? Was he also a soft touch in the family? Because as a NKVD chief...

K. A.: [*she interrupts to turn the conversation]* He was a wonderful man. Polish. A gentleman. You could tell [*she snaps her fingers*] that he was not of Russian *muzhik* stuff. We Alliluyevs loved him a lot. We had heard of course how close he was to the NKVD bosses. As they say today Stalin promoted his career. And that... *[She falters unsure whether to go on.]*

M. K.: As a secret police officer he was a cruel man.

K. A.: Let's talk of something else. After all he is dead. *[Gloomily]*. He was shot in the head. I must say that before my Aunt Nadezhda's death, when she had really become distant from Stalin, she planned to move to Kharkov where Redens was working for the local OGPU. She trusted him and Anna that much, although Anna Alliuyeva was the complete opposite of Nadezhda.

1 Andrei Andreyev, the people's commissar for transportation, later member of the Politburo, Stalin's confidant. He came to the fore during the Great Terror. His wife, Dora Khazan taught at the Industrial Academy. She was one of Nadezhda Alliluyeva's best friends. She had a political career rare for Soviet women: she became a light and then textile industry deputy people's commissar. At the beginning of 1949, during the Soviet anti-Semitic campaign, she was forced into the background. In September of that year she was dismissed from all her posts and later imprisoned. Kostirchenko, 1994, 137.

2 *RGASPI*, fond. 668, op. 1, d. 15. l. 70. It is not impossible that the letter is about notebooks or college books borrowed from her fellow students. It is also possible that the Industrial Academy wanted to organize an exhibition in Nadezhda's Alliluyeva's memory. The institute which in the meantime had been renamed after Stalin strove to keep her cult alive to the end. On October 6, 1940 for example they informed Nadezhda's father, Sergei Alliluyev, that they plan to unveil a relief of her. For this they requested photographs from the family album. *RGASPI*, fond. 668, op. 1, d. 15.

3 Alliluyeva, 1981, 117–118, 120–129.

4 *Iosif Stalin v obyatiakh semyi*, 1993, 45–47, 53–54.

5 *Iosif Stalin v obyatiakh semyi*, 1993, 159.

6 In 1932 there were serious rivalries in OGPU [*Obyedinyonnoye Gosudarsvennoye Politicheskoye Upravlenyie*, United State Political High Command, [later NKVD]. The dissatisfied group was primarily revolting against Yagoda, a key figure in the political police. But Stalin defended him. The losers, including Olsky, were relocated to the civil sphere. Sreyder, 1995, 13–15.

7 Anna Larina, Bukharin's widow, describes how on November 7th 1936, a short while before her husband's arrest they met Anna Alliluyeva on Red Square. "She saw me and said: "Oh we liked N[ikolai] I[vanovich] so much, Nadya and I. It was strange that she talked about herself in the past tense. But so it was: by then all had become past." Larina, 1989, 313.

8 Not long afterwards everything became clear. According to Anna Redens in his new post was not able to speak to Stalin once over the telephone. He simply wasn't connected. Sreyder, 1995, 110.

9 Later I found these stories almost word for word in Yury Dombrovsky's key novel about his exile in Alma-Ata. Dombrovsky,1978, 441–442.

10 *RGASPI*, fond. 668. op. 1. d. 13. l. 83.

11 Simon Petlyura was a Ukrainian nationalist politician, one of the Bolsheviks' main enemies in the Soviet-Russian Civil War.

12 *RGASPI*, fond. 81. op. 3. d. 99.

13 Kravchenko 1946. 130.

14 Bryuhanov-Soskov, 1998, 78.

15 *RGASPI*, fond. 17, op. 120, d. 45.

16 *Reabilitatsia*, 2000, vol. I, 141.

17 *Ibid.*, 296.

18 *RGASPI*, fond. 558, op. 1, d. 5125.

19 Alliluyeva, 1981. 52–55.

20 Yusis was one of the commanders of Stalin's bodyguards, who lost his job to his successor, Vlasik.

21 *RGASPI*, fond. 74, op. 2, d. 38.

22 Alliluyev, 1995, 120.

23 Sreyder, 1995, 101–102, 106–113.

24 The Soviet leaders who did not get married in the tsar's time did not take the official procedure that went with marriage seriously. But after 1945 Stalin required the nomenclature to take measures to rectify the situation.

25 Alliluyeva, 1981. 52.

26 *RGASPI*, fond. 558. op. 4. d. 648.

27 *Ibid.*

28 Alliluyev, 1995, 121, 124.

29 *RGASPI*, fond. 74, op. 2, d. 153.

30 Mikoyan, 1999, 21.

31 *RGASPI*, fond. 668, op. 1, d. 15.

32 Alliluyeva, 1992, 231.

33 *RGASPI*, fond. 668, op. 1, d. 15.

34 *Pravda*, May 14, 1947.

35 *RGASPI*, fond. 668, op. 1, d. 15.

36 *RGASPI*, fond. 668, op. 1, d. 16.

37 *Ibid.*

Organized Famine in the Ukraine

Famine reached the bigger towns in months. According to Ewald Ammende, an eyewitness who published these rare photographs in Vienna in 1935, bread disappeared from the stores overnight in Harkov, Soviet Ukraine's capital at the time.

People were so weakened that they could not even bury their dead.

CHAPTER 27
Fyodor Alliluyev

Maria Korona was the wife of Stalin's brother-in-law, Alyosha Svanidze. From her diary it appears that she was not exactly well disposed towards the Alliluyev family. On March 5, 1937 she noted the number of damaged souls, indeed clinically mad people that existed in Stalin's wider family circle. She came to this conclusion when Yakov Dzhugashvili, Stalin's son from his first marriage, married for the third time without his father's permission. Instead of marrying a "suitable girl from our circle of revolutionaries" whom "everybody would have liked and spoiled," he married Yulia Meltser, a woman who had been married four or five times before. Korona describes the scene when Yasha first appeared at Zubalovo-4 with his wife. "I believe that J[oseph] stayed away deliberately [...] I am sorry that our, anyway not exactly sparkling, company has been added to by such a woman. I am sorry for J[oseph]. It is hard to think on that he is surrounded by the half-witted O[lga] A[lliuyeva], the idiot Fyodor, the not exactly bright Pavel and Nyura, the narrow minded Stan *[Redens—M. K.]*, the lazy Vasya and the weak willed Yasha. Perhaps only Alyosha [Svanidze], Zhenya *[Yevgenia Alliluyeva—M. K.]* and I can be counted as normal of them all. And Svetochka *[Svetlana—M. K.]* who makes up for everything in J[oseph]'s eyes. And then there is the grandfather *[Sergei Alliluyev—M. K.]*, that crotchety yet wonderful old man. That's more or less the whole circle of Joseph's close relatives."[1]

Perhaps this picture is a little too dark. But it is true that members of the Alliluyev family were not completely healthy psychologically speaking. As we know Nadezhda committed suicide. Both of her maternal aunts were treated for years for schizophrenia in closed wards. One of Vasily Stalin's daughters, Svetlana died in a mental asylum, while Anna Alliluyeva had another bout of schizophrenia in the Vladimir Prison and several residents of the House on the Embankment were on the opinion that she had already showed symptoms of it after her husband's arrest. Fyodor Alliluyev also struggled with similar symptoms. Although his relatives never saw any signs of mental illness in him until the Bolshevik terrorist Kamo, who was hailed as a hero in the Soviet Union, stood him against a wall and made as if to execute him as part of a test.[2]

To his misfortune, in September 1917 Joseph Stalin introduced the wild, completely uninhibited Kamo as an old friend of his to the Alliluyev family. It is hardly likely that he mentioned any of the bloody, armed "expropriations" he had planned with him. In other words, "Comrade Koba" was the mastermind behind the famous robberies and the boss working behind the scenes. As far as we know today he never took part in the executions that accompanied these actions.[3] He always gave the dirty work to Kamo, who was often caught and then put into mental asylums as he simulated madness. He was also put on death row once.[4]

After the Bolsheviks took power, Kamo, who appeared from time to time in the Soviet-Russian capital, seemed bored. This was not his scene! During the summer of 1919 he paced the corridors of the Kremlin until he was allowed to select a number of people, commando types with whom—as in the good old days—he could collect money "for the dictatorship of the proletariat" on the other side of the front. Kamo "tested" his people one by one before he set off with these mostly young volunteers to the Caucasus.

One of these "tested warriors" was Yelizaveta Drabkina, who as a young girl had already come close to the pinnacles of power.[5] At the beginning of the 1970s during our conversations in Budapest she told me how the test was done. In a forest clearing near Moscow she was gathered along with other young people and put against the "wall", that is the trees, by armed freebooters who appeared suddenly out of nowhere dressed as white guardists—all this, as it later became clear, at Kamo's orders. The beatings, the sight of blood and the fake executions provoked a terrible nervous reaction in Fyodor Alliluyev, who was also a member of the group. "He wept sobbingly, like a wounded reindeer," recalled Drabkina. He stood next to me, tied to an old oak tree. When the bandits placed the cord around his neck his nose started to bleed, he started to shake, then he fell forward and fainted." He was already physically weak, as he had not fully recovered from the typhoid he contracted at the front. Drabkina told me this terrible story at the Kútvölgyi Hospital in Budapest where she was being treated and condemned the terror and horror involved in the test. A few days later, however, she told the same story as an example of poetic, positive heroism to her students at a Budapest university.[6]

Fyodor Alliluyev was the son of a simple electrician, but in the tsarist regime he could have had a career as a naval officer or a famous intellectual, based on his talents. However, he lost his mind in the grim world of the Soviet-Russian Civil War.

Mikoyan also mentions the event in his memoirs. According to his version, the infinitely suspicious Kamo had already suggested to him in June 1919 that he dress in uniform and surprise the revolutionaries in the town of Lenkoran' and stand them against the wall. "If one of them behaves in a cowardly way, pleads for mercy or starts to rat then execute them," he explained to Mikoyan. Although he did not get permission for staging this action, he still staged the test in a wood close to Moscow. Everybody behaved with courage, except a Polish spy who confessed before the pointed gun that he was agent for Piłsudski. "This action had a terrible effect on one of those present, [...] on Fyodor Alliluyev," adds Mikoyan who is always careful what he writes. Fyodor became "seriously ill" as a result.[7]

Several members of the commando left Kamo after this. Drabkina recalled that news of this sadistic test reached Lenin who was furious and sent a message to Kamo that he never wanted to see him again. But later Lenin seemed to forgive his old favorite. In the April of 1922 the Soviet leader was ill in bed and his doctors urged him to go for a cure in the northern Caucasus. The leader of his guard was to have been Kamo.[8]

It is true that after this strange "test" Fyodor Alliluyev never fully recovered. He lived off a pension and money from relations in a one-room flat, rather poorly, in the "House on the Embankment". Back in his young Petersburg days he had been an unusually educated man, as is proven by his navy officer's diploma. Although he was the son of an electrician, he managed to achieve better results than the young aristocrats around him who were better suited to the milieu of elite training. But after the "drama in the woods" he was never able to use his skills again. He clung to the past, learning languages during the day and reading books on mathematics, history, the military and other subjects during the night up until dawn. ☆

K. A.: Uncle Fedya, my uncle, was two years younger than my father, and despite his illness, he was respected as a very educated man. Everybody thought that he would become a great scholar. But fate had different things in store for him unfortunately. Along with my grandfather he entered the Kamo team. And was the victim of a test.

M. K.: Was your grandfather also present at the test? How did he react to it?

K. A.: He didn't bat an eye![9] But Uncle Fedya *[she sighs]* went nuts a little.

M. K.: What do you mean?
K. A.: He went mad. He had strange fits. The shooting supposedly brought out his epilepsy. Sometimes he was even a little strange with us children too. When we lived in the Kremlin, he would look after me by leaning out of the window with me, on the fourth floor. My mother saw him once from the street and screamed: "Fedya, what in God's name are you doing? What's going on?!" But my uncle just calmly, slowly replied: *[she imitates him]* "Why shouldn't I if little Kira likes it so much." He was dotty. One day my mother was on the telephone to somebody. Uncle Fedya looked at her for a long time and then ran at her and started to strangle her. It was pure luck that a Georgian acquaintance of ours was on hand to pull him off because he had huge hands *[she demonstrates]*.
M. K.: But Fyodor Alliluyev had better days too. Nadezhda, for example, who was studying for university exams, wrote to Stalin: "Imagine, Fedya is helping me study, he still has a good brain. He explained everything just as well as before. We studied for three days, hardly without stopping. We must do something for him. I feel really sorry for him."[10]
K. A.: That must have been later, at the end of the 1920s. He recovered a little bit then. But he was still a strange one. I remember that if something remained on the plates after a meal he would collect it together and eat it. He was never full. If he went out somewhere he could never stand up and say goodbye. Sometimes he was there until after midnight, until one or two. If this happened at ours I had to see to it. "Kira, you're the only one who can do it," I was told. And so it was. I took my uncle by the arm and led him to the door and said kindly to him: "Uncle Fedya, will you come again?" Then he would come to his mind and say goodbye. He always said that of course he would come again. But that wasn't the end, one had to stick to him and push him through the door. I was embarrassed for him.
M. K.: It seems that Fyodor lived for a time in the Kremlin in his mother's flat. Mikoyan also mentions in his memoirs that he paced the corridors, smoking a pipe and sometimes speaking to himself.[11]
K. A.: He also behaved like that when they put him out of the Kremlin. What else can I say about him? He was married for a while. So he didn't have problems *on that score. [She laughs]*. But he was different from other people in that he never felt the heat. Even 30-35 degrees [Celsius]. But he didn't feel the cold either. He never buttoned up or wore a scarf in the coldest weather. This was surely a sign of sickness.
M. K.: Your uncle must have been a good writer. A manuscript survives of a story about how the exiled Stalin escaped from freezing Siberia.[12]
K. A.: A story comes to mind about my "dear relative's" exile. You know when I returned from my own exile to Moscow *[she continues emotionally]* at the beginning I kept in contact with two female teachers who I had met in Shuya. They were older than me and more educated. They both spoke French well. Once we were with Fyodor the four of us, and my uncle started to sing French chansons. They made a trio; Fyodor had a very good ear for languages.
☆ In the 1930s Fyodor Alliluyev was stopped a few times by the Kremlin guard. Although his entry pass had been revoked still wanted to get into his old flat at all costs. But in the second half of the decade it seemed that despite these occurrences his state had improved significantly.[13]

He decided to write his memoirs on his famous family and his meetings with Stalin. The value of this source is increased by the fact that Fyodor, alongside his younger sister Nadezhda, was secretary to the future dictator for nearly a year. In the summer of 1918, he accompanied him to the Tsaritsyn front where Stalin and Feliks Dzerzhinsky made a tour of inspection to examine the reasons for the "Perm catastrophe"—the temporary defeats of the Reds.[14]

Today this affair is dealt with only by a few military historians, yet all subjects in the Soviet empire had to know the story if there were to take part in the obligatory party history seminars. Of Joseph Stalin's Civil War activities this was the one which grounded from many points of view his later rise to power. On this section of the eastern front the Reds were really in trouble. The Third Army, which was composed mainly of red guardists made up of workers from the Urals and Petrograd, suffered one defeat after another from Admiral Kolchak's Siberian snipers and the Cossack cavalry. As a result the people's commissars who were mainly Petrograd party workers suspected all military experts who had formerly been in the tsar's army and demanded that Leon Trotsky, who was already famous nationwide, should travel to the front and examine the reasons for the defeats. But Lenin had a more important job for Trotsky and so Stalin and Dzerzhinsky were sent to the Urals instead.[15]

Fyodor Alliluyev, the mentally ill resident of the House on the Embankment with his niece, Kira, in the mid-1930s.

Joseph Stalin made use of this opportunity to assume *extraordinary powers*[16] after the series of Tsaritsyn defeats—which nevertheless made it possible for Trotsky to push him and Voroshilov who sided with him, into the background. Stalin attempted to remove almost the entire commanding and people's commissar staff of the Third Army.[17] But he did not succeed because this unified "Petrograd company" enjoyed Lenin's and Zinovyev's trust. Trotsky, however, did not at that time pay much attention to Stalin's machinations, although he had dealt rigorously with the commanders and party workers of the eastern front on another occasion.[18]

Stalin then selected a less significant military leader as his target: Stogov, the commander responsible for the evacuation of the troops stationed in Perm. In the former Soviet party archives a notebook survives with Dzerzhinsky's writing which Stalin dictated to the then commander of the Soviet political police the VChK *[Vserossiyskaya Chrezvichaynaya Komissia, All-Russian Extraordinary Committee—M. K.]*. The manuscript reads just like a show trial prosecution file. Nonetheless, despite the fact that Stalin gained no concrete evidence at all from Stogov whom he interrogated several times, he closed the report as follows thus cutting the man's career to shreds: "It is clear that Stogov is either stupid (which is unlikely) or a cunning impostor (which is likely)."[19]

So the person responsible for the temporary series of defeats that the Third Army suffered was found. Stalin also found out that Stogov's father-in-law was an innkeeper, that he "was in contact" with Grand Prince Mikhail Aleksandrovich, the tsar's younger brother. That his mother-in-law had escaped to the whites, while his brother "also had anti-Soviet sentiments". He assembled similar lists of crimes against a few other commanders and people's commissars.[20] And then turned to Lenin with the request that he could establish "a standing investigative committee composed of young [...] workers" with the name Supervisory and Revision Committee to examine similar scandals.[21] Lenin, who also had a tendency to come up with bureaucratic solutions, readily accepted the plan. So in the early spring of 1919 the State Supervisory People's Commissariat was established, and on March 30, Stalin was appointed its head.[22]

In Fyodor Alliluyev's memoirs there is little about this period of the Soviet dictator's life. As the author proceeds in time the text increasingly resembles the hagiographies typical of the Great Terror. On the pages of the manuscript Stalin appears at times as an Olympian god. "During the time of the October revolution Comrade Stalin did not close his eyes for five nights. Finally tiredness got the better of him and he fell asleep sitting at the table. Lunacharsky stepped towards the sleeping Stalin on tip-toe and kissed him on the forehead. Stalin woke up and laughed good-naturedly for a long time at A. V. Lunacharsky." But in addition to the tear jerking moments there are a few interesting human gestures too: "In 1917 and the first half of 1918 Stalin wore civilian clothes and shoes. He only put on the famous military uniform for the first time in August 1918 [...] I remember one episode when the shoemaker brought Comrade Stalin his boots to try. The size was good but they were so tight that he could not pull them on. "When will they be ready?" asked Comrade Stalin. "In five days," came the reply. "Can't it be any earlier?" asked Comrade Stalin. "You can't be serious!" At this Iosif Vissarionovich said reproachfully, "My father could make two pairs of boots in a single day."[23]

In the same manuscript a few "deviator" politicians, who had been executed by then, are mentioned several times. Fyodor Alliluyev, in keeping with the times, writes about them with hate: "Five or six days after Comrade Stalin had arrived, the infamous Slyapnikov *[the people's commissar for employment for the first Soviet government, later leader of the so-called "workers' opposition"—M. K.]* went to the northern Caucasus via Tsaritsyn at the behest of the People's Commissars' Council.[24] This is the man who not long ago was arrested for being an enemy of the people. This well-fed, red-faced man, who recalls a flabby bourgeois, was still a worker until recently. But he learned gentlemanly behavior and looked down and patronized 'the simple people'. Slyapnikov's wagon was completely different inside and out from Comrade Stalin's separate train. It was obvious that its owner lived well; he occupied his own wagon comprised of two salons, with a kitchen in the other wagon in which two, but perhaps even three cooks worked furiously. Slyapnikov's environs was made up of three dozen people, all adjutants, aides-de-camp, and the like."[25]

But this manuscript was not published despite such scenes. Fyodor Alliluyev in his lucid moments knew well that his high-flying brother-in-law loathed his whole family. One of the signs of this was Pyotr Fedoseyev's denunciation of Anna Alliluyeva's memoirs that were published in *Pravda* in May 1947. When Fyodor read the article he noted bitterly: "This whole anti-Alliluyev campaign started with Stalin's knowledge." His words were immediately noted by the agents of the political police.[26] Anna Alliluyeva was imprisoned soon after while Fyodor adopted his older sister's younger son Vladimir.[27]

The united Alliluyevs reacted in a similar way in 1938 when they arrested and executed Anna's husband Stanisław Redens. Sergei Alliluyev then entered the names of his two grandsons, Leonid and Vladimir, into his own identity papers in order to make their life easier. This brave step *de facto* meant that he had adopted them.[28]

1 *Iosif Stalin v obyatiakh semyi*, 1993, 191–192.
2 See page 71 in this book.
3 See page 72 in this book.
4 Smith, 1967, 160, 199–202, 204–206, 257, 345.
5 Alliluyev, 1995, 288.
6 Kornei Chukovsky, the Russian writer who lived a very long life, wrote about the Kamo test in his diary on September 24, 1933. Chukovsky was being treated at the OGPU Hospital, where he met "Lizaveta Drabkina, who was completely deaf. [...] Her mother frequently visited Moscow during the December 1905 uprising. During her travels, she wore Bickford fuses *[detonating fuses—M. K.]* wrapped around her body under her dress, that made her look like an aristocratic dame. Her four-year-old daughter always accompanied her. [...] Drabkina told the story of her

adventures she endured in the Kamo group, and I could not sleep afterwards. The story is fascinating! Kamo's group prepared 'to kill Denikin'. Along with the other youngsters, Drabkina was taken to a forest near Moscow, where whites attacked them. And they were all put against the wall." Drabkina recalled that she had sung the *Internationale* while the whites targeted them. "But there where five in the group who could not stand this, and started to betray their group mates. One by one, they betrayed their comrades. It turned out later that the whole scene was plotted by Kamo, to find out how loyal the members of his revolutionary organization are." Chukovsky, 1995, 84–85.

7 Mikoyan, 1999, 131–132.

8 This was suggested to Lenin by Semyon Ter-Petrosyan [Kamo] himself. *Biograficheskaya Khronika*, 1982, 274–275.

9 It is not impossible that Sergei Alliluyev was not there at all. This scene does not feature in any of his biographies.

10 *Iosif Stalin v obyatiakh semyi*, 1993. 24.

11 Mikoyan, 1999, 361.

12 *RGASPI*, fond, 558, op. 4, d. 663.

13 *Druzhba Narodov*, 1997, no. 4, 79.

14 Spassky, 1958, 99–102.

15 Trotsky, 1964, vol I, 228–229. Due to the work of the censors, all references to this were taken out of the Soviet authors' writings. *Istoricheskie Zapiski*, 1949, no. 30, 31.

16 The Trotsky Papers 1964, I, 134–140, 156–164.

17 He considered them his rivals even back then.

18 Trotsky would decimate retreating troops. He executed divisional commanders and people's commissars who left the front without permission. On other occasions he would threaten well-known party workers fighting in the Third Army with the death penalty. Trotsky, 1964, vol. I, 152–154, 204–211.

19 *RGASPI*, fond. 558, op. 1, d. 5269.

20 *Ibid.*, 459.

21 Stalin, 1947, vol. IV, 186–224.

22 *Soviet Narodnikh Komissarov*, 1999, 453. As of February 1920, the people's commissariat headed by Stalin took up the name "Worker-Peasant Supervision".

23 *RGASPI*, fond. 558, op. 4, d. 663.

24 Two telegrams sent by Stalin dated June 14, 1919 are extant from this trip: they indicate that he was in close working contact with his later political rival: "Urgent government message. Yekaterinodar. To Dunayevsky. Commissar Slyapnikov set off on the 14th in the day. He took money and a van with him. After him come the textiles." *RGASPI*, fond. 558, op.1, d. 3916. The second telegram "Yekaterinodar, or wherever he is: To Rubin, president of the Kuban' Central Executive Committee. As I cannot leave Tsaritsyn, Commissar Slyapnikov has set off to meet you instead." *RGASPI*, fond. 558, op. 1, d. 3917.

25 *Ibid.*

26 Kostirchenko, 1994, 86–87.

27 Alliluyev, 1995, 228.

28 *RGASPI*, fond. 668, op. 1, d. 15.

Next page:
Stalin and Kirov walking on a Moscow street.

Inspecting New Weaponry

Weapons inspection in the mid-1930s. Before long, most of the participants in this event became persecuted during the Great Terror. Among the future victims we can see General Mikhail Tukhachevsky and Ian Gamarnik (x), who was the chief political commissar of the Red Army. On the next picture, there stands behind Stalin Valerian Mezhlauk (xx), the true engineer of the Soviet economy, Molotov's deputy. Soon enough he also became a victim of the purges, together with his two siblings.

CHAPTER 28
Pavel Alliluyev

Of the Alliluyev couple's four children only Pavel had a significant career in the last part of his short life. Although as a youth he had been the odd one in the family. While Fyodor, Anna and Nadezhda all entered grammar school—Fyodor, as we have seen, even went to naval officer school—Pavel, following his father's footsteps, learned to be an electrician and in the best instance a technician. Although he must have been a talented young man, since in addition to having a job, he managed to graduate from high school as a private student.

Before February 1917 only Pavel of the four siblings found his way to the organized workers movement. During the great strike wave of 1913 he also saw the inside of the tsar's prisons. In the First World War he served as a private in several provincial barracks near the Russian capital. This is how after the February 1917 revolution he was elected a member of the Novgorod military Soviet. From this time onwards his life went up and down like a see-saw, the key moments of which gape like a black hole in all the writings about Stalin's relatives so far. What is certain is that after the Bolshevik turn in October 1917 he was dismissed and returned to his old workplace, a Petersburg electric plant. Then he joined the army once again, this time the Red Army—it is possible, although there is no documentation to prove it, that he did so voluntarily. He was able to make use of his technical skills at a sapper unit. Lenin, who liked the Alliluyevs a lot, saw to it that he got to the front, although one did not need any special contacts to do so. But after a time his health deteriorated and at his mother's request—as we saw in Olga Alliluyeva's story, again with the help of Lenin's intervention—he was sent home.[1] Despite this he was soon again in uniform fighting throughout the Civil War: even in those bloody times there were only a few people who can say that they fought on twelve fronts. On two occasions he was awarded the Military Order of the Red Banner for exceptional bravery.[2]

At the end of the fighting he was people's commissar of a small communications unit, then he entered the interior security formations. Here was involved with his fellow soldiers in a cruel liquidation of peasants from Tambov, who refused to turn in their crops during the collection raids and armed themselves. At another time for long months he pursued "counter-revolutionary gangs" over the Central Asian steppes, that is armed groups made up of the various indigenous ethnic groups. "For us, Europeans, this fight is fraught with extraordinary difficulties. We can only liaise with each other *[between the red units that were stationed far apart—M. K.]* by donkeys, camels, and horses. The thermometer sometimes went up to 70 degrees Celsius. There was a lack of good drinking water. Tropical malaria raged among us. Even so we finally reaped a great victory," wrote Pavel Alliluyev in May 1924, in a long appeal against being thrown out of the Bolshevik Party, which read more like an autobiographical short story.[3]

This gentle man, who throughout his life would much rather make peace than confront others, was completely nonplused—just like his younger sister Nadezhda had been earlier—by the party cleansing decisions made by his colleagues. He saw it as professional jealousy, the "arrogance of intellectuals" when faced with a manual worker who had been able to reach higher social status. He also thought that he was a victim of "party opposition" machinations against "the central line".

But the conflict—probably at the intervention of the Bolshevik Party's first man, Joseph Stalin—finally came to rights. In the meantime Pavel Alliluyev was enrolled at an intensive technical course. And at the same time, he was studying at the communications institute which was supported by the Red Army, of which he eventually became a director. Then following the memorandum of his parents' old friend, Klim Voroshilov, he was sent to Weimar Germany as a military commissar.[4] There he carried out military transactions between Moscow and Berlin, which were strictly forbidden by the entente Paris Peace Treaty, in the greatest secrecy.[5]

In the German capital, Aleksandr Orlov, later the NKVD's man in Spain, became one of his superiors. The famous intelligence officer got lots of blood on his hands during the Spanish Civil War.[6] Later he broke with the Stalinist system and escaped abroad under a false name, in order to escape the fate of those Soviet master spies who were charged with and recalled home by Yezhov, the NKVD chief. So in 1938 Orlov, during the Great Terror, escaped sure execution. But he did not join the western intelligence services. It was only after Stalin's death that he went public in the United States, by publishing his memoirs in the American press that created quite a stir.

Pavel Alliluyev.

To our knowledge today, only General Orlov left any personal description of Pavel Alliluyev's years in Berlin: "I remember when he entered my study. I was taken aback at how much he resembled his little sister *[Nadezhda Alliluyeva—M. K.]*. The same proportional features and eastern eyes that looked sadly at the world. After a time I realized that Pavel's nature was also very similar to Nadezhda's. He was a pure, honest and very modest man. I would like to mention one of his characteristics—rare among Soviet *chinovnik*s—he never used a weapon if he realized that his enemy is unarmed. As Stalin was his brother-in-law and Voroshilov his good friend, he had great influence. But he did not make

Stalin's brother-in-law with his children in Berlin.

Pavel Alliluyev (x) in Paris, on the rooftop of the Notre Dame.

this at all felt among his colleagues at the Berlin mission who intrigued against him either for careerist reasons or through misreading his character, not knowing where he came from."

According to Orlov, he himself did not often mention Stalin when he talked to Pavel Alliluyev even though during the Berlin years they became very good friends. "Once he mentioned that Stalin sings hymns when he drinks vodka. At another time he told the following story: in Sochi [...] Stalin ran out of the *dacha* dining room with a contorted face and threw his knife on the ground. He screamed: 'Even in prison I had a sharper knife!'"[7] ✩

M. K.: How did your father's relationship with the Joseph Stalin develop?

K. A.: He called my father 'My little pigeon' as Pavel Alliluyev was a very good-hearted man *[her voice softens]*. Perhaps that is why Stalin always sent him to places where people had not got on with each other. First of all to beyond the Arctic Circle. The collective working there *[geologists—M. K.]* were always fighting. Thanks to my father they made peace with each other. My father was well-intentioned, he was a democratic man to use today's terminology. Not a Soviet bureaucrat! He was given an interesting job in 1937 at the time of Paris World's Fair. My parents had gone to see Stalin and he said: "Pavel! I would like to send you to Paris. You will be *[imitating the celebratory style]* the commissar of the Red Banner award winning Aleksandrov ensemble. We are afraid that members of the ensemble may want to stay in France. But you know how to prevent this from happening." But my father protested: "How can I prevent it. What can I do if someone travels to Paris with this in mind?" "Yes you will be able to," Stalin tried to convince my father. "You have such an unusual nature that everybody listens to you. Nobody will want to get you into trouble." My father consented and went to Paris. In the meantime my mother sought Stalin out: "Joseph, I have never asked anything of you. But now I would ask you to allow me to go to France too." Yezhov was also present at this conversation, and Stalin turned to him: "What do you think Comrade Yezhov, should we let this *little village beauty* out into Europe?" The people's commissar for internal affairs saw that the Master was in a good mood so he said yes. They gave my mother money and a passport. When she returned from Paris she told many stories about her western adventures: "Can you imagine there are white Russian émigrés who seeing the Aleksandrovs, sank to their knees in the theater foyer. Others cried. The ensemble was a huge success. Many people entreated the singers and dancers to stay, promising them the world. But despite this nobody wanted to emigrate." The ensemble later went to Czechoslovakia but nobody tried to stay there either. Stalin was most satisfied: he believed this was all thanks to my father.

☆ We get a completely different picture form this sweet, but seemingly unbelievable account, in Orlov's memoirs concerning Pavel's Paris mission. The general was the representative of the NKVD in Spain at the time. He recalled that Stalin's brother-in-law congratulated him in a warm letter at the end of January 1937 on receiving the Order of Lenin in Moscow. In the post scriptum he requested as if in passing that Orlov arrange for him to travel to Spain too. Orlov did not understand the request and immediately forgot about it. In the September of the same year the two former colleagues met in the French capital. Orlov simply did not believe that Pavel Alliluyev, who had directed the political work at the entire armored formations of the Red Army, was now carrying out lowly jobs in the Soviet pavilion at the World's Fair. Aleksandr Orlov soon found out that Yezhov had ordered the Soviet political police's Paris division to watch Pavel Alliluyev's movements. "I asked him how he had been given this job at all. 'Simple!' he replied bitterly. 'They want me as far away as possible from Moscow. [...] You must know how my younger sister died,' he said hesitatingly and was silent." He informed Orlov that "in recent years great changes had taken place" in Moscow and that is why his political position had weakened too."[8] ☆

M. K.: Following the Tukhachevsky trial your father traveled to the Paris World Fair. It was then that the most vehement purges were taking place in the commanding staff of the Red Army.[9] Didn't Pavel Alliluyev fear that he would also fall prey to this? They could have said for example that he belonged to Tukhachevsky's circle.

K. A.: My father knew everybody accused in the Tukhachevsky trial well. At the beginning of the 1930 many of them had trained at various chief officer and commanding courses in Germany.[10] That is when we lived there too. And they all came to our house. But whether my father had any political connection with them—that I don't believe. Moreover, the circle around Tukhachevsky had members older than my father and nearly all of them had served as officers in the tsar's army, like, for example, Uborevich. The fierce Marshall Yegorov for example, who was later arrested in 1938, had been a colonel in the tsar's army during the First World War. Just like Shaposhnikov who was not put through the *Stalinist meat grinder*, as they would say today. The old, asthmatic, large commanding officer—he became a Marshall in the Second World War—lived very close to us in Zubalovo. But I would not say that he was a good friend of my father's. Believe me, to *them* it mattered that Pavel Alliluyev had come up *through* the ranks. And he was only an ill-fated private in the army of the last tsar. A common past did not unite most of the leaders of the Red Army whom my "dear relative" had executed, every one because he was afraid of a coup.

M. K.: However it did matter to the NVKD that these commanding officers were guests at your parents' house in Berlin. And that when off-duty they also turned up at your home a little later when your father was recalled from Berlin.

K. A.: I will try to remember who came to see us at home in the thirties. *[She shakes her head]*. But no, no I can't remember if Mikhail Tukhachevsky or his friends were our guests. They were more friendly with the Mikoyan family. When we stayed in the Mikoyans' *dacha* at Zubalovo then we met high ranking army officers.

☆ Stalin's order to execute Mikhail Tukhachevsky and his fellow officers as part of the Great Terror had grave consequences, no one would question that today. As a result, not only the high-ranking officer corps was decapitated, but Stalin also pushed the Empire into a severe crisis right at the outset of the Second World War. Stalin, however, who since the beginning of the 1920s tended to favor *preventive expansionism* in his foreign and military policies, originally had similar ideas as Tukhachevsky, who had dreamed of a well-equipped, huge, peacetime army of eleven-million troops, which would enable him to dictate the terms of foreign policies to the neighboring countries, just like in the summer of 1920 during the military campaign against Warsaw.[11] Despite his unsympathetic attitude against Tukhachevsky, Stalin—who had almost imprisoned the general during the campaign against the former tsarist officers in 1930—eventually came to terms with the "Red Bonaparte". In a letter dated May 7, 1932, Stalin made amends with Mikhail Tukhachevsky. Although the "Master" still found the idea of eleven million troops excessive, he would accept a peacetime army of six million. As a result of this temporary compromise, Stalin appointed the general a deputy of the people's commissar for military affairs. Moreover, Tukhachevsky became one of the first five Soviet marshals, and was commissioned with overseeing the military industry. Stalin acknowledged his achievements in successfully modernizing the army, and awarded the general the Order of Lenin in February 1933. In the

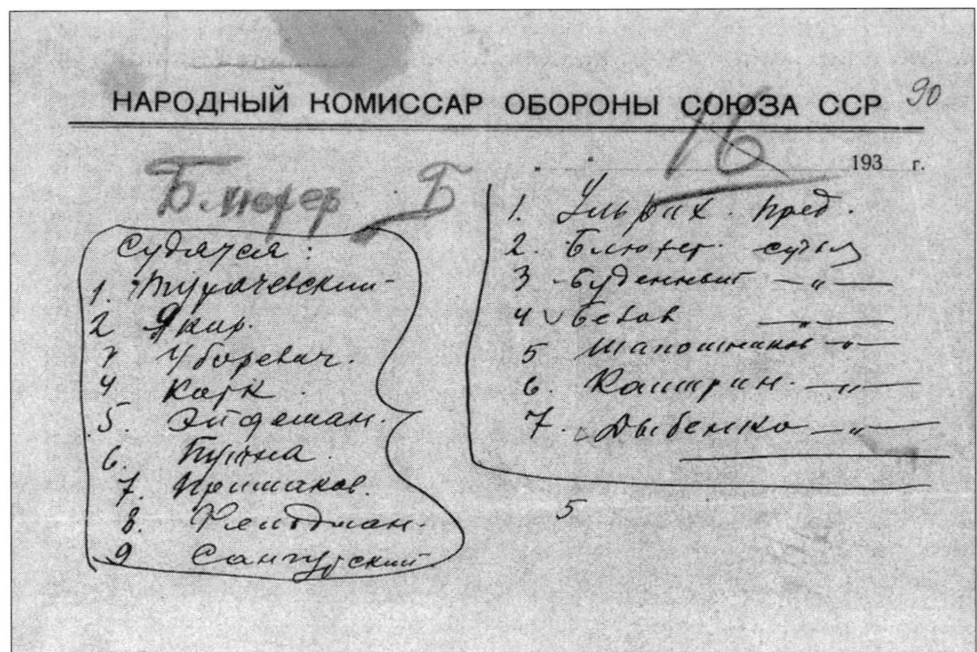

НАРОДНЫЙ КОМИССАР ОБОРОНЫ СОЮЗА ССР 90

16

193 г.

Блюхер Б

Судьи:
1. Тухачевский
2. Якир
3. Уборевич
4. Корк
5. Эйдеман
6. Путна
7. Примаков
8. Фельдман
9. Сангурский

1. Ульрих пред.
2. Блюхер судья
3. Буденный —"—
4. Белов
5. Шапошников —"—
6. Каширин —"—
7. Дыбенко —"—

5

These so far unpublished two pages are taken from Voroshilov's register, which he decorated with a drawing while he discussed with Stalin the fate of the high-ranking commanders of the Red Army.

same year, sitting on a white horse at the official ceremonies commemorating the Seventh of November, he reviewed the military parade.

Then suddenly Tukhachevsky's fate turned again. Following the Kirov assassination, during the political trials that decimated the Soviet elite, the Purge eventually reached the ranks of the army as well. Moreover, Stalin skillfully utilized the opposition between the "conservatives", grouped around Voroshilov and Budenny, and the "reformsists", hall-marked by Tukhachevsky. And when in the spring of 1937 the investigators of the NKVD obtained false testimonies from the former Trotskyist generals—Shmidt, Primakov, and Putna—against Tukhachevsky and his comrades, the young marshal was doomed. Tukhachevsky—who had defeated Admiral Kolchak and, who had been the hero of the campaigns

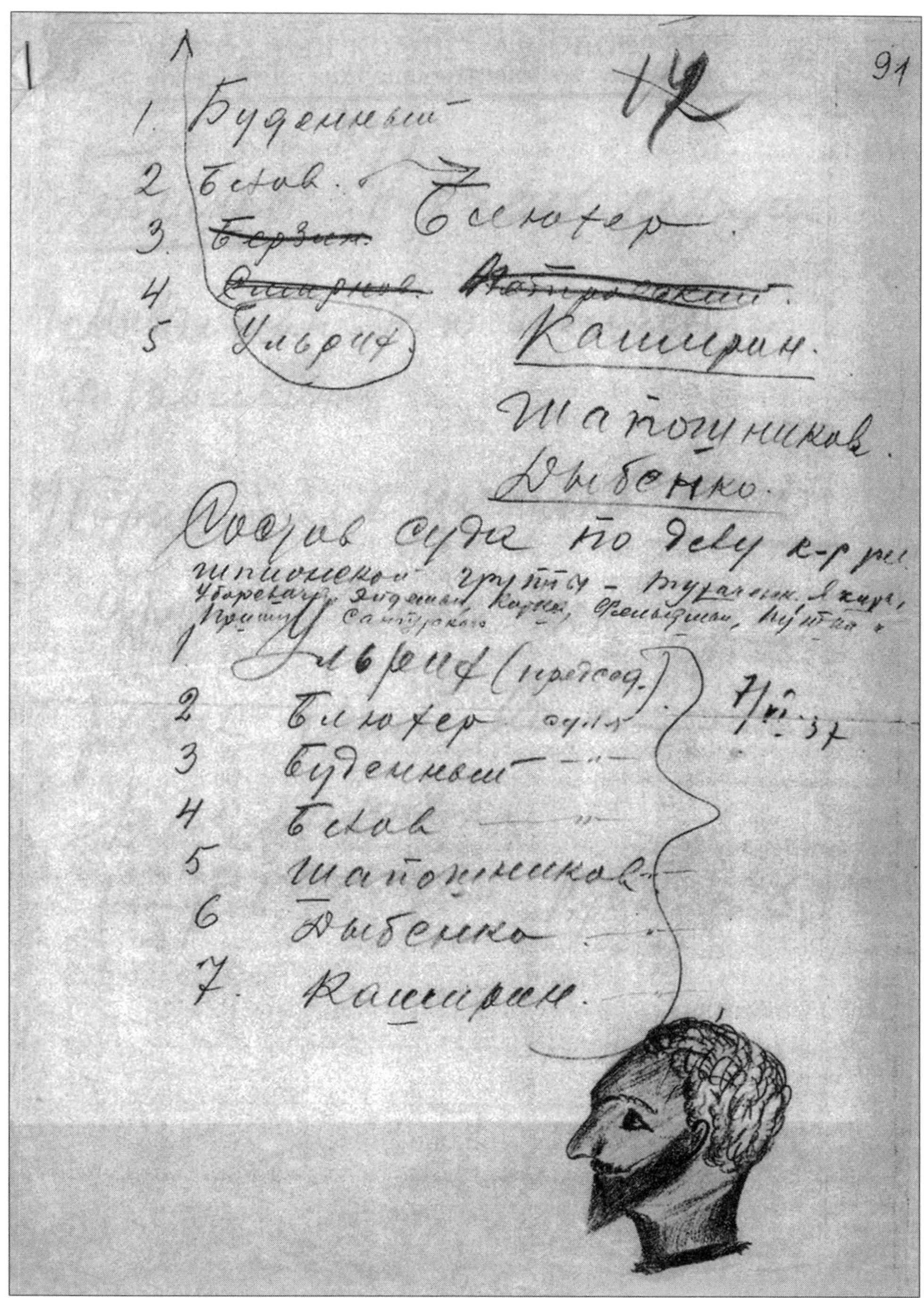

91

1. Буденный
2. Белов.
3. Блюхер
5. Ульрих Каширин.

Шапошников.

Дыбенко.

Состав суда по делу к-р шпионской группы – Тухачевск. Якира, Уборевича, Эйдемана, Корка, Фельдмана, Путна и Примакова

1. Ульрих (председ.)
2. Блюхер судья
3. Буденный –"–
4. Белов –"–
5. Шапошников
6. Дыбенко
7. Каширин.

7/VI.37

A revealing document proving that on July 7, 1937, Stalin and Voroshilov still did not know how many defendants the Tukhachevsky trial would have, and who would be selected to act as judges. During the contrived show trial, which was held behind closed doors, 3,167 high-ranking officers of the Red Army were executed.

against the Whites and the Poles in 1920 on the Western Front—was called back from the position of deputy people's commissar, and appointed commander of the Volga region military district. Soon after Tukhachevsky arrived in the city of Kuybishev, he was arrested on May 22, 1937. Others shared his fate: Iona Yakir, the commander of the Kiev region military district, Robert Eydeman, the commander of the civil defense, Boris Feldman, the number one human resource director of the Red Army, Avgust Kork, the commander of the Frunze Military Academy, and Ieronim Uborevich, the commander of the Belarus region military district were all arrested and subjected to physical and mental torture. Tukhachevsky's files, for example, are still covered with rusty red color bloodstains. It was equally abominable for these commanders, charged with spying for Ger-

According to Yelizaveta Tukhachevskaya, there was no such thing as a "Tukhachevsky conspiracy", but it is true that her brother and his friends criticized official military policies in their friendly meetings.

many and conspiring against the Soviet Union, that in front of the court-martials they had to recite testimonies prepared in advance, with their own former comrades in the audience. Up until now, we had known that Stalin, Molotov, Kaganovich, and Yezhov decided over their fate on June 5, 1937. However, as it is evident from the two pages of Voroshilov's diaries, dated two days later and published for the first time in this book, only two people, Stalin and Voroshilov, put together the list of judges and that of the generals condemned to death. In this version, there was still one more person named among leaders of the "Tukhachevsky conspiracy", and the list of judges was also still under consideration by the two chief executioners, Stalin and Voroshilov. But when on June 11, 1937, at 11.35 p.m., the chief military judge Ulrikh read the death sentence, the name of army corps commander Sangursky was missing from the list. He was executed a year later.[12] ☆

M. K.: But if Pavel Alliluyev evaded the Tukhachevsky affair then why did his fate turn out so tragically? Why did Stalin take offense at him and then…

K. A. [she interrupts in great agitation]: I see that you don't dare ask why Stalin did away with my father!

M. K.: Well if you have the strength then tell me and please don't be angry for upseting you with my questions.

K. A.: Of course I'm not angry. *[Fatigued.]* Lets go through things chronologically. Perhaps I have already mentioned that we could not move into the Kremlin, back to our former apartment when we returned from Germany. After a short wait we got a flat in the "House on the Embankment ". More or less all the relatives lived in that huge house from which *[she laughs bitterly]* the secret police took someone every blessed night during the 1930s. We tried to go on as if nothing was happening at all. Sometimes we gathered together, sang, listened to popular records. That very night we'd had a small gathering. I wish we hadn't… On that night they took Maria Korona away. And her husband Alyosha Svanidze, the older brother of Stalin's first wife. Who was everybody's favorite.

1 Trotsky, 1971, 128–130.
2 Alliluyev, 1995, 18, 22.
3 Alliluyev, 1995, 16–20.
4 Carev-Costello, 1995, 50–51.
5 *Ibid.*
6 *Ibid.*, 306–332.
7 Orlov, 1993, 307–308.
8 *Ibid.*, 309–311.
9 Suvenirov, 1998, 60–133
10 On the intensive military and technical cooperation between the two countries, see Gorlov, 2001, 232–256, 265–286.
11 Tukhachevsky's prophecy in part became reality. Approximately this many people were in service during the last months of the Second World War, in the Soviet Union and across its borders, in the ranks of the Red Army, the special police, the border guard and gulag guard corps, and the various para-military troops.
12 Suvenyirov, 1998, 379.

Stalin's style often resembled the manners of a preacher.

Kliment Voroshilov (1),
Mikhail Tukhachevsky (2),
Nikolai Muralov (3), and
Aleksandr Yegorov (4)
in the early 1920s.

Tukhachevsky's rivals
and debate partners: Bubnov (3),
Budenny (2), Voroshilov (1),
and Unschlicht (4)

Next page:
Mikhail Tukhachevsky's stiff features
did not change over the years.

Below sitting are the army leaders
of the Soviet Union in the 1920s.
From left to right: Uborevich,
Sergei Kamenev, Alksnis, Orlov,
Budenny, Voroshilov, Unschlicht,
Bubnov, Yegorov, Tukhachevsky
and Dibenko. All of them perished
in the late 1930s except for Voroshilov
and Budenny, the masterminds
behind the Great Terror.

Mikhail Tukhachevsky

CHAPTER 29
The Destruction of the Svanidze Family

Georgia, which was under Menshevik political rule and was independent until 1921, was only brought to heel by the Bolsheviks killing tens of thousands of people. While the archive material concerning this remains unpublished it is difficult to establish how personally responsible Aleksei Svanidze—known as Alyosha by his old illegal social demokrat name—was for this tragedy. What is certain is that he, as the new Tiflis government's cultural and then financial people's commissar between 1921–26, who came to power under the protection of the Soviet-Russian Red Army, would have had to sign the decrees which decimated time and again this small mountainous country. We know that during theses campaigns a good few of Alyosha Svanidze's old friends were sent to prison or faced the firing squad.

Earlier Stalin had taken his brother-in-law with him on a special train to Tsaritsyn where in 1918 he was lord of life and death. Or perhaps he ordered his brother-in-law there after sending him on a secret mission to the northern Caucasus. In an until now unpublished document dated June 14, 1918 he certified: "Certificate. I certify that Aleksei Svanidze works for the Council of People's Commissars. As part of his work he is traveling on a mission to Vladikavkaz. We order that the commissars on duty at the station, the station officers, and the other employees of the Transport Commissariat ensure a place for Comrade Svanidze on the wagon kept for representatives of the central authority. That they help him in all ways in order that he reach his destination as quickly as possible. Member of the Council of People's Commissars, Commissar."[1]

In another of Stalin's letters dated March 1921 it becomes clear that he regarded his well-mannered and cultivated brother-in-law as a *tool* during the period that he was negotiating with Georgian intellectuals: "Baku. To Ordzhonikidze. In order to pursue a new policy in relation to Georgian petit-bourgeois circles Svanidze will be very useful to everyone as he has wide-ranging contacts with the intellectuals outside the party. In addition, he could easily be given the position of people's commissar for cultural or foreign affairs. He would in all cases be better than Gegechkori.[2] So I propose that Svanidze be a member of the Revolutionary Committee *[of Georgia—M. K.]*. Inform me of your and the comrades' opinion about this. If you agree, Svanidze can travel over there along with Yenukidze."[3]

Anastas Mikoyan, who was an old friend of Alyosha Svanidze and for a time even his superior, wrote the following on the always gentle and erudite, European mannered financial expert in his memoirs: "He was a respectable, calm, and polite man who did not rush things. He liked to ponder over things and ask others' advice. [...] He was capable of self-control and did not offend others. But at the same time he could not bear it if someone did not care about his own 'noble' self-respect. Svanidze was of noble birth."[4]

This noted financial expert was hailed as a polymath in his circle of friends at the Kremlin. He spent his spare time chiefly studying the antique world. For a time in the thirties he edited the periodical *Vestnik Drevnei Istorii*. He also translated *belles lettres*.[5]

He spent most of his life in exile in Germany, later in the Soviet colony there.

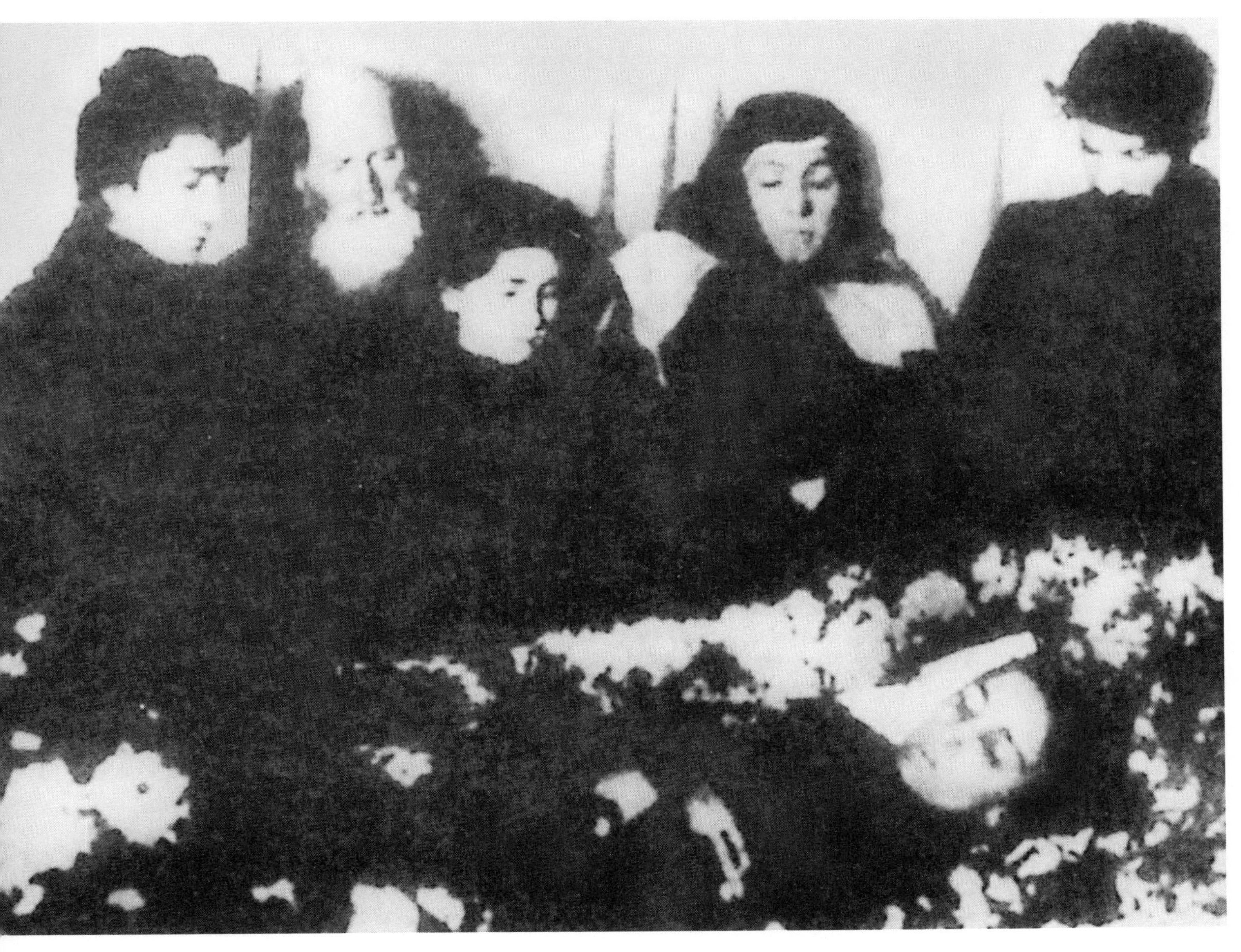

Perhaps because of his *European manners*, he had an aversion to the cruel methods of the Georgian Bolshevik Party leadership that Stalin epitomized in Moscow. Once he let slip to a circle of close acquaintances that "Koba does not like the people. Indeed he despises them. His self-importance will cost the party a lot."[6] But he did not protest against the excessiveness publicly. Even later on, when he worked in high-ranking foreign Soviet delegations and then when he became the vice president of the State Central Bank in Moscow, he obediently subordinated himself to the period of continual terror which bore all the hallmarks of Stalin's hand. In December 1937, despite the dictator's unconditional loyalty to his brother-in-law and old friend, Alyosha Svanidze and his wife Maria Korona were from one day to the next declared enemies of the people and underwent terrible torture in the NKVD's Lubyanka prison. Just a few months before the four men, who were tied by kinship relations as well as being from similar socio-cultural backgrounds, and who understood each other instinctively, had regularly played billiards in the hall of Zubalovo-4. Three of them—Pavel Alliluyev, Stanisław Redens, and Alyosha Svanidze—had no inkling that their lives would soon end tragically. The fourth player, Joseph Stalin, who became

Yekaterina Svanidze, Stalin's first wife, died at a very young age. She was put on the bier in an open coffin, according to the Georgian custom.
The picture shows Keto's family: her parents, sisters, and the seemingly heart-broken husband. Iosif Dzhugashvili, who had not been a kind person before either, started to be really heartless after the funeral. Although he supported the family of his first wife after he became the leader of the Soviet Union, he eventually decimated them during the Great Terror.

intoxicated by the ever-increasing executions, had planned ahead, in a manner that would have put professional criminals to shame, in what way he would strike down on them.

At the beginning of the 1990s, Abdurakhman Avtorkhanov, the old Kremlin expert who had lived for years in Germany, told me at his home near Munich that one of Stalin's most typical "Asian" or "Caucasian" characteristics was "revenge on several generations". The mendacity of his act consisted of behaving sweetly to the victims the day before their arrest. And so it was with most of the members of the Zubalovo circle as well. Avtorkhanov, who is also of Caucasian origin and former Bolshevik Party *apparatchik*, knew the trap situation *from the inside*—the development of which can be clearly traced in Maria Korona's secret diary. This disturbing document, which gives us a glimpse into the pre-war Soviet elite's Orwellian modes of thought, eventually landed in Stalin's private archive, with bits ripped out by an unknown person, after the diarist's arrest.[7]

Maria Korona, the former Tiflis opera singer who was smart, cultured, and well-educated in art history, fell in love with Stalin after the suicide of her best friend Nadezhda Alliluyeva. Despite its platonic nature, she was gripped by powerful emotions, and strove to see the everyday life in the world, and especially the daily lives of the small community at Zubalovo within it, through the eyes of the Great Idol. The woman's manifest adoration was increasingly irritating to her husband who, despite his western learning, was a jealous Georgian, and found it difficult to bear when Maria behaved in an over-emancipated manner with other men. On August 1, 1934 she noted: "I am a little sad and quiet. Such is my mood. On the 28th J[oseph] went to Sochi. Because of Alyosha I wasn't able to see him before his departure. Irritating. Over the last two months Alyosha has continually prevented me from being in Joseph's company. Though how fascinating it is to be be with him!"[8]

The majority of the diary entries are about the intricate relations between "little planets" [Alliluyev, Redens, and Svanidze] that circled the "heavenly body" [Stalin], about the daily life of the Soviet upper leadership. But as the number of acquaintances and friends who disappeared without a trace increased, Maria Korona started to seek the answer to what was happening around them more and more frequently. As nobody, including her husband, spoke to her honestly, she tried to solve the enigma alone. On March 5, 1937 she wrote: "I have not written my diary for more than three months. I have been through much, thought things over, wept, fumed [...] the Trotskyists' trial was a significant event.[9] My soul rages and burns with hate. Executions are not enough. I would like them to be tortured, broken on the wheel, burned alive for their perfidy. They betrayed my country! That rabble currying favor with the party! And how many there were of them! They planned a terrible end to this system. They wanted to eradicate the victories of the revolution, they destroyed our husbands and our children." The diarist later even came to think that the political police were rightfully making people disappear one after another. She was only sorry that she had not uncovered them herself in time.[10]

It seems incredible that Maria Korona, who was known for being independent and very observant, withdrew to her *dacha* on August 7, 1937 in order to bitterly reproach herself for not being vigilant enough when it came to her acquaintances. "I take up my pen, but I have no idea where to start. It is difficult to reconstruct all the events of the recent months. [...] What could have happened, how was it possible that we did not notice that hostile elements have flourished to such an extent among us? [...] As I go down the street I often stare at people,

Maria Korona's best friend, the writer Galina Serebyakova, and her husband, Grigory Sokolnikov, Soviet ambassador to London.

The prison photograph of Sokolnikov, the tertiary defendant of the January 1937 showtrial in Moscow.

observe their features. I ponder where they hid until now, how they masked themselves, those millions of people [sic] who were incapable of accepting the Soviet system because of their social standing or their mental frame. They could not keep up with the workers and poor peasants on the road to socialism and communism. And these chameleons became exposed in all their duplicity in the twentieth year of the revolution. They have neither basic integrity, nor patriotism, not even an instinctive clinging to their state either. To harm, betray, hiss like snakes, hate—they are well capable of. Of everything, only to prevent the world's most just system from flourishing [...] The atmosphere has become intense. Uncertainty and suspicion dominates everywhere. But then, how could that be strange when the acquaintances of yesterday, who lied for many years wearing masks, have become our enemies of today? It is true that the majority of the traitors and saboteurs were always debased people for whom I rarely felt sympathy. So personally I am not disappointed as I never felt affection towards the masked enemy. But what is disgusting is that I met and talked with them at all. And a few of them I even received in my home. This is the background which *[overshadows—M. K.]* this year."[11]

The mass psychosis of this inhuman period seems incomprehensible to us today. Typical to this psychosis is that Maria Korona, who herself was of "bourgeois" and "class alien" origin, thus she suffered prejudice and branding from the outset, tried to "determine" the "enemies of the people" in Soviet society on basis of the same appearances. Sometimes Maria, who was slowly going mad, debated for hours with herself on the Great Idol.

Galina Serebryakova, who had been the wife of two famous party leaders—Serebyakov and Sokolnikov—who were both sentenced at the same January 1937 trial, wrote in her memoirs: "...during those years we all feverishly read Tarle's *Talleyrand* and Zweig's *Fouché*. Alyosha Svanidze often referred to these books. 'We have faced so much adversity in recent years after Nadya's *[Alliluyeva—M. K.]* death. The Kirov murder. Everybody seeing the wolf in everybody else. And I, I don't understand anything, anything,' noted Maria Anisimovna *[Korona—M. K.]*. 'You don't need to understand it. It is not a thing for women,' joked Svanidze. At this Maria Anisimovna raised her sky blue eyes and made a sweet face, making her look very beautiful. She continued, 'Aleksandr believes that Joseph [Stalin] loses a lot [of his appeal] when you get to know him better. That is why he keeps a certain distance between himself and others. I have known him for many years but he remains a big enigma for me. And will remain so.' 'Great people are often even greater actors,' replied Aleksandr Semyonovich *[Svanidze—M. K.]*. 'But let's not talk about these things! These sorts of conversations have become very dangerous recently. Even if we were in the woods.'"[12] ☆

K. A.: It is terrible that Stalin and that S.O.B. Beria, who never liked Alyosha, killed such wonderful people as the Svanidze couple. Maria was a lovely woman. One of the most beautiful women that I have ever met. At the evening we met for the last time, she was wearing a low cut velvet dress, disregarding that it was already chilly. Her fine bust, like alabaster...She threw a light coat over her shoulders, and came over to our stairwell. You will soon see why this detail is important. Her husband Aleksei Svanidze, who everybody knew as Alyosha in the underground movement, which also became his byname, was also a good-looking man, graying at the temples. And he, too, dressed elegantly. That night he was in a good quality gray suit, of western make. *[Proudly.]* Because, like my parents, the Svanidzes had lived for years abroad, so they also had a rich wardrobe.

We were sitting immersed in intimate conversation. Everything seemed so fine... After midnight, at about one, the Svanidze couple stood up and went home. We started to wash up with my mother. We had a funny habit of never leaving dirty dishes in the sink until the next day. There were lots of cups and plates and the washing-up took until three or four in the morning. Then somebody rang the doorbell. Tolya came in, Maria Svanidze's son from her first marriage. Deathly pale he informed us: "They have arrested both of them, my mother and Alyosha. They took them away dressed as they were, in those fine clothes. They were not allowed to go into the dressing room and change and were not permitted to take anything with them."

M. K.: As far as I know the NKVD left Tolya, Alyosha Svanidze's stepson, alone. What happened to him later?

K. A.: I think Anatoly's father was a wealthy manufacturer or a merchant in Tiflis. When his parents divorced, the boy stayed with Maria. He came to love Alyosha, he never spoke of him as the "stern stepfather." After the outbreak of the Second World War, Tolya volunteered for the front and was killed almost immediately. As a Svanidze, even if he was only his stepson, he was an "enemy of the people," and so was sent into the penal battalion. There was another small boy in the Svanidze family. His real name was *Johnreed*, he was named after the author of *Ten Days That Shook the World*. But everybody called him Dzhonik. The relatives loved him, and spoiled and babied him. There is no point in deny-

ing that he was a very clever boy, but Maria and Alyosha went to the extremes when they bragged for years that their little Dzhonik would be Stalin's successor. We wondered why they had to say such things. "They will get in trouble because of this," said my mother, who was a wise woman. And she was right.
M. K.: Did they brag to others, saying that a new ruler is growing up in the Svanidze household?
K. A.: To all and sundry. "What a great mind the child has! A little genius!" This was their mania. "Only he is capable of stepping into Stalin's shoes. When he grows up he will be the leader!" But despite his cleverness little Dzhonik made the impression of an unpleasant boy. He was like all spoiled child prodigies. He was blessed with an extraordinarily good memory: after one hearing he could recite a long poem. He also wrote verses from when he was five on. He drew beautifully, and made some really good little sculptures out of plasticine. His parents taught him German and he sometimes spoke German with them. But he allowed himself too much... You can only imagine what that meant for such a helpless orphan in the detention camps, from where the detainees were transported to the prisons and camps. And then came exile. The world of criminals. Where one struggles for a piece of bread. It is bad enough just to think about

Serebyakov, the one-time Trotskyist and an old friend of the Svanidze family, who became a Soviet statesman from a simple worker, resisted the torture for many months. He finally broke when during an interrogation he was shown his adolescent daughter and told that if he did not cooperate, anything could happen to the girl.

This photograph of Leonid Serebyakov was taken shortly before his execution.

it...After Stalin's death Dzhonik was permitted to return to Moscow and met my mother who had reprimanded him so many times in his childhood. He fell weeping on her neck. "Auntie Zhenya, thank you for scolding me so much then. At home I was brought up in a sterile environment, that was the big trouble. Only when I was in exile could I really learn what life was like..."
M. K.: Various stories have been circulating about Alyosha Svanidze's last hours for many years now. What do you know of them?
K. A.: I don't know much but it seems that he was shot in the head not long after the outbreak of the war. I've heard this from many people. However I can bear witness to the fact that once when my mother met Stalin in a good mood she handed him Maria Svanidze's letter. You know, sometimes people smuggled letters out of the prisons or the Gulag. The unfortunate woman had written that she had to suffer innocently. Her health had deteriorated gravely and that she would die soon. Stalin read the letter and sternly rebuked my mother: "Zhenya, never do that again!"

The picture was most likely taken in Berlin, at the beginning of the 1930s. Sitting in the middle is Maria Korona, and standing next to her is the little Dzhonik. The man standing in the middle of the back row is Alyosha Svanidze.

I believe that this contributed to the fact that after long tortures Maria was eventually executed.

M. K.: Didn't they meet when Dzhonik married Svetlana, the daughter of his parents' executioner? This is something to think about, isn't it?

K. A.: Yes I believe it was then. *[She takes a long pause, thinking hard.]* But perhaps not, it was one or two years earlier. And Svetlana was not just the "daughter of the executioner" as you have said but unlucky Dzhonik's cousin too. They were the same age. After Stalin's death, Dzhonik returned from exile ill, and totally broken. By that time Svetlana was also a distressed woman. After Khrushchev's secret speech he made at the 20th Congress, she was very upset by what had come to light about her father. When she met Dzhonik, their wonderful childhood memories came back to them. And enchanted by this they felt they were made for each other. But I don't know whether they actually got married or not. I don't believe so.

☆ When Stalin heard what role Dzhonik's parents had envisioned for the child, he started to hate with a vengeance not only the Svanidze couple but also the child prodigy. As if a real rival had appeared on the horizon! Other oral history sources also bear witness to this. In the mid-1990s I sought out the old general, Artom Sergeyev, in his *dacha* near Moscow. According to the blind old officer, Joseph Stalin really—as the general said, *rightly*—could not stand the confident Dzhonik. Whenever he saw the child, he mocked him. He was shaken with rage when the little *Johnreed* interrupted adult conversations. And yet the child even dared to debate with the ruler of the country. Once he even boasted to Stalin, "Imagine, I'm going to be an astronomer!" "You will be lucky if you become a swineherd," quipped Stalin his face frowning.[13] As if telling off an opposition spokesman at the party Congress's presidential table.

It would be wrong, of course, to explain the Svandizes' arrest with an "intense rivalry" the dictator felt towards their little boy. There is more to it that Alyosha Svanidze was unfortunate to be one of the Soviet dictator's oldest acquaintances in the Bolshevik elite. The Master of the Kremlin got rid of his old friends almost without exception during the Great Terror because he saw them as unpleasant witnesses to his life. Apart from this, other reasons, still unknown to us, could have driven Stalin when he went after the relatives of his deceased first wife, Yekaterina Svanidze. Lavrenty Beria also intrigued a lot against the family. The complicated relations between the two Georgian politicians can be best summed up by an incident that happened in the autumn of 1932. After the future chief executioner had been appointed General Secretary of the Trans- Caucasusian party committee, while Alyosha Svanidze was named the vice president of the Council of People's Commissars, the "government" of the Trans-Caucasian Federation—the headquarters of both of which were in Tiflis—the latter resigned immediately in protest saying he could not work with Beria.[14]

At the beginning it seemed as if Stalin did not take sides in their disagreement. But after half a decade Beria got the upper hand. In many respects the subsequent fate of the Svanidzes depended on him after their arrest; NKVD investigators spent an unusually long time on unraveling the case—from December 1937 to August 1940. "Comrade Alyosha" was charged with joining the group of Georgian nationalist deviationists in 1922, who were against Stalin—even though exactly the opposite was true. The other charge against him was that in 1929, during the antagonisms within the party leadership, he joined the "right-wing deviationists", led by Bukharin and his associates. And in the meantime he arranged the sponsoring of Trotskyist groups in Spain and spied for Germany.[15] For all these charges, the Military College of the Soviet Supreme Court sentenced Alyosha Svanidze to death. It seems, however, that the Master of the Kremlin wanted to prolong the agony of his former favorite: he was waiting for his brother-in-law to grovel and suggest making a deal with him. This explains that following a protest made by the supreme military judge, Vasily Ulrikh—who was one of the confidants of the Soviet dictator—the court changed the sentence on January 23, 1941 to fifteen years' hard labor. These sorts of corrections were extremely rare—but it seems that Alyosha Svanidze was not willing to go down on his knees to beg his brother-in-law for his life.[16] The enraged Stalin then brought yet another decision through the courts. After Ulrikh filed a new protest, this time against the second sentence, the very same college of the Supreme Court annulled its own former decision on August 20, 1941. The prisoner was shot in the head the same day at Beria's personal orders.[17]

Nikita Khrushchev later came up with two fairly diverse versions concerning Svanidze's death. On October 29, 1962, during his speech at the 22nd Congress of the CPSU, he emphasized that "Svanidze was an old party member, but Beria gave the impression through various artifices that he had been spying on Stalin for the Germans. But in reality he was Stalin's best friend. And then Svanidze was shot in the head. Before he was executed he was handed a message from Stalin to the effect that if he apologizes then he will be spared [...] He responded by asking: 'Why do I have to apologize to him? I have done nothing.' [...] After Svanidze's death Stalin said: 'Well, what a proud man he was! He died without apologizing.' But he never thought for a moment that Svanidze was above all a man of integrity."[18]

In the 1940s, Johnreed Svanidze changed his name to Ivan. But he was unable to forget the past. When he thought of Stalin, the murderer of his parents, and his close relative at the same time, he would always get furious. Still, when he returned to Moscow after Stalin's death, he fell in love with Svetlana, the daughter of the dictator.

The same story in more detail, although with slightly different connotations, is found in Khrushchev's memoirs: "I believe that that quiet and calm Georgian intellectual Alyosha Svanidze was closest to Stalin. [...] He often visited him, I saw him there myself more than once. It was striking how pleased Stalin was when he had a chance to converse with Alyosha. Most frequently they talked about Georgia, its history and culture. I don't remember what qualifications Svanidze had, but he gave the impression of being a cultured and well-read man. Stalin's children also regarded him as a friend. They called him Uncle Alyosha. He slept there often [...] Then all at once he was an enemy of the people. That is, an enemy of Stalin's. [...] Stalin later regularly raised the question of how Alyosha became a spy. I believe they said that he was spying for the English [...] Stalin then approved Alyosha's execution. But it seems that he had misgivings. He said to Beria: 'Tell him for me that if he is sorry for his crimes and confesses everything then we will spare him his life.' After a while Beria reported that Svanidze had been executed. Svanidze had been given Stalin's message before his execution. The prisoner listened and replied: "I have nothing to confess. Why should I repent if I have nothing to hide? I have done nothing bad against the party, the people, or Stalin. I see no reason to ask him to forgive anything." Then he was executed. Later Stalin said: 'What kind of man was Alyosha! His soft intellectual being behaved with rock hardness! [...] What a man!' I don't know how honestly he meant this. But it was true that Svanidze was a clever man. He clearly understood that death awaited him even if he is penitent. At most just a little later on."[19]

Both versions need to be cleared up. From a look at the dates it becomes clear that Stalin by no means sent a message to Svanidze in the hours before his execution but after the Supreme Court's second ruling. Furthermore, Khrushchev maintains that Svanidze confessed nothing, and then somewhere else writes that confessions were extracted from him by torture which he then revoked in the hours before his death.

But Khrushchev does not go on to say that Maria Korona's fate was similarly tragic. On December 29, 1939 the Extraordinary Board of the NKVD sentenced her to eight years imprisonment. Among the charges against her, she was accused for not reporting her husband. She had allegedly condemned the "Soviet government's crime policy"—yet we know from her diary that she had been very enthusiastic about it. She admitted "that she had had terrorist intentions against one of the leaders of the Communist party and the Soviet government *[that is, Stalin—M. K.]*." On March 3, 1942 this same Extraordinary Board changed its earlier decision. It convened at the *Tsentral* in Saratov, which was primarily maintained for political prisoners, and sentenced her to death.

On the same day, in the cellar of the same prison Mariko Svanidze, Alyosha's younger sister was shot in the head. She had worked as a secretary in the Kremlin in the 1930s next to Avel Yenukidze who had been executed during the Great Terror. Stalin's sister-in-law had been spending ten years in the Saratov high security prison when she also sprang to the dictator's mind—he who was slowly being eaten away by evil—who admittedly had loved the woman as his own kin. The third Svanidze sibling, Sashiko "luckily" escaped this fate because she had died of cancer at the beginning of the Great Terror.[20]

In the mid-1920s Stalin happened to visit Tiflis but he did not seek out his first wife's relatives. "Dear Soso, I have been to your house three times but I could not get in," reads Sashiko Svanidze's letter written in Georgian, probably in 1926. "Soso, is it possible that you leave without even looking us up for two minutes?"[21]

But the old connection with the Svanidze siblings was re-established when the three—Alyosha, Sashiko, and Mariko—moved to Moscow and with other Caucasian acquaintances signified a "a little bit of Georgia" to the then still sentimental dictator. That is why the members of the Bolshevik elite living in the "House on the Embankment" were taken completely by surprise by the change in their fate.

☆ According to family legend, Dzhonik—who after his parents' arrest appears in official documents as Ivan—was saved by his nanny from being taken to one of prison-like orphanages established for children of the "enemies of the people". It was sheer luck that his former nanny took in the Svanidze boy who had not been adopted either by close or distant relations. Not even Yakov Dzhugashvili, Stalin's older son, was brave enough to rush to his cousin's aid, even though he himself was brought up mainly in the Svanidze family until the beginning of the 1920s, as his father forgot about him for a long time.

With the passing of time it would seem that Stalin did not feel threatened any longer by his young "rival." But it was only an appearance: in 1945 the state security forces arrested the orphaned son of Alyosha Svanidze and Maria Korona, and following the sentence of the Extraordinary Board he was exposed to forced medical treatment at the prison hospital. The strange charge was that he

The marriage between Svetlana Stalina (who had to change her name to Alliluyeva after the death of her father, on the orders of the party) and Ivan Svanidze did not last long.

was mentally not accountable.[22] Then on August 8, 1948 the Extraordinary Board of the MGB, which replaced the NKVD, sentenced Ivan Svanidze, formerly Dzhonik, to five years in exile. The then twenty-one year-old spent his sentence in Kazakhstan, which came to an end in 1953. But the exile, who worked as a wandering laborer going from construction site to construction site, was not immediately allowed to leave the place of his exile. It was only three years later that he was given permission to depart from the Kazakh steppe for Moscow. This incredibly talented, former child prodigy started his studies at the history department of the Lomonosov University during Khrushchev's thaw at the age of thirty.[23]

Following this forced intermezzo he met his childhood playmate Svetlana Alliluyeva. Shortly before that the dictator's daughter, at the order of the party leadership, had changed her surname from Stalina to Alliluyeva, taking the name of her deceased mother. She submitted her childhood correspondence with her father to the archives of the CPSU Central Committee—many of the letters have been published in this book for the first time. By doing so she signaled to the world how deep the chasm was between the past she wished to overcome and her present.

Svetlana's private life seemed to reflect this turnaround. Not long before seeing Dzhonik again, she had accidentally bumped into Yury Tomsky in the flat of a common childhood friend, the son of her father's former ally and then one of his bitterest enemies. Mikhail Tomsky, who was called a "right wing deviationist", committed suicide in August 1936, escaping his certain arrest. The farewell letter he wrote to Stalin was always widely known as a dignified protest against the dictator's genocidal policies. But not long ago the short text came to light. It revealed how the formerly proud, indeed, haughty trade union leader had a mental breakdown as a result of the persecution, and tried to cast suspicion onto some other, mysterious "right wing deviationist". He hoped that if Stalin learned that others set him against the Master of the Kremlin, he would not harm his family. "If you want to know who those people are who forced me onto the road of the right wing opposition, ask my wife," he wrote to Stalin whom he called "not only the party leader" but "my old comrade-in-arms" in his farewell letter. The Master of the Kremlin was not in Moscow at the time. Kaganovich and Ordzhonikidze, who were substituting for him, entrusted Yezhov with "winding up the affair". The woman confessed to him that it was the former NKVD chief Yagoda who at the end of the 1920s played an active role in organizing the "right wing opposition" led by Rykov, Bukharin, and Tomsky. It is not impossible that Tomsky had planned all this with his wife in advance.[24]

After Tomsky's suicide, who had already been forced to his knees, it would have been logical to leave his family alone. But just the opposite occurred. The enraged Soviet dictator—since Mikhail Tomsky slipped through his hands in an unforgivable way—executed his two older sons and sent his wife to a prison. Soon the teenage Yury Tomsky was also arrested, then spent more than ten years in prison and another nine in exile.[25] He had such terrible experiences during these years—which he recounted to me in Moscow at the beginning of the 1970s—that it made it impossible for him to be happy with Svetlana after the first short reunion. "After a while I did not see the sweet red-pigtailed little girl in her but the pigheaded offspring of the Master. Moreover, she deeply humiliated me as a man by taking me to the best Moscow tailors. She did not like that I still wore my patched old clothes. [...] Finally I realized that we were not a good match and we parted ways."

During her short romance, the Soviet dictator's daughter wanted to make a statement by accepting Yuriy, her childhood friend who had spent most of his life in prisons. Boris Runin, the old writer, was of the opinion in his book that this is why she took the released prisoner with her to Koktebel in the Crimea, to the Writer's Union's rest house favored by Soviet artists: she wanted to demonstrate a generous gesture before the outside world. But the caretaker of the rest house—who earlier would have bowed low before Stalin's daughter—did not dare let the "infanta" and Yury Tomsky in. "On the first day they lived in Svetlana's car on the empty beach and were busy making it comfortable," recalls Runin. The next day a great rumpus broke out as it turned out that Aleksei Kapler was spending his holidays there just then—who, because of a short romance with Svetlana, had spent altogether ten years hard labor in the Gulag.[26] (It is also true that Kapler and Svetlana had tried to renew their romance when they saw each other again at the 2nd Congress of the Soviet Writers' Union in 1954. "But we were incapable of piecing the broken romance together again," complained Kapler bitterly to his old friend, Mikhail Romm, the film director. So they quickly separated again.)

But Joseph Stalin's willful daughter did not give up even after these two failures. After breaking with Aleksei Kapler and Yury Tomsky she took up with another *lagernik*, another former Gulag prisoner: "Now only one man exists for me, that is Dzhonik Svanidze!" she happily informed her acquaintances. But her autobiographical notes say nothing about finding love with her old friend. Although she does recognize Dzhonik Svanidze's wonderful qualities: "Though he suffered from innate neurotic problems, and life had been terrible to him when it pushed him to the abyss from the luxurious circumstances, Ivan Alekseyevich always lived up to the example of his wonderful parents. [...] He inherited a great capacity for work from them. But his health was not up to it: his nerves were not capable of taking a lot and gave up on him. He was an unbearably difficult man as far as his relations were concerned. Although those who were less close to him, his college students, his constituents found him a good hearted, sympathetic, kind person."[27]

Although it soon becomes clear that these two mentally disturbed people—despite their initial attempts—were incapable of getting along. The man made the first move: in the summer of 1959 he filed for divorce. The Soviet laws of the time—in a humiliating manner—meant that the divorcees had to publish their intention to divorce as a notice in the local papers. So the following text was found in the paper *Vechernaya Moskva*: "Svanidze, Ivan Aleksandrovich [Dobrolyubov Street 35, apartment 11.] filed for divorce against Alliluyeva, Svetlana Josifovna [Serafimovich Street 2, apartment 179.]. *[this was the famous-infamous "House on the Embankment"—M. K.]*. The case will be considered by the Timiryazev District People's Court."[28]

1 *RGASPI* fond. 558. op. 1. d. 3904.
2 It is not entirely clear which Gegechkori Stalin is referring to: the former Menshevik foreign minister of Georgia, or his cousin, the famous Bolshevik politician who was gravely wounded in the territorial battles, and in 1921 became the president of the Tiflis Revolutionary Committee.
3 *RGASPI* fond. 558. op. 1. d. 2198.
4 Mikoyan, 1999, 357.
5 Torchinov-Leontuk, 2000, 420.
6 Smerch, 1989, 257.
7 *Iosif Stalin v obyatiakh semyi*, 1993, 156–157.
8 *Ibid.* 156-157.
9 The show trial took place on January 23–30, 1937 in Moscow.

10 *Iosif Stalin v obyatiakh semyi*, 1993, 190–191
11 *Iosif Stalin v obyatiakh semyi*, 1993, 192–193.
12 Smerch, 1989, 254.
13 General Artom Sergeyev actually performed this scene in front of the video camera.
14 I heard a lot about the conflict with Beria by a person who had witnessed them crossing swords. Aleksei Snegov, who on the eve of the 20th Congress of the CPSU congress made notes of Svanidze case for Nikita Khrushchev.
15 *Reabilitatsia*, 2000, vol. I, 300.
16 Volkogonov, 1990, vol. I, 581.
17 *Iosif Stalin v obyatiakh semyi*, 1993, 193–194.
18 *Khrushchev o Staline*, 1989, 61.
19 Khrushchev, 1997, 73–74.
20 *Iosif Stalin v obyatiakh semyi*, 1993, 193–194. Mariko's husband, the talented economist, Nikolai Kipiani, however, remained alive and lived to the end of the 1970s.
21 *RGASPI*, fond. 558. op. 4. d. 676.
22 *Reabilitatsia*, 2000, vol. I, 300.
23 Alliluyeva, 1982, 77.
24 Khlevnuk, 1996, 204–205.
25 Gorelov, 2000, 269, 280–281. In 1950 the exile Tomsky was arrested again for a short time.
26 Runin, 1995, 187–188.
27 Alliluyeva, 1981, 72–77.
28 Tarkhova, 1998, 156.

Sergo Ordzhonikidze and Nikolai Yezhov

Sergo Ordzhonikidze

This picture was taken in Stalin's office in March 1934. The Soviet leaders are glad that the three Bulgarian Communists, Georgy Dimitrov (1), Blagoi Popov (2), and Vasil Tanev (3), who had acted so bravely during their trial in Leipzig, managed to get out of the hands of Hitler and Göring. Among those celebrating their Bulgarian comrades are Wilhelm Knorin (4) and Dmitry Mauinsky (5), the Soviet leaders of, the Comintern, as well as Molotov (6), Kuybishev (7), Ordzhonikidze (8), Stalin, Voroshilov (9), and Kaganovich (10). Three years later, on Stalin's orders and approved by Dimitrov (who in the meantime became the leader of the Comintern), the agents of the NKVD arrested Popov, Tanev, and Knorin. By that time, Kuybishev and Ordzhonikidze had already died, under suspicious circumstances.

Григорий Константинович
ОРДЖОНИКИДЗЕ

ПРАВИТЕЛЬСТВЕННОЕ СООБЩЕНИЕ.

18 февраля в 17 часов 30 минут в Москве, у себя на квартире в Кремле, от паралича сердца скоропостижно скончался Народный Комиссар Тяжелой Промышленности, член Политбюро Центрального Комитета ВКП(большевиков) товарищ Григорий Константинович ОРДЖОНИКИДЗЕ.

Immediately after Ordzhonikidze died, Stalin classified as top secret the true reasons and circumstances of his death. This picture at the home of the deceased could also be taken only by a trusted insider: in this case it was Molotov's (1) brother. Ordzhonikidze's elbow on the catafalque was elevated by a couple of books, so as to cover the place of the wound made by a bullet and avoid any guesses that perhaps it was not a heart attack that killed him, as the official version claimed. The photo shows Zinayda Ordzhonikidze (2), Yezhov (3), Stalin, Zhdanov (4), suffering from a serious headache and wearing a strange black scarf on his head, Kaganovich (5), Mikoyan (6), and Voroshilov (7).

CHAPTER 30
False Medical Reports

News of the early deaths and suicides of leading politicians, military leaders and their relations terrified the population during the Soviet era, who lived in the atmosphere of permanent terror and uncertainty, even though only unverifiable snippets of gossip about all this reached them, the "simple people". Not long after the 1917 Bolshevik takeover a high, almost impassable wall went up around the people living in the Kremlin and the "House on the Embankment ". Only the death of Mikhail Frunze, people's commissar for the military and navy, who supposedly died as the result of a medical malpractice in the autumn of 1925, received some publicity. One of the period's most famous writers, Boris Pilnyak, who had a very convoluted life, wrote a key novel about this affair based on information from Trotskyists entitled *A Story of the Inextinguishable Moon.* But only the first part of the book saw the light of day in the periodical *Novy Mir.*[1]

However, the stifling of news meant that accidental deaths and suicides of a few less well-known military leaders and internal opposition politicians went completely unnoticed. As Joseph Stalin's power increased, stories of strange deaths were increasingly presented *as counter-revolutionary* or *anti-Soviet agitation.* That is why in the mid-1930s the "scare-mongers" were sentenced to eight—more rarely five—years *isolation,* in other words, imprisonment. At the end of the decade this increasingly meant the *highest degree of social defense* or, less euphemistically, death by bullet.

Despite these strict measures, the rulers of the Kremlin were afraid of any news that could be unpleasant for them. That is why they issued a standard official statement about the more "problematic" deaths in order to avoid speculation. The text of the statement was approved by Stalin or one of his associates—probably Molotov or Kaganovich. Every sentence in the text was significant and had a carefully worked out coded message. The relatives and friends of the person who died in mysterious circumstances were watched like hawks by the political police from the day of their burial. And before long the *chorny varon* (paddy wagon) was sent for most of them. But sometimes years went by between the burial and the arrest of relatives. Stalin then waited with enjoyment before doing away with the possible witnesses.

Joseph Stalin often led funeral processions in the 1930s.

Karl Radek, who was known as a sharp observer and a wit, told Maria Joffe, the widow of the Soviet diplomat who committed suicide: "It happened at the beginning of the 1920s [...] After a trying, tense meeting we decided to take a short excursion, have lunch, and rest a little in the fresh air. At that time this happened very rarely. We lay down on the grass in the woody Morozovka Park and started to talk. Then one of us suddenly raised that eternal question: 'What's the best thing in the world?' Kamenev cut in without thinking: "Books!" To which Radek responded, "Nobody can give greater pleasure than a woman, your woman." Bukharin jumped up to say, "Nothing compares to the feeling when you find yourself with thousands of others on the crest of a popular wave." Rykov joked: "What is all this speculation for? We've already finished it all up. We have drunk all this wonderful cognac." Then Stalin said, "The sweetest thing is to devise a plan, then, being on the alert, waiting in ambush for a goo-oo-ood long time, finding out where the person is hiding. Then catch the person and take revenge!"[2]

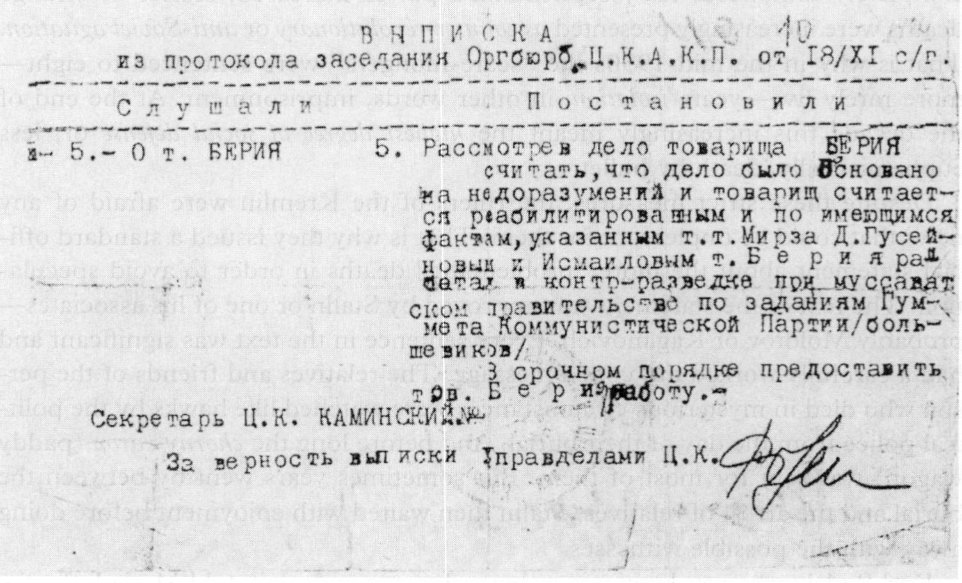

ВЫПИСКА

из протокола заседания Оргбюро Ц.К.А.К.П. от 18/XI с/г.

Слушали	Постановили
5.- О т. БЕРИЯ	5. Рассмотрев дело товарища БЕРИЯ считать, что дело было основано на недоразумений и товарищ считается реабилитированным и по имеющимся фактам, указанным т.т. Мирза Д. Гусейновым и Исмаиловым т. Б е р и я работал в контр-разведке при муссаватском правительстве по заданиям Гуммета Коммунистической Партии/большевиков/ 3 срочном порядке предоставить тов. Б е р и я работу.-

Секретарь Ц.К. КАМИНСКИЙ

За верность выписки Управделами Ц.К.

Lavrenty Beria was Sergo Ordzhonikidze's number one Georgian protégé, and his "eyes and ears" in Tiflis. There are still many unknown details around an allegation that Beria had an important position in the Baku police during the Civil War, under the Azeri government of the nationalist Musavat party. Though these documents, which are published for the first time here, show that Beria was eventually cleared of the charges by a respected body, the cunning politician would certainly have fallen out of Stalin's favor without Ordzhonikidze's support.

This is exactly what happened after the death of the dictator's wife, Nadezhda Alliluyeva in November 1932. Not even a regular police report was filed, just for the sake of formality. It is true that Aleksandra Kanel, the chief doctor at the Kremlin hospital, who had treated the woman for long years, was not willing to sign the medical report saying that the young woman had died of a supposed heart attack. That is why she was later dismissed and her family members were "isolated" so that they could not let the truth out.[3] Even so across the country many people speculated about what happened to the Master's wife on the night of November 8 in 1932. It is not unlikely that the gossipmongers were primarily from Stalin's court. After a while the Soviet dictator learned about this but generally he only took revenge years later. The wives of functionaries who knew Nadezhda Alliluyeva well, were arrested one after the other. He believed that Molotov's, Kalinin's, Andreyev's, Postishev's and Poskryobishev's wives knew

The two close friends:
Stalin and Ordzhonikidze.

too much about the sensitive details of the tragedy. Stalin's wife's relatives were also sent to prison and in front of the firing squad. Two of Nadezhda's doctors, Levin and Kazakov, got involved in the 1938 showtrial and were shot in the head on Stalin's orders. In the summer of 1941 a similar fate awaited the already very old Professor Pletnov, who was originally sentenced not to death but "merely" to long imprisonment.[4] It seems that the officers of the political police initially also wanted to implicate Stalin's doctor, Professor Vladimir Vinogradov in one of the "conspiracy cases" they made up during the Great Terror.[5] But they had to wait with this for a long time, until the beginning of the 1950s.[6]

This 1932 script, based on a false medical statement, was dusted down by Joseph Stalin less than five years after his wife's death when the Kremlin went into mourning because of another "heart attack". In February 1937 Grigory [Sergo] Ordzhonikidze's heart "suddenly stopped", as the obituaries put it. The

Stalin places the urn containing the ashes of Valeryan Kuybishev into the Kremlin Wall. Following the sudden death of Kuybishev in 1935, rumors spread about the possible causes of it.

Soviet tyrant's good old friend and one of his most loyal comrades, a living manifestation of the system, had just celebrated his fiftieth birthday. Great national celebrations were organized to honor him. Settlements, *kolkhoz*es, community houses were all named after the hot-tempered politician who, as a simple bone setter, had directed enforced industrilization in the years of the *pyatiletka*s, the first Soviet five-year plans.

Paradoxically, Ordzhonikidze's position weakened at precisely the time he was most glorified.[7] The continual attacks from behind the scenes forced him to withdraw gradually into the background. And following a bitter exchange with Stalin, he eventually shot himself in the heart at home with a revolver.[8] But typically of the time and its protagonists, the legend still goes that in reality the NKVD agents executed Sergo at his dictator friend's behest. During our conversations in Moscow, several of his contemporaries said this as if it were actual fact, indeed his stepdaughter, who entered adulthood at around the time of his death, also said the same. Eteria Ordzhonikidze was even willing to repeat her assertion in front of a video camera, citing her mother.

The suspicion that fell on the doctors of the Soviet leaders who lived in the Kremlin and the "House on the Embankment " was sometimes generated by the relatives of the deceased themselves. From this perspective, the letter written by the widow of Valeryan Kuybishev to Molotov is quite typical. Olga Lezhova lists by name the doctors whom she thought were responsible for her husband's death, who died of a heart attack. Among them were the Austrian Epiger, Metallikov, the supervisor of the Kremlin hospital, and Levin, who was later implicated in the show trial of 1938. The widow mentions that Kuybishev spent four days on a train between Tashkent and Moscow following a tour of inspection to central Asia at the end of 1934, and that he was not accompanied by a doctor.[9] In spite of this, many supposed that Kuybishev was a victim of malpractice ordered by Stalin himself. (One of them was Varvara Sidorova, his close colleague, who kindly let me study her unpublished memoirs.)

But the heart attack of Kuybishev's former foremost rival, Sergo Ordzhonikidze caused even more speculation, even though rumors spread in much narrower circles during the frightened atmosphere of the Great Terror, than after the death of Stalin's wife. Nonetheless, Aleksandr Solovyov, who moved about in the Soviet leadership circles at ease and was surprisingly well informed, dared write in his diary on February 19, 1937: "Last night Ordzhonikidze shot himself in his flat. They say that one of his relatives *[his older brother Papulia who lived in Tiblisi—M. K.]* has been arrested as an enemy of the people. He therefore protested to Comrade Stalin but to no avail. He accused him of tyranny and unlawfulness. He was not willing to accept responsibility *[for the events—M. K.]*, as a member of the Politburo. Comrade Stalin lost his temper, there was a big argument. Ordzhonikidze informed him that he would protest. With that he left. And shot himself that evening. Terrible. Ordzhonikidze was the party favorite."[10]

A few days later, on March 5, 1937 the Master of the Kremlin felt it necessary to take a swipe at his dead friend at the Central Committee meeting. Those assembled—nearly two thirds of whom did not survive the end of the following year—at the end of the several days long meeting unanimously proposed arresting Nikolai Bukharin and Aleksei Rykov. The members of this important council stepped to the podium one by one, beating their chests, saying that they had not been "vigilant" enough and had not noticed in time the enemy that had slipped in amongst them. But Stalin was not self-critical. Indeed in his speech he attacked Sergo Ordzhonikidze as if he were sitting there alongside the other Politburo members. "People should not be selected in this way. Here among others there is Comrade Sergo, who was one of the first in the Politburo, one of the best. He was the highest ranking economics leader. And yet [...] he suffered from the same sickness *[as the other "gullible" party leaders—M. K.]*. He was capable of sticking by someone, stubbornly stating his loyalty to him. He backed this person although the party, the Central Committee had warned him against it." In this speech Stalin also accused him of handling cases in a "noble manner, in a courtly way", of patronizing "numerous scoundrels", and of being overconfident. The Soviet dictator later removed these passages from the minutes. However, his statement—just a short time after Ordzhonikidze had actually passed away—points to the political death of his former good friend.[11] In the following years "the hot tempered, good Sergo" as he was known by his circle was

Sergei Kirov's wife says a final goodbye to her murdered husband on December 2, 1934. "Hey cucumber, red tomato, Stalin killed Kirov in a corridor of the Smolny," went the *chastushka* (ditty). After a while no one dared to sing this song, as it was worth at least eight years in prison.

increasingly pushed to the back of the Soviet pantheon. An indication of this was that in the 1940s numerous settlements that had been named after him were given back their original names.[12]

The revaluation of the political career of the Bolshevik leaders who had stood in Stalin's way did not come to the knowledge of the public from one day to the next. The Master of the Kremlin did not want to give grounds for further gossip. That is why in February 1937, the best known doctors in the country signed, along with Grigory Kaminsky, the people's commissar for health, an official medical report issued by the party leadership and the government which explains Ordzhonikidze's death as a result of an old and grave heart disease. Three years later an anniversary calendar, a huge amount of copies of which were published, provided a brazen political explanation. It read that Ordzhonikidze "fought an indefatigable struggle against the enemies of the people, the followers of Trotsky and Bukharin. The betrayals and intrigues of this gang of spies and murderers hastened his death."[13]

A few dozen people in the know and the Kremlin personnel of course guessed that it was not Sergo's body that had failed him, although he really had struggled with heart problems for years, but—like in the case of Nadezhda Alliluyeva—had been killed by a revolver bullet. But the well-informed were not around to see who would be Stalin's next victim as, to use the expression of the time, "they were taken out of circulation" by the NKVD's operative section. Some two years later these members of political police also suffered the same fate at the hands of the new generation that had stepped into their place, which now obeyed the orders of Lavrenty Beria, Yezhov's successor, one of the main protagonists in the Great Terror.[14]

In the meantime almost every one of Sergo's relatives were either sent into prison or exile.[15] The secretaries, bodyguards, and chauffeurs of the hitherto praised politician were also executed. The same fate awaited nearly all the leaders of the Soviet industrial-military complex, which had been supervised by Ordzhonikidze for years. One after the other the signatories of the false medical report were imprisoned. Grigory Kaminsky, who had protested against the policy of terror, was arrested at the Central Committee meeting held in the summer of 1937, in the presence of his colleagues who were scared to death. The "disappearance" of witnesses went on right up until 1952. Then, as a *cadenza* to the affair, Stalin picked out several professors who had once treated Ordzhonikidze or had signed the medical report to play the role of defendant in the major doctors' plot trial he was preparing.[16]

☆ These two strange deaths and their consequences must be taken into account when reading Pavel Alliluyev's obituaries. Let us remember that in the Alliluyev family, Pavel was closest to his little sister Nadezhda. In addition he was Ordzhonikidze's immediate colleague and close friend. All this was enough for Stalin to see his brother-in-law living on borrowed time."

"After Alliluyev returned *[from a confidential German mission—M. K.]*, he became commissar at the armored main division of the People's Commissariat for Military Affairs," recalled Lidia Shatunovskaya. "If we keep in mind how significant this branch of service was at that time, it is clear that Stalin trusted him completely. But around 1937 [...] Joseph Stalin started to liquidate the military leadership systematically. And then Pavel became a serious obstacle in his path. [...] If they did not get rid of him it would not have been possible to destroy all his friends and comrades before his very eyes, the whole commanding staff of the armored divisions. It would have been hard to arrest Pavel him-

The military delegates of the 16th Congress of the Bolshevik Party, in the company of Tukhachevsky (1), Gamarnik (2), Molotov (3), Voroshilov (4), Stalin, Kalinin (5), Kaganovich (6), and Budenny (7). This was the group of people Pavel Alliluyev felt comfortable with, but which was almost completely destroyed in the first year of the Great Terror.

self as an "enemy of the people". After all, everyone knew he was the Master's brother-in-law. At that time old Sergei Alliluyev, Pavel and Nadezhda's father was still alive, and Stalin counted on him to some extent. That is why Pavel had to be got rid of secretly, without fuss and with no publicity."[17]

☆ Among the events leading up to the death of Nadezhda's favorite brother, there is an important moment which researchers generally neglect. By the summer of 1938, at the orders of Stalin and Voroshilov, a large part of the commanding staff of the Red Army had been arrested. Most of them—many thousands of people—had been executed. So there was a great vacuum, the result of which was that not much more than twenty-year-old commanders of platoons, squadrons, and battalions found themselves making huge leaps in rank in a very short time to become commanders of regiments, divisions, and even army corps. As a result discipline in the vast Red Army was very lax. Moreover, almost every imprisoned high-ranking officer had the lives of several dozen comrades in arms on their conscience; whom they betrayed during the interrogations, under the impact of physical and mental torture, or even while they were still free they made accusations at party meetings or denounced secretly in writing. The endless cycle of these purges meant that before soon even the privates started to call their superiors "spies" and "saboteurs". One could sometimes hear such comments at party or Komsomol meetings as well.[18]

The ensuing situation threatened not only the discipline within the army and its military efficiency, but also the life of the still free officers of the completely decimated Red Army. That is why several high-ranking commanders and commissars, who belonged to Stalin's inner circle and had earlier accepted readily his policies, wrote two letters of protest. The authors—Pavel Alliluyev, Georgy Savchenko, Dmitry Pavlov, Kirill Meretskov, and Grigory Kulik—sent one of the petitions to Klim Voroshilov and the other a little later to Stalin. Unfortu-

Dmitry Sukhanov led Malenkov's secretariat for many long years. Flashing his excellent memory, he told me at the very end of the 1990s in an interview that Stalin was willing to slow down the machinery of the Great Terror only when it seemed that the Soviet Empire was going to become uncontrollable. But as this idea was suggested to him by someone else, in this case actually initiated by a group of high-ranking officers, he would never forgive them. Joseph Stalin ordered Malenkov to investigate the circumstances in which the letter of the "Group of five" was written, remembered Sukhanov.

nately, these documents, so important for understanding the Stalinist terror, have still not come to light. But their content can be reconstructed from the confession of General Pavlov who was appointed commander of the western front before the outbreak of the German-Soviet war, and then shortly afterwards arrested in July 1941. He dictated it before his execution to the prosecutor.[19]

It seems that the rare daring of this step was originally initiated by Georgy Savchenko, commissar for the artillery high command. At the Supreme Military Council's meeting in the summer of 1938, the courageous man explained to the members of the Politburo that the relaxation in discipline in the Red Army was in direct proportion to the string of arrests. "After this—recalls Pavlov in his confession—myself and Savchenko were required to put this in writing. Kulik *[commander of the artillery high command, later marshall—M. K.]* was the main author of the text. Its content was debated by several Red Army commanders: apart from me there were Kulik, Savchenko, and Meretskov *[Red Army chief of staff in 1940—M. K.]*. Then Kulik took the next step, he called me, Alliluyev and Savchenko and proposed we compose the document together. We the four of us put the text together in letter form. We sent it to Voroshilov but his secretariat informed us that the people's commissar would not even read our letter and requested us to withdraw it. At this Kulik called us together again on a Sunday. We made some changes to the letter and sent it to the General Secretary of the Central Committee *[to Stalin—M. K.]*, with a copy to Voroshilov. The letter argued that the main forces of the counter-revolution had already been liquidated within the army yet the arrest of its commanders continued. Indeed, to such an extent that the army might start to disintegrate. [...] These circumstances, we wrote at the end of the letter, could weaken the fighting spirit of the army if war broke out. Finally we requested that they *[the party leaders—M. K.]* make the necessary decisions. We believed that as a result of our petition, the government would reduce the arrests." Suffering physical and mental torture, Pavlov eventually signed a paper that the prosecutors demanded from him, which read that by this move, Pavel Alliluyev and the others had intended to protect the "the conspirators hiding in the Red Army".[20]

To the amazement of their colleagues the five military leaders were not arrested immediately. It is true that they had a bit of luck. By the summer of 1938 the Great Terror, even if it had not lost its drive, was winding down somewhat. "Soon there'll be nobody to arrest," said Stalin's henchmen indignantly. A lot fewer proscriptive lists were issued compared to the previous months. The reason for this was primarily that the Extraordinary Board of the summary justice *troikas*—comprised of local party leaders, the representatives of the NKVD and the public prosecution—had fulfilled their regional execution quotas, indeed surpassed them, in the preceding months. Despite the high mortality among the prisoners, and the ensuing rapid turnover, neither the prisons nor the death camps had any vacancies, even though the NKVD staff worked hard to execute as many people as possible. Apart from the usual shot in the head, they also tried cutting off heads with axes and experimented with using poison gas—like in the town of Ivanovo-Voznesensk, among others, as it has recently become clear. They also executed the "enemies of the people" by dousing them with hoses in minus thirty degree Celsius and thus literally turning them to ice.[21]

It is true that earlier—in the years of the "total collectivization" and the Civil War—even greater numbers had died. But the Great Terror, which also took the life of millions, was different from the earlier carnages in that Joseph Stalin also wanted to "replace" the complete ruling elite. As a result, however, the continent-size Soviet Empire slowly became ungovernable and gravely vulnerable to possible attacks from abroad. This is why at the beginning of 1939, almost inevitably, a temporary thaw followed, and the party leadership suddenly stood up against the "over-zealous" NKVD, although from behind the scenes it was always Stalin and his associates who generated the Great Terror. It is not impossible, that experiencing the discontent of his favorite commanders, Stalin, who sometimes gladly played the "good tsar" role, clandestinely encouraged his old creation Kulik to submit a written complaint with his colleagues to the people's commissar for military affairs. On the other hand, it was well-known that the Master of the Kremlin was never pleased by spontaneous, not previously agreed on, protests. So he took a careful note of the names of the complainants, and in the following years, he sent them one by one into the cogwheels of his liquidation machine. At first Pavel Alliluyev, Stalin's brother-in-law died unexpectedly in September 1938. According to his relatives and friends he was poisoned. Two and half years later in the spring of 1941, Kirill Meretskov was arrested and imprisoned, his spine was broken during a torture session by the execution gang known as body mechanics *(telomekhaniki).* Merkulov, who was second in rank in the Soviet political police, himself tortured one of the Red Army's most talented officers, Meretskov, against whom more than forty of his colleagues had confessed earlier. (In the meantime Merkulov took pleasure in playing the cultured man, and several Soviet theaters performed his plays.) Then during the German attack on Moscow, the physically broken Meretskov was suddenly released from prison, and reactivated as a military officer. When Stalin received him, he cynically asked the general: "How are you? You don't look well." Later he even became a marshall. But he lived the rest of his life as an invalid.[22]

But the showdown against the "recalcitrant" military leaders went on. In June 1941, when there were hardly any experienced commanders left in the Red Army—who learnt their trade during the Soviet-Russian and then the Spanish Civil Wars—Georgy Savchenko was arrested along with several dozen other chief officers. Then in October he was executed without trial on Beria's written orders. In July it was Dmitry Pavlov's turn.[23] Together with a couple of other generals, he was blamed by Stalin for Hitler's unexpected military attack on the Soviet Union—putting an end to the dictator's imperfect preventive war plans.[24]

Of the five only Grigory Kulik lived through the second month of the Soviet-German war a free man. Perhaps Stalin hesitated for so long on whether or not to liquidate the commander of the Soviet artillery because the nonqualified marshal, who took the place of the executed Tukhachevsky and his circle, had been part of his immediate circle for more than twenty years. He must have treated him like a capricious lord would do with a bad servant. After receiving the petition written by Pavel Alliluyev and the others Stalin never forgot to make Kulik feel that he had a knife to his throat. To emphasize his point further, in March 1939, rather like in a bad thriller, the marshal's wife was abducted in the open street. The woman, who was famed for being dissolute and wearing wonderful gowns, was riddled with bullets in the cellars of the inner Lubyanka prison without any trial.[25] Her desperate husband turned to Stalin for protection. The dictator, after a long paternal scolding, during which he expounded why a Red commander should not bind his life to a "nympho female spy", he suggested that Kulik marry again as soon as possible. The soldier thanked him for his "tough lesson" and breathed a sigh of relief because he understood that the Master would let him to live. Stalin, who interfered with increasing cruelty in the private lives of his circle over the years, awarded Kulik by personally appearing at his wedding, although earlier he had never honored anyone else in that way. And together they sang heartily at a table groaning with drinks along with veteran Red cavalry, forgetting all else.[26]

But after the outbreak of the war, Grigory Kulik's career came to an end. It became clear that in a world of air battles and armored battles the deep voiced, aggressive and vulgar commander was good for nothing. Once he even lost his own flank and spent days in an unranked uniform hiding behind the German lines until the commando sent to rescue him saved him. On another occasion he sent a great deal of food on a reserve plane serving all the army commanders to his wife far into the interior. In the absence of a replacement plane he could not get to his troops in time in the town of Kerch which was surrounded by Germans. Seeing this series of mishaps, Stalin, as the commander-in-chief, demoted the marshal to brigadier general in February 1942, something which had never happened before. At the same time he ordered his dismissal from his post as deputy defense people's commissar and expelled him from the Central Committee. Two years later this body, which convened only once throughout the entire war, dealt with the "Kulik affair" in a special issue on its agenda. The marshal was expelled from the party. Although the several times demoted military leader was by no means less prepared than his former Civil War fellows Voroshilov and Budenny, he became the Red Army's "punching bag" later to be pummeled by all and sundry.[27]

The deeply offended artillery officer even hastened his own demise: he made many biting remarks about Stalin to his acquaintances. The Master of the Kremlin, in turn, had an opportunity to link the general's behavior to the summer 1938 events when Kulik "rebelled" against him with Dmitry Pavlov, Pavel Alliluyev, and others. The fate of Grigory Kulik was therefore sealed: on the basis of informers' reports he was arrested in 1947 with two other generals, then after a three year inquiry and dreadful torture he was executed.[28]

Thus the careers of all five came to a similar end. After the composition of the two letters, independent of their talents and dispositions, they never again regained the trust of the Master. In Stalin's eyes, Pavel Alliluyev committed one additional "crime" when in the months of the Great Terror he stood by his arrested colleagues. This is certainly why he was the first one to go. ☆

M. K.: At the height of the purges, in under barely two years, Stalin seized three family heads of his hitherto populous kinship. First of all he preyed on Alyosha Svanidze. Then on your father Pavel Alliluyev. And finally he had Stanisław Redens, Anna Alliluyeva's husband, taken away.

K. A.: Yes, that's right. In that order. *[she sighs]* As far as my father is concerned he decided in the summer of 1938, affected by the great disturbances, to pay more attention to his health. He gave up smoking and went to rest in Sochi where he took thermal baths. He had skin eruptions probably from nerves. If I recall right he spent twenty-four or twenty-eight days at the seaside. My father came home rested. He was unrecognizable. He arrived one late afternoon, lovely and tanned. We talked for a long while and only sat down to supper at around half past nine. Then my father went to bed, because he was going to work the next day. I slept in late the next morning but my then seven-year-old brother recalls that my father was still in a good mood. He sat him on his knee and praised him for growing such a lot in a month. Then he said goodbye and went down the stairs. We lived on the eighth floor but he went on foot, because he thought it did his heart good.

[Increasingly quietly] At two in the afternoon the phone rang. Someone reproachfully asked my mother: "Yevgenia Aleksandrovna, in God's name what did you give your husband to eat that has made him so ill?" My mother grew alarmed: "What did I give him? Eggs and coffee. And a cheese sandwich. Why? Has something happened to Pavel? Should I come over?" "No, don't! What for? We'll take your husband to the Kremlin hospital and ring you from there." My mother became very upset. She waited for the call for hours, but the telephone was silent. Then she decided to go to the hospital. She was received by a female doctor: "Why didn't you come earlier? Your husband was waiting for you, he wanted to say something. But he's dead now." They deliberately hadn't rung. So that my father could not tell us what had really happened.

M. K.: This really wasn't an ordinary food poisoning or heart attack as the official report said.

K. A.: [whispering] I don't believe my father died from food poisoning or a sudden heart attack either. Later when my mother and Aunt Anna, my father's younger sister, came out of prison they said: "Pavel was murdered. They poisoned him." They could have done it easily. Even more so given that they had a poison laboratory. I believe it existed not only under Nikolai Yezhov but under Genrikh Yagoda *[the former NKVD chief—M. K.]* too. It might have been in existence since the late 1920s. It was operated by the OGPU in the greatest secrecy. We did not know about it then, the papers have written about it not long ago. It was strange that my father was buried so quickly. Then he was exhumed for an autopsy. And of course *[sarcastically]* they found nothing suspicious.

M. K.: The same thing happened to Sergo Ordzhonikidze. But his corpse was not autopsied, they were satisfied with the false medical report.

K. A.: But the report about his death also said, like in my father's obituary, that he died of heart disease… I remember how much my father wept for Sergo, who once came to see us in Berlin when he was treated by German doctors. They became good friends and were later colleagues. Both of them were much preoccupied with tanks and armored vehicles. Sometimes they called each other late at night. They were both Stalin's favorites but then he turned on them.

By the way, "my dear relative" never came to see us after my father's death. He didn't come to his funeral either. But I remember Voroshilov, he was there. He stood by the coffin, completely broken. And I remember a lot of uniformed chief officers. It was an official funeral, his bier stood in what is today GUM *[in the club in the building of the biggest Moscow store opposite the Kremlin—M. K.]*. Like Nadezhda Alliluyeva's coffin five years before. And everybody who was there all said the same: "My God, to die so young! He could have lived longer!"

M. K.: What role did that petition in which he protested along with four colleagues to Stalin and to Voroshilov about the mass arrests in the summer of 1938 play in his death?

K. A.: I heard about this petition later from my mother. But my father did not only do this during those times. Before he sent the petition you mentioned to "my dear relative" he regularly sought him out in the Kremlin and demanded the release of his employees who had been arrested one after another by the NKVD. Although they had worked abroad for years *[under Pavel Alliluyev, carrying out confidential work—M. K.]*, my father trusted them, and he fought for them. He argued to Stalin: "Arrest me too, as I am in solidarity with them…" "I will arrest you precisely when I no longer trust you," answered Stalin. And he acted: most of my father's colleagues were released. And this did not happen with others so these exceptions became widely known. They said that many innocent people were held in the Lubyanka. If they let these ones out then the others cannot be guilty either. Probably Stalin had enough of this. And he took steps against my poor father *[she breaks down crying]*.

1 Topolyansky, 1996, 95–98.
2 Joffe, 1978, 33–34.
3 Kanel, 1989, 495.
4 Topolyansky, 1996, 99–100. This highly respected scientist was accused of sadistically sexually harassing his female patients.
5 Yagoda, 1997, 21.
6 Gereben, 2000, 569–570, 579–581, 583, 588, 590–591.
7 Khlevnuk, 1996, 178.
8 Khlevnuk, 1993, 118–129.
9 *RGASPI*, fond. 82, op. 1, d. 5095.
10 *Nyeizvestnaya Rossia*, 1993, 192.
11 *Stalinskoye Politbyuro*, 1995, 153–155.
12 Of the towns bearing Ordzhonikize's name, one became Dzandzhikan and the other Yenakievo. The Sergo settlement regained its old name of Kadievka and Ordzhonikidzegrad became Bezhica etc.
13 *Kalendar Spravochnik*, 1941, 28.
14 Tucker, 1997, 532–533; Suvenirov, 1998, 223–225, 288–290.
15 *Reabilitatsia*, 2000, vol I, 63–64. Nikita Khrushchev mentioned this in his speech he made in front of party workers in Leningrad on May 7, 1954. "For Beria, it was enough to imprison someone for only a year, to keep him there for life. He imprisoned Konstantin Ordzhonikidze *[Sergo's younger brother—M. K.]* originally for five years, yet he spent twelve years in solitary confinement." *Ibid.*, 140.
16 On what happened to them, see Gereben, 2000, 579–582, 590–592.
17 Shatunovskaya, 1982, 214–215.
18 Suvenirov, 1998, 298–308. 324–341.
19 Bobrenev-Ryazantsev, 1993, 182–183.
20 At the court hearing before his execution Pavlov, in his last speech, withdrew all the confessions forced out of him. *Ibid.*, 182–183. 186–191.
21 Petrus, 1953, 125, 179–181.; Boykov, 1957, 169–173, 374–378; Sreyder, 1995, 5, 184–224.
22 Meretskov, 1968, 97; Bobrenyev-Ryazantsev, 1993, 181; Suvenirov, 1998, 215.
23 Smirnov, 1997, 18–19.
24 1941 god, 1998, vol. II. 455–468. 472–473.
25 Stolyarov, 1997, 272–273.
26 Bobrenev-Ryazantsev, 1993, 199–205.
27 *Voyenno-Istorichesky Zhurnal*, 1993, no. 12, 16–21.; *Izvestia CK KPSS*, 1991, no. 2, 197–201.
28 Smirnov, 1997, 180–188; Pikhoya, 1998, 49–52.

CHAPTER 31
Yevgenia Alliluyeva

Yevgenia Alliluyeva.

After Pavel Alliluyev's death people shunned his widow. According to Yevgenia's friend, Lidia Shatunovskaya, the unfortunate woman was kept under house arrest for a month. But Kira does not remember this although she also knows that her mother was being slandered and talked about in Stalin's circles. In my interview with her she spoke indignantly of how the Soviet party leaders "circled" the lone Yevgenia Alliluyeva, regarding her as easy prey. Among them was Lavrenty Beria who had been loathed by the Alliluyev family for ages, who after Pavel Alliluyev's death came to head the People' Commissariat for Internal Affairs, with increasing influence in the Kremlin.

The good family friend Shatunovskaya even believes that Stalin himself had his eye on Yevgenia: "he shamelessly made an unmistakable proposal to Pavel Alliluyev's widow, that [...] she be his 'housekeeper'. She herself told me." The memoir writer remembers well that her friend rejected the idea with dignity. As a result Stalin hated her passionately.[1] Kira Alliluyev remembers this a little differently. But she admits that after her father's death this could have played a decisive role in the family's fate. ✫

K. A.: The estrangement between my mother and Stalin did not happen from one day to the next. The break down in relations was linked not only to the circumstances of Pavel Alliluyev's death. As I have mentioned, new faces appeared around Stalin and his half-orphaned children, after Nadezhda Alliluyeva's death. First of all they got rid of Svetlana's governess *[the cultivated, refined Karolina Till—M.K.]*. Then Beria found Stalin a Georgian housekeeper. Who was "by chance" a distant relation of his. She was called Sashiko.

M. K.: Aleksandra Nikashidze,[2] who was a relative of Beria's wife. She was not intended as a concubine.

K. A.: *[laughingly protests]* That would show how bad Beria's and Stalin's taste was. Do you know what an ugly woman she was? Rough faced, long-nosed, and wide-hipped. Sharp, dark features. I don't understand why Svetlana said in her memoirs that she was quite a pretty woman.[3] "My dear relative" liked blondes, like Georgians generally. The very beautiful ones. What would he have done with that nightmare? Sashiko's role was rather to tell Beria everything that was happening around Stalin.

M. K.: And how did the Alliluyev family react to this?

K. A.: All of us were enraged because Joseph entrusted little Svetlana to such a woman. But we tried to keep quiet about it in Stalin's presence. Because he really didn't like us to judge his decisions. But there must have soon been some problem with Nikashidze. After my father's death, Beria probably turned up at my mother's as a result. His voice was sweet as honey. *[She imitates]* "Yevgenia Aleksandrovna, it would be good if you were Stalin's *housekeeper*. And guide Svetlana's upbringing. You are the most suitable person for this job." My mother did not tell us then. And absolutely did not boast to us that Lavrenty even tried to court her. She just got out of it as quick as she could.

M. K.: I am not at all surprised that the famed womanizer Lavrenty Beria liked your mother. She is very beautiful in the photographs you laid on the dining table.

K. A.: *[proudly]* A Russian beauty. Red-cheeked, full bosomed. A charming, button-nosed woman. But more people noticed her for her sharp mind and her quick tongue. Not long after my mother was released she told me in a shaky voice how she had reacted to Beria's suggestion. *[She performs her mother's monologue]* "When I went home after the conversation, I realized that I must escape from them. I must save my children. Beria would have pressed an agreement out of me. It would have been easy to persuade Stalin that I should move in with him in the Kremlin. After all, we were relatives. And Joseph really liked me in those days. But if I agreed then one fine day Beria would poison Stalin and put the blame on me. Then we would all be destroyed." When my mother told me this, I understood why she married Molochnikov so quickly.

M. K.: We have not talked about him yet.

K. A.: They had met in Germany at the end of the 1920s. My mother worked in the personnel section of the Soviet commercial office in Berlin. She received colleagues newly arrived from Moscow, who she then showed around the German capital. Molochnikov was among them, a very well-built, elegant man, and from my mother's part of the world. "My God, are you from Novgorod too?" my mother cried, when she flicked through his papers. Then she pressed the newcomer to tell her more about his family. "I am Jewish," he blurted out immediately. "Or half-Jewish. My mother is Russian." He complained that during the tsarist period, he could not get good work as a result and ended up at cemetery where he patched together all sorts of grills. My mother pitied him and made friends with him. It seems that it was then that the spark was lit... Molochnikov got into great trouble at the end of the 1930s. His wife was arrested. He remained alone with his two children. In the meantime we also became half-orphaned, my two younger brothers and I. Then my mother decided that she would move in with Molochnikov and bring the five children up together.

M. K.: Did your mother talk this over with you?

K. A.: If my mother decided something then she never told us in advance. When she unexpectedly got married I was in Sochi on holiday, imagine, *[laughing]* in an elegant sanatorium named after my father's old friend Klim Voroshilov, established for chief officers.

☆ The "first Red officer"—this was at that time Klim Voroshilov's official *epitheton ornans*. In the second half of the 1930s the sanatorium bearing his name was a frequent site of arrests. Voroshilov often planned these arrests in advance first with Yezhov and then with Beria and then gave the order to the intendeted victim to go and rest at the sanatorium. As there was no need to fear any armed opposition from the comrades of the victim. So even the bravest became easy prey for the NKVD commandos that arrived from the capital. It is not surprising that the Red officers after a while were wary of the order that used to be a great privilege. During the short thaw in 1939–40 some of the chief officers languishing in prisons and camps regained their freedom—including the marshall-to-be Konstantin Rokosovsky. At Stalin's order, who was again playing the "good tsar," the best doctors tried to nurse the released prisoners back to health.

The Voroshilov sanatorium was perfect for this. The sea facing walls of its five huge buildings were made of thick glass. The rooms were allocated in strict military hierarchy order. Accordingly, provisions were also different for various ranks. In the mid-1930s a separate building planned along modern lines was built for the Red Army's highest-ranking commanders. On its terrace they used the popular treatment of the time: special filters and mobile reflectors were used to give doses of sunshine. Voroshilov and his circle were taken to the beach in a separate lift, which could not be used by the many guards or staff.[4] ☆

Georgy Pyatakov, an old acquaintance of the Alliluyev family, sitting next to the pipe-smoking Stalin, his old rival.

Pyatakov's photograph taken in prison.

K. A.: I had been to the sanatorium before. It has just come to my mind that Svetlana, Stalin's daughter once lived close by. She had a small girl with her. *[Marfa Peshkova, Gorky's granddaughter—M. K.]*

One day Svetlana came to see me: "Kira, Papa has arrived and asks you to visit us." I was happy to accept, I had a quick lunch and then went across to them. The path leading to the house was strange in a sort of rhombus shape *[she demonstrates]*. As I ran up it, suddenly, out of nowhere, the Stalin villa appeared built on the highest hill in the area. On the path I saw Joseph Stalin. *[She performs the dialogue with a Georgian accent]* "Good day, Iosif Vissarionovich," I greeted him. "I am not he!" protested the man. "Well then, who are you?" I asked bursting with curiosity. "The gardener," he replied. "I am Georgian. We Georgians all look the same in old age."

I went on and there stood Stalin. I couldn't believe my eyes. I asked him: "Are you sure you are Iosif Vissarionovich?" "Of course I am, why do you ask?" he said, shrugging his shoulders. "I have just met your gardener…" I would have started to tell the story but Stalin interrupted me and said exactly what his double had: "You know, we Georgians all look the same in old age…"

So "my dear relative" asked me for supper. In the meantime he questioned me about what was happening in Moscow. "What are our common acquaintances doing? And primarily what was with my mother?" At that time I had no idea that he was curious about my mother and not me. Svetlana did not guess why her father had invited me to supper either. Why me! Whatever the case, he pressed me to stay the night as it was dark by then. But I said that they would put me out of the sanatorium if I stayed out until morning. "Rules are rules," he said with a mischievous smile. "Well then, go in peace. But let me give you someone to accompany you!" But I didn't want anyone, God knows who to come with me. I did not think of myself as some grand dame. Well I snatched from the table two huge pears. *[She laughs]* They were like two huge hand grenades. And I wandered home on the dark, bushy path.

I spent my holidays in the same sanatorium also in 1939. But at that time Stalin was not living nearby. When my stay ended I went back to Moscow, I opened the apartment door, stepped into my room, and *[she takes a long pause]* saw a strange boy. It was Nikolai Molochnikov's son whom I knew already, but not very well. "What are you doing here?" I asked him. "I live here," he replied. He told me that my mother had married his dad. Stalin, however, had been informed about it already.

M. K.: And that's why he was so furious.

K. A.: Yes, he was furious. The others were too. I remember how enraged Anastas Mikoyan was, with whom we lived during the summers in Zubalovo before the war, that my mother had remarried barely nine months after my father's death. "I will never respect Yevgenia again," he announced. After this my mother *[in 1954—M. K.]* explained that she had got married because Beria's proposal had really frightened her. Molochnikov was, as they say, *right at hand.*

M. K.: I do not want to pry about the intimate details of your mother's life. But many people noticed that Maria Korona, Alyosha Svanidze's wife, wrote the following entry in her diary: "November 4, 1934 [...] J[oseph] joked with Zhenya. He teased her saying that she had got even plumper, and was very affectionate towards her. Since I've come to know the full story, I've watched them carefully, to see how they behave with one another."[5] We know that the diarist was hopelessly in love with Stalin. That is why she reacted very sensitively if his attention turned to another woman. Even so it is hard to misunderstand her observations.

K. A.: I don't completely rule out that Stalin...I have thought about this too... *[she is embarrassed]*. But I cannot say for certain that he had already tried his luck with my mother in 1934. I was not there. *[Almost gaily]*. I wasn't standing over

Yevgenia Alliluyeva (x) and her daughter, Kira (xx) relaxing at the sanatorium named after their good friend, Voroshilov.

her...And anyway very few people could resist Stalin. He behaved like the willful Master of all of us. After Nadezhda's death all the women in his circle tried to please him. But to that extent?

At the same time *[she grimaces nervously]* why should this diary entry be such material evidence? Maria Korona was not standing over her either. And *[she laughs again]* Stalin would have found it difficult to be alone with my mother. We always puttered about her....And I don't believe that my mother, as a woman, had any need of a relationship the emphasis of which was not on the spiritual. Look, I will tell you something intimate about her. I wouldn't have brought it up if you hadn't read from the diary. Despite her sensual exterior Yevgenia Alliluyeva was as cold as ice her whole life. That is precisely why she was careful not to arouse men *unnecessarily*.

But I do know, and I've mentioned it already, that after my father's death my mother was besieged. Beria once received a hard slap from her because he tried to feel her up. But after the war he struck back—to all the Alliluyevs...

M. K.: It is noteworthy that not only you, but the Redens and Svanidze families all hated Beria...

K. A.: My father simply did not think he was human. My mother was disgusted by him. She spoke of her low opinion of him several times to Stalin. *[She plays*

Yevgenia Alliluyeva loved dressing elegantly, and she was always surrounded by clouds of perfume She was eager to tell people her opinion right in their face. She liked spending her time abroad, and made no secret of the fact that she preferred to stay in Berlin, instead of Moscow. As long as Stalin liked the wife of his brother-in-law, "the beautiful Zhenya" could enjoy his protection. This picture was taken at the Berlin airport.

out the dialogue.] "Be careful with him Joseph! That dangerous man is capable of deceiving you!" "But he did good operative work in the *chekist* period," said Stalin. "That is why I still think of him as an invaluable colleague." "One day it'll turn out what sort of operative things your Lavrenty did," my mother went on. "And what a rotten man he is. Imagine Joseph, your Beria hit me not long ago. He snuck up to me, jumped up like a billy goat and butted me with his forehead with all his might. Strange things can come to light about a man like that."

But "my dear relative" just laughed. He enjoyed it when my mother was sarcastic about his loyal servant. But he never warned Beria to leave the Alliluyev family alone. It didn't occur to him. Later many things came out about Beria. But unfortunately only after Stalin's death.

M. K.: And it was possible to say things like that to Stalin?

K. A.: [raises her hand and proudly points to Yevgenia's photo] It seems that my mother had certain privileges in Stalin's court. For example, after a performance at the Bolshoi Theater, she once said to him: "Iosif Vissarionovich! Why do we go everywhere by car? I would like to walk with you a little." Stalin was glad to oblige and the whole company set off towards the Kremlin. On foot! The guards nearly went mad. But they could do nothing.

On another occasion *[December 5, 1936—M. K.]* my mother received an invitation to an event in which Stalin gave a lecture on the new Soviet constitution which was named after him and credited to him *[in reality it was composed by the soon to be executed Nikolai Bukharin, Karl Radek, and others]*.[6] And as this was a very important event in the life of our "socialism-building Soviet people", *[she bursts into a laugh]* my mother had some lovely new clothes made for herself. But as usual the seamstress was late. Imagine, minutes before the opening of the ceremony her dress had to be altered!

I warned my mother not to be late. You could hear a fly buzzing when Stalin paused in his speech. Nobody even dared cough. But my mother, did she listen to me? She smoothed down her hair and stormed off. Wonderfully dressed in a cloud of perfume. Stalin, of course, noticed when she entered the chamber late and at the first opportunity reproached her: "Zhenya, you were late for my lecture!" "How did you notice? You were in the middle of giving an official speech!" my mother said. "But I saw someone moving through the rows. I have eagle eyes, after all I am a mountain dweller. I knew that only Zhenya would dare do that to me. Even before I was certain I had known who it would be. Nobody else would tempt Providence like that!"

M. K.: Whatever you have said, these stories indicate a great deal of coquetry...

K. A.: But why shouldn't she have flirted with anyone? She was a lovely woman. She was afraid of nothing and no one. Not even of being criticized.

But there was, for example, Polina Zhemchuzhina, the wife of Molotov, the head of the Soviet government at that time. At receptions she always clung to Stalin. She really *went for him.* And once he even praised her perfume. "It seems that Soviet perfume is not in the least inferior to the best western brands," mumbled Stalin in a satisfied way from under his mustache. The maniacally vain Zhemchuzhina's face lit up. Before the war, this branch of the light industry *belonged to her* for a long time, as they said in those days. But my mother, who was present just laughed in Stalin's face: "It shows Joseph that you don't understand feminine wiles. That is the newest product from Chanel. I brought a bottle for Polina from Paris."

There was an awkward silence. Then Stalin said turning to my mother: "How elegant you are today, Zhenya! You always wear nice clothes. It would be good if you dressed Soviet women. Think about it..." "But I can't sew!" laughed my mother. "There are other people who sew even the buttons onto my blouses. That is not a job for me." Polina Zhemchuzhina got visibly sick at this, perhaps because she *supervised* the garment industry as well, or perhaps she was simply jealous of my mother.

1 Shatunovskaya, 1982, 207.
2 More recently the name "Nakishidze" appears in some writings. Torchinov-Leontyuk, 2000, 354–355.
3 But Khrushchev was of the same opinion in his memoirs: "After the death of Nadezhda Sergeyevna *[Alliluyeva—M. K.]*, for a while I saw a young, beautiful, typically Caucasian woman at Stalin's residence. She tried to hide from us. Her eyes flashed, and then that's it, off she went. Then they said that this woman is Svetlana's governess." Khrushchev, 1997, 22.
4 Barmin, 1997, 322.
5 *Josif Stalin v obyatiakh semyi*, 1993, 158.
6 "I am going away now. I have done everything on the constitution *[with its text—M. K.]*. You do not require my agreement for anything further. I have made the rough draft. All the best to you, Kalinich!" writes Bukharin to Mikhail Kalinin in the postscript to an undated letter. *RGASPI*, fond.78, op.1, d.616.

CHAPTER 32
Vladimir Prison Years

Whatever was behind the banter between Yevgenia Alliluyeva and Joseph Stalin, it all came to an end in the autumn of 1939. The Master of the Kremlin broke off with his relatives and his old circle of acquaintances from one minute to the next—that is, with those whom he had shown any mercy during the Great Terror. But the apple of the dictator's eye, little Svetlana, remained the link between him and the Alliluyev family.

After the outbreak of the war, however, the Soviet dictator's circle changed once more and this time finally. Stalin, who always tended to theatrical solutions like a capricious director, gave less and less time to his daughter. This was partly because he believed that the Alliluyev family, and the Jews they were in contact with, had a bad influence on Svetlana. Stalin even summoned his daughter and warned her not to trust in Yevgenia Alliluyeva as it was not impossible that she had had something to do with her husband's, Pavel Alliluyev's death. Svetlana, who was scared by her father and who had lived through a few serious traumas—the worst being when Stalin arrested and sent to the Gulag her first great love Aleksei Kapler—did not dare argue with her father. After a while she did write a letter to her father in "Auntie Zhenya's" defense. "Papa, regarding Zhenya, perhaps the reason you doubt her is that she got married too quickly," we read in her letter dated December 1, 1945. "And why? She said something to me about it although I did not ask about it. I will certainly tell you when you come back from the cure[1] *[from the Black Sea—M. K.]*, as it is terrible and somehow unpleasant to harbor such antipathy for someone. Apart from this, this is a matter of principle and has not only to do with Zhenya's family. Remember what people have said also about me to you... And who? The devil take them!"[2]

Stalin's reply is not among his papers. It is not certain that he even argued with Svetlana as he would have thought this beneath him. But one can see from the letter that seven years after Pavel Alliluyev's death there was always someone trying to defame Yevgenia. It is also certain that Svetlana was thinking of Lavrenty Beria and the political police in general in her letter, who saw "enemies of the people" or spies in everybody if they were close to the Master of the Kremlin and his family.

This was a vicious circle: Stalin ordered the state security apparatus to watch the Alliluyevs and their friends, as he wanted to prove that Anna and Yevgenia, the sister and sister-in-law of his dead wife, were surrounded by Zionists.[3] That was how he tried to demonstrate how profound the international Jewish conspiracy was in the Soviet Union. Although after a while Stalin himself also believed this nonsense because he wanted to believe it. The state security investigation officers, who had come from the ranks of the NKVD, tried to outdo each other in the tasks they were given. They took informers' reports, bugged telephone conversations, snippets of confessions taken under extreme duress, to their leader who impatiently awaited the end result. The aim was to prove before the world that professional American spies and Moscow Jewish (consequently Zionist) intellectuals in their pay—with the famous actor Solomon Mikhoels at their head—were planning to spy and undertake terrorist acts, by getting close to Joseph Stalin's daughter, Svetlana, via Yevgenia Alliluyeva and her family. Through her they would then get right to the first man in the Soviet Empire.[4]

Viktor Abakumov, the commander of SMERSH, the infamous military counter-intelligence agency, later minister for State Security.

In the original script of the planned showtrial, the MGB *[Ministerstvo Gosudarsvennoi Bezopasnosti, which replaced the NKVD—M. K.]* intended to make Isaak Goldstein, the chief of the Moscow Economic History Institute—who had been a militant in the Bund, the Jewish Socialist party, at the beginning of the century—the link between Yevgenia Alliluyeva and the members of the alleged American and Zionist spy network. He was chosen because Yevgenia Alliluyeva had known him since 1929 (other sources say since 1930) when they had worked together at the Soviet commercial office in Berlin. They renewed their friendship in 1943 when Yevgenia and her family returned, after being evacuated, to Moscow.[5]

Today it is almost impossible to know when Goldstein came into the sights of the Soviet political police to be selected as a crown witness at the show trail. He was arrested on December 19, 1947. This was three days after Yevgenia Alliluyeva was forced to confess in the cells of Lubyanka that her old Berlin acquaintance, that is Goldstein, "harbors hostile attitudes" towards the Soviet system and "defames Soviet reality."[6]

The unfortunate man was at first not willing to make such a confession. In December 1947 and January 1948 he was interrogated for a total of sixty-nine hours. He collapsed under duress and signed the interrogation transcript which stated that the Jewish Anti-Fascist Committee, which had been established in August 1941 and included famous writers, publicists, actors and scholars, "had become a nest of western agents".[7]

In reality, exactly the reverse was true. According to the several volumes of documents that are now accessible, for three years after the war—until it was outlawed—the organization had been openly controlled by direct orders from the Soviet political police. Some of its activists had for years written their reports under assumed names for the "agency" and the other members of the committee felt obliged to help the NKVD—later renamed the State Security Ministry—in Soviet information gathering and counter espionage activities.[8]

The political police's leaders knew this well. But they were also clear that Stalin was expecting them to *expose* people. Furthermore, there was no group which was as suited to this role as the Soviet Jewry. Since the end of the nineteenth century there were several huge waves of emigration, fleeing the tsarist empire, and, therefore they had relatives in many western countries. And they continually and feverishly sought their relatives among the holocaust survivors of the Soviet Jews. After the invasion of the Soviet Union they had wanted to help in the struggle against Fascism so, apart from the military equipment, vehicles, ammunition etc. sent through official Soviet channels to Moscow, aid parcels were also sent to the beleaguered population. This really important activity was viewed even more suspiciously because two leaders of the Jewish Anti-Fascist Committee, Solomon Mikhoels and the poet Itsik Feffer, who had been appointed by the political police *[in secret reports he was known as Zorin, that is, "Dawn"—M. K.]*, had toured America for six months in 1943.[9]

The agreement concerning the hundreds of tons of aid was that they would distribute it, regardless of ethnicity, to all Soviet peoples and that American Jewish leaders would not set foot in the Soviet Union during these years. Despite this, the authorities said it was undeniable that the Soviet Jewry was in contact with the western powers. As proof, the political police leaders told Stalin that Moscow Zionists under the influence of Americans had "latched onto" Svetlana Alliluyeva's husband, Grigory Morozov. Allegedly, through him

74

Сов.Секретно

Экз.№ 1-й

СПИСОК

заключенных ОСОБОГО КОНТИНГЕНТА, содержащихся во Владимирской ОСОБОЙ тюрьме МГБ СССР

По состоянию на 10 ноября 1951 г.

Фамилия, имя и отчество	Год рожд.	Когда, кем и на какой срок осужден.
№ 3 Орджоникидзе Константин Констант.	1896	30.Х1.46 г. Особым Совещанием при МГБ СССР за незаконное хранение оружия и как социально-опасный элемент на 10 лет тюремного заключения.
№ 15 Аладжаджян Петр Степанович он же Аладжани Пиетро Стефано.	1894	28.У1.47г. Особым Совещанием при МГБ СССР, по ст. 58-4, 58-11 УК РСФСР на 10 лет тюремного заключения.
№ 21 Молочников Николай Владимирович	1899	29.У.48г. Особым Совещанием при МГБ СССР, по ст.19-58-1"а", 58-10 ч.1 и 58-11 УК РСФСР на 25 лет тюремного заключения.
№ 22 Аллилуева Евгения Александровна	1898	29.У.48г. Особым Совещанием при МГБ СССР, по ст.58-1"а", 58-10 ч.2, 58-11 УК РСФСР на 10 лет тюремного заключения.
№ 23 Аллилуева Анна Сергеевна	1896	29.У.48г. Особым Совещанием при МГБ СССР, по ст. 58-10ч.2, 58-11 УК РСФСР на 5 лет тюремного заключения.

- 2 -

75 2

№ 27 Майнерс Вольфган Иоганн	1908	14.УШ.50г. Особым Совещанием при МГБ СССР, по ст. 58-6ч.1 УК РСФСР на 25 лет тюремного заключения.
№ 28 Вадильо Мартинас Эвелио	1902	3.Ш.51г. Особым Совещанием при МГБ СССР, по ст. 58-6ч.1, 58-10ч.1 УК РСФСР на 20 лет тюремного заключения.
№ 29 Меньшагин Борис Георгиевич	1902	12.1Х.51 г. Особым Совещанием при МГБ СССР, по ч.1 Указа Президиума Вер. Совета СССР от 19.1У.1943 г. на 25 лет тюремного заключения.

НАЧ ВЛАДИМИРСКОЙ ТЮРЬМЫ МГБ СССР
ПОДПОЛКОВН[ИК] /ЖУРАВЛЕВ/

ЗАМ НАЧ ВЛАДИМИРСКОЙ ТЮРЬМЫ МГБ СССР
МАЙОР:- /ПАВЫГИН/

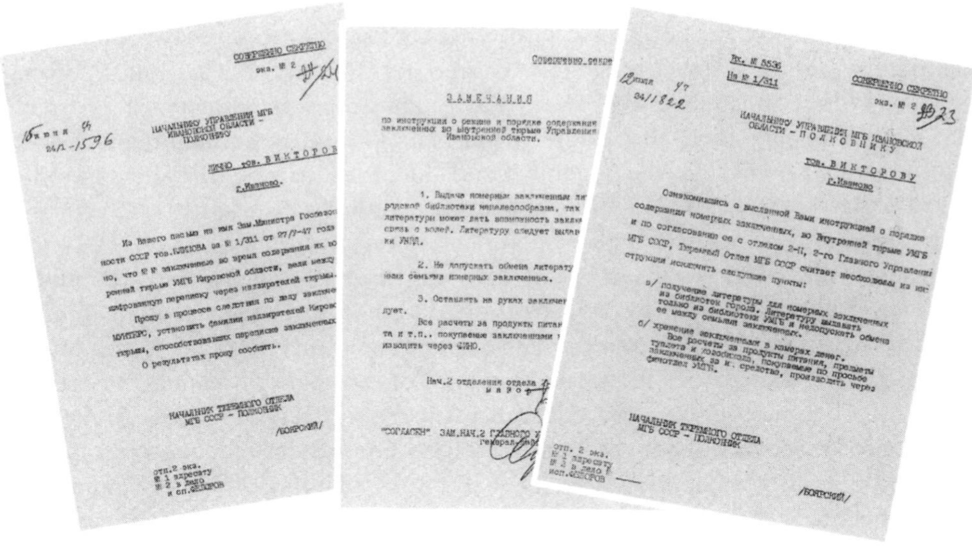

Documents listing the prisoners of the high-security prison in Vladimir, which only a couple of years ago were still classified top secret. Among the numbered prisoners—to whom the guards were not allowed to speak—we can see the members of the Alliluyev and Ordzhonikidze families.

they wanted to inform the Master of the Kremlin of the complaints of the Soviet Jewry.

It did not bother either Stalin or the political police that Svetlana had in the meanwhile divorced Morozov in May 1947. The man was not even told of this. Vasily Stalin, who disdained the law, simply asked his little sister to give him her identity booklet and tore them up. The local police made out a new ID on Svetlana in which she appears as single. Therefore, the accusation concerning Morozov should have been dropped in the Alliuyev case, but the detectives simply demanded more information from the detainees, about the influence they, the enemy Zionist circles, had on Stalin's daughter, through mediation of the Alliluyev family and her husband.[10]

In reality all that had happened was that people detained in the case, similarly to people of other nationalities in the Soviet Empire, sometimes gossiped about the Kremlin inhabitants, including the private lives of Stalin and his children. Sometimes there was a grain of truth in the gossip which sometimes got out to the West, although it was by no means certain that it was through "Jewish channels". At the beginning of December 1947, one or two bits of inside information appeared in the American press. It was probably this that caused the great anger and fright on the part of the Soviet dictator, who was not used to publicity. He decided to push the investigation against the Alliluyev family and their Jewish acquaintances. The informers' reports had been ready for some time, which stated that an extremely bitter Yevgenia Alliluyeva and her sister-in-law, Anna Alliluyeva, complained more and more frequently to their acquaintances in the "House on the Embankment" about Stalin's insolence to them and their relatives.

The Master of the Kremlin also learned via a similar roundabout way, although a lot later, that in December 1946 there was a family party in Yevgenia Alliluyeva's house at which the hostess had introduced Svetlana and her husband to Isaak Goldstein. This led to Yevgenia's arrest on December 10, 1947. The accusation was that "she had held anti-Soviet meetings in her apartment for years". At the same time her second husband Nikolai Molochnikov also went to prison and so did her daughter from her first marriage, Kira Alliluyeva. Even so the "House on the Embankment" inhabitants were surprised when on January 29, 1948 Anna Alliluyeva, Stalin's sister-in-law was arrested for "counter-revolutionary agitation".[11]

Members of the Alliluyev family suffered cruel mental torture and their acquaintances terrible physical torture from the two investigating officers, Colonels Komarov and Likhachev and their subordinates. Even among Stalin's executioners they were infamous for their cruelty. So much so that in 1955, during the time of the Khrushchev "Thaw" both of them were brought before the military courts in Leningrad and sentenced to death. But this did not make the *infection known as the struggle against cosmopolitanism* disappear from the mindset of the Soviet population. In the 1940s, this was a euphemism for persecuting Jews that gradually became official state policy.[12]

During the interrogations the pair of colonels were in their element. As it later became clear in their trial they were on permanent phone contact with Stalin, who had them on string, even while they were taking confessions, saying how far advanced they were in unwinding the conspiracy. Sometimes they asked him how far they should go with the torture. In Lidia Shatunovskaya's case, for example, the dictator decreed: "You may use physical force but don't cause visible injuries on the prisoner..."[13]

Komarov's and Likhachev's favorite method was to make prisoners sign a prepared false confession during torture sessions. In this way the circle of those under suspicion grew ever wider. At the end of 1947 and the beginning of 1948, among Yevgenia Alliluyeva's friends and acquaintances who were put behind bars was the above-mentioned Lidia Shatunovskaya, a theater historian, and her husband, the physicist Lev Tumerman, as well as Esfir Gorelik, a teacher of political economy. Her husband, Brigadier General Andrei Khrulyov, was one of the key figures in the Soviet military leadership. Suprisingly he was not arrested and even kept his deputy ministerial post in the Defense Ministry. However, Colonel-General Georgy Uger, the commander of the Soviet airforce's radar network, was put in Lubyanka, as was Rebekka Levina, deputy director of the Moscow Economic History Institute, and Tatyana Fradkina, technical translator and former employee of the Soviet commercial office in Berlin, whose eight-year Gulag exile had ended not long before this.[14]

The investigating officers intended them all as either accused or key witnesses in the same show trial. Then for some reason Stalin dropped the idea of the "Alliluyev trial" although not for good. At his orders, certain elements of the script, indeed the confessions of the accused were inserted into the operative, and then the early investigating phase of the "doctors' plot" case which ran parallel with the Alliluyev case and other anti-Semitic showdowns. This is why Yevgenia Alliluyeva's friends from the "House on the Embankment ", who had been arrested at the end of the 1947 and beginning of 1948, were not released from prison. Indeed, one by one they themselves, their acquaintances and relatives were brought to trial behind closed doors. There were some who received eight or ten years, others twenty years security prison sentences on charges of "Zionist subversion".[15]

But the detectives encountered difficulties with the Alliluyev family. According to a shrewd observation made by one of their fellow defendants, Yevgenia Alliluyeva, "the daughter of a Novgorod pope, and Anna Alliluyeva, whose father was an old Petrograd Bolshevik worker, could not in any way be accused of Zionism. Not even by the State Security Ministry." Nevertheless, Yevgenia got ten years for anti-Soviet agitation and propaganda.[16] Anna got five for the same. Stalin could not, and did not, want to forgive them for their statements: "A. S. Alliluyeva stated that Stalin is becoming more and more unbearable as he gets older. He liquidates anyone who is unpleasant for him. Such a dictator has not been seen in Russia before." Anna Alliluyeva served out her sentence. Then the authorities sentenced her to another five years although she had by then become seriously schizophrenic in solitary confinement.[17]

Compared to them Kira Alliluyeva can consider herself fortunate. The investigating officers could have declared her a spy but they did not: after six months solitary confinement she was exiled for five years. Her mother and aunt, however, were taken to the harsh Vladimir Prison. Later others joined them from among the defendants sentenced to prison during the "Alliluyev" investigation. Among them was Nikolai Molochnikov, Yevgenia's second husband.

His father was a famous disciple of Tolstoy. As a result, after 1917 the son had been declared a class-enemy. But from the end of the 1920s, after Nikolai Molochnikov had been recruited as an informer, he had quite a career, perhaps due to the help of his patrons. First he was sent to Berlin to the Soviet commercial office. At the time of his arrest he worked for the Iron Foundry Ministry, which belonged to the military industry complex, as a research institute chief constructor. But his career as an informer did not help him. Especially as informers were regular players in showtrials. Molochnikov's investigators had an easy time, during the investigation he snitched on his friends and all his relations including his wife, Yevgenia. So he became Komarov's and Likhachev's favorite. He enjoyed special privileges during the investigation and later as a prisoner as well. Then in 1955, when the two sadistic colonels came before the courts, Molochnikov again testified but this time against them. He reported in detail how cruelly they had treated their innocent prisoners.[18] ☆

M. K.: Lidia Shatunoskaya writes of Nikolai Molochnikov that he was the NVKD *plant* in the Alliluyev family.[19]

K. A.: [indifferently] It's possible. Molochnikov and my mother were released at the same time but they did not live together again. My mother never told me the details. It is true that from the start of her marriage to Molochnikov my mother was a "black sheep" in the eyes of Stalin and the "agency."

M. K.: But then it is obvious that Molochnikov was placed in the Alliluyev family on Stalin's orders. Yet he was angry at her for marrying him? Where's the logic in it?

K. A.: Since when have you been seeking logic in the acts of "my dear relative"?
M. K.: And why did Stalin's showdown against Yevgenia Alliluyeva take so long? He grabbed her only in December 1947. And Anna's aunt even later; she was arrested in the following January.
K. A.: [very tense] He harassed us in the meantime too. He had imprisoned Leonid, Anna Alliuyeva's son, during the war. Even though he was a schoolboy he was accused of conspiracy. Then co-tenants were put in Anna's apartment. Of course, you are right that years passed simce he had a falling out with my mother and Anna. But Stalin made up for the delay. He took us through the hell of hells. Me included.
M. K.: Please speak about your years in prison!
K. A.: Let posterity know about my mother's sufferings instead. After she came out of prison in 1954 she told me a lot about what happened inside. It seems that she had to get it all out of her system.

But wait! I haven't told you yet that I was at home when they arrested my mother, have I? Two men rang the bell. They didn't say what they wanted. "Mom, two comrades want you," I shouted to her, and went into my room where I was memorizing a part. After a while I came out. By then the house search was in full swing. I went as white as a sheet. My mother went past me into the hall. Proudly, head held high. She pulled me to her and said something like: "It seems one can't escape prison and beggardom!" This is an old Russian saying. Obviously she was saying that Stalin had finally got us. Then she ran out. Ran straight to the railing to throw herself off, but the officers grabbed her from behind.

They took her to Lubyanka, to one of the foulest interrogation cells in the inner prison. They did not beat her, but kept threatening to really hurt her. This torment must have been very humiliating for her. Then they sentenced and took her to the Vladimir maximum security prison. According to my mother's recollections the first years were the worst. She wanted to die again. She realized that they would never let her out of that special prison. But in the Vladimir *Tsentral*—it was named that back in tsarist times—it was impossible to commit suicide. My mother's every step, every move was watched. She was surrounded by guards, one of them was always pacing outside her cell and peeping in through the spy hole. But you know what a maximum security prison is… Even so my mother intended to do away with herself. While walking, as after a while she was sometimes allowed out to the prison yard, she searched for glass shards in the gravel. She bent down for them and hid these tiny slivers of glass. Then she swallowed them in her cell to make her stomach bleed. She believed that this would kill her.

But one day she heard a very soft knock from the neighboring cell. My mother knew Morse code as she had worked in the Novgorod telegram office during the Bolshevik revolution. She answered at once: she introduced herself to her cell neighbor and said she had no wish to live any more. Then the reply came:

"I am Polish and have been here a long time. I can tell from your words how much you despair. Now you are completely despondent. But believe me it won't always be like this. I will teach you what you must do to get out of this state. First of all, exercise every single day! Do not leave out a single one! And recite poetry out loud so you don't forget how to speak. Because if you are silent for too long your facial muscles will grow slack. Finally, try to learn some sort of trade in your cell."

My mother accepted everything the Polish prisoner had advised. She asked for many technical books—strangely enough the prison inmates could receive better and better books and periodicals seemingly without limit[20], and in the course of the years she had become an agricultural specialist. She believed that after her long imprisonment she would have to spend the rest of her years far away in the north, near the Arctic Circle. That is why she read masses of books about animal husbandry, especially about reindeer. In the meantime, she calmed down and to the end of her life was very grateful to her fellow Polish prisoner.

M. K.: Who could that person have been?

K. A.: Unfortunately I don't remember the name. Although my mother spoke about him a lot and always with affection.

M. K.: The Stalinist system was in the final analysis, to quote my former teacher, the historian Viktor Dalin, who spent long years in the Gulag, "a mental asylum of continent size", worthy of a Gogol novel. This professor spent more than one and a half decades in the Gulag and jail and studied the French Revolution even there. But even if we accept Dalin's choice of words, I still don't understand how it was possible that the prisoners of the Vladimir security prison had so many privileges, quite uncharacteristic in the Soviet system. Yet at the same time they were not allowed to talk to their guards, who addressed them not by name but by number and led them along the corridors—two guards behind them and two in front—like the numbered prisoners in the Bastille during Louis XIV's reign. Did they treat them like this because the *Vladimiris*—amongst whom were a German general, an army officer who had been arrested in Budapest, high ranking Soviet party functionaries, members of the Ordzhonikidze and Alliluyev families—were chosen to be defendants or witnesses in the great trials that were being prepared? Did they want to "conserve" them so that they could be at hand at any time? Some of them were not spoken a word to for four-five years: in effect the guards just gestured to them. But the food was sometimes brought from the best restaurants in town so that they would not weaken. If someone arrived from the Gulag with scurvy they immediately brought them vegetables and vitamins. To some they even offered paper and work. Indeed, if necessary, they were given books, dictionaries and maps from the public library in Moscow. Do you understand this? Because I don't…

K. A.: [shrugs her shoulders] I don't know the answers to these questions. Not even vaguely. Although I heard a lot from my mother about the strange procedures in the VladimirPrison. For example, medical provision was excellent. But during the examination in the cell the doctors were not allowed to ask questions about the history of the illness lest they find out who they were examining.

M. K.: They communicated with the patient through the guards?

K. A.: Yes, which of course was completely stupid. I remember my mother saying that the prisoners in special cells—they were in a separate wing with guards at every turn of the stairs—were allowed to walk for a whole hour in the yard. And after a while they could even request foreign language books. My mother often used this privilege. I don't know if you know but she was a great linguist. She spoke German, English, and French. And due to her secondary school studies, she could read Greek and Latin. In Vladimir she read the classics of world literature in the original. She often told me that is why she did not lose her mind. Although sometimes her nerves went to pieces. Then she went into obstruction.

M. K.: How?

K. A.: She grabbed her tin plate and beat on the door. "I am Alliluyeva!" she cried. "Understand, I am Alliluyeva. Innocently sentenced!" *[She begins to cry]*

M. K.: Let's finish the conversation, I don't want you to get sick…

K. A.: Quite the opposite, it is a relief to finally say all this to someone. I would like to go on. *[She is silent for a long time and then continues rapidly]* So then the

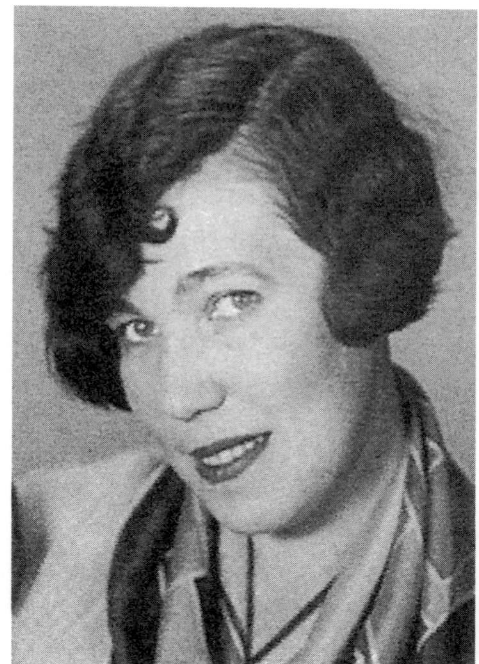

Yevgenia Alliluyeva before her arrest, and after the years she spent in solitary confinement in the Vladimir prison.

prison warden or his political deputy would have my mother summoned and would start to shout at her. "What do you think you're doing?!" But my mother was not afraid of them, in that respect she did not change after her arrest.
M. K.: In what respect did she change?
K. A.: I was then living in Moscow. On April 2 in 1954 somebody rang me up and said I should go for my mother and Aunt Anna. To be honest, at first I thought that somebody was playing a late April Fools joke on me. After that I felt as if I had wings and literally flew to them. But when I saw them my great joy was shattered. I could see that poor Aunt Anna was not herself and that my mother had become a shrunken old woman. She was no longer the beautiful woman she had been before her arrest. And at the beginning even her speech was faltering as if she had a stutter. Later she said it was because she had not spoken to anyone for so long and no one had spoken to her either. Imagine, the two poor old women had no idea that Stalin had died. They believed it was thanks to "our dear relative" that they had been released. "What do you think, made Joseph pull himself together?" asked my mother. At which I said with caution that the secret police officers noted our every word and that in the life of the Soviet Union great changes had taken place. That is why they had been let out.

At our very first meeting it became clear that my mother and aunt still hated Lavrenty Beria. But luckily by then he was no longer alive because my mother would have really given him a piece of her mind. Over the following days I talked a lot with my mother, we interrupted each other with our stories, what had happened to us since we had last met. I told her that Beria had come spying on me. He put a friend of mine onto me, whom the swine had broken mentally and physically.

1 At that time Stalin had already been a frequent visitor to the sanatoriums of northern Caucasia and the Black Sea coast to have his arthritis and his deformed hand treated in the greatest secrecy. Buber-Neumann, 1995, 175.
2 *Iosif Stalin v obyatiakh semyi*, 1993, 96.
3 Kostirchenko, 1999, 85–86, 88–89.
4 Shatunovskaya, 1982, 238–239, 247–248, 314, 319–321.

5 Gereben, 2000, 365.
6 Goldstein was probably telling the truth when during one interrogation he confessed that he had met Solomon Mikhoels, the "Jewish King Lear", in the Autumn of 1946, and that he asked him about the philo-Semite Alliluyev family. *Nepravedny Sud*, 1994, 5. In the text the name of Kira Alliluyeva appears mistakenly. Moreover, this valuable publication on the Jewish trial also gives her father's name (Pavlovna) wrong.
7 *Evreysky Antifashistsky Komytyet*, 1996, 318, 319, 362, 375.
8 For further details see some recently declassified sources, the publications *Evreysky Antifashistsky Komytyet*, 1996; and *Nepravedny Sud*, 1994.
9 Redlich, 1982, 108–112.
10 *Nepravedny Sud*, 1994, 6. After Stalin had read the confessions and come to the conclusion that information about him reached Mikhoels, he ordered the actor's liquidation.
11 Kostirchenko, 1994, 89.
12 Pikhoya, 1996, 75–78.
13 Shatunovskaya, 1982, 252–270, 279–292, 295, 300–314.
14 *Ibid.*
15 Kostirchenko, 1994, 92–94.
16 The prosecution had fourteen witnesses against her, including her own daughter, Kira and her second husband, Molochnikov. *Reabilitatsia*, vol. I, 2000, 71.
17 Shatunovskaya, 1982, 346.
18 Kostirchenko, 1994, 88.
19 *Ibid.*, 156–159.
20 The prison's inmate librarian, who had been the mayor of Smolensk during the German invasion, recalls that it was only in the second half of the 1950s that subscriptions for literary periodicals were allowed. Menshagin, 1988, 106–107.

According to members of the Alliluyev family still alive, Beria was constantly inciting Stalin from behind the scenes against his sister-in-law, Anna.

Lavrenty Beria

The career of Lavrenty Beria (x), who was born into a poor Western Georgian family, had a peaceful course at the beginning. Before he turned into a sadistic police chief, he graduated from a technical high school, and was planning to make a career as an architect. During the Soviet-Russian Civil War, however, he became involved in politics. In the 1920s he was the infamous commander of the OGPU in Georgia, in the early 1930s he became the head of the local party organization, and before soon, the "governor" of all of Caucasia.

These two rare pictures show Beria with two of his influential supporters: Voroshilov (X) and Mikoyan (XX).

The cunning Georgian Beria knew all too well that in Moscow he could trust only his fellow militiamen.

CHAPTER 33
"He was an Evil Man, the Wretch"

In the second half of the 1940s, right until his arrest in 1951, Viktor Abakumov stood at the head of the Soviet political police, that is the State Security Ministry. He, who had only a few years of schooling and was a warehouseman turned goon, was the leader of the SMERSH *[Smerty spionam, death to spies—M. K.]*, the Soviet military counter-intelligence, famous for its cruelty.[1]

The dictator's young minion—whom Beria helped during the Great Terror and who, as a result, saw him as a role model—personally interrogated Yevgenia Alliluyeva. He also threatened Anna Alliluyeva, who was imprisoned not long afterwards, that he would break all her bones if she did not sign the prepared confession that incriminated many others. Once he interrogated even Kira Alliluyeva, although the young actress was given only a supporting role in the "Zionist conspiracy" affair.

The boorish Abakumov personally gave orders to Komarov and Likhachev, who tried to get more out of Yevgenia Alliluyeva and her supposed accomplices in Lubyanka. But in the summer of 1951, Joseph Stalin ordered the members of the Abakumov circle, who had suddenly fallen from favor, arrested.[2] Abakumov, Komarov, and their fellows who had attacked their prisoners viciously and were militantly anti-Semitic, were replaced by interrogators from the Soviet party center and Comsomol leadership. Stalin personally selected the new interrogators on the basis of their personnel files. But the questions remained the same. Stalin wanted answers to why the former inhabitants of the "House on the Embankment " conducted "Zionist agitation" directed from the West and on whose orders. The charge against Abakumov and his associates was that they obstructed the process of investigation.[3]

One of the victims of the police chief's insatiable lust was Zoya Fyodorova, the celebrated and beautiful diva. By blackmailing her, Beria managed to enlist the actress in the network of the NKVD agents. He also tried to seduce her, but the woman showed great integrity and rejected his approach. She was already in love with a high-ranking American naval officer assigned to the American embassy in Moscow, and she gave birth to their daughter. (The picture shows her in the military uniform of the American officer.) Zoya Fyodorova spent many years on the Gulag.

Officially, the case of the Alliluyevs—which was closed in 1949 with the accused receiving first degree sentences—was still linked to Abakumov's name. Despite this, Anna and Yevgenia's living relatives—who, independently of their various opinions of the Stalinist system, all loathe even the memory of the Komarov-type investigating officer—interestingly enough rarely blame Abakumov. But even today they feel terror at the name of Lavrenty Beria. This is partly explained by the fact that Viktor Abakumov was a still unknown provincial NKVD officer when Beria, at Stalin's orders, personally participated in the campaign against Alyosha Svanidze and Stanisław Redens. He even was directly linked to their executions.

In addition, at the end of the 1930s Joseph Stalin used Beria when he wanted to humiliate the Alliluyev family's female members who were still free. According to Kira Alliluyeva, the dictator knew that the solitary women could not bear the pasty-faced NKVD chief. They had heard the contemporary rumors that Beria and his loyal adjutant, Colonel Sarkisov, regularly hunted down women in the center of Moscow. They would pursue unsuspecting beautiful women walking down the street, indeed sometimes underage girls as well. They would create a situation whereby the victim was usually too afraid to refuse another rendezvous.[4]

Of course, there were some who tried to say no to Beria. Zoya Fyodorova, one of Stalin's favorite film actresses, sex symbol of the age, met the chief of the Soviet secret police several times at his office and home. The signs are that she allowed him to recruit her hoping she could get her father released from prison. But in the meantime she fell in love with an American navy officer working in Moscow and had his child. Beria, who was mad with jealousy, ordered his fortunate rival out of the country and sent the beautiful actress to the Gulag as a dangerous spy.[5] We also know of cases where a few women who had suffered rape and humiliation at Beria's hands committed suicide. One husband, a much decorated military officer wanted to kill Beria in revenge. But somebody reported him and he was executed without trial as a terrorist. A pilot, a Hero of the Soviet Union persuaded his humiliated wife to escape to the countryside. But Beria's men were watching them and in the end the man, who filed a complaint at the Central Committee, was sent to a dungeon at a Soviet camp.[6]

Many of the chief executioner's victims—like the period's other great diva, Tatyana Okunevskaya, the film actress—have since written down the story of their forced relations with the disgusting Beria. Their testimonies unanimously reveal that Beria first collected detailed information on the women he had selected to be his concubines.[7] If it became clear from these "background studies" that the woman had a relative in the Gulag or prison then the NKVD chief implied that for services rendered he would release the person in question.[8]

The lascivious Lavrenty Beria spent most of his leisure time chasing women.

But he generally did not keep this promise. For example, he lied to Okunevskaya in 1941 saying that he would release her beloved father and grandmother from prison. Yet he already knew that both of them had been executed two years before. In addition, Beria especially enjoyed it if the husband or fiancé was present at these rendezvous. At the end of the 1970s, M., a famous composer told me with wringing his hands, his voice broken with sobs, that Beria had asked him to play Chopin as background music while he was in the next room "having tea" with the composer's wife. The woman, a novice mezzo-soprano in the Moscow Bolshoi Theatre, was deeply in love with her young husband. Yet Beria after a long struggle was able to have her because he managed to find out that her husband was a distant relation of Paderewski, the world famous Polish pianist, and first president of the independent Polish state. So the composer was a potential spy. While he blackmailed the husband by telling him that his wife was, on her mother's side, a Volga German. In 1941, this ethnic group was exiled to forced labor camps in the Soviet Union, so the woman believed that she would find herself in Yakutia or Kolima if she did not give in. The couple wanted to die in order to escape this situation. But only the woman managed to throw herself off the balcony of their ninth floor flat, out of desperation. The man got frightened and stayed alive—if one can call the vegetating wreck that was left of him a living being. (According to his doctor and adjutant, Beria contracted venereal disease from a prostitute at the end of the war at one of his Moscow flats that the NKVD transformed into a trysting place.)[9]

It seems that Beria planned a similarly terrible and perhaps an even more pitiful role for Boris Gorbatov, the much decorated Stalin Prize writer and one of the leaders of the Soviet Writers' Union. Beria demanded that this favorite of the Soviet elite, should spy on his own wife, Tatyana Okunevskaya. He had to accept that the NKVD chief had earlier seduced and then deceived her. In the meantime his political police found out that the actress, who hated the Stalinist system, had secretly rented a flat in the suburbs of Moscow and was there meeting Marshall Tito's—by then denounced by Stalin—Moscow ambassador. In order to make things easier for Beria, Gorbatov, on orders from the Lubyanka, took from his wife the little pistol she always carried, and did not leave her for a minute until she was taken away from their home.[10]

Tatyana Okunevskaya in an elegant white dress, shortly before her arrest. The second picture was taken in the Gulag, while the third in the early 1960s, many years after her release from the prison camp. A popular actress during Stalin's time, she was seduced and deceived by Beria, who had promised to release her father and grandmother from prison. She still hates the one-time boss of Lubyanka, although admits that he was a talented and cunning politician.

But there were women who rendered services to Beria for careerist reasons or greed. They also calculated that if they got pregnant from him they would with his help get out of their small rented rooms and in needy war time obtain the *pay*, the special food ration that were only for the Soviet elite. All Moscow talked of how Beria usually provided a trousseau and married off to one of his obedient employees the women that he got tired of, or at least the ones he got pregnant. ☆

K. A.: That scum, Beria even tried to get me. It seemed to really annoy him that an Alliluyev girl was still free. It all started when he met my friend Valyusha by chance, she had moved to Moscow from Tashkent before the war because they had arrested and executed her father at home. I remember her mother well. She was a fat, kind woman, she lived and died for her Valya... Who was anyway to be pitied, a typical poor girl. Once I gave her my winter coat. She often came to see us in the "House on the Embankment ", I always gave her food and drink. *[Sarcastically]* Well she was grateful all right... "Well, just you wait!" I would say of her in prison, and afterwards in exile "If I get out you'll get it from me!"

After six months solitary confinement I was released, and after Stalin's death I was allowed to move back to Moscow. Then I went immediately to Valya, who had no clue that I knew about her snitching. She received me kindly, but I did not beat about the bush but got straight to the point: "Valya! Why did you grass on me?" She started to defend herself. "Oh God, it is a complicated story!" And she told me how she was ensnared. The acting school which we attended was near the Bolshoi Theater, Valya was a lovely, blonde girl—I'll show you her photograph—one day she was going home. She always walked right across the center of Moscow. Perhaps because she never had money for the streetcar.

Unfortunately, Beria caught sight of her somewhere around the Kuznetsky Bridge. That scum always peered out his car when he went on the prowl. Almost every day. He ordered his adjutant to pursue the little blonde. He, a colonel.... *[hesitates]*. Wait he had a Caucasian name. I think he was a distant relative of Mikoyans...

M. K.: No, that was Lyudvigov, the head of Beria's secretariat. You are thinking of another Armenian called Sarkisov. After Beria's arrest he pretended he was mad. That's why he was not executed.

K. A.: Yes, Sarkisov. I heard many bad things about him. Anyway Valya only saw that this adjutant type gets out of a huge, curtained black car. In a silky voice he called out to her:

"My poor child! How young you are and so pale! Won't you let me help you? Wouldn't you like to come with me? I'll invite you to a good lunch and if you want you can even have a bath at my house."

I don't understand how Valya could have agreed, but she said that the man spoke to her so kindly and paternally that she didn't think there was anything wrong. On top of that, she would have loved a bath, because they hadn't had hot water for days. Anyway, I don't understand it, but Valya agreed to play the game. She allowed the officer to take her to a nearby villa where she really did have a bath, ate a good lunch and then lay down to read. Then somebody stepped into the beautifully furnished, half-lit room. "I immediately knew it was Beria," said Valya, "because the light fell on his pince-nez."[11] Everybody in the whole country knew that only Lavrenty Beria wore them among the leaders.

You can imagine what happened. Beria went over to Valya and sat on the edge of the bed. He started to sweet talk her but they were only the usual cheap compliments:

"What lovely cherry lips you have! A figure like Venus." He did not hesitate long and bedded her. Afterwards he guizzed her about her background and the people she knew. And when he knew that she was my friend he persuaded her to spy on me and report everything about me. And our family. After I was arrested, Komarov summoned Valya and dictated to her a string of lies about me.

M. K.: What happened to her later?

K. A.: God punished her well. She didn't become an actress but died very young of cancer. Poor thing!

M. K.: Are you really capable of feeling sorry for someone who informed on you for so long?

K. A.: I am sorry for everyone who is denied at such a young age the right to live. *[A very long pause. Only the wall clock breaks the frozen silence.]*

M. K.: Kira Pavlovna, you were an actress when you were young. Then you worked for a long time as a production manager and then as a director. I am sure you know better than me what you would like to say to close our conversation.

K. A.: We haven't said anything yet about my meeting with Vasily Blyukher, who was commander of the Far-Eastern Special Army. But this story can perhaps shed some light on Joseph Stalin's *Asian character*. How cunning he was! After what happened to me and my mother I can compare him to an eastern despot. In solitary confinement I recalled how softly and flatteringly "my dear relative" spoke to people and how he watched what effect his words had on them. Then he attacked just when you expected it least. Just like a Central Asian desert scorpion. My mother also kept saying that "if Joseph acts like he likes someone then they are done for." He was an evil man, the wretch... *[Long pause]*

M. K.: Did you realize this only after Nadezhda Alliluyeva's death?

K. A.: I believe he was evil already before. But perhaps he was better at covering his feelings as a young man. Outwardly.

So as I have mentioned, "my dear relative" once urgently summoned Vasily Blyukher from the Far East. My father knew Blyukher well. They had a work connection. You know that in the mid-1930s Pavel Alliluyev was a sort of chief people's commissar for the armored divisions, so they had corresponded officially. That day they had some meeting in the Kremlin where Blyukher was also present. During the break my father telephoned us to say that there would be

In the first row from the left: Vasily Blyukher (1), Lazar Kaganovich (2), Joseph Stalin, and Sergo Ordzhonikidze (3). All four of them were good friends of Pavel Alliluyev who died under suspicious circumstances.

This rare picture shows Blyukher (x), Kaganovich (xx), and Stalin.

a big reception after the meeting. And he added: "Do come! Stalin made a special invitation to both of you."

My mother and I both quickly got changed and went over the bridge. We passed the place where poor Volodya Sakhurin shot Nina Umanskaya and then himself. We got there quickly, since the "House on the Embankment " was opposite the Kremlin. But we had a surprise encounter during this short trip. We bumped into Klim Voroshilov. He looked very unfortunate, running off somewhere with his neck well wrapped up. My mother started to ask what was the matter. He said he had a bad cold. When we arrived at the reception, my mother immediately told Stalin: "Imagine Joseph, we saw poor Klim Yefremovich, he looks terrible." To this Stalin replied "That man is always imagining he's ill. Always whining. He has just left, excusing himself as ill. But forget him!" This was typical of Stalin. He liked to ridicule others. He even made fun of his best friends, for example, Voroshilov.

In the meantime, my father introduced Vasily Blyukher to my mother: "Zhenya, this is my good friend from the Far East." They started to speak about how my father had traveled to see him by train with the singer Leonid Utesov, our Odessan Maurice Chevalier. And how Stalin had praised Blyukher in front of the whole company at the meeting earlier the day: "My best Soviet military leader" is how he described Blyukher. He drank to his health and then smashed the champagne glass to the ground, laughing.

M. K.: Is it possible that Voroshilov had left the reception greatly offended because he was jealous of Blyukher's successes?

K. A.: Certainly. But later Klim got the better of him. He became the "first Red officer" as we sang of him in Zubalovo, while Blyukher had his nemesis. He was lured to Moscow from the Far East and, as I heard, he was arrested en route. One of his eyes was gouged out during torture. Then he was executed. Others say, such as Blyukher's widow, that Beria and his colleagues beat him to death.[12] Well, so much for the sort of fate that awaited anyone whom Stalin called "my best Soviet military leader".

1 Abakumov took over the post from his predecessor, Vsevolod Merkulov, on May 4, 1946.
2 Pikhoya, 1998, 78–87.
3 Stolyarov, 1997, 43, 47–61.
4 Beria, 1999, 317–318.
5 Sopelnak, 1998, 29. After Stalin's death, Fyodorova was released. But the "agency" continued to watch her every step with eagle eyes. And when her daughter considered emigrating to America Fyodorova was brutally murdered in her Moscow flat.
6 *Pamyat'*, 1980, vol. III, 406–411.
7 Alekseyeva, 1996, 28–34, 45–50, 80–85, 128–132, 151–155, 175–179, 202–205.
8 Okunevskaya, 1998, 67, 80–81, 139–140, 175–176.
9 Stolyarov, 1997, 249–260.
10 Okunevskaya, 1998, 224–228, 243–245.
11 And Molotov, too.
12 New research evidence suggests that Blyukher was in fact beaten to death after he had to undergo the long tortures of the sadistic Beria. Suvenirov, 1998, 310.

The Twilight of the Dictator

His Yugoslav guest in the mid-1940s, Koča Popović, described Stalin in the following words: "His shoulders are extremely narrow and sloping, as if deformed. When he smiles, you can see his irregular yellow teeth."

The party congress meetings were always trying for Stalin, but he gradually realized that with each congress, he becomes even more powerful. He noted once on a piece of paper that "it would be great to have fights more often. After the fight, one may become truly respected, damnation." During the 19th Party Congress held in November 1952, he nevertheless looked like a lone wolf. He even left the keynote speech to his protégé, Malenkov.

Following the Second World War, Stalin's personality cult started to take irrational forms.

During the May Day parade in May, 1953, people marched under the black-bordered picture of Stalin. Under the pictures, however, many people were laughing happily.

BIBLIOGRAPHY

Abramovich, R., "Sfinks Stalin (Novaya kniga o Staline.)", *Sotsialistichesky Vestnik,* 21 (1935).

—, "Chingis-Khan 20-ovo veka", *Sotsialistichesky Vestnik,* 12 (1949).

Adamova-Slyozberg, O., "Put'", in *Dodnes tyagoteyet. Zapiski vashei sovremennitsi* (Moscow: Sovietsky Pisatel, 1989).

Ayvazyan, S., *Istoria Rossii. Armyansky sled* (Moscow: Kron-Press, 2000).

Alekseyeva, N., *Lavrenty Beria v moyei zhizni* (Moscow: Sovremennik, 1996).

Alliluyev, S., "Vstrechi s tovarishchem Stalinim", *Proletarskaya Revolyutsia,* 8 (1937).

—, *Proydenny put* (Moscow: OGIZ, 1946).

Alliluyev, V., *Khronika odnoi semyi: Alliluyevi – Stalin* (Moscow: Molodaya Gvardia, 1995).

Alliluyeva, A., *Vospominania* (Moscow: Sovietsky Pisatel, 1946).

Alliluyeva, K., "V dome na naberezhnoy", in *Konets veka* (Moscow, 1992).

Alliluyeva, S., *Twenty Letters to a Friend,* translated by Priscilla Johnson MacMillan (New York: Harper and Row, 1967).

—, *Only One Year,* translated by Paul Chavchavadze (New York: Harper and Row, 1969).

—, *Tolko odin god* (New York and Evanston: Harper Colophon Books & Row Publishers, 1970).

—, *Dvadtsaty pisem k drugu* (New York: Russkaya Kniga, 1981).

—, *The Faraway Music* (New Delhi: Lancer International, 1984).

—, *Dalyokaya muzika* (New York: Liberty Publishing House, 1988).

—, *Kniga dlya vnuchek. Puteshestvie na rodinu* (New York: Liberty Publishing House, 1991).

—, "O zapade, o Rossii, o sebe", *Vremya i mi* 142 (1999).

Andreyev, A. A., *Vospominania pisma* (Moscow, Izdatelstvo Politicheskoi Literaturi, 1985).

Andreyeva, O. V., *"Ya vsyo zhe zhiv..." Pisma, iz nevoli* (Moscow: Izdatelstvo MPI, 1990).

Andreyevsky G., *Moskva 20–30-ie godi* (Moscow: published by the author, 1998).

Antonov-Ovseyenko, A., *The Time of Stalin: Portrait of a Tyranny,* translated by George Saunders (New York: Harper and Row, 1981).

—, *Portret tirana* (Moscow: Gregori Peydzh, 1994).

—, *Teatr Iosifa Stalina* (Moscow: Gregori-Peydzh, 1995).

—, *Vragi naroda* (Moscow: Intellekt, 1996).

Arkomed, S. T., *Rabocheye dvizhenie i sotsial-demokratsia na Kavkaze* (Geneve: Chaulmontet, 1910).

Aronson, G., "Stalinsky protsess protiv Martova", *Sotsialistichesky Vestnik,* 7–8 (1939).

—, *Rossia nakanune revolyutsii. Istoricheskie etyudi* (Madrid: Planeta–LAN, 1986).

Aroseva, N., *Sled na zemlye* (Moscow: Izdatelstvo Politicheskoi Literaturi, 1987).

Aroseva, O. A. and V. A. Maksimova, *Bez grima* (Moscow: ZAO Izdatelstvo Tsentrpoligraf, 1999).

Arsenidze, R., "Iz vospominany o Staline", *Novy Zhurnal,* 72 (1963).

Artyom (F. A. Sergeyev), *Stati, rechi, pisma* (Moscow: Izdatelstvo Politicheskoi Literaturi, 1983).

Avalov, Z., *Nezavisimosti Gruzii v mezhdunarodnoi politike. 1918–1921 gg.* (New York: Chalidze Publications, 1982).

Avtorkhanov, A., *Tekhnologia vlasti. Process obrazovania KPSS. herki)* (Munich: Izdanie Tsentralnovo Obyeginenia Politicheskih Emigrantov iz SSSR, 1959).

—, *Stalin and the Soviet Communist Party: A Study in Technology of Power* (New York: Praeger, 1959).

—, *Proishozhdenie partokratii* I–II (Frankfurt-am-Main: Possev Verlag, 1973).

—, *Tekhnologia vlasti* (Frankfurt-am-Main: Possev Verlag, 1976).

—, *Zagadka smerti Stalina (Zagovor Beria)* (Frankfurt-am-Main: Possev Verlag, 1981).

Babichenko, D., " 'Literaturny front.' Istoria politicheskoi tsenzuri 1932–1946 gg. Sbornik dokumentov", in *Entsiklopedia rossiyskih dereven* (Moszkva, 1994).

Bagirov, M., *Iz istorii bolshevistskoi organizatsii Baku i Azerbajiana* (Moscow: OGIZ, 1948).

Bakhov, A. S., *Na zare sovietskoi diplomatii. Organi sovietskoi diplomatii v 1917–1922 gg.* (Moscow: Izdatelstvo Mezhdunarodnie Otnoshenia, 1966).

Banac, I., *With Stalin Against Tito: Cominformist Splits in Yugoslav Communism* (Ithaca: Cornell University Press, 1988).

Barbusse, H., *Stalin. A New World Seen through One Man* (New York: MacMillan, 1935).

—, *Stalin. Chelovek, cherez kotorovo rasskrivayetsya novy mir* (Moscow: Khudozhestvennaya Literatura, 1936).

Barmine, A., *One, Who Survived. The Life Story of a Russian under the Soviets* (New York: Putman, 1945).

—, *Sokoli Trotskovo* (Moscow: Sovremennik, 1997).

Batumskaya demonstratsia 1902 goda (Moscow: Partizdat, 1937).

Bazhanov, B., *Vospominania bivsevo sekretarya Stalina* (Paris–New York: Tretya Volna, 1983).

—, *Bazhanov and the Damnation of Stalin* (Athens: Ohio University Press, 1990).

Baykalov, A., "Moi vstrechi s Iosifom Dzhugashvili", *Vozrozhdenie,* 3–4 (1950).

Berezhkov, V., *At Stalin's side: his interpreter's memoirs from the October Revolution to the fall of the dictator's empire* (New York: Birch Lane Press, 1994).

—, *Ryadom so Stalinim* (Moscow: Vagrius, 1998).

Beria, L., *K voprosu ob istorii bolsevistskih organizatsii v Zakavkazye. Doklad na sobranii tbilisskovo partaktiva 21–22 iulya 1935 goda* (Moscow: Gosudarstvennoe Izdatelstvo Politicheskoi Literaturi, 1952).

Beria, S., *Moi otets – Lavrenty Beria* (Moscow: Sovremennik, 1994).

—, *Beria, My Father: Life Inside Stalin's Kremlin* (London: Duckworth, 2001).

Bernov, Y. and A. Manusevich, *V krakovskoi emigratsii. Zhizn I deyatelnoct V. I. Lenina v 1912–1914 gg.* (Moscow: Izdatelstvo Politicheskoi Literaturi, 1988).

Bezimensky, L., *Gitler i Stalin pered skhvatkoi* (Moscow: Veche, 2000).

—, *Operatsia "Mif", ili skolko raz khoronili Gitlera* (Moscow: Mezhdunarodnie Otnoshenia, 1995).

Bezirgani, G., "Koba i Kamo", *Perspektivi,* 6 (1991).

Bibineishvili, V., *Za chetverti veka* (Moscow: Molodaya Gvardia, 1931).

Bibliografia russkoi revolyutsii i grazhdanskoi voyni (1917–1921), edited by Postnikov, S. P. (Prague: Rusky Zakhranichni Historiky Arkhiv v Prahe, 1938).

Bil li Stalin agentom Okhranki? Sbornik statei, materialov i dokumentov, edited by Felstinsky, Y. (Moscow: Terra-Knizhny Klub, 1999).

Bistroletov, D., *Puteshestvie na kai nochi* (Moscow: Sovremennik, 1996).

Bobrenev, V. A. and V. B. Ryazantsev, *Palachi i zhertvi* (Moscow: Voennoe Izdatelstvo, 1993).

Bogdanova, N., *Moi otets, menshevik* (St. Petersburg: Nauchno-Informatsionny Tsentr Memoriala, 1994).

Bohlen, C., *Witness to History. 1929–1969* (New York: W. W. Norton & Co., 1973).

Boykov, M., *Lyudi sovietskoi tyurmi. Konveyer* I (Buenos Aires: Sembrador, 1957).

Bolsheviki. Dokumenti po istorii bolshevizma s 1903 do 1916 gg bivsevo Moskovskovo Okhrannovo Otdelenia (New York: Telex, 1990).

Bolshevistskaya fraktsia IV Gosudarstvennoi Dumi. Sbornik materialov i dokumentov, (Leningrad: Gosudarstvennoe Sotsialno-Ekonomicheskoe Izdatelstvo, Leningradskoe Otdelenie, 1938).

Bolshevistskoye rukovodstvo. Perepiska. 1912–1927 (Moscow: Rosspen, 1996).

Borin, A., *Zakon i sovest'. Za kulissami izvestnih sobity* (Moscow: Izdatelstvo Politicheskoi Literaturi, 1991).

Bourbina, M. and M. Jakobson eds., *Guide to the Boris I. Nicolaevsky Collection in the Hoover Institution Archives* (Stanford: The Hoover Institution on War, Revolution and Peace, 1989).

Bryukhanov, B. B. and Y. N. Shoshkov, *Opravdaniu ne podlezhit. Yezhov i yezhovshchina 1936–1938* (St. Petersburg: "PF", 1998).

Broido, V., *Lenin and the Mensheviks. The Persecution of Socialists under Bolshevism*, (Boulder, CO.: Westview Press, 1987).

Brutskus, B. D., *Sotsialisticheskoye khozyaistvo. Teoreticheskie misli po povodu russkovo opita* (Paris: Poiski, 1988).

Buber-Neumann, M., *Mirovaya revolyutsia i stalinsky rezhim. Zapiski ochevidtsa o deyatelnosti Kominterna v 1920–1930-h godah* (Moscow: AIRO-XX, 1995).

Budnitsky, O. V., *Terrorizm v rossyskom osvoboditelnom dvizhenii: ideologia, etika, psikhologia (vtoraya polovina XIX – nachalo XX veka)* (Moscow: Rosspen, 2000).

Bugai, N., *L. Beria – I. Stalinu. „Soglasno vashomu ukazaniu…"*, (Moscow: AIRO-XX, 1995).

Bugai, N. and A. Gonov, *Kavkaz: narodi v eselonah (20-60-je godi)* (Moszkva, Insan, 1998).

Bukharin, N., *Selected Writings on the State and the Transition on Socialism* (Armonk: M. E. Sharpe, 1982).

—, *Töprengések a szocilaizmusról* (Budapest: Kossuth Könyvkiadó, 1988).

Bukovsky, V., *Moskovsky protsess* (Paris–Moscow: Russkaya Misl–Izdatelstvo MIK, 1996).

Bulgakova, Y., *My Life with Mikhail Bulgakov* (New York: Ardis Publishers, 1983).

—, *Dnevnik Yeleny Bulgakovoi* (Moscow: Knizhnaya Palata, 1990).

Carev, O. and J. Costello, *Rokovie illyuzii. Iz arkhivov KGB: Delo Orlova, staliskovo mastera shpionazha* (Moscow: Mezhdunarodnie Otnoshenia, 1995).

Carr, E., *The Interregnum, 1923–1324* (New York: MacMillan, 1954).

Carrère d'Encausse, H., *Stalin: Order Through Terror* (New York: Longman, 1981).

Conquest, R., *The Great Terror. Stalin's Purge of the Thirties* (New York: The MacMillan, 1968).

—, *Bolshoi Terror* (Florenz: Edizioni Aurora, 1974).

—, *The Harvest of Sorrow: Soviet Collectivization and the Terror-Famine* (New York: Oxford University Press, 1986).

—, *Stalin and the Kirov Murder* (New York: Oxford University Press, 1989).

—, *Stalin: Breaker of Nations* (New York: Viking, 1991).

Chernenko, K., *I. V. Stalin v sibirskoi ssilke* (Krasnoyarsk: Kraevoe Izdatelstvo, 1942).

Chervakova, I., "Pesochnie chasi. Istoria zhizni Irini Gogua v vosmi kassetakh, pismakh I kommentariakh", *Druzhba Narodov*, 4 (1997).

Chkhalova, V., *Chkhalov bez grifa „Sekretno"* (Moscow: Poligrafresursi, 1999).

Chuyev, F., *Tak govoril Kaganovich* (Moscow: Otechestvo, 1992).

Chukhovsky, K., *Dnevnik. 1930–1969* (Moscow: Sovremenny Pisatel, 1995).

—, *Dnevnik. 1901–1929* (Moscow: Sovremenny Pisatel, 1997).

Churchill, W., *The Second World War* (Boston: Houghton Mifflin, 1986).

—, *A második világháború* (Budapest: Európa Könyvkiadó, 1989).

Dallin, D., *From Purge to Coexistence: Essays on Stalin's and Khrushchev's Russia* (Chicago: Henry Regnery, 1986).

Dambyan, T., "Rekviem po Yakovu Dzhugashvili", in *Razvedchiki i shpioni* (Moscow: Izdatelskj Dom XXI. Vek – Soglasie, 2000).

Daniels, R., *The Conscience of the Revolution: Communist Opposition in Soviet Russia* (Cambridge, Harvard University Press, 1960).

Dedijer, V., *The Battle Stalin Lost: Memoirs of Yugoslavia, 1948–1953* (New York: Viking, 1971).

Delo provokatora Malinovskovo (Moscow: Respublika, 1992).

Deportirovannie v Kazakhstan narodi. Vremya i sudba, edited by Anes, G. (Almati: n. p., 1998)

Deutscher, I., *Sztálin. Politikai életrajz* (Budapest: Európa Könyvkiadó, 1990).

—, *Stalin: A Political Biography* (London: Penguin Books, 1991)

—, *Russia in Transition and other Essays* (New York: Coward-McCann, 1957).

Deyateli SSSR i revolyutsionnovo dvizhenia Rossii (Moscow: Sovietskovo Entsiklopedia, 1989).

Djilas, M., Conversations with Stalin (San Diego: Harcourt, Brace and World, 1962).

—, *Találkozások Sztálinnal* (Budapest: Magvető Könyvkiadó, 1989).

—, *Litso Totalitarizma* (Moscow: Novosti, 1992).

Dirksen, H von, *Moscow – Tokyo – London. Twenty Years of German Foreign Policy* (Oklahoma: Norman, 1952).

Dombrovsky, Y., *Fakultet nenuzhnih veshchei* (Moscow: Sovietsky Pisatel, 1989).

—, *The Faculty of Useless Knowledge* (London: Harvill, 1997).

Drugaya voyna 1939–1945 (Moscow, Rossyszky Gosudarstvenny Gumanitarny Universitet, 1996).

Dubinsky-Mukhadze, I. M., *Ordzhonikidze* (Moscow: Molodaya Gvardia, 1963).

—, *Saumyan* (Moscow: Molodaya Gvardia, 1965).

Dumyatsky, J., "Za polyarnim krugom", *Komsomolskaya Pravda*, 1929, XII, 21.

Dvinov, B., *Ot legalnosti k podpolyu (1921–1922)* (Stanford: The Hoover Institution of War, Revolution and Peace, Stanford University, 1968).

Dyakova, Y. L. and T. S. Bushuyeva, *Fashistsky mech kovalsya v SSSR. Krasnaya Armia i Reyhsver. Taynoye strudnichestvo. 1922–1933. Neizvestnie dokumenti (Moscow: Sovietskaya Rossia, 1992).*

Dzhugashvili, G., *"Ded, papa, mama i drugie"*, Druzhba Narodov, 1993, 6.

Eastman, M., *Stalin's Russia and the Crisis in Socialism* (New York: W. W. Norton & Co., 1940).

Ekonomicheskaya kontr-revolyutsia v Donbasse. (Itogi sakhtinskovo dela) (Moscow: Yuridicheskoye Izdatelstvo NKJU RSFSR, 1928).

Elwood, R., *Roman Malinovsky: A Life without a Cause* (Newtonville: Oriental Research Partners, 1977).

—, *Inessa Armand. Revolutionary and Feminist* (Cambridge University Press, 1992).

Enver, H., *With Stalin: Memoirs 8* (Tirana: Nentori, 1981).

Esaiashvili, V., *Perepiska gruzinskih kommunistov s V. V. Leninim* (Tbilisi: Sabchota Sakartvelo, 1966).

Fainsod, M., *How Russia is Rules* (Cambridge: Harvard University Press, 1963).

Felstinsky, Y., *K istorii nashei zakritosti* (London: Overseas Publications Interchange, 1988).

—, *Razgovori s Bukharinom* (New York: Telex, 1991).

Fesenko, A. and T. Fesenko, *Russky yazik pri sovietakh* (New York: Published by the authors, 1955).

Frunze, M. V., *Neizvestnoye i zabitoye* (Moscow: Nauka, 1991).

Galagan, L. and D. Trifonova, *Kremlyovskie deti* (Moscow: Lirius, 1995).

Gavrilovich, i., *Ocherki po istorii viborgskoi partorganizatsii gor. Leningrada* (Leningrad: Lenpartizdat, 1933).

Gefter, M., *Iz tekh i etikh let* (Moscow: Progress, 1991).
Geifman, A., *Revolyutsionny terror v Rossii. 1894–1917* (Moscow: Kron Press, 1997).
—, *Russia under the Last Tsar: Opposition and Subversion 1897–1917* (Oxford: Blackwell, 1999).
Geller, M., *Mashina I vintiki. Istoria formirovania sovietskovo cheloveka* (London: Overseas Publication Interchange, 1985).
Genrikh Yagoda. Narkom vnutrennikh del SSSR, generalny sekretar gosudarstvennoi bezopasnosti. Sbornik dokumentov (Kazan': n.p., 1997).
Gereben, Á., *Művészet és hatalom. Orosz írók a XX. Században* (Budapest: Akadémiai Kiadó, 1998).
—, *Antiszemitizmus a Szovjetunióban* (Budapest: PolgArt, 2000).
Girenko, Y., *Stalin – Tito* (Moscow: Izdatelstvo Politicheskoi Literaturi, 1991).
Ginzburg, Y., *Krutoi marshut* (New York: Possev–USA, 1985).
Gnegin, J. A., *Katastrofa i vtoroye rozhdenie* (Amsterdam: Izdatelstvo Fonda Imeni Gercena, 1977).
—, *Vikhod iz labirinta* (Moscow: Memorial, 1994)
Golubovich, V., "Stalin v godi solvichegodskoi i vologdskoi ssilok", *Istorik Marksist,* 1 (1940).
Gorelov, O., *Zugzvang Mikhaila Tomskovo* (Moscow: Rosspen, 2000).
Gorlov, S., *Sovershenno sekretno: alyans Moskva–Berlin. 1920–1933 gg. (Voyenno-politicheskie otnoshenia SSSR-Germania)* (Moscow: Olma-Press, 2001).
Gribanov, S., *Khronika vremyon Vasilia Stalina* (Moscow: Geya Iterum, 1999).
Gromov, Y., *Stalin. Vlast i iskusstvo* (Moscow: Izdatelstvo Respublika, 1998).
Gronsky, I., *Iz proshlovo… Vospominania* (Moscow: Izvestia, 1991).
Grunt, Y., *Godi borbi* (Moscow: Izdatelstvo Vsesoyuznovo Obshchestvo Politkatorzhan I ssilno-poselentsev, 1933).
Holmes, L., *Stalin's School. Moscow's Model School No. 25. 1931–1937* (Pittsburg: University of Pittsburg Press, 1999).

Iosif Stalin v obyatiakh semyi. Iz lichnovo arkhiva (Moscow: Rodina, 1993).
Iosif Vissarionovich Stalin. Kratkaya biografia (Moscow: Gosudarstvennoye Izdatelstvo Politicheskoi Literaturi, 1951).
Iremaschwili, J., *Stalin und die Tragödie Georgiens* (Berlin: Volksblatt-Druckerei, 1932).
Ivanova, G., *GULAG v sisteme totalitarnovo gosudartsva* (Moscow: MONF, 1997).
Ivanova, L., *Vospominania. Kniga ob ottse* (Paris: Atheneum, 1990).
Ivanov-Razumnik, R. V. *Tyurmi i ssilki* (New York: Izdatelstvo imeni Chekhova, 1953).
Ivinskaya, O., *V plenu vremeni. Godi Borissom Pasternakom* (Paris: Fayard, 1978).
Iz arkhiva L. O. Dan (Amsterdam: Stichting Internationaal Instituut voor Sociale Seschiedenis, 1987).
"Iz perepiski CK RSDRP (1912–1914 gg.)", *Istorichesky Arkhiv,* 2 (1960).

Kahan, S. *The Wolf of the Kremlin* (New York: William Morrow & Co., 1987).
Kalendar spravochnik (Moscow: OGIZ–Sotsialno-Ekonomicheskoye Izdatelstvo, 1941).
Kamenev, Y., *Ob A. I. Gertsene i N. G. Chernishevskom* (Petrograd: Knigoizdatelstvo „Zizn i Znaniye", 1916).
Kaminsky, V. and I. Vereshchagin, "Detstvo i yunosti vozhdya", *Molodaya Gvardia,* 12 (1939).
Kan, A. *Nikolai Bucharin und die skandinavische Arbeiterbewegung* (Mainz: Decaton Verlag, 1993).
Kanel, N., "Vstrecha na Lubyanke", in *Dodnes tyagoteyet* (Moscow: Sovietsky Pisatel, 1989).
Kapitsa, P., *Pisma o nauke. 1930–1980* (Moscow: Moskovky Rabochy, 1989).
Karyagin, V., *Diplomaticheskaya zhizn za kulissami i na stsene* (Moscow: Mezhdunarodnie Otnoshenia, 1994).
Kemp-Welch, A., *Stalin and the Literary Intelligentsia, 1928–39* (New York: St. Martin's Press, 1991).
Ken, O. N. and A. I. Rupasov, *Politburo CKVKP (b) I otnoshenia SSSR s zapadnimi sosednimi gosudarstvami (konets 1920–1930-kh gg.)* (St. Petersburg: Evropeisky Dom, 2000).
Kennan, G., *Russia and the West under Lenin and Stalin* (Boston: Little, Brown & Co., 1961).
Khlevniuk, O., *Stalin i Ordzhonikidze. Konflikti v Politbyuro v 30-ye godi* (Moscow: Rossia Molodaya, 1993).
—, *In Stalin's Shadow: The Career of "Sergo Ordzhonikidze,* translated by David Nordlander (Armonk: M. E. Sharpe, 1995).
—, *Politburo. Mekhanizmi politicheskoi vlasti v 1930-ye godi* (Moscow: Rosspen, 1996).
Khorkodina, T., *Istoria otechestva i arkhivi 1917–198-ye gg* (Moscow: RGGU, 1994).
Khrabrovitsky, A., "A. I. Kuprin v 1937 godu", *Minuvsheye,* 5 (1988).
Khrushchev, Nikita, *Vospominania. Izbrannie fragmenti* (Moscow: Vagrius, 1997).
Khrushchev o Staline (New York: Telex, 1989).
King, D., *The Commissar Vanishes: The Falsification of Phootographs and Art in Stalin's Russia* (New York: Metropolitan Books, 1997).
—, *Retusált történelem* (Budapest: PolgArt, 1997).
Kirilina, A., *Rikoshet ili skolko chelovek bilo ubito vistrelom v Smolnom* (St. Petersburg: Znanie, 1993).
Kislitsin, S. A., *Variant Sirtsova. Iz istorii formirovania soprotivlenia v sovietskom obshchestve v 20–30-e godi* (Rostov-on-Don: published by the author, 1992).
Knight, A., *Beria. Stalin's First Lieutenant* (Princeton: Princeton University Press, 1993).
—, *Who Killed Kirov? The Kremlin's Greatest Mistery* (New York: Hill and Wang, 1999).
Knishevsky, P., *Dobicha. Tayni germanskikh reparatsii* (Moscow: Soratnik, 1994).
Koch, S., *Double Lives: Spies and Writers in the Secret Soviet War of Ideas Against the West* (New York: Free Press, 1994).
—, *Kettős szerepben. Az értelmiség elcsábítása* (Budapest: XX. Század Intézet, 2000).
Kollektivizatsia i krestyanskoye soproteivlenie na Ukraine (noyabr 1929-mart 1930 gg) (Vinnitsa: Logos, 1997).
Konchalovsky-Mikhalov, A. and A. Lipkov, *The Inner Circle: An Inside View of Soviet Life under Stalin* (New York: Newmarket, 1991).
Korolyov, Y., *Kremlyovsky sovietnik* (Moscow: Olimp, 1995).
Korshunov, M. and Terekhova, V., *Tayna tayn moskovskikh* (Moscow: Slovo, 1995).
Korzhikhina, T., *Izvolte bit blagonadozhni!* (Moscow: Rossysky Gosudarstvenny Gumanitarny Universitet, 1997).
Kostishin, D. N., " 'Nebolshoye pismetsa' iz gromadnoi fabriki lzhi (k istorii falsifitsirovannoi perepiski Lenina so Stalinim)", *Kentaur* 5–6 (Kentaur).
Kostiuk, H., *Stalinist Rule in the Ukraine: A Study of the Decade of Mass Terror* (New York: Praeger, 1961).
Kostirchenko, G., V *Plenu u krasnovo faraona. Politicheskoye presledovanie yevreyev v SSSR v posledneye stalinskoye desyatiletie. Dokumentalnoye issledovanie* (Moscow: Mezhdunarodnoye Otnoshenie, 1994).
—, *Taynaya Politika Stalina* (Moscow: Mezhdunarodnoye Otnoshenie, 2001).
Kot, S., *Conversations with the Kremlin and Dispatches from Russia* (London: Oxford University Press, 1963).
Kotelenets, Y. A., *V. I. Lenin kak predmet istoricheskovo issledovania* (Moscow: Izdatelstvo Rossyskovo Universiteta Druzhbi Narodov, 1999).
Kravchenko, V., *I Choose Freedom. The Personal and Political Life of a Soviet Official,* (New York: Charles Scribner's Son, 1946).
Krawchenko, B., *Social Change and National Consciousness in Twentieth-Century Ukraine* (London: MacMillan, 1985).
Krestanskie istorii: rossyskaya derevnya 1920-kh godov v pismakh i dokumentakh, edited by Kryukov, S. S. (Moscow: Rosspen, 2001).

Kristof, L., "B. I. Nicolaevsky. The Formative Years. Revolution and Politics in Russia", in *Essays in Memory of B. I. Nicolaevsky* (Bloomington: Indiana University Press, 1972).

Krivitsky, V., *Ya bil agentom Stalina* (Moscow: Sovremennik, 1996).

Krotkov, Y., *The Red Monarch: Scenes form the Life of Stalin* (New York: W. W. Norton & Co., 1979).

Kumanev, G., *Ryadom so Stalinim: otkrovennie svigetelstva* (Moscow: Bilina, 1999).

Kumanev B. and I. Kulikova, *Protivostoyanie: Krupskaya–Stalin* (Moscow: Nauka, 1994).

Kun, M., *Bukharin. Yevo druzya i vragi* (Moscow: Izdatelstvo Respublika, 1992).

—, " 'Szóltak nekem, hogy én fogok tolmácsolni Sztálinnak...' Beszélgetés Oleg Trojanovszkijjal", *Kritika*, 4 (1997).

Kuusinen, A., *Before and after Stalin: A Personal Account of Soviet Russia from the 1920s to the 1960s* (London: Joseph, 1974).

Lakoba, N., *Stalin i Hashim (1901–1902 gg.) Nekotorie epizodi iz batumskovo podpolya* (Sukhum: Abkhazkoye Partynoye Izdatelstvo, 1934).

Larin, Y., *Za neprerivnoye proizvodstvo* (Moscow: Molodaya Gvardia, 1989).

Larina, A. (Bukharina), *Nezabivayemoye* (Moscow: Izdatelstvo APN, 1989).

—, *This I Cannot Forget: The Memoirs of Nikolai Bukharin's Widow* (New York: W. W. Norton and Co., 1993).

Lavrenty Beria. 1953. Stenogramma iyulskovo plenuma CK KPSZSZ i drugiye dokumenti (Moscow: Mezhdunarodny Fond Demokratsia, 1999).

Lebina, N. B., *Povsednevnaya zhizn sovietskovo goroda: normi I anomalii. 1920/1930 godi* (St. Petersburg: Izdatelstvo Kikimora, 1999).

Ledovsky, A. M., *SSSR i Stalin v sudbakh Kitaya* (Moscow: Pamyatniki Istoricheskoi Misli, 1999).

Leggett, G., *The Cheka: Lenin's Political Police* (Oxford: Clarendon, 1981).

Lemeshev, S., *Put k iskusstvu* (Moscow: Iskusstvo, 1968).

Lenin, V. I., *Biograficheskaya khronika,* II (Moscow: Izdatelstvo Politicheskoi Literaturi, 1971).

—, *Biograficheskaya khronika,* X (Moscow: Izdatelstvo Politicheskoi Literaturi, 1975).

—, *Biograficheskaya khronika,* XI (Moscow: Izdatelstvo Politicheskoi Literaturi, 1976).

—, *Biograficheskaya khronika,* XII (Moscow: Izdatelstvo Politicheskoi Literaturi, 1982).

—, *Polnoye sobranie sochineny,* 48 (Moscow: Izdatelstvo Politicheskoi Literaturi, 1965).

—, *Neizvestnie dokumenti 1891–1922* (Moscow: Rosspen, 1999).

"Leningradskoye delo", edited by Demidov, V. I. and V. A. Kutuzov (St. Petersburg: Lenizdat, 1990).

Leonhard, W., *Child of the Revolution* (London: Overseas Publications Interchange, 1984).

—, *Betrayal of the Hitler–Stalin Pact* (London: Overseas Publications Interchange, 1989).

Levine, I., *Stalin* (New York: Cosmopolitan Book Corporation, 1931).

—, *Life of Stalin: A Symposium* (New York: Worker's Library Publishers, 1930).

Likhachev, D., *Vospominania* (St. Petersburg: Logos, 1997).

—, *Reflections on the Russian Soul: A Memoir* (Budapest: Central European University Press, 2000).

Litvin, A. L., *Krasny i bely terror v Rossii. 1918–1922 gg.* (Kazan: Tatarskoye Gazeto-zhurnalnoye Izdatelstvo, 1995).

Loginov, V., *Teni Stalina. General Vlasik i yevo soratniki* (Moscow: Sovremennik, 1999).

—, *Lubyanka 2. Iz istorii otechestvennoi kontr-razvedki* (Moscow: Izdatelstvo Obyedinenia Mosgorarkhiv, 1999).

Ludwig, E., *Stalin* (New York: Putnam, 1942).

Lunacharsky, A., *Revolutionary Silhouettes,* translated by Glenny, M. (New York: Hill and Wang, 1968).

—, *Emlékképek* (Budapest: Kossuth Könyvkiadó, 1988).

Lyons, E., *Moscow Carrousel* (New York: Alfred A. Knopf, 1935).

—, *Assigment in Utopia* (New York: Harcourt, Brace and Company, 1937).

—, *Stalin, Czar of All the Russians* (Philadelphia: J. B. Lippincott, 1940).

Makharadze, F., *Ocherki revolyutsionnovo dvizhenia v Zakavkazye* (Tiflis: Gosizdat Gruzii, 1927).

Maksimenkov, L., *Sumbur vmesto muziki. Stalinskaya kulturnaya revolyutsia 1936–1938* (Moscow: Yuridicheskaya Kniga, 1997).

Maryamov, G., *Kremlyovsky tsenzor. Stalin smotrit kino* (Moscow: Konfederatsia Soyuzov Kinematografistov, Kinotsentr, 1992).

Martov, O., *Pisma. 1916–1922* (New York: Chalidze Publications, 1990).

Maser, W., *Der Wortbuch. Hitler, Stalin und Zweite Weltkrieg* (Munich: Olzog Verlag, 1994).

McNeal, R., *Stalin's Works: An Annotated Bibliography* (Stanford: The Hoover Institution on War, Revolution and Peace, 1967).

—, *Stalin: Man and Ruler* (New York: New York University Press, 1988).

Menshagin, B., *Vospominania. Smolensk... Katyń ... Vladimirskaya tyurma...* (Paris: YMCA-Press, 1988).

MCHK. Iz istorii moskovskoi chrezvichaynoi komissii 1918–1921, edited by Alidin, V. I. (Moscow: Moskovsky Rabochy, 1978).

Menshikov, M. A., *S vintovkoi i v frake* (Moscow: Mezhdunarodnie Otnoshenia, 1996).

Meretskov, K., *Na sluzhbe narodu* (Moscow: Voyenizdat, 1968).

—, *Serving the People,* translated by Devid Fidlon (Moscow: Progress Publishers, 1971).

Merridale, C., *Moscow Politics and the Rise of Stalin: The Communist Party in the Capital, 1925–1932* (New York: St. Martin, 1990).

Mikoyan, A. I., *Tak bilo. Razmishlenia o minuvshem* (Moscow: Vagrius, 1999).

Mikoyan, N., *S lyubovyu i pechalyu (Vospominania)* (Moscow: Terra-Knizhny Klub, 1998).

Moyseyev, I., *Ja Vospominayu... Gastrol dlinnoyu v zhizni* (Moscow: Soglasie, 1996).

Moshentseva, P., *Tayni kremlyovskoi bolnitsi* (Moscow: Kollektsia „Sovershenno sekretno", 1998).

Moskalev, M., *Russkoye Buro CK Bolshevistskoi Partii. 1912-mart 1917* (Moscow: OGIZ-Gospolitizdat, 1947).

Nakanune voyni. Materiali soveshchania visshevo rukovodyashchevo sostava RKKA 23–31 dekabrya 1940 g., edited by Zolotaryov, V. A. (Moscow: Terra, 1993).

Narimskaya khronika. 1930–1945. Tragedia Spetspereselentsev. Dokumenti i vospominania, (Moscow: Russky Put', 1997).

Narimskaya ssilka. 1906-1917. Sbornik dokumentov i materialov o ssilnikh bolshevikakh (Zapadno-Sibirskoye Knigoizdatelstvo, Tomskoye Otdelenie, 1977).

Nepravedny sud. Posledny Stalinsky rasstrel, edited by Naumov, V. (Moscow: Nauka, 1994).

NKVD i polskoye podpolye 1944–1945. (Po osobim papkam I. V. Stalina) (Moscow: Institut Slavyanovedenia i Balkanistiki—RAN, 1994).

Neizvestny Bogdanov. A. A. Bogdanov i gruppa RSZDRP „Vperyod". 1908–1914 gg., (Moscow: IC Airo-XX., 1995), II.

Nekrasov, N. F., *Beria: Konets Karyeri* (Moscow: Izdatelstvo Politicheskoi Literaturi, 1991).

Nekrasov, V., *Trinadtsat „zeleznikh" narkomov. Istoria NKVD–MVD ot A. I. Rikva do N. A. Shcholokova. 1917–1982* (Moscow: Izdatelstvo Versti, Gosudarstvennaya Firma Poligrafresursi, 1995).

Nenarokov, A. P., *Vostochny front 1918* (Moscow: Nauka, 1969).

Nicolaevsky, B. *Power and the Soviet Elite: "The Letter of an Old Bolshevik" and Other Essays* (New York: Praeger Publishers, 1965).
—, *Taynie stranitsi istorii* (Moscow: Izdatelstvo Gumanitarnoi Literaturi, 1995).

Okunevskaya, T., *Tatyanin den* (Moscow: Vagrius, 1994).
Olitskaya, Y., *Moi vospominania* I–II (Frankurt am Main: Possev Verlag, 1971).
Ordzhonikidze, Z., *Put bolshevika. Stranitsi iz zhizni G. K. Ordzhonikidze* (Moscow: Izdatelstvo Politicheskoi Literaturi, 1967).
Orlov, A., *The Secret History of Stalin's Crimes* (New York: Random House, 1953).
—, *Taynaya istoria stalinskikh prestupleny* (Moscow: Izdatelstvo Vremya i Mi, 1983).
Ormos, M., *Hitler* (Budapest: Polgár Könyvkiadó, 1997).
Ortenberg, D., *Stalin, Shcherbakov, Mekhlis i drugie* (Moscow: MP Kodeks, Obyedinnyonnaya Redaktsia MVD Rosszii, 1995).
O Sergo Ordzhonikidze, edited by Seyranan (Moscow: Izdatelstvo Politicheskoi Literaturi, 1986).
Osokina, E. A., *Ierarkhia potreblenia. O zhizni lyudei v usloviakh stalinskovo snabzhenia. 1928–935 (Moscow: Izdatelstvo MGU, 1993).*
Ostrovsky, A., "Rodstvennie svyazi pervoi zheni Stalina", *Iz Glubini Vremyon*, 1997, 7.
—, "Predki Stalina", *Genealogichesky Zhurnal*, 1 (2001).
—, *Kto stoyal za spinoi Stalina?* (St. Petersburg: "Neva" and Moscow: Olma, 2002).

Pavlova, I. O., *Stalinizm: stanovlenie mekhanizma vlasti* (Novosibirsk: Sibirsky Khronograf, 1993).
—, *Mekhanizm vlasti i stroitelstvo stalinskovo sotsializma* (Novosibirsk: Khronograf, 1993).
Payne, R., *The Rise and Fall of Stalin* (New York: Simon & Schuster, 1965).
Pervoye sovietskoye pravitelstvo. Oktyabr 1917–iyul 1918 (Moscow: Izdatelstvo Politicheskoi Literaturi, 1991).
Petrov, N. V. and K. V. Skorkin, *Kto rukovodil NKVD. 1934–1941. Spravochnik* (Moscow: Zvenya, 1999).
Petrus, K., *Uzniki kommunizma* (New York: Izdatelstvo imeni Chekhova, 1953).
Pikhoya, R., *Sovietsky Soyuz: istoria vlasti 1945-1991* (Moscow: RAGSZ, 1998).
Pipes, R., *Formation of the Soviet Union: Communism and Nationalism 1917–1923* (Cambridge: Harvard University Press, 1964).
— ed., *Revolutionary Russia* (Cambridge: Harvard University Press, 1968).
—, *Russia Observed: Collected Essays on Russian and Soviet History* (Boulder: Westview, 1989).
Pisma I. V. Stalina V. M. Molotovu 1925–1936 gg., Sbornik dokumentov (Moscow: Rossia Molodaya, 1995).
Politburo i tserkov 1922–1925 gg., edited by Petrovky, N. (Novosibirsk–Moscow: Sibirsky Khronograf–Rosspen, 1997).
Pomper, P., *Lenin, Trotsky and Stalin. The Intelligentsia and Power* (New York: Columbia University Press, 1990).
Popova (Cederbaum), T., *Sudyba rodnikh I. Martova v Rossii posle 1917 goda* (Moscow: ZAO IC Zhurnala Rossia Molodaya, 1996).
Prazhskaya konferentsia RSDRP. Stati i dokumenti (Moscow: Partizdat CK VKP /b/, 1937).
Pribitkov, V., *Apparat* (St. Petersburg: VIS, 1995).
Protokoli soveshchania rasshirennoi redaktsii Proletaria. Iyun 1909 g. (Moscow: Partizdat, 1934).
Prut, I., *Nepoddayushchysya. O mnogikh drugikh I koe-chto o sebe* (Moscow: Vagrius, 2000).

Radek, K., *Portreti i pamfleti* (Moscow: Sovietskaya Literatura, 1933).
—, *Portraits and Pamphlets* (New York: Robert M. McBridge, 1934).
Rancour-Leferrière, D., *Psikhika Stalina* (Moscow: Progress-Akademia, 1966).
—, *The Mind of Stalin: A Psychoanalytic Study* (New York: Ardis Publishers, 1988).
Randall, F., *Stalin's Russia: An Historical Consideration* (New York: Free Press, 1965).
Rapoport, L., *Stalin's War Against the Jews: The Doctor's Plot and the Soviet Solution* (New York: Free Press, 1990).
Rasskazi starikh rabochikh Zakavkazya o velikom Staline (Moscow: Molodaya Gvardia, 1937).
Rasstrelnie spiski, Moskva, 1937–1941 (Moscow: Obshchestvo Memorial–Izdatelstvo Zvenya, 2000).
Razgon, L., *Nepridumannoye. Povest v rasskazakh* (Moscow: Slovo, 1991).
Reabilitacia: Kak eto bilo. Dokumenti prezidiuma CK KPSS i drugie materiali. Mart 1953.–fevral 1956 (Moscow: Mezhdunarodny Fond Demokratia, 2000), I.
Redlich, S., *Propaganda and Nationalism in Wartime Russia: The Jewish Anti-fascist Committee in the USSR. 1941–1918.* (Boulder: East European Monographs, 1982).
Reiman, M., *The Birth of Stalinism: The USSR on the Eve of the "Second Revolution"* (Bloomington: Indiana University Press, 1987).
Repressii protiv polyakov i polskikh grazhdan (Moscow: Zvenya, 1997).
Revvoyensoviet respubliki. 6 sentyabrya 1918 g.–28 avgusta 1923 g., edited by Nenarokov, A. P. (Moscow: Izdatelstvo Politicheskoi Literaturi, 1991).
Ribalkin, Y., *Sovietskaya voyennaya pomoshch respublikanskai Ispanii (1936–1939)* (Moscow: Liro-XX, 2000).
Richardson, R., *The Long Shadow. Inside Stalin's Family* (London: Little, Brown and Co., 1993).
Rieber, A., "Stalin, Man of the Borderlands", *The American Historical Review*, 106 (2001).
Rikov, A. I., *Izbrannie Proizvedenia* (Moscow: Ekonomika, 1990).
Rogov, A., "Na revolyutsionnoi rabote v Baku", *Katorga i ssilka*, 1927, 6.
Romanovsky, N., *Liki stalinizma. 1943–1945* (Moscow: n.p., 1995).
Rosenfeldt, N., *Knowledge and Power. The Role of Stalin's Secret Chancellery in the Soviet System of Government* (Coppenhagen: Rosenkilde and Bagger, 1978).
—, *Stalin's Special Departments: A Comparative Analysis of Key Sources* (Copenhagen: Institute of Slavonic and East European Studies, 1989).
Roslyakov, M., *Ubystvo Kirova. Politicheskie i ugolovnie presztuplenia v 1930-h godakh* (St. Petersburg: Lenizdat, 1991).
Rozanov, M., *Zavoyevateli belikh pyaten* (Frankfurt-am-Main: Possev Verlag, 1951).
Rozental, I., *Provokator Roman Malinovsky. Sugba i vremya* (Moscow: Rosspen, 1996).
Rubtsov, Y., *Alter ego* Stalina (Moscow: Zvonnitsa-MG, 1999).
Runin, B., *Moyo okruzhenie. Zapiski utselevsevo* (Mocow: Vozvraschenie, 1995).
Russky Berlin. 1921–1923 (Paris: YMCA-Press, 1983).

Sabsovich, L. M., *SSSR cherez 15 let* (Moscow: Izdatelstvo Planovoye Khozyaistvo, Gosplan SSSR, 1929).
Salisbury, H., *900 dney. Blokada Leningrada* (New York: Harper & Row Publishers, 1969).
—, *Moscow Journal: The End of Stalin* (Chicago: Chicago University Press, 1975).
Samoylov, F., *Po sledam minuvshevo. Vospominania starovo bolshevika* (Moscow: Izdatelstvo Stary Bolshevik, 1934).
Sekreti Gitlera na stole u Stalina. Razvedka i kontrrazvedka o podgotovke germanskoy agressii protiv SSSR. Mart-ijuny 1941 g. (Moscow: Mosgorarkhiv, 1995).
Semyonov, J., "Teoreticheskaya razrabotka V. I. Leninim natsionalnovo voprosa", *Narodi Azii i Afriki*, 4 (1960).
Serebyakov, G., *Smerch* (Moscow: Izd. DOSAAF SSR, 1989).
Sharagin, (Ozerov) A., *Tupolyevskaya saraga* (Frankfurt-am-Main: Possev Verlag, 1971).

Shatunovskaya, L., *Zhizn v Kremle* (New York: Chalidze Publications, 1982).
Shepilov, D., *Neprimknuvshy* (Moscow: Vagrius, 2001).
Shrayer-Petrov, D., *Druzya i teni* (New York: Liberty, 1989).
Shreyder, M., *NKVD iznutri. Zapiski chekista* (Moscow: Vozvrashchenie, 1995).
Shweitzer, V., *Stalin v turukhanskoi ssilke* (Moscow: Moldaya Gvardia, 1943).
Sirotinsky, S., *Mikhail Sergeyevich Frunze* (Moscow: Izdatelstvo Voyenny Vestnik, 1928).
Sistema ispravitelno-tudovikh lagerei v SSSR. 1923–1960 (Moscow: Zvenya, 1998).
Sitz, I., *Dnevnik „velikovo pereloma" (mart 1928–avgust 1931)* (Paris: YMCA Press, 1991).
Skoryatin, V., *Tayna gibeli Vladimira Mayakovskovo* (Moscow: Zvonnitsa-MG, 1998).
Skryabina, Y. *Stranitsi zhizni* (Moscow: Izdatelstvo Progress-Akademia, 1994).
Slavko, T., *Kulatzkaya Ssilka na Urale. 1930–1936* (Moscow: Mosgorarkhiv, 1995).
Slusser, R., *Stalin in October: The Man Who Missed the Revolution* (Baltimore: Johns Hopkins University Press, 1987).
Smirnov, N., *Vplot do visshei meri* (Moscow: Moskovsky Rabochy, 1997).
Smith, E., *The Young Stalin. The Early Years of an Elusive Revolutionary* (New York: Farrar, Straus and Giroux, 1967).
Sofinov, P., "Permskaya katastrofa i likvidatsia yeyo posledstvy", *Istoricheskie Zapiski,* 30 (1919).
Solomon, G., *Sredi krasnikh vozhdei* (Moscow: Sovremennik–Rossinform, 1995).
Solonevich, I., *Rossia v kontslagere* (Moscow: Redaktsia zhurnala Moskva, 1999).
Solovyov, A., "Tetradi krasnovo professora. 1912–1941", in *Neizvestnaya Rossia* (Moscow: Mosgorarkhiv, 1994), 4.
Solovyov, M., *Zapiski sovietskovo voyennovo korrespondenta* (New York: Izdatelstvo imeni Chekhova, 1954).
—, *Kogda bogi molchat* (n.p.: published by the author, 1963–1964).
Sopelnyak, B., *Smert v rassrochku* (Moscow: Izdatelstvo Geya, 1998).
Sotman, A., *Kak iz iskri vozgorelos plamya* (St. Petersburg: Molodaya Gvardia, 1935).
Souvarine, B., *Stalin. A Critical Survey of Bolshevism* (New York: Longmans, Green & Co., 1939).
Soviet Narodnikh Komissarov SSSR. Soviet Ministrov SSSR. Kabinet Ministrov SSSR 1923 1991. Entsiklopedichesky spravochnik (Moscow: Izdatelstvo Obyedinenia Mosgorarkhiv, 1999).
Sovietskoye rukovodstv. Perepiska 1928–1941 (Moscow: Rosspen, 1999).
Spassky, A., *Tretya armia* (Perm: Permizdat, 1958).
Spiridovich, *A. I., Istoria bolshevizma v Rossii, ot vozniknovenia do zakhvata vlasti. 1883–1903–1917.* (New York: Orfej, 1986).
Stalin, I. V., *Sochinenia,* I (Moscow: Gosudarstvennoye Izdatelstvo Politicheskoi Literaturi, 1946).
—, *Sochinenia,* II (Moscow: Gosudarstvennoye Izdatelstvo Politicheskoi Literaturi, 1946).
—, *Sochinenia,* III (Moscow: Gosudarstvennoue Izdatelstvo Politicheskoi Literaturi, 1946).
—, *Sochinenia,* IV (Moscow: Gosudarstvennoye Izdatelstvo Politicheskoi Literaturi, 1947).
—, *Sochinenia,* VIII (Moscow: Gosudarstvennoye Izdatelstvo Politicheskoi Literaturi, 1948).
—, *Sochinenia,* XIII (Moscow: Gosudarstvennoye Izdatelstvo Politicheskoi Literaturi, 1951).
—, *Sochinenia,* I (XIV) (Stanford: The Hoover Institution on War, Revolution and Peace, 1967).
—, *Sochinenia,* II (XV) (Stanford: The Hoover Institution on War, Revolution and Peace, 1967).
Stalin and His Generals: Soviet Military Memoirs of World War II (New York: Pegasus, 1969).
Stalin and Stalinism, edited by Dallin, A. and B. Patenaude (New York: Garland, 1992).
Stalinism: Its Impact on Russia and the World, edited by Urban, G. R. (Cambridge: Harvard University Press, 1986)
Stalinism: Its Nature and Aftermath: Essays in Honor of Moshe Lewin (Armonk: M. E. Sharpe, 1992).
Stalin v vospominniakh sovremennikov i dokumentakh epokhi, edited by Lobanov, M. (Moscow: Novaya Kniga, 1995).
Stalin. Sbornik statei k pyatidesyatiletiu so dnya rozhdenia (Moscow–Leningrad: Gosudarstvennoe Izdatelstvo, 1930).
Stalinskoye Politburo v 30-ye godi. Sbornik dokumentov (Moscow: AIRO-XX, 1995).
Starkov, B., *Dela i lyudi stalinskovo vremeni* (St. Petersburg: Izdatelstvo Sankt-peterburgskovo Universiteta Ekonomiki i Finansov, 1995).
Sto sorok besed s Molotovim. Iz dnevnika Feliksa Chuyeva (Moscow: Terra, 1991).
Stolyarov, K., *Palachi i zhertvi* (Moscow: Olma-Press, 1997).
Stopani, A., *Iz proshlovo. Stati i vospominania iz istorii bakinskoi organizacii i rabochevo dvizhenia v Baku* (Baku: Gosizdat, 1923).
Strick-Strickfeldt, W., *Against Stalin and Hitler: Memoir of the Russian Liberation Movement, 1941–1945,* translated by David Footman (London: MacMillan, 1970).
—, *Protiv Stalina i Gitlera. General Vlasov i Russkoye Osovoboditelnoye Dvizheniye* (Frankfurt-am-Main: Possev Verlag, 1975).
Sudoplatov, P., *Spetsoperacii. Lubyanka i Kreml* (Moscow: Kollekcia „Soversenno sekretno", 2001).
Sukhomlinov, A., *Vasily, sin Vozhdya* (Moscow: Kollekcia „Soversenno Sekretno", 2001).
Suny, R., "A Journeyman for the Revolution: Stalin and the Labour Movement in Baku, June 1907–May 1908", *Soviet Studies,* 3 (1972).
Suvenirov, O., *Tragedia RKKA 1937–1938* (Moscow: Terra, 1998).
Sverdlov, Y., *Izbrannie proizvedenia,* I (Moscow: Gosudarstvennoye Izdatelstvo Politicheskoi Literaturi, 1957).

Talakvadze, S., *K istorii Kommunisticheskoi patrii Gruzii* (Tiflis: Istpart, 1925).
Tarkhova, L., *Zalozhniki Kremlya* (Moscow: AST-Pressz, 1998).
Taylor, S., *Stalin's Apologist. Walter Duranty. The New York Times' Man in Moscow* (New York–Oxford: Oxford University Press, 1990).
Ter-Vaganyan see Vaganyan
The Alliluyev Memoirs: Recollections of Svetlana Stalina's Maternal Aunt Anna Alliluyeva and Her Grandfather Sergei Alliluyev (New York: G. P. Putman's Sons, 1968).
The Okhrana. The Russian Departmnet of Police: A Bibliograpy, edited by Smith E. (Stanford: The Hoover Institution on War, Revolution and Peace, 1967).
The Stalin Revolution: Foundations of Soviet Totalitarianism, edited by Daniels, R. (Lexington: D. C. Heath, 1972).
The Stalinist Terror in the Thirties: Documentation from the Soviet Press, edited by Levytsky, B. (Stanford: The Hoover Institution on War, Revolution and Peace, 1974).
The Trotsky Papers 1917–1920 (The Hague: Mouton & Co., 1965).
The Trotsky Papers 1920–1922 (The Hague–Paris: Mouton & Co., 1971).
Tikhonov, V. A., V. S. Tazhelnikova, and I. F. Yuskin, *Lisenie izbiratelnikh prav v Moskve v 1920–1930-ye godi. Novie arkhivnie materiali i metodi obrabotki.* (Moscow: Izdatelstvo Obyedinenia Mosgorarkhiv, 1998).
Tokaev, G., *Betrayal of an Ideal* (Bloomington: published by the author, 1955).
Tolmachev, A., *Kalinin* (Moscow: Molodaya Gvardia, 1963).
Topolyansky, V., *Vozhdi v zakone. Ocherki fiziologii vlasti* (Moscow: Prava Cheloveka, 1996).
Torchinov, U. A. and A. Y. Leontyuk, *Vokrug Stalina. Istoriko-biograficheskу spravochnik* (St. Petersburg: Filologichesky Fakultet Sankt-peterburgskovo Universiteta, 2000).

Torkunov, A. V., *Zagadochnaya voyna: koreisky konflikt 1950–1953 godov* (Moscow: Rosspen, 2000)

Trifonov, Y., *Another Life: The House on the Embankement,* translated by Glenny, M. (New York: Simon & Schuster, 1986). "Otblesk kostra", in *Smerch* (Moscow: Izdatelstvo DOSAAF SSSR, 1988).

Trotsky, L., *History of the Russian Revolution,* translated by Max Eastman (Ann Arbor: University of Michigan Press, 1932).

—, *Stalinskaya Shkola Falsifikatsii. Popravki I dopolnenia k literature epigonov* (Berlin: Granit, 1932).

—, *My Life. An Attempt at an Autobiografy* (London: Penguin Books, 1971).

—, *The Stalin School of Falsification* (New York: Pathfinder, 1972).

—, *Portreti revolyutsionerov* (Moscow: Moskovsky Rabochy, 1991).

—, *Stalin* I–II (Vermont: Chalidze Publications, 1985).

—, *Életem* (Kossuth Kiadó, Budapest, 1988.)

—, *Stalin* I–II (Moscow: Izdatelstvo Politicheskoi Literaturi, 1990).

Troyanovsky, O., *Cherez godi rasstoyania. Istoria odnoi semyi* (Moscow: Vagrius, 1997).

Tucker, R. *Stalin as Revolutionary, 1879–1929: A Study in History and Personality* (New York: W. W. Norton & Co., 1992).

—, *Stalin. Put k vlasti 1879–1929. Istoria i lichnost* (Moscow: Progress, 1997).

Tutukin, S. V. and V. V. Selokhayev, *Marksisti i russkaya revolyutsia* (Moscow: Rosspen, 1996).

Ulam, A., *Stalin: The Man and His Era* (Boston: Beacon, 1989).

Ulyanovskaya, N. and M. Ulyanovskaya, *Istoria odnoi semyi* (New York: Chalidze Publications, 1982).

Uratadze, G., *Vospominania gruzinskovo social-demokrata* (Stanford: The Hoover Institution on War, Revolution and Peace, 1968).

Vaganyan, V., *Dve stati otklononnie redaktsiyei zhurnala "Pod Znamenem Marksizma"* (Moscow: published by the author, 1927).

—, *O natsionalnoi kulture* (Moscow–Leningrad: Gosudarstvennoye Izdatelstvo, 1927).

Valentinov, N., *Novaya ekonomicheskaya politika i krizis partii posle smerti Lenina* (Stanford: The Hoover Institution on war, Revolution and Peace, n. d.).

—, *Nedorisovanny portret* (Moscow: Terra, 1993).

Vasilyeva, L., *Kremlyovskie zheni* (Moscow: Vagrius, 1995).

—, *Deti Kremlya* (Moscow: Atlantida, 1996).

Vasilevsky, A., *A vezérkar élén* (Budapest: Zrínyi Katonai Kiadó, 1975).

Vereshchak, S., "Stalin v tyurme. Vospominania politicheskovo zaklyuchonnovo", *DNI,* 1, 22, 24 (1928).

Vetoskin, M., „Stalin v sibirskoi ssilke", *Istorichesky Zhurnal,* 1 (1940).

Vinogradov, V. K., V. P. Gusachenko, and O. I. Nazheskin, *Sekreti Gitlera na stole u Stalina. Razvedka I kontrrazvedka o podgotovke germanskoi agressii protiv SSSR. Mart–iyun 1941 g.* (Moscow: Mosgorarkhiv, 1995).

Vinogradskaya, P., *Sobitia I payatnie vstrechi* (Moscow: Izdatelstvo Politicheskoi Literaturi, 1968).

Vishnevskaya, G., *Galina. Istoria zhizni* (Chimkent: MP Aurika, 1993).

Vladinsky, I. A., "'Vrach i evo patsient' (Vospominania I. A. Vladinskovo o J. V. Staline)", *Golosa Istorii,* 2 (1992).

Vlaszt i hudozhestvennaya inteligentsia. Dokumenti CK RKP/b/–VKP/b/, VCSK–OGPU–NKVD o kulturnoj polityike 1917–1953 (Moscow: Mezhdunarodny fond Demokratia, 1999).

Volkogonov, D., *Triumf i tragedia* I–IV (Moscow: Izdatelstvo APN, 1989).

Voronsky, A., *Za zhivoi i myortvoi vodoi* (Moscow: Federatsia, 1931).

—, *Izbrannaya proza* (Moscow: Khudozhestvennaya Literatura, 1987).

Voslensky, M., *Nomenklatura. Gospodstvuushchy klass Sovietskovo Soyuza* (London: Overseas Publications Interchange Ltd., 1990).

Vsesoyuznoye soveshchanie o merakh uluchshenia podgotovki nauchno-pedagogicheskikh kadrov po istoricheskim naukam. 18–21 dekabrya 1962 g. (Moscow: Izdatelstvo Nauka, 1964).

Wolfe, B., Three Who Made a Revolution. A Biographical Study (New York: Delta Book, 1964).

Yakovlev, A., *Omut pamyati* (Moscow: Vagrius, 2000).

Yaroslavsky, Y., *O tovarishche Staline* (Moscow: OGIZ, 1939).

Yelagin, Y., *Ukroshchenie iskusstv* (Hermitage: Tenafly, 1988).

Yevreysky Antifashistsky Komitet v SSSR 1941–1948. Dokumentirovannaya istoria (Moscow: Mezhdunarodnie Otnoshenia, 1996).

Yoffe, Maria. *Odna noch. Povest o pravde* (New York: Izdatelstvo Khronika, 1978).

Zelikson-Bobrovskaya, C., *Za pervie 20 let. Zapiski ryadovovo podpolshchika* (Moscow: Izdatelstvo Stary Bolshevik, 1932).

Zhordania, N., *Moya zhizn* (Stanford: The Hoover Institution on war, Revolution and Peace, 1968).

Zhukov, Y., *Tayni Kremlya. Stalin, Molotov, Beria, Malenkov* (Moscow: Terra-Knizhny Klub, 2000).

1941 God v dvuh knigah (Moscow: Mezhdunarodny Fond „Demokratia", 1998).

INDEX

Page numbers in Italics refer to illustrations.